CW01304302

Acadamh Ríoga na hÉireann   An Chartlann Náisiúnta
An Roinn Gnóthaí Eachtracha

Cáipéisí ar Pholasaí Eachtrach na hÉireann

Imleabhar VI

1939 ~ 1941

Eagarthóirí
Catriona Crowe
Ronan Fanning
Michael Kennedy
Dermot Keogh
Eunan O'Halpin

Royal Irish Academy   National Archives
Department of Foreign Affairs

Documents on Irish Foreign Policy

Volume VI

1939 ~ 1941

EDITORS
Catriona Crowe
Ronan Fanning
Michael Kennedy
Dermot Keogh
Eunan O'Halpin

First published in 2008 by
Royal Irish Academy
19 Dawson Street
Dublin, Ireland

All rights reserved

A catalogue record for this title is available from the British Library

ISBN 978-1-904890-51-5
EAN 9781904890515

Publishing consultants
Institute of Public Administration, Dublin

Design by Jan de Fouw
Typeset by Carole Lynch
Printed by ColourBooks, Dublin

Contents

	Pages
Editors and Editorial Advisory Board	vii
Abbreviations	viii
Preface	ix
Introduction	xi
List of archival sources	xxii
Biographical details	xxiii
List of documents reproduced	xxxiv

Documents

1939	1
1940	129
1941	422

Appendices

1	Destruction of files and documents dating from 1938 to 1940 by the Department of External Affairs, 25 May 1940	459
2	Months of the year in Irish and English	467
3	Glossary of Irish words and phrases	468
4	List of Irish missions abroad 1939-1941	469
5	Calendars for years 1939, 1940, 1941	471

Index	475

Editors

Ms Catriona Crowe
(Senior Archivist, National Archives)

Professor Ronan Fanning MRIA
(Professor Emeritus of Modern History, University College Dublin)

Dr Michael Kennedy
(Executive Editor, Documents on Irish Foreign Policy Series,
Royal Irish Academy)

Professor Dermot Keogh MRIA
(Professor of History, University College Cork)

Professor Eunan O'Halpin MRIA
(Professor of Contemporary Irish History, Trinity College Dublin)

Assistant Editor
Dr Kate O'Malley (Royal Irish Academy)

Editorial Advisory Board

(In addition to the Editors)

Mr Patrick Buckley (Royal Irish Academy)

Ms Julie Connell (Department of Foreign Affairs) (from August 2007)

Mr Ciaran Madden (Department of Foreign Affairs) (from August 2007)

Mr Tony McCullagh (Department of Foreign Affairs) (from August 2006 to August 2007)

Ms Jean McManus (Department of Foreign Affairs) (from August 2007)

Mr Adrian O'Neill (Department of Foreign Affairs) (from September 2005 to August 2007)

Mr Charles Sheehan (Department of Foreign Affairs) (from August 2006 to August 2007)

Ms Maureen Sweeney (Department of Foreign Affairs)

Abbreviations

The following is a list of the most commonly used abbreviated terms and phrases in the volume, covering both documents and editorial matter. Other abbreviations have been spelt out in the text.

DFA	Department of Foreign Affairs collection, National Archives, Dublin
DT S	Department of the Taoiseach, S series files, National Archives, Dublin
NAI	National Archives, Dublin
TD	Teachta Dála (Member of Dáil Éireann)
TNA	The National Archives (formerly the Public Record Office), Kew, London
UCDA	University College Dublin, Archives Department

Preface

The National Archives Act, 1986, provides for the transfer of departmental records more than thirty years old to the National Archives of Ireland for inspection by the public, unless they are certified to be in regular use by a Department for administrative purposes, or unless they are certified as withheld from public inspection on one of the grounds specified in the Act. The bulk of the material consulted for this volume comes from the records of the Department of Foreign Affairs (previously the Department of External Affairs) and the Department of the Taoiseach, all of which are available for inspection at the National Archives of Ireland at Bishop Street in Dublin. Other material comes from the holdings of the University College Dublin Archives Department and The National Archives, Kew, London. The Department of Foreign Affairs documents in the National Archives of Ireland have been made available to researchers since January 1991.[1]

The concept of a multi-volume series of documents on Irish foreign policy was put forward in 1994 by the Department of Foreign Affairs. Mr Ted Barrington, then the Political Director of the Department of Foreign Affairs, brought the proposal to a meeting of the Royal Irish Academy's National Committee for the Study of International Affairs of which he was then a member. The then Tánaiste and Minister for Foreign Affairs, Mr Dick Spring, sanctioned the proposal, which was also welcomed by the Director of the National Archives of Ireland, Dr David Craig, whose permission was necessary for the publication of material in his care. The Royal Irish Academy agreed to become a partner in the project when Council approved its foundation document on 3 April 1995.

The main provisions of that document are:

- that the project's 'basic aim is to make available, in an organised and accessible way, to people who may not be in a position easily to consult the National Archives, documents from the files of the Department which are considered important or useful for an understanding of Irish foreign policy';
- that an Editorial Advisory Board, comprising representatives of the Department, of the Academy and of the National Archives, in addition to senior Irish academics working in the fields of modern history and international relations, would oversee decisions on publication;
- that the series would 'begin at the foundation of the State and publish volumes in chronological order' and that the basic criterion for

---

[1] The Department of Foreign Affairs was known as the Department of External Affairs from December 1922 to 1971. From January 1919 to December 1922 the Department was known as the Department of Foreign Affairs or the Ministry of Foreign Affairs (see DIFP Volume I for further details).

the selection of documents would be their 'use or importance in understanding the evolution of policies and decisions'.

These arrangements found public expression in the 1996 White Paper on foreign policy, *Challenges and Opportunities Abroad* (16.48), which provided that–

> As part of the Government's desire to encourage a greater interest in Irish foreign policy, it has been agreed that the Department of Foreign Affairs, in association with the Royal Irish Academy, will publish a series of foreign policy documents of historic interest. It is hoped that this initiative will encourage and assist greater academic interest in the study of Irish foreign policy.

Provision for the project was first included in the Department's Estimates for 1997 and a preliminary meeting of what became the Editorial Advisory Board, in Iveagh House on 10 April 1997, agreed that an assistant editor should be appointed in addition to the editors nominated by the National Committee for the Study of International Affairs: Professors Ronan Fanning, MRIA, Dermot Keogh MRIA and Eunan O'Halpin MRIA. Dr Michael Kennedy was appointed in June 1997 when work began on the selection of documents. Dr Kennedy was in January 1998 designated as executive editor, and is responsible for the direction and day-to-day running of the Documents on Irish Foreign Policy (DIFP) project. At the meeting of December 2003 of the DIFP Editorial Advisory Board the important contribution of the National Archives to the Documents on Irish Foreign Policy project was officially recognised and the National Archives formally became a full partner to the DIFP project. Accordingly, Ms Catriona Crowe, Senior Archivist at the National Archives, who had attended meetings of the editors since June 1997 and who was de facto a fifth editor of DIFP, was formally appointed an editor of the DIFP series.

The first volume, *Documents on Irish Foreign Policy I*, covering the period 1919 to 1922, was published in November 1998 in the run-up to the eightieth anniversary of the founding of the Department of Foreign Affairs in January 1919. Subsequent volumes have been published at two-yearly intervals with volume VI being published in November 2008.

Introduction

This volume of selected documents, the sixth in the Documents on Irish Foreign Policy (DIFP) series, runs from September 1939 to January 1941. Commencing as war began in Europe, it covers seventeen months of grave crisis for Irish foreign policy makers, months in which an invasion of Ireland by either belligerent became a real possibility. Neutrality, hitherto aspirational, had to be implemented in practice. Ireland did not wish to be dragged unwillingly into war.

The execution of foreign policy in Dublin, particularly during the war years, was the product of the close working relationship between a small group of senior officials in the Department of External Affairs: Secretary of the Department, Joseph Walshe; Assistant Secretary, Frederick H. Boland; Legal Adviser, Michael Rynne and Private Secretary to Walshe and custodian of the Department's secret archives, Sheila Murphy. Under the political direction of the Taoiseach and Minister for External Affairs, Eamon de Valera, the four led Ireland's diplomatic service through the war. The Department of External Affairs sought to protect Ireland's sovereignty by emphasising the state's neutrality to the belligerent powers. Missions abroad – in particular those in London, Berlin, Washington and Ottawa – were central to this process. While Irish diplomats in these capitals were required to report on the events unfolding around them, their primary duty was to protect Ireland's national interests – in short, to protect Ireland's international sovereignty as expressed by neutrality. Preventing invasion, preserving neutrality and independence in wartime, became the overriding theme of Irish foreign policy in September 1939 and would remain so until May 1945.

The choice of documents for DIFP VI was challenging for the series editors. Research in 2005 and 2006 for DIFP V had for the first time shown the full extent of the May 1940 destruction of the records of the Department of External Affairs. The editors knew that many essential records central to the explication of Irish foreign policy in the opening nine months of the Second World War had been destroyed on the orders of Eamon de Valera when it was feared that a German invasion of Ireland was imminent. Readers will notice the scarceness in DIFP VI of confidential reports from London from September 1939 to May 1940. They will also be aware of the paucity of information on the specifics of British-Irish relations over the same months. To overcome partially the loss of Irish documents, the editors have included a strictly limited number of British documents from the National Archives, Kew, London. In choosing these documents they have endeavoured to elicit Irish perspectives alone, including documents where Irish views were reported verbatim or where direct speech was reported. From May 1940 the run of material in the Department of Foreign Affairs archives appears to be intact and the editors have not seen the need to undertake further the exceptional inclusions from non-Irish sources necessary for the first nine months covered by the volume.

Documents on Irish Foreign Policy, Volume VI, 1939–1941

* * *

September 1939 saw brisk activity in the Department of External Affairs to bolster and consolidate Ireland's declared policy of wartime neutrality. DIFP VI elucidates the legal and geopolitical basis of neutrality using memoranda drafted by the Legal Adviser at External Affairs, Michael Rynne. While missions abroad reported international reactions to the outbreak of war and speculated as to future possibilities, Rynne and his senior colleagues in headquarters in Dublin divided their responsibilities.

Assistant Secretary Frederick H. Boland was central to the management and development of the policy of neutrality from Dublin. Not only had External Affairs to implement urgently and in a period of crisis an entirely new and untried foreign policy, they also had to plan for possible emergencies including their own evacuation from Dublin, the safety of the Dublin diplomatic corps should hostilities break out in Ireland and how to keep the Irish diplomatic service functioning should Ireland be occupied by belligerent forces.

The Secretary of the Department, Joseph P. Walshe, shuttled between Dublin and London in the early months of the war seeking to ameliorate the increasingly fraught nature of the British-Irish relationship. The maintenance of workable relations between neutral Ireland and belligerent Britain is one of the central themes in DIFP VI. Walshe acted as de Valera's *éminence grise* during his missions to London, so much so that British officials often thought that Walshe was the Minister for External Affairs. Yet at every critical juncture between September 1939 and January 1941 de Valera took personal control of Irish foreign policy. The reader will observe this at such key moments as the appointment of Sir John Maffey as British Diplomatic Representative in Dublin in September 1939, Dublin's efforts in early 1940 to gain clemency for those convicted of IRA bombings in Britain, and also the British offer in June 1940 of Irish unity in return for immediate Irish entry into the war. At less critical moments Walshe returned to London to undertake policy on behalf of his minister. Walshe's long report to de Valera of his visit to London in the days just after the outbreak of war (document No. 15) provides a crucial insight into the development of British-Irish relations in late 1939 and shows Walshe acting on his minister's behalf in conveying to London de Valera's often cited 'certain consideration' for Britain.

Two significant developments in September 1939 were the communication to belligerent governments of an *aide mémoire* regarding restrictions on the use of Irish territorial waters on 12 September 1939 (document No. 19) and the appointment of a British Diplomatic Representative in Dublin – agreed by the government on 22 September. Until the appointment of Sir John Maffey there had been no British diplomatic presence in Ireland. With tensions rising between Dublin and London over Ireland's neutrality – in particular because of Ireland's refusal to allow the Royal Navy use of naval facilities – the *aide mémoire*, essential to the exposition of neutrality and which formalised the refusal of facilities in legal terms, was one of the first problems to face the new British Representative. Maffey was to have no honeymoon period.

Introduction

In London, Irish High Commissioner John Dulanty, under pressure from Winston Churchill – now First Lord of the Admiralty – and from British propaganda accusations that German submarines were using Irish waters for refuelling operations, sought to counter strong political opinion in support of the British appetite for naval facilities in Ireland. However important Dulanty had been in developing British-Irish relations up to September 1939, Maffey's appointment changed the nature of Irish contact with the British government and administration. De Valera could now deal with London directly through Maffey. While Dulanty's reports for much of late 1939 have not survived, the continuing central importance to British-Irish relations of his role in London in 1940 both in communicating Dublin's foreign policy and in reporting on affairs in wartime Britain is clearly apparent.

As in the case of Dulanty, Irish diplomatic representatives remained posted to belligerent states throughout the war. It became increasingly difficult for diplomats to take up new postings and for Dublin to fill vacancies, as was to be the case regarding the appointment of new ministers to Berlin and the Holy See. Communications with Dublin were frequently more difficult than before, the security of diplomatic bags was sometimes in doubt, but reports got through nonetheless, often after delays due to wartime restrictions. Confidential reports from William Warnock and later Con Cremin in Berlin, from Michael MacWhite in Rome and from Seán Murphy in Paris and Vichy provide a picture of the war in Europe that is not always available from other English language sources.

Warnock's Berlin reports reveal the swiftness of the German *blitzkrieg* in Poland in September 1939. The obliteration of Poland provoked little overt comment in Dublin. Walshe sent a strictly official, curt note to the Polish Consul General in Dublin which merely acknowledged that a state of war existed between Poland and Germany. By contrast, reports from Berlin and Geneva from December 1939 show considerable Irish interest in the 'Winter War' between Finland and Russia. Irish sympathy for the Finns is evident, but so too is the realisation that Dublin could do nothing to support Helsinki.

The 'Phoney War' passed with no direct threat to Ireland beyond British pressure and propaganda over the war in the North Atlantic. The months from September 1939 to May 1940 allowed the Department of External Affairs to organise to meet the exigencies of the European conflict and to set out the parameters of neutrality. For Irish diplomats, the most sensitive and dangerous period of the Second World War was without doubt the summer of 1940. The German invasion of France and the Low Countries on 10 May, the eventual fall of France on 22 June and the advance of German forces to the French coast concentrated Irish minds on the possibility of a German invasion of Ireland as part of, or as a diversionary raid leading to, an invasion of Britain.

Irish diplomats in Paris, Berlin, Rome and Geneva sent regular reports to Dublin on the progress of the war in western Europe. As the summer of 1940 progressed, the speed of the German advance across France and the Allies' inability to check the Wehrmacht in France and Norway was a common theme in their reports to Walshe in Dublin. Despatches from the Irish

Documents on Irish Foreign Policy, Volume VI, 1939–1941

Legation in Berlin show how the pressures of war affected ordinary people in Germany and how, from a German perspective, a German victory seemed inevitable in the summer of 1940. Michael MacWhite in Rome was less sanguine as to Italy's prospects after she entered the war on 10 June 1940. From the United States, Robert Brennan informed Dublin on how American opinion was turning increasingly pro-British and bellicose.

British Prime Minister Neville Chamberlain's resignation and replacement by Winston Churchill on 10 May saw British-Irish relations, already tense, take a turn for the worse. In 1938 Churchill had criticised the return of the ports at the time of the signing of the Anglo-Irish Agreement. He failed to appreciate the reasons for Ireland's neutrality and had never fully accepted Irish independence. The fall of France reignited the war in the Atlantic, placing Ireland on the front line of naval conflict through the summer of 1940. The war at sea, the threat of a German invasion and the threat of a British invasion to retake the ports and to deny Ireland to Germany posed imminent threats to Irish foreign policy makers throughout the summer of 1940.

As Britain's situation worsened following the withdrawal from Norway, the evacuation from Dunkirk and the fall of France, its Irish policy became more dramatic. Former Dominions Secretary Malcolm MacDonald arrived in Dublin on 17 June talking up the possibility of a German invasion of Ireland to de Valera and offering Irish unity at an early date in return for immediate Irish abandonment of neutrality and participation in the war. These proposals were contained in a communication received from MacDonald on 26 June. The extant documents show increasing pessimism in Dublin in the summer of 1940 as to the outcome of the war. Walshe's gloom was reinforced by reports received from his colleagues abroad. At times appearing close to exhaustion, Walshe's belief in Britain's 'inevitable' defeat was balanced by Frederick Boland's cool-headedness. Above all de Valera, supported by the advice of Boland, Rynne and other senior civil servants, believed that Ireland would only suffer by involvement in the war and that, as a small state, her own national interests would hold little weight in the event of either a British or a German victory. The MacDonald offer of unity was rejected by de Valera, a view subsequently confirmed by a unanimous decision of the government on 27 June and communicated to London on 4 July.

The MacDonald mission led to press reports of a possible British-Irish defence agreement, a view immediately squashed by missions abroad on Dublin's explicit orders, with Brennan in Washington placing particular emphasis on this point to journalists and congressmen. Talks regarding a British-Irish trade agreement were ongoing and what Walshe referred to as Ireland's 'position of benevolent neutrality' towards Britain continued, but no formal position over defence was ever under consideration. External Affairs was closely involved in containing the fallout from a number of damaging British activities in the aftermath of the MacDonald mission as British officers on intelligence missions were picked up on Irish territory by Irish security forces and Walshe had occasion more than once to contact Maffey about alarming movements of British forces in border regions of Northern Ireland.

Introduction

While defence policy is outside the scope of the DIFP series, it is clear that the Department of External Affairs and Irish Military Intelligence (G2) operated with increasing closeness and synchronicity from the outbreak of the Second World War. The security threat posed by Germans remaining in Ireland and plans to counter a German invasion of the country were common issues for both departments. Amidst the tension of the crucial months of May and June 1940 Walshe at External Affairs and Colonel Liam Archer, the Director of the army's intelligence section, G2, worked together developing British-Irish relations at official and military level during a period where relations at the highest political level between de Valera and Churchill were increasingly fraught. G2 in effect reported to External Affairs on all aspects of intelligence and security having an external bearing, including the activities and conduct of foreign diplomats in Ireland and their contacts with groups and individuals representing various strands of Irish political opinion.

The fruits of this growing relationship were evident in the defence staff talks of 23 and 24 May 1940 at which Irish and British officials and military met to agree a common strategy to counter a German invasion of Ireland, and in later liaison talks involving senior officers from British forces based in Northern Ireland with Irish military and officials and with de Valera. External Affairs was also closely involved in the largely unsuccessful attempts by the Defence Forces to obtain quantities of modern weapons from Britain for the defence of Ireland.

The threat of a British invasion did not diminish outright after the May talks and British-Irish relations remained difficult for the remainder of 1940. De Valera made it clear that Ireland would fight against any country that invaded her territory, a view repeated emphatically by Irish diplomats, particularly in Britain, Canada and the United States.

Seán Murphy's 18 June 1940 despatch describing his and his staff's departure from Paris to Vichy (document No. 194) records the trials of diplomatic representation in time of war. His later despatches reveal how his relations with Walshe deteriorated rapidly in the second half of 1940. Murphy sought to explain to Walshe that the Secretary could not dictate policy in relation to France based on his personal beliefs and certainly could not tell Murphy and his colleagues how they were to conduct themselves. This strong difference of opinion came to a head in December 1940 and ended when Walshe conceded to Murphy that he had not tried to dictate how Murphy should deal with the French authorities.

Murphy, Cremin and Count O'Kelly de Gallagh, who kept an Irish office open in Paris, also had to deal with an increased number of consular cases. The war brought difficulties for Irish people in France. In the course of the research for DIFP VI a number of significant consular cases came to light and the editors have included aspects of them in this volume. While James Joyce was by 1940 a writer of international fame, Samuel Beckett, resident in France for the duration of the Second World War and involved with the French Resistance, was less well known. Joyce sought assistance from Irish diplomats for his daughter Lucia to enable her to travel and Beckett and his family in Dublin were able to stay in contact through the good offices of the Irish mission in Vichy. The needs

Documents on Irish Foreign Policy, Volume VI, 1939–1941

of these two men were mirrored in the cases of many Irish people who remained in France and in the other countries at war in Europe.

In Geneva, and later in Berne, Frank Cremins provided useful parallels for Ireland from the stance of neutral Switzerland and reported the final chapters in the decline of the League of Nations as his former colleague Seán Lester sought to preserve the remnants of the ailing international institution in his capacity as its Acting Secretary General. Ireland retained only a token faith in the League of Nations during the Second World War. The Irish office at Geneva was closed in 1940 and Cremins transferred to Berne as Ireland's first representative to Switzerland. Berne was the only new mission opened in Europe during the period covered by this volume. As Chargé d'Affaires in Berne, Cremins was an important conduit of information to Dublin on how neutral Switzerland managed her wartime external relations. Cremins' office also became an important link in the chain of communications between Dublin and its missions abroad as lines of transmission worsened with the continuing war and with Germany's increasing dominance over western Europe.

Edouard Hempel, the German Minister to Ireland, had continually emphasised to Walshe since before the outbreak of hostilities that Germany had no intention of violating Ireland's neutrality. Though Dublin considered the immediate German threat to have declined as July 1940 ended, 17 August 1940 saw the extension of the German blockade of Britain and the waters around Ireland. Irish merchant vessels had already been subjected to German attacks and as the blockade intensified further incidents occurred. By Cabinet decision Irish vessels were to remain unarmed. Warnock in Berlin protested strongly to the German foreign office after the attacks and attempted to explain the vital importance to Ireland of trade with Britain. The difficulty of supplying Ireland during wartime was never far from the minds of policy makers in External Affairs and involved considerable contact with the newly established Department of Supplies. Walshe was friendly with John Leydon, the Secretary of the Department of Supplies, and had worked closely with Leydon and his minister, Seán Lemass, during the 1938 British-Irish trade agreement negotiations.

While the threat to Irish shipping grew, it was at least anticipated owing to German warnings transmitted through Hempel. Proximity to Britain during the Battle of Britain and the Blitz brought a new threat to Ireland. On the early afternoon of 26 August 1940 two German aircraft dropped bombs in County Wexford, opening a new chapter in Irish-German relations. While German aircraft had been overflying Ireland since the early summer of 1940 despite Irish protests to Berlin, this was the first time bombs were dropped and fatalities occurred. Dublin took as strong a line as possible with Berlin on the attack and though compensation was eventually paid, other attacks were to occur. Though these bombings were later agreed to have been mistakes, they began nine months of sporadic attacks that culminated in the bombing of the North Strand in Dublin on 30–31 May 1941, an attack that left thirty-four people dead.

Although Dublin lodged protests in response to all German bombings of Irish territory and at German overflights, Walshe and Boland handled relations

Introduction

with Germany carefully. In their discussions with Hempel both men took pains to explain de Valera's specific interpretation of neutrality, though Walshe could at times appear gushing, if not unctuous towards the German Minister. A most serious event, one which tested Irish-German relations to the limit, was Germany's attempt in December 1940 to fly in extra staff for her mission in Dublin. Hempel attempted to gain Dublin's agreement to fly in three diplomats, known to be military advisers with an intelligence role, to Shannon airport. De Valera refused and tensions heightened as the possibility of Germany using Dublin's refusal as a pretext for an invasion increased. Though Germany eventually backed down, a subsequent series of German bombings along Ireland's east coast left some wondering if the raids were other than a mistake.

Neither had the threat from Britain diminished during this period. November and December 1940 saw Churchill again call for the return of the Treaty ports to Britain and a British propaganda campaign in the United States increased pressure on Ireland to abandon neutrality. Attempts by Dublin to highlight Irish concerns, such as partition and neutrality, fell on deaf ears in the United States in this climate. Brennan had, since his appointment to Washington in 1938, assiduously courted Irish-America but he lacked high-powered contacts on Capitol Hill and within the Roosevelt administration. He was unable to make in-roads into the increasingly pro-British mindset in the United States, a mindset that now had little time for Ireland's neutrality and had no inclination to appreciate the reasons behind Ireland's stance.

In contrast to Brennan in Washington, Irish High Commissioner in Ottawa, John Hearne, had excellent high-level contacts in Canada. Hearne's diplomatic skills were put to great effect as he sought to explain Ireland's neutrality to his Canadian audience. His explanations of neutrality were patiently tolerated, but despite his good relations with Prime Minister Mackenzie King, Canadian opinion remained resolutely unsupportive of Ireland's stance.

From London Dulanty reported how Britain was bearing up during the Blitz and he sent his own eyewitness reports of life in the British capital under the constant threat of German attack. Warnock tried to report as frequently as possible on day-to-day life in Berlin, but the constraints of reporting by insecure code telegram make his confidential reports much less explicit than the detail Dulanty could report to Dublin verbally or by courier. Murphy in Vichy was under the same constraints as Warnock, but he used couriers where possible to return vivid reports to Walshe.

In his dealings with the Madrid authorities Irish Minister to Spain Leopold Kerney began to act increasingly without specific reference to External Affairs, though he considered he was always acting on general orders from Dublin. This was particularly so when it came to the 'escape' of Frank Ryan from Spain into German hands. Kerney's contacts with the Spanish and the German secret service ensured Ryan's handing over to German agents, but he was less than comprehensive in reporting the event to Dublin (document No. 277). Kerney was to remain in Spain until 1946; though he and his superiors did not always see eye-to-eye, he endeavoured to harness the diplomatic opportunities which his position in the murky world of wartime Madrid presented.

Irish relations with the Holy See, a state also on the frontline of the European conflict, underwent a significant upset in 1940 as Minister to the Holy See William J. B. Macaulay left Italy for an extended trip to the United States in June on Italy's entering the Second World War. Macaulay eventually resigned in 1941. Colman O'Donovan, who represented Ireland as Chargé d'Affaires until Thomas J. Kiernan was appointed Minister to the Vatican in 1941, replaced him in Rome. O'Donovan, acting largely on Walshe's instructions, undertook the delicate negotiations surrounding the agreement that John Charles McQuaid would be appointed Archbishop of Dublin in 1940.

DIFP VI closes in January 1941. The month saw German bombs again drop on Irish territory and saw Britain begin to tighten the economic screws on Ireland. German bombing was later shown to be due to the errors of the Luftwaffe, but Britain's policy was deliberate and deadly serious, seeking to punish Ireland further for not giving up neutrality, allowing use of the Treaty ports and joining the war effort. Political and economic pressure on Ireland from London would continue through 1941, but Germany's decision to invade Russia in July 1941 changed the nature of the war in Europe and by moving the war on the land to the east made Ireland's position somewhat less difficult. In retrospect it is apparent that by January 1941 the worst crisis of the war was over for Ireland, but as the final documents in DIFP VI show, this was in no way obvious at the time.

Records of the Department of Foreign Affairs, and other archival sources
Until the passage of the National Archives Act (1986), government departments in Ireland were under no compulsion to release their archives. The Department of the Taoiseach, however, has voluntarily released material since the mid-1970s. The Department of Foreign Affairs records have been released on an annual basis since 1991.

In the late 1920s the Department of External Affairs established a numerical registry system for filing its papers. Under this system a list of subject categories corresponding to the main areas of the department's work was drawn up and each subject category was assigned a unique number code. For example the number code 26 was allocated to files and papers dealing with the League of Nations. Individual files within each number category were assigned a unique sub-number. File 26/95 deals with the Irish Free State's candidature for the League of Nations Council in 1930. This registry and filing system, known colloquially as 'number series' files, was further developed in the mid-1930s. The existing two-digit prefixes had the number 1 added to them with, for example, the previous 26 series becoming the 126 series and so on. A further development took place in the late 1930s with the 1 being replaced by a 2, thus 126 became 226.

The most sensitive information held by the Department of External Affairs was kept in the Secretary's Files series. This collection began in the 1920s, with files being designated S with a number following (not to be confused with the separate Department of the Taoiseach S Series files). In later years A and P series were created, as well as a PS series for the Private Secretary to the Secretary. These series were held under lock and key in the Secretary's

Introduction

office and were only made available to lower ranking officials under certain conditions. The S Series was a target for widespread destruction during the wartime invasion scares of 1940.

Material generated in Irish missions abroad is held at the National Archives in Dublin in the Embassies Series collection. For the late 1930s and early 1940s this material covers the missions in London, Washington, Geneva, Brussels, Ottawa, Berne, the Holy See, Paris, Berlin, Madrid and Rome. Due to weeding and wartime destruction the Embassies Series is very patchy for the inter-war years. The collections for Madrid and Paris are the most complete. The archives of the Irish Legation in Berlin were almost completely destroyed after a bomb hit the chancellery during an air raid in 1943. Unfortunately, the majority of files of the Irish Embassy in London (Irish High Commission from 1923 to 1949) were shredded in the 1950s. Similarly, very little survives from the Washington Embassy for the period covered by this volume. Where files do survive there is an understandable degree of overlap with Headquarters' number series files.

The main files from the Department of the Taoiseach (known from 1922 to 1937 as the Department of the President of the Executive Council, or simply 'the Department of the President') are known as the 'S-files' series. They begin at S1 and progress numerically (S1, S2, S3 etc.) in a roughly chronological order. In contrast to the 1920s, when foreign policy matters appeared regularly on the agenda of the Executive Council and Cabinet, with de Valera as President of the Executive Council and Minister for External Affairs from 1932 to 1948 there was a tendency for the members of the government to leave foreign policy decisions solely to him.

Readers of Volume VI will notice that both government minutes and cabinet minutes are published. While in common parlance the government and the cabinet are considered to be the same body, there was a difference between the two. The government was the term given to members of the government meeting under the functions devolving upon it by provision of the Constitution or the law. The cabinet was the name given to the government meeting to decide matters of policy as the main policy-making organ of the state. The distinction between government decisions and cabinet decisions was abolished with the commencement of the Eighteenth Government on 9 March, 1982.

The editors have reproduced three documents from The National Archives, Kew, London. The first (document No. 37) is a report from Maffey to Eden of his initial weeks in Dublin; the second (document No. 193) and third (document No. 198) are MacDonald's account of his meetings with de Valera.

Editorial policy and the selection of documents
The executive editor is responsible for the initial wide choice of documents. These documents are then assessed periodically by the five editors in order to select the most appropriate documents for publication. Documents are prioritised in terms of importance on a one to five scale and are processed by the editors in geographical and thematic tranches. The documents in this volume are presented in chronological order based on date of despatch. The text of documents has been reproduced as exactly as possible. Marginal notes and annotations have generally been reproduced in footnotes; annotations

Documents on Irish Foreign Policy, Volume VI, 1939–1941

have however sometimes been reproduced in the body text when to have reproduced them as footnotes would have reduced the clarity of the document from the reader's point of view. Where possible the authors of marginal notes have been identified. There have been no alterations of the text of documents nor have there been any deletions without indication being given of where changes have been made. Nothing has been omitted that might conceal or gloss over defects in policymaking and policy execution. With the exception of twenty-five documents from files which were located in the London Embassy in the autumn of 2005 and which were released to the public in 2006, all material reproduced was already open to the public at the relevant repository.[1]

At some points in the text the footnotes refer to documents that were 'not printed'. Either the document referred to could not be found or the document was either routine or repeated information found elsewhere in the documents selected and so was not printed. Where it was impossible to decipher a word or series of words, an ellipsis has been inserted or the assumed word inserted with an explanatory footnote. Spelling mistakes have been silently corrected, but capitalisation, punctuation, signatures and contemporary spelling have in the main been left as found in the originals and have been changed only where the sense is affected. Additions to the text appear in square brackets. Original abbreviations have been preserved and either spelt out between square brackets or explained in the list of abbreviations. Where a sender has signed a document, either in original or copy form, the word 'signed', in square brackets, has been inserted. A similar practice has been followed with initialled or stamped documents, with the word 'initialled' or 'stamped' inserted in square brackets as appropriate. In all cases without an insertion in square brackets, the signature or initials were typed on the original document and are reproduced as found. Where an unsigned copy of a letter is reproduced, the words 'copy letter unsigned' have been inserted in square brackets. The editors have at all times tried to confirm the identity of the senders and recipients of unsigned letters, and in cases where identity is impossible to establish a footnote has been inserted to that effect. In correspondence, English was the working language of Irish diplomats. It is evident from the archives that written communication in Irish was only used for documents of symbolic national importance, although Irish was the spoken language of a number of diplomats, particularly Joseph Walshe, and many officials were bilingual.

In the weeks leading up to the outbreak of the Second World War foreign missions were instructed to send 'situation reports' to Dublin in Irish on the

---

[1] The guidelines of the Department of Foreign Affairs state that

There may be no alteration of the text, no deletions without indicating the place in the text where the deletion is made, and no omission of the facts which were of major importance in reaching a decision. Nothing may be omitted for the purpose of concealing or glossing over what might be regarded by some as a defect of policy.

However, certain omissions of documents are permissible to avoid publication of matters that would tend to impede current diplomatic negotiations or other business.

In addition, the above guidelines are to be interpreted in conjunction with the obligations laid out in the National Archives Act (1986) and the Freedom of Information Act (1997), the provisions contained in which are to be regarded as taking precedence.

Introduction

likelihood of war breaking out as seen from their particular post.

In correspondence, the Irish language was otherwise more commonly used for salutations and in signatures. In many cases there was no consistent spelling of gaelicised names and in the DIFP volumes many different spellings of the same name and salutation in Irish occur. These have not been standardised and are reproduced as found.

The authors of the documents reproduced tended to refer to Britain as 'England' or made no distinction between the two geographical entities and the editors have not thought it necessary to insert (sic) at all relevant points throughout the volume.

Acknowledgements

The editors would like to thank all those who were involved in the production of Volume VI of the Documents on Irish Foreign Policy series. The assistance of the following is particularly acknowledged.

At the Department of Foreign Affairs: Dermot Gallagher, Secretary General of the Department; Julie Connell; Clare Hanratty; Ciaran Madden; Tony McCullough; Jean McManus; Andrée Kearney; Adrian O'Neill; Charles Sheehan and Maureen Sweeney.

At the Royal Irish Academy: Professor Nicholas Canny, President of the Academy, and his predecessor, Professor James Slevin; Patrick Buckley, Executive Secretary of the Academy; Professor Howard Clarke, Secretary of the Academy; James McGuire (Managing Editor) and Dr James Quinn (Executive Editor) of the Academy's Dictionary of Irish Biography and Dr Kate O'Malley of DIFP.

At the National Archives: Dr David Craig, Director, for his generosity in providing access to the facilities and collections; Ken Hannigan, Keeper; Aideen Ireland, Mary Mackey and Tom Quinlan.

At the University College Dublin Archives Department (School of History and Archives): Seamus Helferty, Ailsa Holland, Kate Manning and Orna Somerville.

At the Institute of Public Administration: Eileen Kelly; Hannah Ryan and Tom Turley.

We would also like to thank Commandant Victor Laing of Military Archives, Cathal Brugha Barracks, Dublin, Professor John Horne, Trinity College Dublin, Helen Litton, and our typist, Maura O'Shea.

We would like to thank the MacWhite family for permission to consult and reproduce material from the papers of Michael MacWhite held at the University College Dublin Archives.

Samuel Beckett's letter of 23 January 1941 to Count O'Kelly de Gallagh (NAI DFA Paris Embassy Miscellaneous Papers, Box 40), No. 406 below, is reproduced by kind permission of the Estate of Samuel Beckett, c/o Rosica Colin Limited, London.

Catriona Crowe
Ronan Fanning
Michael Kennedy
Eunan O'Halpin
12 June 2008

List of Archival Sources

National Archives

Department of Foreign Affairs
2006 release (2006/39 series)
Confidential Reports
   219 Series
Embassies Series
   Berlin Embassy
   Holy See Embassy
   Madrid Embassy
   Ottawa Embassy
   Paris Embassy
   Washington Embassy
Legal Adviser's Papers
Number Series Files
   200 Series
Secretaries Files
   A Series
   P Series
   S Series

Department of the Taoiseach
S Series
Government and Cabinet Minutes
2001 release (2001/6 series)

University College Dublin Archives

Eamon de Valera papers (P150)
Michael MacWhite papers (P194)

The National Archives, Kew

PREM Series
   PREM 1 and PREM 3

Biographical Details

This list gives priority to the main Irish ministerial, diplomatic and administrative figures who appear in the text. Key foreign figures have also been identified, but generally in less detail. Minor figures, or people who receive only an occasional mention, have been identified in the text in footnotes.

Aiken, Frank (1898-1983) TD; educated at Christian Brothers School, Newry; succeeded Liam Lynch as Chief of Staff of the IRA (April 1923) and issued the cease-fire orders which ended the Civil War; Minister for Defence (1932-39); Minister for Lands and Fisheries (June-November 1936); Minister for the Coordination of Defensive Measures (1939-45); Minister for Finance (1945-48); Minister for External Affairs (1951-54 and 1957-69); Minister for Agriculture (March-May 1957); Tánaiste (1965-69).

Andrews, John Miller (1871-1956) Northern Ireland Minister of Labour (1921-37); Northern Ireland Minister of Finance (1937-40); Prime Minister of Northern Ireland (November 1940-May 1943).

Archer, Colonel Liam (1900-1969) Director of G2 (Military Intelligence) (1932-41); Assistant Chief of Staff of the Irish Defence Forces (1941-48); Chief of Staff (1948-52).

Avenol, Joseph (1879-1952) Secretary-General of the League of Nations (1933-40).

Beckett, Samuel (1906-1989) Nobel Prize winning (1969) Irish writer, poet and dramatist who had settled permanently in Paris prior to the outbreak of the Second World War and who joined the Resistance in 1940.

Bewley, Charles Henry (1888-1969) Educated at Park House, Winchester and New College, Oxford; called to the Bar in 1914 and to the Inner Bar in 1926; Trade Representative to Germany (1921-23); Minister to the Vatican (1929-33); Minister to Germany (1933-39).

Boland, Frederick H. (1904-1985) Educated at Merchant Taylor's School, London, Catholic University School, Dublin, Clongowes Wood College, Co Kildare, Trinity College Dublin, King's Inns, Dublin, Harvard University, University of Chicago and University of North Carolina; entered Department of External Affairs (1929); Junior Administrative Officer (1930-31); First Secretary, Paris Legation (1932-34); Head of the League of Nations Section of the Department of External Affairs (1934-36); Principal Officer in charge of foreign trade section, Department of Industry and Commerce (1936-38); Assistant Secretary, Department of External Affairs (1938-46); Secretary, Department of External Affairs (1946-50); Ambassador to Great Britain (1950-55); Permanent Representative/Ambassador to the United Nations (1956-64).

Documents on Irish Foreign Policy, Volume VI, 1939–1941

Brennan, Robert (1881-1964) Educated at Christian Brothers School, Wexford; Sinn Féin Director of Publicity (1918-20); Under-Secretary, Department of Foreign Affairs (7 February 1921-21 January 1922); organiser of the Irish Race Conference (Paris, January 1922); anti-Treaty propagandist during the Civil War; General Manager, the Irish Press (1931-34); Secretary, Washington Legation (1934-38); Acting Chargé d'Affaires, Washington (March-September 1938); Minister to the United States of America (1938-47); Director of Broadcasting, Radio Éireann (1947-48).

Chamberlain, Neville (1869-1940) British Conservative politician; Chancellor of the Exchequer (1923-24 and 1931-37); Prime Minister (1937-40); Lord President of the Council (1940).

Churchill, Winston S. (1874-1965) First Lord of the Admiralty (1939-40); Prime Minister (1940-45); Minister of Defence (1940-45).

Conway, John Mary (1896-1988) Educated at St Mary's College, Rathmines, and Belvedere College, Dublin; Department of Defence (1923-30); Department of External Affairs, Dublin (1930-35); Vice Consul, New York (1935-39); Consul, New York (1939); Secretary, High Commission, Ottawa (1939-47); Consul, Chicago (1947-54); Representative to the United Nations (1955-56); Consul General, New York (with personal rank of Minister Plenipotentiary (1959-61)) (1955-61).

Craig, Sir James (later **1st Viscount Craigavon**) (1871-1940) MP (Westminster and (from 1921) Northern Ireland parliaments) (1906-40); leader of the Ulster Unionist Party (1921-40); first Prime Minister of Northern Ireland (1921-40).

Cremin, Cornelius 'Con' (1908-1987) Educated at St Brendan's Killarney, University College Cork, and at Athens, Rome, Munich and Oxford; Third Secretary, Department of External Affairs (1935-37); First Secretary, Paris (1937-43); Chargé d'Affaires ad interim, Berlin (1943-45); Chargé d'Affaires ad interim, Lisbon (1945-46); Counsellor, Headquarters, Dublin (1946-48); Assistant Secretary, Department of External Affairs (1948-50); Minister Plenipotentiary/Ambassador to France (1950-54); Ambassador to the Holy See (1954-56); Ambassador to Britain (1956-58); Secretary, Department of External Affairs (1958-63); Ambassador to Britain (1963-64); Ambassador to the United Nations (1964-74).

Cremins, Francis T. (1885-1975) Clerical Officer, General Post Office (1900-22); Higher Executive Officer, Publicity Department, Department of External Affairs (1922-25); Higher Executive Officer, Department of Lands and Fisheries (1925-29); Head of League of Nations Section, Department of External Affairs (1929-34); Permanent Representative to the League of Nations (1934-40); Chargé d'Affaires, Berne (1940-49).

Coyne, Thomas (Tommy) (1901-1961) Educated at Clongowes Wood College, Co Kildare, University College Dublin and King's Inns, Dublin; Private Secretary to Minister for Home Affairs/Justice (1923-29); seconded to the Department of External Affairs (1929-34) and served as Secretary, Holy

Biographical Details

See Legation (1929-32), and assistant to the Irish Free State Permanent Delegate to the League of Nations (1932-34); Principal Officer, Department of Justice (1934-39); seconded to the Department of Defence for six months; Deputy Controller of censorship (1941-46); Assistant Secretary, Department of Justice (1946-49); Secretary, Department of Justice (1949-61).

Cudahy, John Clarence (1887-1943) Served in the United States Army during the First World War; Ambassador to Poland (1933-37), United States Minister to Ireland (1937-40); United States Ambassador to Belgium (1940).

de Valera, Eamon (1882-1975) TD; born in New York, brought to Ireland in 1885 by an uncle; educated at Bruree National School, Co Limerick, Christian Brothers School, Charleville, Co Cork, Blackrock College, Co Dublin, the Royal University of Ireland, Dublin, and Trinity College Dublin; teacher of mathematics at Rockwell College, Co Tipperary, and Blackrock College, Co Dublin; Commandant of the Third Battalion of the Dublin Brigade of the Irish Volunteers during the 1916 Rising; imprisoned in England (1916-17); elected for East Clare (July 1917), elected President of Sinn Féin (October 1917); imprisoned in England (1918-19); returned unopposed for East Clare and elected for East Mayo in the 1918 General Election, also elected for North Down (1921-27) and South Down (1933-38) to the Parliament of Northern Ireland; President of Dáil Éireann (1 April 1919-9 January 1922); whilst in America from 11 June 1919 to 23 December 1920 de Valera referred to this post as 'President of the Irish Republic'; opposed the Treaty; served with the Third Dublin Brigade of the Republican Forces during the Civil War; announced re-organisation of Sinn Féin (January 1923); arrested by Irish Free State troops and imprisoned (August 1923-July 1924); TD for Clare (1923-59); resigned Presidency of Sinn Féin (March 1926), founder of Fianna Fáil (May 1926); became leader of the opposition in Dáil Éireann (August 1927); President of the Executive Council and Minister for External Affairs (1932-37); President of the Council of the League of Nations and Acting President of the Assembly of the League of Nations (1932-33); Taoiseach and Minister for External Affairs (1937-48); Minister for Education (September 1939-June 1940); Minister for Local Government (August 1941); Taoiseach (1951-54 and 1957-59); President of Ireland (1959-73).

Dobrzyński, Wacław Tadeusz (1887-1962) Polish Consul General in Dublin (1929-54).

Dulanty, John W. (1881-1955) Born in Liverpool; educated at St Mary's School Failsworth, and Manchester University; joined British Civil Service (1914); successively Examiner, Board of Education, and Principal Assistant Secretary, Ministry of Munitions; Assistant Secretary to the Treasury (1918); awarded CB and CBE; Managing Director of Peter Jones Ltd (1919-26); Irish Trade Commissioner in London (1926-30); Irish High Commissioner in London (1930-49); Ambassador to Britain (1950).

Eden, Anthony (1897-1977) British Conservative politician; Minister for League of Nations Affairs (1935); Secretary of State for Foreign Affairs (1935-38);

Secretary of State for Dominion Affairs (1939-40); Secretary of State for War (1940); Secretary of State for Foreign Affairs (1940-45 and 1951-55); Prime Minister (1955-57).

Ferguson, Robert Campbell (1880-1945) Educated at Queen's College, Belfast; Ministry of Labour (1920-22); transferred to the Irish Free State Department of Labour (1922); Department of Industry and Commerce (Trade and Industries Branch) (1923-32); Assistant Secretary, Department of Industry and Commerce (1932-39); Secretary, Department of Industry and Commerce (1939-45).

Franco Y Bahamonde, Francisco (1892-1975) Spanish general; head of insurgent government in Spain (1936); Chief of State (1936-75).

Gallagher, Frank (1893-1962) Author and journalist; member of the Irish Volunteers (1913-16); parliamentary correspondent at Westminster for the *Cork Free Press* (1917); worked under Robert Erskine Childers on the publicity staff of the first Dáil Éireann (1919-21); Editor, *Irish Bulletin* (1920-22); personal secretary to Eamon de Valera (1927-28); Editor, *Irish Nation* (1928-30); Editor, *Irish Press* (1931-36); Deputy Director, Radio Éireann (1936-39); Director, Government Information Bureau (1939-48 and 1951-54); books include *Days of Fear* (1928), *Four Glorious Years* (1953) and *Indivisible Island* (1957).

Gascoyne-Cecil, Robert, Viscount Cranborne (1893-1972) Secretary of State for Dominion Affairs (1940-February 1942 and September 1943-July 1945); Secretary of State for Colonial Affairs (February-November 1942); Lord Privy Seal (November 1942-September 1943).

Gray, David (1870-1968) American journalist, lawyer and soldier; United States Minister to Ireland (1940-47); married (1914) to Mrs Maude Livingston Hall Waterbury, an aunt to Eleanor Roosevelt.

Hambro, Carol J. (1885-1964) Norwegian journalist and politician; President of the Assembly of the League of Nations (1939-46).

Harding, Sir Edward J. (1880-1954) Assistant Secretary, Colonial Office (1921-25); Assistant Under-Secretary, Dominions Office (1925-30); Permanent Under-Secretary, Dominions Office (1930-39).

Harrison, Major General James M. R. (1880-1957) Commandant of the Royal School of Artillery (1932-4); Commandant 2nd Anti-Aircraft Division (1936-9); Lieutenant Governor of Jersey (1939-40); Chief Liaison Officer between British forces in Northern Ireland and the Irish Defence Forces (1940-1).

Hearne, John Joseph (1893-1969) Educated at Waterpark College, Waterford, and University College Dublin; called to the Bar (1919); Assistant Parliamentary Draftsman (1923-29); Legal Adviser, Department of External Affairs (1929-39); called to the Inner Bar (1939); High Commissioner to Canada (1939-49); Ambassador to the United States of America (1950-60).

Hempel, Edouard (1887-1972) German Minister to Ireland (22 June 1937-8 May 1945).

Biographical Details

Horan, Timothy Joseph (1912-1975) Educated at University College Cork, entered the Department of External Affairs in 1938 as Third Secretary; Consul, New York (1942-45); Acting Head of Consular Section, Department of External Affairs (1945-56); First Secretary, Madrid (1946-47); First Secretary, Paris (1947-49); Counsellor, Department of Foreign Affairs (1949-52); Chief of Protocol (1952-55); Minister to Argentina (1955-59); Assistant Secretary (1959-60); Minster to Switzerland (1960-62); Ambassador to Spain (1962-67); Ambassador to Sweden (and, concurrently, Finland) (1967-73); Permanent Representative to the United Nations at Geneva (1973-75).

Hore-Belisha, (Isaac) Leslie, 1st Baron Hore-Belisha (1893-1957) Secretary for War (1937-40).

Hull, Cordell (1871-1955) United States Secretary of State (1933-1944); awarded Nobel Peace Prize for 'co-initiating the United Nations' (1945).

Hyde, Douglas (1860-1949) Irish language scholar; co-founder and President (1893-1915) of the Gaelic League; member of Seanad Éireann (1925-38); President of Ireland (1938-45).

Inskip, Thomas Walker Hobart (later **1st Viscount Caldecote**) (1876-1947) British Conservative politician; Minister for Co-ordination of Defence (1936-39); Secretary of State for Dominion Affairs (January-September 1939); Lord Chancellor (1939-40); Secretary of State for Dominion Affairs (May-October 1940).

Joyce, James (1882-1941) Irish poet, novelist and playwright; educated at Belvedere College and University College Dublin; lived in Trieste (1904-14), Zurich (1914-18) and Paris (1920-41); major works include *Dubliners* (1914), *A Portrait of the Artist as a Young Man* (1916), *Ulysses* (1922) and *Finnegan's Wake* (1939).

Kerney, Leopold Harding (1881-1962) Irish Consul, Paris (1919-22); Irish Republican Envoy in Paris (1923-25); Commercial Secretary, Paris Legation (1932-35); Minister to Spain (1935-46).

Lemass, Seán (1899-1971) TD; educated at O'Connell Schools, Dublin; took part in the 1916 Rising and the War of Independence; opposed the Anglo-Irish Treaty; interned during the Civil War; elected to Dáil Éireann (1924); founder member of Fianna Fáil (1926); Minister for Industry and Commerce (1932-39, 1941-48, 1951-54 and 1957-59); Minister for Supplies (1939-45); Tánaiste (1945-48, 1951-54 and 1957-59); Managing Director, *Irish Press* (1948-51); Taoiseach (1959-66).

Lester, Seán (1888-1959) Educated at Methodist College, Belfast; news editor of the *Freeman's Journal* (1916-23); joined the Department of External Affairs (1923); head of Publicity Office (1923-25); head of the League of Nations Section (1925-29); Irish Free State Permanent Representative to the League of Nations (1929-34); League of Nations High Commissioner in Danzig (1934-37); Deputy Secretary General of the League of Nations (1937-40); Secretary General of the League of Nations (1940-46).

Leydon, John (1895-1979) Educated at St Mel's College, Longford, and St Patrick's College, Maynooth; entered the British Civil Service (1915); served in the War Office and the Ministry of Pensions; returned to Ireland (1923); Assistant Principal Officer, Department of Finance (1923-27), Principal Officer (1927-32); Secretary, Department of Industry and Commerce (1 May 1932-1939 and 1943-55); Secretary, Department of Supplies (1939-46).

McCauley, Leo T. (1895-1974) Educated at St Columb's College, Derry, and University College Dublin; lecturer in classics (University College Dublin); Department of Finance (1925-29); transferred to the Department of External Affairs (1929); Chargé d'Affaires, Berlin (1929-33); Chargé d'Affaires, Holy See (1933-34); Consul General, New York (1934-46); Assistant Secretary, Department of External Affairs (1946-49); Ambassador to Spain (1949-54); Ambassador to Canada (1955-56); Ambassador to the Holy See (1956-62).

MacDonald, Malcolm (1901-1981) British Labour politician; Parliamentary Under-Secretary, Dominions Office (1931); Secretary of State for Dominion Affairs (November 1935-May 1938 and October 1938-January 1939); Minister for Health (1940-41); son of James Ramsay MacDonald (Prime Minister of Great Britain (1924, 1929-31 and 1931-35)).

McElligott, James J. (1893-1974) Educated at Christian Brothers School, Tralee, and at University College Dublin; entered the Civil Service in 1916 as a first division clerk, dismissed after seeing active service in the 1916 Rising; imprisoned in Stafford Jail; joined the staff of the *Statist* in London in 1919, Acting Editor (1920), Managing Editor (1922); returned to Ireland in 1922 to take up position as Assistant Secretary, Department of Finance (1922-27); Secretary, Department of Finance (1927-53).

MacEntee, Seán (1889-1984) TD; educated at St Malachy's College, Belfast, and Belfast Municipal College of Technology; took part in the 1916 Rising; elected for South Monaghan (1918-21); took part in the War of Independence; opposed the Anglo-Irish Treaty; took part in the Civil War; founder member of Fianna Fáil (1926); Joint-Treasurer of Fianna Fáil (1926-32); Minister for Finance (1932-39 and 1951-54); Minister for Industry and Commerce (1939-41); Minister for Local Government and Public Health (1941-48); Member of the Council of State from 1948; Minister for Social Welfare (1957-61); Minister for Health (1957-65); Tánaiste (1959-65).

MacMahon, General Peadar (1893-1975) General Officer Commanding, Curragh Training Camp (1922-24); Chief of Staff of the Defence Forces (1924-27); Secretary, Department of Defence (1927-58).

MacWhite, Michael (1882-1958) Served in the French Foreign Legion (1914-18); Secretary, Irish delegation to Paris Peace Conference (1920); Irish Representative to Switzerland (1921-23); Permanent Representative to the League of Nations (1923-28); Irish Minister to the United States of America (1928-38); Irish Minister to Italy (1938-50).

Biographical Details

Macaulay, William J. Babbington (1892-1964) Educated privately; Royal Navy (1914-18); Inland Revenue (1918-25); Secretary, Irish Legation, Washington (1925-30); Consul General, New York (1930-34); Minister to the Holy See (1934-40).

Machtig, Sir Eric (1889-1973) Assistant Under-Secretary, Dominions Office (1936-39), Deputy Under-Secretary, Dominions Office (1939), Permanent Under-Secretary, Dominions Office (1940-48).

Mackenzie King, William Lyon (1874-1950) Prime Minister of Canada (1921-6, 1926-30, 1935-48).

Maffey, Sir John Leader (later **Lord Rugby**) (1877-1969) Educated at Rugby and Christ's College, Oxford, entered the Indian civil service (1899); Political Agent, Khyber (1909-14); Deputy Commissioner, Peshwar (1915); Deputy Secretary to the Foreign and Political Departments, Government of India (1915-16); Private Secretary to the Viceroy (1916-20); Chief Commissioner, North West Frontier (1921-23); Governor General of Sudan (1926-33); Permanent Under-Secretary of State for the Colonies (1933-37); Director, Imperial Airways (1937-39); British Representative in Ireland (1939-49).

Moynihan, Maurice (1902-1999) Educated at Christian Brothers School, Tralee, and at University College Cork; entered the Department of Finance (1925); Secretary to the Government (1937-48 and 1951-60); Secretary, Department of the Taoiseach (1937-60); Governor of the Central Bank of Ireland (1961-69); brother of Seán Moynihan (q.v.).

Moynihan, Seán (1891-1964) Educated at Christian Brothers School, Tralee; Secretary to Eamon de Valera (1929); Assistant Editor, *Irish Press* (September 1931-March 1932); Secretary to the Government (1932-37); Assistant Secretary, Department of Finance (1937-52); brother of Maurice Moynihan (q.v.).

Murphy, Matthew (1890-1967) Entered the civil service in 1913 and served in various departments including Education, Inland Revenue, National Health Insurance and Defence; joined the Department of External Affairs in 1925; Passport Control Officer, New York (1925-29); Consul, New York (1929-33); Consul, Chicago (1933); Consul, San Francisco (1933-47); Chargé d'Affaires, Buenos Aires (with personal rank of Minister Plenipotentiary) (1947-55).

Murphy, Seán (1896-1964) Educated at Clongowes Wood College, Co Kildare, and University College Dublin; solicitor; Secretary, Irish mission to Paris (1920); Representative of the Irish Free State in Paris (1923); Administrative Officer, Department of External Affairs (1925-27); Assistant Secretary, Department of External Affairs (1927-38); Minister to France (1938-50); Ambassador to Canada (1950-55); Secretary, Department of External Affairs (1955-57).

Murphy, Sheila Geraldine (1898-1983) Dáil Éireann publicity department (1921-22); Secretariat of the Provisional Government (1922-23); Private Secretary to the Irish High Commissioner in London (1923-26); Private Secretary to Secretary, Department of External Affairs (1926-46); Archivist,

Department of External Affairs (1933-46); Second Secretary, Political and Treaty Section, Department of External Affairs (1947-49); First Secretary, Cultural Relations Division, Department of External Affairs (1949-51); First Secretary, Political Division, Department of External Affairs (1952); First Secretary, Irish Embassy, Paris (1952-59); Counsellor and Head of Economic Section, Department of External Affairs (1960-62); Assistant Secretary, Department of External Affairs (1962-64).

Nunan, Seán (1890-1981) Born in London; member of the Irish Volunteers, fought in the 1916 Rising; Clerk of Dáil Éireann (1919); Secretary to Eamon de Valera (1919-21); Registrar of the Dáil Éireann loan in the USA (1919-21); Consul General, New York (1932-38); First Secretary, London (1938-41); Consul General, Washington (1941-46); Consul General, New York (1946-47); Minister to the United States of America (1947-50); Assistant Secretary, Department of External Affairs (1950); Secretary, Department of External Affairs (1950-55).

O'Byrne, Patrick J (1893-1982) Connacht Rangers (1916-22); Department of Defence (1923-26); Secretary, Irish Trade Office, Brussels (1926-29); High Commissioner's Office, London (1929-31); Clerk, Legation to the Holy See and to Rome, and High Commissioner's Office, London (1931-34); Assistant to the Permanent Representative, Geneva (1934-36); Assistant to the Secretary, Paris (1936-40), Secretary, Madrid (1940-42); Assistant to the Chargé d'Affaires, Lisbon (1942-44); Second Secretary, Lisbon (1944-46); Chargé d'Affaires ad interim, Lisbon (1947-48); Second Secretary, Rome (1948-50); Secretary, The Hague (1951-58).

O'Ceallaigh, Seán Thomas (1883-1966) TD; educated at O'Connell Schools Dublin; took part in 1916 Rising; Ceann Comhairle (Speaker) of Dáil Éireann (1919); Irish representative to the Paris Peace Conference (1919) and representative in Paris (1919-22); opposed the Anglo-Irish Treaty; Sinn Féin Envoy to Italy; Sinn Féin Envoy to the United States of America (1924-26); founder member of Fianna Fáil (1926); Minister for Local Government and Public Health (1932-39); Tánaiste (1937-45); Minister for Finance (1939-45); President of Ireland (1945-59).

O'Connell, Kathleen (1888-1956) Personal Secretary to Eamon de Valera (1920-1956).

O'Donovan, Colman John (1893-1975) Educated at St Aloysius' College, Glasgow; Second Class Clerk, India Office (1913-16); Intelligence Officer, Dublin Brigade of the IRA (1920-21); Assistant Trade Representative, Brussels (1922-26); Department of Industry and Commerce (1926-30); First Secretary, Irish Legation, Washington (1930-33); First Secretary, Irish Free State Legation, Berlin (1933-35); First Secretary, Irish High Commission, London (1935-38); Irish Legation, Holy See (1938-40); Chargé d'Affaires, Holy See (1940-42); Chargé d'Affaires, Irish Legation, Lisbon (1942-45); Department of Local Government (1945-50); Minister to Belgium (1950-53).

O'Kelly de Gallagh, Count Gerald (1890-1968) Educated at Clongowes Wood College, Co Kildare; Sinn Féin envoy to Switzerland (1919-21); Irish representative to Belgium (1921-29); Minister Plenipotentiary to France

Biographical Details

(1929-35); Special Counsellor at Paris and Brussels Legations (1935-48); Chargé d'Affaires at Lisbon (1948-68).

Ontiveros, Juan Garcia Spanish Minister to Ireland (1939-45).

Pope Pius XII (Eugenio Pacelli) (1876-1958) Cardinal Secretary of State (1930-39); elected Pope Pius XII (1939-58).

Ryan, Frank (1902-1944) Educated at St Colman's College, Fermoy, and University College Dublin; interned during the Civil War; editor of *An Phoblacht* (1929-33); founder member of Republican Congress (1934); fought on the Republican side in the Spanish Civil War (1936-37), was wounded, and recuperated in Ireland; returned to Spain and was captured by Nationalist forces, 1 April 1938; sentenced to death, later commuted to thirty years hard labour. In August 1940, under the aegis of the Irish minister in Madrid, Leopold Kerney, Ryan was secretly released into the custody of German military intelligence. A plan to land him and the IRA's Seán Russell in Ireland by U-boat in August 1940 collapsed when Russell died at sea. Ryan died in Dresden.

Ryan, Dr James (1891-1970) TD; educated at St Peter's College, Wexford, Ring, Co Waterford, and University College Dublin; medical doctor; took part in the 1916 Rising; opposed the Anglo-Irish Treaty; founder member of Fianna Fáil (1926); Minister for Agriculture (1932-47); Minister for Health and Social Welfare (1947-48 and 1951-54); Minister for Finance (1957-65); Member of Seanad Éireann (1965-69).

Rynne, Michael Andrew Lysaght (1899-1981) Educated at Crescent College, Limerick, Our Lady's Bower, Athlone, Clongowes Wood College, Co Kildare, University College Dublin, and King's Inns, Dublin; Assistant Legal Adviser, Department of External Affairs (1932-36); Head of League of Nations Section, Department of External Affairs (1936-39); Legal Adviser, Department of External Affairs (1939-50); Assistant Secretary, Department of External Affairs (1951-53); Ambassador to Spain (1954-61).

Skelton, Oscar D. (1878-1941) Canadian Under-Secretary of State for External Relations (1925-41).

Stephenson, John (1893-1948) Assistant Secretary, Dominions Office (1936-39); Assistant Under-Secretary, Dominions Office (1939-40); Deputy Under-Secretary, Dominions Office (1940-42).

Twomey, Daniel R. (1886-1968) Secretary, Department of Agriculture (1934-47).

Walshe, Joseph Patrick (1886-1956) Educated at Mungret College, Limerick, and University College, Dublin; former Jesuit seminarian and teacher at Clongowes Wood College, Co Kildare; solicitor; served on the Irish delegation in Paris (November 1920-January 1922); Secretary to Dáil Ministry of Foreign Affairs (February 1922-August 1922); Acting Secretary, Department of External Affairs (September 1922-August 1927); Secretary, Department of External Affairs (August 1927-May 1946); Ambassador to the Holy See (May 1946-September 1954).

Warnock, William (1911-1986) Educated at High School, Dublin, and Trinity College Dublin; Third Secretary, Department of External Affairs (1935-38); First Secretary, Berlin (1938-39); Chargé d'Affaires ad interim, Berlin (1939-43); First Secretary, Department of External Affairs, Dublin (1944-46); Chargé d'Affaires en titre, Stockholm (1947-50); Envoy Extraordinary and Minister Plenipotentiary to Switzerland (1950-54); Assistant Secretary, Department of External Affairs (1954-56); Envoy Extraordinary and Minister Plenipotentiary to the Federal Republic of Germany (1946-59); Ambassador to Germany (1959-62); Ambassador to Switzerland (1962-64) and, concurrently, Ambassador to Austria (1963-64); Ambassador to India (1964-67); Ambassador to Canada (1967-70); Ambassador to the United States of America (1970-73); Ambassador to Switzerland (1973-76).

Wood, Edward, Viscount (later **1st Earl Halifax**) (1881-1959) British Conservative politician; Viceroy of India (1926-31); Lord Privy Seal (1935-37); Lord President of the Council (1937-38); Foreign Secretary (1938-40); British Ambassador to Washington (1941-46).

List of Documents Reproduced

1939

No.	Title	Main Subject	Date	Page
1	Memorandum, Rynne to Walshe	'Irish neutrality in practice'	1 Sept.	1
2	Letter, Warnock to Walshe	Berlin on the eve of war	2 Sept.	5
3	Confidential report, Cremin to Walshe	Paris on the eve of war	2 Sept.	6
4	Confidential report, Cremins to Walshe	Situation in Switzerland	2 Sept.	7
5	Confidential report, Kerney to Walshe	Spanish neutrality	2 Sept.	7
6	Confidential report, Seán Murphy to Walshe	Situation in Paris	4 Sept.	8
7	Confidential report, Kerney to Walshe	Spain's attitude towards outbreak of war	5 Sept.	10
8	Confidential report, Brennan to Walshe	US opinion on the outbreak of war	5 Sept.	10
9	Memorandum, Rynne to Walshe	'Furtherance of neutrality policy'	5 Sept.	11
10	Cabinet minutes	Appointment of British diplomatic representative in Dublin	6 Sept.	12
11	Confidential report, Brennan to Walshe	Meeting with Lord Lothian	7 Sept.	12
12	Confidential report, Brennan to Walshe	US neutrality	7 Sept.	13
13	Letter, Boland to Warnock	Communications with Berlin	8 Sept.	13
14	Memorandum, Kerney to Walshe	'Ireland's attitude in European War'	9 Sept.	14
15	Memorandum by Walshe	Mission to London	undated, Sept.	15
16	Confidential report, Brennan to Walshe	US neutrality	11 Sept.	20
17	Confidential report, Cremins to Walshe	Situation in Geneva	11 Sept.	21
18	Cabinet minutes	Belligerent Naval Craft	12 Sept.	23
19	Aide mémoire to belligerent states	Restrictions on use of Irish territorial waters	12 Sept.	23

List of documents reproduced

No.	Title	Main Subject	Date	Page
20	Letter, Boland to Kerney	Spanish neutrality	14 Sept.	24
21	Confidential report, Warnock to Walshe	Opinion on war in Berlin/situation in city	14 Sept.	24
22	Memorandum, Kerney to Walshe	Frank Ryan	14 Sept.	26
23	Letter, Walshe to Dobrzyński	German invasion of Poland	15 Sept.	27
24	Memorandum, Rynne to Walshe	Emergency powers	15 Sept.	28
25	Confidential report, MacWhite to Walshe	Government and public opinion on war in Rome	15 Sept.	31
26	Memorandum, Rynne to Walshe	'The maintenance of Neutrality'	16 Sept.	32
27	Confidential report, Brennan to Walshe	Lack of news on situation in Ireland	16 Sept.	34
28	Telegram, External Affairs to Macaulay	Ireland's neutrality	19 Sept.	35
29	Letter, Chamberlain to de Valera	Appointment of Maffey and need for close contact	19 Sept.	35
30	Letter, Dulanty to Hore-Belisha	Equipment for Irish Defence Forces	19 Sept.	36
31	Letter, Maurice Moynihan to MacMahon	Matters arising from neutrality	21 Sept.	36
32	Government minutes	British diplomatic representative in Ireland	22 Sept.	37
33	Letter, de Valera to Chamberlain	Appointment of Maffey	22 Sept.	37
34	Confidential report, Kerney to Walshe	Wartime measures in Spain	22 Sept.	38
35	Confidential report, Warnock to Walshe	War on eastern front/domestic conditions in Germany	22 Sept.	39
36	Letter, Warnock to Boland	Censorship and communications	22 Sept.	41
37	Memorandum, Maffey to Eden	Meetings with de Valera and Walshe	24 Sept.	41
38	Letter, Chamberlain to de Valera	Sir John Maffey	25 Sept.	48
39	Memorandum, Rynne to Walshe	Proposed statement by de Valera in Dáil	26 Sept.	48
40	Memorandum by Rynne	Basis of Irish neutrality	undated, Sept.	53
41	Telegram, Walshe to Brennan	Inform State Department of Irish neutrality	29 Sept.	60

Documents on Irish Foreign Policy, Volume VI, 1939–1941

No.	Title	Main Subject	Date	Page
42	Telegram, Walshe to Seán Murphy	Sir John Maffey	30 Sept.	60
43	Confidential report, Warnock to Walshe	Russo-German Pact	30 Sept.	60
44	Telegram, External Affairs to Cremins	Irish declaration of neutrality	4 Oct.	62
45	Telegram, Brennan to Walshe	United States neutrality legislation and Irish neutrality	4 Oct.	62
46	Confidential report, O'Donovan to Walshe	Ireland and Poland	4 Oct.	62
47	Memorandum, Kerney to Walshe	Frank Ryan	5 Oct.	63
48	Confidential report, Warnock to Walshe	German domestic and foreign policy	7 Oct.	64
49	Confidential report, Matthew Murphy to Walshe	Attitudes towards European war on US west coast	9 Oct.	65
50	Letter, Warnock to Boland	Appointment of Irish Minister to Berlin	9 Oct.	67
51	Letter, Boland to Warnock	Instructions on what to report from Germany	10 Oct.	68
52	Letter, Seán Murphy to Walshe	Impressions of situation in France	12 Oct.	69
53	Letter, Warnock to Boland	Appointment of Irish Minister to Berlin	17 Oct.	71
54	Minute by Boland	Radio broadcast from Hamburg concerning Ireland	19 Oct.	71
55	Memorandum, Rynne to Walshe	British press and neutrality	20 Oct.	72
56	Confidential report, Warnock to Walshe	General report on affairs in Germany	21 Oct.	72
57	Aide mémoire, Brennan to Hull	United States shipping and Irish ports	25 Oct.	74
58	Confidential report, MacWhite to Walshe	Overview of options for Italian foreign policy	25 Oct.	74
59	Letter, Boland to Warnock	Irish Minister to Berlin/great interest in Warnock's reports	26 Oct.	76
60	Confidential report, Warnock to Walshe	German attitudes towards Ireland	26 Oct.	77
61	Confidential report, Kerney to Walshe	Spanish-Irish trade negotiations	26 Oct.	78

List of documents reproduced

No.	Title	Main Subject	Date	Page
62	Minute, Boland to Sheila Murphy	Appointment of Slovak Consul to Ireland	26 Oct.	80
63	Memorandum, Cremins to Walshe	Forthcoming session of League Assembly	27 Oct.	81
64	Telegram, Walshe to Hearne	Instructions re Irish neutrality policy	31 Oct.	83
65	Minute by Walshe	Meeting with Hempel re safety of Irish shipping	1 Nov.	84
66	Confidential report, Hearne to Walshe	The basis of Irish neutrality	8 Nov.	85
67	Confidential report, Cremins to Walshe	View from Geneva on European geopolitics and developments in war	11 Nov.	87
68	Memorandum, Hearne to Walshe	Development of Irish-Canadian relations	14 Nov.	88
69	Letter, Brennan to Walshe	Combat zones in the Atlantic and Irish shipping	14 Nov.	91
70	Confidential report, Warnock to Walshe	German concerns re shipment of contraband through Ireland	14 Nov.	93
71	Telegram, Brennan to Walshe	Protest to State Department is front page news	14 Nov.	94
72	Confidential report, Kerney to Walshe	Views on war at diplomatic reception in Madrid	16 Nov.	94
73	Telegram, Brennan to Walshe	US shipping and war zone	16 Nov.	95
74	Letter, Walshe to Leydon	Transhipment, US shipping and Irish neutrality	18 Nov.	95
75	Confidential report, Warnock to Walshe	German propaganda/events in Poland/Austria/Bohemia and Moravia	21 Nov.	96
76	Report, Kerney to Walshe	Frank Ryan	21 Nov.	98
77	Confidential report, Brennan to Walshe	Sino-Japanese relations	22 Nov	99
78	Letter, Walshe to Hearne	Overview of Irish foreign policy with instructions for action in Canada	29 Nov.	100
79	Report, Warnock to Walshe	Shipping between Ireland and Britain	30 Nov.	102
80	Confidential report, Brennan to Walshe	Russian invasion of Finland	1 Dec.	103

Documents on Irish Foreign Policy, Volume VI, 1939–1941

No.	Title	Main Subject	Date	Page
81	Confidential report, Warnock to Walshe	Russian invasion of Finland	2 Dec.	103
82	Minute, Walshe to Rynne	Forthcoming session of League of Nations Assembly	4 Dec.	105
83	Confidential report, Warnock to Walshe	Overview of German foreign and domestic policies	6 Dec.	105
84	Letter, Walshe to Maurice Moynihan	Wartime British-Irish trade	7 Dec.	107
85	Telegram, de Valera to Hambro	de Valera unable to attend League of Nations Assembly	8 Dec.	107
86	Memorandum by External Affairs	20th Assembly of the League of Nations	8 Dec.	107
87	Confidential report, Brennan to Walshe	Visit to Boston	12 Dec.	108
88	Memorandum, Rynne to Walshe	Neutrality and recruitment for belligerent armies	12 Dec.	110
89	Report, Cremins to Walshe	Finnish appeal to the League of Nations	12 Dec.	112
90	Confidential report, O'Donovan to Walshe	Italo-German relations	13 Dec.	113
91	Letter, Boland to MacWhite	Appointment of Slovak Consul in Dublin	13 Dec.	114
92	Telegram, Walshe to Hearne	Instructions re communication of Irish neutrality to Canadians	13 Dec.	115
93	Confidential report, Warnock to Walshe	Public opinion and attitudes in Germany	14 Dec.	115
94	Report, Cremins to Walshe	Russo-Finnish War/expulsion of Russia from League of Nations	15 Dec.	118
95	Letter, Boland to MacWhite	Appointment of Slovak Consul in Dublin	15 Dec.	119
96	Letter, Walshe to Dulanty	Case of Barnes and Richards (Coventry bombings)	19 Dec.	119
97	Confidential report, Dulanty to Walshe	Case of Barnes and Richards (Coventry bombings)	21 Dec.	120
98	Aide mémoire, Hearne to Skelton	Explanation of neutrality policy	22 Dec.	121
99	Report, Kerney to Walshe	Frank Ryan	23 Dec.	122
100	Report, Kerney to Walshe	Frank Ryan	27 Dec.	123
101	Confidential report, Brennan to Walshe	Appointment of Taylor as United States Vatican Representative	27 Dec.	125

List of documents reproduced

No.	Title	Main Subject	Date	Page
102	Confidential report, Macaulay to Walshe	Consistory of Cardinals	28 Dec.	125
103	Memorandum, Rynne to Walshe	Case of Barnes and Richards (Coventry bombings)	30 Dec.	127
104	Telegram, External Affairs to Warnock	Civilian traffic by sea between Ireland and Britain	30 Dec.	128

1940

No.	Title	Main Subject	Date	Page
105	Statement by Cremins	Russian invasion of Finland	1 Jan.	129
106	Confidential report, Warnock to Walshe	Christmas and New Year in Berlin	3 Jan.	129
107	Memorandum, Boland to Walshe	Establishing diplomatic relations with Portugal	3 Jan.	131
108	Draft letter, Walshe to Dulanty	Establishing diplomatic relations with Portugal	3 Jan.	132
109	Confidential report, Warnock to Walshe	Resignation of Hore-Belisha, war in Finland, food supplies, press reports on Ireland	13 Jan.	133
110	Memorandum, Rynne to Walshe	Change of Constitution and international treaties	19 Jan.	135
111	Confidential report, Hearne to Walshe	Irish-Canadian relations, explaining neutrality in Canada	24 Jan.	137
112	Telegram, External Affairs to Washington Legation	Case for reprieve for Barnes and Richards (Coventry bombings)	26 Jan.	140
113	Letter, Kerney to Walshe	Frank Ryan	26 Jan.	141
114	Confidential report, Dulanty to Walshe	Possible attempt to kidnap Maffey	26 Jan.	141
115	Confidential report, Dulanty to Walshe	Appointment of Minister to Berlin	27 Jan.	141
116	Letter, de Valera to Eden	Case for reprieve for Barnes and Richards (Coventry bombings)	29 Jan.	142
117	Minute, Boland to Walshe	German religious persecution in Poland	29 Jan.	143
118	Letter, Walshe to Dulanty	Ammunition supplies for Defence Forces	1 Feb.	144

Documents on Irish Foreign Policy, Volume VI, 1939–1941

No.	Title	Main Subject	Date	Page
119	Minute, Walshe to Dulanty	Draft letter to Neville Chamberlain	2 Feb.	145
120	Letter, de Valera to Chamberlain	Case for reprieve for Barnes and Richards	2 Feb.	146
121	Telegram, Washington Legation to External Affairs	Case for reprieve for Barnes and Richards	3 Feb.	146
122	Letter, de Valera to Chamberlain	Case for reprieve for Barnes and Richards	5 Feb.	146
123	Confidential report, Dulanty to Walshe	Case for reprieve for Barnes and Richards	6 Feb	147
124	Note for file by Walshe	Case for reprieve for Barnes and Richards	7 Feb.	148
125	Memorandum by Rynne	British intentions in regard to Ireland	7 Feb.	149
126	Confidential report, Warnock to Walshe	Executions of Barnes and Richards	8 Feb.	155
127	Letter, Walshe to Ontiveros	Frank Ryan	23 Feb.	156
128	Telegram, Walshe to Hearne	Basis of Irish neutrality	26 Feb.	156
129	Confidential report, MacWhite to Walshe	Negative impact of IRA bombings on Irish prestige internationally	27 Feb.	157
130	Cabinet minutes	Irish participation in New York World's Fair	28 Feb.	158
131	Confidential report, Warnock to Walshe	*Altmark* incident, German industry, possibility of hostilities in western Europe	2 Mar.	158
132	Letter, Walshe to Dulanty	Anti-Irish press campaign in USA	2 Mar.	160
133	Extracts from annual report	Irish Consulates in the United States	6 Mar.	161
134	Confidential report, Brennan to Walshe	David Gray	7 Mar.	162
135	Confidential report, Matthew Murphy to Walshe	Meeting with Wei Kuo Chiang	7 Mar.	163
136	Letter, Macaulay to Walshe	Appointment of Archbishop of Dublin	8 Mar.	163
137	Confidential report, Warnock to Walshe	Conclusion of peace in Finland, affairs in Bohemia and Moravia	16 Mar.	164

List of documents reproduced

No.	Title	Main Subject	Date	Page
138	Memorandum by John Leydon	British-Irish trade relations	19 Mar.	165
139	Confidential report, Dulanty to Walshe	Situation in Finland	20 Mar.	166
140	Confidential report, Macaulay to Walshe	David Gray	20 Mar.	167
141	Memorandum by Maurice Moynihan	Trade discussions with Britain	21 Mar.	167
142	Confidential report, MacWhite to Walshe	David Gray	21 Mar.	168
143	Memorandum by Maurice Moynihan	Trade discussions with Britain	28 Mar.	168
144	Memorandum, Walshe to de Valera	Trade discussions with Britain	29 Mar.	169
145	Despatch, de Valera to Eden	Trade discussions with Britain	29 Mar.	169
146	Minute by Maurice Moynihan	Trade discussions with Britain	29 Mar.	170
147	Confidential report, Kerney to Walshe	Conversation with Spanish foreign minister	29 Mar.	170
148	Minute by Maurice Moynihan	Trade discussions with Britain	4 Apr.	171
149	Confidential report, Cremins to Walshe	German invasion of Denmark and Norway	10 Apr.	171
150	Confidential report, Dulanty to Walshe	Trade discussions with Britain	10 Apr.	175
151	Confidential report, Cremins to Walshe	German invasion of Denmark and Norway	12 Apr.	176
152	Letter, Walshe to Kerney	Propaganda in Spain in relation to partition	12 Apr.	178
153	Confidential report, MacWhite to Walshe	Italo-German relations	15 Apr.	179
154	Memorandum by Nunan	Anti-de Valera cartoon in the *Daily Mirror*	17 Apr.	181
155	Annual report	Berlin Legation (1939-40)	19 Apr.	181
156	Cabinet minutes	Trade negotiations with Britain	19 Apr.	186
157	Confidential report, Warnock to Walshe	German invasion of Denmark and Norway	20 Apr.	186
158	Letter, Kerney to Walshe	Frank Ryan	23 Apr.	186
159	Memorandum, Rynne to Horan	Irish refugee policy	23 Apr.	188

Documents on Irish Foreign Policy, Volume VI, 1939–1941

No.	Title	Main Subject	Date	Page
160	Confidential report, Dulanty to Walshe	Irish refugee policy	26 Apr.	188
161	Minute by Maurice Moynihan	British-Irish trade discussions	29 Apr.	189
162	Minute by Kerney	Frank Ryan	29 Apr.	190
163	Notes by Kerney	Frank Ryan	30 Apr.	190
164	Memorandum, Walshe to de Valera	Alleged unfriendly references to Ireland in German radio broadcasts	30 Apr.	190
165	Memorandum, Walshe to de Valera	British-Irish trade discussions	1 May	192
166	Minutes	British-Irish trade discussions	1 May	193
167	Confidential report, MacWhite to Walshe	Italy moving towards entering conflict on German side	2 May	197
168	Confidential report, Warnock to Walshe	German victory over British forces in Norway	4 May	198
169	Report, Walshe to de Valera	Meeting with Eden on British-Irish relations	6 May	200
170	Confidential report, Seán Murphy to Walshe	German invasion of the Low Countries	11 May	203
171	Instructions, External Affairs to all missions	Action to be taken in the event of emergency	11 May	203
172	Confidential report, Seán Murphy to Walshe	War in France and the Low Countries	14 May	208
173	Confidential report, Dulanty to Walshe	Meeting with Neville Chamberlain	14 May	209
174	Confidential report, Brennan to Walshe	United States views on the German advance in western Europe	14 May	211
175	Telegram, External Affairs to Warnock	Taoiseach's speech in Galway on invasion of Belgium and the Netherlands	15 May	212
176	Letter, de Valera to Chamberlain	Role of Chamberlain in strengthening British-Irish relations	15 May	212
177	Telegram, MacWhite to External Affairs	Situation in Italy tense	15 May	213
178	Confidential report, Macaulay to Walshe	Pessimism in Vatican regarding European situation	18 May	213
179	Confidential report, Warnock to Walshe	German view that war has finally begun	18 May	214

List of documents reproduced

No.	Title	Main Subject	Date	Page
180	Confidential report, Seán Murphy to Walshe	Bleak outlook in France as German forces advance	18 May	215
181	Confidential report, Brennan to Walshe	American political and public opinion on war in Europe	21 May	216
182	Minutes	Meeting between Irish representatives and representatives of British Service Departments and the Dominions Office	23 May	217
183	Minutes	Meeting between Irish representatives and representatives of British Service Departments and the Dominions Office	24 May	222
184	Telegram, External Affairs to Warnock	Defence of Ireland from external attack	28 May	227
185	Confidential report, Warnock to Walshe	German advances in western Europe	28 May	227
186	Telegram, Warnock to Walshe	Taoiseach's speech in Galway on invasion of Belgium and Netherlands	30 May	229
187	Confidential report, Seán Murphy to Walshe	German military intentions in France	3 June	229
188	Confidential report, O'Donovan to Walshe	Appointment of Archbishop of Dublin	3 June	230
189	Confidential report, Brennan to Walshe	Change in United States official policy on the war in Europe	11 June	230
190	Draft Letter, Walshe to Leydon and Ferguson	Production of military ordnance in Ireland	12 June	231
191	Memorandum, Walshe to de Valera	German questioning of Irish neutrality	17 June	232
192	Memorandum by Rynne	Appreciation of the war situation	17 June	233
193	Note by MacDonald	MacDonald-de Valera conversation	17 June	234
194	Confidential report, Seán Murphy to Walshe	Journey from Paris to Ascain	18 June	244
195	Telegram, Macaulay to External Affairs	Appointment of Archbishop of Dublin	19 June	249
196	Memorandum, Walshe to de Valera	'Britain's inevitable defeat'	21 June	249
197	Confidential report, Seán Murphy to Walshe	French capitulation	21 June	250

xliii

Documents on Irish Foreign Policy, Volume VI, 1939–1941

No.	Title	Main Subject	Date	Page
198	Note by MacDonald	MacDonald-de Valera conversations	23 June	252
199	Memorandum by Rynne	Appreciation of the war situation	24 June	260
200	Memorandum by Rynne	Suggested action in intensified emergency	24 June	261
201	Telegram, External Affairs to Macaulay	Italian entry into Second World War	25 June	263
202	Confidential report, Hearne to Walshe	Views on the war situation	26 June	264
203	Cabinet minutes	Irish reply to British proposals for a united Ireland	27 June	266
204	Memorandum by Maurice Moynihan	Irish reply to British proposals for a united Ireland	27 June	266
205	Confidential report, Hearne to Walshe	Canadian interest in Irish affairs	27 June	267
206	Confidential report, Seán Murphy to Walshe	De Gaulle – French capitulation	28 June	268
207	Memorandum by Walshe	Résumé of talks between de Valera and MacDonald	28 June	269
208	Memorandum, Walshe to de Valera	Comments on British proposals for a united Ireland	1 July	271
209	Memorandum, Walshe to de Valera	Developments in the war situation	1 July	272
210	Letter, Rynne to Walshe	The 'Region of War' theory and the cession of Northern Ireland	1 July	275
211	Confidential report, Brennan to Walshe	United States views on Britain's war effort	3 July	277
212	Telegram, Walshe to Warnock	Countering German views on Irish neutrality	4 July	278
213	Letter, de Valera to Chamberlain	Irish reply to British proposals for a united Ireland	4 July	278
214	Telegram, External Affairs to all missions	Irish determination to remain neutral	5 July	279
215	Confidential report, Dulanty to Walshe	Irish reply to British proposals for a united Ireland	5 July	280
216	Memorandum by Walshe	Meeting with Hempel: German attitude towards Ireland	6 July	281

List of documents reproduced

No.	Title	Main Subject	Date	Page
217	Confidential report, Dulanty to Walshe	Irish reply to British proposals for a united Ireland	8 July	281
218	Confidential report, Seán Murphy to Walshe	France's international position, past, present and future	8 July	283
219	Confidential report, Brennan to Walshe	American public opinion forecasts British defeat	9 July	286
220	Confidential report, Seán Murphy to Walshe	British attack on French fleet at Mers-el-Kebir	10 July	287
221	Memorandum, Walshe to de Valera	Neutrality and Ireland's international position	11 July	289
222	Telegram, Walshe to Brennan	Explaining Ireland's neutrality in the USA	11 July	292
223	Telegram, External Affairs to Warnock	German questioning of Ireland's neutrality	13 July	293
224	Telegram, Seán Murphy to External Affairs	Interview with French foreign ministry official on British attack on French fleet	15 July	293
225	Memorandum, Walshe to de Valera	Ireland's position vis-à-vis the international situation	15 July	294
226	Letter, Archer to Walshe	Interception of radio transmissions	15 July	297
227	Letter, Walshe to de Valera	Interview with Maffey re anti-Irish propaganda in the British press/illicit British activities in Ireland	15 July	297
228	Telegram, External Affairs to Brennan	Explaining Ireland's neutrality in the USA	16 July	299
229	Letter, Walshe to Dulanty	Representations to Dominions Office on illicit British activities in Ireland	17 July	300
230	Memorandum by Walshe	Visit of Hempel/German intentions in regard to Ireland	18 July	300
231	Telegram, Warnock to External Affairs	German intentions in regard to Ireland	20 July	302
232	Telegram, External Affairs to Warnock	German and British intentions in regard to Ireland	20 July	302
233	Telegram, External Affairs to MacWhite	Inquires as to attitude of Vatican towards totalitarian states and Vichy France	20 July	302
234	Telegram, Walshe to Brennan	Explaining Ireland's neutrality in the USA	21 July	303

Documents on Irish Foreign Policy, Volume VI, 1939–1941

No.	Title	Main Subject	Date	Page
235	Telegram, Walshe to Hearne	Irish determination to remain neutral	21 July	304
236	Telegram, Walshe to Seán Murphy	Maintaining close touch with Papal Nuncio to obtain views of French Right	22 July	304
237	Telegram, Brennan to External Affairs	Difficulties of explaining Irish neutrality in USA	23 July	305
238	Confidential report, Dulanty to Walshe	British-Irish trade relations	23 July	305
239	Draft confidential report, Dulanty to Walshe	British propaganda and military intentions in regard to Ireland	23 July	306
240	Confidential report, Dulanty to Walshe	Mining of St George's Channel/ British-Irish trade relations/ equipment for Defence Forces	24 July	307
241	Confidential report, Dulanty to Walshe	British-Irish trade relations	25 July	308
242	Telegram, Cremins to External Affairs	Avenol's resignation as League of Nations Secretary General	26 July	309
243	Confidential report, Dulanty to Walshe	British intentions in regard to Ireland	27 July	309
244	Telegram, Seán Murphy to Walshe	Courtesy visit to French foreign minister	28 July	310
245	Letter, Walshe to de Valera	Supply of military equipment to Ireland	29 July	311
246	Confidential report, Kerney to Walshe	Frank Ryan	29 July	312
247	Letter, Walshe to Gray	United States press propaganda hostile to Ireland	31 July	314
248	Confidential report, Brennan to Walshe	German intentions in regard to Britain and US support for Britain	1 Aug.	314
249	Memorandum by External Affairs	Meeting between de Valera, Maffey and Harrison	2 Aug.	315
250	Telegram, External Affairs to Warnock	Luftwaffe sinking of the SS *Kerry Head* off Cork coast	2 Aug.	316
251	Confidential report, Dulanty to Walshe	Anti-Irish propaganda in the British press	5 Aug.	316
252	Memorandum by Aiken	Meeting between de Valera, Maffey and Harrison	6 Aug.	317

List of documents reproduced

No.	Title	Main Subject	Date	Page
253	Telegram, External Affairs to Seán Murphy	Rumour in Vichy of German invasion of Ireland	8 Aug.	317
254	Confidential report, Seán Murphy to Walshe	Franco-German co-operation	8 Aug.	318
255	Letter, O'Byrne to Seán Murphy	Samuel Beckett	8 Aug.	318
256	Memorandum by Walshe	'Have we a guarantee against invasion from the German government?'	9 Aug.	319
257	Memorandum by Walshe	Meeting with Hempel	9 Aug.	320
258	Memorandum by Walshe	'Has Britain guaranteed not to invade us?'	9 Aug.	320
259	Confidential report, Dulanty to Walshe	Activities of Charles Tegart	9 Aug.	321
260	Letter, Brennan to Scott	Rationale for Ireland's neutrality	12 Aug.	322
261	Memorandum, Gallagher to de Valera and Walshe	Shortwave transmission of news bulletins in Morse	12 Aug.	322
262	Memorandum, Gallagher to de Valera	Establishment of a high-speed Morse station	12 Aug.	323
263	Telegram, External Affairs to Seán Murphy	Receipt of reports from Ascain	15 Aug.	325
264	Cover letter and memorandum by Walshe	Impact of German blockade of Britain on Irish trade and shipping	19 Aug.	325
265	Letter, Walshe to de Valera	Impact of German blockade of Britain on Irish trade and shipping	19 Aug.	329
266	Confidential report, Dulanty to Walshe	Battle of Britain/conditions in London	19 Aug.	330
267	Confidential report, Dulanty to Walshe	Battle of Britain	19 Aug.	332
268	Confidential report, Brennan to Walshe	John Cudahy	20 Aug.	332
269	Confidential report, Warnock to Walshe	References to Ireland in the German press	20 Aug.	333
270	Memorandum, Walshe to de Valera	British request for civilian pilot training in Ireland/transhipment of goods	21 Aug.	334
271	Confidential report, Dulanty to Walshe	British-Irish trade relations/transhipment	23 Aug.	335

Documents on Irish Foreign Policy, Volume VI, 1939–1941

No.	Title	Main Subject	Date	Page
272	Telegram, Warnock to External Affairs	Luftwaffe sinking of the SS *Kerry Head*	23 Aug.	337
273	Telegram, Seán Murphy to External Affairs	Conditions in Paris	23 Aug.	337
274	Confidential report, Dulanty to Walshe	Life in London/Neville Chamberlain's health/munitions production	24 Aug.	337
275	Telegram, Kerney to External Affairs	Frank Ryan	24 Aug.	339
276	Telegram, External Affairs to Warnock	Luftwaffe bombing of areas in Wexford (Campile)	26 Aug.	339
277	Confidential report, Kerney to Walshe	Frank Ryan	26 Aug.	339
278	Confidential report, Seán Murphy to Walshe	Conditions in Paris	27 Aug.	343
279	Letter, Walshe to Ryan	Release of Frank Ryan	27 Aug.	346
280	Telegram, External Affairs to Warnock	Luftwaffe bombing of areas in Wexford (Campile)	28 Aug.	347
281	Telegram, External Affairs to Seán Murphy	Dealing with Irish citizens in occupied areas	29 Aug.	347
282	Memorandum by Walshe	Response of British troops in Northern Ireland in the event of a German invasion of Ireland	30 Aug.	348
283	Telegram, External Affairs to Warnock	Impact of German blockade of Britain on Irish trade and shipping	30 Aug.	348
284	Telegram, External Affairs to Brennan	Luftwaffe bombing of areas in Wexford (Campile)	30 Aug.	350
285	Confidential report, Brennan to Walshe	American war propaganda	3 Sept.	350
286	Telegram, External Affairs to Warnock	Sinking of *Kerry Head*/ Campile bombing	5 Sept.	351
287	Telegram, Warnock to External Affairs	Allied bombing raids on Germany	5 Sept.	351
288	Telegram, External Affairs to Warnock	Dealing with Irish citizens in occupied France – possible German facilitation	6 Sept.	351
289	Memorandum by Rynne	Transhipment	6 Sept.	352
290	Notes by Kerney	Frank Ryan	10 Sept.	354

List of documents reproduced

No.	Title	Main Subject	Date	Page
291	Memorandum by Boland for Aiken	Impact of German blockade of Britain on Irish trade and shipping	11 Sept.	354
292	Telegram, Warnock to Walshe	Dealing with Irish citizens in occupied France – possible German facilitation	11 Sept.	355
293	Telegram, Warnock to Walshe	Campile bombing	14 Sept.	355
294	Memorandum, McElligott to Maurice Moynihan	Trade agreement with Britain	19 Sept.	356
295	Letter, Boland to O'Connell	Trade agreement with Britain	19 Sept.	359
296	Note with covering letter, Boland to Brady	Trade agreement with Britain	19 Sept.	360
297	Telegram, External Affairs to Kerney	Frank Ryan	19 Sept.	361
298	Letter, O'Kelly de Gallagh to Seán Murphy	Consular cases of Irish citizens in France	20 Sept.	361
299	Telegram, Seán Murphy to External Affairs	Franco-German tensions between Vichy and Occupied France	23 Sept.	363
300	Cabinet minutes	Trade agreement with Britain	24 Sept.	363
301	Telegram, O'Donovan to External Affairs	Archbishops of Dublin and Galway	25 Sept.	364
302	Telegram, External Affairs to Warnock	Campile bombing	26 Sept.	364
303	Letter, Hearne to Walshe	Events in Canada	26 Sept.	365
304	Telegram, External Affairs to O'Donovan	Archbishop of Dublin	26 Sept.	366
305	Telegram, External Affairs to Warnock	Campile bombing	27 Sept.	366
306	Telegram, O'Donovan to External Affairs	Archbishop of Dublin	30 Sept.	367
307	Telegram, O'Donovan to External Affairs	Archbishop of Dublin	4 Oct.	367
308	Confidential report, Dulanty to Walshe	London Blitz	5 Oct.	368
309	Statement by External Affairs	Campile bombing	8 Oct.	370
310	Memorandum by External Affairs for de Valera	Establishment of Legation in Berne	undated, Oct.	370

xlix

Documents on Irish Foreign Policy, Volume VI, 1939–1941

No.	Title	Main Subject	Date	Page
311	Confidential report, Cremins to Walshe	Presentation of credentials at Berne	11 Oct.	371
312	Letter, Walshe to Dulanty	Exchange of meteorological data with Britain	17 Oct.	372
313	Letter, Walshe to de Valera	British military intentions in regard to Ireland	18 Oct.	373
314	Memorandum by Rynne	Ireland's continued membership of the League of Nations	21 Oct.	375
315	Telegram, Seán Murphy to External Affairs	Destruction of documents	22 Oct.	378
316	Letter, de Valera to Cranborne	Appointment to the Dominions Office	23 Oct.	378
317	Letter, Walshe to Maurice Moynihan	Measures to be taken by External Affairs in the event of an invasion/maintenance of communications with outside world	25 Oct.	379
318	Confidential report, Dulanty to Walshe	London Blitz	25 Oct.	380
319	Telegram, External Affairs to Warnock	Need for more detailed reporting from Berlin	1 Nov.	382
320	Telegram, External Affairs to Kerney	Avoiding upset to Spanish government	5 Nov.	382
321	Telegram, Warnock to Walshe	Conditions and opinions in Germany	5 Nov.	382
322	Telegram, Warnock to Walshe	German maritime blockade and British-Irish trade	6 Nov.	383
323	Telegram, Colman O'Donovan to External Affairs	Archbishop of Dublin	7 Nov.	383
324	Telegram, Walshe to Brennan	Anti-Irish propaganda in the US	7 Nov.	384
325	Telegram, de Valera to conference of the American Association for the Recognition of an Independent Irish Republic	Explanation of Irish neutrality	8 Nov.	384
326	Telegram, Brennan to Hearne	Explanation of Irish neutrality	9 Nov.	385
327	Memorandum by Archer	Possible diplomatic offensive by Britain in the US against Irish neutrality	9 Nov.	386
328	Telegram, Walshe to O'Donovan	Archbishop of Dublin	11 Nov.	386

l

List of documents reproduced

No.	Title	Main Subject	Date	Page
329	Telegram, Brennan to Walshe	Explanation of Irish neutrality	11 Nov.	387
330	Telegram, External Affairs to Irish Legations in Ottawa, Geneva, Rome, Madrid, Vichy	De Valera's reply to Churchill over latter's call for British use of Treaty ports	12 Nov.	387
331	Letter, Walshe to Gray	Role of British fleet in the protection of Ireland and Irish waters	12 Nov.	387
332	Telegram, Walshe to Seán Murphy	Calls for more regular reports	12 Nov.	389
333	Telegram, Walshe to Warnock	Impact of German blockade on Britain on Irish trade and shipping	13 Nov.	389
334	Memorandum by Walshe	Churchill's call for British use of Treaty ports	13 Nov.	389
335	Telegram, Hearne to Walshe	Anti-Irish press campaign in Canada	14 Nov.	391
336	Letter, Cremins to Lester	Cessation of representation to the League of Nations	14 Nov.	391
337	Telegram, External Affairs to Kerney	Anti-Irish press campaigns in USA and Britain dying down	16 Nov.	392
338	Telegram, Warnock to Walshe	Impact of German blockade of Britain on Irish trade and shipping	16 Nov.	392
339	Telegram, Walshe to Cremins	Instructions as to reporting from Berne	18 Nov.	392
340	Telegram, Walshe to Brennan	Move to explain policy on ports to US audiences	18 Nov.	393
341	Telegram, Seán Murphy to Walshe	Politics and public opinion in France	18 Nov.	393
342	Telegram, Brennan to Walshe	Queries regarding arguments proposed for use in the US to explain and defend Irish neutrality	19 Nov.	394
343	Telegram, Walshe to Brennan	Replies to queries regarding arguments to be used in the US to explain and defend Irish neutrality	21 Nov.	395
344	Letter, Hearne to Walshe	Explaining and defending Ireland's neutrality in Canada	22 Nov.	395
345	Telegram, Walshe to Seán Murphy	Request for information on French political landscape	25 Nov.	399

Documents on Irish Foreign Policy, Volume VI, 1939–1941

No.	Title	Main Subject	Date	Page
346	Telegram, Walshe to Brennan	American views on Irish refusal to allow Britain use of Treaty ports/David Gray	26 Nov.	399
347	Confidential report, Dulanty to Walshe	Hitler-Molotov meeting/war in the Balkans	26 Nov.	400
348	Memorandum, Boland to Walshe	Ireland's financial contribution to the League of Nations	26 Nov.	400
349	Letter, Seán Murphy to Joyce	Lucia Joyce	26 Nov.	402
350	Confidential report, Dulanty to Walshe	Professor Lindemann and Churchill	27 Nov.	402
351	Confidential report, Dulanty to Walshe	Exchange of meteorological data with Britain	27 Nov.	402
352	Letter, Walshe to Seán Moynihan	Emergency arrangements in External Affairs	27 Nov.	404
353	Confidential report, Brennan to Walshe	US views on world war	28 Nov.	404
354	Telegram, Walshe to Seán Murphy	Visit to Paris	28 Nov.	406
355	Minute by Walshe	Ireland's financial contribution to the League of Nations	30 Nov.	407
356	Telegram, Seán Murphy to Walshe	Political developments in France	1 Dec.	407
357	Telegram, Walshe to Brennan	American views on Irish refusal to allow Britain use of Treaty ports	2 Dec.	408
358	Confidential report, Seán Murphy to Walshe	Political developments in France	3 Dec.	408
359	Telegram, Walshe to Brennan	American views on Irish refusal to allow Britain use of Treaty ports	4 Dec.	411
360	Telegram, Kerney to Walshe	Frank Ryan	5 Dec.	411
361	Telegram, Walshe to Brennan	Treaty ports and Battle of the Atlantic	5 Dec.	411
362	Telegram, Brennan to Walshe	Treaty ports and Battle of the Atlantic	6 Dec.	412
363	Telegram, External Affairs to Warnock	Securing German permission for Murphy to visit Paris	7 Dec.	412
364	Telegram, Walshe to Brennan	Treaty ports and Battle of the Atlantic	9 Dec.	413

List of documents reproduced

No.	Title	Main Subject	Date	Page
365	Telegram, Brennan to Walshe	Treaty ports and Battle of the Atlantic	10 Dec.	413
366	Telegram, Walshe to Brennan	Sovereignty, Treaty ports and neutrality	12 Dec.	414
367	Letter, Archer to Walshe	Frank Ryan	12 Dec.	414
368	Telegram, Cremins to Walshe	Visits to members of diplomatic corps in Berne	13 Dec.	415
369	Telegram, Warnock to Walshe	Treaty ports/bombing raids on Britain/Irish Legation in Berlin	15 Dec.	416
370	Memorandum by Walshe	Meeting with Maffey on aspects of British-Irish relations	17 Dec.	416
371	Telegram, Brennan to Walshe	American views on Treaty ports	18 Dec.	417
372	Memorandum, Hempel to Walshe	Staff requirements for German Legation	19 Dec.	418
373	Telegram, Boland to Warnock	Staff requirements for German Legation	19 Dec.	419
374	Telegram, Warnock to Walshe	Staff requirements for German Legation	24 Dec.	420
375	Telegram, Warnock to Walshe	Air raids on Berlin	24 Dec.	420
376	Memorandum, Rynne to Walshe	Plans for propaganda abroad in the event of invasion	30 Dec.	420

1941

No.	Title	Main Subject	Date	Page
377	Telegram, Walshe to Hearne	Explaining Ireland's wartime stance to Irish-Canadians	1 Jan.	422
378	Telegram, Walshe to Warnock	Dropping of bombs by German aircraft on Irish territory	2 Jan.	422
379	Memorandum by External Affairs	German request to increase Dublin Legation staff	3 Jan.	423
380	Memorandum by Walshe	Dropping of bombs by German aircraft on Irish territory	3 Jan.	425
381	Telegram, Walshe to Warnock	Dropping of bombs by German aircraft on Irish territory	3 Jan.	426
382	Memorandum by Walshe	Dropping of bombs by German aircraft on Irish territory	4 Jan.	427

liii

Documents on Irish Foreign Policy, Volume VI, 1939–1941

No.	Title	Main Subject	Date	Page
383	Telegram, External Affairs to O'Donovan	Dropping of bombs by German aircraft on Irish territory	6 Jan.	427
384	Memorandum by Walshe	German request to increase Dublin Legation staff	6 Jan.	428
385	Letter, Seán Murphy to Kerney	Treatment of Irish citizens in German-occupied territory	6 Jan.	429
386	Telegram, Brennan to Walshe	Meeting with Krock on Irish neutrality and the ports/Joseph Kennedy prepared to visit Ireland	6 Jan.	429
387	Letter, Cremins to Seán Murphy	Lucia Joyce	7 Jan.	430
388	Telegram, Walshe to Seán Murphy	Need for frequent reports from France	7 Jan.	431
389	Memorandum by Walshe	Dropping of bombs by German aircraft on Irish territory	7 Jan.	431
390	Memorandum by Walshe	German request to increase Dublin Legation staff	7 Jan.	432
391	Telegram, Warnock to Walshe	Dropping of bombs by German aircraft on Irish territory	7 Jan.	432
392	Telegram, O'Donovan to Walshe	Statement by Rector of Irish College, Rome	9 Jan.	433
393	Telegram, Seán Murphy to Walshe	Need for frequent reports from France	13 Jan.	434
394	Letter, Seán Murphy to Cremins	James Joyce/Lucia Joyce	13 Jan.	434
395	Letter, Boland to Coyne	Attitude of Italian Minister to Irish press	13 Jan.	436
396	Telegram, External Affairs to Warnock	German intentions in regard to Ireland	16 Jan.	437
397	Memorandum, Walshe to MacMahon	Emergency planning regarding possible invasion of Ireland	16 Jan.	437
398	Memorandum by Walshe	Gray's views on American attitude to Ireland	17 Jan.	439
399	Telegram, Seán Murphy to Walshe	Internal political events in France	20 Jan.	441
400	Letter, Cremins to Seán Murphy	Death of James Joyce/position of Lucia Joyce	20 Jan.	441
401	Memorandum by Boland	Matters arising should Ireland become involved in hostilities	21 Jan.	442

List of documents reproduced

No.	Title	Main Subject	Date	Page
402	Memorandum by Department of the Taoiseach	Matters arising should Ireland become involved in hostilities	22 Jan.	444
403	Telegram, Walshe to Brennan	Raising of a loan for Irish government in USA	22 Jan.	445
404	Letter, Brennan to Walshe	Possibility of American entry into war	23 Jan.	445
405	Telegram, Walshe to Seán Murphy	Position of French Commercial Attaché	23 Jan.	446
406	Letter, Beckett to O'Kelly de Gallagh	No difficulties regarding personal circumstances	23 Jan.	447
407	Telegram, Walshe to MacWhite	Need for more reports on conditions in Italy	24 Jan.	448
408	Memorandum by External Affairs	Questions affecting External Affairs which would arise in the event of an invasion	28 Jan.	448
409	Draft by Rynne	Note to be sent to foreign governments in the event of an invasion	undated, Jan.	450
410	Telegram, Walshe to Brennan	Transhipment and neutrality	28 Jan.	451
411	Telegram, MacWhite to Walshe	Italian attitude towards Ireland	29 Jan.	451
412	Telegram, Brennan to Walshe	United States attitude towards Irish loan and Lend-Lease	30 Jan.	451
413	Telegram, Brennan to Walshe	United States attitude towards Irish loan and Lend-Lease	30 Jan.	452
414	Telegram, Brennan to Walshe	United States attitude towards Irish loan and Lend-Lease	30 Jan.	452
415	Telegram, Warnock to Walshe	Dropping of bombs by German aircraft on Irish territory	30 Jan.	452
416	Memorandum by Walshe	Dropping of bombs by German aircraft on Irish territory	30 Jan.	453
417	Confidential report, Dulanty to Walshe	British attitude towards Ireland changed for the worse/British food supplies	30 Jan.	454

1939

No. 1 NAI DFA Legal Adviser's Papers

Memorandum entitled 'Ireland's Neutrality in Practice'
from Michael Rynne to Joseph P. Walshe (Dublin)
(Secret)

DUBLIN, 1 September 1939

Ireland's Neutrality in Practice

1. The neutrality policy of the Government will have to be put into practice should the present crisis develop into a general war. It seems desirable, therefore, to set down some clear propositions with regard to our practical duties and rights as neutrals. Up to the present, a certain lack of accuracy has been noticeable in many statements and discussions on the subject of Ireland's position in wartime, due to ignorance of the generally settled concepts and norms of the international law doctrine of neutrality.

For instance, it is remarkable how widely accepted is the fallacy according to which Irish neutrality must inevitably collapse once we permit a belligerent Great Britain to buy cattle here. On the other hand, matters which almost certainly contain implications of direct concern to the Government's neutrality policy (such as the matter of shipping war risks insurance) are apt to be examined mainly from a merely technical or economic point of view.

2. Undoubtedly the enforcement of the Government's policy of absolute neutrality cannot be achieved without severe inconvenience and even financial loss to many interests in this country, but, in practice, we may nevertheless be pleasantly surprised to find that a certain measure of 'business as usual' will be possible and permissible. In any case, it is clear that the policy must be rigorously administered by every branch of the State service in order to avoid at any cost the civil disorder and tragic consequences to our future as a nation of a slip into belligerency on either side.

3. The first aspect of the matter to call for our attention must, therefore, be that which relates to the *duties of a neutral*.

These are chiefly three:-
   (1) to oppose any act of hostility which one belligerent may attempt against another *on our neutral territory* (including the territorial sea);
   (2) to refrain from any act of such a kind as to interfere with the military operations of one of the belligerents against another *outside* our territory; and
   (3) to maintain the most complete impartiality in our relations with the two belligerents, abstaining from any action which might amount to *auxiliary aid* to one of the combatants.

4. The foregoing are only general principles. We must endeavour to work out their practical application.

In the first place, the Irish Government will be expected by the warring Powers to oppose the performance of any acts here in Ireland, whether on land or sea (3 mile limit), which would constitute *the preparation, accomplishment or continuation of a warlike operation* of one of the belligerents against another.

5. Without going into all the examples of such warlike, neutrality-contravening acts, we may note at this point:
    (1) that the international law governing such examples consists of a number of rules that have been almost as honoured in the breach as in the observance,
    (2) that a neutral State is only expected to oppose breaches of its neutrality under those rules by all the means in its power.

That is to say, that while we may in practice find that a number of the rules under the first principle of neutrality laid down in paragraph 3 above may be broken freely in our case, we may, on the other hand be able to oppose their breach in an adequate manner without the use of force.

6. One of the strict rules under the first principle of neutrality which would be most likely to give the Government trouble, should it be infringed by the British forces, is *the rule that a neutral State must not permit its ports, harbours or coastal waters to be used as bases of the ships of a belligerent State.*

This means that, in general, we would have to resist, by protest, boycott or otherwise, the occupation of our ports by the British in wartime. We could not, and would not, of course, allow them to take on munitions at an Irish port. We would protest against (if we could not actually prevent) the British or other fleets from sheltering behind one of our islands or headlands in order to ambush their enemy's shipping or battleships.

If the fact of having depots of petrol, etc. at certain points on our coast appeared to be leading to breaches of our neutrality, the Government would have to close down such depots, failing any other means of asserting the State's neutrality at those points.

According to Articles 10 and 26 of the Hague Convention of 1907, which contain principles still almost universally recognised, any step that the Government might take in order to prevent a clear breach of Ireland's neutrality would have to be regarded as a lawful act by all the belligerents and not as an act of war. In other words, we could not be accused of being a belligerent simply because we used all our forces to assert our status of a neutral.

7. Another rule of law which our Government will almost certainly be expected to enforce will be that whereby *a neutral must not permit a belligerent to recruit troops on its territory*. This will mean in our case that (i) *we ought to forbid our citizens to join the British Army*, (ii) prevent our ships from being used to bring *large numbers* of British subjects back to their military units.

The law even on these points has been so infringed in the past that it is not altogether clear. But, at least, it would be safer to confine ourselves for a start to a policy of facilitating the quick return of reservists (of all nations) *at an early stage* of the hostilities and at no stage to knowingly permit Irish citizens to leave the country for service abroad. Our eventual attitude to these matters may be stricter or laxer depending on the reactions of the belligerents. On the main issue, namely, the question of foreign recruiting here, the Government will, of course, continue to be adamant.

8. A third rule of neutrality which may give rise to difficulties in Ireland in view of the very divergent outlook of the people on our political relations with Great Britain, is the rule that *a neutral State must not allow any preference for one belligerent rather than for another to appear officially and must endeavour to keep the expression of any such preferences among the public within the bounds of international courtesy.* In practice, this will no doubt entail the curbing, if not the censorship, of all Irish newspapers and published matter and a strict control of the rights of free speech and public meeting. The official aspect of the matter will be best met by a strict censorship of our wireless stations.

9. With regard to the nationals of belligerent States who may find themselves here, after the outbreak of hostilities, the Government will have the duty of seeing that they do nothing to endanger the country's neutrality. *Nationals of belligerent States who reside in Ireland must not be allowed to do acts liable to imperil our status any more than Irish nationals or foreigners belonging to other neutral States will be allowed to do them.* This does not, of course, mean that we must lock up all foreigners (i.e. 'belligerent' foreigners), but we must not favour them unduly. We are bound to keep them all under observation and control, or take the consequences of their misconduct.

10. Besides the rules affecting the ships, troops and nationals of belligerents, there is a generally accepted rule about aeroplanes to the effect that *a neutral State ought not to permit the military aircraft of a belligerent to overfly or land on its territory.*

Whether this will mean that we will be bound to have recourse to force against belligerent planes which overfly Ireland and refuse to descend after signals, is a matter than can be left in abeyance, as the law is not very clear on it (although Holland shot down planes during the last war); but *we must make it known that we propose to intern military planes which land on our territory until the war comes to an end.*

The matter of the publicly-owned planes of belligerents is one that may also be left in abeyance for the present, even if we should express our desire that foreign planes of all descriptions avoid Ireland after a war has broken out.

11. The duties of a neutral State necessarily connote duties on the part of its subjects or citizens to conduct themselves 'neutrally'. If an Irish citizen voluntarily joins one of the belligerent armies he cannot plead his citizenship against the enemy belligerents. For that reason, *the Government might do well to warn Irish citizens on the outbreak of war that they must forfeit their right to the protection of the Irish State once they become members of any belligerent force.*

12. Citizens of Ireland who propose to continue to deal commercially with the belligerent States, or their citizens, should likewise be warned not to overstep the bounds set to such commercial dealings by international law.

The position is briefly this:-
(1) Citizens of neutral States are free to trade with the belligerents, to whom they may sell anything (even arms and munitions – which a neutral *Government* may not sell) *on their own territory,*
(2) but it must be remembered that the belligerent State opposed to the State which buys from the neutral State, or its citizens, may impose the sanction of contraband at any time and on almost any kind of merchandise, and

(3) citizens of a neutral State are compromising their country's neutrality once they endeavour to run a blockade. *Hence the Government will not have to forbid trade with any belligerent whose ports are not effectively blockaded by the enemy, but they may have to warn Irish citizens to insist on sales for cash so that they will not be at a loss should their cargoes be sunk or otherwise treated as contraband.* These are matters which may not call for attention unless and until the seas over which Irish trade is principally carried become dangerous for shipping.

13. Finally, among our duties as a neutral will be that of seeing to it *that this country is not used by either belligerent as a centre of espionage*. This may entail a number of precautions of a preventive kind, directed not only against belligerent aliens here but also against our own nationals and those of neutral States.

14. The foregoing paragraphs give some idea of the *duties* which will fall on us in wartime. Ireland's rights as a neutral may now be considered equally briefly. In the first place, however, we must observe that even our neutral rights are affected by our duties as a neutral, so that it would be incorrect to imagine that on assuming the status of a neutral in wartime we will be able to carry over all our peacetime rights.

Certainly, we will continue to preserve our full rights of sovereignty throughout the territory which is under our own jurisdiction, and as a result of that *we may afford as much hospitality as we like to the nationals of belligerent states. But not to their troops.* We will also have *a right to forbid the belligerent States to recruit here*, simply because we have a duty not to allow our citizens to be recruited for service abroad.

We will have, for example, the right to refuse to recognise the capture by a belligerent war vessel of an enemy vessel should that capture take place in our waters, merely because we are bound by our neutral status to refuse any belligerent the right to conduct war operations on our territory.

15. Nearly all the rights of neutrality are corollary to duties and proceed from a theory of national sovereignty which is recognised to justify strong measures. That is to say, *we will be expected to be firm in the enforcement of our neutral rights and we will be legally entitled to be as drastic as circumstances demand.*

16. In time of war, just as in peace-time, *we will be entitled to exercise our sovereign rights to admit, or refuse admission to foreign war-vessels which desire to use our harbours.* Our duty will be to exercise that right impartially. We will not be required to refuse admission (as did, e.g., Holland in 1914) to all foreign war vessels, but if we concede the right of entry to ships of one belligerent we must not deny it to the ships of the other. If we do decide to admit such ships at all, we must permit them only to purchase necessary provisions or make essential repairs: we must not let them embark arms or munitions of war.

17. Another right which we may have some difficulty in enforcing against one or other of the belligerents will be the right to correspond freely with our diplomatic representatives abroad. A natural complement to this right *is that which we will possess of forbidding the official representatives of any of the belligerents from interfering with our neutrality here.* The Government must not of course interfere with the normal activities of diplomats accredited to Ireland by belligerent states and still expect to enjoy the right to freely correspond with their own representatives abroad, but they will have to see to it that those activities do not overstep the limits of ordinary

diplomatic representation. *At the beginning of hostilities no action is likely to be called for under this head except that of providing sufficient police protection for the foreign Legations and Consulates in Dublin and elsewhere in the country and making sure that our communications to the Irish offices abroad are not being hindered unlawfully.*

18. In a general resumé of this sort it is scarcely necessary to attempt an examination of all the possible states of fact which if they were to materialise would give us special rights to protest or claim compensation against one or other belligerent. Enough has been said to give a general indication of our position and, it is submitted, to demonstrate that it is neither a difficult position to attain nor to maintain. Undoubtedly, in practice, Irish ships may be sunk and even Irish territory invaded or attacked. But unless we should fail to take the normal action by way of protest or otherwise, our position of neutrality will not have been sacrificed in principle. *The main consideration must, therefore, be to take all the essential steps at an early opportunity after the outbreak of a war to define beyond any possible doubt a position of strict neutrality. Exceptions, to that general declaration if any are to be permitted, might be carefully considered during the course of the hostilities and when possible and desirable admitted in practice.*

Such exceptions should not be defined in words at the beginning of a war when all the belligerents as well as all Irish people will expect to be presented with the fait accompli of Irish neutrality in accordance with the publicly stated policy of the Government.

[initialled] M.R.

No. 2 NAI DFA 219/4

Letter from William Warnock to Joseph P. Walshe (Dublin)
(32/33)

BERLIN, 2 September 1939

Today (Saturday) we are waiting in a feeling of rather anxious expectancy. It now seems inevitable that war will break out between Germany and the allies of Poland. I understand that the British Embassy has as yet received no reply to Mr. Chamberlain's message, but that it is expected that the British Ambassador[1] will be 'asking for his passports' this evening, though on the German side there does not appear to be any desire to hasten matters in this respect. The Polish Ambassador[2] is still here, and is in communication with the Foreign Office as usual.

As from last night anti-aircraft precautions have been taken. Street lighting has been suspended until further notice, and vehicles travelling at night are required to mask their headlights. Petrol as well as food is very strictly rationed.

The people generally seem to be in a state of doubt. There is no great enthusiasm for war, but at the moment the average citizen feels that if war comes he must do his part for his country no matter what sacrifice that may entail. If Germany is attacked, not only national socialists, but all Germans will be in equal danger.

You have probably seen in foreign newspapers that Germans are now forbidden by law to listen in to foreign wireless stations. The spreading of news received from foreign stations will be severely punished, possibly with death penalty.

---

[1] Sir Nevile M. Henderson (1882-1942), British Ambassador to Germany (Apr. 1937-Sept. 1939).
[2] Józef Lipski (1894-1958), Polish Ambassador to Germany (1934-9).

It has been obvious to me during the last few days that it would be advisable if each of our Legations were furnished with a wireless set of high selectivity. In our case, for example, we have no other means of obtaining up-to-date news.

[signed] W. WARNOCK

No. 3 NAI DFA Paris Embassy 19/34A

Confidential report from Con Cremin to Joseph P. Walshe (Dublin) (P19/34) (Copy)

PARIS, 2 September 1939

I attended the session of the Chamber this afternoon at which M. Daladier[1] read a declaration of the Government in regard to the present situation. The declaration reviewed the efforts made by the French for peace during the past 20 years and in particular those made during the past few years, referred to the exchange of letters last week-end between M. Daladier and Herr Hitler, characterised as a lie the German contention that Poland had rejected the proposals published on 31st ulto. which, the President of the Council claimed, had never been submitted to Poland, made a reference to the various efforts made in the last few weeks by persons in authority and in particular the 'noble efforts of Italy' and said that the French Government did not even now at the eleventh hour despair of some peaceful solution being found. He went on to deal with the outstanding events of German foreign policy in the last four years and with particular reference to the contrast between Herr Hitler's words and his actions in regard to Austria, Sudeten Germany, Czechoslovakia and finally Poland, asserted that it is impossible to place any reliance whatever in what he says. He emphasised the closeness of the co-operation at present between Great Britain and France and read the text of the message which the French Ambassador at Berlin[2] was yesterday instructed to deliver on the same lines as that presented by the British Ambassador. He emphasised that France is determined to observe her obligations and for that purpose has mobilised, but maintained that France has mobilised only in defence of what she considers to be right and because the destruction of Poland would only make inevitable the subsequent destruction of herself, that French people have no hate for any nation or people and none against the German people. This latter statement as well as the reference of M. Daladier to the brutality of the invasion of Poland were greeted with enthusiastic applause.

The declaration contained no announcement of definite action on the part of France; although the Government has emphatically reiterated its intentions of observing its obligations towards Poland it appears to be postponing making a declaration of war on Germany apparently in the hope that some peaceful settlement may be found even at this late hour.

The Government's declaration in the Chamber seems to be received with unanimous approval and at certain stages was warmly applauded.

[stamped] (Signed) C.C. CREMIN

---

[1] Edouard Daladier (1884-1970), French Prime Minister and Minister for National Defence (1938-40).
[2] Robert Coulondre, French Ambassador to Germany (1938-9).

No. 4 NAI DFA 219/7

> *Confidential report from Francis T. Cremins to Joseph P. Walshe (Dublin)*
> *(S.Gen. 1/1) (Confidential)*
>
> GENEVA, 2 September 1939

With reference to previous minutes regarding the general situation, and especially to my minute of the 31st August,[1] I have to state that shortly after the despatch of my telegram yesterday morning rumours that the Germans had crossed the Polish frontiers at 5.45 a.m. began to circulate and some time later it was confirmed that the expected emergency had actually arisen. The 8.30 a.m. wireless news give no indication that hostilities had begun. General mobilisation in Switzerland was proclaimed to take effect from today.

Public opinion remains calm, but it is certainly shocked at the outcome of the negotiations, and at the manner of the aggression. To-day 'La Suisse' has a large heading
> 'Rome propose un règlement européen – la France accepte', with a despatch from Havas agency as follows: 'Paris 1er (Havas) – Le Gouvrnement français a été saisi, ainsi que plusieurs autres gouvernements d'une initiative italieene tendant à assurer le règlement des difficultés européennes. Après en avoir délibéré, le gouvernement français a donné une réponse positive'.

A news item in these terms was also given in the Radio-Paris wireless news at 8.30 a.m. There is much speculation as to what if anything this vague announcement means. The reference in the 'Temps' of Paris shows blanks indicating that it had been censored.

Most people now are satisfied that a European war has practically begun, but even now I hear many hopes that it may not even yet be too late for some settlement. Certainly, the continuance of efforts for a just settlement would be approved. Germany probably hopes to have achieved, militarily, something decisive before the States allied to Poland get going, and that those States may then be prepared to listen to German claims, rather than take part in a general war. Most people however seem to think in terms of a fight to a finish as being the only possible, and probable, solution, as in the war of 1914-18, in Spain, etc. Nevertheless, occasions may present themselves in the course of hostilities in which the Germans may be more disposed than they are at present to listen to reason. Any efforts by peacemakers to take advantage of such occasions would I imagine be generally approved here.

[signed] F.T. CREMINS
Permanent Delegate

No. 5 NAI DFA 219/6

> *Extract from a confidential report from Leopold H. Kerney to Joseph P. Walshe*
> *(Dublin)*
> *(S.S. 27/6) (Secret)*
>
> SAN SEBASTIAN, 2 September 1939

With reference to your secret minute of 24th August,[2] my last telegram[3] was sent from here at 11 a.m. on 1st September and outbreak of hostilities between Germany

---

[1] See DIFP V, No. 354.
[2] See DIFP V, No. 348.
[3] Not printed.

and Poland became known here at 1 p.m. the same day. The 'situation' code[1] does not appear to meet the situation which has now arisen and I presume therefore that there will be no object in utilising it for future daily wires relating to the situation.

I feel that your chief anxiety, in so far as information from this Legation is concerned, will be to know the attitude which Spain is likely to adopt as the situation develops. The general desire here is undoubtedly in favour of neutrality. The official attitude is one of reserve but appears to encourage the idea of Spanish neutrality.

[matter omitted]

My own impression of the Spanish attitude is that strict neutrality will be preserved so long as Italy may remain outside the conflagration but that this position may undergo modification from the day on which Italy enters the war.

[signed] L.H. KERNEY
Aire Lán-Chómhachtach

No. 6 NAI DFA Paris Embassy 19/34A

Confidential report from Seán Murphy to Joseph P. Walshe (Dublin)
(Copy)

PARIS, 4 September 1939

1. The difference in time in the expiration of the British and French ultimatum to Germany was explained on the French radio last evening as being due to a deliberate concertation between the British and French authorities who wished to give Herr Hitler every opportunity of making a peaceful arrangement possible. St. Brice in this morning's *Journal* states that the reasons which prompted this difference must remain secret but are certainly good ones. He contends that in the rejection of both ultimatums by the Germans, there were different nuances which, in his opinion, were nothing less than a manoeuvre to separate France and England. When replying to the British Ambassador Herr von Ribbentrop[2] handed him a long memorandum endeavouring to place the responsibility for the war on England on the ground that it was her granting of a free hand to Poland that encouraged her to resist. In his reply to M. Coulondre he developed the thesis that Germany was very sorry to see her hope of living on good terms with France deceived, that Germany did not consider that France had any responsibility in the present conflict and suggested that England had refused to admit the Italian mediation which France was disposed to accept.[3] The comment of St. Brice is that such an interpretation is quite fantastic as France as well as England always considered that the general settlement suggested by Mussolini could only be considered if Germany began by ceasing hostilities, withdrawing her troops and accepting a free discussion with a fully independent Poland. His judgment is that it is Germany who ruined the work of conciliation which Mussolini carried out unceasingly and that

---

[1] See DIFP V, No. 348.
[2] Joachim von Ribbentrop (1893-1946), German Ambassador to Britain (1936-8), German Foreign Minister (1938-45), found guilty at the Nuremberg War Crimes Trial and hanged in October 1946.
[3] See No. 4.

Italy can now see that a general war has been deliberately sought by Germany, and provoked by her. This latter opinion is also that of Bailby[1] in *La Jour* who suggests that Hitler 'who wanted his war and now has it' must be very sorry that he did not bring it about a year earlier when French preparations were less ready.

2. There were conflicting accounts on Friday and Saturday as to the French attitude towards the Italian mediation alluded to by Mr. Chamberlain and Lord Halifax on Saturday evening. While the radio (which is of course subject to a strict censorship) stated that the French reply delivered on Friday was one of acceptance of such mediation, one of the correspondents of the semi-official *Le Petit Parisien* of Saturday claimed en passant that the Italian mediation was inacceptable.

3. Cardinal Verdier[2] has announced that he intends to deliver a broadcast to the world today over the French system protesting against the barbarity of the Germans in bombing Czestochowa,[3] the Polish Lourdes. Cardinal Lienart (of Lille) addressed a message to his diocese in connection with the German mobilisation in which he stated that 'at the moment the German aggression against Poland risks unloosening on the world another war. We desire to condemn loudly the injustice of which the present leader of Germany has been guilty. If in spite of the efforts of the Holy Father, Sovereigns and the Heads of States, Governments and the peoples attached to peace, the violent attacks against the independence of Poland should continue, France would enter into the struggle strong in right and resolved to reduce to impotence the unjust aggressor'.

4. M. Daladier spoke over the radio to the French people last evening. He asserted inter alia that 'the issue of peace rested in the hands of Hitler: he has desired war' and that 'the cause of France is identical with that of justice. It is that of all peaceful and free nations; it shall be victorious'.

5. Most of the press reports on the neutrality of the 'neutral' states, Holland, Denmark, the Baltic States, Switzerland and Belgium. The report as to the neutrality of Japan is reproduced prominently. All the press announces that Turkey will be on the side of France and Great Britain. There is an absence of press comment as to the positions of Rumania and Italy.

6. Although I have seen no comment on the subject yet it is not unlikely that French opinion will be somewhat disappointed with the tenor of President Roosevelt's speech this morning. The *Jour* which apparently had not available when going to press the text of the speech prints a Havas despatch from Washington (as does *Le Matin*) suggesting that President Roosevelt is preparing to give effect to his policy which consists in preventing U.S. participation in the war and the grant to France and Great Britain of the greatest possible measure of material and moral support. The *Journal* which prints most of the text of the speech underlines that section in which President Roosevelt said that he could not of course compel people to take up mentally a neutral attitude in regard to the conflict.

7. M. Daladier is reported in some of the press to have informed the Finance Commission of the Chamber that the Government intends to remain in Paris and to share whatever risks exist with the population which remains behind.

The atmosphere in Paris is very normal except for the fact that the city is rather

---

[1] Léon Balby, editor of *La Jour*.
[2] Cardinal Jean Verdier (1864-1940), Archbishop of Paris (1929-40).
[3] The southern Polish town of Czestochowa was occupied by German forces on 3 September 1939 and renamed Tschenstochau.

empty and that at night practically all street lighting is extinguished. Restaurants have been ordered to close at 11 p.m. There is as yet relatively little evidence of extensive military activity in the city.

[stamped] (Signed) SEÁN MURPHY

No. 7 NAI DFA 219/2

> Confidential report from Leopold H. Kerney to Joseph P. Walshe (Dublin)
> (S.S. 27/6) (Confidential)
> SAN SEBASTIAN, 5 September 1939

SPAIN'S ATTITUDE IN EUROPEAN WAR

I enclose copy of to-day's 'Voz de España' giving the text of the declaration of Spain's strict neutrality made yesterday evening by radio and published in the Boletin Oficial of 5th September. You will notice that this affirmation of neutrality relates to the war which exists between England, France and Poland on one side and Germany on the other; it may still be an open question as to whether this strict neutrality would be affected in any way by the eventual inclusion of Italy amongst the belligerent powers.

Spain's trade with Germany must naturally be affected by the war; Spain is still in Germany's debt and this debt has been reduced by considerable exports of iron-ore and other raw materials; the Foreign Minister in Burgos recently remarked in the course of a conversation with one of my colleagues that it would be an excellent thing if exports of iron-ore to Germany became impossible because in that case they would certainly go to England and France and consequently strengthen Spain's financial position.

[signed] L.H. KERNEY

No. 8 NAI DFA Washington Embassy Confidential Reports 1938-9

> Confidential report from Robert Brennan to Joseph P. Walshe (Dublin)
> (108/47/39) (Copy)
> WASHINGTON, 5 September 1939

There is no doubt but that the opinion of America is almost entirely against Germany in the present war. Even before war was declared or before Germany had invaded Poland, the Gallup Poll published the result of a poll taken on the question of Germany's territorial claims, and it showed that 83% of Americans were against even Danzig going to Germany. The invasion of Poland by Germany is denounced on all sides. If there are any who think Germany was justified, their voices are not heard. The case presented by Great Britain justifying her action in making war on Germany is almost universally accepted here; even the few who previously had something to say for Hitler and Germany have now come to the conclusion that Hitler must be insane.

On the other hand, there has arisen a surprising volume of opinion to the effect that America must keep out of this war, together with warnings against propaganda from one side or the other. President Roosevelt, in his radio address to the

Nation on Sunday night, pledged himself to use every effort to keep America neutral. Generally speaking, the press of the country endorses his stand.

Nothing else is talked of here but the war situation. Wherever one goes, there is a radio at hand giving forth the latest bulletins, and most of the radio stations are kept going all night. Practically every programme is interrupted three or four times to give the latest bulletins. While it is stressed by the announcers that the news is strictly neutral, it is to be noticed that there are at least six broadcasts from London and Paris to one from Germany.

It is, of course, impossible to prophesy, but many people think that notwithstanding the obvious desire of the President and Congress and the people to keep out of this war, the United States will eventually be found on the side of England and France.

[stamped] (Signed) ROBT. BRENNAN

No. 9 NAI DFA Legal Adviser's Papers

Memorandum from Michael Rynne to Joseph P. Walshe (Dublin)
(Copy) (Secret)

DUBLIN, 5 September 1939

re Furtherance of Neutrality Policy

Although the war has been in existence for only two days, yet one has the impression, speaking to various members of the Dublin public, that the vital necessity of the Government's policy of neutrality is not being fully appreciated. This is probably due to two main causes, (if we ignore that of merely personal 'pro-British' or 'pro-German' sentiments) namely (i) the fact that no air raids have as yet been made on British territory so as to illustrate to our people what a modern war really means, and (ii) that our newspapers are not only not pointing out to their readers the undoubted advantages of our position, but are actually publishing and emphasising matter of a most tendentious character from unneutral sources.

2. As an example of the type of journalism which is undermining the public's morale at the present very critical moment, I attach a copy of last night's 'Evening Mail'. I have 'censored' the paper in red ink so as to draw attention to its objectionable features.

3. It is submitted that unless a strong censorship is rigorously imposed on the Press at once, public opinion may get entirely out of control with extremely unfavourable reactions on the Government which in the best interests of the country have adopted the neutrality policy. Apart from that aspect of the matter there is, of course, the danger of divided (or 'unneutral') opinions to public order here. We in the Department must take account of the difficulties that may result in regard to our relations with the diplomatic representatives of the various belligerents, if our newspapers continue to stress foreign war-propagandist 'news' items on prominent pages.

4. Much of the foregoing is true of the official wireless news bulletins from Athlone which still relies entirely on Reuter etc. The Belgian stations take news from all the others; at 11 p.m. last night they quoted the Irish 10.30 news.

5. Our press censorship might also be advised to take example from Belgium and other neutral countries. Even the United States (judging from its radio broadcasts)

are obviously endeavouring to remain strictly objective regarding the present state of war in Europe.

6. I attach a few suggested 'Rules for Press Censorship'[1] in order to indicate what appears to be lacking at present.

No. 10 NAI CAB 2/2

Extract from the minutes of a meeting of the Cabinet
(G.C. 2/95) (Item 1) (S. 11417)

DUBLIN, 6 September 1939

APPOINTMENT OF A BRITISH DIPLOMATIC REPRESENTATIVE

It was decided that the Minister for External Affairs should reopen with the British Government the discussion as to the appointment in Ireland of a British Diplomatic Representative.

No. 11 NAI DFA Secretary's Files P2

Confidential report from Robert Brennan to Joseph P. Walshe (Dublin)
(108/48/39)

WASHINGTON, 7 September 1939

I paid my duty call yesterday on the new British Ambassador, Lord Lothian.[2] In the course of a general conversation arising out of the war situation, he asked me what it was that Mr. de Valera had said exactly in the Dáil, and he quoted his recollection of the press report of same to the effect that Mr. de Valera had said that Ireland 'would remain neutral as long as possible'. I told him that I had a message to the effect that the Irish Government had declared its neutrality and that the German Government had promised to observe same.

He asked me what the qualification in Mr. de Valera's statement meant and I told him I did not know. He then asked if this would prevent our allowing the British to use Cobh as a naval station, and I said that I imagined such action would be a violation of our neutrality.

He went on to give me a picture of Hitler attributed to Dr. Jong,[3] the great German psychologist, to the effect that as a man Hitler has no special qualities either mentally or physically, but that he has become the subconscious soul of a Germany which considered itself down-trodden and humiliated when it was capable of being the greatest country on earth and that when he assumes this role, he talks like one inspired. He never does any work of any kind and his end will be suicide.

The Ambassador has had a very favourable press here so far.

[signed] ROBT. BRENNAN

---

[1] Not printed.
[2] Philip Henry Kerr, 11th Marquess of Lothian (1882-1940), British Ambassador to the United States of America (Aug. 1939-Dec. 1940).
[3] Dr Carl Gustavus Jung (1875-1961), Swiss psychologist and founder of analytical psychology.

1939

No. 12 NAI DFA Washington Embassy Confidential Reports 1938-9

> *Confidential report from Robert Brennan to Joseph P. Walshe (Dublin)*
> *(108/49/39) (Copy)*
>
> WASHINGTON, 7 September 1939

On September 5th, President Roosevelt signed three Proclamations, the first, proclaiming the neutrality of the United States, the second, embargoing arms shipment to belligerents, and the third, embodying rules for United States citizens travelling by sea. The text of these Proclamations is attached hereto.[1] It is agreed that these Proclamations are in accordance with the existing United States Law. A few days ago it was definitely stated that the Administration were not in favor of trying, at the moment, to persuade a reconvened Congress to change the Neutrality Laws because they feared that an acrimonious debate on the subject at the moment would do more harm than good, and that Congress itself might not even now endorse the views of the Administration. However, today it is stated by sources close to the Administration that a special session of Congress may be convened for next week with a view to having the arms embargo removed.

So far as the man in the street can see, there seems to be little change in the opinion of those who voted against the Administration's policy in this matter, though Representative Sol Bloom,[2] who sponsored the Bill embodying the removal of the arms embargo, has stated that many of the Congressmen who voted against his measure have now changed their minds.

The section of the Press which supports the Administration on this matter now openly state that it is the duty of America to allow the French and British to obtain here all the munitions they can take on the cash and carry principle, because they are fighting against the aggressor for a continuance of the way of life which Americans hold dear. The opponents of the measure consider in the main that the removal of the arms embargo will be a definite step towards the ultimate embroilment of America in the war.

[stamped] (Signed) ROBT. BRENNAN

No. 13 NAI DFA 217/33

> *Letter from Frederick H. Boland to William Warnock (Berlin)*
> *(Copy)*
>
> DUBLIN, 8 September 1939

Dear Warnock,

I hope that this letter will reach you safely. We haven't come to any definite conclusion here as to how we are going to communicate with you in future, and we shall be glad to receive any observations on the matter which you have to make. You may like to talk to the authorities in Berlin about it. In the meantime, perhaps you would be good enough to send your reports and official correspondence to the Minister at the Holy See for transmission here in his bag.

---

[1] Not printed.
[2] Sol Bloom (1870-1949), Member of Congress (1920-49), Chairman of the Foreign Affairs Committee of the House of Representatives (1938).

I hope you received the bank drafts for $5,000 which we sent you. Please acknowledge their receipt when you are writing.

I should be glad if when you are writing you would give us full particulars of the German censorship regulations in so far as they would affect your official correspondence with the Minister for the Holy See, or with any of our other missions in Europe with whom we might ask you to communicate officially. If there are any Irish nationals left in Germany we should be glad if you would keep in as close touch with them as possible, and let us know when you are writing how they are etc., so that we may be able to answer any enquiries we may get from their relatives and friends.

I am sending you with this letter an official minute with regard to an Order made here obliging all Irish ships to fly only the Irish flag.[1] We should be glad if you would bring the Order at once to the notice of the German authorities and send us through Macaulay any observations they may have to make about it.

I presume that Dr. Mahr,[2] the Director of the National Gallery, is still in Germany. You might let us know what, precisely, he intends to do. I should, perhaps, tell you that a large number of German nationals normally resident here are trying to get back to their own country, and in our own interest, as well as theirs, we are doing our best to help them.

I hope you are keeping well and not finding the isolation too depressing. Once we get a regular system of communication established however, we will be able to keep in constant touch with you.

Yours sincerely,
[stamped] (Signed) F.H. BOLAND

No. 14 NAI DFA Madrid Embassy IP/1/2/1

Memorandum from Leopold H. Kerney to Joseph P. Walshe (Dublin)
(S.S. 27/6) (Copy)

SAN SEBASTIAN, 9 September 1939

Ireland's Attitude in European War

I learned by the Radio on 2nd inst. that Ireland had decided to observe strict neutrality.

I enclose cutting from to-day's 'Voz de España'; this is a message from London dated 8th September stating that the British Minister for Information has announced the creation of a British naval base on the south coast of Ireland, and others elsewhere; I gather that Spanish ships proceeding to Ireland would have to put in there.

I do not accept this report as being correct; there was no reference to it by Radio-Éireann at 10.30 p.m. on 8th September. It does not fit in with Irish neutrality and therefore could only be correct if there had been a violation of that neutrality by England, and, consequently, a state of war between England and Ireland.

The latest communication received by me from you was sent from Dublin on 28th August and delivered here on 1st September.

---

[1] Not printed.
[2] Adolf Mahr (1887-1951), was in fact Director of the National Museum of Ireland (1934-9), Nazi *Ortsgruppenleiter* (local group leader) in Ireland (1934-8).

1939

Postal correspondence necessarily suffers delay; a personal letter addressed to me from Dublin on 31st August reached St. Jean de Luz on 7th September and another posted on 1st September was delivered there on the 8th September.

The Irish newspapers of 1st and 2nd September have reached me to-day, 9th September.

No. 15 UCDA P150/2571

Memorandum by Joseph P. Walshe entitled 'Visit of the Secretary of the Dept. of External Affairs to London, 6th to 10th September, 1939'
DUBLIN, undated, but September 1939

I arrived in London on Thursday morning, the 7th September. I went to the Dominions Office with the High Commissioner about 10.30 to see the Secretary of State for Dominion Affairs. Mr. Eden was in his usual cheerful form, and when I told him you had sent me over to have a very frank talk with him he said there was nothing he wished for more, as he really wanted to understand Ireland, particularly in view of the disaster that had come upon the world. In his new post he would give his earnest attention to Irish matters. The following represents as closely as I can recollect what I said to him:

1. Mr. de Valera wished to assure Mr. Eden that he was very glad to hear of his appointment to the Office of Dominions Secretary. He was particularly glad to resume in a more important sphere the friendly relations which had been established between them at Geneva.[1] Mr. de Valera had asked me to convey to Mr. Eden his very real sympathy for the British Government and people in their hour of trial. His attitude vis-à-vis the British Government was that he wished to be as friendly as he could, and to go as far as possible to assist Great Britain while maintaining the essentials of neutrality. It would take some little time to settle down to a regime of essential neutrality. At the beginning there were bound to be difficulties and confusion.
2. My Minister felt that this war would lead to a new world order. He hoped very much indeed that the British Government, and especially Mr. Eden, would realise the immense importance of Ireland's position in the English speaking Catholic world, and the possibility of her playing a friendly role in the relations between the British and American peoples. A proper understanding of Ireland would be possible if only a certain flexibility were introduced into the attitude hitherto maintained by the Dominions Office in our regard. Every advance in the forms of Irish freedom, and our legitimate demands for the settlement of the paramount issue of unity had been met by an unbelievable narrow-mindedness and rigidity of outlook.
3. Mr. de Valera felt that these matters had now assumed a character of the very gravest import to both countries. He had in the past, for obvious reasons, opposed the appointment of a British representative to Dublin. But in the perilous circumstances which had suddenly arisen, he felt that the appointment could no longer be delayed. The British representative in Dublin would be able by direct observation of Irish conditions, and by close contact with Mr. de Valera and the

---
[1] From June to December 1935 Eden was Minister without Portfolio for League of Nations Affairs. He met de Valera often in Geneva during this time.

Department of External Affairs, to keep his Government accurately informed. He would thus put his Government, and indirectly ours, in a position to secure an early and rapid solution of immediate and remote difficulties. Mr. de Valera hoped that in that way a close mutual understanding could soon be reached.

4. Mr. Eden would have learned from his officials that our Dáil and Senate, as well as the very great majority of our people, including the ex-Ascendancy Irish Times group, regarded essential neutrality as a vital necessity for internal peace and for good relations with Great Britain. Any other attitude would provide troubled waters in which internal and external enemies of friendship between the two countries would not hesitate to fish.

5. Mr. de Valera would be glad to give whatever help was possible on the humanitarian side. Evacuation camps and hospitals for the permanently disabled, similar to those established in Switzerland during the Great War, were suggested, but this would naturally be a matter for discussion between the Ambassador in Dublin and the Irish Government.

6. Mr. de Valera realised the particular difficulties arising from the nature of our Southern and Western Coast, and the possibility of submarines taking refuge in our shallow waters while waiting for their targets. He would propose making a declaration that all submarines be forbidden entry into Irish waters, and that naval surface craft would be granted asylum in accordance with international usage. That would enable our armed forces to take measures against the only submarines likely to appear in our waters and to give the customary help to the only surface craft which were similarly situated. I proposed to discuss the form of the declaration with the competent authorities in London. It should be couched in the fewest possible words.

7. It would help very greatly towards an immediate good understanding if Great Britain recognised in some formal way our neutrality. The sentimental response would be immediate and widespread and would contribute to a generally favourable reception for the appointment of a British Ambassador in Dublin. Such recognition would furthermore be taken as a decent gesture, and a renunciation of any further desire to belittle our independence. At this hour of unparalleled [———][1] we should not allow the good relations between our peoples to be sacrificed to prejudiced devotion to precedents. Apart from our mutual relations, the relations between Dublin and Belfast were bound to benefit by the appointment of an Ambassador. We could, if necessary, find a new method for making the appointment. A very desirable corollary to the appointment would be the raising of Mr. Dulanty's post to ambassadorial rank. Mr. Eden was aware of the services beyond all praise of the High Commissioner in the cause of friendship between the two countries, and Mr. de Valera wished to say that the importance of his position would not be in any way diminished by the presence of a British Ambassador in Dublin.

8. Several important politico-technical questions had been raised by his people, and were awaiting solution. I would briefly mention them so as to put him *au courant*
    (a) Coast Watching. Our organisation was complete, but we wanted more Planes. (I understood we had several Anson[2] Planes on order.) We wanted

---

[1] Word left out in original.
[2] Avro Anson, British twin-engine monoplane, a derivative of a civilian model. The Irish Air Corps flew the Anson as a coastal reconnaissance aircraft during the Second World War.

more submarine chasers. It should be possible to get instant delivery of all armaments ordered. There had been very serious delays. Wireless apparatus for our Planes had not yet been delivered.

(b) Our rearmament, which was very much in their interest as well as in our own and arose out of their difficulties rather than ours, was going to cost a great deal of money. I felt that with all the credits they were giving to remote countries they might well wipe out the last relic of our financial past and drop the annual payment of £250,000.

(c) We intended to ask for an expert to destroy mines and torpedoes when an emergency arose.

(d) The interrogation of the crews of merchant vessels would be a matter for the officials of the Embassy (who should inform at any rate the civilians).

(e) We intended to intern any crews of German submarines who might be obliged to land on our shores.

(f) Directions to ships about routes and other matters could be given by officials of the Consular section of the Embassy.

(g) We wanted to let our German aliens go home, but we were being held up by red tape in some London department.

9. Finally, Mr. de Valera urged upon Mr. Eden the necessity of helping us to be friendly. He should keep Lord Craigavon out of mischief. The anti-Catholic pogroms had already begun. Such manifestations would create adverse opinion in America. Mr. Eden should ask his people to avoid all possible propaganda in Ireland. We should be left to look after our own public opinion.

10. Some step must be taken immediately towards unity. That was the fundamental and supreme issue. If it were settled, possibilities of real cooperation would be opened up. Perhaps (and this I said on my own initiative) if the real big view could now at last be taken, there would be the possibility of a joint guarantee of Ireland's neutrality by Great Britain and the United States.

Mr. Eden expressed great pleasure at getting the foregoing message from you. He said he was very new to the whole business, but, he repeated, Ireland was the most important part of his job and he would do everything possible to help. I mentioned Lord Perth[1] as the type of Ambassador which in your view was most fitting. He did not seem to agree. Perth was old, and besides they had given him a job in the Publicity Section.

Mr. Eden had to go to a meeting of the War Cabinet at 11.30. It was almost that hour. As I left him, he said he would talk to his colleagues, especially to the Prime Minister, at once about the whole matter, and he would see us again in the afternoon.

In the late afternoon we went to the D.O. again. This time Mr. Eden had with him the Duke of Devonshire,[2] Sir E. Harding, and Sir Eric Machtig (who is now principal Assistant Secretary). Mr. Eden asked me straight away whether I had any

---

[1] Lord Perth, Sir Eric Drummond (1876-1951), Secretary General of the League of Nations (1919-33), British Ambassador to Italy (1933-9).

[2] Edward William Spencer Cavendish (1895-1950), 10th Duke of Devonshire, Under-Secretary of State, Dominions Office (1936-40).

objection to the presence of the others. I had to say that I was very pleased indeed to have them there, but I made up my mind that there was going to be no progress until I met him alone again. He said that the P.M. was very pleased indeed to hear Mr. de Valera's message, and he had promised to give immediate consideration to the appointment of a 'United Kingdom Representative'. They could not call him an Ambassador or Minister. That would embarrass them enormously, especially in view of their difficulties with South Africa. It would make their whole position in Parliament and in the country very difficult indeed just now. I replied that now was surely the best possible time. Parliament was accepting much more difficult measures without a murmur. I knew, of course, and regretted very much that Sir Edward Harding at least would regard the appointment as being against all proper precedents. But even Sir Edward Harding should take a broader view at such a critical moment. Mr. Eden went on to say that he couldn't see why we would not accept a High Commissioner. I referred him to the precedent of the British High Commissioner in Egypt, which was very much present to the minds of my Government and our people. In Egypt, the High Commissioner[1] exercised complete control over a puppet Government. We could not accept the title. He then suggested 'Special Representative'. This I also rejected out of hand. A 'Special Representative' so called would be regarded as having been sent for the special purpose of forcing us out of our essential neutrality.

Finally, the matter was dropped and 'United Kingdom Representative' seems to be their sticking point.

We then came to the Submarine declaration. Harding had the audacity to suggest that we should specifically exclude German submarines. I told him that I did not quite understand what he was driving at, but he was certainly trying to make us violate our neutrality from the start. I spoke with a certain amount of heat, and Eden turned to Harding impatiently, waived him aside, and said 'no no' under his breath. I told them that the formula must be all-embracing. Mr. de Valera believed, and I understood correctly, that the formula would be a help to them. It was decided that I should see the Deputy Chief of the Naval Staff, Admiral Phillips,[2] as soon as possible to discuss the matter with him. Harding didn't say any more during this meeting.

With regard to the recognition of our neutrality, Eden said that it would make enormous difficulties of every kind for them. He mentioned South Africa again, but I waited for our next private meeting to resume the discussion on this matter. They would see at once about facilities for our German aliens. There must be proper supervision during their passage to England, and they should be handed over by our police to theirs at Dublin or Holyhead. I did not object.

They would do their best about the armament orders and were talking to the people concerned. Eden would immediately look for the proper type of representative.

After this interview, which on the English side bore all the marks of Harding's inspiration, I decided to have a further frank talk with Eden. I arranged it early on

---

[1] The post of British High Commissioner to Egypt and Sudan ceased to exist in 1936. Sir Miles Lampson (1880-1964), the last official appointed to the post in 1934, immediately became British Ambassador to Egypt (1936-46) after the ratification of the Anglo-Egyptian Treaty of Alliance, 1936.

[2] Admiral Sir Tom Phillips (1888-1941), Deputy Chief of the Naval Staff (1939-41).

Friday morning (8th Sept.) before the High Commissioner had come to the office. I suggested to the latter that it might be easier for Eden to take in good part all I was going to say to him if there were no witness. The High Commissioner was slightly hurt at the idea of being left out, and he thought that Eden would not be affected by his presence. So we saw him again for about an hour before the Cabinet met at 11.30.

I began by saying that I had been very tired the previous morning after a trying journey, and I had perhaps not given him as complete a background of our position as he would wish to have. He responded at once, and said that I was to talk with the greatest possible freedom. He wanted to have the complete picture and I was to have no hesitation in saying exactly what I thought. I spoke more or less as follows: The new Representative would be useless for both sides if he did not understand our fundamental attitude towards Great Britain. We regarded ourselves as a nation just as old, and just as good as the British nation. We were not an ex-colony, and I was afraid that his allusions to South Africa indicated that he himself was starting from false premises. We were a mother country, just as Great Britain was, and the one thing that wounded us most was to be treated as an ex-colony or as a Dominion. That course had unfortunately been invariably adopted by the Dominions Office for the twenty years I had been in contact with them. I had myself made suggestion after suggestion to them long before our present Government came into office which if they had been met with any breadth of outlook would have prevented a lot of our present difficulties from arising. But I had always found Sir Edward Harding so exposed[1] to every expression of equality, and so determined to keep us in a subordinate position, that I had to conclude that his mentality made him completely unfit to deal with any self-respecting country. The extent of his interest in Ireland was probably measured by the fact that during some twenty years he had passed only two afternoons in our country. I believed he was very largely responsible for the bad advice upon which the British Government had been acting in our regard.

A very early opportunity should be sought, perhaps in connection with the new appointment to Dublin, to refer to Ireland publicly as a separate nation and a mother country with a history as venerable as that of Britain herself, and therefore entitled to special treatment. The British were always asking us to advance towards them, but they refused to recognise the things which meant most for us. Economic concessions were of small value compared with an open and frank recognition of our separate nationhood. We were a proud people, and we refused to shorten our memories to suit them. He had said that we had long memories, but he must remember that what were mere incidents in Britain's long career of conquests were fundamental changes in our social and national life affecting the whole destiny of our people. We remembered the past which they wanted us to forget, largely because its effects were present to us in our daily lives. I spoke of our devotion to our language by symbolising our determination to restore our nation to its full life. I mentioned again and again the absolute need of ending the unity question. He said he thought we had begun the agitation too suddenly. I replied that that was a matter of opinion. Their duty at any rate was perfectly clear.

At the end of this conversation, I thought it wise to mention the possibility of the Services getting their head with regard to the use of our ports, and I enlarged

---

[1] Walshe may have meant 'opposed'.

what a disaster that would be for all concerned. Eden said, the Services could not act independently of the Cabinet.

My brief account of what took place at this meeting may give the impression that I drove Eden a little too hard. That is not so. I spoke all the time very objectively, and in the most friendly way. When I had finished, Eden told me that he was really grateful, and he appeared to be sincere in saying this. He would take the greatest possible care in selecting the new Representative and he would repeat to him all I had said in the course of that conversation. I could also assure Mr. de Valera that he would keep all these things in mind in dealing with Ireland.

The first result of this talk came late in the evening in the form of a personal and secret message from Machtig to me, acting no doubt on Eden's instructions, that although Harding was not going to South Africa for some considerable time,[1] he would be fading out of the D.O. in a few weeks and Machtig will take charge.

No. 16 NAI DFA Washington Embassy Confidential Reports 1938-9

Confidential report from Robert Brennan to Joseph P. Walshe (Dublin)
(108/51/39) (Copy)

WASHINGTON, 11 September 1939

The original document drawn up by the State Department for the signature of the President on the 5th September, proclaiming the neutrality of the United States, began as follows 'Proclaiming the neutrality of the United States in the war between Germany and France; Poland; and the United Kingdom, the British Dominions beyond the seas and India'. In order to get over any difficulty about Ireland, the term 'Northern Ireland' was omitted. The President, himself, changed the wording (see cutting herewith)[2] knocking out 'the British Dominions beyond the seas' and adding 'Australia and New Zealand'. This was due to the fact that Canada and South Africa had not then declared war.

At first it was thought that because of this, arms could be shipped to Canada if Canada did not declare war. The State Department, however, held that when Great Britain declares war, the whole Empire is at war, and that the Dominions have no say in this. What they have a say in is whether they will participate and to what extent. They quote regarding this view Ernest La Pointe, Minister of Justice and Attorney General of Canada who is reported to have stated in the Canadian Parliament that Canada had powers to refuse to participate in any war, but that if Great Britain was at war it was nonsense to say Canada could be neutral. The Canadian Parliament had the right to sever their connection with the British Empire, and that was the only way they could remain neutral. They quoted also one of the South African Ministers to the same effect and also Professor Berriedale-Keith.[3]

[stamped] (Signed) ROBT. BRENNAN

---

[1] In 1939 Harding was appointed High Commissioner to Basutoland, the Bechuanaland Protectorate, Swaziland, and to the Union of South Africa. He took up the post in January 1940.
[2] Not printed.
[3] Professor Arthur Berriedale Keith (1879-1944), Chair of Sanskrit and Comparative Philology and later lecturer on the constitution of the British Empire at the University of Edinburgh (1914-44).

No. 17 NAI DFA 219/7

Confidential report from Francis T. Cremins to Joseph P. Walshe (Dublin)
(S.Gen. 1/1) (Confidential)

GENEVA, 11 September 1939

With reference to previous reports regarding the general situation,[1] I have to state, for the information of the Minister, that public opinion remains calm here, and, as was to have been expected, the spirit and morale of the people continues high. It is clear that all steps have been taken by the authorities to carry out and maintain the policy of the strictest neutrality, but it is manifest also that the general sympathy of the population is with the country which is regarded as offering resistance to aggression. Generally speaking, the newspapers present reports of political and military events with the greatest objectivity, which does not however prevent the commentaries from being occasionally surprisingly outspoken.

With attention for the most part now focussed on the east of Europe, there is not much at present in the situation to excite opinion here. If and when however, and it may be in the near future, Germany is in a position to turn her eyes seriously westwards, I have no doubt that the situation may again be serious for small countries at the ends of the Maginot line. The position of Roumania may also prove to be interesting.

So far as Geneva is concerned, life is naturally much quieter than usual, with so many men withdrawn for military service. There is no shortage of food, and people are using their reserve stocks of those commodities such as sugar, rice, certain cereals, etc. which have been temporarily withdrawn from the market. The restaurants function as usual. Petrol has been rationed during the past couple of weeks – sixty litres a fortnight are allowed – and apparently this will be continued, and since yesterday automobiles are not permitted to circulate on Sundays or holidays, exceptions being of course provided for. There have been no blackouts at night so far, but the lighting of the town has been reduced, and France, across the lake, seems to settle down each evening into complete darkness.

I am sending with separate minutes copies of the multifarious laws and decrees which are being brought into force by the Federal Authorities to meet the situation in which Switzerland finds itself.[2] These bear on many subjects, for example, neutrality and maintenance of neutrality; organisation of war economy; use of wireless stations; limitation of exports; insurance of transports against war risks; prices and cost of living; grinding of corn, etc.; provisional rationing of petrol and oil; entry of aliens, etc. etc. The bringing into force of compulsory service for work of national importance is especially interesting. This has been rendered necessary of course by the withdrawal of labour for military service.

I am told that the Federal people are in a much better position than they were during the previous war to make provision for all the possibilities, and that they are this time putting immediately into practice the lessons which they learned during the period 1914-1918. It has been arranged that much of the provisioning of the country will be effected through Italy, but naturally that arrangement might have to be modified if Italy entered the war.

---

[1] See No. 4 and DIFP V, Nos 351 and 354.
[2] Not printed.

The League and the International Labour Office continue to function as best they can, but it is clear that there will be, almost immediately, further reductions of staff and large economies. At present the Institutions, like the Government representatives here, are waiting on events. I presume that I will shortly receive instructions on the various points which I raised in previous minutes. I am sending you a diplomatic bag today, though I do not know when it is likely to reach you. I understand that it will go from here to Basle. I have received no correspondence from Dublin since the war commenced, but for the past couple of days, newspapers and private letters are dribbling in.

There have been 600 or 700 people of British nationality, and many of other nationalities, stranded here for the past week or so. There are also 3 or 4 Irish, Mrs. Reid, of Elgin Road, Dublin, and her son Noel Reid, and a Miss de la Hoide and a Miss Lecky-Watson of Dublin. Mr. W. McConnell of Dublin was here until Saturday when he left to return to Dublin by Germany and Holland. He had been in Germany and Budapest when the war broke out. The British Consul here – Mr. Livingston – has arranged with the French authorities for a special train which will leave Geneva on Wednesday, 13 September at 2.06 p.m. and run direct to a French port. The journey will take from 36 to 48 hours, and I understand that a boat will be available to take the travellers to England. The Irish will also travel on this train as the British Consul will include them in the general visa which he has arranged for the party instead of the individual military visas at first insisted upon for all travellers by the French authorities. Before accepting people with Irish passports the Consul asks me to vouch for the persons concerned. This is a precaution against I.R.A. activities. He states that the precautions being taken are very stringent. Mr. Peter Mortished, son of Mr. Mortished,[1] will also travel with the party as he is returning to college in Dublin. The British Consul advances money where necessary to pay fares, subsistence, etc., on a signed undertaking being given to refund the amounts later.

The outbreak of war has disillusioned many people here: the leftists who feel that Russia has let them down, and those who held that it was only necessary to stand up to Hitler to preserve peace. There are few now who would seriously argue that once a nation like Germany was allowed to re-arm, a constructive – Article 19 – policy, in addition to a strong – Article 16 – policy, became immediately necessary.[2] It was a question for the Powers chiefly concerned of treating with Germany and others, in time, or eventually having to fight them. This constructive policy was always urged at Geneva by the Minister. Some people continue to argue that armed resistance should have been put up in September last, but the progress in Poland in a week is some indication of what the fate of Czechoslovakia would have been with its defences turned by the annexation of Austria and its Slovaks and the rest; apart from the better state of general preparedness which the interval has brought to the Western Powers.

[signed] F.T. CREMINS
Permanent Delegate

---

[1] R. J. P. Mortished (1891-1957), an Irish official of the International Labour Office (1929-45).
[2] Cremins was referring to Articles 16 and 19 of the Covenant of the League of Nations.

1939

No. 18 NAI CAB 2/2

> *Extract from the minutes of a meeting of the Cabinet*
> *(G.C. 2/97) (Item 2) (S. 11419)*
> DUBLIN, 12 September 1939

Belligerent Naval Craft: Draft Communication

Consideration was given to a draft communication to belligerent Governments regarding the position of their naval and air craft, submitted by the Minister for External Affairs.[1]

General approval was given to the draft subject to any drafting amendments that may be decided upon by the Minister for External Affairs.

No. 19 NAI DFA Secretary's Files A75

> *Aide mémoire to British, French and German governments regarding*
> *restrictions on the use of Ireland's territorial waters*
> DUBLIN, 12 September 1939

The Government of Ireland, in order to ensure and maintain the neutral status of Ireland during the present state of War in Europe, have decided to place immediate restrictions on the use of Ireland's territorial waters, ports and roadsteads by vessels of war, whether surface or submarine craft, belonging to the belligerent Powers. They intend, moreover, to prohibit the entry into Irish jurisdiction of belligerent military aircraft.

2. The Government of Ireland propose to apply, generally, to belligerent surface war vessels the rules laid down in Convention (No. XIII) concerning the rights and duties of neutral Powers in naval war, which was signed at the Hague on the 18th October, 1907. Accordingly, they have decided to prohibit within the territorial waters, ports and roadsteads of Ireland, all warlike operations on the part of any belligerent vessel armed for war, including belligerent surface vessels which are not naval war vessels, but which carry armaments other than armaments of a purely defensive character. The right to sojourn within the territorial waters, ports or roadsteads of Ireland will be prohibited until further notice to all such belligerent vessels armed for war. Exception may be made only in certain well-recognised cases of distress or necessity for periods of time not exceeding, as a general rule, a period of twenty-four hours.

3. The Government of Ireland have further decided, in accordance with the practice of other neutral Governments, to prohibit to all belligerent submarines armed for war the right to navigate or sojourn in Irish territorial waters, ports or roadsteads. Exception may be made only in cases where such submarines are forced to enter Irish waters due to severe damage amounting to disablement. In such cases, belligerent submarines must navigate on the surface and display conspicuously their national flag and other identification marks. Such submarines, in the event of salvage, will be interned until the cessation of the hostilities.

4. The Government of Ireland, relying on the principle enunciated in Article 1 of the International Convention for Air Navigation, 1919, whereby the air space above

---

[1] See No. 19.

the territory and territorial waters of a State shall be recognised as within its complete and exclusive sovereignty, propose to prohibit all military aircraft belonging to the belligerent Powers from entering the jurisdiction of Ireland

5. Pending the making of appropriate Orders to give effect to the aforementioned proposals, the Government of Ireland desires to make them generally known to the .... Government. The text of the Orders will be duly forwarded as soon as the Orders are made.

No. 20 NAI DFA 219/2

Letter from Frederick H. Boland to Leopold H. Kerney (San Sebastian)
(Copy) (219/2)

DUBLIN, 14 September 1939

With reference to your minute (S.S. 27/6) of 7th inst.,[1] I should be glad if you would be good enough to forward the text of the neutrality Decree published in the 'Boletin Oficial' on the 5th September. If the Decree is not too long, perhaps you could furnish us with a translation of it.

It will be very useful if you can arrange to report fully from time to time on Spain's neutrality policy and the legislative and other measures taken to give effect to it.

If there is an official censorship in force in Spain, we would be interested to know the details of its application to the official telegraphic and postal correspondence of the diplomatic missions.

[stamped] (Signed) F.H. BOLAND
Rúnaí

No. 21 NAI DFA 219/4

Confidential report from William Warnock to Joseph P. Walshe (Dublin)
(43/33)

BERLIN, 14 September 1939

It is still difficult to grasp that a great war is in progress, even after ten days of general hostilities. The population here had been more or less led to believe that there would be no war. Now that it has started, the blame is thrown on Germany's enemies, particularly Great Britain. France is regarded as Britain's dupe.

Food is strictly rationed, but the amounts available are at the moment quite adequate. I can speak from experience, as only today has the Foreign Office arranged that I be supplied with greater quantities than those laid down for the ordinary German citizen. The diplomatic missions were asked to send in estimates of their requirements. My requests have been satisfied in practically all details.

I am entitled to receive 300 litres of petrol per month. Permanent heads of mission receive double that amount. I think that 300 litres per month will well suffice – my car is a Ford V8 – as there is now little enticement to long journeys. The use of motor-cars by private persons has practically ceased. Persons who travel by car attract considerable attention, and usually unfavourable criticism.

---

[1] Not printed.

Berlin and all other cities are 'blacked out' each night. Each house is required to have a cellar prepared for use during air-raids, and many houses have sandbags as protection against splinters and shrapnel. Most of the people have gas-masks. We are clearing out a cellar in the Legation, but we have not yet bought any sandbags, nor have any of us got gasmasks. If, however, events show that raiding aeroplanes can reach Berlin we shall have to obtain both sandbags and gasmasks. So far, there have been two alarms, but no enemy aircraft reached the city. Polish reports of air-raids on Berlin are ridiculous. On the second occasion, British raiders came as near to Berlin as Hanover, which is only about an hour's flying distance away.

The population has quickly adapted itself to the new circumstances. The average citizen feels that it is up to him to do his part, because if Germany loses the present struggle, she will emerge in a state of complete chaos, perhaps even worse than in 1918. It is a great mistake for the British to think, at least in the early stages of the war, that they can drive a wedge between the German Government and the people. The Germans make no secret of the fact that they have always regarded themselves as a soldier-nation. Adolf Hitler took full account of this when building up the National Socialist Party; he knows and understands his people. The man-in-the-street is profoundly and reverently thankful to him for having brought Germany once more to a position of military greatness. As long as I have been living here I have noticed that news-films showing units of the armed forces draw enthusiastic applause at all times.

The rapid advance of the German Army on the Eastern Front surprised everybody. It is as yet too early to judge whether the Polish withdrawal across the Vistula was in the nature of flight before the strong German forces or whether it was in reality a strategic retreat, as the Poles now claim. I understand from journalists of neutral countries that the Poles were guilty of indescribable barbarity in the German areas of West Prussia and Posen (the 'Corridor') before they retreated. Germans were murdered out of hand, and their bodies disfigured in an abominable way.

Great Britain is singled out as the 'villain of the piece' by the German propagandists. The attitude towards France is quite different – almost commiserating in fact. In the early days of the war many people had persuaded themselves that France would not come in at all. 'What', said they, 'do we want from France? And what do they want from us? The Führer has already assured France that our frontier in the west has been fixed for all time. He would never have ordered the construction of the magnificent fortifications which we now have in the west if he felt that the frontier would eventually be pushed forward. How can it be said that we threaten France?'

It has now become obvious that France has every intention of taking part in the war. The hope is still encouraged that after the final defeat of Poland the British and French will retire gracefully, and will be glad to cut their losses.

It is prohibited by law to listen-in to foreign broadcasting stations. This law is rigidly observed, so that enemy attempts to reach the attention of the German people by wireless propaganda are without avail. I find it difficult to hear either Athlone or the new Irish experimental short-wave station distinctly. Most evenings they are both completely blotted out by interference from other stations. I can receive British and French stations quite well. My experience is that Italian and

Russian stations are much the best for news. The stations in the belligerent countries devote so much time to propaganda that it is hardly worth while listening to them at all. The news-bulletins from Athlone are excellent, but, as I said before, I have difficulty in hearing them.

All theatres and places of amusement are still open, and life in Berlin is by no means unpleasant. As the city is hundreds of miles from the Western front, it has not been considered necessary to evacuate the population.

We Irish are extremely popular at the moment. Until the last moment there were doubts expressed as to whether we would come in on Great Britain's side. Once our position had been made clear, our neutrality was given full publicity over the wireless and in the newspapers. Disappointment was felt that the Union of South Africa joined the enemy front. That came as somewhat of a surprise, particularly to the members of the South African Legation here. So far as I could judge, the members of the Legation were, without exception, strongly in favour of neutrality.

I hope that we shall soon have a more direct way of communicating with you than that through Rome. Our activities are, of course, rather curtailed, but even so the closer touch we have with the Department the more satisfactory for all concerned.

[signed] W. Warnock

No. 22 NAI DFA Secretary's Files A20/2

Extract from a memorandum from Leopold H. Kerney to Joseph P. Walshe (Dublin)

San Sebastian, 14 September 1939

Further to my minute of 1st inst.,[1] I telephoned to Burgos on 9th inst. and asked for the Minister for Foreign Affairs. Barcenas came to the 'phone; he enquired as to the purpose of my telephone call; I told him that the Minister had requested that I should telephone to him; he said the Minister was busy and again asked what was the matter I wished to discuss. I replied – 'Ryan'; he asked me to hold the line; a couple of minutes later Beigbeder's[2] Chef de cabinet (Barcenas' son) came to the 'phone and said that the Minister had not yet got a reply, but hoped to have one in two or three days' time. I said that I would wait to hear from the Minister.

The Duchess of Tetuan[3] is cooperating with me and taking a very friendly interest in Ryan; in full agreement with myself, she went to Burgos and was able to pay a visit to Ryan on 12th September, Beigbeder having given her the necessary special authorisation and also providing her with an official car to go from Burgos to the prison. It would be good policy to allow it to appear in the press that the Duchess of Tetuan visited Frank Ryan in Burgos Central Prison and is anxious to assist in securing his release at an early date, knowing that his continued imprisonment causes much concern in Ireland.

On 13th September the Duchess gave me an account of her visit to Burgos; Beigbeder told her that he had brought Ryan's case to Franco's notice 'à plusieurs

---

[1] Not printed
[2] Juan Beigbeder Atienza (1888-1957), Spanish Foreign Minister (Aug.-Oct. 1939).
[3] Blanca O'Donnell, the Duchess of Tetuan.

reprises', but that Franco had given no decision; she asked him whether it would be advisable for her to see Franco, and he replied that 'anything more that might be done would be all to the good.' I have asked her to seek an audience with Franco as soon as possible, and she intends to do so through the medium of Beigbeder. She expects to leave for Madrid in the car of the Finnish Minister on 18th September but will return from Madrid to Burgos at any moment if she can get an appointment; if this can only be fixed after her return to San Sebastian I have offered to put my car at her disposal for any such visit to Burgos. I have also asked her to make a point of seeing Fusset,[1] but not before her audience with Franco, Ryan's chief enemy from the start, and whose mind was poisoned against him by Gunning[2] and others; Hodgson[3] did his best to prejudice Fusset (and also Lopez Pinto)[4] against Ryan, as being a dangerous communist and an assassin; the Duchess has been given all necessary arguments by me, and she has herself formed a very favourable impression of Ryan from her conversation with him; she has even discussed with him ways and means of cooperating later on in bringing Spain and Ireland closer together; Ryan told her (in confidence, of course) that he had made a mistake in going to Spain, but that he could not make any confession of that kind before a Tribunal. The importance of her cooperation with me lies in the fact that she enjoys the esteem and friendship of the present Minister for Foreign Affairs, that, as daughter of the former Duke of Tetuan, she is practically certain to be given an audience by Franco, and that, as a Spaniard, she can stress the importance, from the Spanish point of view, of doing as we want.

The Director of the prison in Burgos told the Duchess that she could visit Frank Ryan there as often as she wished; I have prepared a parcel of foodstuffs etc. for him, and she will take this to the prison, probably on 18th September, on her way through Burgos to Madrid.

[signed] L.H. Kerney

No. 23 NAI DFA 241/89

Letter from Joseph P. Walshe to Wacław Tadeusz Dobrzyński (Dublin) (Copy)

Dublin, 15 September 1939

Sir,

I am directed by the Minister for External Affairs to thank you for your communication of the 11th September, in which you informed him of the existence of a state of war between Poland and Germany.

---

[1] Martinez Fusset, Franco's principal legal advisor.
[2] Thomas Gunning, Irish Brigade volunteer in the Spanish Civil War. Gunning remained in Spain after the conflict ended and encouraged the Spanish authorities to execute Ryan.
[3] Sir Robert Hodgson (1874-1956), British Agent to Nationalist Spain (1937-9), British Chargé d'Affaires to Spain (1939).
[4] General José Lopez-Pinto Berizo (1876-1942), Spanish Nationalist General.

No. 24 NAI DFA Legal Adviser's Papers

*Memorandum on the Emergency Powers (No. 5) Order 1939
from Michael Rynne to Joseph P. Walshe (Dublin)
(Copy) (Secret)*

DUBLIN, 15 September 1939

1. We are asked to reply immediately to the Secret minute dated 14th September,[1] which we have received from the Controller of Censorship[2] in regard to the draft of an Order to be entitled the Emergency Powers (No. 5) Order, 1939.
2. We are not asked to comment on the draft Order, and there is probably no reason why we should want to. In accordance with the usual practice adopted by the Parliamentary Draftsman in drafting such Orders, no penalties are set out for contraventions of the Order. Hence, it would appear that the very effective penalty of closing down an Irish newspaper's offices for a period of time cannot be resorted to where such a newspaper's proprietors or editors have disobeyed a prohibition imposed by an 'authorised person' under the Order.
3. The Controller of Censorship does not ask us to put forward any constructive suggestions as to 'the matters arising in our Department' which we might desire to have dealt with positively in Irish newspapers. The reason for that may be that the Order, as now drafted, is mainly repressive in character, although Article 5, paragraphs (2), (3), (4), (5) and (6) refer to requests by the Government for the publication of official documents in Irish newspapers.
4. What we are specifically asked to do is to give definite particulars of matters, objectionable from the point of view of our Department, the publication of which we desire to have *prohibited*.
5. It is submitted, however, that this Department, unlike other Departments of State, has a positive as well as a negative policy in regard to censorship. Insofar as we will want to continue our normal peacetime policy of averting as far as possible all causes of offence to friendly States, their rulers and peoples, our future policy will be negative. But, if the Department is to fulfil the special duty laid upon it in the present emergency, to ensure and maintain the status of neutrality vis-à-vis all the belligerent States, it is clear that a public opinion must be built up in this country favourable to Irish neutrality at once. A purely negative Press censorship policy will not achieve this end. A positive newspaper campaign would go far to do so.
6. We may assume that, notwithstanding the broad lines of the new draft Order, it will be possible for the Controller of Censorship to exert considerable influence on what goes into the Press as well as on what must be kept out of it. No doubt, he or some other 'authorised person' will address representatives of the leading dailies from time to time in order to advise them how best to avoid having their journals fall victims to the Censor's scissors. That being so, it is suggested that all the arguments in favour of neutral status should be urged upon newspapermen who should be prevailed upon to present and 'feature' them constantly.
7. Even from the standpoint of newspaper proprietors, the foregoing suggestion should commend itself. Newspapers are now being confronted with enormous

---

[1] Not printed.
[2] Tommy Coyne (1901-1961), Controller of Censorship (1941-6). See biographical details in DIFP IV, p. xxiii.

difficulties. They are likely to lose a large amount of their advertising matter, to find their paper supplies severely restricted, and, on top of those disadvantages, they will be asked to sacrifice much of the material which they have to buy on a permanent contract basis from British controlled Press agencies. Any proposals of a constructive nature may be expected to be welcomed, and if this Department can supply material as well, having, of course, some news value, there is no doubt that the newspapers will prefer that method of approach than the way of the scissors.

8. Between the alternatives of 'putting over' the neutrality policy peaceably now or having to impose it later on by force (or relinquish it altogether), the Government have scarcely any choice. There can be no question as to which is the more expedient plan. This is especially the case as far as the Department of External Affairs is concerned. Unless the public are quickly rendered 'neutral-minded', the Department is going to find a quite disproportionate share of its official time taken up by apologies and 'explanations' to the belligerent Governments.

9. The Press is the greatest potential ally available at the present time in the campaign to establish the neutrality principle firmly once for all in this country. And, once that principle is really supported at home by the vast majority of Irish people, the difficulties that it may involve vis-à-vis foreign States will be fewer and easier to adjust.

10. It is accordingly submitted that we might reply to the Controller of Censorship's minute in terms which will not only furnish him with a complete catalogue of the topics which we would prefer to have prohibited, but also with a list of matters that we would like to see emphasised.

11. Among the first class of matters, namely, the prohibited matters, we will, no doubt, mention all references to Heads of States, whether direct or indirect, in printed or pictorial form, in newspapers or on posters, which might be liable to give offence to such Heads of States or their representatives (if any) here. Also, similar references to foreign Governments, peoples, armies, customs, religions, ways of living, etc. We might even propose, for greater safety, that no newspaper posters containing more than the name of the relevant journal should be allowed. And we might, perhaps, recommend the prohibition of ribbon headlines. Such prohibitions form part of the normal regulations in force in some States. The Swiss papers, for instance, appear to avoid sensational headlines, and, during the present emergency, newspaper vendors are forbidden to shout the contents of their wares. In France, 'Stop Presses' are prohibited.

12. On the positive side, however, it is thought that we should be more detailed in our recommendations. We might, for instance, suggest that Irish newspapers be generally informed in the following sense regarding the Government's neutrality policy:-
- (a) Neutrality is the only logical policy for Ireland which neither lost nor gained by the Peace Treaties, 1919. For, notwithstanding propaganda to the contrary, the truth appears to be that the present war is being waged between the 'have' and the 'have not' States.
- (b) Neutrality is the only decent attitude for a Christian country like this to adopt at the present time. Ireland has, since the creation of the Irish State, used all her endeavours to establish tolerance and goodwill at home and to further peace efforts abroad.

(c) The difficulties of neutrality have been exaggerated. There are certainly great difficulties for States close up to the firing line, such as Denmark for example, but experience has shown that those difficulties have the effect of drawing the people of neutral States closer together precisely in favour of the preservation of their neutrality.

(d) The cost of neutrality is nothing like the cost of war. If some people are suffering materially now, it is due not to their own country's neutrality, but to the war which is taking place elsewhere. Were Ireland at war, that suffering would be increased a hundredfold. This is a time of individual readjustment everywhere.

13. Even using the limited sources at their disposal, Irish newspaper editors should be able to convey to the public:-

(a) The fact that this is not a 'world war' like that of 1914-1918. That means that every country is consulting its own best interests, which nearly always results in the decision to remain neutral. A list of those countries which have declared their neutrality should be published prominently from day to day. New additions to the list should be given larger headlines than the 'war news'.

(b) The incidental 'horrors of war' should be pointed out, even if the 'atrocity' stories are eliminated. Thus, news of famine, disease, high living costs and food shortage consequent on the war and coming from the countries at war ought to get full publicity with suitable editorial comment.

(c) All attempts to bring about peace, especially those emanating from the Vatican and neutral countries such as Catholic Belgium, should be described in as much detail as possible. When the British agencies do not give such particulars at the time, they should be sought out some days later in the appropriate Continental journals. The demand for 'hot' news will, no doubt, fall off as a result of the censorship. News will be welcome whenever it is available and after some days the time-lag will not be very noticeable, because regular.

14. It is going to be difficult to explain to the Controller of Censorship how we would wish to have the Irish papers controlled in regard to the more subtle kind of anti-neutrality items which the 'Irish Times' has been publishing recently. The general tone of such items is favourable to the idea of neutrality, but, by damning it with faint encouragement, leaves on the reader's mind the impression that Ireland cannot remain neutral for long. Perhaps, if you were to speak personally to the Chief Press Censor and to illustrate your remarks by references to the offending items, the Department's view might be easier to appreciate.

15. No attempt to deal with the positive aspect of the Department's view on Press censorship is being made here. Only a few general ideas are given so as to draw urgent attention to the fact that merely suppressive measures (or the method of providing 'antidotes' in the form of pro-German reports) would not meet our needs. On the repressive side, we would simply require that neither pro-British nor pro-German matter should go into the papers as such. On the positive side, we will have to ask for the deliberate creation by Press propaganda of a neutrally-minded public opinion here in the shortest possible time.

No. 25 NAI DFA 219/6

Confidential report from Michael MacWhite to Joseph P. Walshe (Dublin)
(Confidential) (Copy)

ROME, 15 September 1939

If it were not for the disappearance of motor traffic from the streets and the scarcity of foreigners in public places, the aspect of Rome at the moment has all the appearances of normality. The Café habitués are in their usual places from six to eight every evening and late comers will have to be satisfied with the less fashionable resorts, off the main thoroughfares. It would be difficult to tell from the faces of the people that their next door neighbours are fighting a desperate war in which they themselves may be plunged at any moment.

Despite this superficial calm there is immense activity behind the screen from which the public gaze is excluded. There was a public announcement that two classes were to be called to the colours on the third of September. They had eight days' notice and an extra day of grace was given them to show that there was neither haste nor anxiety – less so even than if it were for any army manoeuvre. Since then, however, no further classes have been called, as such, but thousands of individuals get their marching orders overnight to present themselves at their battalion headquarters within twenty-four hours. In this fashion, without any outcry, the effective of perhaps two or three other classes are now under arms.

Large reinforcements sail almost daily from North Africa and Sardinia. The naval and air mobilisation was completed some time ago. Since the fourth of September Italian munition factories are working on a twenty-four hour schedule and at the beginning of this week Factory heads received orders to ignore the clauses of the law governing the conditions of labour of which Fascist leaders are so proud.

There is a scarcity of many articles of prime necessity. The sale of coffee has been forbidden altogether and large money prizes are being offered to chemists and others who can provide an artificial substitute for tea and coffee. Sugar is only obtainable occasionally and only then at an abnormal cost. Bicycles are no longer obtainable and those ordering same are told they must wait three months for delivery. In accordance with the policy of re-assuring the public, automobiles may be allowed to run again, but the price of gasoline has been increased from 3.50 lire to 8 lire per litre. Only very few Italians can afford to pay this price so the apparent concession turns out to be a Greek gift.

It is now reported on good authority that hospitals in the North East of Italy near the Yougoslav frontier, have been evacuated and put in readiness for the reception of refugees, it is said, but what refugees? It would appear as if they are being prepared in anticipation for national requirements. Now that Hitler has control of most of Poland, can it be that he invites the Duce to help himself to Yougoslavia? Whether this be so or not, it is certain that Italy is preparing for war as discreetly as possible.

In a recent article Gayda[1] admitted as much and added that this country would play an important role in the European struggle if, when, and where its best interests would be served thereby. He did not say on which side, as that will depend on

---

[1] Virginio Gayda, Italian journalist and editor of *Il Giornale d'Italia*.

whether France and England are ready and willing to pay the high price the Duce demands. Hitler, who realises the danger of a long war, would not hesitate, perhaps, to bid higher, even though he may not be in a position to honour his signature on the day of reckoning.

If Italy were to place herself on the side of England and France at the moment, Hitler's cause would be irretrievably lost, for the Balkan States are awake to the Duce's slightest gesture and his support of the allies would set the armies of Roumania, Yougoslavia and even Hungary, marching against Germany. They are held back now from helping Poland because of their fear of being attacked from behind.

Even if Italy decides that her best interests are served by remaining neutral and wishes to do so, the day might come when the Allies would force her to show her colours, for one thing is certain, that if this war lasts for three years, there will be no neutrals. It is even doubtful that many will be regarded as such at the end of three months. It may be, and there are military experts who hold the opinion, that Italy by remaining neutral is a greater asset to Germany than if the two armies were fighting side by side. There are no fortifications of any consequence on the old Austro-Italian frontier and if, by any chance, a French army were able to crash its way into Northern Italy, the seat of Italian industry would be in their hands, and the back door to Germany within easy reach.

From the naval and economic angle, even without any military disaster, Italy would be in a very embarrassing position. She would be cut off from her supplies of food and raw materials – oil, wool, cotton, steel, copper, etc. She could not hope for any supplies from her North African Colonies as they are not self supporting. She could hardly hope to get the mastery of the Mediterranean without which she would be completely isolated. The Suez Canal would be closed and so also would the Dardanelles and, in all likelihood, British Colonial troops would attempt to seize Ethiopia from the Italian garrison which would be then cut off from the mother country. All this would lead a realist to conclude that the Duce, by remaining neutral, for the time being, is acting with good judgment and common sense. He holds some excellent cards in his hands, but if he raises the stakes beyond the reach of the other players he may find himself in the same predicament as many an old time gambler in an American mining camp.

[signed] M. MacWhite

No. 26 NAI DFA Legal Adviser's Papers

Memorandum from Michael Rynne to Joseph P. Walshe (Dublin)
(Copy) (Most Secret)

Dublin, 16 September 1939

The maintenance of Neutrality

It is becoming increasingly obvious that the maintenance of our neutrality is going to involve us, practically every day, in difficult decisions of policy. I have been considering one such 'daily problem' (re messages received from 'Cabot')[1] since yesterday. The *legal* answer to that problem is, as usual, quite easy to find. But, if

---

[1] Short Empire 'C-Class' Flying Boat: 'Cabot' had served with Imperial Airways under the registration G-AFCU until 1939 when it began military service with the RAF as V3138.

we want to stay out of war, we must not tie ourselves to the strict law, and yet we cannot embark with safety on a policy of applying the law to one belligerent and waiving it in favour of another.

2. What are the essential *facts* of our position?

Although the question-mark is only too evident, one may hazard the following reply:-

i) The Germans want us neutral. They know that, if we were not so, we would be on England's side at this early stage of the war. Towards the end of the war, after a German victory was practically certain, Germany might prefer to have us on her side. The essential is that, at present, Germany prefers us neutral, because

   a) we represent at least one State of the Commonwealth which does not believe in the righteousness of Britain, of which British propaganda is trying to convince the world;
   b) our neutrality may inconvenience Britain's blockade policy;
   c) our neutrality, preventing the stampeding of the population into the British block, may be hoped to serve as a slight distraction to a belligerent Britain.

Of these three reasons, I think that 'reason a)' is self-sufficient. The moral effect of our declared neutrality is worth so much to Germany that she will not want to disturb our *status quo*.

ii) The British are resigned to our neutrality on certain terms. They know that, if we were not neutral to a fairly considerable extent,

   a) encouragement would be given to the pro-German element here which might eventually carry the day. To prevent such a possibility, Britain would have to 'lend' us troops that she could ill afford. How much better to let the country be held 'benevolently neutral' by an Irish Government plus a small Irish Army and Police. Should those means fail, the matter can always be reconsidered;
   b) a neutral island (whose neutrality has been promised respect by Germany) just next door has its advantages for Britain as an evacuation area, base hospital and centre of espionage, *or*, perhaps, counter-espionage;
   c) if we went 'loyal' to all appearances, we might be expected to insist on our pound of flesh in Ulster at a very awkward time. That might mean 1914 and 1916 all over again. 'The Irish cannot be trusted' – 'The Irish will always have a grievance'.

3. To conclude, given that the above premises are all fairly well-founded, we may take the view that our neutrality suits both belligerents at the moment. The Germans are so pleased that they have promised to recognise the status we have assumed, but the British are holding back for terms. In parenthesis, it may be remarked that neither belligerent is in the least likely to respect our 'neutral rights' in practice – but there we will be no worse off than any other small neutral country.

4. The main problem, therefore, that appears to confront us now is not a day-to-day problem (such as the 'Cabot' messages), but the question of what terms we will concede to Britain for what *quid pro quo*. This may not be realised as yet (which is the reason for this note) by our Government; it is, however, fully appreciated in Great Britain. By conveying the impression that they are 'disappointed' by our

attitude to the present war, the British are succeeding in conveying a menace to our integrity. Yet, it is clear, by hypothesis, that our attitude suits them just now. Why, then, do the British pretend to resent our neutrality, as exemplified by their reception of our recent Aide-Memoire?[1] Admitted that Irish neutrality and the Aide-Memoire represent a technical breach in the moral solidarity of the Empire, does not the real reason of Britain's lack of cordiality lie in her determination to extract good 'terms' from us?

5. The suggestion made here is that we stiffen up our give-and-take policy at once vis-à-vis the British. We know they are prepared to recognise our neutrality, therefore, should we not initiate at once a plan to obtain that recognition in formal terms precisely as we were accorded it by the Germans? It would seem not only absurd but distinctly dangerous to concede to a belligerent, whom we regard as a potential invader and who refuses to recognise us as a neutral country in a formal way, special privileges contrary to every ordinary rule of international neutrality law. But, granted a formal recognition such as the Germans gave us, the position might be different. We would be safer from invasion, inasmuch as Britain would find it harder to justify the invasion of a country whose neutrality she had agreed to respect.

The object is worth struggling for. The struggle might begin now with a stiff refusal to permit the 'Cabot' to use the Foynes radio station for un-neutral purposes, and might be followed up by a strong complaint against such incidents as the newspaper interview of the British airmen who landed on our waters. That incident can only be interpreted as an attempt to embroil us with the Germans, thus destroying our neutrality and landing us into the war. It was a complete letdown of the give and take policy – 'perfidious Albion' at her worst. How can the Government possibly be expected to be helpful at the present critical time (when the Treason Act is being availed of) if the British do not take Irish neutrality more seriously than that? The best and, indeed, the only solution from every point of view is that the British recognise and publish their recognition of our complete neutrality forthwith. We will then consider ways and means of co-operating as far as we can *within the limits of technical neutrality*. Otherwise, it may not be possible to guarantee a peaceful Ireland, so essential to Britain's immediate future.

No. 27 NAI DFA Washington Embassy Confidential Reports 1938-9

Confidential report from Robert Brennan to Joseph P. Walshe (Dublin)
(108/54/39) (Copy)

WASHINGTON, 16 September 1939

We are almost completely at a loss concerning information about current events in Ireland. We have to depend on very scanty reports in the American press. The Irish newspapers, which were usually necessarily seven to ten days late, are now received considerably later.

I have not been able to pick up the Irish short wave broadcast and neither has anybody here including the Consuls.

The Norwegians have adopted a very clever device. Every night the Norwegian Broadcasting Station sends out a short wave summary of the news of the day, and

---

[1] See No. 19.

information which is intended for Norwegian vessels on the high seas. This message is picked up by a press agent in New York by arrangement. He translates the message and mimeographs same, sending it out to stated addresses by air mail the same night in Norwegian and English. This means that the Norwegian Consuls and certain personages who are interested in Norwegian events receive the news in most cases on the following morning. I do not know whether such a thing is possible considering the weakness of our short wave station.

I am constantly asked questions bearing on the Irish Government's policy and on Irish events and, unfortunately, I am not able to give any replies beyond such replies as would be based on the scanty news in the American press. For instance, several people including newspaper men asked me what changes had occurred in the Irish Cabinet, and I was unable to reply because up to this morning, when a partial list was given in the New York Times, the only information was that Mr. de Valera had reshuffled his Cabinet.

[signed] ROBT. BRENNAN

No. 28 NAI DFA Holy See Embassy 20/34

Telegram from the Department of External Affairs to William J.B. Macaulay (Holy See)
(No. 38) (Personal)

DUBLIN, 19 September 1939

Please notify Vatican officially of Ireland's neutrality telling Chargé d'Affaires Berlin to inform German Government if he has not already done so.

No. 29 UCDA P150/2548

Letter from Neville Chamberlain to Eamon de Valera (Dublin)

LONDON, 19 September 1939

My dear Prime Minister,
Sir John Maffey has reported to me the substance of his talk with you last week in Dublin[1] and I am very glad indeed to have had this opportunity of establishing more direct contact with you.

Your suggestion that the United Kingdom representative in Dublin should have the name, and presumably the status, of Minister would raise most contentious issues for us here and is one which it would not be possible for me to accept. I hope therefore that you will see your way to help by accepting a solution which, in fact, represents a compromise between our respective points of view. The title 'Representative' would seem to be well suited to an appointment such as this which is essentially an emergency arrangement intended to meet a temporary but urgent situation.

At a time of crisis when so many questions of great moment to our two countries require urgent handling on a basis of most close and intimate understanding, it causes grave anxiety to me and to the War Cabinet that there should be no adequate representation of the United Kingdom in Dublin. The need for closer contact will grow more and more pressing. You may rely on us to operate it in such a

---

[1] Not printed.

manner as to cause you as little difficulty as possible and, having that assurance from me, I greatly hope that you will feel able to agree to my suggestion.

On the more general questions which are of immediate concern I think it better to leave it to Sir John Maffey to explain to you what we have in mind. The submarine menace at the present time is one of the outstanding problems engaging our thoughts and energies. So far as we can judge we have no reason to be dissatisfied with the success of our counter measures. But these measures are hampered in many ways, and the position may rapidly deteriorate unless we press on, using all available means with the utmost determination. In this sphere of activity problems may suddenly arise the solution of which would be of vital moment to this country and which would also naturally involve the interests of Éire. For that reason, I attach great importance to full mutual understanding of the special problems which the war has created for both of us, and to reaching some line of agreement as to how these difficulties can best be discussed and adjusted.

Kind regards
Yours sincerely
NEVILLE CHAMBERLAIN

No. 30 NAI DFA 2006/39

Letter from John W. Dulanty to Leslie Hore-Belisha (London)
(Copy)

LONDON, 19 September 1939

Dear Secretary of State,

Adverting to my letter of 7 September, my Government have written me urging the great necessity for an immediate delivery of the several equipments shown on the enclosed list.[1]

Although not unmindful of your difficulties let me entreat your personal help towards meeting our extremely urgent needs.

Yours sincerely,
(Sgd.) JOHN W. DULANTY

No. 31 NAI DFA Legal Adviser's Papers

Memorandum from Maurice Moynihan to General Peadar MacMahon
(Dublin) copied to the Department of External Affairs
(Copy)

DUBLIN, 21 September 1939

I am directed by the Taoiseach to inform you that he proposes when the Dáil meets on Wednesday to deal in a comprehensive survey with the special problems of this country arising out of the present situation with special reference to such matters as neutrality, finance, essential commodities, etc., military preparedness, unemployment, etc., and to indicate the steps which have been taken or which are contemplated by the Government to deal with the problems which have arisen.

For this purpose he wishes to be supplied at a *very early date* with a statement

---

[1] Not printed.

from your Department covering the various matters with which it is or will be dealing and in particular the following:-
1. Problems that arise in preserving our neutrality as a relatively small country while powerful neighbouring States are at war.
2. The necessity for being prepared to deal with any demands from belligerents on any side, the acceptance of which would involve infringement of our neutrality.
3. Illustrations by reference to problems presented to neutral countries (a) in the war 1914-1918 and (b) in the present war.
4. The necessity for avoiding any action which by giving assistance to belligerents on either side in their war-like operations could reasonably be interpreted as a breach of neutrality.
5. The necessity for being prepared as far as practicable against the danger, however remote, of attack from any quarter.
6. The censorship of communications and Press censorship with reference to 4 above.
7. Light restrictions with reference to 4 and 5 above.
8. The necessity for certain minimum military preparations within our resources.

I am also to request that you will be good enough to enumerate in detail the special emergency measures which it has been found necessary to take in your Department by way of (a) Government orders and (b) ministerial and subsidiary orders, and to indicate in each case the reasons which have rendered such measures necessary.

Signed – M. Ó MUIMHNEACHÁIN
Rúnaí

No. 32 NAI GOV 3/3

Extract from the minutes of a meeting of the Government
(G. 2/86) (S. 11417)

DUBLIN, 22 September 1939

1. *Diplomatic Representative in Ireland*
The appointment of a British Diplomatic Representative in Ireland was approved.

2. *Diplomatic Representative in Ireland*
The appointment of Sir John Maffey as British Diplomatic Representative in Ireland was approved.

No. 33 UCDA P150/2548

Letter from Eamon de Valera to Neville Chamberlain (London)
(Copy)

DUBLIN, 22 September 1939

My dear Prime Minister,
I received your letter of September 19th, and have had another talk with Sir John Maffey.[1]

---

[1] See No. 29.

My colleagues and I, in the circumstances, are prepared to accept the 'Representative' you propose. For a long time we have felt that it would greatly make for speed and efficiency if we had here an Ambassador or Minister from Britain to be a counterpart of our High Commissioner in London. We were aware that there would be certain difficulties on your side in the making of such an appointment, and did not consequently press the matter, although we were convinced that that was the wise policy to follow.

I have explained to Sir John Maffey the difficulties which the acceptance of your proposal will involve for us. He will I am sure make clear to you how much, in my opinion, will depend on the character of the person chosen to inaugurate the service. I have already informed my colleagues that I believed that Sir John Maffey has the experience and understanding necessary to make it a success.

I remain,
my dear Prime Minister,
Yours sincerely,
[signed] EAMON DE VALERA

I would like you to know how much I sympathise with you in your present anxieties. E. de V.[1]

No. 34 NAI DFA 219/2

Confidential report from Leopold H. Kerney to Joseph P. Walshe (Dublin)
(S.S. 27/6)
SAN SEBASTIAN, 22 September 1939

Spanish Neutrality

With reference to your minute 219/2 of 14th inst.,[2] the text of the neutrality decree published in the 'Voz de España' of 5th September,[3] and of which I forwarded you a copy on that date, was a faithful reproduction of the decree as published in the 'Boletin Oficial' of 5th September, and of which I sent you a copy on 16th September.[4]

It is a somewhat remarkable fact that no special measures of a legislative or military nature have so far been taken in Spain in connection with the war in Europe; I am alive to the importance of advising you promptly of any development which may be observed in either sphere.

Progress is being made with the building of machine-gun blockhouses on the main road between here and the frontier, and in some places what appear to be communication tunnels have been bored through rocks; the machine-gun nests are plainly visible on the roadside, but they are now being camouflaged; they are of course for defensive purposes only and work was begun on them as far back as July.

There are no special troop movements and no evidence so far of any intention to mobilise in defence of Spanish neutrality.

---

[1] Postscript by de Valera.
[2] See No. 20.
[3] See No. 7.
[4] Not printed.

The official military censorship which exists in Spain has nothing to do with the European war; it came into being during the civil war and its continued existence merely tends to prove that its suppression would be a risky experiment for the present regime. The official postal and telegraphic correspondence of diplomatic missions is respected as a rule, although mistakes occur and envelopes are sometimes opened; all letters pass through the hands of the military censor who puts his stamp on all envelopes, even when not opened. Letters addressed in my name, without indication of my representative position, have been opened by the censor; in such cases I have never protested, because the censor could not be expected to know the head of each mission by name; when properly and fully addressed, my correspondence reaches me unopened, so far as I am aware.

The fact that telegrams in code are sent by you to me and by me to you shows that there is no telegraphic censorship for diplomatic missions.

Telephonic conversations are habitually tapped, but this again concerns the internal rather than the external situation.

[signed] L.H. KERNEY

No. 35 NAI DFA 219/4

Confidential report from William Warnock to Joseph P. Walshe (Dublin)
(43/33)

BERLIN, 22 September 1939

The rout of the Polish armies came much quicker than anyone expected. The invasion of East Poland by the Russians finally settled the matter.

The fact that Poland's allies did not raise a finger to assist her has called forth sarcastic comment among the general public here. German official circles always maintained that Poland would have behaved in a much more 'sensible' manner if left alone, and would have come to some kind of agreement long ago had it not been for the interference of Great Britain. It was often asked what Great Britain could do to help Poland in a practical way: we have now seen that Great Britain was completely powerless to assist. Even if Poland had accepted the most far-reaching claims imaginable from Germany, she would have been spared the humiliation and the terrible destruction which she has suffered since the war began less than three weeks ago. The renewed British assurances of support for Poland are looked on here as shameful hypocrisy, and praise of the Polish resistance in Warsaw is regarded as the height of cynicism. In short, Poland is presented as the victim of British intrigue. It was intended by Germany's opponents, as formerly in the case of Czecho-Slovakia, that Polish resistance should make it necessary for the Germans to keep a strong force on the East Front, but, unfortunately for the allies' plans, the Polish armies have been annihilated, and the whole Polish state battered to pieces in a couple of weeks. All this time the Allies have done next to nothing in the West, beyond dropping propaganda leaflets (in my opinion a waste of time and paper at the present juncture) over parts of Western Germany, and making an unsuccessful air-raid on Wilhelmshaven and Cuxhaven.

Unfortunately for us, one of the members of the crew of a British machine, which crashed during the raid in Wilhelmshaven, is an Irishman. The men interned were interviewed over the wireless on Sunday evening last, and prominence was given to a Mr. Slattery from Tipperary.[1] The interview was re-broadcast on Monday.

People are waiting to see whether Poland's allies, in view of their protests of loyalty, will now declare war on Russia. If they really do intend to restore Poland, they will have to do so. It is confidently expected that they will shirk this issue. In fact, in spite of the fact that the rest of the world expects the war to drag on for years, hope still persists here that the Western Powers will come to terms. It is believed in many quarters that Russia and Japan will settle their differences in the near future.

One power, however, causes the Germans some anxiety, and that is the United States of America.

Despite allegations to the contrary, the morale of the civil population is very high. At first there were grumblings concerning food-rationing, but no significance could be attached to that. I can well imagine that there is a certain amount of complaining at the present time even in Ireland, where food is plentiful. The inconveniences of food-cards and 'black-outs' are now accepted as part of everyday life. The vast majority of the population are, of course, pedestrians, and therefore the restrictions on petrol-consumption and the use of motor-vehicles are exceedingly popular with the man-in-the-street. Officially inspired articles in the press assure the public that the food supply is safe, even though they will have to do without delicacies. Now that Russia and all Central and South-Eastern Europe are open to Germany, there does not appear to be any reason to doubt this, except that after a few years the problem of payment may raise difficulties. Before the war started a great part of Germany's trade was with countries outside Europe. The British will very probably succeed in stopping a considerable portion of this. The figures for 1938 in terms of RM. 1,000 were:-

	Imports	*Exports*
Europe	3,403,485	3,965,182
(Foodstuffs	1,410,247)	
(Raw materials	892,400)	
Overseas	2,628,307	1,644,717
(Foodstuffs	964,896)	
(Raw materials	1,099,053).	

Neutral countries outside Europe who normally have a large trade with Germany are very concerned as the result of the British blockade. As in our own case, their trade may be brought to a standstill. The Brazilian Ambassador informs me that his country is at present at a loss to know how to continue trading with this country. All the South American countries, with the exception of Ecuador, had a favourable trade balance with Germany in 1938, and consequently the threatened falling-away of this trade is a severe blow to them economically.

I shall close with the question uppermost in the minds of all Germans for the past fortnight:- 'If there really is to be war in the West, when is it going to start?'

[signed] W. Warnock

---

[1] Airman L.M. Slattery, one of three RAF airmen captured during the above-mentioned raid on 4 September 1939.

No. 36 NAI DFA 217/33

> *Letter from William Warnock to Frederick H. Boland (Dublin)*
> *(Copy)*
> BERLIN, 22 September 1939

Dear Mr. Boland,

I was very glad to receive your letter of the 8th September,[1] which arrived here yesterday (21st inst) with some later correspondence.

The German Post Office does not censor letters addressed to the Legation, nor, so far as I am aware, does it open correspondence sent by us. We can send our correspondence for the Department to any address you wish. So far as I can find out here, the German Post Office places no difficulty in our way. The obstacle seems to be the British postal authorities. We receive the Irish newspapers, though irregularly, and occasionally I receive personal letters from Ireland.

Could you arrange permission through the International Postal Union for us to use mailbags in our correspondence with the Legation at the Holy See? I am sure that the Union would assist us.

I duly received the bank drafts for $5,000.

I informed the Foreign Office of the new order obliging our ships to fly the Irish flag, and no other: Mr. O'Donovan telephoned from Rome early in the month about it, and I took action at once. I asked for observations or comments, but so far I have received no questions.

Dr. Mahr, the Director of the National Gallery,[2] and Dr. Reinhard,[3] the Director of Forestry, are still in Germany. Both of them wish to return to Ireland.

We are feeling in splendid form at the Legation. The Foreign Office arranged for us to get supplies of food, so we have no anxiety on that score. We are hoping that supplies will hold out well. If things disimprove, we may have to ask for your co-operation in sending out food to the starving garrison.

Please remember me to Mr. Walshe and to the Department in general.

Yours sincerely,
[signed] W. WARNOCK

P.S. The Foreign Office have just phoned to say that the Under-Secretary of State wishes to see me on Monday. I shall report the interview through Rome.[4]

[initialled] W.W.

No. 37 TNA PREM 1/340

> *Memorandum by Sir John Maffey to Anthony Eden (London)*
> DUBLIN, 24 September 1939

Owing to much travelling it has not been possible to turn these notes into a report proper. They are submitted in diary form and perhaps in this way give the better

---

[1] See No. 13.
[2] Mahr was in fact Director of the National Museum.
[3] Dr Otto Reinhard, appointed Director of Forestry to the Irish Free State (1935). Recalled to Germany in March 1938, Reinhard returned to his post in Ireland in May 1938. He left permanently for Germany at the outbreak of the Second World War.
[4] Handwritten postscript by Warnock.

picture of the personalities and problems concerned. There are many points in the notes which need consideration or action, but these can be sorted out in the Department.

Wednesday, 20th September.
I did not arrive in Dublin till the evening, my journey via Stranraer and Belfast having taken nearly twenty-four hours from London owing to various delays. I established touch with Mr. Walshe, Secretary for External Affairs, by telephone and was told that Mr. de Valera would see me that same evening at 8 p.m. if convenient. Mr. Walshe came to drive me round.

I was alone with Mr. de Valera from 8 p.m. till 9.45. After our first greeting I handed him Mr. Neville Chamberlain's letter.[1] I said that I understood that our Prime Minister had addressed him as 'Dear Prime Minister' and that I had learnt that this was not the mode of address which found favour. If incorrect it was an unintentional mistake. He smiled and said that he did not mind and gave me a constitutional lecture, which I did not follow entirely, explaining why 'Prime Minister' was inappropriate. Dominions Office should note this. 'President' is not a good alternative, since the President is President Hyde. 'Mr. de Valera' is the best solution.

After asking me whether the letter was germane to our discussion he proceeded to open it with extraordinary difficulty, holding it close to his nose. The reading of it was even more laborious. He obviously made no progress and kept looking away. Finally he said: 'Excuse my difficulty in reading. My sight is very bad and my trip to America, which I have had to cancel, was intended to benefit my eyes'.

I asked if I might read it out aloud to him and he gratefully accepted.

When I had finished, he at once turned on the old arguments as to why 'Minister' was a possible title for a United Kingdom agent in Dublin and why 'Representative' was impossible. He is a difficult man to interrupt. But interrupt him you must. He shows no resentment when this happens and his nimble mind is quickly lifted on to the new line you have started.

However, to start with he had a good run on the old scent.

Though he fully saw our difficulties, etc., etc., he could not face the danger and embarrassment resulting from a new and unusual title applied to a new British post. To do so would be to more than undo any possible good results. Every action he took in any matter affecting neutrality or relationship with Great Britain was watched by most critical eyes. He was known to be pro-British in sentiment on the question of the war. No doubt, half or more of his people shared this sentiment. But it was a delicate balance. A clumsy step on his part would lose him much of that support. The striking German successes in the war had produced a good many waverers. That was the way of the world. However, he said, early successes do not mean everything. The way in which suspicion could be excited and susceptibilities aroused in Ireland was beyond belief. For instance, a most natural and proper suggestion had been put forward that some of the women and children evacuated from danger zones in England should be offered hospitality in Éire. It had at once provoked outspoken opposition, as suspicion was aroused that there was 'something behind it'.

---

[1] See No. 29.

It was now time for me to intervene. I said that Mr. Chamberlain was concerned somehow or other to find a practical solution to a very grave problem, which would day by day grow more insistent. Éire was pursuing a path of neutrality. She had proscribed submarines in her waters and we acquiesced.[1] But the whole thing was in reality an empty gesture. The last war and German methods generally showed plainly what might and what probably would happen in the secret places of the Irish coast. Already tongues were beginning to wag. The President must surely see that unless a closer relationship was established in Dublin, unless the Admiralty felt that through that relationship they had established a real liaison with and source of information in the Irish system of watch and ward, any happenings off the Irish coast would start a justifiable outcry and our two Governments would meet in headlong collision simply because we had not established reasonable contacts and collaboration. The same considerations applied to other questions.

The President agreed to this but said that the solution proposed was not acceptable. His Government was not strong enough to take such a step and risk the consequences. If he went, who would come in? There was a delusion in some peoples' minds that if he went a government of the right would come in. This was utter nonsense. The only alternative to his government was a government of the left.

I intervened again to say that if he could swallow the word 'Minister' it seemed difficult to see the enormous difference between that and the term 'Representative'. A stand on that point would make it look as if a side issue was being exploited in order to gain a point in the constitutional game. This stung. He exclaimed that any such view was quite unjustified. He could assure me that there was no such thought in his mind. And after all, if it came to a question of quibbles, what were the objections to using the term 'Minister' for a post which would, like that of a High Commissioner, be mainly diplomatic in character. I said that if the King appointed a Minister it could only be done by the procedure applicable to foreign countries, by exequatur, etc. The King could not appoint a Minister to himself.

He then went off on the line that he would not expect the same formal methods of appointment to be applied in this case. Let the name be Minister or Ambassador, and he could explain away to his people the difference in the accrediting on the score that it was a post established to balance his High Commissioner in London and that the appointment was of a special character as from Government to Government. I said that we only knew one way of appointing a Minister and a Minister to us had a certain defined meaning. However, in his reply to Mr. Chamberlain's letter he could explain the difficulties and make his suggestion. I gave no encouragement to the idea, though it may not be as repellent to some people as it is to others. Therefore I did not kill it then and there.

I went on to make one or two other points. I said that if representation here in some form was to be arranged it could not be long delayed. A debate in the House of Commons might at any moment reveal the natural anxiety in England at seeing other countries, enemy countries too, represented in Dublin, while we with our old traditions and our many links to-day, commercial, cultural and social, were not represented at all. As it would be doubly difficult for him to act after such a debate, he would no doubt bear that in mind.

---

[1] See No. 19.

I also said that in times of grave emergency it was important for London to know what was in *his* mind. Did we know at present? We had our doubts. He fully agreed as to this and said where Mr. Dulanty succeeded and where he failed, though I had not intended my comment to be a criticism of Mr. Dulanty.

Having so far failed to get any sign of yielding to the request put forward in Mr. Chamberlain's letter, I turned the conversation in search of a consolation prize. Whatever happens on the question of a representative, the problem of *liaison* with our Admiralty in regard to watch and ward along the coast and the difficulties to be anticipated from the Éire policy of neutrality remain to be tackled. They would be greatly helped by the presence of a representative. But they cannot be allowed to drift, even if we have no representative. I therefore put the Admiralty difficulty to the President and said: 'It is obvious beyond all dispute that there must be liaison and information. Otherwise your neutrality will be non-operative and will be a positive danger to us. Do you agree to the appointment in some unobtrusive way of a liaison officer representing the Admiralty and having under him in the watch and ward service three or four men, Royal Navy Irishmen preferably, who will be his active agents in promoting the efficiency of your coastal service?'.

After some consideration Mr. de Valera said that he thought such an arrangement possible. And I said: 'If a submarine is reported in your territorial waters what happens?'. He said: 'Information of its whereabouts will be wirelessed at once, not to you specially. Your Admiralty must pick it up. We shall wireless it to the world. I shall tell the German Minister of our intention to do this.' (I am certain *his* wish is to make it thoroughly unhealthy for a German submarine to use Irish waters.)

I said: 'You realise that on receipt of such information our destroyers, if available, would attack wherever the submarine happened to be'. He said: 'We do not want you to take action in our territorial waters.' I said: 'It will happen and you will have to turn the blind eye'. He did not know what to say to this except that if they had information they should find it easy to lie up outside and deal with the enemy. I said that there was too many a slip between the cup and the lip. A submarine could create many perils once having dived out of view.

He said that they needed swift patrol boats, and gear of various kinds in order to deal with these matters themselves. I agreed and said that the Admiralty would certainly help. A patrol of civil aircraft would also greatly help him to gain his objective. He was interested in this suggestion.

He spoke of the delay in the supply of anti-aircraft guns and said that though he understood it the delay gave a bad impression in Éire. Could we not hurry matters up?

More than once he asked that these military and naval requirements which are to serve the British should not be charged up against Éire at a high price. I must emphasize his repeated request for consideration in this matter of price. He said that people think they are out of the war and do not approve of the expenditure. Besides, with falling tariffs, we are hard-hit financially. A low scale of prices is of great moment to us.

He turned now to the general questions arising under Éire's neutrality.

He had put in the ban on submarines to please us. To balance that he had put a ban on military aircraft. I said that he must not suppose that the ban on our submarines meant nothing to us. Submarines were a weapon in anti-submarine measures. However, we accepted the ban because obviously, broadly speaking, it was to our advantage.

He then reverted to military and naval aircraft. Cases had already occurred of their alighting in the territorial waters of Éire. I said that it would happen again. This upset him somewhat and he asked why. I said: 'Because, no longer having the facilities of the Irish coast, they have to take a longer flight out and back and this lands some of them like "exhausted birds" on your shores. I hope you will go slow with any specific rules about aircraft'. Then he said: 'Shall I leave out all mention of submarines? But I have already communicated with the German and French Governments'. I suggested fuller consultation with London. The whole fabric of neutrality was beginning to look healthier from our point of view. Indeed, at the moment it seems to be in a tangle and the longer it remains so the better. Still an attempt will be made to introduce rules or make a statement. I suggested a vague formula (vide my instructions), viz., a neutrality in general accordance with the practice of international law and a specific formula as to submarines. But the difficulty over the submarine point persists in his mind if he cannot balance it in some way to prove his basic neutrality.

I gathered from Mr. Walshe that any mention at present of facilities at Berehaven would upset the applecart.[1] As progress was being made by me on certain other lines, I thought it best not to jeopardise this progress at present and I hope the First Lord[2] will understand this. Action at Berehaven would undoubtedly shake the President's position. If such action is vital we shall have to take it. But we must think twice and count the gain and the loss.

Generally speaking, he revealed to me a much warmer pro-British attitude than on the last occasion. I am sure that he greatly appreciated the fact that Mr. Neville Chamberlain had written a personal letter to him. The more that kind of thing can be done, the better.

But, apart from that, in his actions he is definitely showing a bias in our favour, and we must be most careful not to deflect it.

He spoke of his Red Cross campaign. Of course, it is entirely neutral in constitution and aims but everyone knows that it is only the British who can benefit.

He said: 'Recruiting is active here for the British forces. We place no obstacle whatsoever in the way. I believe there are as many men recruited here now as in 1914 in spite of all Redmond's[3] big talk. But you would help us and help yourselves if the men did not come into Éire in uniform'.[4]

It is again one of those unreasoning prejudices to which attention must be paid. He had no particular feelings himself about it, except in so far as here lay a source of possible trouble. Perhaps the War Office and Admiralty will take note of this in an understanding spirit.

I now rose to leave and most surprisingly he said: 'I am turning over in my mind the question of "Minister" or "Representative"'. I shall make a choice after

---

[1] A marginal note in type at this point reads: 'No coup de main'.
[2] Winston Churchill was appointed First Lord of the Admiralty and became a member of Chamberlain's War Cabinet on the outbreak of the war.
[3] John Redmond (1856-1918), MP (1880-1918), leader of the Irish Parliamentary Party (1900-18). Redmond was an enthusiastic exponent of the recruitment of Irish volunteers to fight in the British forces during the First World War.
[4] Marginal note by Anthony Eden: 'I agree A.E.'.

discussion with my constitutional lawyers. I want to examine the case for each of them from every point of view'. This was much more forthcoming than anything I had dared to hope for and shows that some of the seed sown has not been wasted. However, it may well all be reversed again before I leave Dublin.

As I left the room he led me to his black map of Éire with its white blemish on the North East corner and said: 'There's the real source of all our trouble'. He could not let me go without that.

Thursday, 21st September.
I lunched with Mr. Walshe at his house to-day. He tells me that the President has come on surprisingly in the matter of a Representative and he anticipates that the thing will go through.

A letter is being drafted by the President and Mr. Walshe is to see it to-day.[1]

Mr. Walshe and I had some further discussion on the subject of neutrality legislation, and it looks as if the matter will be left in a vague condition for the present. We can ask for nothing better. To emphasise the facilities which the Éire Government has given Mr. Walshe quoted to me the case of the 'Cabot' (Imperial Airways) Flying Boat which spotted a submarine 70 miles outside Foynes. Foynes repeated the Cabot's message to the Admiralty *en clair*. It was agreed by the President that if such a thing happened again the message should be forwarded, but by code. This indicates helpfulness. I told Mr. Walshe that I had warned the President that if one of our destroyers heard of a submarine in Irish territorial waters it would certainly attack and that the only help for it was a 'blind eye'. Mr. Walshe seemed to accept the situation – if silence is acceptance.

He asked for help in regard to the attitude of Mr. Dyce (Board of Trade or Food Control in London) who was refusing to buy Irish cattle here and would only buy it in the English market by weight. The Irish farmers are on strike about this and ask for the cattle to be bought and paid for in Éire. Great feeling apparently.

Mr. Walshe said that the President had discussed again with him the difficult question arising under neutrality in regard to our planes alighting in Irish limits. He was thinking about transferring any such plane to the Government of Éire, who need aircraft for purposes useful to us. As regards the crews, he was considering the possibility of releasing them or of retaining them in Éire service as they need pilots. All this is very nebulous at present. But the problem will arise and London must be ready with their arguments, though it by no means follows that they will be accepted.

To-night Mr. Walshe dined with me and in our talk afterwards he showed himself less happy as to the President's latest thoughts on the subject of representation. He has gone back to his apprehensions and the draft reply to Mr. Neville Chamberlain is getting more and more controversial. The President meets his Cabinet to-morrow (22nd) at 11 a.m. and will put the matter to them.[2] Mr. Walshe thinks that I must go over the ground again with Mr. de Valera and try and pull him back to where he was yesterday.

Friday, 22nd September.
Mr. Walshe tells me that the President is still thinking it over. The difficulty now is the name 'United Kingdom Representative'! The United Kingdom includes

---

[1] See No. 33.
[2] See No. 32.

Northern Ireland! Hence the objection. I said that we on our side obviously could not announce it as anything else. The President is holding a special meeting of his Cabinet to-day[1] and will see me after that.

Finally the time fixed was 8 p.m.

22nd September (later).
I was asked to see Mr. de Valera at 8 p.m. and he gave me a letter to Mr. Neville Chamberlain[2] and told me that it contained acceptance in principle of his request. I said that our Prime Minister would greatly appreciate this helpful attitude, etc., etc.

Mr. de Valera asked me to give a verbal message from him to the Prime Minister on the subject of the use of the term 'Ambassador' or 'Minister' to designate the post at a later appropriate date. He did not wish the term 'United Kingdom Representative' to be regarded as other than temporary. He hoped I should emphasize to the Prime Minister the genuineness of the difficulties in which the use of this name involved him. He said that no doubt the incumbent would be referred to as 'United Kingdom Representative' over here but that in Éire they would speak of him as 'British Representative' in common parlance. His residence also should, if possible, not be labeled 'United Kingdom'. I said I thought these points would present no difficulty.

He then went over some of the old ground in regard to neutrality. He repeated a phrase he has used before:- 'I do not want Irish freedom to become a source of British insecurity.' This *dictum* may have its uses in the course of the war.

He spoke again of the critical eyes which watched his every step in the matter of neutrality. There were members of the I.R.A. established in Berlin. He noted in a recent issue of the 'Standard' – an Irish newspaper – a criticism of his form of neutrality as compared with the correct and rigid neutrality of Holland. In fact, he was prejudiced in favour of the British and this *was* duly noted by his critics. Still, he must try to be fair to Germany. There were some things he could not do. A suggestion had been made that the Athlone broadcast should occasionally be switched over to Droitwich to mislead German submarines. This was a trap to which he could not give his assent.

He desired me to emphasize two matters in London and to have action taken if possible:-
  (a) The return to Éire in uniform of Irishmen who had joined our fighting forces should be stopped. It caused trouble and that trouble would 'snowball'. He gave us this advice knowing that it was friendly and helpful advice. We shall get more recruits by adopting it.
  (b) A new Controller was operating in London in the matter of Irish cattle imports in a manner very prejudicial to Irish farmers. He would only pay for deadweight in the place where the cattle were slaughtered. It was impossible to trace the cattle of individual farmers in that way. A great agitation was developing and he asked for a readjustment of the methods employed to be considered without delay.

In the matter of essential supplies from Éire to England, he suggested better co-ordination of industrial effort. There was a closing down of business in certain

---
[1] See No. 32.
[2] See No. 33.

directions in Éire. Yet these activities might serve a purpose taking a long view of our needs.

I had been given a copy of a statement made by the Captain of the s.s. 'Inverliffey', carrying the flag of Éire and sunk in the Channel by a German submarine.[1] The idea was that this would impress Dublin. Before I left I was told by the Admiralty that the action could not be regarded as abnormal, since the 'Inverliffey' carried contraband of war, viz., petrol. I refrained, therefore, from attempting to make any great use of this incident and merely handed the paper to Mr. Walshe.

Mr. de Valera asked that our Representative should not employ secret service funds and methods in Dublin. It was a small world there and everything would be known. He and his Government would be quite frank and outspoken with us.

Mr. de Valera spoke of his high hopes of future association and bade me a most friendly good-bye.

(Sgd.) J.L. MAFFEY
24/9/39

No. 38 UCDA P150/2548

Letter from Neville Chamberlain to Eamon de Valera (Dublin)
LONDON, 25 September 1939

My dear de Valera,

I was very glad to have your letter of the 22nd September[2] and I want to thank you for agreeing to accept the name 'Representative' which I suggested. I have seen Sir John Maffey who has explained to me the difficulties in which this will involve you and I appreciate all the more on this account your readiness to meet me.

I am very glad to learn from your letter that, in your opinion, Sir John Maffey's qualities will enable him to make a success of his service and he has accordingly been appointed and will take up his new duties as soon as possible.

May I add my warm thanks also for the personal note in your postscript. It is a satisfaction to me that you so thoroughly understand my past and present anxieties and your sympathy is very welcome.

Yours sincerely
NEVILLE CHAMBERLAIN

No. 39 NAI DFA Legal Adviser's Papers

Memorandum from Michael Rynne to Joseph P. Walshe (Dublin)
(Copy)
DUBLIN, 26 September 1939

Re Taoiseach's Proposed Statement to Dáil – Mr Moynihan's Minute of 21st September

I have examined the questions set out in Mr. Moynihan's minute of 21st

---

[1] The vessel, an oil tanker, had capacity for 13,000 tons of gasoline and, although registered at Dublin, was managed by Andrew Weir and Co of London, Glasgow and Middlesbrough. *Inverliffey* was sunk by gunfire from U-38 on 11 September 1939. All forty-nine crew survived.
[2] See No. 33.

September,[1] the replies to which are intended to provide the Taoiseach with the material for a speech in the Dáil when it meets tomorrow.

Only the first four questions would appear to require the attention of this Department in a general way. Primarily they are questions which must depend for detailed answers on those State Departments responsible for administering ordinary laws and emergency orders which, taken together, enable the Government to deal with problems arising out of the present war situation. Insofar as existing legislation (including emergency orders) may affect our position in international law as a neutral State, this Department is, of course, concerned. It is our task to deal directly with the various belligerents and to satisfy them, if necessary, that the State is able and willing to maintain its neutrality.

2. The Minister for External Affairs has not so far made any emergency orders, nor is this Department responsible for administering any statutes or orders relevant to the present situation. Because of the Department's particular function of directly dealing with the belligerents, however, we have a special interest in what the Taoiseach may decide to communicate to the Dáil on Wednesday. If he were to deal to any extent with the many hypothetical problems which seem to flow from the Government's neutrality policy, this Department would almost certainly find itself involved in a series of embarrassing diplomatic explanations and elaborations. Even if the Taoiseach's speech merely resumed in considerable detail the history of how certain neutrality problems were disposed of during the last few weeks, this Department might likewise find itself in the position of having to give supplementary facts to those belligerent Governments which are, at the moment, inclined to take Ireland's neutrality for granted. The comments and criticisms of Deputies regarding the steps already taken to establish and preserve our present status might result in placing this Department, and the Government as a whole, in the highly vulnerable position of having to explain in minute detail the particular brand of neutrality adopted by this country. So far as we know, no other foreign Minister nor head of State of a neutral country has felt bound to render account of the operation of the neutrality policy to Parliament since this war began. Many of the Parliaments of such countries have by now virtually ceased to function. The President of the United States of America provides an apparent exception to this rule, but only an apparent one. In the case of the United States, the neutrality policy has been resubmitted to Parliament with the definite view to having it modified. The circumstances attending President Roosevelt's recent action, and those indicated in regard to the Taoiseach's proposed speech to the Dáil, are, therefore, quite dissimilar.

3. Mr. Moynihan's first question covers almost the whole field of international relations, as well as bearing on a considerable part of the State's internal administration. Fortunately, most of the problems to which the question refers have not yet arisen and, it is to be hoped, may never arise. Compared, for instance, with the neutral status of Holland, Belgium and Denmark, which is being outraged almost daily (and nightly) by the British naval and air forces, our neutrality during the last three weeks has suffered relatively negligible interference.

4. Certain problems of neutrality, such as the Irish merchant shipping problem, which was expected to give trouble, as well as the problem of keeping our newspapers and periodicals more or less 'neutral' in tone, were anticipated by the

---

[1] See No. 31.

Government and dealt with summarily in appropriate Emergency Orders. Other problems which have materialised only partially, such as the problem of the use of our waters by belligerent warships and submarines, and the invasion of our airspace by belligerent military aircraft, have been partially dealt with, or are being considered by the interested Departments with a view to dealing with them by further Emergency Orders. No doubt, the Taoiseach will be advised of this latter type of problem by each of the Departments at present engaged in providing a remedy for it. But, from the point of view of this Department, practical difficulties might be avoided if the Dáil were not invited to discuss prospective Emergency Orders which may have to undergo last-minute alterations to meet circumstances as they arise. For example, until the Dáil (and people) can be confronted with the *fait accompli* of an Emergency Order to compel Irish merchant shipping to light up at night (instead of blacking out as at present), it might be a mistake to dilate on the international law whereby neutral merchant ships are expected to flood light their national colours after dark. At the moment, no final decision has been come to regarding the display of Irish neutral colours on our ships by night. The same applies to a large number of other problems which still await a definitive and, perhaps, an *ad hoc* ruling. To mention only one such problem, there is the question as to whether Imperial Airways crews should be allowed to use the Foynes radio station for the purpose of transmitting naval information to Great Britain. In that regard, the Dáil could only be informed that the intention was to prevent such unneutral use of our Foynes transmitter – but such may not ultimately prove to be the case when a decision is taken.

5. It is difficult to enlarge on Mr. Moynihan's second query. Undoubtedly, the Government must be prepared to deal with all demands from belligerents on both sides, whether or not those demands seem to involve the infringement of our neutrality. In the event of belligerent demands involving infringement of our neutrality, the Government cannot lawfully comply with them. If they do so, the Government are going to lay themselves open to a charge of dereliction of their international duty to conduct themselves as the Government of a neutral State. Possibly, this question has been set down in the belief that a neutral State has certain rights *per se*. That is not, however, the case. Ireland's 'rights' are chiefly represented by the Government's theoretical right to take defensive action (or merely to protest) when *Ireland's duty to behave neutrally* has been rendered difficult or impossible by an outside Power.

6. If, in the present emergency, the Government decide, in what appears to them to be the best interest of the country, to concede to the demands of any one belligerent, notwithstanding that they thereby deviate somewhat from their international duty to remain strictly neutral, it might be well not to inform the Dáil of what must be regarded as quite exceptional concessions.

7. Up to the present, the necessity contemplated by question (2) has not given very much trouble in practice. The anticipated arrangement with regard to the re-export of American maize from Ireland to Great Britain might come under the matters envisaged by the question, but a case can be made for that in international law, and, in any event, the facts of the matter may not come to light, if not expressly brought to the notice of Dáil Éireann.

8. Short of summarising several hundred pages of international law text-books, it would be impossible to illustrate by reference to *all* the neutral countries (in two

different war-situations) *all* the problems of neutrality. In general, we will, no doubt, endeavour to keep our policy in line as far as we can with that of such small States as Belgium, Holland and Denmark. It should, however, be remembered that most of the European neutral countries find themselves surrounded by rival belligerents. Ireland's geographical position is almost unique in Europe in that she has as her immediate neighbours two belligerents which are fighting as allies in the present war. Moreover, whereas other neutral countries have been compelled by circumstances and enabled by their previous experience to deal with their particular neutrality problems in a comprehensive manner, this country has taken, so far, scarcely any overt steps to establish in law the status for which the Taoiseach declared himself in favour as far back as February last.

9. Any reference to 'illustrations' in the Dáil drawn from the neutrality laws of other countries would, therefore, be likely to give rise to questions from Opposition Deputies as to how this country was reacting to particular states of fact. It is, accordingly, submitted that as few comparisons as possible should be made between the Government's neutrality programme here and the practice of neutrality in other countries which are in but few respects similar to our own.

10. To take only one example, no neutral country, as far as we know, intends during the present hostilities to take so strict a line with belligerent submarines as we do. In the last war, Spain alone approached our contemplated stringency in that regard. On the other hand, there is no example of a State in this or any other war (except ourselves) intending to repatriate the crews of belligerent military aircraft which may land upon the neutral national territory.

11. The fourth question set out in Mr. Moynihan's minute (the last question with which we have to deal), appears to be a kind of converse to question (2). Unlike that question, however, the duty which is imposed by international law upon the Government to observe strict neutrality seems to be fully recognised here. Nevertheless, it might be well to advise the Taoiseach to consider the desirability of not going into too much detail about the necessity for avoiding unneutral action, unless to warn individuals against the abuse of freedom of speech and to advise newspaper editors that the continued freedom of the Press will depend largely on their own moderation and respect for Ireland's position of neutrality. Beyond that, there would seem to be but little which can be said in the Dáil on this question that would not entail diplomatic 'explanations' by this Department sooner or later.

12. One rather un-neutral situation which, in the words of Mr. Moynihan's question, 'could reasonably be interpreted as a breach of neutrality', might be brought to the Taoiseach's notice, even though he may not wish to encourage any discussion of it in the Dáil. That is the situation in regard to the registration of foreign merchant ships in Irish ports. The law as it now stands enables the ship of any State of the British Commonwealth to be registered here by virtue of the British Commonwealth Merchant Shipping Agreement, 1931. Insofar as such ships may be entirely or mainly owned by persons who are not Irish citizens, the situation (even in peace-time) is completely anomalous, and inasmuch as all the States of the British Commonwealth are at present belligerents, the situation is completely 'unneutral'. Certainly, the Government have gone some way towards adjusting the position by the provision (Article 5) in the recent Emergency Powers (No. 2) Order, that no ship may be registered in an Irish port without the specific sanction of the

Minister for Industry and Commerce. That, however, does not get over the fact that our Registry still comprises a disproportionately large number of ships the ownership of which is entirely, almost entirely or mainly in the hands of persons who are the subjects of a belligerent State. Until this situation is cleared up – if necessary, by causing all belligerently-owned passenger and merchant vessels to leave our shipping register – the Government are open to the charge of acting so equivocally as to be suspect of conduct unbecoming to a neutral.

13. Perhaps, when we are replying to Mr. Moynihan's minute containing all the above mentioned and other questions, we might submit the view that, although we appreciate the motives underlying the questions, we feel that they are so framed as to seem to incline towards an unduly pessimistic view of Irish neutrality. The experience of the last three weeks has not demonstrated to this Department (which is so largely responsible for the maintenance of the neutrality policy) any unforeseen difficulties in the preservation of our present status. On the contrary, such minor difficulties as have so far arisen have been duly overcome, and, owing to a certain measure of good-will displayed by all belligerents in our regard, we may hope to continue to remain a neutral State without undue effort. Public opinion, as far as our Department is in touch with internal affairs, would seem to be taking the Government's policy as sensible and practicable and the doubts so often expressed some weeks ago as to the possibly brief duration of Ireland's neutrality are much less heard.

14. In short, it might be a pity if the Taoiseach were to convey to the Dáil by any statement he might now make on neutrality, the possibility – however remote – of our not being able to remain permanently out of the war. After all, the Government's policy has stood the test of one month of hostilities in which all the British Dominions and our two nearest neighbours are involved. No difficulty has arisen in those four weeks which has not been solved or which cannot be solved. The only factors lacking at present before the Government can express entire satisfaction with the working of their policy are the formal acts of recognition of Irish neutrality on the part of all the belligerent Powers, none of whom (except Germany) have so far expressed themselves in this connection. Irish neutrality is none the less an accepted fact, and a workable policy in the opinion of all realistic people at home and abroad.

15. Having passed the Emergency Powers Act, 1939, Dáil Éireann is not entitled to demand the right to review the policy of neutrality while the emergency still subsists. If that policy requires implementation from time to time, the Government will be carrying out the expressed will of the Oireachtas by simply making the necessary Emergency Powers Orders.

16. With regard to the reference in the final paragraph of Mr. Moynihan's minute to '(b) ministerial and subsidiary orders' rendered necessary in this Department by the present emergency, we need only advert to the Travel Permit regulations which the Department has found it necessary to make in respect of travel between this country and Great Britain. The necessity for the regulations originated with the British Government, which desired, for various reasons (*inter alia* that of preventing an exodus of British subjects of military age and an influx of undesirable aliens) to control travel in and out of Great Britain. The system as now established is working well, being to some extent assimilated to the usual passport system set

up by the Department to meet normal conditions of travel out of Ireland. As both the officers of the Department who are chiefly responsible for the Permit regulations are absent on sick leave, it is not possible to provide full details of the system today. It may, however, be possible to procure further particulars, if required, before the Dáil assembles tomorrow.

No. 40 NAI DFA Legal Adviser's Papers

Memorandum by Michael Rynne entitled 'Neutrality'
(Copy)
DUBLIN, undated, but September 1939

NEUTRALITY

1. *Essentials of Neutrality*
   The essentials of neutrality are:-
   (a) An impartial attitude towards belligerents on both sides of the conflict.
   (b) Acquiescence in this attitude by both belligerents.
   (c) Ability to take such action as may be necessary to defend neutrality.
   (d) The first two essentials have already come into existence, in fact and according to International Law, in this country, the position being briefly this:

2. *Impartial Attitude*
   The present position of this part of Ireland regarding neutrality, or any other matter relating to its Sovereign Rights, is the same as that of every other Sovereign State. Every Sovereign State is a master of its own resolutions and the question of remaining neutral or not is, in the absence of a treaty stipulating otherwise, one of policy and has no relation to International Law.

   All Sovereign States which do not expressly declare the contrary, by word or action, at the commencement of a war are regarded as neutral, and the rights and duties arising from neutrality come into existence and remain in existence, through the mere fact of a State taking up a duty of impartiality, and using all the means at its disposal not to be drawn into the war by either set of belligerents. A special assertion of intention to remain neutral is not legally necessary on the part of neutral States. Many States are neutral in the present war who did not so far consider it necessary, as far as I know, to make any public pronouncement to that effect, e.g. the South American Republics.

3. *Recognition by Belligerents*
   A belligerent who, at the outbreak of war, refuses to recognise a third State as a neutral, does not violate neutrality by that action alone, because neutrality does not come into existence in fact and in law until both belligerents have acquiesced expressly or tacitly in the attitude of impartiality taken up by third States. But the Law of Nations, in its present development, objects to a would-be neutral State being forced into war, and a belligerent who refuses to recognise it as neutral violates International Law, although not neutrality. The fact remains that both sides in the present European conflict have acquiesced in our attitude of neutrality, hence, as I have said, the first two essentials of our neutrality are accomplished facts.

4. *Ability to take such steps as may be necessary to defend neutrality*
   Impartiality towards belligerents on both sides excludes such assistance and succour to one of the belligerents as is detrimental to the other, and, further, such injuries to one of the belligerents as benefit the other. In addition, it includes active measures on the part of a neutral for the purpose of preventing belligerents from making use of neutral territories and neutral resources for their military and naval purposes, and of preventing either of them from interfering with his legitimate intercourse with the other. The duty of impartiality excludes, in addition, all facilities whatever for military and naval operations of the belligerents, even if granted to both belligerents alike. It has thus become a recognised principle of International Law that a neutral State must take all measures in its power, including force if necessary, to preserve its neutrality. If a neutral is unable or unwilling to use the means at its disposal to preserve its neutrality, a belligerent is, in certain circumstances, entitled, for the purpose of self-preservation, to occupy any portion of the neutral's territory.
5. *Position of Small States during the World War*
   It is well known that some small States, such as Belgium, Greece and Persia, had their neutrality violated during the World War. The difficulties which other small States had in preserving their neutrality is, however, not so generally known. The original German plans provided for the invasion of Holland as well as Belgium. The Dutch, however, recognising the general and particular nature of the International situation, modernised and increased both their army and fortifications just before the war. The Germans, then, in view of the changed situation due to improved Dutch armaments, decided the probable Dutch resistance would more than counterbalance the advantages of invading Holland and changed their plan. During the whole period of the war, the Dutch had 450,000 troops and considerable naval forces on a war footing. Yet, in 1918, they again narrowly escaped German invasion.

   Switzerland also found it necessary to ensure her neutrality by mobilising and keeping two to three hundred thousand troops under arms for the whole period of the war.

   Demark, Norway and Sweden were not so directly threatened but they found common action, amounting almost to an alliance, combined with the full mobilisation and increase of their defence services, essential to the preservation of their neutrality and of their rights as neutrals. All neutral States suffered severely in their economic, commercial and industrial activities. They were left without essential imports and, in many cases, actually short of food, as a result of a conflict in which they took no part.
6. *Precautions taken by some small European States in present emergency*
   (a) *Belgium*
      The Belgian Cabinet, at a meeting on 1st September decided that, in view of Belgium's policy of neutrality and of the present international situation, further military measures would be necessary to ensure her security and respect of engagements undertaken by her.

      It was reported on 25th September that the Belgian army had manned the frontier forts along her German border to full strength. It was stated that, since shortly after the outbreak of war, Belgium has proceeded with complete mobilisation measures, so that the country now has an efficient

army of nearly 750,000 under arms. This force is superior to the Belgian army of 1914 and the Belgian frontier forts, constructed on the same lines as the Maginot Line, although not so elaborately, are more formidable obstacles than the pre-war system of isolated fortresses.

A joint Belgo-Luxemburg Committee discussed on September 7th the measures to be taken to protect the population of the Grand Duchy in case of danger. The Belgian delegation promised 'the fullest and most fraternal support' to Luxemburg in case of emergency.

The Belgian Government asked parliament for special powers and a special credit of 2,000,000,000 francs (about £11,000,000).

(b) *Netherlands*

Mobilisation of the Netherlands army and navy was carried out on 29th August, a few days before the invasion of Poland. The Government announcement stated:

'To be fully prepared for all responsibilities should an armed conflict in Europe break out, and, notwithstanding the fact that there is still hope, Holland has decided to guard its neutrality on all sides and against all parties. The Government has, therefore, thought it necessary to order mobilisation of the army and navy without further delay'.

The order affecting the army includes the reservist classes from 1924 up to and including 1939.

The Government appealed to the nation to bear its burden and meet all difficulties as calmly as possible.

The Queen, in a broadcast message, stated that, should a conflict break out, Holland will maintain a strict neutrality to all sides and with all the means at her disposal.

(c) *Denmark*

The Danish Government, on September 1st, called up five classes of men, totalling 40,000. Parliament met on the same night to pass several urgent emergency measures.

Previously, only 8,000 men were under arms, equivalent to one year's supply of recruits. The Navy had a further 2,000. It is claimed in official circles that an army potential of 100,000 trained men could, in case of necessity, be mobilised in 24 hours. Arrangements are complete to call up members of the Auxiliary Services for civilian assistance and defence.

Officially the view is taken that Denmark's neutrality is an accepted fact, strengthened by the non-aggression pact with Germany. The fact remains, however, that since the German Minister at Copenhagen re-emphasised Germany's intention not to infringe Denmark's neutrality, defensive measures have been redoubled.

While Ministers and Government officials maintain close reserve to avoid giving offence to any Great Power, precautionary measures are being taken as far as possible, e.g. piles of sandbags for the protection of doors and windows were placed outside the building which houses the Danish Admiralty, Ministry of War, Home Office and also outside other Government buildings. The same applies to buildings like the Thorvaldsen Museum, to shield the Museum against possible harm.

(d) *Switzerland*

The Swiss Federal Council decided on 28th August to proceed with the full Swiss frontier mobilisation. This involved calling to the colours between 80,000 and 100,000 men.

It was announced on September 1st that general mobilisation would take place on the following day. On 11th September it was reported that Switzerland had completed her general mobilisation and has now between 500,000 and 600,000 well trained and well equipped men under arms to defend her neutrality.

7. *Geography and National Defence*

National defence problems are primarily affected by geography. To quote a recent writer on Canadian Defence Policy: 'The permanent bases of the external relations of practically every country in the World find their origin in geography'. Continental European States maintain large armies and build fortifications to ensure the security of their land frontiers. Insular Powers, such as Great Britain and Japan, depend principally on Naval Power for the protection of their territories and interests. Many Powers maintain both armies and navies because they have land frontiers as well as overseas territories and interests to protect.

With the exception of Belgium, all Continental European States maintain a naval service for local coast defence and for the effective control and preservation of the neutrality of their territorial waters.

8. *Problems arising from the geographical position of this country*

Éire, notwithstanding the Six-County border, still has nearly all the elements of an island in matters of national defence. With the exception mentioned, it can only be invaded from overseas, and even to reach the Six-Counties, any forces except those already there, must come from overseas. It follows that the defence of Ireland must be considered in relation to questions of navies and sea-power. It is generally agreed that naval strategic measures fall naturally into two main categories; first those of a military character – using the term in its broadest sense – and second, those of an economic character, undertaken with object of weakening the enemy's power by striking at his resources. For naval operations suitable harbours or bases are the paramount need. Such harbours or bases must be situated in central and controlling positions.

No harbours in Western Europe are so centrally situated for this purpose as those of Ireland. Operations in any portion of the North Eastern Atlantic can be conducted more easily from Irish ports than from those of any other country. Irish coasts and harbours also directly control the entrances to the English Channel and the Irish Sea. To a somewhat less extent the Irish Coast is a suitable centre from which to direct operations towards the Bay of Biscay and the areas West and North of Scotland. United States troops coming to Europe in 1918 were practically all landed at Brest or ports further south in the Bay of Biscay. For the protection of those troops while in the Eastern Atlantic against a possible cruiser raid by the Germans, it was considered necessary to station a squadron of battleships at a suitable centre. Berehaven was selected by the Americans as the most central and suitable base for the purpose of protecting troops destined, not for Ireland or England, but for France.

Many Irish harbours, e.g. Cobh, Berehaven, Galway, Killary, Lough Swilly, are sufficiently deep, naturally sheltered and commodious enough to accommodate a great fleet and, in addition, are easily navigated and can be protected against attack with comparatively little expenditure. Generally, they provide in their natural state many of the facilities which other countries have only been able to provide, indifferently, after very large expenditure.

The development of new weapons, such as aeroplane and submarine, has largely increased the difficulty of protecting or even maintaining naval bases in narrow waters exposed to such attack. These developments have still further enhanced the value of the Southern and Western Irish harbours.

Of the World's sea communications, 75 per cent are centred in the North Atlantic and it is estimated that more than half the World's traffic passes through the ocean gateway bounded on the North by the South Irish Coast and on the South by the Brittany Peninsula and then proceeds through the still narrower gateways of the English Channel or St. George's Channel. Not only does practically all British traffic pass through those gateways, but also almost all French, Dutch, German, Scandinavian and Baltic traffic. Admiral Mahan,[1] who is considered one of the greatest authorities on these matters, from an English point of view, said: 'Ireland, by geographical position lies across and controls the communications of Great Britain with all the outside world .... save the North Sea'. He also said: 'Communications dominate war; broadly speaking, they are the most important single element in strategy, political or military. In its control over them had lain the pre-eminence of sea-power as an influence upon the history of the past and in this it will continue, for the attribute is inseparable from its existence'.

The great crisis of the World War, from the point of view of the Allies, was due to the activity of German submarines and this form of warfare was waged in its most intensive form, and from the German viewpoint, with most successful results, in the waters surrounding Ireland. The importance and intensity of the submarine war in Irish waters, and around Cobh in particular, is described by Admiral Sims,[2] Wartime United States Commander in Europe. In his book he states: 'The far flung steamship lanes which bring Britain her food and raw materials from half a dozen continents focus in the Irish Sea and English Channel, therefore, the submarines ... merely used to hover round the extremely restricted waters west and south of Ireland'. In an official report he stated: 'There is reason for the greatest alarm about the issue of the war caused by the increasing success of the German submarines ... Most of the ships are sunk to the Westward and Southward of Ireland'. Admiral Sims then went on to state that in this case and other reports he urged 'that the United States should immediately assemble all her destroyers and other light craft and send them to the port where they could render the greatest service in the anti-submarine campaign, viz. Queenstown'.

---

[1] Alfred Thayer Mahan (1840-1914), United States Navy officer and military historian known for his writings on geopolitics and naval power.
[2] William Sowden Sims (1858-1936), Admiral, United States Navy. The reference is to *The Victory At Sea* (New York, 1920), Sims' memoir of his service in Europe during the First World War.

9. *British opinions as to the strategic importance of Ireland's geographical position*
   Some expressions of opinion given by responsible British officers as to the position of Ireland in the event of a war in Europe in which Great Britain would be involved serve to illustrate further the strategic importance of Ireland's geographical position.

   Major General Bird,[1] in 'The Direction of War' (1925) under the heading 'Flanking Position' states: 'Ireland, which lies to the West of Great Britain, is so placed that, if held by a hostile nation, British trading ships sailing westwards and south-westwards would be liable to attack for many days after leaving British ports, and also when returning to them. The British would also be compelled to take far more extensive precautions for the security of their western coastline. Hence, in the wars between the French and English, the former, on more than one occasion, endeavoured to stir up rebellion in and gain possession of Ireland. Further, were the ports on the south and west of Ireland to be even closed to British sea and aircraft, the power of the British to deal with enterprises launched from the west or south against Great Britain or her commerce would be much reduced'.

   Boycott,[2] in 'Elements of Imperial Defence' says: 'England holds the key to the sea gates of Europe'. (She held the fortified Irish ports when this was written.) 'Lines of communication in the Atlantic tend to centralise in an area lying roughly between Cape Clear, Milford Haven, Land's End and Ushant and it was in this area that German submarines became firmly established and did most damage. Submarines and aircraft based on Cherbourg and Brest would make this area even more dangerous than the German submarines were able to do from their bases on the Belgian coast.'

10. *Naval forces maintained in Irish Waters during World War*
    During the whole period of the World War considerable British, and during its later stages, considerable American Naval forces were based on, and exclusively used Irish Ports and Harbours. In January, 1918, the following mixed British and United States detachments, under a British Commander, were based on Cobh alone:

    1   Light Cruiser,
    37 Destroyers,
    4   Torpedo Boats,
    10 Sloops,
    9   Sweepers,
    1   Decoy Ship,

    as well as numerous smaller and auxiliary craft, such as depot and supply ships, tugs, submarine chasers, etc.

      These forces, and others based on Berehaven and Lough Swilly, were engaged in the following duties:-
      1. Keeping channels leading from Irish harbours and on the routes used by Irish Coastal shipping and shipping proceeding to English and Scottish

---

[1] Major General Sir Wilkinson D. Bird (1869-1943). The reference is to his work *The direction of war: a study and illustration of strategy*, 2nd ed. (Cambridge, 1925).

[2] A.G. Boycott, member of the Royal Air Force Education Service; author of *The Elements of Imperial Defence: a study of the geographical features, materials, resources, communications, and organisation of the British Empire* (Aldershot, 1939).

Harbours swept clear of mines and patrolled. All were, it is believed, usually swept daily.
2. Performing the same duties on the great trade routes off the North and South Irish Coasts.
3. Protecting, as necessary, the entrance to Irish Harbours and War Anchorages by the use of nets, booms and protective minefields.
4. Finally, the flotillas of destroyers and all kinds of auxiliary patrol, and submarine-hunting craft, based on Cobh, Berehaven, Lough Swilly, Rosslare and other Ports in the South and West of Ireland, fought out the intensive submarine war in the waters off the Irish Coast known as the 'Western Approaches' of the Queenstown Command.

11. *Dangers that our neutrality may be violated*

It will be seen, from the preceding paragraphs what an important part Ireland, because of its occupation by the British and its strategical importance, played in the World War. In the words of Major General Bird: 'were the ports in the South and West of Ireland to be even closed to British sea and aircraft, the power of the British to deal with enterprises launched from the West or South against Great Britain or her commerce would be much reduced'.

In the British Government's proposals for Irish peace in August 1920, the following passage occurred: 'Great Britain lives by sea-borne food; her communications depend upon the freedom of the great sea routes. Ireland lies at Britain's side across the sea-ways North and South, that link her with the Sister Nations of the Empire, the markets of the world and the vital sources of her food supply. In recognition of this fact, which nature has imposed and no statesmanship can change, it is essential that the Royal Navy alone should control the seas round Ireland and Great Britain'. May not similar arguments be used again before the termination of this war?

As explained in the Memo on Contraband of War, page 3,[1] even the clearest and most emphatic treaties have been unable to withstand the pressure of necessity, because every treaty is based on compromise and none are framed to meet the ultimate strain of war. When a State found itself fighting with its back to the wall, it preferred life to the observance of its promises. Naturally its lawyers explained the justification but the fact remained. As Sir Edward Grey[2] has said: 'The Navy acted and the Foreign Office had to find the argument to support the action'. The fact is that, in time of peace States agree to certain legal rules by which they refuse to be bound when urgent self-interest dictates a contrary course. History is strewn with such broken treaties.

The difficulty which some small States had in maintaining their neutrality during the last year is explained in Para. 5. All the virtues were not on one side and all the iniquities on the other in this respect. Both sides to the conflict violated the neutrality of small and weak States when it suited their purpose to do so and the same thing has happened in every major war.

---

[1] Not printed.
[2] Sir Edward Grey, 1st Viscount Grey of Fallodon (1862-1933), Foreign Secretary (1905-16).

No. 41 NAI DFA 227/100

Code telegram from Joseph P. Walshe to Robert Brennan (Washington DC)
(No. 219) (Personal) (Copy) (205/11)

DUBLIN, 29 September 1939

Cable immediately date on which you informed State Department of our neutrality and whether acknowledgment received. If you did not inform them in writing do so immediately and insist on written acknowledgment very urgent cable text of acknowledgment. Follow neutrality debate very closely and make sure no step taken by State Department ignoring our neutrality by implication or otherwise. Watch in particular delineation of belligerent areas in relation to trading. This whole matter is of gravest importance for us.

No. 42 NAI DFA Paris Embassy 48/2

Code telegram from Joseph P. Walshe to Seán Murphy (Paris)
(No. 51) (Copy)

DUBLIN, 30 September 1939

Sir John Maffey has been appointed as British Representative to Ireland. His appointment indicates that our relations approximate to these existing between two sovereign but friendly neighbouring states. He completes the diplomatic channels of communication of which the High Commissioner constitutes the other. If asked questions you may reply in the foregoing words.

No. 43 NAI DFA 219/4

Confidential report from William Warnock to Joseph P. Walshe (Dublin)
(43/33)

BERLIN, 30 September 1939

The latest Russo-German pact,[1] resulting from the obliteration of Poland, must be considered as a success for both sides, in spite of the fact that British propaganda (as I hear it over the wireless) is naturally enough trying to show that all the gains have been on Russia's side.

The German newspapers this morning are jubilant at the final downfall of the British 'encirclement' plans. The man-in-the-street quite realises that Russia may in time prove to be a dangerous neighbour, but there is not the slightest likelihood of the Russians giving any trouble at the present time, nor is there any reason to suppose that they will turn against Germany before the war is over. Their pre-1914 frontier did, of course, reach further into Poland than the new one, but, as far as territory is concerned, they can occupy themselves elsewhere, where the neighbours are less powerful, as, for instance, in the Baltic. At some future time the Russians may be in a position to challenge German sea supremacy in the Baltic, now that they have secured bases in Esthonia; such speculations, however, have little practical value just at present.

---

[1] The German-Soviet Boundary and Friendship Treaty was signed on 28 September 1939.

I presume that you have seen in the press maps showing (1) the provisional demarcation line agreed on by the German and Russian armies, and (2) the frontier definitely fixed in the Moscow agreement. Under the second arrangement Germany retains control of the Vistula, a matter of great strategic importance in any eventual war between the new neighbours.

In terms of great elation the people here are being informed (as is usual on such occasions) that the settlement now reached will more or less last for ever, and that Germany and Russia are resolved for the future to settle all their differences by negotiation. War between them is said to be unthinkable. Economically, one country is the complement of the other, and the continuance of trade and industry are assured, so we are told. The joint declaration made by the two Governments regarding the continuance of the war is spoken of as a 'peace ultimatum'.

The man-in-the-street, though he is cut off from foreign propaganda, does not necessarily accept everything given in the press and wireless as Gospel truth. Gradually he is beginning to realise that the war may not, after all, be over in a few months. He had already had to suffer a severe rationing of food. It is worth while, however, noting a few things which he feels about the war:-

(1) The Russians will twist and turn according as they think their interests change, but there does not appear to be any plausible reason why they should come to the assistance of Great Britain and France.

(2) No matter how strong the British consider their Navy to be, it has been amply demonstrated that German submarines can do a lot of damage to British shipping. It will take more than declarations by Mr. Churchill to drive German submarines from the seas.

(3) The British blockade is, no doubt, a handicap to commerce, but now that new Russian and Eastern European avenues of trade have been opened up, the difficulties will be to a large extent overcome. Existing stocks of food and essential war materials are said to be sufficient to last for some years.

(4) The Allied Armies and Air Forces are not as well equipped as the German, nor can they put as many men in the field. It is not believed that the number of trained aircraft pilots available on the other side can be compared with the number actually on service here. In an effort to bring the war to a speedy conclusion, it is probable that mass air-attacks will be made on important centres in Great Britain and France.

(5) German Air Defence will be well able to deal with Allied attacks from the air.

(6) Allied attacks on the Siegfried Line will be unavailing.

(7) Nobody believes that the British attack is directed merely against Hitler and National Socialism. It is well known that Great Britain can never endure the thought that another nation should become stronger than herself, and that she should lose her position of world pre-eminence.

(8) If Germany loses this war, the consequences will be even graver than that of the last. Germany, as we know it, will disappear. It is ridiculous to expect a 'just peace' from any victor.

The appointment of a British special representative to Dublin is looked on by some newspapers as an attempt by the British to bring pressure to bear on Ireland. There is no suggestion, however, that we shall acquiesce in British demands. The attitude to us remains as friendly as ever.

Isolation makes me feel the lack of up-to-date Irish news, but the wireless news-bulletins from Athlone are a great help.

[signed] W. WARNOCK

No. 44 NAI DFA 227/87

Code telegram from the Department of External Affairs to Francis T. Cremins (Geneva)
(No. 19) (Copy)

DUBLIN, 4 October 1939

Please communicate formally to the Secretary General of the League[1] that Ireland intends to maintain neutrality in the present war. It will not be necessary to refer to belligerents by name nor to mention any dates as was done in the case of the Argentine notification forwarded with your minute S.Gen.1/1 of the 14th September.[2]

No. 45 NAI DFA 227/100

Code telegram from Robert Brennan to Joseph P. Walshe (Dublin)
(Copy)

WASHINGTON, 4 October 1939

Your telegram 219.[3] I made appropriate representations to State Department yesterday morning and Mr. Moore said no one can predict how neutrality legislation will go and under second clause American ships could visit Ireland because she is neutral. However combat areas are defined Ireland will suffer like other north European neutrals since the seas surrounding her are combat areas.

No. 46 NAI DFA 219/5

Confidential report from Colman O'Donovan to Joseph P. Walshe (Dublin)
(MP 30/39) (Confidential)

HOLY SEE, 4 October 1939

Within the past week or so the question of the attitude of Ireland towards the fate of Poland has arisen several times in the course of discussions on the war which I have had with Irish priests here. In view of the common faith and similar past of the two countries it was natural enough that the topic should arise, but I did not observe any tendency to argue that there was anything that Ireland could have done to save Poland from her fate.

A few days ago, however, the Rector of the Irish College[4] told me that he had come into possession, under a pledge of secrecy, of information which caused him to suggest to me that it might be desirable that we should prepare ourselves to meet criticism that Catholic Ireland had been found wanting in the moment of Catholic Poland's trial. I told Dr. MacDaid that it was difficult for me to take any

---

[1] Joseph Avenol.
[2] Not printed.
[3] See No. 41.
[4] Mgr Denis McDaid, Rector of the Irish College in Rome (1939-51).

action in such a matter without knowing the source or the nature of the information which he had received. He said that he would try to release himself from the pledge of confidence and would see me again when he had done so.

I have since received by post the enclosed anonymous message[1] written across a newspaper article about the surrender of Warsaw and the end of Polish resistance. The message itself and the method of its transmission bear the familiar stamp of the crank and I should not ordinarily think it worthy of notice. I mention it now merely because it, and the conversations to which I have referred may be the outcrop of a sentiment, more or less widely felt, which it would be well to take under notice.

I introduced the matter casually in my conversation with Mgr. Montini[2] at the Vatican yesterday, and said that I did not see what, in her position, Ireland could have done beyond raising funds for the relief of sufferers in Poland and that I understood that a fund had in fact been started. Mgr. Montini agreed with my remarks, saying that Ireland was neutral and had entered into no engagements with Poland, but he thought it should be a good thing to publish the news of the fund and any other such news (e.g. resolutions of sympathy, if any) in the OSSERVATORE ROMANO. He would see that full publicity was given to anything of the kind that I would send him. I therefore telegraphed to you today making that suggestion.

[signed] C.J. O'Donovan

No. 47 NAI DFA Secretary's Files A20/3

Memorandum from Leopold H. Kerney to Joseph P. Walshe (Dublin)
(S.S. 10/11)

San Sebastian, 5 October 1939

Frank RYAN. Your 244/8A

I called at Burgos Prison on Monday morning, 25th September, and spent about half an hour in conversation with Frank Ryan; the Director informed me that the missing parcel of clothes had arrived and that Ryan had written thanking me; the books, however, were lying in the Director's office, pending a reply from Madrid to Ryan's written request to be allowed to have these, this being in accordance with the requirements of prison regulations; the parcel of foodstuffs left by the Duchess of Tetuan, at my request, on Wednesday evening 20th September, was also being given to him, though Ryan told me that he had not yet seen it.

I left 150 pesetas with the Director for Ryan and obtained the usual receipt.

Ryan looked if anything better than last time; he was as bright as usual and assured me that he was feeling well and hardly bothered at all with his heart; he said the prison doctor was being changed, and of course it has to be seen what the new doctor will be like. Ryan showed no signs at all of impatience and he accepts his position philosophically, although he confessed that it cast a shadow over him now and again when he reflected on the fact that as time passed his parents were becoming more aged but he was not worrying at all about himself. I told him briefly how matters stood and that we had now to wait until we could get a

---

[1] Not located.
[2] Mgr Giovanni Battista Montini (1897-1978), assistant to the Cardinal Secretary of State (1933-44), Archbishop of Milan (1954-63), elected Pope Paul VI (1963-78).

decision from the very top; this brought about a reference to Fusset whom Ryan knew to have been very ill-disposed towards him. (N.B. Fusset is a close friend of Franco and was with him all through Franco's recent triumphal tour in Galicia).

He was aware of events in the outer world, his source of information being a privileged fellow-prisoner of high standing.

He asked me to send him foodstuffs only *once a month* so as to be less of a charge on his friends; he particularly asked that his sister should approach Peadar O'Donnell[1] as he did not think it right that he should be a cause of expense to his family, whom he had not consulted before going to Spain. Spanish food would be good enough, 'anything good enough for a horse', he said, but condensed milk (sweetened) was the most desirable thing, even if nothing else could be got; unfortunately, condensed milk is unobtainable in Spain, and I fear it will be soon impossible for me to get any in France.

He was eager to have news of his two brothers who are doctors in England and to know how they are faring under present circumstances.

The visit of the Duchess of Tetuan had pleased him greatly and had been a big surprise; he enjoyed his talk with her.

I told him that I would call again when on my way to reopen the Madrid Legation.

[signed] L.H. KERNEY

No. 48 NAI DFA 219/4

Confidential report from William Warnock to Joseph P. Walshe (Dublin)
(43/33)

BERLIN, 7 October 1939

I attended yesterday to hear the Chancellor's speech at the Reichstag. You will have seen the contents in the press long before you receive this minute, and therefore there is scarcely need for me to refer to the text.

Those of us who had hoped for something really new were, I am afraid, sorely disappointed. Nevertheless, it is difficult to see how it could have been otherwise. There was a suggestion that a kind of Polish Protectorate might be set up some time, but in such a way that the resulting state 'should not be a danger to either Russia nor Germany'.

People have now become accustomed to the Russian alliance, but it is becoming increasingly obvious to them what price has to be paid. The Soviet Government has now obtained a right to have air-bases as near as Latvia. This has given everybody to think.[2] As I am writing, the result of the Soviet negotiations with Lithuania is not known. I do not know if you listen-in to the Moscow news-bulletins. It appears from them that the Russians have 'Sovietised' right up to the new frontier. They have thrown landlords and shopkeepers into prison, and have set up workers and peasants councils in all districts. This fact is not generally known among the people here. The Chancellor said, of course, in his speech that the new

---

[1] Peadar O'Donnell (1893-1986), Irish left-wing republican and author; volunteered with Frank Ryan to fight with the International Brigades in Spain.
[2] This sentence is reproduced exactly as in the original.

alliance represented a turning-point in German foreign policy, but it will take some time to make everybody accustomed to it. With the excellent propaganda services at their disposal, the Government may succeed. I have heard some grumbling that the Germans had all the trouble of conquering Poland, and the Russians simply had to walk in, and that they are bringing things too far, with their forward drive in the Baltic; nevertheless, the man-in-the-street prepares to wait and see, or at any rate, to hold his tongue. It is not at all clear whether Russia is prepared to give military aid to Germany.

I understand from the Turkish Ambassador[1] that his country is very anxious to keep out of the conflict. He said to me that there was scarcely a man among their middle-aged population who had not been through at least two campaigns. All they wanted now was to be able to build up their country in peace.

The Taoiseach's most recent references in the Dáil to our desire to remain neutral were given both in the press and over the wireless.

Among the general public there is a feeling that a general war can be averted, on the grounds that Germany, with Russia, is so powerful that Great Britain and France would not have any reasonable hope of victory. This is, however, a case of the wish being father to the thought, even though the German-Russian combination (assuring Russian military aid) appears on paper to be almost invincible. The feeling in diplomatic circles is extremely pessimistic.

I hear that the Propaganda Ministry is anxious to have Dr. Maloney's book on the forged Casement Diaries translated and published here.[2] Madame Maud Gonne MacBride's 'Servant of the Queen' is ready for issue; this was, however, translated as a private venture of the German publisher.[3] At first the Ministry withheld its sanction for the translation of 'Servant of the Queen', as the English publishers are Jewish, but once the responsible official had read the book he immediately gave permission.

[signed] W. WARNOCK

No. 49 NAI DFA 219/8

Confidential report from Matthew Murphy to Joseph P. Walshe (Dublin) (58/M/39)

SAN FRANCISCO, 9 October 1939

(Through the Minister Plenipotentiary)
A month's duration of European hostilities finds the Pacific Coast States assuming a detached air, bordering on indifference as to the ultimate fate of Europe. A similar attitude prevailed during the various crises which have occurred in Europe for some time, and is due to the fact that the people of the Western States maintain an aloofness not only from foreign affairs, but even from developments in the Eastern States.

During the week preceding and following the outbreak of hostilities, intense interest was displayed in radio and press despatches. The press on the whole is

---

[1] Hüsrev R. Gerede (1886-1962), Turkish Ambassador to Germany (1939-42).
[2] William J. Maloney, *The Forged Casement Diaries* (Dublin, 1936).
[3] Maud Gonne MacBride (1866-1953), Irish nationalist. The reference is to her book *Servant of the Queen: reminiscences* (London, 1938).

pro-British and pro-French in its editorial comment, and while maintaining a desire for neutrality, favours the repeal of the Arms Embargo. Mr. William R. Hearst[1] maintains his isolationist policy, and opposes the repeal of the Arms Embargo.

The press generally is facetious in its reference to the recent and suddenly developed friendship between Germany and Soviet Russia. Mr. Hearst, who is uncompromisingly hostile to Communism, informed me that he considered the pact between those countries the most unfortunate thing which happened in European affairs since 1918.

The San Francisco 'Chronicle', (Independent Republican), sent its Foreign Commentator to Germany early in August to cover the Nuremberg Nazi Congress. When the latter was cancelled, he was instructed to remain in Berlin and report on the crisis. Mr. Paul Smith, Managing Editor, informed me that he received a cable in code eight hours before the war broke out, from Mr. Ross, then in Berlin, to the effect that there would be no European war.

I attended a function held at the Golden Gate International Exposition, at which most of the Foreign Consuls in San Francisco were present, and gathered that they were adopting the policy of avoiding discussing the European crisis with Americans. Captain Fritz Wiedemann, German Consul General, appeared very nervous and depressed. It is generally known he was close to Reichsfuehrer Hitler when in Germany, and is reported to have always advised against taking any steps which would bring about war. It is also stated that Foreign Minister von Ribbentrop clashed with the Reichsfuehrer over Captain Wiedemann, and was responsible for the latter being sent to his present post. Captain Wiedemann is reported to have stated that his only hope now is that his advice to his Chief proves to have been wrong.

Shortly after war broke out, Captain Wiedemann received a telegram purporting to have come from the Secretary of the Olympic Club, San Francisco, of which he is a member. The telegram alleged that 165 members of the Club had declared their intention of resigning unless Captain Wiedemann tendered his resignation as a member. The Consul General immediately telegraphed his resignation, and later learned that the telegram was a hoax, and had not been sent by the Secretary of the Club. At the unanimous request of the Board of Directors, Captain Wiedemann withdrew his resignation. The Consul General has a very likeable personality, and has made, since coming to San Francisco, quite a number of friends whom he still retains. He has, however, kept very much to himself during the past month. The San Francisco 'Chronicle' editorially condemned the sending of the telegram referred to, and called it a 'dirty trick'.

There are three groups of organized Germans in San Francisco, as follows:
(1)   The United German Societies, numbering 77.
(2)   The German-American League of Culture.
(3)   The German-American Bund, a Nazi organization.

In my report numbered 81/M/38, dated the 6th October, 1938, I reported the disturbance which attended the annual German Day celebrations held last year. The German Consul General, Baron von Killinger, addressed that meeting, which was picketed by Communists, and resulted in serious rioting. The 1939 celebrations were held last week, but the German Consul General was not present, nor were any Nazi

---

[1] William Randolf Hearst (1863-1951), American newspaper publisher.

flags displayed. The Mayor of San Francisco attended, and his stand against America being drawn into the European war was loudly applauded. So also was a reference made by a Judge of German descent to the fact that Germans were in the front ranks 'which kicked the British out of the United States'. The proceedings were reported as being orderly, and there was no picketing.

The German-American League of Culture is known to be a Communist organization, and its San Francisco branch has attacked Captain Wiedemann on many occasions, and has frequently picketed the German Consulate General. Nothing has been heard of it recently, but the National Convention held at Cleveland on the 4th September requested the recall of Captain Wiedemann, and called upon the German people 'to over-throw Hitler as the destroyer of the reputation of Good Germans'.

The German-American Bund is considered the official Nazi Party Organization in the United States. I enclose report of its meeting held last week from which it appears it concentrated most of its energy against the Jews, the Democracies, and is working for American Neutrality.[1]

A feature writer of the San Francisco 'News' (Scripps-Howard publication) reports that propaganda sheets are being sent from Hamburg to the San Francisco Irish, with a view to lining them up with Germany. I have not seen a copy of the circular, and have not met any Irish or Irish-American in San Francisco who received one.

The San Francisco 'Chronicle', reporting on Reichsfuehrer Hitler's speech on the 6th instant, heads the editorial 'Brigand States his Terms. Hitler States he will be Content with his Loot'. The editorial states that Britain and France cannot settle with Hitler except on his own terms, which would reduce them to the position of third rate Powers henceforth by the grace of Nazidom.

Other Western comment is made by the Portland (Oregon) 'Oregonian', which states, 'The address indicates that Hitler wants war if he cannot have what he wants, which is dominance of the continent, through negotiation'.

Relative press clippings are enclosed.[2]

[signed] M. MURPHY

No. 50 NAI DFA 217/33

Letter from William Warnock to Frederick H. Boland (Dublin)
(43/33)

BERLIN, 9 October 1939

Dear Mr. Boland,
With your minute of the 29th August you sent us a letter to be forwarded to Mr Charles Bewley. In view of the uncertain conditions at the time, I returned it in our mailbag No. 98, as so far as I am aware Mr. Bewley was then in Dublin. It occurs to me now that the mailbag may have gone astray, as we have not yet received the relevant receipted schedule from the Department. Mr. Bewley is at the moment in Berlin, staying at the Hotel Russischer Hof, but I have no idea how long he intends to remain here. He left Dublin about the middle of September.

---

[1] Not printed.
[2] Not printed.

If any of our correspondence to you is missing, I shall send you duplicates.

On two occasions recently at the Foreign Office officials have asked me when the new Irish Minister is expected to arrive. Dr. Woermann, Under-Secretary of State, mentioned that it would be a sign of the good relations existing between us if the new Minister could come soon. I have, however, always avoided this question, as I read a few weeks ago in the 'Irish Times' that there were difficulties as regards the Letters of Credence. I should much appreciate your guidance in this connection. I should be glad of a hint as to whether I am likely to be alone for some time to come (assuming that the war is long drawn-out). I am thinking of domestic matters concerning my residence in the Legation premises. This brings me to another point.

The competent official of the Foreign Office has asked me – verbally – when we are going to make up our minds about the Legation building. We have now been holding them off for several years, and at last they are showing signs of impatience. I think that, even if we do not purchase, the Ministry of Finance, which controls the property, would be willing to allow us to remain on as tenants under a new agreement after the end of next year, when the present lease expires. We held them off for another while by telling them that we would have to wait for the new Minister's opinion. That was two months ago, and the effect has now worn off somewhat.

We are right in the middle of the new diplomatic quarter, and I think that it will be a tragedy if we let the house go. We have frontages in the Drakestrasse and the Rauchstrasse. New Legations are being built all around us, and when they are completed our neighbours will be as follows:

(1) *Drakestrasse*
    Hungary, Yugoslavia, Norway, Portugal, Spain, and Denmark round the corner.
(2) *Rauchstrasse*
    Papal Nunciature, Cuba, Finland, Netherlands, Roumania, Switzerland.

Nearby in the Tiergartenstrasse are, or will be, Argentine, Chile, Iran, Italy, Japan, Turkey.

Furthermore, the Drakestrasse is easily reached from the business quarters of the city.

I should value your advice in one thing more than any other, and that is, in the writing of reports, because I am not at all sure as to what matters interest you particularly.

Please accept my best wishes for the Department.

With kind regards,
Yours sincerely,
[signed] W. Warnock

No. 51 NAI DFA 219/4

> *Letter from Frederick H. Boland to William Warnock (Berlin)*
> *(Copy)*
>
> Dublin, 10 October 1939

You referred, in a recent report I think, to the fact that, not only the general attitude in Germany, but Press and wireless allusions also were friendly to Ireland.

You should make a particular point of reporting systematically to the Department on all references to Ireland and the policy of the Irish Government, particularly in the matter of neutrality, made in the German papers or on the German wireless. You should draw the attention of the Department to every such allusion, furnishing the text if possible. You should also continue to report to the Department as frequently as possible on the general public attitude to Ireland as evidenced by the conversations which you and Miss Walsh[1] may have with individuals, or by expressions of opinion which may reach your ears.

You will have seen from the text of the Dáil Debates which I sent you some days ago that there was some discussion in the Dáil about an allusion to Ireland stated to have been made in the 12.15 a.m. English broadcast from Hamburg station on 12th, 13th or 14th September. The allusion which was referred to in particular by Deputy McGilligan[2] was to the effect that the 'blacking out' arrangements in Dublin indicated a disposition on the part of the Irish Government to 'shelter under Mr. Chamberlain's umbrella'. The German Minister here was rather upset about this allusion, and telegraphed to Berlin about it. He was apparently informed in reply that no trace of such an allusion could be found in the scripts of the English talks given from Hamburg on any of the dates mentioned. If you have any information about this particular allusion, we would be glad to receive it, but, of course, it is not necessary for you to do anything about the matter officially.

[stamped] F.H. BOLAND

No. 52 NAI DFA 219/6

Letter from Seán Murphy to Joseph P. Walshe (Dublin)
(Copy)

PARIS, 12 October 1939

A Chara,
With reference to our telephone conversation yesterday I have the honour to state that I would have sent you reports of my personal impressions of the situation here were it not for the fact that the delay in the post puts them completely out of date. It was for that reason that I confined myself to giving the views of the French Press which I felt however late in arriving would constitute a record of French public opinion. Henceforth however I will send you a weekly report of my impressions or oftener if the circumstances should warrant it.

The big events of the last eight days have been the German Peace offensive, the Chamberlain speech on the peace offensive and the speech of Daladier.

With regard to the German Peace offensive as I have already reported the French press turned down any peace proposals from Hitler. The Communist party was the only element in France prepared to consider peace proposals and their attitude resulted in the dissolution of the party by decree.

Chamberlain's speech was favourably received by the French press but one

---

[1] Ms Eileen J. Walsh, Secretary to the Irish Legation in Berlin.
[2] Patrick McGilligan (1889-1979), Fine Gael TD, Minister for External Affairs (1927-32), Professor of International Law at University College Dublin. See biographical details in DIFP III, p. xxiv.

heard questions being asked in all sections of French life as to whether there was not a possibility that Chamberlain might consider peace terms at this stage. I read Chamberlain's speech very carefully and I confess I found it difficult to find ground for this French apprehension. However there is no doubt it existed.

Yesterday evening I met quite by accident Mr. Percy Phillip who is the European correspondent of the New York Times. He is regarded as a very good newspaperman and was very well in with Bonnet.[1] He told me he had recently visited the Maginot line at the invitation of the French Government. He said that the line was very interesting. He had gone down in one section of it 115 metres by electric light. Below they saw a complete world. There was a light railway, munitions dumps, hospital stations, Officers messes, etc. He said they had been with the French advance posts in No Man's land. The advance was about 30 to 40 Kilometres. He had no doubt that if the Germans made a serious attack the French would not try to hold on but would retreat to the Maginot line. The advance was merely to show that France was really at war with Germany. Phillip said the real interest for him was his talk at lunch with some officers of the reserve who had been called up for duty. Officers of the reserve are of course a much better guide to public opinion than those of the regular army, as they have left professions and business and are generally suffering loss. He asked them what they thought of Hitler's proposals and they replied to a man that if any French Government dared to negotiate with Hitler the army would take control of the country at once. They were determined that this time it would be seen through to the end, and there would be no more political armistice such as 1918. They were worried by Chamberlain's speech and hoped there was no danger of England letting up at this stage.

Daladier's speech was completely approved by all the French press as indicating the attitude of the ordinary French citizen. As far as the press here report it seems that the speech was well received in England and all the neutral countries. Even the German press it is alleged stated that 'the speech was not as bad as was expected.' From all I can hear the speech represents the attitude of the man in the street towards the war. Everyone seems anxious to put an end to the constant disturbances in Europe and are prepared to pay a very high price to secure stability.

The other question of interest is the attitude of Russia towards the Baltic countries. As you know Estonia, Latvia and Lithuania have already accepted the Russian conditions. I met the Lithuanian Minister[2] the other day and he said after the example of Poland that they had no alternative but to accept the Russian terms and hope for the best. I should say that the Minister has always been very left in his views. I think however he feels that his country is in for a very bad time.

The Finns as far as one can gather are prepared to resist Russia's demands. Whether that attitude will continue remains to be seen.

In conclusion I think that the French are prepared to see their war through to the bitter end whatever the cost. They consider themselves better prepared and better equipped than ever before. They have abundance of food and apparently oil supplies.

---

[1] Georges-Étienne Bonnet (1889-1973), French politician (Radical-Socialist Party); Finance Minister (1937-8), Foreign Minister (1938-9), member of the Vichy National Council (1941).
[2] Jurgis Baltrusaitis (1873-1944).

They are very impressed by the organisation and equipment of the English troops that have already arrived here and they are glowing in their praise of the English Air Force.

Is Mise le meas,
(Sgd) Seán Murphy

P.S. May I have a copy of this in due course please

SM

No. 53 NAI DFA 217/29

> *Letter from William Warnock to Frederick H. Boland (Dublin)*
> *(13/39) (Confidential)*
> Berlin, 17 October 1939

I beg to inform you that numerous newspapers, both in Berlin and all through the provinces, have published a report from Amsterdam to the effect that the newly nominated Irish Minister cannot take up his appointment in Berlin, in view of the fact that his Letters of Credence should, in the ordinary way, be signed by the British King.

[signed] W. Warnock

No. 54 NAI DFA 205/4

> *Minute by Frederick H. Boland*
> Dublin, 19 October 1939

The German Minister told me on 9th October that he has taken up with Berlin the question of the ———[1] broadcast from the Hamburg station on 14th of September to which reference had been made by Mr. McGilligan in the Dáil and which had occasioned a certain amount of comment here.[2]

He had a reply from Berlin to the effect that the scripts of all the English talks given from the Hamburg station round about the dates mentioned had been carefully examined and no trace of any allusion to Ireland, either derogatory or otherwise, had been found in them. Herr Hempel said that the telegram he had received asked him to obtain further particulars with regard to the station from which, and the date and time at which, the alleged broadcast was supposed to have been made, whereupon further enquiries would be instituted. I thanked Herr Hempel for his communication, and said that, if any further particulars with regard to the supposed broadcast were brought to our notice, we would furnish them to him.

[initialled] F.B.

---

[1] Word missing in original.
[2] See Dáil Debates vol. 77, col. 195 (27 Sept. 1939). Deputy P.S. Doyle questioned de Valera (on McGilligan's behalf) on the content of alleged broadcasts from Hamburg.

Documents on Irish Foreign Policy, Volume VI, 1939–1941

No. 55 NAI DFA Legal Adviser's Papers

Memorandum from Michael Rynne to Joseph P. Walshe (Dublin)
(Secret) (Copy)

DUBLIN, 20 October 1939

Re British Newspaper Stories concerning Irish Neutrality

I spoke to Colonel Archer with regard to the extract from the British newspaper 'Daily Telegraph' of the 9th October which he sent you on the 12th October. I asked if we had any official report of the incident referred to by the newspaper, and mentioned that the phrase 'Who are we neutral against?' had gone all around the United States press.

2. Colonel Archer replied that from such reports as the Department of Defence had received, no State official had behaved precisely in the manner alleged by the British newspaper, and that the 'account' was simply a combination of two stories, viz.:- (i) the story of a forced landing on the East coastal waters at an extremely early stage,[1] and (ii) the story of a similar landing on Western waters more recently.[2] In the first case some social contact took place, but no statement concerning Irish neutrality had been made; in the second case no conversations of a friendly character took place between our protection officers and the belligerent aviation officers.

3. Colonel Archer's idea in sending you the extract (even though he expected you would have seen it anyway) was that you might, perhaps, think it well to bring it to the notice of Sir John Maffey when a suitable occasion presented itself. Colonel Archer is of opinion that unless the British authorities are prepared to close down on the publication of such highly impolitic (and false) newspaper stories, we will be absolutely compelled to intern the next British aircraft and crew that may fall into our hands.

4. The above opinion of Colonel Archer concerning the danger to our special brand of neutrality of irresponsible newspaper-propaganda seems to correspond exactly with that which I submitted in a minute of the 16th September under the heading 'The Maintenance of Neutrality'.[3]

No. 56 NAI DFA 219/4

Confidential report from William Warnock to Joseph P. Walshe (Dublin)
(43/33)

BERLIN, 21 October 1939

The press is full of accounts of the prowess of the German submarine commanders, and their successful campaign against the British Navy and Mercantile Marine.

---

[1] On 3 September 1939 two British seaplanes made a forced landing at Skerries, to the north of Dublin, and one seaplane made a forced landing at Dún Laoghaire harbour, to the south of Dublin. The landings were due to bad weather and all aircraft were later permitted to depart when conditions improved.

[2] On 14 September 1939 a British flying boat made a forced landing in Ventry Harbour, Kerry. The aircraft left after a local mechanic fixed an engine fault. The landing came to de Valera's attention as he was meeting Sir John Maffey.

[3] See No. 26.

The news is received enthusiastically by the people, who consider with great satisfaction that the British fleet is completely powerless in the North Sea; one newspaper writes that the stage has now been reached when it is definitely dangerous for a British warship to put out into the North Sea at all.

Though you in Dublin may find it difficult to believe, I may say that the majority of the people were absolutely shocked when they heard that Mr. Chamberlain had rejected the Chancellor's peace offer. They entirely reject any British mention of obligations to Poland. If Britain had obligations to Poland and if she really intended to keep them, why, they ask, did she not give the Poles assistance in time? The only attempts Britain made to relieve pressure on Poland were (a) an unsuccessful air-raid on Wilhelmshaven, and (b) the distribution of some millions of pamphlets from aeroplanes, in other words, practically nothing.

About a fortnight ago a rumour of an armistice and the fall of the British Government spread through Berlin. It was received with great rejoicing. Several people enquired of the Legation for confirmation of the report, and seemed surprised that we knew nothing about it. The official denial, which blamed the British Secret Service for the rumour, brought bitter disappointment.

As well as the sinking of the 'Courageous' and the 'Royal Oak', the Germans claim that in addition they have sent the 'Ark Royal' and the 'Repulse' to the bottom, and have put several craft out of action.[1] It is stated that the efficacy of the air attack against naval units has been amply demonstrated.

The submarine Commander who sunk the 'Royal Oak' in the harbour of Scapa Flow has been feted in Berlin for the past few days.[2] His act of cool daring has raised fresh enthusiasm for the Navy, and in particular for the submarines.

Nobody seems to have any idea of the new dread means of destruction mentioned by the Chancellor in a recent speech at Danzig. I have heard it said that it may be an exceptionally powerful explosive which was tried out once in Spain with marked success. One bomb filled with this explosive is said to have destroyed an entire village. It is thought that it may have been used in the torpedoes which accounted for the 'Courageous' and the 'Royal Oak', both of which were supposed to be proof against attack by submarines.

Several members of the former German colony in Ireland have called at the Legation since their return with the special party last month. Some of those who have lived for some years in Ireland do not seem to have yet become settled down, and so far as I can see, would be glad to be back. I have heard from one source that the authorities here would on the whole have preferred that they should have remained on in Ireland. Even though some of the party were of military age, the necessity for the enlistment of all the available man-power of the State in the Army is remote, as for the present Germany has only a comparatively short front in the West to defend. The circumstances are completely different to those of 1914.

The feeling is still maintained that France has no enthusiasm for the war into which she has been forced by Great Britain. Soldiers returning from the West Front bring stories of notices posted on French positions worded something like: 'Shoot

---

[1] HMS *Courageous* was sunk by U-29 (17 Sept. 1939). HMS *Royal Oak* was sunk by U-47 (14 Oct. 1939). The commander of U-47 misidentified HMS *Pegasus* (a flying-boat tender) as HMS *Repulse* and claimed a hit. Neither *Ark Royal* (sunk by U-81, 13 Nov. 1941) nor *Pegasus* were sunk on this occasion.
[2] Kapitänleutnant Gunther Prien (1908-41), commander of U-47.

over there, where the English are'. The much publicised French offensive in the Saar region seems have been of no military importance.

The Anglo-French-Turkish Agreement[1] has undoubtedly caused disappointment in German political circles, but official comment has so far been meagre and restrained, and is confined to pointing out to Turkey that Great Britain can give her practically no effectual assistance, whereas Turkish help is extremely valuable to the British. Turkey is regarded as the successor to Abyssinia, Czecho-Slovakia, and Poland.

There have been no references of importance to Ireland in the press recently, with the exception of the matter to which I alluded in my confidential minute of 17th inst.[2]

[signed] W. WARNOCK

No. 57 NAI DFA 227/100

Aide mémoire from Robert Brennan to Cordell Hull (Washington)
WASHINGTON, 25 October 1939

Sir:
I have the honour to inform you that my Government is seriously concerned over the proposal that sailings of United States ships to Irish ports should be suspended.

As I had the honour to inform you in my Note of the nineteenth of September, 1939, Ireland has declared her neutrality in the present conflict in Europe.[3] I should like to emphasize moreover that apart from Ireland's neutral status, most of Ireland's seaboard is removed from the center of European hostilities. This fact has been fully demonstrated since hostilities commenced. American ships have made frequent sailings from Irish ports to home ports during recent weeks for the purpose of carrying passengers and goods.

I am to assure you that the Irish Government sees no reason to anticipate any circumstances which would render perilous or impossible the continuance of such sailings. My Government trusts that the Government of the United States will take a similar view in this regard.

Accept, Sir, the renewed assurances of my highest consideration.
[stamped] (Signed) ROBT. BRENNAN

No. 58 NAI DFA 219/6

Confidential report from Michael MacWhite to Joseph P. Walshe (Dublin)
(Confidential)
ROME, 25 October 1939

Due to the Soviet penetration in Western and South Western Europe Italy has been presented with a series of problems not all of which are political. Some to which she attaches much importance are of a moral, social, religious and historical order. Since

---

[1] A fifteen-year pact of mutual assistance between the three powers, signed on 19 October 1939 at Ankara.
[2] See No. 53.
[3] Not printed.

its inception in 1922 Fascism has never ceased to defend and glorify Roman tradition which is Western and Christian against Bolshevism which is Asiatic and Pagan.

The Duce has appeared, at all times, as the defender and perpetuator of the glories of ancient Rome with its constitution and laws and, likewise, as the champion of the greatness of Christian Rome with its great moral heritage. It cannot be gainsaid that he has restored religion to the schools and rendered to the Catholic Church much of the influence that it enjoys in Italy today. On the other hand Italian Catholics are amongst the most loyal supporters of the regime. It is only natural, therefore, that the Italian conception of the State should revolt against all the ideologies and cultures that are opposed to Roman tradition.

In the presence, therefore, of the new fact of the collusion of Nazi Germany which is largely inspired by anti Christian ideas and Soviet Russia, which would replace the civilisation of Rome by that of Moscow, Italy finds herself at the crossroads. She must either range herself on the side of doctrines which are contrary to Roman tradition in which she will have to renounce an important part of her spiritual and her moral heritage, or by refusing to follow the new doctrines as exemplified by the Rome-Berlin axis, she may be able to conserve integrally her glorious traditions.

In view of the foregoing it may be asked which road is Italy going to follow? So far she has made no concession to Bolshevik ideology. The 'Regime Fascista', a newspaper directed by Farinacci,[1] an extremist member of the Fascist Grand Council, affirms that Italians have always been and will always remain anti Communist. The 'Corriere Padano', which is owned by Air Marshal Balbo,[2] a moderate member of the Fascist Grand Council, has taken a more aggressive stand towards Moscow. Writing of the Soviet Commissar for Defence it says: 'Voroshiloff, and his companions, like all carrion in Bolshevik Russia, do not interest us in the slightest. We were born anti Communist and wish to remain so. We refuse a grain of esteem, or an ounce of sympathy to the Bolsheviks who are the models of gross bestiality, living monsters who are serving the most infamous undertaking of human deceit, cruelty and degradation which has ever been recorded by natural history.'

It is true that four issues of the 'Padano' containing similar attacks on Bolshevism, and what it stands for, were seized by the police, nevertheless we have here two expressions of opinion from which one may reasonably conclude that Fascist Italy is not likely to take a stand that would coincide with the policy of Hitler since he took Stalin to his bosom.

There was a further indication of this attitude in the manifestation which took place at Madrid a week or ten days ago on the occasion of the presentation of the credentials of the Italian Ambassador to General Franco. In the speeches exchanged it was made clear that neither Italy nor Spain were likely to follow the example of Germany in renouncing the anti Comintern pact, the poles of which would seem today to be fixed at Rome and Madrid. In his reference to Italo-Spanish solidarity Franco's plea in 'defense of Catholic and Western civilisation' appears to be significant.

---

[1] Roberto Farinacci (1892-1945), Secretary General of the Italian Fascist Party (1925-6) and senior advisor to Mussolini.
[2] Italo Balbo (1896-1940), Minister for Aviation (1929-33), Governor of Libya (1934-40).

Nevertheless, in this critical hour in the history of Europe, Italy remains, officially at least, the ally of Germany, and while England and France are extremely affable and courteous and make every endeavour to gain the good will of the Duce, the bitterness created by the Sanctions has not yet faded from his memory. He watches every move on the military and diplomatic chessboard, always silent and inscrutable. He would like to play a role, but time is on his side. As a neutral, Italy is rapidly restoring her economic fences. Everybody profits thereby. By peaceful methods she may achieve what is now an aspiration, by participation in the war on either side, she may lose the gains of the last eighteen years.

The Anglo-Franco-Turkish Agreement which received strong Italian opposition last May when discussions were taking place on the return of the Sandjak of Alexandretta to Turkey came as no surprise to Italy. It has been mildly criticised by Gayda, more for forms sake than anything else, as it preserves Italian influence in the Balkan instead of opening the South East of Europe to Soviet penetration which would, otherwise, have been the case. It is, however, slightly to Italy's disadvantage in so far as her prestige in the Mediterranean is concerned, as it reinforces the allied position. The French are now showing more confidence in the continuation of Italian neutrality and are withdrawing troops from the frontier and discontinuing the 'black-out' in the border region.

[signed] M. MacWhite

No. 59 NAI DFA 219/4

Letter from Frederick H. Boland to William Warnock (Berlin)
(Copy)

Dublin, 26 October 1939

Dear Warnock,

I have your letter 43/33 of the 9th October.[1]

I do not think any of your correspondence to us is missing. We received about a week ago the bags which you despatched round about the time of the outbreak of war. They came to us via New York. I shall have enquiries made and shall let you know if there is any indication that correspondence despatched by you has not been received.

As you surmise in your letter, there are difficulties about accrediting a Minister to Germany in present circumstance. However, the Taoiseach himself is anxious that the Minister-designate (Dr. Kiernan)[2] should get to Berlin as soon as possible, and we may find some means of enabling him to take up duty about the end of the year. As we told Herr Hempel at the time, it was not contemplated in any event that Dr. Kiernan would be able to take up duty earlier than about the middle of November. For the moment it is better that you should not say anything to the German people about any constitutional difficulty in the way of accrediting a Minister.

We are going into the question of the Legation building, and I hope to send you a minute about it in the course of the next week or so.

---

[1] See No. 50.
[2] Dr Thomas J. Kiernan (1897-1967), Director, Radio Éireann (1935-41); Minister, Holy See (1941-46). See biographical details in DIFP IV, p. xxvi.

We have read all your reports since the outbreak of war with great interest, and generally speaking, I think I am right in saying that they have given us just what we wanted. What we like to hear about is how the German people themselves – the individual Germans whom you meet casually every day – feel about the war. Secondly, we are always interested to get reports either of press or purely individual comment about this country and its policy in relation to the conflict. In the third place, we welcome information about German foreign policy and the attitude of German opinion towards it, particularly in such contexts as the expansionist tendencies of Soviet Russia, the neutrality of Italy, the position in the Balkans, and so on. Reports about administrative and other measures taken by the German Government in connection with the war – food rationing, war trade agreements, blockade policy and a hundred and one other things – are always of interest.

The great thing is to send plenty of reports. The more information we get the more we like it.

Kindest regards,
Yours sincerely,
[stamped] (Signed) F.H. BOLAND

No. 60 NAI DFA 219/4

Confidential report from William Warnock to Joseph P. Walshe (Dublin)
(43/33)

BERLIN, 26 October 1939

With reference to your minute of the 10th October,[1] I beg to state that I did not hear the broadcast from Hamburg mentioned in a recent debate in Dáil Éireann. News bulletins are given at all times of the day, and it is impossible to listen to them all. The first I heard of the alleged 'Hamburg broadcast' was a reference to it in the report of a Dáil debate given one evening from Athlone.

Ever since then I have endeavoured to listen to as many of the German bulletins as possible, and have so far heard no mention of Ireland which could be described as unfriendly. On the 22 inst. reference was made to the economic troubles caused to us by the war, and particularly to the lack of the raw materials needed by our industries. Quotations were given from Dáil debates. Listeners were given to understand that the disturbance of our commercial life has been brought about by British war methods.

On the 23rd inst. it was reported in the press and over the wireless that an explosion had taken place in Mountjoy Prison. It was suggested that an attempt had been made to rescue I.R.A. prisoners.[2]

It was stated on the 25th inst. that the British Government were taking repressive measures against numerous Irish citizens in England.

I know one of the journalists who are at present editing the English news bulletins given from the wireless stations. He tells me that in the last few weeks no unfavourable reference has been made to us. According to him, they have no wish to offend us, but rather the opposite. I asked him if he knew anything about the

---

[1] See No. 51.
[2] On 22 October 1939, using an improvised explosive device smuggled into the prison, some prisoners blew open a door but were promptly detained while still within the complex.

'Hamburg' broadcast. Unfortunately he could give me no information in the matter, as he was not, at that time, employed on this work.

As I stated in previous minutes, the general attitude to us is very friendly. I must confess, however, that interest in us springs from the fact that we are traditional opponents of Great Britain. There is always the hope that we will take up arms again, and worry the British in the rear. The less-thinking section of the population cannot understand why we have not done so already. The I.R.A. activities since January have been given great publicity, and many people have mentioned them sympathetically to me in ordinary conversation.

The following experience of one member of our colony is rather typical. He had called to see me, and after having left the Legation, was looking around for a taxi – not an easy task during a 'black-out'. A short distance away he came across two policemen, and asked their assistance. They noticed from his accent that he was a foreigner, and enquired as to his nationality. When he told them that he was Irish, they clapped him on the back in a most friendly way, exclaimed 'Bomb-throwers!' and went off in opposite directions to look for a taxi. In a minute or so both returned, each with a taxi!

At the present moment everything anti-English is grist to the propaganda mill; consequently I shall be very surprised indeed if anything is said or done which might annoy us. The public is continually told of the unscrupulous ways and means of the British Secret Service, and in this connection a few articles have appeared regarding the efforts made during the war by Mr. Findlay,[1] the British Minister to Norway, to secure the betrayal of Sir Roger Casement. I understand that the Propaganda Ministry is keen on having Dr. Maloney's book on the forged Casement diaries translated and published.

Some recent press cuttings are attached.[2]

The question of news bulletins reminds me that I often receive the transmission from the new experimental short-wave station at Athlone. I should be very grateful indeed if you would be good enough to ascertain for me the evenings on which this station works, and whether more than one wavelength is used. At present the wireless is my only hope of obtaining up-to-date Irish news, as the newspapers are usually at least a fortnight late.

[signed] W. WARNOCK

No. 61 NAI DFA Madrid Embassy 15/20A

Memorandum from Leopold H. Kerney to Joseph P. Walshe (Dublin)
(M.15/20A) (Copy)

MADRID, 26 October 1939

Trade Negotiations

With reference to your minute 207/48 of 5th inst.[3] and further to mine of 23rd inst.,[4] I was able to have an interview with Mr. Pan de Soraluce to-day.

The Political Director at the Ministry for Foreign Affairs is the Count de Casas

---

[1] Sir Mansfeldt de Cardonnel Findlay (1861-1932), British Minister to Norway (1910-23).
[2] Not printed.
[3] Not printed.
[4] Not printed.

Rojas; the two main branches under his control, dealing with both political and trade matters, concern themselves with Europe and America; Pan de Soraluce is the head of the former section (the post he held before the war) and the Viscount de Mamblas is at the moment (pending further imminent changes at the Foreign Office) head of the American section.

Now that the Government Departments have again gathered together in Madrid, the intention is to re-organise the work of the administration, to return to the methods of former days, to proceed in a more methodical way than has hitherto been possible and to establish some sound basis for the negotiation of trade agreements generally. There is now once more an inter-Ministerial Committee functioning; it meets ever other day from 5 p.m. till 10 p.m. This Committee has met three times so far, and has only been able to give a close examination to 3 items on the lengthy agenda down for consideration. Meanwhile, Casas Rojas has had to absent himself, and his work devolves on Pan de Soraluce, who is extremely occupied. He and I are on very friendly terms from the old days, and he has assured me more than once that he feels a greater sympathy for me than for any other chief of Mission here.

During my conversation of half an hour with Pan de Soraluce, we agreed that the main purpose of my visit was to ascertain his impressions on the broad principles of my proposals; you will understand therefore that these impressions, important though they are, do not commit his Government in any way, and that they could not do so under the circumstances; he will consult his colleagues in due course, as soon as may be possible, and then ask me to call and see him again; meanwhile I told him that this first conversation was merely for the purpose of exploration, and that I did not propose to follow it up, as yet, with any written note or aide-memoire.

The following were my proposals:

1. A payments agreement on a 2 to 1 basis (on the lines of our agreement with Turkey), a Spanish Bank centralising operations.

2. Private compensation agreements on a similar basis to be encouraged, without excluding individual enterprise outside such agreements.

Pan de Soraluce (we might abbreviate his name to Pan in future, as his name will constantly crop up and may have to figure in telegrams) was favourably impressed, and thought it should be possible to come to an agreement quickly on these lines; he saw no objection to the principle, but of course could not commit himself definitely at this stage. The fact remains that he views these proposals favourably as a basis for discussions.

I made it quite clear to him that we could not return to a system of quotas for oranges or other produce, but that, on the other hand, there was practically an open market for Spanish goods in Ireland, with scarcely any limitations. I also pointed out the desirability of disposing of the following matters (which I number consecutively for convenience in subsequent reference thereto) so as to make the way smooth for a trade agreement.

3. The 'blocked' account of the Irish Government in the Banco Hispano Americano, Madrid, should be released without delay.

4. The 'Clonlara' and 4 other vessels of the Limerick Steamship Co. should be taken off the black list without delay.

5. The 'frozen' pre-war credits, estimated to amount to £8,000 at the very outside, should be taken into consideration in connection with the proposed agreement.

6. Frank Ryan should be released.

Pan made a written memo of all these things, this in itself being an indication of his intention to have them considered; moreover, he took the same view of them as I did. He promised to have the matter of our 'blocked' account examined at once, and he did not protest at my describing the 'blocking' of this Government account to be intolerable. He promised to take up at once with 'Comunicaciones Maritimas' the question of the Limerick Steamship Company. He did not commit himself in any way with regard to the 'frozen' credits; but made a note of my estimate of the total maximum amount.

When I told him that another obstacle in our path was the fact that an Irishman was held prisoner in Spain, he began to explain to me the difference between untried prisoners in concentration camps and the others; I interrupted to let him know that this particular man was in Burgos Prison, and had in fact been sentenced to death, at least once, whereupon he exclaimed – 'Is it the famous – ?', and I replied 'The very same.' We did not mention Ryan's name, but he was apparently familiar with the case, although I had never had occasion to bring it to his direct notice; he agreed with me that the absence of a satisfactory solution could only continue to poison relations between Ireland and Spain, and he also made a note of this; he asked me if I had seen the 'assesseur juridique' (i.e. Fusset) whose consent would be necessary; I told him, in confidence, that Fusset had been seen, that he was well-disposed, that the Minister himself was in favour of Ryan's release, and that I was hoping his case would receive attention at the Cabinet Meeting the same afternoon.

Pan asked me what classes of goods we wanted to export to Spain; I told him that I could not say anything definite until I heard further from you; if we omitted eggs and seed potatoes I feared the volume of our exports would be small, and we had an easy market for these elsewhere under present circumstances; he remarked that it might perhaps be possible to do something in the way of eggs, but not to the same extent as formerly; I mentioned woollen goods as being likely to be included in any list we might put forward; I also told him that we would like to send some whiskey to Spain, say to the value of £5,000 or so, and chiefly for the purpose of putting ourselves in a good starting position if circumstances were to become more normal later on; he thought whiskey would be classified as being 'de luxe', but possible some nominal quantity might be admitted as 'a symbolic import'.

L.H. KERNEY

No. 62 NAI DFA 227/23

Minute from Frederick H. Boland to Sheila Murphy (Dublin)
DUBLIN, 26 October 1939

Private Secretary to the Secretary.

I think you said that we had been approached by the Slovak Government with a view to the appointment of a Slovak Consul here.

Other things being equal, there might perhaps be no reason for withholding the *de facto* recognition of Slovakia which the acceptance of a Consul would imply; but the matter is by no means free from difficulties. In the first place, although so far as I know there has been no declaration of war between Great Britain and Slovakia, relations have obviously been broken off between the two countries, and Britain is apparently treating Slovakia for all practical purposes as a part of Germany. This situation may cause us some embarrassment if we have to approach King George in connection with the exequatur.

Apart from that difficulty, there is the question whether, knowing as we do the views of the British Government about the presence of the German Minister here, it would be prudent on our part to add to our difficulties by receiving a Consul from Slovakia. Whatever the position is between Britain and Slovakia, it would not be difficult for the British to find ground, in such an appointment, for raising difficulties. If Britain and Slovakia are at war, it would be somewhat tactless on our part to choose this particular juncture for establishing relations with Slovakia. On the other hand, if the relation between Britain and Slovakia is not that of belligerents, the Slovak Consul would certainly be charged with acting as a channel of communication for the German Minister. According to recent press reports, the Slovak Consul in London has apparently ceased to act under the instructions of his Government and has denounced Germany for invading Slovakia. The British Consul at Bratislava, who had been exequatured, a few weeks before, was withdrawn by the British Government on the outbreak of war.[1] Under the Agreement between Slovakia and Germany, the commission of any consul for Slovakia appointed here would, I gather, be granted by the German Government.[2]

On the whole, I think that we should try to evade the issue and prevent the appointment of a Slovak Consul here at the present juncture, if it is practicable to do so.

[initialled] F.B.

I agree.
J.P.W. 23/11/39

No. 63 NAI DFA 226/31

Extract from a memorandum from Francis T. Cremins to Joseph P. Walshe
(Dublin)
(Ass./20) (Confidential)

Geneva, 27 October 1939

I have received your telegram as follows (27/10/39):-
'23 Your telegram 19 Please report by wire what Assembly agenda is likely to be. In our view it should be confined to administrative and routine work necessary to keep League in being. Political initiatives would be embarrassing to us and probably other neutrals as well. Can you say what views Scandinavian and other neutrals are taking re holding of Assembly session.'
In reply I sent the following telegram (27/10/39):-
'20 Your telegram 23 Agenda, Budget, Report of Committee on Economic, Social, Affairs, Council elections, Court elections, Technical Cooperation with China. Court elections probably postponed. There will be probably no general debate. Your view as expressed fully shared by Secretariat and by all members neutral and

---

[1] Marginal note by Murphy: 'See Hansard 9/10/39'.
[2] Marginal note by unidentified hand: 'No'.

belligerent with which Secretariat is in touch. All energies being directed to avoid political initiatives and Secretariat confident this is general desire and that it will be attained. League acting as neutral organisation in all its activities. Scandinavian and neutrals generally in favour of session. Mr. Colijn[1] mentioned as possible President.'

On receipt of your wire, I saw Mr. Lester and discussed the matter with him. He confirmed what was the general understanding here, that the session of the Assembly in December would be confined to administrative and routine matters, that is, to non-political matters, and that in fact the agenda, even as regards these questions, would be restricted to a very few items. I indicated the principal items in my minute of the 11th October,[2] but that has not yet reached you. Mr. Lester assured me that he is satisfied from all the contacts which he and the Secretary-General have been making that it is the general desire that no political matter should be raised at the Assembly. Everybody desires that the League machinery should be kept going on technical work and studies during the period of the war, although it is realised that some different sort of institution may be established at the end of the war.

From my discussions with Mr. Lester and with some of my colleagues here, it is clear that many Governments are anxious that nothing should arise at the Assembly which would be of embarrassment to neutral countries, and especially to the Swiss Government, and that therefore everything possible should be done in order to avoid any political initiatives. I learn from a colleague that the Swiss Government were particularly anxious that no political issues should be raised. It is therefore altogether in the interest of the League that there should be no trouble. I am told that the British and French are in complete agreement with this and are doing all they can to co-operate, and their attitude is expected to be effective if, for example, Poland desires to raise the Polish question. No one here thinks it at all likely that the representative of Poland – if indeed Poland sends a delegation, which is, I understand, doubtful – would be prepared to act against the advice of the British and French Governments in this matter. Any attempted intervention would be wholly ineffective, and there is the further consideration that it would be regarded as nothing but ironical that Poland should now seek the aid of the League, after, when it was the case of other aggressed States, declaring openly that she would in future take no part in political discussions in the Council or the Assembly, and refusing only last year to pose her candidature for the Council on the same grounds. She further withdrew her permanent delegation from Geneva because she had decided to confine her League activities to purely technical questions. And I need hardly recall also, in this connection, Poland's own settlement of the Teschen question by force and her appeal, by force, to a peaceful settlement of certain difficulties with Lithuania. For these reasons, but especially because of the attitude of the British and French Governments, it is regarded here as extremely unlikely that, if Poland sends a delegation, her representative will endeavour to raise in the Assembly any political issue. This is the opinion here notwithstanding the communications from the Polish Government on the subject of the partition of Poland (document C.349.M.264.1939.VII). No action by the League is requested in these communications.

[1] Heindrikus Colijn (1869-1944), Prime Minister of the Netherlands (1925-6 and 1933-9).
[2] Not printed.

There is one point about Poland to which I should draw attention, namely, the question of the recognition of the credentials of a Polish delegation. I have discussed this point with Mr. Lester, and with a colleague to whom it had also occurred, and who had mentioned it to the Secretary-General. The view taken, which I share, is that it is highly improbable that anyone, even Russia, will raise objection. The Polish Government is still recognised by other Governments, and is in a totally different position from that of, for example, Czecho-Slovakia, whose Government – including M. Beneš – had resigned and had not been constitutionally replaced. If it happened that the Czechs desired representation at the Assembly, it is fairly certain that they could not and would not be accepted. But it is thought that they have no such intention, and I understand that the influence of Britain and France would be thrown against any such idea. I presume that in the unlikely event of any serious question arising regarding Polish credentials, the Irish Delegation should support the maintenance of the *status quo* which I feel satisfied would be the wish of the majority even from the point of view of neutrality. It is hardly conceivable however that the question would be brought to a vote of the Assembly. The rule (Par.4, Rule 5, Rules of Procedure of the Assembly) is as follows:-

'Any representatives to whose admission objection has been made shall sit provisionally with the same rights as other representatives, unless the Assembly decides otherwise'.

No. 64 NAI DFA Secretary's Files P4

Code telegram from Joseph P. Walshe to John J. Hearne (Ottawa)
(No. 16) (Copy)

DUBLIN, 31 October 1939

Secretary writing you on general neutrality situation as requested 12th October. Important to convey, whenever appropriate, following indisputable facts, one, in deciding for neutrality Government were exercising sovereign rights as were Governments of Canada or France when declaring war; two, in state of national sentiment and interest no other policy possible here at outbreak of war; three, after two months' hostilities Irish churches, press and people are virtually unanimously in favour of indefinite maintenance of policy. You need not unduly emphasise that from legal standpoint no general enactment yet made equivalent to formal declaration of neutrality. Ireland's position however officially notified to all belligerents and to European Governments in direct diplomatic relations. An extensive code of emergency law achieved during recent weeks under which neutrality policy being effectively administered. Emergency measures relate Irish neutral shipping and trade, military and political censorship, aliens (including aliens formerly exempt), currency and prices problems, supplies and rationing, etc.

The most important measures remaining to be made will concern, one, naval and air forces of belligerents, to which provisions of Hague Convention (No. XIII) 1907 and other generally accepted rules of international law will apply; two, will penalise unneutral acts committed by persons in jurisdiction. Meanwhile Government have formally indicated to belligerents their intentions in first foregoing matter. You may, therefore, assume where incidents such as that referred to in your paragraph one occur without protest Irish Government consider no infringement of law or neutrality policy committed. In connection with Kerry incident,[1] you should read Article 22, paragraph 2, of the Proces-Verbal, 1936, relating to Part IV of London Naval Treaty, 1930. Crew of Greek merchantmen were presumably landed in accordance with that Treaty provision, humanitarian object of which appreciated by Irish Government. In general, Irish Government desire exclusion belligerent submarines from Irish waters and are prepared to use every means at their disposal to enforce.

No. 65 NAI DFA 241/113

Minute by Joseph P. Walshe of a meeting with Edouard Hempel

Dublin, 1 November 1939

The German Minister called to see me this morning, and I took the opportunity to speak to him about his letter of the 24th October warning us as a neutral State not to allow our citizens to travel on English or French ships. I told him that our Government would be placed in an impossible position if our citizens could not use the chief means available for them to travel between here and Great Britain. Such a position would be in complete contradiction with that accepted by him and his Government in all our conversations on Irish neutrality which took place between him and myself and between him and my Minister prior to and subsequent to the outbreak of war. I realised that his letter was based on a general instruction issued to all German Ministers in neutral countries and not one issued to him in relation to the particular difficulties (so frequently explained to him) of the Irish Government. I now wished to inform him that the sinking of ships carrying passengers between Great Britain and Ireland would provoke such an outcry in this country against Germany that the maintenance of our neutrality would become almost impossible. I felt therefore that it was not the intention of the German Government to apply this rule to the special circumstances existing between Ireland and Great Britain, and I asked him to urge upon his Government in the strongest possible fashion not to include passenger traffic between Ireland and Great Britain in their general instruction. I referred to the very bad effects created by the sinking of the 'Leinster'[2] at the end of the Great War. Whatever excuse there was then, there could not possibly be any excuse for taking similar measures now. The German Minister told me he would get into touch with his Government as soon as he could, though he again emphasised how difficult it was for him to communicate with his Government at all, and he urged upon me the necessity of using our own channels of communication through our Chargé d'Affaires in Berlin in order to bring the matter with all possible speed to the attention of his Government. The German Minister quite agreed that we could not give any publicity to his letter of the 24th October even through private channels to the Companies concerned, and he further agreed that a serious situation would be created by the sinking of passenger ships between Great Britain and Ireland.

[1] On 3 October 1939 U-35 torpedoed the Greek steamer *Diamantis* off Land's End, having taken the twenty-eight members of the crew onboard prior to sinking the ship. The crew members were ferried ashore close to Ventry harbour, Kerry.

[2] On 10 October 1918, the Royal Mail Steamer *Leinster* was hit by three torpedoes from U-123 and sank outside Dublin Bay. The official death toll was 501.

We have sent cabled instructions to our Chargé d'Affaires in Berlin to inform the German Government in the foregoing sense.

No. 66 NAI DFA Secretary's Files P4

Confidential report from John J. Hearne to Joseph P. Walshe (Dublin)
(14/11)

OTTAWA, 8 November 1939

I have the honour to report as follows:-

I duly received your cable of the 31st of October[1] containing a summary of certain facts of the situation at home. I am very grateful for it. I note that you are writing to me on the general neutrality situation as requested in my minute of the 12th of October.[2]

You state in your cable (as I have decoded it) that the Government have formally indicated to belligerents their intention of applying the provisions of the Hague Convention (No. 13) 1907 and other generally accepted rules of international law. I should be glad to be informed as to whether Canada is one of the belligerents with whom you have communicated or will communicate in that sense.

I note your direction to me to convey the following facts, namely, that (1) in deciding for neutrality, the Government were exercising a sovereign right; that (2) in the state of national sentiment and in the national interest no other policy was possible at the outbreak of the war; and that (3) after two months' hostilities, the people of Ireland are virtually unanimously in favour of the indefinite maintenance of the policy of neutrality. You will be glad to know that I had already been emphasising points (1) and (2). I am grateful for the instructions contained at (3), as there has been a general feeling here that the neutrality of Ireland in the war would be of temporary duration owing to the proximity of Ireland to the scene of the conflict and in particular her proximity and relations with the United Kingdom. The most emphatic view I heard expressed recently on our present national policy was that of Mr. Grattan O'Leary, the editor of the Ottawa Journal. At a dinner party given by Baron Silvercruys,[3] Belgian Minister, on November the 3rd, in honour of the birthday of the King of the Belgians (at which the Governor-General attended), Mr. O'Leary stated very strongly to me that Ireland could not continue to remain neutral in the war. I did not have an opportunity of having a long conversation then but I am taking occasion to talk generally with him, as well as in the particular sense of your cable, as soon as I can.

I have found very little tendency to dispute the right of Ireland as a sovereign State to be and to remain neutral. And in the most sympathetic quarters the policy itself of neutrality, as distinct from the right to be neutral, is well understood, and is not the object of adverse comment at any rate not to me or to my colleague Mr. Conway.[4] But here and there, however, we have in more recent weeks found criticism of the policy itself. It is invariably based upon the belief that the European

---

[1] See No. 64.
[2] Not printed.
[3] Baron Robert Silvercruys (1893-1971), Belgian Minister to Canada (1937-44), Ambassador to Canada (1944-5).
[4] John M. Conway, Secretary, Irish High Commission, Ottawa.

War is a war of Christianity against paganism. Those who criticise our neutrality policy to us do so on the ground that a great Catholic country like Ireland cannot logically remain aloof from a war which our critics regard as a war to smash an anti-Christian German ideology and to smash at the same time the doctrine of force as an instrument of political action whether in the domain of domestic or foreign affairs. I have been taking the view, which I have not hesitated to express in conversation with others, that the Irish people as a whole are completely out of sympathy with, and opposed to Nazism in theory and in practice. I have at the same time emphasised the fact that the Irish Parliament is solid behind Mr. de Valera's Government, and that no alternative Government is possible in Ireland on a pro-war programme. I should be very grateful however for an authoritative statement from you containing a full exposition of the situation in so far as 'national sentiment' and 'national interest' (your cable) are concerned. It would, for example, be of great help if I had in a few sentences the answers which you consider I should give to questions like the following:- 1. Is there any considerable body of opinion in Ireland which is pro-German in the present war? 2. Is the neutrality policy based on a determination of the Government and people to remain out of all wars and to make Ireland virtually a member of the group of countries who have made neutrality, so far as they can do it, a permanent feature of their foreign policy? 3. How far are the war slogans, for example, 'Christianity gets Paganism', 'A war to put an end to force as a political method', etc., accepted in Ireland as in any way summing up the issues involved? 4. How far is the neutrality policy determined by the Anti-Partition policy of Mr. de Valera's Cabinet? The replies to questions of that kind would, I think, provide sufficient amplification of the expression 'national sentiment' in your cable of the 31st of October. Perhaps you could send me also a statement on the question as to how the 'national interest' is best served by the neutrality policy.

I have a fear that you may think I should be able to answer queries of that kind without asking for instructions. I am anxious, however, in a situation which is so grave at home and so delicate here, that any thing I may say, however privately, should be covered by more authority than my own view, for, notwithstanding the closeness of my association with the Minister's frame of mind and your own, there may be some danger that even in so short an interval as three months I may be out of touch, if not with the general trend of things, at any rate with day-to-day developments and tendencies of opinion of which, at so great a distance, I could have no knowledge.

There is yet another series of questions that have been put to us. For example the following:- Would Ireland stand in with Great Britain if the war were being waged at full intensity and Great Britain and France were, in fact, losing? What would her attitude be if the United States became a belligerent on the side of the Allies? I have been giving no answers to these hypothetical questions except the answer that the attitude of our people to situations of the kind referred to would be determined as the national interest required if and when occasion arises. I am sure that our neutrality policy has been decided upon apart from the alignment of belligerent countries, that it is a decision based upon an active determination to keep out of wars undertaken by other States in their own interests, or interests conceived to be their own, a decision not directed against any particular State or group of States. I have been putting it to myself that our external policy remains primarily, as it was before war broke out, a peace with all nations' policy which we are resolved to pursue no matter what countries are at war. And I have been assuming that nothing short of an attack on our country would deflect us from that course. If you consider that the views set down in this paragraph are generally sound perhaps you would be so good as to approve them.

[signed] JOHN J. HEARNE

No. 67 NAI DFA 215/211

Extract from a confidential report from Francis T. Cremins to Joseph P. Walshe (Dublin)
(S.Gen. 1/1) (Confidential)

GENEVA, 11 November 1939

[matter omitted]
It is clear that Italy, which, before war actually broke out, was rather happy to lend its support to the German-Soviet pact, on the score that any stick was good enough to beat France and Britain with, is now becoming alarmed at the increase of Soviet power in Europe – in Poland and the Baltic – and at the possibility of greater Russian penetration in a region which Italy regards as part of her own sphere of influence, the Balkan peninsula. In this connection I attach an extract from a sheet circulated daily by 'Telepress',[1] an agency here under Italian influence. This extract, headed 'Rome contre Moscou', is an indication that official Italy is now taking openly a stand against the menace of Soviet Russia. This menace provides the possibility of eventual complications in Italo-German relations. Even in Germany itself, whilst the main German purpose is now to win the war, many thinking Germans must be exercised in their minds at the price which Germany is paying in Poland and the Baltic, and on the Roumanian frontier, for Russian support, and at the divergencies between the policies so labouriously worked out in 'Mein Kampf' and the present situation. Many people hold that Germany's policy in regard to Russia has brought about the encircling which she had been at pains to avoid. It could no doubt be Russia's policy to assist Germany to the point of enabling her to keep resisting, in order that both sides might be exhausted at the end, but few believe that it could ever be her policy to bring into being a preponderating Germany. Just as the Poles were all the time confused by the uncertainty caused by Soviet mobilisation in their rear, so Germans must wonder whether the time will not come when at a critical moment the Russians will let them down. It is useless to speculate, but the developments will be interesting to watch. The German-Soviet pact may eventually prove to be one of the deciding errors of the war. In the meantime, Italy is clearly becoming anxious, and is endeavouring to consolidate her position in the Balkan area. A settlement of some of the Bulgarian claims would help, but this is difficult to realise, as Roumania, the State chiefly concerned, fears that any territorial concessions would open the way to Hungarian claims to Transylvania. Roumania is pressing for the constitution of a neutral block of Balkan States with the help of Italy, but Roumania is in a weak position, with

---

[1] Not printed.

Hungarian eyes on Transylvania, Russian on Bessarabia and Bulgarian on the Dobrudja.

The view prevails here that things are on the verge of livening up on the Western front. In Balkan circles the view seems to be held that for the moment the Balkan countries are safe. The Finns here naturally remain anxious, although, as compared with last week, the tension for them has somewhat lessened. Even the Finnish situation is somewhat obscured by that now developing on the Belgian and especially on the Dutch frontier. The Belgians and Dutch here have become in the last few days extremely anxious, and they seem to expect a German attack, at least on Holland, at any moment. The view is held that the Germans cannot remain still indefinitely, and that they will try for a success with overwhelming force in the hope that they might be able to consolidate any position gained, during the period of forced inactivity in Winter. In Switzerland, it is not now seriously thought that the Germans will strike at both ends of the Maginot line simultaneously, but at the same time the Swiss authorities are taking new precautions, and are recalling to the colours as from Monday, 13 November, various classes which had not been retained. They are taking steps particularly to strengthen at once their active defence against air attack. I am told that at Berne, while all precautions are being taken, the view prevails that this country need not feel too anxious so long as Italy refrains from entering the war on the German side. Hope grows that Italy will not fight on the side of Germany.

No. 68 NAI DFA 219/49

Memorandum from John J. Hearne to Joseph P. Walshe (Dublin)
(14/12) (Copy)

OTTAWA, 14 November 1939

I have referred in previous reports to the absence of comment upon Ireland in the Canadian Press since the commencement of hostilities. I have also referred to the fact that the exchange of official representatives with Ireland, Australia, New Zealand and South Africa has been defended here by the Prime Minister as part of a policy of closer co-operation between Canada and those countries for the successful prosecution of the war. At the Remembrance ceremony on Armistice Day representatives of Canada, the United Kingdom, Australia, New Zealand, South Africa and Ireland (in that order) laid wreaths on the Cenotaph as a group. The Prime Minister represented Canada, and Australia and New Zealand were represented by members of the Air Training Missions of those countries. This is the only occasion in the year on which the United Kingdom High Commissioner, the Accredited Representative of the Union of South Africa and the High Commissioner for Ireland precede the representatives of other countries. The reason is that the Remembrance ceremony is regarded as 'a family affair'. The doyen of the corps (Baron Silvercruys, Belgian Minister) was prevailed upon by Sir Gerald Campbell[1] (so the latter told me) to consent to the arrangement on that ground. But apart from the Remembrance ceremony and the reason given by the Canadian

---

[1] Sir Gerald Campbell (1879-1964), British High Commissioner in Canada (1938-41), later Director-General of British Information Services in New York (1941), British Minister at the Embassy in Washington (1941-5).

Government for the exchange of representatives with Ireland etc. at the present time there appears to be a settled policy of staging down our position as a neutral country. The result is a blackout of Ireland in public speeches (in most of which the 'unity of the Empire' is emphasised) in the newspapers, and even in the conversation of official people. No member of the Cabinet has initiated any conversation with us on the question of our attitude to the war. I have been the guest of Mr. King on three occasions and on two others he and I were guests of the same host (the Governor General and the Belgian Minister). On none of these occasions (on all of which we had some general conversation) did he refer to our neutrality policy. On Wednesday the 8th November when we dined at Laurier House he gave us (as second guests of honour, Mr. and Mrs. Meyer being the guests of honour) an exceptionally kind welcome and took us over the house. He spoke of his disappointment that Mr. de Valera had to postpone his visit to Canada adding that Mr. de Valera had many warm friends in the Dominion. But he did not refer to the war. While we were at dinner, the news came of the Buergerbrau bomb explosion at Munich.[1] Mr. King related the news to his guests. (Captain Balfour, British Under-Secretary of State for Air, almost cheered). That was Mr. King's only reference to the war during the evening. He made none to our neutrality policy in conversation with us. He does not invite references to the subject. Any conversations I had with him upon it were initiated by me. When I paid him an official call on September the 24th he spent most of the time explaining his own position along the same lines as his public speeches. I told him that no Irish Government would have taken any course other than that taken by the present Government and that the Parliament and people were solid behind the Government's decision. I also said that Mr. de Valera and Mr. Chamberlain had been very closely in touch during the past two years. I referred to the Taoiseach's telegram to Mr. Chamberlain during the Munich crisis last year; and referred to the similarity between its terms and those of his own (then recent) telegram to Herr Hitler. Mr. King beamed all over. I said that I was sure that Mr. de Valera's present attitude which was a continuation of his peace policy was well understood in London. Mr. King's only comment was: 'I hope so'. He then continued to explain his own attitude. He went so far as to say that his war policy was a continuation of the fight for liberty traditional in his own family since the Mackenzie 'Rebellion'. On a subsequent occasion I explained to him the connection between the bombing incidents in England for some months prior to the war and Mr. de Valera's neutrality policy as stated about the same time. He seemed enormously interested. It apparently had not occurred to him that any group of Irishmen, however small, would want to be against Great Britain in the war and would consequently regard neutrality as a departure from the 'England's difficulty' doctrine.

Dr. Manion is the only man of standing in the Canadian Parliament who has so far very definitely defended our attitude. He is a wholehearted supporter of the war policy of Mr. King's Government. He came to see me (returning my official call) on the 26th October. He remained longer with me than any other caller except

---

[1] On 8 November 1939 an attempt was made to assassinate Hitler at the Beurgerbrau during celebrations to mark the 1923 'Munich Putsch'. A bomb left by Johann Elser near the podium at which Hitler addressed his audience exploded eight minutes after Hitler had departed. The explosion killed eight people and wounded sixty-five.

the Apostolic Delegate. On that occasion he said that he fully understood the position Ireland had taken up. No one, he said, who remembers 'the savage treatment of Ireland by Britain' can fairly criticise our neutrality policy. I thought it right to say at that stage that our policy was not directed against Great Britain. I repeated, as I have done to many others, the Taoiseach's statement that he would not permit Ireland to be used as a basis of attack on Great Britain.

I am submitting the foregoing observations as they are with a view to drawing the distinction which exists between the official Canadian attitude to us as Irish representatives and personally on the one hand and to the policy of neutrality on the other. The attitude to us is of the warmest, the attitude to present national policy is of the most reserved. (I informed Mr. Skelton in the sense of your cable of the 31st October[1] and we will have a further general talk when I receive your note on the general neutrality situation.) If it is possible to get over to the Canadian people a clear impression that our policy is not directed against Great Britain that will clear the air. The one thing we cannot be here is anti-British, especially at the present time. I think it right, therefore, whenever I can, privately, to emphasise that our neutrality policy is not evidence of hostility to Great Britain. Neither does it (I have said) represent a purely negative frame of mind on the war itself. It is a positive and active peace policy steadily pursued in a most difficult set of circumstances regardless of the war slogans of one side or another: I have not of course used phrases like 'the war slogans of one side or the other'. Last evening I addressed the Queen's University (Kingston) Alumni Association. That was my first address in the presence of the press. I took the line of the Taoiseach's speeches on certain parts of the Constitution: the Christian Commonwealth line. I did not (and shall not in public, except on your instructions) deal with any controversial matter. But I have received invitations to address all kinds of bodies, some very important. I declined to address the Catholic Youth of Canada at their rally here two Sundays ago. I told the organizers that an address by me at the moment might do more harm than good to interests we all had at heart. They understood. I am invited again and again to broadcast (coast to coast) by the Canadian Broadcasting Corporation. The Director, Mr. Gladstone Murray, is a Scotsman who is very friendly to us. He asked me once more today. I put him off for a few weeks. I have been invited also by the Canadian Club, which is (Dr. Skelton tells me) the body the Taoiseach would have addressed (Parliament not in session) had he come here in October. It is the best platform in Canada. I have put them off until next year. I have done the same to the Rotary Club. But I have already accepted the invitation of the Irish Historical Society to be their chief speaker on the 16th March and to speak also at their banquet on St. Patrick's Day. On Saturday next I am to address the Canadian Catholic Women's Association (at the Chateau Laurier) which is one of the biggest Catholic organisations in the world. I could not get out of it especially as the Archbishop of Ottawa is to preside and the new Catholic Chaplain General of the Canadian Overseas Armies, Monsignor Neligan, Bishop of Pembroke, is to attend. They wish me to speak on 'Citizenship' as one of the activities of this huge organization is devoted to the study of the relations between the citizen and the State. I am taking again the Christian Commonwealth line following texts already approved by you during the past few years.

---

[1] See No. 64.

I would submit that talks of that kind might form a basis for a cultural foreign policy for Canada. I do not think (subject to your views) that we can get very far here along the line of strong and reiterated public or private references to our neutrality in the war. It would be taken as a criticism of Canada's participation. It would be resented by the Government and the people generally – although many of the latter would defend it – and it would make the Department of External Affairs nervous of our public appearance. It would, in addition, result in our exclusion from social contacts with people with whom – whatever their politics – we should be upon good and even intimate personal relations. The proper course, it seems to me, would be to emphasise the cultural aspects of our history and our hopes for the future. We should in other words emphasise the premises from which a neutral policy follows as a natural conclusion. It is for that reason that I request in my minute of the 8th instant[1] an amplification of the expressions 'natural sentiment' and 'national interest' in your cable of the 31st October.[2]

If a course along the lines just stated should commend itself to you the most workmanlike method of carrying it out would, I think, be to have the actual text of a number of talks prepared in Dublin and transmitted to me to be delivered on occasions (not too frequent) which you might perhaps allow me to choose. If there is not the time in the Department in present circumstances to prepare actual texts perhaps short sketches of talks might be sent to me. Or if you preferred to instruct me as to the things I should not say or the subjects I should not refer to that would be another way. Should you take the view that it is not desirable for me to pursue what I have called a cultural foreign policy at all for the present and that it would be better not to speak in public until later on I am sure you will instruct me in that sense. Addresses by official representatives are a usual feature of life in Ottawa which is a meeting place for innumerable Canadian organisations. I do not urge the necessity for my falling into line with that custom at the present difficult time. On the other hand I do not shirk the duty, if you feel it is, now above all, a duty which our representative here should perform. I should like, however, to perform it with credit and something in the nature of outstanding success. And it is because I do not feel that my own knowledge of Irish history is sound enough and that I do not know what line of approach to the development of a cultural foreign policy would most commend itself to you that I am asking you to help me in the way I have indicated.

Dr. Skelton expressed his regret to me today that he was unable to come to my address to the graduates of Queen's. He was good enough to say that he had heard it was a great success.

(Sgd) JOHN J. HEARNE

No. 69 NAI DFA 227/100

Letter from Robert Brennan to Joseph P. Walshe (Dublin)
(N/39)

WASHINGTON, 14 November 1939

In accordance with your instructions contained in cables Nos. 235, 236 and 238,[3] I called to the State Department on Monday, the 13th of November, and interviewed

---
[1] See No. 66.
[2] See No. 64.
[3] None of the above printed.

Mr. Berle,[1] the Assistant Secretary of State, on the matter of shipping and air services to Ireland. The result I have reported in my cable No. 201 of the 13th of November.[2]

Mr. Berle told me, as I had been previously informed, that the zones were fixed because of the charts showing points where ships had been attacked. He added, however, that if Irish ports had been kept open the suspicion that American ships were carrying goods which might be transhipped to England would invite attack by German submarines. I asked him if an undertaking were given by the Irish Government that such transhipment would not take place would it have any effect. I explained that I had no instructions to ask a question of the kind. He replied that he would not say it would not have any effect, but that America was very chary about entering into any arrangements of the kind in Europe. Later, Mr. Stewart of the European Division, said that in that case it might be necessary to get the German Government to give an undertaking not to attack American ships travelling to Ireland which did not carry goods for transhipment.

On the question of the air service to Foynes,[3] I pointed out that there was no case for restricting this service because flying boats were not subject to the same danger as surface craft which could be attacked by submarines. Mr. Berle said there was something to be said for that, but that in any case there would have been no service to Foynes for the winter. Later I saw Mr. Burke, Head of the Division of International Communications, on the same matter. He said there was a good case for opening Foynes and he would do his best in the matter.

I have not seen the charts showing points where ships were attacked. Would it be possible for you to prepare such charts? They might well show that routes from New York to Cobh and more likely Galway are safer than some areas outside the present combat zones.

I enclose a copy of the map prepared by the State Department showing the combat zones, also a copy of the Neutrality Act in which the combat zones are defined, and copy of a Proclamation by the President.

A couple of hours after I returned from the State Department, I had a ring from Mr. Fitzmaurice of the International News Service. He asked if I had seen Mr. Berle at the State Department, and if it was in connection with shipping to Ireland. I told him that I could not give out anything on the subject, and that such information should be obtained from the State Department. He than contacted Mr. McDermott, Chief of the Division of Current Information, and Mr. McDermott told him it was all right. I then told Mr. Fitzmaurice and later Mr. Birding of the Associated Press the object of my visit to the State Department as well as the arguments in favour of restoring the services to Ireland. Clippings enclosed.

[signed] ROBT. BRENNAN

---

[1] Adolf Augustus Berle Jr (1895-1971), Assistant Secretary of State (1938-44), later Ambassador to Brazil (1945-6).
[2] Not printed.
[3] From 1939 to 1945 Foynes, Co Limerick, was a base for transatlantic flying boat services.

No. 70 NAI DFA 219/4

Confidential report from William Warnock to Joseph P. Walshe (Dublin)
(43/33)

BERLIN, 14 November 1939

I beg to report that in the course of a conversation which I had yesterday with Dr. Rüter,[1] he said that the German Foreign Office felt that they had been relieved of a certain amount of worry in that the United States Government had included Ireland in the 'war area'. It seems that Germany was afraid that, if our west coast were declared not to be in the war zone, munitions and other contraband goods would be consigned by United States firms to Great Britain through Ireland.

The German Minister at Dublin has reported home that timber from Baltic countries has been imported into Northern Ireland through Dublin. I believe that he also brought the matter to your attention. The Germans would, of course, like us to prohibit transactions leading to the re-export of contraband. Their control ships have so far let ships bound for Ireland through without delay, but if the re-export of wood continues they will have to be much more strict in future.

I hear that you have suggested a 'clearing' arrangement for payments between the two countries. Dr. Rüter was none too sure that this would be practicable, as our dealings in foreign currency have until now been conducted through London. I said to him, however, that at least two of the Irish banks have always had connections with the Guaranty Trust of New York, and that direct dealings with Holland or Switzerland could be established. The question of transfer would arise in any case, whether or not a 'clearing' was negotiated.

Before the outbreak of war, Dr. Rüter was in charge of the section dealing with trade with members of the British Commonwealth of Nations. At present he is mainly engaged in studying the economic measures taken in these countries, and in considering plans to combat the British blockade. The position with regard to Egypt and Irak is not at all clear. While both countries have broken off diplomatic relations with Germany, neither of them appear to have actually declared war, so that it is not certain whether goods consigned, say, to Alexandria may be regarded as goods consigned to an enemy.

It is hoped to turn most of the trade of the Balkan and Scandinavian countries to Germany. At present it is difficult for them to trade with anyone else.

Germany feels that she can eventually control a large portion of the total European trade. She is ideally situated for this purpose, and is undoubtedly the great industrial and commercial country on the Continent; she considers that she has a right to the leading place.

Ever since the end of the Polish campaign there has been an air of unreality about war from the military point of view, as nothing much is happening in that line, but those responsible for the country's economic adaptation to the new circumstances are working literally night and day. Officials of the Foreign Office state that the effects of the British blockade have been minimised, and that Germany can hold out for an indefinite period in a trade war.

[signed] W. WARNOCK

---

[1] German Foreign Office official in charge of Irish-German trade.

No. 71 NAI DFA 227/100

Telegram from Robert Brennan to Joseph P. Walshe (Dublin)
(No. 203) (Copy)

WASHINGTON, 14 November 1939

Your telegram 201[1] my protest to State Department is front page news in New York and Washington papers. Reporters in the first instance got news from State Department. Associated Press accounts summaries give my representation as follows (1) Ireland is neutral (2) Ireland's trade is hit, particularly the imports of wheat, maize, fertilisers, (3) American ships trading Irish ports have been unmolested. (4) No more danger Irish ports than Norwegian or Mediterranean.

No. 72 NAI DFA 219/2

Confidential report from Leopold H. Kerney to Joseph P. Walshe (Dublin)
(M.19/4)

MADRID, 16 November 1939

Reception by Franco's Wife

Further to my report of 13th November,[2] the reception on 15th November was attended by the wives of the German and Belgian Ambassadors and by those of 7 Ministers. Tea was served at three tables – Sra. de Franco with Germany, Belgium and Holland at one, a Spanish lady (Marquesa de Clenzia) with Ireland, Hungary and Norway at a second, and another Spanish lady with Uruguay, Paraguay and Cuba at the third. There were two empty seats, the wife of the Greek Minister having fallen ill at the last moment, and the American Ambassadress being absent for some unknown reason.

The Italian Ambassadress and the wives of the Egyptian, Turkish, Roumanian and Yugoslavian Ministers are not in Madrid at present. You will notice that only neutral States were represented as well as Germany; the Norwegian Ministress ascertained from the Protocol that there was to be a second similar reception to which the British and French Ambassadresses &c. would be invited.

At Mrs. Kerney's table, the Norwegian spoke her opinions openly, said that she had no longer any sympathy for the Germans and laid much blame on Germany, who she said had turned everyone against her. The Hungarian (wife of a General) said Hungary was very uneasy, but hoped her neutrality would be respected by Germany to whom she supplied much food. The Marquise de Clenzia's sympathies seemed to be similar, but she was more reserved. The Uruguayan was also critical of Germany.

The reception lasted from 5 p.m. till 6.30 p.m.

The Norwegian Ministress, who has lived for many years in Spain and has many friends here, told Mrs. Kerney on the way home (they were in the same car) that she was much disillusioned and 'désabusée' by the present state of affairs here, where, she said, they were copying German methods in their treatment of prisoners and suspects as well as in other ways; she thought the Diplomatic Corps were badly treated and objected to no special arrangements being made for providing

---

[1] Not printed.
[2] Not printed.

them with foodstuffs, coal etc. This lady used to be ardently pro-Franco and her husband did his very best to induce his Government to recognise latter at an early stage.

No. 73 NAI DFA 227/100

> Telegram from Robert Brennan to Joseph P. Walshe (Dublin)
> (No. 205) (Copy)
> WASHINGTON, 16 November 1939

My despatch 197.[1] President yesterday in press conference indicated there would be no change in zone as a result of our protest. He had sympathy with neutral countries but protection of lives and ships of nationals was first consideration. He indicated also transfer to Panama or any American country would be barred because it would be unfair to put sister republics in a different position from United States. Asked if ships could be transferred to Irish registry President smiling said a good offer might be considered. Sanction has been given to transfer of several ships to register of Norway and other countries.

No. 74 NAI DFA 227/100

> Letter from Joseph P. Walshe to John Leydon (Dublin)
> (Copy)
> DUBLIN, 18 November 1939

Dear Leydon,
I have your letter of the 16th November[2] relating to correspondence, etc. about the exclusion of Ireland from the 'combat area'. I quite understand that your Department would not wish to encourage a development which might involve us in contraband difficulties. At the same time, my Minister is so anxious to obtain the fullest possible recognition of the United States for our neutrality that he feels our exclusion from the 'combat area' would be an advantage altogether outweighing the inconveniences of having to take measures to prevent contraband trading by the American ships which would enter our waters. I do not think there is any conflict there. The State Department seem to be fully alive to the dangers of trans-shipment and re-export, and the Assistant Secretary of State mentioned transshipment as one of the considerations weighing with the American Government against the exclusion of Ireland. Even if only one or two American ships a month came here, the principle of recognition would be sufficiently established.

As you know, my Minister wishes to stop contraband trade in any form which could be regarded as a departure from the particular kind of neutrality which circumstances enable us to observe. He would be very worried indeed if any basis were given to public rumour that we were not observing that neutrality. He believes that our ability to face any crisis that may arise during the war depends on maintaining the general goodwill of the people, which has been secured by the manner in which our neutrality has been observed so far. You can therefore

---

[1] Not printed.
[2] Not printed.

understand that small and occasional departures from the present neutrality routine which would give rise to the belief that they were part of a system, would do just as much harm to public opinion as if that conclusion were justified.

I gathered from a chat with Cudahy yesterday evening, and indeed from all we have heard from Brennan, that there is no chance of our being excluded from the 'combat area'.

Yours sincerely,
[stamped] (Signed) J.P. WALSHE

No. 75 NAI DFA 219/4

Confidential report from William Warnock to Joseph P. Walshe (Dublin)
(43/33)

BERLIN, 21 November 1939

The German attempt to divide Great Britain and France by propaganda, or at all events to persuade the German people that France's heart is not in this war, seems to have been given up for the present. I asked an official of the Foreign Office recently if they really believed that the Daladier Government is so weak that anti-English propaganda would influence the French people to any extent, and he replied quite unhesitatingly that he did not. He said that on the contrary, he felt that the French Government is in a very strong position.

Propaganda has now taken a new line. The French Government is represented as having no policy of its own at all, except to follow blindly to where they are led by the British. The visit of the French Minister of Finance[1] to London last week is interpreted as meaning that France is in a serious position financially, and that she is insisting on receiving financial aid from Britain at once. In order to obtain this she has had to surrender her economic freedom, and to join the co-ordinating committee set up by the British to control supplies. The 'Deutsche Allgemeine Zeitung' says that 'doubtless the golden chains with which French economics and finance are tied to the "City" will under the political influence of British financial circles bind France's trading freedom even tighter.' The establishment of the Allied committee is taken as a proof of the telling effect which the German Navy is having on deliveries to England.

It is further reported that the French Air Force is to be placed under British control, and that Mr. Churchill has asked for a more active co-operation from the French Navy in carrying on the blockade against Germany. In other words, Great Britain is asking everything from France, and giving next to nothing in return. German observers have seen no trace of British Soldiers in the front lines on the Western Front; the French 'poilu' is, of course, expected to do all the fighting there.

It is hotly disputed that the 'Simon Bolivar', the big Dutch liner which sank in the North Sea a few days ago, went down as the result of striking a German mine.[2] It is thought to be a poor compliment to the efficiency of the over-rated British

---

[1] Paul Reynaud (1878-1966), French Minister of Finance (1938-40), French Prime Minister (March-June 1940).
[2] The Dutch liner *Simon Bolivar* was en-route from Holland to the West Indies with 397 passengers when it was sunk in the North Sea on 18 November 1939. Later reports agreed that the ship had hit a German mine.

Navy if mines could have been laid comparatively close to the English coast by German mine-layers. Just as in the case of the 'Athenia',[1] Great Britain, without one vestige of proof, is endeavouring to throw the blame on Germany, and to poison neutral opinion.

The Baltic Germans are being settled in the old Polish 'Corridor' and in the Posen district. The Poles planted there since 1920 have been removed to the purely Polish territory, and their houses and farms are being given to the German immigrants. The houses in the towns are said to be in poor condition. Poles never had a high reputation for cleanliness and order, and the war made things worse. About 40,000 have been repatriated from Esthonia, and 70,000 from Latvia. About 20,000 have already been accommodated in Dantzig and West Prussia (the 'Corridor') and it is hoped to settle at least 70,000 in the Posen province. The majority of the elderly people will be settled within the old Reich, mainly in institutions.

The borders of the new Polish state or protectorate, whichever may be the correct title, do not seem to have been definitely determined. The German Ministry of the Interior has appointed a 'Regierungspräsident' (a position not unlike our City Manager) in Lodz, which would indicate that this city is to be incorporated in the Reich, even though it was not inside the German frontiers in 1914. Cracow is at present the residence of the Governor-General, but there are suggestions that it, too, may be incorporated. The Governor-General received a delegation in Zakopane a few days ago from the Gorals (a Tatra mountain-folk), who expressed their loyalty to Germany, and rejoiced that the days of Polish oppression of minorities were now at an end. It is thought that Cracow, Zakopane and the adjacent mountain district may be eventually taken over as German territory.

The inclusion of a restoration in Austria among the stated war-aims of the Allies has caused great anger. It is pointed out that both Britain and France had already accepted the 'Anschluss' in March 1938 and that it is now rather late in the day for them to change their minds. English newspapers of the 13th March 1938 and following days are quoted to show the enthusiasm with which the Anschluss was greeted in Austria. Articles in the 'Observer' written by Mr. Garvin[2] soon after the event are cited to show that leading persons in Britain were satisfied that the union of Germany and Austria was just – and final. Mr. Ward Price, the well-known English journalist, and M. Jules Sauerwein, the equally well-known French journalist, are quoted as eye-witnesses of the spontaneous demonstrations of joy which broke out all over Austria at the time. The very mention of a separate Austria is regarded as an attack on German unity.

It is admitted that there have been disturbances in the Protectorate of Bohemia and Moravia. Nine Czech students have been executed, and the polytechnic institutes have been closed for three years. It is almost impossible in Berlin to get any reliable news about the Protectorate, as permission for entry into or exit from the Protectorate is rarely given. I have had no opportunity to go there myself, but an Irishman who passed through Prague early in September told me that he had seen

---

[1] On 3 September 1939 *Athenia* was sunk off the Rockall Bank by German U-boat U-30 commanded by Leutnant Fritz-Julius Lemp. Germany initially refused to admit that her forces had sunk the liner. Survivors were landed in Galway and Irish military intelligence (G2) learned from them that a German torpedo had sunk *Athenia*.

[2] James Louis Garvin (1868-1947), editor and manager of *The Observer* (1908-42).

cases of Germans being jostled in the streets. While I have no idea at the moment of the extent of the discontent, I feel quite sure that the Germans have the situation well in hand from the military point of view. It is obvious that a revolt would have no chance of success. No doubt the Czech nationalists are well aware of this. The occasional outbursts are intended to keep national feeling alive, and to prevent peaceful penetration by Germany.

There have been few direct references to us in the last few days, save that it is reported that our unemployment figures have gone up appreciably as a result of the war.

[signed] W. WARNOCK

No. 76 NAI DFA 219/2

Report from Leopold H. Kerney to Joseph P. Walshe (Dublin)
(M.10/11)

MADRID, 21 November 1939

Frank RYAN. Your 244/8B

I had a conversation with the Foreign Minister[1] on Monday 20th November and took the opportunity to refer to this matter. The Minister reached for a portfolio containing papers which he said were for discussion with Franco the following day; one of these was a memorandum relating to Ryan – apparently the one whose existence I have already reported; I had only a brief glance at it, but attached to it were numerous press cuttings which I had supplied to Blanca O'Donnell; he produced it to prove that he was not overlooking the matter; he said that he saw Franco every Tuesday and I even gathered that he had raised this question on every such occasion, but so far without success; the moment was not yet perhaps quite ripe, there were about 80,000 judgments pending but there would be measures of clemency and he was going to seize the first such opportunity; Fusset and others could now be relied on; and he remarked, laughingly, that he was organising a 'complot'; there were about 400 foreign prisoners in all; he did not think there would be time to obtain satisfaction ahead of the proposed trade agreement. When I asked him what on earth could account for Franco's hesitation, he revealed to me that there was not in fact unanimity in Ireland on this question, and that Franco had received a great many letters from Ireland saying that Ryan was a dangerous man and begging Franco not to release him; I pointed out, as I had done on other occasions, that Ryan had political enemies, but that, even supposing it to be true that he were a dangerous character, it was scarcely logical that Franco should be expected to hold as prisoner in Spain an Irishman who might be deemed to be dangerous in Ireland; I asked Beigbeder to use the argument that, if there was any gaoling to be done where an Irishman was concerned, the gaoler ought really to be de Valera rather than Franco. I pointed out once more that de Valera (we were talking in a friendly intimate way, omitting titles) was anxious to secure the release of Ryan, as an Irishman with a national record, quite irrespective of the fact that, once back in Ireland, he might conceivably be an opponent of the Government in every way; that possibility did not in the slightest affect the

---

[1] Ramón Serrano Súñer (1901-2003), brother-in-law of Franco, Spanish Foreign Minister (1940-2).

Government's attitude in this matter; I went on to explain to Beigbeder the mistaken policy of the I.R.A. in Ireland, as it would be a preparation for anarchy if violence were tolerated whilst peaceful methods were available. I suggested in fact that Ryan's outlook might very well approximate to that of the I.R.A., so that our concern for his fate was completely disinterested and inspired by higher motives.

Beigbeder gave me the interesting piece of information that it had been found that there was no truth whatever in the accusation which had been framed against Ryan of having commanded firing squads.

It is clear now that the opposition to Ryan's release comes from Ireland and is of that secret underhand nature which I have feared all along; and which can only have received an impetus from the occasional publicity resorted to by Ryan's friends.

Knowing that the Foreign Minister and others near him are anxious to secure her brother's release and that I myself have this case constantly in mind and will lose no opportunity that may present itself, I trust that Miss Ryan will arm herself with whatever further patience may be necessary; I hope to be able to visit Burgos on Sunday 3rd December, to bring Ryan some things which he needs and to let him know that we are hammering away and hope to succeed, sooner or later.

[signed] L.H. KERNEY

No. 77 NAI DFA Washington Embassy Confidential Reports 1938-9

Confidential report from Robert Brennan to Joseph P. Walshe (Dublin)
(108/63/39) (Copy)

WASHINGTON, 22 November 1939

Ever since the Japanese invasion of China began,[1] relations between the United States and Japan have been anything but cordial. The sinking of the U.S. Gunboat PANAY in December 1937 by Japanese aeroplanes[2] had a decidedly bad effect here, and ever since instances of maltreatment of American citizens in China by Japanese soldiers have not tended to improve the atmosphere. Quite recently, Mr. Joseph C. Grew, the United States Ambassador to Japan, gave great offense in Tokyo by denouncing Japan's policy in China, and only this week, Mr. Sumner Welles, Acting Secretary of State, said that the United States was taking serious notice of indignities heaped on U.S. citizens in Tientsin[3] by the Japanese Authorities there.

Early this year, the State Department denounced the Trade Treaty of 1911 with Japan and this expires next January. At the same time, the Senate voiced a demand that an export embargo be placed on Japan. As the bulk of her war munitions come from the United States, it is clear that if such a policy were carried out, not merely would the campaign in China be jeopardized, but the whole economic structure of

---

[1] In 1937, during the Second Sino-Japanese War, Japan launched a full-scale invasion of China, occupying Shanghai, Nanjing and Southern Shanxi.
[2] On 12 December 1937 Japanese aircraft sank the United States gunboat *Panay* on the Yangtze River outside Nanjing, killing three sailors. Japan claimed the attack was a mistake, apologised and paid compensation. However the attack caused United States public opinion to turn against Japan.
[3] Tientsin or Tianjin is the third largest urban area in China. In July 1937 it fell to Japan during the Second Sino-Japanese War.

Japan might be endangered unless Japan chose to establish closer relations with Russia. Wall Street would not like the embargo, of course, since quite apart from the heavy American investments in China, the trade between the United States and Japan amounts to nearly five hundred million dollars annually. The State Department does not relish the prospect of Japan and Russia getting closer together and, consequently, they do not want the question of the embargo to be revived. There are intimations this week that the pressure indicated by the statements of Ambassador Grew and Mr. Welles is the forerunner to a bid for a new commercial treaty with Japan which would not only safeguard the present trade but would also involve the protection of United States interests in China. Mr. Fred Essary, the well informed Washington correspondent of the BALTIMORE SUN deals with the matter in the cutting enclosed.[1]

Some observers here are inclined to think that one of the big considerations behind this move is to lessen any tension there may be in the Pacific so as to give the United States a freer hand in the event of intervention in Europe.

[stamped] ROBT. BRENNAN

No. 78 NAI DFA 219/49

Letter from Joseph P. Walshe to John J. Hearne (Ottawa)
(Secret) (Copy)

DUBLIN, 29 November 1939

Your reports have been read with great interest.[2] The last received here is dated the 28th October.[3] Unfortunately our means of communicating with you at length is still very slow. The American lines, as you know, are now ceasing to call at Irish ports, and you must expect despatches to take some weeks to get to and from Ottawa.

Since your earlier reports the situation in the Canadian Press seems to have improved. J.B. McGeachy's articles from Dublin in the 'Winnipeg Free Press' must have helped to inform public opinion of the real situation here. While making the usual mistakes made by foreign correspondents, he succeeds in giving quite a good picture. The general feeling amongst our people is anti-Hitler because of his persecution of Christians and Jews. At the same time, the struggle is regarded as essentially one between two imperialisms for which Hitler's antics provide the immediate occasion. Britain's propaganda about small nations is received with scepticism and, as you know, always will be in this country until her new leaf has been turned over a little more completely. The tact of Herr Hempel, the German Minister, has deprived our neutrality of a lot of the problems which would otherwise have made it very difficult to observe. There has been no attempt by submarines against the normal commerce between these two islands, and that is a matter for satisfaction to the British as well as to ourselves. No doubt the British Government regret our neutrality for sentimental reasons, but we believe that they are slowly becoming as convinced as we are that Ireland's neutrality is an advantage for them. It has produced a feeling of contentment in this country, because it

---

[1] Not printed.
[2] See Nos 66 and 68.
[3] Not printed.

is a very clear proof to all shades of Nationalist opinion that our independence is genuine. That contentment has reacted on our people in America, and no doubt has been at least a small factor in bringing about the repeal of the arms embargo. From the point of view of the State, the Taoiseach regards neutrality as a very precious consolidation of the present Nationalist position. In his view, the loss of our neutrality through our fault would bring chaos at home, trouble with the British, and incidentally would have its corresponding reactions in the United States. There is no voice whatever raised in this country in favour of going into the war. Those who occasionally speak behind the scenes in favour of such a course are not regarded as friends of this country or friends of continued good relations between this country and Great Britain.

Two and half months' experience has made it clear that neutrality, contrary to the view of a lot of our sceptics, can be maintained in practice. The arrival of a German submarine at a remote Kerry village with a captured crew on board did not astonish public opinion here.[1] Failing to find a neutral vessel on board which the captured crew might be placed, the submarine commander was obliged to make for the nearest neutral coast. He ran 36 hours on the surface before reaching Kerry, and he entered and left the little bay on the surface. There has been no question of the British occupying the Treaty ports. Any proposal to do so would at once be rejected by the Government, and any attempt to take them by force would be resisted. There is no shadow of division of opinion on this matter. The recent stand of the Finns against a similar demand by Russia has strengthened the resolution of our people never to yield on this vital question of sovereignty. The British and some of our Canadian friends may argue the submarine menace could be more easily crushed by the British if they could operate from Bantry and Cobh, but they could equally argue that Germany's military forces could be more easily crushed if the British were in occupation of Antwerp and Rotterdam. Abstention from acts of this kind is the price that Great Britain has to pay for the establishment of a regime of right and justice in the world. In the face of what she is preaching with regard to other small nations we do not believe that she will make any attempt to violate our sovereignty.

With regard to the question of unity, it cannot be said that any progress has been made in recent months. The Taoiseach has been overwhelmed with work immediately connected with the war situation. He has not been able to devote very much time to the unity issue. There is a feeling in the country, though not universally shared, that it is essential to continue the agitation during the war. There is no doubt in the mind of anyone that we should not allow the issue to be forgotten. A certain propaganda is being maintained, and the restoration of the unity of Ireland should constantly be in the minds of our representatives abroad as one of the aims for which they should endeavour to obtain the goodwill of the Government and people of the country to which they are accredited. If Britain would really put into practice in relation to Ireland her fine sentiments about freedom and justice the sentimental response amongst all Irishmen would be enormous, but she is still in the hands of a hopelessly narrow-minded and incompetent Civil Service in so far as her relations with the Dominions are concerned – and the hope that Mr. Eden can break through the darkness is not very good.

---

[1] See footnote 1, p. 84.

The Government found it necessary to take a strong stand against the practice of the hunger-strike amongst political prisoners. The majority of these latter gave up the struggle at a relatively early stage, but a few persisted until their lives were in real danger. The Government then decided to release them so that they would take food. It is believed that hunger-striking in our prisons is now at an end.

The policy of the revival of the language is to be pursued with ever-increasing vigour. The Taoiseach and the Government generally realise that the lot of small nations is going to be ever more difficult. If the present war is followed by a close European federation, our national distinctiveness will depend on the language more than on any other factor for its continued assertion. The Taoiseach is therefore very anxious indeed that all our representatives abroad and their Irish-born staffs should regard a knowledge of the language and pride in it as essential fundamentals for the pioneering work in which they are engaged.

The Taoiseach is beginning to wonder when a Canadian High Commissioner will be appointed to Dublin.[1] From every point of view, the sooner the appointment is made the better. Sir John Maffey is getting on very well here. His presence has made what might have been a difficult situation between the two countries a relatively easy one, and all our difficulties in regard to neutrality and trade are being smoothed out. His Naval Attaché, Captain Greig,[2] has been most useful in putting an end to all the stupid rumours about the adventures of submarines in Irish bays and harbours. For a time every public-house around the coast had its pet submarine captain attached to it by the local imagination, but investigation has shown that there was not one single case in which the story could be verified. The same is true of the supply of petrol to submarines about which local imagination was equally fertile.

[stamped] (Signed) J.P. WALSHE

No. 79 NAI DFA 241/113

Report from William Warnock to Joseph P. Walshe (Dublin)
(25/39)

BERLIN, 30 November 1939

I beg to refer to your telegram No. 82 of the 3rd November[3] regarding passenger traffic between Ireland and Great Britain, and to state that I brought our Government's view to the attention of the Foreign Office at once.

I was assured that the German Government is very friendly disposed towards us, and would give full consideration to our interests. The warning against the use of British and French passenger boats had been addressed to all neutral countries, and therefore must be regarded in general terms. In time of war, however, conditions are liable to change rapidly, and at this early stage the German Government is anxious not to appear to bind itself to any attitude which might in altered circumstances work out unpleasantly or disadvantageously.

---

[1] On 31 December 1941 Canadian Prime Minister Mackenzie King appointed John Hall Kelly (1879-1942) as Canadian High Commissioner to Dublin. Mr Kelly died in 1942 and was replaced by John D. Kearney.
[2] Captain Alexander B. Greig took up his post in Dublin in November 1939.
[3] Not printed.

I pointed out that leaving the question of the right to sink enemy vessels out of consideration altogether, it would raise great indignation in Ireland if any of the regular passenger ships were sunk as a result of German action, and that German prestige in Ireland would suffer irreparably; in short, that it would be very much against their own interests.

I had a long conversation concerning this and kindred matters yesterday afternoon with Dr. Lohmann of the Legal Section, who is the official dealing with the legal questions (including contraband) arising out of the war. He insisted once more on Germany's good will towards us, and said that the delay in letting us have a reply was due to drafting difficulties. They are obviously reluctant to give anything which might be construed as a written guarantee concerning their future conduct of the war. I reminded him that we have now been waiting for four weeks.

I understand that pressing reminders have also been received in the Foreign Office from the German Minister in Dublin.

[signed] W. WARNOCK

No. 80 NAI DFA Washington Embassy Confidential Reports 1938-9

Confidential report from Robert Brennan to Joseph P. Walshe (Dublin)
(108/68/39) (Copy)

WASHINGTON, 1 December 1939

Today I called on the Minister for Finland[1] to express my sympathy with him in his country's plight.[2] He said he appreciated my action very much, that Ireland's long struggle for freedom had been an inspiration to his people.

He told me that he foresaw this event, that is the attack by Russia on Finland, as far back as the time when the British first opened negotiations with Russia. That act, he said, brought Russia back into Europe.

No. 81 NAI DFA 219/4

Confidential report from William Warnock to Joseph P. Walshe (Dublin)
(43/33)

BERLIN, 2 December 1939

The news of the Russian advance into Finnish territory was not revealed to the German public until quite late on the 30th November, and even then it was reported as if the matter was not serious, and as if there were still a good chance of a peaceful settlement. The news bulletins gave full reports of Molotov's[3] broadcast speech after the breaking off of diplomatic relations, and emphasised the passages in which he hinted that the Western Democracies had been endeavouring to stiffen the Finnish attitude. The offer by President Roosevelt of mediation by the United States was not reported at all until this morning, and then only in an obscure place

---

[1] Hjalmar Johan Procopé (1889-1954), Finnish Minister to Washington (1939-45), Foreign Minister (1924-6, 1927-31).
[2] On 30 November 1939 Russian forces invaded Finland through Karelia, beginning the 'Winter War' which lasted to March 1940.
[3] Vyacheslav Mickhaylovich Molotov (1890-1986), Russian Foreign Minister (1939-49).

in the newspapers. Military operations were scarcely mentioned, except that Russian aeroplanes had flown over Helsinki and Viborg, and had dropped 'some bombs on military objects'.

Several people to whom I have spoken, and who know the real state of affairs, have expressed their disgust at the Russian action. Relations between Germany and Finland have hitherto been exceptionally friendly, particularly before the conclusion of the Russo-German Pact. The Olympic Games were to have been held in Helsinki next year, and thousands of Germans hoped to go there for a week or so during the Games.

The official attitude will doubtless be that Finland lies within the Russian sphere of influence, that Russia cannot endure provocation on this important stretch of frontier, that Britain and France have been looking for another Poland, and that in any case the dispute concerns no one but Russia and Finland. The public will possibly sympathise with their old friends, but at the moment I do not think that the Government will be much affected by this – unless the Russians attempt to spread out further than Finland, into either Norway or Sweden; in that case even the most plausibly-tongued expert of the Propaganda Ministry will be hard put to it if he wishes to explain that the Russians are Germany's friends, and that they will not do anything at all which might harm Germany's interests.

I have often referred to the people's pride in the Navy. The Navy's popularity has been still further enhanced this week by the report that Lieutenant-Commander (Kapitanleutnant) Prien, whose submarine entered Scapa Flow and torpedoed the 'Royal Oak' at her anchorage, claims to have sunk a cruiser of the 'London' class. The British deny the claim. Mr. Winston Churchill, however, has been found wrong so many times that nobody here gives the slightest credence to communiqués issued by the British Admirality. About once a week Mr. Churchill announces that the German submarine danger has now been overcome, and on the next day the U-boats come into the news again. Lieutenant-Commander Prien, who certainly seems to be a gallant and capable officer, has become a national hero.

The press reports that we are going to establish a small fleet of motor-torpedo-boats and armed cutters to defend our coasts. It is pointed out that the great activity at sea of the belligerents has compelled us to this step. The wireless adds a report that the boats will be assisted by aeroplanes in their watch. Our preparations are taken to mean that we doubt the ability of the British to keep even the seas around their own coast clear.

The newspapers this morning carry reports that German women and children have been interned under inhuman conditions in the British Colony of Southern Rhodesia, whose Governor, Sir Herbert Stanley,[1] is said to be a Jew. As a reprisal for this, British women in Berlin, who were until now allowed to remain at liberty, have been arrested. Some at least were released again soon after detention, though I know that others are still in custody.

Newspaper cuttings referring to Ireland are enclosed.

[signed] W. WARNOCK

---

[1] Sir Herbert Stanley (1872-1955), Governor of Rhodesia (1935-40).

No. 82 NAI DFA 226/46

> Handwritten minute from Joseph P. Walshe to Michael Rynne
> DUBLIN, 4 December 1939

I phoned Mr. Cremins at 11.30. He informed me that the Secretariat were discussing the procedure relating to the calling of the Assembly. Would they have a new session of the 19th Assembly; would they call the 20th Assembly 1939; or would they call an extraordinary Assembly outside the normal series? Mr. Cremins will phone when a decision has been taken. No doubt the British and French Governments are being sounded as to the advisability of having an Assembly at all. They are principally involved. If there is an assembly the T.[aoiseach] will go.

J.P.W.

No. 83 NAI DFA 219/4

> Confidential report from William Warnock to Joseph P. Walshe (Dublin)
> (43/33)
> BERLIN, 6 December 1939

Neutral observers here are awaiting with great interest the action, if any, which Germany proposes to take should other powers give material assistance to Finland in her struggle against the Russian invaders. I think that we may take it for granted that Germany will not idly stand by if either Great Britain or France send large numbers of aeroplanes, or big supplies of munition to Finland; Germany fears that the Allies might utilise the Finnish situation to advance their influence in Scandinavia, and to foment intrigues against her.

The tone of recent press articles shows that Sweden and Norway are being watched very closely. It is obvious, of course, that any Allied help to Finland must pass through these countries. Both of them are having an anxious time, torn as they are between wishes to preserve their absolute neutrality on the one hand, and on the other to protect themselves from being engulfed by Russia. Germany will not tolerate their co-operating with the Allies. Even though Russian policy is always, to say the least of it, something of a mystery and full of surprises, it seems fairly certain that, if they are successful in Finland, the Russians will be sorely tempted to 'free the workers' of Norway and Sweden, too. I think myself, however, that at this point Germany would be forced to intervene. She imports large quantities of Swedish ore – the Swedish mines are, in fact, her surest source of supply – and could not view with equanimity the passing of such a convenient store of this precious raw material into Russian hands, or under Russian control. They do not wish to see them under British control, either. In view of the Russo-German treaty the Russians might halt at the Finnish frontiers of their own accord. It is hardly likely that they would wish to test the new German friendship to breaking point just yet, even though they know that the Germans are prepared to acquiesce in many things rather than run the risk of a war on two fronts.

Strange as it may seem, the Allies will also suffer if Germany does not fairly soon call a halt to Russian expansion around the Baltic. If Russia's aggression is not checked, they will be forced to declare war on her.

In spite of the official attitude, private opinion here is strongly in sympathy with Finland, and some people with whom I come in contact resent strongly – outwardly, at all events – any suggestion that Germany must share some of the responsibility for present happenings.

Long reports appear concerning the organisation of an army under the French General Weygand[1] in Syria. It is stated that the British and French are aiming a stroke at the Russian oilfields in Baku, one of the richest oil-bearing districts in the Soviet Union. This is given as a further proof that the Allies are endeavouring to spread the war out as much as possible, and to involve more and more nations, knowing that they cannot hope to defeat Germany as matters stand at present.

A diplomat recently transferred here from Brussels tells me that in the Low Countries there is still great anxiety. The defences on both sides of the present Western Front are so perfect that it is almost natural to expect that one of the opposing parties will attempt to cut through either Belgium or Holland.

Recent speeches by Dr. Funk,[2] the Minister for Economics, in which he exhorted his hearers to save money, are regarded in some quarters as intended to correct the present tendency to buy up all kinds of articles. Memories of inflation are still fresh in everyone's mind. Now a new committee headed by Field-Marshal Goering,[3] has been established to guide war economy. Final decisions will rest with the Field-Marshal himself.

Field-Marshal Goering is extremely popular with the people. It is becoming hard to keep trace of his many activities, each of which, Germans assure me, he takes very seriously. He is, to name some of his offices: Minister for Air, Commander-in-Chief of the Air Force; Prime Minister of Prussia; President of the Reichstag; Special Commissioner for the Four Year's Plan; Chairman of the Council for the Defence of the State; Chief Forester; and Chief of Hunting and Game-Keeping, together with his new position as supreme director of war economy.

The general public is slowly beginning to realise that the war is likely to last a long time. The present bitter weather (the temperature has not been above freezing point, even at mid-day, in Berlin for the past ten days, and we have had cold spells intermittently since November) has made people think. Fuel is scarce, and even where it is still available, the quality is poor, and then comes a further difficulty, namely, that of transport; the number of lorries or other conveyances available is very limited, and labour is scarce owing to the large number of men mobilised for service with the armed forces. The question of clothes is not yet serious, but everybody is wondering what it will be like next winter.

[signed] W. Warnock

---

[1] General Maxime Weygand (1867-1965), Marshal Foch's Chief of Staff (1918-40), appointed Supreme Allied commander in May 1940.
[2] Walther Funk (1890-1960), German Minister for Economics (1937-45), President of the Reichsbank (1939-45).
[3] Reichsmarshall Hermann Goering (1893-1946), Commander in Chief of the Lufftwaffe (1939-45) and Hitler's chosen successor from 1939 to 1945. Goering was sentenced to death at the Nuremburg Trials but committed suicide by swallowing a cyanide pill before the sentence could be carried out.

No. 84 NAI DFA 207/150

Letter from Joseph P. Walshe to Maurice Moynihan (Dublin)
(207/150) (Copy)

DUBLIN, 7 December 1939

With reference to your minute (S.11393) of the 17th November,[1] relative to the development of this country's foreign trade in the circumstances of the present war, I am directed by the Minister for External Affairs to say that the proposals made in the memorandum attached to your minute seem to turn mainly on questions of supply, shipping and foreign exchange, which are outside the immediate province of this Department.

The aspect of the proposals which is of direct concern to this Department is the question of the effect which the proposed development of our trade would have on our relations with the present belligerents, particularly Germany. An increase in the volume of our normal trade with Britain is less likely to lead to difficulty with Germany than a change in its character. It is virtually certain that the German Government would take strong exception to any development here such as the production for export of munitions or similar war supplies which were not previously manufactured in this country or the re-consignment to Britain of foreign goods imported ostensibly for use in this country. The German Government would not have the same grounds for objecting to an increase in the volume of our cattle, pig, poultry and other normal exports, and, in view of what is known of their attitude, it is considered unlikely that a mere increase in the volume of our normal exports would cause them to alter their present policy towards our trade with Britain.

[stamped] (Signed) J.P. WALSHE
Rúnaí

No. 85 NAI DFA 226/46

Telegram from Eamon de Valera to Carl J. Hambro (Geneva)
(Copy)

DUBLIN, 8 December 1939

Telegram received. Regret impossible for me to go to Geneva. You know how I sympathise with Finland but cannot see how League can act effectively in the matter.

No. 86 NAI DFA 226/46

Memorandum by the Department of External Affairs on the 20th Assembly of the League of Nations
(Copy)

DUBLIN, 8 December 1939

Draft Notice for the Press

Ireland will be represented at the 20th Assembly of the League, which opens on Monday, 11th December, by Mr. Frank Cremins, Permanent Delegate to the League of Nations.

---

[1] Not printed.

Points which might be communicated to the Press:
No important action can result from the meeting of the Assembly.

Finland herself wants an immediate favourable settlement with Russia. She does not want to antagonise Russia to the point of making her own position irreparable. She is unlikely to ask the League for anything more than a general expression of sympathy. She may ask the League to persuade Russia to adopt a conciliatory attitude towards her.

The Scandinavian States do not want to antagonise Russia. They also are anxious for immediate negotiations. The Baltic States will probably absent themselves from the Assembly. The Balkan States will not do anything to increase the menace of Russia in their regard. Only the South American States are likely to talk about the 'big stick', but they are not sufficiently strong to secure effective action.

It is unlikely that any Minister for Foreign Affairs will be present. In fact, so far no Cabinet Minister has been spoken of in relation to the delegations, except one from Ecuador who happens to be on a holiday in Europe at the present moment.

Britain and France, though they may condemn Russia at the Assembly, have not given up all hope of separating her from Germany, and are therefore unlikely to press for action of any kind. There is just a remote possibility that the Western Powers may lose all hope of separating Russia from Germany and may endeavour to rope in the small nations into a sanctions resolution against Russia for the purpose of involving them eventually in the war with both Germany and Russia which would be likely to follow such a threat. But this is mere speculation, and the eventuality is most unlikely.

No. 87 NAI DFA Washington Embassy Confidential Reports 1938-9

Extracts from a confidential report from Robert Brennan to
Joseph P. Walshe (Dublin)
(108/69/39) (Copy)

WASHINGTON, 12 December 1939

My visit to Boston was very successful and I made a great many contacts which will, I hope, be useful as time goes on. I was the guest of the Clover Club of Boston, an organization which is confined to a few hundred members, consisting mainly of Irish and Catholic business and professional men. The Society has been fifty years in existence, and one of its earliest members was John Boyle O'Reilly.[1]
[matter omitted]

After the breakfast I went to the Consulate and had a look around. Everything seemed to be in good shape.

It had been arranged that I should see Mr. John T. Hughes[2] at this stage, but we were already behind in our time schedule and I had only time to shake hands with him, but arranged I should have a talk with him later in the day which I did. Mr. Hughes wanted to explain that he did not wish to embarrass the Government by

---

[1] John Boyle O'Reilly (1844-90), poet and novelist; transported to Australia in 1868 for involvement with the Irish Republican Brotherhood but escaped to America in February 1869.

[2] John T. Hughes (1871-1945), Boston lawyer; a strong supporter of Irish republicanism and a founder member of the American Association for the Recognition of the Irish Republic.

his recent cable about the prisoners, but that he felt that if a tragedy had occurred it would have had disastrous effects on Irish opinion here. We had a long talk about Irish affairs generally. He seemed to be hurt because he had not seen some recent Irish visitors to Boston including Mr. Seán Moylan.[1] He explained that the reason why he had not been more active in the matter of the de Valera Reception Committee was, firstly, because his health was not good and, secondly, because he thought there was no necessity for him to take a prominent part because he was satisfied that the Reception would have been the biggest thing ever held in Boston.

From the Consulate we proceeded to the Mayor's office where I was cordially received by His Honor and shown over the City Hall. Thence we proceeded to the residence of Cardinal O'Connell.[2] His Eminence, who on the previous day had celebrated his 80th birthday, was very affable, and the interview instead of lasting the customary fifteen or twenty minutes, took the greater part of an hour, a circumstance which was commented on favourably by the members of the Reception Committee. The Cardinal expressed his great satisfaction that Ireland was neutral. He said that Ireland was very fortunate at the present time in having a Government with such patriotic, broadminded, unselfish and cultured gentlemen. This he attributed to the fact that the standards had not been corrupted in Ireland. The picture in America was otherwise. Here the pro-British element were trying to involve America in war and quite apart from that they were setting up false standards. He had just been reading a book on J. Pierpont Morgan[3] in which this gentleman was lauded to the skies. In the Cardinal's opinion, Morgan and his like were merely heirs to the robber Barons; they were lauded because they managed to rob the people to the extent of many millions while unfortunate Irishmen, for whom of course there was no excuse except the bad example set, were jailed for doing something similar on a much smaller scale. When I mentioned the fact that the Catholic Church was now recognized almost universally in America as a great stabilizing influence, he said he resented the patronizing attitude which produced this thought and he had no desire to see the Church regarded as a sort of moral policeman for the robber Barons. To the gentlemen present he said, its about time we, the Irish, raised our heads in this country and let one and all know that the standards we hope to achieve are ingrained in us because of our faith and tenacity, and that we are in the forefront of the best elements in America today. It is time that an end was put to the claim of any mental or moral superiority on the part of the Anglo-Saxons. The Cardinal asked me many questions about Ireland which I was able to answer, and altogether the general atmosphere of the audience was very pleasing and warm-hearted. His Eminence, at the close, presented me with a replica of the medal given to him on the occasion of his Golden Jubilee. During the audience he was accompanied by his Secretary, Monsignor Minehan.

Subsequently we visited Harvard University where President Conant[4] received us and expressed his disappointment that Mr. de Valera had been unable to carry out his visit. Under the guidance of Dr. Jerome Green and Dr. Corcoran Thom we

---

[1] Seán Moylan (1888-1957), Fianna Fáil TD for North Cork (1932-57), Minister for Lands (1943-8) and Minister for Education (1951-4).
[2] Cardinal William Henry O'Connell (1859-1944), Archbishop of Boston (1907-44).
[3] John Pierpont Morgan (1837-1913), American financier, banker and philanthropist.
[4] Dr James Bryant Conant (1892-1978), President of Harvard University (1933-53).

made a tour of the College premises. One of the Professors in the Anthropologic Section, whose name I cannot find at the moment, recalled his very pleasant experiences in Ireland while a member of the Anthropological Expedition[1] and he expressed deep appreciation for the financial help given by the Irish Government and for the assistance generally given by all and sundry connected with the work.

Afterwards we proceeded to the State House where in the absence of Governor Saltonstall,[2] who was in Washington for the Gridiron Dinner, we were received by the Acting Governor, Mr. Cahill[3] and Mr. David J. Lynch of the Governor's Staff.

At luncheon, Mr. Sheehan had arranged that I should meet several of those who had been active in the Irish movement from 1916 onward.
[matter omitted]

In the afternoon we visited Boston College where we were received by Father Keyes, S.J., and Father Murphy, S.J., the latter being the Gaelic Professor in the College.

In the evening I was the guest of honour at the Clover Club Dinner and the speakers all paid high tribute to Ireland and to myself. I sat between the President of the Club and the Mayor. The latter told me of his pleasant experiences on his recent visit to Ireland and said he had made a promise to his wife that they would visit Ireland every year. He did not know how he was going to manage it now while the war was on, but he would probably fly to Lisbon. My speech was very well received. It was on the lines of recent speeches dealing mainly with the progress of events in Ireland under a National Government.

On Sunday morning, accompanied by several members of the Clover Club Committee and by Mr. O'Riordan and Mr. Sheehan, we attended High Mass in the Cathedral. Owing to a mistake in the arrangements the Cardinal was elsewhere.
[matter omitted]

No. 88 NAI DFA Legal Adviser's Papers

Memorandum from Michael Rynne to Joseph P. Walshe (Dublin)
(Copy)

DUBLIN, 12 December 1939

Neutrality and recruitment for belligerent armies

1. Before proceeding to examine the above-indicated question, the following distinction must be made between:
   (1) The right of a neutral State to prevent belligerents from setting up recruiting offices in its territory, and

---

[1] A reference to the field study undertaken in the west of Ireland in 1932 by Harvard archaeologists and anthropologists under the direction of Professor Earnest Hooten. The project received funding from the Rockefeller Foundation and from the Irish Government. Best known of the team were anthropologists Conrad M. Arensberg (1910-97) and Solon T. Kimball (1909-82) for their book *Family and Community in Ireland* (Harvard, 1940) and for Arensberg's *The Irish Countryman: an Anthropological Study* (London, 1937). Professor William Lloyd Warner was directly responsible for Arensberg's and Kimball's research and, through contacts with de Valera, for the Taoiseach's endorsement of the project.
[2] Leverett A. Saltonstall (1892-1979), Governor of Massachusetts (1939-45), United States Senator (1945-67).
[3] Horace T. Cahill, Lieutenant Governor of Massachusetts (1939-45).

(2) The duty, if any, of a neutral State to prevent its nationals from taking service in belligerent armies.

2. International law is clear and uncontroverted in regard to the aspect of the matter mentioned first above. Not only has a neutral State the right to prevent by every means in its power the setting up of recruiting offices in its territory by a belligerent Power, but it has actually a duty to do so, vis-à-vis the enemy of such a belligerent. As this aspect does not arise at present, it is unnecessary to argue it here. The law is as stated.

3. With regard, however, to the other aspect of the question, namely, the point whether citizens of a neutral State may be permitted to join belligerent armed forces, the law is not so certain. Many authorities take the strong line (e.g. Fauchille)[1] that in these modern times, when mercenary armies have practically ceased to exist, a neutral State ought never to allow its citizens to enrol for service abroad. On the other hand, there is the moral weight of a Hague Convention behind the opposing view that neutrality is not affected by the enlistment in belligerent forces of a neutral's citizens. Article 6 of Convention (No. V) respecting the Rights and Duties of Neutral Powers and Persons in War on Land, signed at The Hague, 18th October, 1907, is as follows:-

'The responsibility of a neutral Power is not engaged by the fact of persons crossing the frontier separately to offer their services to one of the belligerents'.

4. It is obviously difficult to decide between the two conflicting theories referred to above. The fact that the 1907 Convention was adopted without reservation by practically all the States represented at the Hague Conference is evidence that most of them did not feel in a position to curb the zeal of neutral citizens to participate in warlike operations, provided that those citizens first of all departed from their home countries. But, alternatively, it must be recognised that if modern writers are tending to an opposite view it is because they observe a trend away from the 1907 Convention in the legislative theory and practice of modern States.

5. Realistically viewed, there can be no doubt that the armies of to-day are very unlike those of thirty years ago. In 1907 there were comparatively few conscript armies and still a fair number of small professional ('mercenary') armies. Nowadays, with so many new States adding to the number of separate armies, the proportion of professional armies even in peace-time, has become relatively quite insignificant. When war is declared in this era, whole nations mobilise under systems of virtual compulsion. It may, therefore, be argued that when men leave their neutral home countries (assuming they are not already mobilised there, which, in the vast majority of cases, they are) they are very deliberately associating themselves with a belligerent national cause.

6. There may appear to be an answer to this manner of viewing the question in the curious fact that only two important States (Great Britain and the U.S.A.) have legislated expressly to prevent their nationals joining foreign armies. That argument is fallacious.

The very change in the character of modern wars which makes it necessary for entire male populations, even of neutral countries, to rally to the flag, renders legislation against taking service with foreign nations entirely superfluous. In this

---

[1] Paul Fauchille (1858-1926), authority on international law, author of the four volume *Traité de Droit International Public* (Paris, 1921-6).

connection one may observe that both Great Britain and the United States still profess a certain respect for the old-fashioned idea of 'voluntary service'.

7. Many countries (probably all States with a conscription law) impose stringent penalties on their male citizens who endeavour to travel abroad during wartime without very special permission. Some countries go a step farther and impose further penalties on such citizens when the purpose of their desertion is that of engaging in a foreign army. These penalties usually apply whether the mother-country is at war or merely neutral.

A very usual way to deal with cases of desertion for foreign enlistment is that of depriving the guilty person of his nationality. Examples of such legislation may be found in the Roumanian Nationality Law of 1924, and the Yugoslavian Nationality Law of 1929 and other modern codes and, notably, in the French Civil Code (among older codes) where naturalised Frenchmen are made liable to loss of French nationality for the offence of enlisting abroad.

8. On the whole, however, one many conclude by stating that we, in this country, are not likely to be accused of a definite breach of the neutral status which we have taken up, if we continue to allow our citizens to travel to England or Northern Ireland to enlist there in the British Forces. We have, of course, no municipal law against foreign enlistment, such as the British themselves have (the United States legislation does not count as it appears to be more or less in abeyance) and our nationality law does not provide for deprivation of Irish citizenship, even in the case of naturalised persons who virtually forswear allegiance by taking service out of Ireland.

No. 89 NAI DFA 226/46

Report from Francis T. Cremins to Joseph P. Walshe (Dublin)
(S.7/40)

GENEVA, 12 December 1939

I have to forward the enclosed copies of the communiqués which were issued to the Press by the Secretariat after yesterday's and today's meetings of the Special Committee for the examination of the Finnish appeal.

I do not know in what form journalists picked up accounts of the meetings which were private. I considered it well to say that I supported M. Unden's[1] proposal, as it was altogether a question solely of bringing about conciliation and the cessation of hostilities. M. Unden did not propose any time limit. He said merely that an immediate reply should be asked for, as the Committee would be sitting only a few days. It was in the subsequent brief discussion that a time limit 'tomorrow evening' was inserted, as several members thought that the word immediate was not sufficiently definite. M. Unden said that the Finns also were anxious that such a telegram should be sent.

The telegram was also addressed to the *two* parties, in accordance with the usual procedure. The communiqué issued by the Secretariat omitted to state this – a very unfortunate oversight. This apparently gave the impression that Russia was being singled out exceptionally.

---

[1] Bo Osten Unden (1886-1974), Swedish Minister for Foreign Affairs (1924-6, 1945-62).

The telegram was a normal attempt to bring about a settlement of the dispute under paragraph 3 of Article 15 of the Covenant which begins:- 'The Council/Assembly shall endeavour to effect a settlement of the dispute'.

My statement of this morning was for the purpose of indicating that I was on the moderate side. The South Americans are pressing hard for a definite recommendation from the Assembly to the Council to expel Russia under paragraph 4 of Article 16. The Scandinavians do not support this. They would prefer a milder wording, such as a request from the Assembly, in a separate report, asking the Council to consider the Argentine proposal as that proposal comes within the competence of the council.

Many delegations here seemed to expect that Ireland would as a matter of course be all out for expulsion. As I have not yet received instructions in the matter and in view of our attitude as explained on the telephone, I considered that it was desirable that I should give some indication that we would take full account of the views of the neighbouring States. Also that this indication could best be given in a private meeting.

[signed] F.T. CREMINS

No. 90 NAI DFA 219/5

Confidential report from Colman O'Donovan to Joseph P. Walshe (Dublin)
(MP 39/39) (Confidential)

HOLY SEE, 13 December 1939

Whilst the Communiqué issued after the Grand Council meeting of the 7-8th inst. does not appear to say anything very new or momentous it cannot be regarded as having left positions unaltered. The most significant passages are those referring to the Balkans and to relations with Germany. The former would appear to contain a warning to Russia, and perhaps also to Germany, of direct Italian interest in the Danube-Balkan basin. As regards Italo-German relations the Communiqué says that they remain 'as they were fixed by the Pact of Alliance *and by the exchange of views which took place – before and after – at Milan, Salzburg and Berlin'.*

The passage underlined above obviously contains the whole meat of the message. It is true that the public has been told nothing of what transpired at the meetings in question, but news manages to travel here as elsewhere and the Italian public has by now become expert at reading between the lines of official pronouncements. It will therefore no doubt conclude that relations with Germany have been modified in a way of which they may be informed later if and when the need arises.

What happened at the meetings referred to has been a well-kept secret, though it became known at an early stage that a rift had appeared in the lute. On his return from his last visit Count Ciano[1] was not to be seen for five days. The American and other Ambassadors who wished to see him were told that he was too busy, when everyone knew that he was spending the greater part of his time on the beach at Ostia. The truth appears to be that he required some time for reflexion and

---

[1] Gian Galeazzo Ciano (1903-44), Italian Foreign Minister (1936-43), son-in-law of Benito Mussolini; executed for treason on 11 January 1944.

re-adjustment of ideas after the shock of his last encounter with Herr Hitler.

I was given some days ago what I believe to be a reliable account of what happened on that occasion. According to my informant Herr Hitler gave Count Ciano a hysterical description of the treatment of the German minority by the Poles ('The man actually believes his own Propaganda Department' Ciano is said to have reported to Mussolini) and said that he would stand it no longer. He would wipe out the Poles. Ciano vainly tried to dissuade him from violent action and finally told him that if he was determined to take that course Italy would have to modify her position. Hitler enquired why, and Ciano replied that if Poland was attacked England and France would fight and it was Italy which, to start with at any rate, would have to bear the brunt of their attack. At this point, the account continues, Hitler lost all restraint and screamed at his guest for a quarter of an hour as they walked in the garden of his retreat. He held forth in the most violent language:- 'Du bist ein Esel, und dein Sohn ein Esel!'[1] England would not fight over Poland. Herr Ribbentrop, who was a very intelligent man and who knew England and the English people, was certain of it. And without England France could do nothing. But Ciano was not to be moved.

Unless the war extends to the Balkans it seems certain that Italy will be very slow to depart from her position of non-belligerency. Whilst the papers give great prominence to the protests of neutrals and the damage done to their trade by the Franco-British blockade nothing is said – at least in the papers – about the serious interference with Italian shipping at Gibraltar where their ships have been held up for as much as ten or twelve days and mails and other cargo impounded. It may be that as a result of the recent discussions between Count Ciano and the British Ambassador a way will be found of reducing the delays, but it is not thought that the control will be relaxed. Some days ago the entire mails for all countries on the 'Saturnia'[2] were seized at Gibraltar and retained.

[signed] C.J. O'Donavan

No. 91 NAI DFA 227/23

> *Letter from Frederick H. Boland to Michael MacWhite (Rome)*
> *(227/23) (Copy)*
>
> Dublin, 13 December 1939

With reference to your minute It/487/39 of the 5th October, the Minister has decided, after due consideration, that the establishment of a Slovak Consulate here would not be opportune in present circumstances.[3]

If you can avoid giving the Slovak Minister a definite reply to his enquiry it would be preferable to do so. If the giving of a definite reply is unavoidable, the Slovak Minister[4] may be informed in the sense of the foregoing paragraph. It is preferable not to give the Slovak Minister any reasons for the decision, but if

---

[1] While the wording means little more than 'You are a fool', the telling insult was the use of 'Du' instead of 'Sie' to an adult who was neither a relation nor a friend, the form usually being reserved for children.
[2] *Saturnia* was an Italian liner which entered service in 1927 and sailed the North Atlantic and the South Atlantic until the 1960s.
[3] Not located.
[4] Dr Zvrskovec, Slovak Minister in Rome.

you feel obliged to do so you may tell him that the view was taken that the formal recognition of Slovakia, and the establishment of a Slovak Consulate here would, having regard to the circumstances of the present conflict and the avowed aims of the belligerents, be hardly consistent with this country's attitude of strict neutrality.

I should, perhaps, add, for your information, that the Slovak Minister to Germany[1] approached our Chargé d'Affaires in Berlin about this matter on the 19th September. The Chargé d'Affaires is being sent a copy of Mr. Zvrskovec's letter to you and of this minute.

[stamped] (signed) F.H. BOLAND

No. 92 NAI DFA 219/49

> Code telegram from Joseph P. Walshe to John J. Hearne (Ottawa)
> (No. 26) (Copy)
>
> DUBLIN, 13 December 1939

Your report 14/12.[2] Agree that best line about neutrality say nothing about it and assume needs no apology from you. Its maintenance is vital for us. Is the most important proof the people have had of reality of our status. My letter twenty-ninth November deals with it at length. Agree completely your line cultural and social talks especially Ireland's past and what she is trying in present. Will send you material sometimes but rely on you to make use of local sources. Kenny has very good Irish library. You could keep off politics altogether and talk exclusively history, race, Irish pagan and Christian monuments, revival of language, its literary past, relation with other languages, methods used in revival. Anglo-Irish literature, writers of Irish-Canadian origin etc. Your personal letter received yesterday.[3]

No. 93 NAI DFA 219/4

> Confidential report from William Warnock to Joseph P. Walshe (Dublin)
> (43/33)
>
> BERLIN, 14 December 1939

The public is feeling very pleased at a recent order by the rationing authorities. It has been officially announced that, as a special concession for Christmas, certain spices and cooking ingredients may be purchased without a corresponding number of coupons being cut from one's ration card. Furthermore – and this has given great pleasure – women will be allowed to buy one pair of stockings additional to those (six pairs per annum) to which they are entitled to purchase under the textile control scheme referred to in my minute of the 17th November.[4] I am sure that there is no need for me to explain that the severe rationing of stockings has been accepted with rather bad grace by the ladies. The patriotism of even the

---

[1] Dr Mateas Chernak (1903-55), Slovak Minister in Berlin (1939-45).
[2] See No. 68.
[3] Not located.
[4] Not located.

most enthusiastic women has been severely taxed. Men will be permitted to buy an extra tie for Christmas.

The war has had a peculiar effect on Christmas shopping. Money is being freely spent, for two reasons; firstly there are people who feel that in war-time there is always a danger of inflation, and that there is no point in saving, and then there are others who are buying up all they can outside the rationing schemes in order to provide against a possible scarcity in the future. And in any case more money changes hands during the Christmas season than at any other. This year, however, one is at a loss to know what to buy as Christmas presents for one's friends. Articles made of cloth, handkerchiefs, and the like, or anything for which one requires a certificate, are completely out of the question. I am told that sales of books have already reached record figures. An acquaintance of mine engaged in the editorial section of Berlin's biggest publishing firm, the Scherl Verlag, tells me that in spite of the large number of books sold already, he has orders for nearly as many again, but owing to labour shortage only a limited number of the publications ordered can be supplied before Christmas. The trouble which the average purchaser is up against is that even though there are still ten days to go before the 'Heiliger Abend' (the evening of the 24th December, when the main celebration takes place here in Germany) the best books have been bought up long ago.

The sports and general outfitters, who in the ordinary way would be doing a busy trade in ski-ing clothes, are suffering badly. No distinction is made in the rationing scheme for sports clothing, and even the few people who will be in a position to take winter-sports holidays this season will prefer to make the best of their old outfits.

As regulations stand at present, no business may dismiss any employee on the grounds that trade has decreased. If the position is so bad that the proprietor decides to close down altogether, he will lose his right to trade. Schemes are under consideration in order to help employers by granting loans at low rates of interest, or in certain cases, by a moratorium. The regulations are very satisfactory from the worker's point of view – they were mainly designed for his benefit – and he is thankful for having a Government which looks after him so well. The British unemployment figures, and their increase since the outbreak of war, are alluded to every day in the press. Industry in Germany is busily occupied, but it is obvious that some trades, for example shipping firms hit by the blockade and retail shopkeepers, cannot keep open indefinitely under existing conditions. The large department stores, the clothiers in the fashionable streets and the boot-and-shoe shops will find it extremely difficult to make even their overhead expenses on the small amount of goods which they are entitled to sell to customers under the rationing schemes.

There was a rumour in circulation at the beginning of the month that St. Stephen's Day would not be a holiday this year in view of the extra work necessary in war-time. The report raised a storm of protests and grumbling, and now an official denial has been issued. This has given rise to a further rumour: that it was originally intended to cancel the holiday, but that in order to test public opinion, the report was at first circulated unofficially, and that the general feeling was so strongly against the proposal that the Ministry of the Interior was forced to abandon it. The second rumour may well be true.

The safe return of the North German Lloyd liner 'Bremen'[1] to its home port, is hailed with great joy, and is regarded as a further proof of the powerlessness of the British at sea. In the early days of the war reports were spread by British agencies that the liner had been captured, then we were told that she had changed her registration on the high seas, then that she was in Iceland, but now she is safe at home again, while the British 'Queen Mary',[2] and the French 'Normandie'[3] are still at New York, afraid to sail for Europe. The statement by the British Admiralty that one of their submarines could have sunk the Bremen off Norway on the last stage of her voyage is commented on very sarcastically. The fact is, says the German official version, that the submarine was sighted in good time by escorting aircraft, and was forced to dive for safety. Neutral circles here are full of praise for the successful arrangements made to bring the vessel home.

The figures given by the British for shipping tonnage lost owing to German naval action are said to be much lower than the actual amount sunk. Some of the ships said to have struck mines were, according to the Germans, torpedoed when actually in British convoys. The same can be said for 'collisions'. On the other hand, the British claim to be sinking from two to five German submarines per week is laughed at. The British, it is said, make a great fuss about 'spots of oil'. Some of the British accounts of the sinking of submarines are given, though with comment, over the German wireless. Last week the British reported that the pilot of an aeroplane of their coastal command had sighted a German U-boat, and swooped down at once, dropping a ton of bombs. He summoned destroyers to the scene by wireless. They arrived at once from nowhere, and dropped depth charges. After all these preparations a spot of oil was seen on the surface. All the trouble for a spot of oil!

News from Finland is still given very cautiously. The communiqués of the Finnish Army are reported regularly, but practically no comment on the situation from Finnish sources is printed, whereas extensive quotations are given from the Moscow newspapers. Reports of the League of Nations meetings at Geneva were used only to demonstrate the inefficiency of the League. The Government apparently hope to keep the attention of the public away from Finland. A few days ago a rather strongly worded warning addressed to the Northern countries was issued by the official news agency. It was stated that in recent years they had shown tendencies to associate with anti-German powers and movements, and had shown great readiness, under pleas of 'common democracy', to listen to propaganda directed against Germany. So far Germany has shown exemplary patience, as she has many ties, commercial and cultural, with the Scandinavian lands. It is about time, however, that these countries re-considered their position.

We have not figured much in the news recently, except that our Government's decision to ban the wearing of foreign military uniforms was given both over the wireless and in the newspapers. It always used to puzzle Germans, who in any case found it hard to understand what our constitutional position was, to see British

---

[1] The German liner *Bremen* was launched in 1929. On its way to Bremerhaven it was spotted by the British submarine *Salmon* but her captain decided not to attack and the *Bremen* arrived safely on 13 December.

[2] The British liner *Queen Mary* was launched in 1936. She arrived in New York after the outbreak of war and remained there until converted into a troopship in 1940.

[3] The French liner *Normandie* was launched in 1932. After the outbreak of war it was docked beside the *Queen Mary* and it too was converted into a troopship.

uniforms in evidence now and then in Ireland. The decision is popular, too, with the few Irish people who live here.

The inauguration of a news service in Irish from the German short-wave wireless stations is a sign of what I might call propaganda friendliness towards us. As against that I have to record the fact that they have shown little consideration of our commercial interests as far as the treatment of ships by the contraband control is concerned.

I enclose some press cuttings.

[signed] W. WARNOCK

No. 94 NAI DFA 226/46

Extracts from a report from Francis T. Cremins to Joseph P. Walshe (Dublin) (Ass./20)

GENEVA, 15 December 1939

With reference to the Assembly, I have to confirm the following telegram which I sent to you last night:-

'39 Assembly accepted Report Resolution, Declarations abstention interpretation noted. Switzerland China Bulgaria three Baltic States abstained. Scandinavian States abstained so far as related framework sanctions system. Belgium Netherlands made declarations interpreting assistance Secretariat technical services not implying any collective action. No actual vote necessary after declarations. Council adopted resolution this evening taking cognisance Assembly resolution and finding Union Soviet Socialist Republics had placed itself outside League and consequently no longer member League. China Yugoslavia Greece abstained Finland abstained voting on own appeal.'

[matter omitted]

It was a tense week for the delegates of many countries, and everybody was glad when it was over. There were no incidents. The ordinary public were not admitted to any of the meetings of the Assembly, but representatives of international associations were admitted. The procedure throughout was cleverly managed, and the ordinary rules were waived where considered desirable.

The Polish delegate spoke both at the Committee of 13 and in the Assembly, all members having the right to attend the Committee. His remarks were for the most part directed to the Finnish question but he referred to Poland as well, though in fairly restrained language. A copy of the provisional minutes of yesterday's meeting of the Assembly will be found with the documents.

The Assembly was adjourned, not closed. The Secretary General was authorised until the next session, to convene the Bureau, and the latter body was given power to decide any question which the Supervisory Commission or the Secretary General might submit to it.

The Finnish delegation are I think convinced that they have got as much as possible out of the Appeal. When the Report and Resolution were adopted they expressed their profound gratitude. Nevertheless, it was clear all the time that they were not so much concerned with the question of the expulsion of the U.S.S.R. from the League, as with the question of positive aid for Finland. It remains now to be seen what positive aid will be forthcoming from the different countries.

[matter omitted]

No. 95 NAI DFA 227/23

> Letter from Frederick H. Boland to Michael MacWhite (Rome)
> (227/23) (Copy)
>
> DUBLIN, 15 December 1939

My dear MacWhite,

Reading over our official minute of the 13th December on the subject of the recognition of Slovakia and the establishment of a Slovak Consulate here,[1] I am not sure that the reference to our neutrality in the second paragraph quite explains the nature of our difficulties in this matter.

As you may well imagine our principal difficulty is that a Consul would have to be exequatured and if we were to move for the issue of an exequatur to a Slovak Consul in present circumstances, the effect might be to embarrass political relations between ourselves and the British. That is precisely the kind of thing we want to avoid because, of course, the neutrality policy connotes an effort to keep our relations with both sets of belligerents as free from difficulties as possible. It is in this sense that the reference to our position of neutrality in the official minute of the 13th December is to be understood. On the other hand, of course, nothing can be said to the Slovak Minister about the difficulties connected with the issue of the exequatur. That is why the concluding sentence of the second paragraph of our official minute is worded rather vaguely.

All this emphasises the desirability of avoiding giving any reasons to the Slovak Minister if it is possible to do so.

Yours sincerely,
[stamped] (Signed) F.H. BOLAND

No. 96 NAI DFA Secretary's Files S113

> Draft instructions from Joseph P. Walshe to John W. Dulanty (London) (Copy),
> with covering letter from Joseph P. Walshe to Kathleen O'Connell (Copy)
> (Dublin)
>
> DUBLIN, 19 December 1939

Dear Miss O'Connell,

I enclose a draft instruction to be sent to-morrow to Mr. Dulanty if the Taoiseach approves. Would you be good enough to bring it to his notice as soon as you get the opportunity.

Yours sincerely,
[unsigned]

DRAFT INSTRUCTION.

Dear High Commissioner,

The Taoiseach would like you to make further representations concerning the case of Barnes and Richardson.[2]

---

[1] See No. 91.

[2] Peter Barnes (1908-40) and James Richards (aka McCormick) (1911-40) were sentenced to death by hanging after they were found guilty of planting the bomb that exploded in Coventry on 25 August 1939 which killed five people. Richards admitted to being a member of the IRA while Barnes maintained he had no link with the organisation. Both men were executed on 7 February 1940.

This is not a case of ordinary crime. It is vital to the good relations between the two countries that the attitude of the British Government should not be finally determined without very serious consideration of the political background in which the activities of the I.R.A. in England are taking place. It would be unwise to ignore the very obvious fact that these young men believe that they are acting in the interests of Ireland when they employ such methods. It is perfectly clear that they do not intend to kill or even to injure. Their object in causing material destruction is to bring to the notice of the British Government in that forceful way the continuing dismemberment of Ireland. Whatever disapproval one feels for their methods, the sincerity of their intentions cannot be doubted. The Irish Government are convinced that the execution of these men would have very serious repercussions. Instead of acting as a deterrent, it is likely to produce a series of reprisals and assassinations the ultimate consequences of which it is impossible to foresee. The execution cannot be productive of any good and cannot in any way further the interests of law and order. When men are inspired to wrong-doing by the existence of a fundamental national injustice and suffer penalties therefor, their countrymen's feelings are bound to be moved in their favour, and the British Government should ask themselves whether it would be wise to lose the element of good understanding now existing between the two countries by considering only the wrong committed by these men while forgetting their motives and the circumstances in which the wrong was done.

You could write a formal note to Mr. Eden in the sense of the foregoing paragraph before asking for an interview. Meanwhile, the Minister wishes you to use every influence available to you in order to prevent the execution, which he believes would be the beginning of a new train of bitterness and strife between our two peoples.

Yours sincerely,

No. 97 NAI DFA Secretary's Files S113

Confidential report from John W. Dulanty to Joseph P. Walshe (Dublin) (No. 77) (Secret)

LONDON, 21 December 1939

Further to our recent conversations with regard to the death sentences recently passed on James Richards and Peter Barnes for the Coventry explosion, Mr. Eden told me today that Sir John Anderson[1] had said that when the appeal in those cases reached him he would consider it with a special care. This consideration however would be limited to purely legal aspects. If there were other considerations it would be for Mr. Eden to put them forward.

The latter asked me to assure An Taoiseach that he was fully alive to the political side of this unfortunate Coventry outrage both for the Irish Government and for their own. He would therefore be most willing to present any case which the Irish Government felt like submitting and would go fully into the matter with Mr.

---

[1] Sir John Anderson, 1st Viscount Waverly (1882-1958), Joint Under-Secretary for Ireland, Dublin Castle (1920-2), Lord Privy Seal (1938-9), Home Secretary (1939- 40), Chancellor of the Exchequer (1943-5).

Chamberlain. We would appreciate of course that this was in no sense a promise that anything could be done but it was a definite undertaking to see what could be done.

[signed] J.W. DULANTY
High Commissioner

No. 98 NAI DFA Ottawa Embassy File 850

> *Aide mémoire from John J. Hearne to Dr Oscar D. Skelton (Ottawa)*
> *(Copy)*
>
> OTTAWA, 22 December 1939

Aide-Mémoire

1. The Irish Government's neutrality policy has produced a feeling of contentment in the Country because it provides a clear proof to all shades of nationalist opinion that independence is an established fact. That contentment has reacted on our people in the United States and has had its measure of favourable influence on the issue of the repeal of the arms embargo. A departure from the policy of neutrality, of our own doing, would bring chaos at home, trouble with the United Kingdom, and unwelcome consequences in the United States. There is no body of opinion in the country in favour of going into the war. Those who occasionally speak behind the scenes in favour of such a course are not regarded as friends of Ireland and of continued good relations with Great Britain.
2. Experience has so far shown that, contrary to the view of some, neutrality can be maintained in practice.
3. There has been no question of the British Forces occupying the 'Treaty ports'. The occupation of those ports would be regarded as a violation of the sovereignty of the Irish State and any attempt to do so by force would be resisted. The respect shown by Great Britain for Ireland's right to be neutral and to maintain her neutrality in practice gives added moral strength to Great Britain's stand for Poland and Finland. There are, no doubt, many who feel that the German submarine
[page missing in original]
But investigation has shown that there was not a single case in which the story could be verified.
6. The Irish Government are hoping that the appointment of an Irish representative in Canada will be reciprocated very soon. They feel that, from every point of view, the early appointment of a Canadian representative in Ireland is eminently desirable.
7.(1) In the sphere of internal politics, the Government have found it necessary to take a strong stand against the practice of the hunger-strike amongst political prisoners. The majority of the prisoners gave up the struggle at a relatively early stage, but a few persisted until their lives were in real danger. The Government then decided to release them so that they would take food. It is believed that hunger-striking in Irish prisons is now at an end.
   (2) The problem of national unity, always a major issue, is the subject of the Government's constant study and care. Mr. de Valera has again emphasised

(Dec. 12th)[1] his view that the use of force to secure the reintegration of the national territory would, if unsuccessful, result in throwing everything into the melting pot again. 'My Government' he said 'is as conscious of the cruel wrong of partition as any body of men, but they have the responsibility of knowing where they are going before they lead their country in that direction.'

(3) The Government are concentrating upon the revival of the national language as one of the things essential to the restoration of our national life. They are satisfied that the lot of small nations is going to be ever more difficult if the war is followed by a close European Federation, our national distinctiveness will depend for its continuance upon the Irish language more, perhaps, than any other factor.

No. 99 NAI DFA Secretary's Files A20/3

Report from Leopold H. Kerney to Joseph P. Walshe (Dublin)
(M. 10/11)

MADRID, 23 December 1939

Frank RYAN.

Referring to my minute of 14th November,[2] Mr. de Champourcin handed to me at 11.45 p.m. on 20th December a certified copy of the sentence, and thereby proved his worth; this copy is dated 1st Dec. and also gives information up to the commutation of the death sentence on 12th November 1939. I am retaining this document here, but enclose copy[3] (correcting where possible the very numerous misspellings and errors in typing) and also a slightly summarised translation made by myself.

Mr. de Champourcin says that, if we could disprove alleged proved facts, we could appeal for revision, but he believes that it may be less difficult to secure a pardon, using Falange and Serrano Suñer as the most powerful intermediaries; I will examine this question with him again. Meanwhile, *if* it should be true that Ryan indulged actively in propaganda against Franco during his convalescence in Ireland – and I suppose this is likely – then there is no case for appeal; *if* it should not be true, I would suggest that a certified declaration be made, say by the Press Information Bureau or by the Department to the effect that an examination of the daily newspapers published in Dublin between March 1937 and the date of Ryan's return to Spain shows that no activities of his were reported during that period, and that, therefore, no activities of a public nature could have taken place.

Baron de Senaller[4] (see my report 7th Dec.)[5] called on 21st Dec.; I gave him a letter for the Director of Prisons with which he hopes to obtain permission to send

---

[1] De Valera had made this point strongly, in the presence of delegates holding opposing views, at the annual Fianna Fáil Árd Fheis at the Mansion House, Dublin, on 12 December 1939.
[2] Not printed.
[3] Not printed.
[4] A friend of Kerney's confidante, the Duchess of Tetuan, and known to Ms Maisie Donnelly, Kerney's secretary, de Senaller – a lawyer, formerly a lieutenant in the Tercio – knew Colonel Casado, 'auditor de guerra' in Burgos, from whom he expected to get a copy of Ryan's sentence for Kerney.
[5] Not printed.

Ryan the books received from Miss Ryan; he will study the sentence to see whether, in his opinion, a case could be made for revision.

I saw the Foreign Minister at 1 p.m. on 21st Dec. and handed him a copy of the sentence; he took it saying this would be something new to show Franco; I called his attention to the fact that no crimes were charged against Ryan, that the case was a clean one and I added that others similarly circumstanced had already been released (this may or may not be true); I told him also that Ryan was by no means the 'destacado politico'[1] or outstanding politician that he was represented to be.

It was necessary, for the purposes of a death sentence, to attach an exaggerated importance to Ryan's prominence in Ireland as a politician, seeing that the Nationalist spirit of justice is supposed to make a distinction between ringleaders and their misguided followers; the fact that Ryan returned to Spain made his case worse, but his great crime was his propagandist work against Franco in Ireland. An 'extremist Republican' means one thing in Ireland, and quite a different thing in Spain – deep green in one country, deep red in the other – and the minds of the Judges will have been prejudiced by the description.

The only Irish informer referred to in the accompanying document is Jane Brown.[2] If I am not mistaken, Miss Jane Brown was repatriated by the Paris Legation in December 1937, having reached Paris from Barcelona via Marseilles; she left Barcelona on 8th Dec. After her return to Ireland she was in a position to curry favour with the Spanish nationalists and the declaration which she appears to have made, and which should have sealed Ryan's fate, must have been made in Ireland, as she did not return to Spain. She was rewarded by Franco with a medal – so much I know – and this medal must have been sent to her in Ireland. I do not know when Ryan returned to Spain, but presume this was prior to her departure from Barcelona. She is a trained nurse.

[signed] L.H. KERNEY

No. 100 NAI Madrid Embassy CON 4/7/22 No. 2

Extracts from a report from Leopold H. Kerney to Joseph P. Walshe (Dublin) (M. 10/11) (Copy)

MADRID, 27 December 1939

Frank RYAN. Your 244/8B

I left for Burgos at 9.30 a.m. on Sunday 24th December, accompanied by Fr. Mulrean;[3] we reached the Prison at 1.30 and remained there till 3.30, arriving back in Madrid at 9 p.m. The road from Burgos to the Prison, about 3 miles, is in shockingly bad condition, and had to be covered at snail-pace.

There were several hundred women outside the prison entrance; we squeezed our way through them and gained admission; leaving Fr. Mulrean with the

---

[1] Literally an 'exceptional politician'.
[2] Jane Brown from Enfield, Co Kildare, had been in the service of a Spanish noble family and during the civil war in Spain had lost all her belongings, including her Irish passport. With aid from British consular officials she made her way to Paris and onwards to Ireland with the assistance of the Irish Legation in Paris in December 1937.
[3] Official chaplain to the Irish Brigade during the Spanish Civil War.

Director, I was accompanied by a sub-warder to the chief-warder's office; whilst waiting for Ryan, the sub-warder told me that numerous cards had come addressed to him and he was much impressed by this; they heaped up apparently to about nine inches in height; and, referring to Ryan, the sub-warder remarked – 'Es un caballero'! (He's a gentleman!).

[matter omitted]

FRANK RYAN'S SENTENCE. Further to my telegram of 21st[1] and my minute of 23rd December,[2] I was given the following information on 24th December by Frank Ryan, to whom I showed a copy of his sentence, as translated by me.

1. He left Spain on 4th March 1937, but his actual arrival in Ireland was delayed till the end of the month.
2. He left Ireland to return to Spain on 16th or 17th June 1937.
3. He took no part whatever in any public demonstrations against Franco whilst in Ireland.
4. The only public meeting in which he took part during this period was an anti-British demonstration on 'Coronation Day', 12th May 1937, on which occasion he had his nose broken; that meeting did not concern itself with Spain.
5. During the above period, he took part in two private meetings in Dublin, to which invitation was by ticket, the purpose of these meetings being to commemorate those who had been killed in Spain.

Frank Ryan's own statement will of course not be accepted as disproof of alleged 'proved facts'; any corroboration which can be obtained by you, say from the examination of newspaper files, should be of value, and might accelerate a pardon, if not revision of the sentence.

Another point is that Ryan refused to sign the confession attributed to him, because of mistakes therein; there had been an interrogation lasting 9 hours; it was inevitable that the interpreter should make some mistakes; the interpreter tried to explain this to the presiding Judge, who would not listen to him and lost his temper, whilst Ryan announced his willingness to put his signature to a true declaration. The fact is, then, that the confession is not signed by him and is not acknowledged by him as being exact.

During the trial, he was accused of having done propaganda work, during his convalescence, in London, Liverpool and Glasgow – although you will note that he was sentenced for propagandist activities *only in Ireland*; however, Ryan says that he paid no visit at all to Liverpool or Glasgow, and that he paid only one visit to London 'for a day or two', and did not act as a propagandist on that occasion.

I have no doubt that you are acting on the suggestion made in my telegram. Once I have whatever statement you may be able to send me, I will again see Champourcin, with whom I discussed this case from 7 till 9 p.m. on 26th December; he happens to be a friend of the General Director of Prisons, whose name (Colonel Maxim Cuervo) Ryan asked me particularly to note, and who may perhaps accede to our wishes in regard to delivery of correspondence &c.

I saw Beigbeder on 26th December but he had no fresh news to give me about Ryan's case; his chef de cabinet, Juan de las Harcehas (son of the former Under-Secretary) was Consul in Palestine till last July and had heard much there about

---

[1] Not printed.
[2] See No. 99.

Ryan from a friend of his, a Franciscan priest at Gethsemane,[1] who had been wounded in 1916 and who subsequently entered holy orders.

[signed] L.H. KERNEY

No. 101 NAI DFA Washington Embassy Confidential Reports 1938-9

Extracts from a confidential report from Robert Brennan to Joseph P. Walshe (Dublin)
(108/71/39) (Copy)

WASHINGTON, 27 December 1939

The action of President Roosevelt in deciding to appoint Mr. Myron C. Taylor[2] as a Representative at the Vatican is the outcome of a long series of negotiations extending over the past two or three years. It is explained officially that Mr. Taylor while having the status of an Ambassador will not have the rank of such. The ostensible reason for the appointment is that the President and the Pope can work more easily to bring about that international peace which both so ardently desire. Simultaneously with his message announcing the appointment of Mr. Taylor, the President issued a peace message addressed to the Head of the Protestant Churches in America, and the Head of the Jewish Church.

Spokesmen for the White House are anxious to dispel the idea that this step means the resumption of diplomatic relations with the Vatican. I learned on good authority that this is correct for the moment. There has been some criticism from the ultra Protestant sections.

The objection to the resumption of diplomatic relations is twofold. Firstly, it might create an out-cry amongst the anti-Catholic elements in the South who still are really bigoted against Rome but whose spokesmen base their objection on the grounds that freedom loving Americans dislike the idea of church and State being linked as in Vatican City. The other objection is that if there were a Papal Nuncio here he would have to be Dean of the Diplomatic Corps as he is in the European and South American countries where the Vatican is officially represented.

[stamped] (Signed) ROBT. BRENNAN

No. 102 NAI DFA 219/5

Confidential report from William J. B. Macaulay to Joseph P. Walshe (Dublin)
(MP 42/39) (Confidential)

HOLY SEE, 28 December 1939

With reference to the correspondence concerning the rumour of an approaching Consistory, I have made some enquiries and gather that the position is as follows.

The creation of new Cardinals will be postponed until the Spring because His Holiness intends to appoint Archbishop Spellman[3] and most likely the next

---

[1] Marginal note by Kerney: 'Fr Eugene'.
[2] Myron Charles Taylor (1874-1959), Personal Representative of the President of the United States to Pope Pius XII (1939-50).
[3] Archbishop Francis Joseph Spellman (1889-1967), Archbishop of New York (1939-67), elevated to Cardinal in 1946.

Archbishop of Chicago, whoever he may be. To have created Mons. Spellman a Cardinal so shortly after his elevation to New York would have seemed very precipitate and cause further adverse comment in regard to him. By this postponement and the creation of one other American Cardinal there will be less grounds for criticism. It is said that Archbishop Curley[1] may well be made a Cardinal instead of the Archbishop of Chicago. It is certainly true that the Archbishop of Baltimore got a very good reception at the Vatican when he came here this year after so long an absence. I think his chances of a Red Hat are much greater than those of Archbishop Glennon of St. Louis,[2] who is said to be 'too old'. This seems a strange objection when one considers the ages of some of the Cardinals created for the Curia.

There appears to be a probability of either Mons. Robinson[3] or Fr. Gemelli[4] being made Cardinal. Against the former is the suggestion that being the first Nuncio to Ireland his creation might be regarded as a precedent for his successors and in view of difficulties in the past over the retirement of Nuncios in Spanish speaking countries the Holy See is anxious to avoid such a situation arising again anywhere else. There is no Franciscan Cardinal at present and if Fr. Gemelli should be created, Monsgr. Robinson would have to wait at least, as two Franciscans could scarcely be made Cardinals at the same Consistory. However, there appears to be no one available to take Fr. Gemelli's place a President of the Pontifical Academy. Furthermore although his relations with the late Pope were exceedingly close, it is not known what these are with the present Pontiff.

The British are still working for an English Cardinal in Curia, there being none since the death of Cardinal Gasquet.[5] There has been considerable exchange of letters between King George and His Holiness and between Lord Halifax and the Cardinal Secretary. Britain as the leading belligerent of the Allies and in view of the Holy Father's open antipathy to the Nazis must loom large in the eyes of the Vatican in these days. I do not know whether the creation of Monsgr. Robinson would satisfy the British Government, so far it appears to be Mons. Godfrey,[6] Apostolic Delegate to England, who is suggested by them. On the other hand Mons. Robinson has many friends in England, important in official and social circles and in the Vatican there is great respect for the English nobility Catholic or not.

I fear I must express my regret that Mr. O'Donovan approached the Father General of the Jesuits in connection with Monsgr. Robinson. Any canvassing on our part would do nothing but harm. The best way in my opinion (and it is not only my opinion) is to impress on the Cardinal Secretary at every opportunity, our admiration of our Nuncio and our appreciation of the great work he has done for the Holy See and the Church in Ireland. This I have not failed to do.

[signed] W. MACAULAY

---

[1] Michael Joseph Curley (1879-1947), Archbishop of Baltimore (1921-47).
[2] Cardinal John Joseph Glennon (1862-1946), Archbishop of St. Louis (1903-46).
[3] Paschal Charles Robinson O.F.M. (1870-1948), Apostolic Nuncio to Ireland (1929-48).
[4] Father Agostino Gemelli O.F.M. (1878-1959), founder of the University of the Sacred Heart, Milan, and President of the Pontifical Academy of Sciences (1936-59).
[5] Cardinal Francis Aidan Gasquet O.S.B. (1846-1929).
[6] Cardinal William Godfrey (1889-1963), Apostolic Nuncio to Britain (1938-53), Archbishop of Liverpool (1953-6), Archbishop of Westminster (1956-63), elevated to Cardinal in 1958.

No. 103 NAI DFA Secretary's Files S113

> *Memorandum from Michael Rynne to Joseph P. Walshe (Dublin)*
> (Secret)
> DUBLIN, 30 December 1939

Re Coventry Explosion Sentences

I showed Mr. O'Donoghue, Attorney-General's Department,[1] the High Commissioner's Secret minute No. 77 of the 21st December in the above matter.[2]

I explained that we did not consider it practicable nor desirable that the Government's case for a reprieve should be based exclusively on legal grounds. Mr. Dulanty's minute indicates, indeed, that the Government's case, (which is to be put forward by Mr. Eden in the British Cabinet), should rest solely on considerations of a non-legal character.

Mr. O'Donoghue agreed that our case must mainly rely on political arguments, it being obvious that the final authority on the various points of law and evidence involved would be the British Court of Criminal Appeal whose judgment on the issues confronting it would doubtless be regarded as conclusive by the British Home Secretary. He added, however, that if the Government felt that they should advert to various aspects of the Birmingham Court proceedings, when drafting their case for the British Government, they might thereby strengthen that case.

From such reports as are available of the Court proceedings it would appear that they could not be regarded as entirely free from bias in regard to the two men sentenced to death. Particularly unfair was the admission during the trial of the statements of the two women prisoners which on the application of their counsel were read out in full to the Court. At the suggestion of prosecuting counsel, the Judge directed that the trial should proceed against all the five persons accused, including Richards and Barnes, so that the admission of the women's statements must have undoubtedly influenced the jury in their verdict against the male prisoners. The fact that the trial judge on two occasions during the proceedings mentioned to the jury that the women's statements were not to be regarded by them as constituting evidence against persons other than the women themselves can scarcely be argued to justify the admission of the statements. The judge was surely expecting too much of a jury chosen from the inhabitants of Birmingham, (a town not very distant from Coventry and one which has suffered extremely from I.R.A. attacks), when he asked them to utterly ignore the full import of statements which were virtually directed against two of the accused men. The statements in fact contained practically all the evidence procurable to substantiate the serious charges brought against those men. Either the statements should have been ruled out by the judge or the trial of the women should have been conducted separately from that of the men.

Apart from this major objection, to which reference might be made in the Government's case for a reprieve of Richards and Barnes, there may be some other

---

[1] Philip O'Donoghue (1896-1987), legal assistant to the Attorney General (1929-59), one of the drafters of the 1937 Constitution of Ireland; called to the Inner Bar (1939), appointed Irish member of the European Commission of Human Rights (1965), Judge of the European Court of Human Rights (1971-80).
[2] See No. 97.

points that we could endeavour to make on the seeming partiality of the Birmingham trial. Mr. O'Donoghue considers, however, that it would be distinctly inadvisable to attempt to found any elaborate criticism of the Court proceedings on mere newspaper reports thereof. He thinks, moreover, that most of the really tenable arguments to be drawn from the conduct of the trial will be made by defending counsel at the Court of Criminal Appeal. If that Court dismisses the appeal, it will mean that even the most telling legal arguments have been tried and have failed.

I agree, therefore, with Mr. O'Donoghue's view that the Government ought not to be advised to overstress the legal aspects of their case, whether the case is to be submitted at once or whether it is to be held over until we learn that the appeal has been dismissed. Doubtless, the political case will be prepared at a very early date.

When it is in draft, I would suggest that it be submitted to the Attorney-General for the addition thereto, in an appropriate place, of a reference to the unfair admission at the Court proceedings of the women's statements as evidence.

[initialled] M.R.

No. 104 NAI DFA 241/113

Code telegram from the Department of External Affairs to William Warnock (Berlin)
(No. 102) (Personal) (Copy)

DUBLIN, 30 December 1939

My telegram 91.[1] Assurances reported in your minute of 30th November[2] are considered as satisfactory as can be expected. No need to press further.

---

[1] Not printed.
[2] See No. 79.

1940

No. 105 NAI DFA 226/46

Statement by Francis T. Cremins to the League of Nations Assembly Committee of Twelve on the Russian invasion of Finland

GENEVA, 1 January 1940

I desire to make one or two observations regarding the attitude of my Government in this important matter. First of all, I wish to say that the statements made at the Assembly of 1934 by the Irish representative, Mr. de Valera, defining the attitude of the Irish Government towards the entrance of the U.S.S.R. to the League,[1] and the statement made at the Assembly last year by the Irish delegation defining the attitude of the Irish Government in matters of a political nature which come before the League, retain all their meaning.[2]

The appeal of Finland which is now being considered by this Session of the Assembly is not at all a simple matter. The wrong done to Finland is in no sense obscure, and, in ordinary times, most States would, I imagine, have no difficulty in formulating a policy. But in these times which bristle with difficulties for many States, it is no simple matter for a State which is situated far from the scene of action easily to fix its attitude, in view of the general complexities of the situation and of the conflict of interests which exists for many countries.

In general, I may say that the instructions which I have received in connection with the Finnish appeal is to take very fully into account first the views and requirements of Finland, but also of those States which are her neighbours and especially the Scandinavian States. That is one of the reasons why I was happy to support yesterday M. Unden's appeal that the first act of this Committee should be an attempt to bring about conciliation and the cessation of hostilities.

No. 106 NAI DFA 219/4

Confidential report from William Warnock to Joseph P. Walshe (Dublin)
(43/33)

BERLIN, 3 January 1940

The Christmas and New Year holidays passed over quietly this year, owing to the war. The Christmas dinner suffered on account of the rationing restrictions, but it would be a mistake to accept the reports of it given in the London wireless broadcasts, which tried to give the impression that the Germans had next to nothing to eat. As I mentioned in earlier reports,[3] the rations were increased for Christmas,

---

[1] See DIFP IV No. 236.
[2] Not printed.
[3] See No. 93.

and even though few were able to eat until the indigestion stage, most people got enough in some way or another. Many of my acquaintances have said to me that they find that they can live quite well on smaller portions than they used to have formerly. On Christmas Day I dined with a friend in quite an ordinary restaurant in the Kurfürstendamm, the main street in the West of the city, and we were given an excellent helping of goose (the national dish for the Christmas), without even having to produce ration-cards, as fowl, like fish, is still free from restriction.

The usual merry-making in the streets on New Year's Eve had to be abandoned on account of the 'black-out', and severe warnings were given by the police against over-indulgence in alcohol.

The Chancellor did not hold the usual New Year reception for the Heads of the Diplomatic Missions, but the Heads of Missions were invited to call and enter their name in the visitor's book in the Presidential Chancellory, and I duly did so.

The naval battle of the estuary of the River Plate took up a lot of space in the newspapers just before Christmas.[1] At first, naturally, we were given accounts of what was reported as the 'Admiral Graf Spee's' significant victory against a superior force. The report of the ship's destruction was compressed into a few lines, but these were followed a day or so afterwards by a violent attack on the Uruguayan Government, who were accused of partisanship with Great Britain. Criticism of Uruguay has commenced again since the internment of the 'Tacoma', the German ship which took the crew of the 'Admiral Graf Spee' on board before it was blown up at sea.

As a compensation for the loss of the pocket battleship, the public is given reports of big German air victories. The fact that British sources state that the reports are grossly exaggerated does not in the least take away from the propaganda value of these reports, as nobody here gives any credence to the war news supplied by the British Ministry of Information.

Several articles have appeared in the press describing the development of Russia's transport system in recent years. It is stated that considerable quantities of goods can be brought to Germany by sea from Leningrad, or through Tailinn or Riga. Agreement has already been reached with Russia concerning new frontier control pacts for land traffic. These articles are undoubtedly intended as a reply to British assertions that the Russian system of communications is so bad that Germany can never hope to get anything like as much from Russia as she would wish, that the rolling stock is insufficient and in bad condition, etc. It is felt here that the Germans will, in their own interests, give considerable help to the Russians in building up a modern system of transport, and that the more important railway lines will soon be in a position to carry as much traffic as required.

The mutiny in Derry Gaol[2] and the attack on the Magazine Fort in Dublin[3] received great attention in the German press. There were also references to the

---

[1] The reference is to the battle of the River Plate of 13 December 1939 in which a force of British cruisers engaged the German pocket battleship *Graf Spee*. Though Captain Langsdorff of the *Graf Spee* scored a greater success in terms of damage to British vessels, he was ultimately forced to scuttle his ship in Montevideo harbour.
[2] The revolt of thirty-nine republican prisoners on 25 December 1939.
[3] On 23 December 1939 the IRA raided the Irish Defence Force's main ammunition store at the Phoenix Park in Dublin. A large quantity of ammunition and weapons was stolen, though most was later recovered.

Taoiseach's Christmas address to the United States, which was quoted to point out a few home truths to the British. The measures taken to recover the stolen munition are also featured prominently.

An interesting article on Ireland appeared recently on the front page of the Frankfurter Zeitung. It was written by Walter von Dewall, who was, until the end of August last, their London correspondent. Mr. von Dewall wrote a series of articles on Ireland a few years ago. He has some friends in Dublin, among them Mr. District Justice Lennon. In his article Mr. von Dewall explained carefully to his readers that they must not expect that, because she is anti-British, Ireland would automatically support Germany. It must be remembered that Irish people see parallels between their own history and that of Poland. Nevertheless a wise censorship controls the press so well that war news is given objectively. The writer says: 'There are, of course, infringements, but it can be said, to Ireland's honour, that the Irish press maintains its neutrality much more honestly than that of many other neutral states. Nor is even the "Irish Times" an exception'.

The German press has made no comment on the incident at the Magazine Fort, but it has interested its readers so much that events are being extensively watched.

Some press cuttings are attached.

[signed] W. WARNOCK

No. 107 NAI DFA 217/38

Memorandum from Frederick H. Boland to Joseph P. Walshe

DUBLIN, 3 January 1940

Secretary,

I have had a discussion with Mr. Seán Moynihan on the financial considerations involved in the suggestion that Mr. Kerney, the Minister in Spain, should also be accredited to Portugal. So far as the Department of Finance is concerned, there is no difficulty.

2. The Legation at Madrid is kept fairly busy, but it could certainly take on the extra work of representing us in Portugal without additional staff. A separate Legation in Lisbon would be difficult to justify. The prospects of trade development between the two countries are slight, and the Consular work of a Legation in Lisbon would not be considerable. On the other hand, there are probably many people who would like to see closer relations established between this country and Portugal. Portuguese development in the sphere of social policy and organisation has aroused a great deal of interest in this country; Portugal is, I believe, part of the Irish province of at least one religious order (the Dominican), and Portugal, as a neutral state on the Atlantic seaboard, is confronted by many of the problems in relation to the war which we are facing ourselves. If therefore we could, at little expense, utilise our existing Legation in Spain to establish direct contact with the Portuguese Government, it would be worth while doing so.

3. The expense involved would hardly exceed £250 per annum, covering the payment to the Minister of a separate representation allowance of £150 per annum in respect of Portugal and provision for, say, four visits to Lisbon during the year, each of about one week's duration. The Department of Finance are prepared to agree to the inclusion of a provision on these lines in the Estimates for 1940-41. The

allowance of £150 may be somewhat on the low side, but I have no doubt that the Department of Finance will be prepared to reconsider it if experience shows that it is inadequate.

4. If the Minister is disposed to proceed at once with Mr. Kerney's accreditation to Portugal, the next steps would be (a) to move the Department of Finance for formal sanction for the inclusion of the necessary provision in next year's Estimates, and (b) at the same time, to seek the Portuguese Government's consent to the arrangement and their 'agrément' to Mr. Kerney. When we were establishing diplomatic relations with Belgium by accrediting the Minister in Paris to Brussels, the matter was submitted formally to the Government. I assume that the precedent will be followed in this case.

5. Probably the best procedure for raising the matter with the Portuguese Government would be to ask the High Commissioner to approach the Portuguese Ambassador in London. No doubt, the first question which will occur to both the Ambassador and the Portuguese Government is whether, and if so in what manner, Portugal would be expected to reciprocate Mr. Kerney's appointment by sending somebody here. The joint accreditation of the Portuguese diplomatic representative in London would not, of course, be acceptable to us, and that makes it difficult to us to press for the early appointment of a Portuguese Minister in Dublin. We would probably have to be content therefore with expressing the hope that the Portuguese Government may find it possible at some not too distant date to send a diplomatic representative to Éire, making it clear at the same time that the joint accreditation of the representative in London would not be acceptable, but that, on the other hand, we would raise no strong objection if the Portuguese Government felt unable to make any appointment for the present. I attach a draft minute to the High Commissioner on these lines.[1]

[initialled] F.H.B.

No. 108 NAI DFA 217/38

Draft letter from Joseph P. Walshe to John W. Dulanty (London)
DUBLIN, 3 January 1940

I should be glad if you would be good enough to arrange to see the Portuguese Ambassador as soon as possible and tell him that, with a view to the establishment of closer relations between Ireland and Portugal, whose progress under Dr. Salazar[2] has aroused great interest and admiration in this country, the Government are anxious that the Irish Minister in Spain should also be accredited to Portugal. The Government hope that this step would serve to promote closer trade, cultural and other relations between Ireland and Portugal which, as two great Catholic countries very similarly circumstanced in relation to the present conflict, have much in common.

Please ask the Ambassador to ascertain as soon as he conveniently can whether this arrangement would be agreeable to the Portuguese Government, and if so, whether Mr. Kerney would be *persona grata*. A brief *curriculum vitae* of Mr. Kerney is enclosed.[3] You should tell the Ambassador that Mr. Kerney would continue to reside in Madrid and that, for the present at least, it would not be the intention to

[1] See No. 108.
[2] António de Oliveira Salazar (1889-1970), Portuguese Prime Minister (1932-68).
[3] Not printed.

maintain a separate chancellery in Lisbon. Mr. Kerney would maintain contact with the Portuguese Government by means of personal visits.

We understand that the proposed arrangement would not be unprecedented so far as Portugal is concerned and that, for example, Turkey is represented by the same Minister in Madrid and Lisbon.

In considering the suggested arrangement, the Portuguese Government will no doubt be anxious to know whether they would be expected to reciprocate at once by sending a Portuguese Minister to Dublin. On this point, you might say to Señor Monteiro[1] that we appreciate that it would not be practicable for the Portuguese Government to reciprocate our action by action on precisely similar lines. Even if there were not the difficulty arising from the fact that the Portuguese representative in London has the status of an Ambassador, there would still be the point that, as we have always been opposed to the accreditation to Ireland of representatives who are also accredited to Britain, the Government could not consistently fall in with such an arrangement in the case of Portugal. The Government would gladly welcome a Portuguese Minister in Dublin, and they hope that the Portuguese would be able in due course to make such an appointment; but, in the special circumstances, the Government would understand if the Portuguese Government felt unable to make such an appointment at once.

No. 109 NAI DFA 219/4

Confidential report from William Warnock to Joseph P. Walshe (Dublin)
(43/33)

BERLIN, 13 January 1940

The resignation of Mr. Hore-Belisha from his position as British Secretary of State for War was the subject of long and numerous articles in the German press, but the public were warned that they need not expect that any change will be noticeable to British War policy. Emphasis is laid on Mr. Chamberlain's letter to Mr. Hore-Belisha on the day of his departure from office.

The resignation is a slight loss to German propaganda. Jewish influence in Great Britain and France is claimed to a large extent for the war, and the fact that the British War Minister was a Jew was a very valuable aid to the discussion. The press has been endeavouring, as happens in all countries during war-time, to ascertain as many dark 'facts' as possible regarding the career of the politicians on the opposite side. Mr. Hore-Belisha is alleged to have been born in a ghetto in Morocco, and to have been frequently concerned in shady business transactions, and generally speaking, to be 'a typical Jewish adventurer'. In that the war is not going well for Great Britain he has decided to make a temporary disappearance so as to be in a safe place if disaster comes. In the meantime he will remain active behind the scenes. A cartoon shows Mr. Chamberlain whispering: 'Good-bye Leslie, come in by the back door in future'.

It is felt that Mr. Chamberlain's personal prestige will suffer greatly, and some observers suggest that he will not be able to retain the position of Prime Minister very much longer, and that this time next year will see a completely altered British Cabinet.

---

[1] Armindo Monteiro, Portuguese Ambassador to Britain (1937-43).

The attitude of the Scandinavian countries to the proposed British and French assistance to Finland is still being sharply watched, and it has not yet been clarified. The arguments that Norway and Sweden are bound, as members of the League of Nations, to allow aid for Finland to pass through their territory, is discussed as being irrelevant, in that the League of Nations is a moribund – if not dead – institution. The question for Germany is a simple one; are the Northern Countries going to allow the British and the French to make use of their territory or not? The much advertised schemes of 'help for Finland' are no more than attempts on the part of the Allies to gain a foothold in Scandinavia.

The announcement that Britain intends to limit her imports of foodstuffs in order to be in a better position, from the point of view of shipping and foreign currency, has caused more sarcastic amusement here. In recent years British propagandists have been sneering at statements by German leaders that 'guns are more important than butter'; now Great Britain is unashamedly following the same policy.

I referred in a previous report[1] to the bitter cold which we are enduring in Berlin. The problem of fuel is very acute as the waterways, which convey most of the city's coal supply, have been frozen over for three weeks. The passenger train service has been reduced to make room for goods trains carrying coal, and all cheap fares have been cancelled until further notice. London reports that owners of block flats have been ordered to operate the control heating apparatus on no more than two days per week are incorrect. There is a new regulation of this nature in respect of warm water supplies but it does not extend to central heating. The intense cold has damped people's enthusiasm about the progress of the war; very likely, however, spirits will go up again when a thaw sets in.

The food position is deteriorating. Fresh vegetables are impossible to obtain. In other years there used to be big imports of vegetables about this time of the year. This winter raw materials for industry are regarded as being more important. I hear from reliable enough sources that the decision to withdraw fresh milk from sale has brought in unexpectedly large stocks of butter, and that at the present rate, Germany's butter supply will hold out for years. Since the outbreak of war, full milk is supplied only to children, and to the sick and infirm. The newly acquired areas in Poland will, it is hoped, produce abundant supplies of foodstuffs. Agricultural produce will also be available in Russia and in the Baltic countries – if Germany can arrange some method of payment. Coffee and tea (and substitutes for them) are becoming very scarce, and in this respect the members of the Diplomatic Corps are beginning to feel the pinch, as the bonded supplies of tea and coffee in the free port at Hamburg, where we usually buy, seem to be running low, and the neighbouring countries prevent the export of these commodities. The Food Control Office has arranged that limited supplies of tea be supplied to us by one particular shop. The price per lb. Is RM.12 (over £1.4.0 at the official rate of exchange)! Cheaper qualities have been sold out. Soap and soap products are unobtainable with the exception of a new standard 'unity soap', which is supposed to serve for all purposes from washing one's face to scrubbing the floor (but soap is now too precious to use for scrubbing). On the whole the population is taking the difficulties in good spirits. Most of them got enough practice in the last war. This time they are at least protected against profiteering.

---

[1] See No. 106.

Figures published a few days ago by the Italian Government show that eighty percent of the German speaking population in the former Austrian regions in Northern Italy have opted for return to Germany. Friends of the German Consul General in Milan tell me that the proportion was over ninety per cent in the purely German areas, and that the Italians had purposely extended the area for option in order to reduce the percentage for the combined provinces. The press has not much to say about the matter, as the whole question of the definite cession of the South Tyrol to Italy called up many bitter and unpleasant memories. The final decision to transplant the population was most unpopular. It is proposed to settle the migrants in Styria, Carinthia, and in the Tyrol.

As the enclosed cuttings show, there are frequent references in the press to Ireland, but few of them are of any special interest, save that some of the reports (not those from Dr. Petersen) show a tendency to sympathise with the 'I.R.A.'. A well-known journalist said in confidence to me the other day that he had reason to believe that the Propaganda Ministry is disappointed with the general attitude of the 'Irish Press'. I replied that they must remember that we are a neutral country, and that, from my own regular reading of the Irish newspapers, I did not think that Germany had any reason for complaint. This matter was never mentioned to me at the Foreign Office, nor do I intend to raise it. Even if there is any truth in my informant's suggestion, I doubt that the Foreign Office will mention it just yet. If I hear anything further indirectly, I shall report it to you at once.

[signed] W. WARNOCK

No. 110 NAI DT S8814B

Memorandum from Michael Rynne to Joseph P. Walshe (Dublin)
DUBLIN, 19 January 1940

The Change of Constitution and International Treaties concluded prior thereto
1. The coming into operation of the Constitution over two years ago meant the disappearance from international, as well as constitutional (or 'internal'), existence of Saorstát Éireann and the coming into being of Ireland (Éire). Whether that is to say that a new State was created by the new Constitution or whether it simply meant that a new name was conferred on an existing State, is not of vital significance in regard to the binding-force of those international agreements to which Saorstát Éireann formerly *was* and Ireland now *is* a party.
2. But if it be assumed that no new State was created in 1937 or, at least, that no new *international* entity came to be recognised then, the matter of the pre-1937 treaties raises no issue whatever. The treaties originally made by the State, Saorstát Éireann, naturally continue to bind that State under any other name. There is no modern precedent to a contrary effect. Where States have changed their names in recent time the most they have done in the international sphere has been to notify other States of the change without, however, referring in any way to their continuing respect for obligations undertaken in the past. For example, Persia on changing its name to Iran some few years ago notified the Secretary General of the League of Nations of that fact, without adverting in any way to its intention to continue to adhere to the League Covenant. We followed a similar procedure during 1938 in regard to the League and to those States where we were directly represented.

3. It seems fairly clear that, from the point of view of other States, no new international person was created by the new Constitution. That impression may have been conveyed by the procedure, already referred to, whereby we merely announced a change of name. It was, no doubt, strongly reinforced by the fact that we did not recall and reaccredit our representatives abroad. Moreover, those Governments which studied the Constitution must have concluded from the very absence of any reference therein to the transfer of international obligations to a new State, that there was no intention to create a new State, at least for international purposes.

4. Thus, arguing that no new State has been established, we may rest assured that no valid objection can be taken (or is likely to be taken) to Ireland's participation in any particular treaty concluded by representatives of Saorstát Éireann, simply on account of the new name of the Irish State.

5. Arguing, on the other hand, that a new State has in fact and in international law been created, we may still assert the indubitable right of Ireland to operate treaties made on behalf of Saorstát Éireann. The rules governing the succession of States enable us to claim that Ireland, as the lawful successor of Saorstát Éireann, is entitled to inherit the latter's contracts, rights and liabilities vis-à-vis foreign States. Properly speaking, if it were generally accepted that 'Ireland' is an entirely new State, the Government, through the Minister for External Affairs, should undertake the gigantic task of informing all the other Governments of the world of the precise treaties now regarded as binding on the new State, although concluded or brought in by the old predecessor-State. In 1922, a similar situation confronted the Government of Saorstát Éireann. It was then more or less reluctantly decided to ignore strict international rules and to work all useful or appropriate old United Kingdom treaties while neglecting the unsuitable ones. Other States gradually began to recognise what treaties were being honoured in practice by Saorstát Éireann and what treaties of a purely 'British' character were not being applied.

6. Plenty of examples can be found of States (Italy, Spain, etc.) which in recent years have entirely altered their Constitutions, and yet adhere to all their former treaties. Only States which have increased their territories in fact (e.g., Italy, Germany, etc.) appear to have had to notify foreign States regarding the application of *certain* old treaties, affected by the territorial changes, but never regarding *all* old treaties.

7. In the particular case that we have to deal with (the Transatlantic Air Agreement)[1] there would seem to be no reason at all why it should receive exceptional treatment from any other State. We may moreover advise the Minister of the important fact that, since the Constitution came into force, we have notified no country of a change in our mutual treaty relations due to the new condition of affairs, and that no foreign country has at any time since 1937 challenged Ireland's right to participate in any agreement concluded for Saorstát Éireann prior to that date.

[initialled] M.R.

---

[1] A reference to the 1935 agreement between Ireland, England and Canada to establish a transatlantic commercial air service.

No. 111 NAI DFA 219/49

Confidential report from John J. Hearne to Joseph P. Walshe (Dublin)
(14/28)

OTTAWA, 24 January 1940

I have the honour to refer to recent conversations with Dr. Skelton on the subject of Mr. Hall Kelly's appointment and some other matters.

We discussed the reasons for your suggested change in the status of official representatives in Dublin and Ottawa. I referred to your general policy of assimilating the status of such representatives to that of diplomatic agents in the international sense. Dr. Skelton understood that, of course, but he was anxious to know why you made the approach at this particular time. I said that you had emphasised to me again and again recently the necessity of making our status as a sovereign, independent State clear in connection with our policy of neutrality and in matters of this kind, the matters which were themselves the very criteria of sovereignty. He asked whether the I.R.A. situation had anything to do with it. I said I had no doubt that our domestic peace might ultimately depend upon our being able to show our own people as a whole the character and extent of our achievements in the constitutional field. I said it would have been a magnificent thing for us, both from the national and the international standpoint, if the Canadian representative in Dublin and the Irish representative in Canada could have been accorded a status equal to Sir John Maffey's, a status which – whatever the title of the agent might be – would not be distinguishable, in any material respect, from that of a Minister Plenipotentiary. I cannot tell you how deeply sympathetic Dr. Skelton was, but you need no assurance on that score. Canadian public opinion, however, is not moving rapidly in these matters. 'Canada', Dr. Skelton said, 'is not ready'. I might add in this connection that Mr. King is known (by some of us) to be turning over in his mind the prospects of an immediate general election. Mr. Hepburn's[1] recent attack upon him for not prosecuting the war vigorously enough, i.e., for not being 'Empire' enough, is regarded as having given Mr. King the opportunity he has been seeking for an appeal to the country at an earlier date this year than was anticipated. Mr. King will take no such risk to his prospects in the Province of Ontario (and, indeed, elsewhere) as might be involved in his adoption now of a forward constitutional policy in the matter of 'inter se' relationships.[2] I reserve for the moment my view on the likelihood or otherwise of Mr. King moving to abolish the appeal to the Privy Council. The Privy Council itself has still to pronounce on the recent decision of the Supreme Court of Canada. That Court has merely decided that the Canadian Parliament has the legal power to abolish the appeal. With Mr. Justice Davies' dissentient judgment, saving Provincial rights, on the record, the question of the policy of abolition may give pause to a Prime Minister soon to seek

---

[1] Mitchell F. Hepburn (1896-1953), Premier of Ontario (1934-42); an opponent of MacKenzie King who felt that Canada should be doing more to support the war effort.

[2] Meaning 'between or amongst ourselves' in Latin and used in Commonwealth terms to denote the international unity of the Dominions and Britain as one unit. Britain held that relations between Dominions were intra-Commonwealth, and not international, relations. Ireland strongly opposed this view and in the 1920s succeeded in establishing many precedents against the British position.

the suffrages of all – including the opponents of abolition – on his war programme.

You will have observed that the Canadian representative in South Africa is going as a High Commissioner. Mr. David Meyer[1] has informed me that when he was appointed Accredited Representative of the Union here the Canadian Government stipulated that their agent in South Africa would be a High Commissioner.

I spoke to Dr. Skelton about references in certain Canadian newspapers to Ireland. A typical caption is 'Irish turmoil'. They give all the bad news and little else. There have been some rather cruel cartoons. Even when the Toronto 'Globe and Mail' recently, in a subleader, made the correction I asked them to make with regard to Mr. McAree's articles (the question of the ports), the subleader was, in parts, a very bad exposition of the constitutional and international position with regard to our neutrality. The Editor-in-Chief sent me a charming letter thanking me for the correction. His exposition (in the subleader) of the situation with regard to the ports was admirable. But he did not appear to see anything wrong, e.g. with publishing in the same article, statements like the following:-

> 'the King's enemies would be perfectly justified in attacking one of the King's dominions even though it elected to remain neutral.'

Again:-

> 'when the King declares war or makes peace each of his Dominions is in a state of war or peace. On the other hand, participation in war depends entirely on the action taken by the Government of Éire, etc.'

Statements like the latter are, of course, based on the Constitution of 1922. I have written to Mr. McIntosh (the Editor-in-Chief) to the effect that I will go into this matter with him when I come to Toronto. He seems friendly enough personally but the tone of his paper is not friendly.

Dr. Skelton told me that they themselves found it extremely difficult to get the correct angle on Canadian affairs over in the United States press. It was impossible, he said, to keep track of press errors and to stop tendentious articles. The only way to deal with the problem, he added, is to issue positive material themselves. They try, in other words, to prevent mistakes from being made, or, at any rate, to reduce the margin of error, by issuing official statements.

Dr. Skelton asked me how our shortwave news service was getting on. I told him the position as already reported to you. He said that the idea was excellent and he encouraged our perseverance. We should, I submit, pick out a more suitable waveband for broadcasts to Canada and step up the power of the station. Dr. Skelton told me that Canada is now seriously thinking of having a shortwave news service. He thinks its value would be enormous.

I think it might be a good thing if we made one or two official statements here on our position and policy with regard to the war. Maurice Walshe's article in the 'Saturday Evening Post' of the 13th January has been widely read. Several people mentioned it to me, friends came to the office with copies of it days after we had seen it. The Toronto 'Globe and Mail' came out with a slashing attack upon its anti-British tone in a long editorial entitled 'Anti-British Neutrality'. It labelled the article as anti-British propaganda, and called upon the authorities here to stop the

---

[1] Dr David de Waal Meyer, South African Trade Representative to Canada, later Accredited Representative of the Union of South Africa to Canada.

importation of undesirable literature of that kind. I think that if our neutrality policy is given an anti-British interpretation here that will do us harm. I am sending you a pamphlet on Canada and United States Neutrality written by the Editor of 'Saturday Night' where our neutrality is referred to without bias as within our legal rights and an accomplished fact. But not everyone is as enlightened as Mr. Sandwell.[1] Perhaps you would consider sending me a brief statement which I could make sometime about St. Patrick's Day. If you permit Mr. Conway to go to Halifax for the celebrations there on that day perhaps he could make a similar statement at the same time. The statement might deal shortly with e.g. our constitutional position with regard to peace and war and the reasons for our present policy. I emphasise, but must not exaggerate, the importance of this. On the whole we have not a great deal to complain of so far as criticism is concerned, and nothing at all to complain of in the best quarters. I am thinking, however, of the newspapers. I feel it would be a good thing for us to give them one clear, positive and persuasive statement of our whole position. I would not submit to you that we should go on repeating it but just that we put ourselves on record once in some official way. I do not know whether you would wish also to add something about the internal situation at home, something that would beat down on phrases like 'Irish turmoil'. Our friend John Steele[2] in a shortwave broadcast on 'The European Scene' from London a fortnight or so ago gave two minutes out of ten to President Hyde's reference of a constitutional issue to the Supreme Court. He had some nice things to say about Article 26 of the Constitution being an ingenious Irish contribution to the solution of problems peculiar to countries governed under written Constitutions.[3] I mention this as an example (not a good example, perhaps, but it is to hand) of how news of the country can be made to illustrate life and conditions in Ireland at the present time. No doubt that is what your shortwave news broadcasts are doing: but we do not get them here. Senator McGuire (Toronto) and Mr. Leddy (Saskatoon) came together to see me yesterday, the latter to invite me to Saskatchewan University. They both said that the question people are mostly asking them (who are regarded as, and in fact are representative Irish Canadians) is 'What's wrong with Ireland, why isn't she in the war?' I explained the position to them and they went away entirely satisfied. (I followed the lines of your previous instructions.) They are splendid types of men, well to do, and in high standing. Senator McGuire organized Toronto Irishmen behind the Mansion House Conference in 1919.

I hope you will not think that I am laying too much emphasis on my submission that we should issue an official statement, or that I should say something in public along the lines suggested. In my broadcast I avoided political issues altogether as you directed and that was wise on that occasion. I feel, however, more and more the need for a clear-cut positive line. It would confirm our friends in their faith in the present national leadership and it might help to bring journals now not favourable a little nearer to us. I hope (when I move out of Ottawa) to get in touch personally with the editors and others who control the policy of those journals. The press here in Ottawa want me to keep them right. Mr. Grattan O'Leary, e.g.

---

[1] Bernard K. Sandwell (1876-1954), editor of *Saturday Night*, a liberal Canadian general-interest magazine.
[2] BBC journalist based in London with whom Walshe was in correspondence and who later often took an anti-Irish line, apparently inspired by the Ministry of Information.
[3] The Article dealing with the reference of Bills to the Supreme Court.

asked me on the 13th January at our house to draw his attention to anything we do not like in the 'Journal'. He apologised for the map to which we took exception and agreed it was a bad mistake made through inadvertence. Many have told me that the press has improved in tone generally towards Ireland since our arrival and that editors are gradually realizing that there is an Irish mission in Ottawa taking note of what is said and quietly drawing attention to any mistakes about the facts of current Irish history. I thought it right to ask the Minister for Finance, through Dr. Skelton, to delete from the print of his broadcast speech last week, on the 200,000,000 dollars Canadian War Loan, a reference to the Irishman who asked whether a certain fight was a private fight or could anyone join in. Mr. Ralston[1] gladly deleted the reference and expressed his gratitude to me (Dr. Skelton had supported me). Mr. Ralston had meant no harm, of course (he is a good friend of ours), but on the other hand, I thought it right to have attention drawn (without fuss) to the reference in a speech of such importance by a member of the Cabinet.

Let me add two more instances which would appear to show the necessity for a positive interpretation of our position. In a recent broadcast from Toronto, a sort of 'cavalcade' of events of the year 1939, the compàre said 'February 1939: Premier de Valera announces that Éire will support the mother country in the event of war'! Again, in the Canadian Hansard for the 17th March 1939 I find the following:

'National Defence:

Attitude of Mr. De Valera and Canadian Departmental Estimates'.

On the orders of the day:

MR. DANIEL McIVOR (Fort William): I should like to direct a question to the Minister of National Defence (Mr. MacKenzie) with the view that the estimates of his department might be cut down. As Mr. De Valera has now decided to fight alongside of Great Britain, do we now need to spend as much on national defence?

Hon. IAN MACKENZIE (Minister of National Defence): I greatly appreciate that splendid Hibernian contribution to national defence.

These examples show how events and speeches can be misinterpreted. Our answer to these statements might, perhaps, be a short account of Mr. De Valera's Statements on his neutrality policy before and since the outbreak of war.

[signed] JOHN J. HEARNE

No. 112 NAI DFA Secretary's Files S113

Code telegram from the Department of External Affairs to the Irish Legation, Washington DC
(No. 11) (Personal) (Copy)

DUBLIN, 26 January 1940

Please endeavour secure intervention of State Department and President in favour of reprieve of death sentence on Barnes and Richards. You should consider whether indirect approach through influential persons who understand the situation or direct approach to State Department the more efficacious. You can say execution of these men for political crime bound to cause a wave of sympathy here and in America and to increase difficulties already very great for Governments concerned.

---

[1] James Layton Ralston (1881-1948), Canadian Minister for Finance (1939-40), Minister for National Defence (1940-4).

You should point out necessity in the general interest of pressing for removal of the root cause of all these dangers – Partition.

No. 113 NAI DFA Secretary's Files A20/3

> Letter from Leopold H. Kerney to Joseph P. Walshe (Dublin)
> (M. 10/11)
>
> MADRID, 26 January 1940

Frank Ryan. Your 244/8B

I would suggest the desirability of making it known through the medium of the Spanish Minister in Dublin, that any action by me here on Ryan's behalf has been taken in accordance with your wishes and instructions; this would give a fresh opportunity for the Spanish Minister to report to his Government in the matter.[1] There may still be a lingering doubt here as to whether my attitude is governed by personal motives; recently Casa Rojas asked me, somewhat casually, whether my talk with him about Ryan was to be taken as official; moreover, Champourcin (who has, I think, certain friendships about which I find it discreet not to enquire) makes this same suggestion to me, and I should not be surprised if he had heard some doubt expressed and which should be dispelled.

No. 114 NAI DFA 2006/39

> Confidential report from John W. Dulanty to Joseph P. Walshe (Dublin)
> (No. 6) (Secret) (Copy)
>
> LONDON, 26 January 1940

I hear today from Sir Eric Machtig that the Police authorities in London have received information as to the possibility of an attack by the I.R.A. on Sir John Maffey. They are well aware of and appreciate the steps already taken by us in order to guard against the possibility of such an attack but it seems to them right that they should pass to us this information which is to the following effect.

It is said that the I.R.A. chiefs have decided that one of the first steps to be taken when they start hostilities will be to kidnap Sir John Maffey and that there is grave danger that he might be killed at once, although for the moment at least the decision is that he should be held as a hostage for the release of any I.R.A. leaders who may be captured.

They point out that they are not of course in a position to assess the reliability of this information.

No. 115 NAI DFA 2006/39

> Confidential report from John W. Dulanty to Joseph P. Walshe (Dublin)
> (No. 8) (Secret) (Copy)
>
> LONDON, 27 January 1940

Mr. Eden asked me to see him last evening.

He referred to a conversation which he had with me a few days ago when I told him in reply to his question that I thought my Government were considering

---

[1] See No. 127.

the question of sending without further delay a Minister to Berlin. I told him that I thought the position was being explored with a view to finding a procedure for such an appointment which would obviate any matter of Credence. It would, as I understood the matter, be for the time being at any rate an appointment mid-way between that of a fully accredited Minister and that of a Chargé d'Affaires.

Mr. Eden said that neither he nor the Foreign Office were aware of any intermediate grade between that of Minister and Chargé d'Affaires. What the Foreign Office would prefer would be to leave matters exactly as they are. In view of what I had already told him as to the urgent need for some really competent person to look after our interests he saw that this course could not be adopted. At considerable length he begged us to consider making the new appointment for the time being in the rank of Chargé d'Affaires. He was afraid any other course would have very serious consequences for them.

Both he and Mr. Chamberlain had done what they could to keep the relations of the two countries on a good footing. They were most anxious to continue that state of affairs. He thought for example they had been helpful on trade matters.

When they, Canada, Australia, South Africa, and New Zealand, accepted our new Constitution as not being fundamentally incompatible with the principles of the British Commonwealth they did feel that there was still a thread or link of association – however tenuous that might be – between ourselves and the members of the Commonwealth in that the King would still be used as an organ in this particular procedure of appointment of Ministers abroad. From their point of view he could not stress the seriousness of the matter if even this slight thread were broken. Any description containing the word Minister would make a most serious position for them.

The conversation lasted for more than an hour and I think there is no doubt that Mr. Eden was very worried about the matter. He had been in consultation with Lord Halifax and with Mr. Chamberlain and was sending an urgent message to the United Kingdom Representative in Dublin.

No. 116 NAI DFA Secretary's Files S113

Letter from Eamon de Valera to Anthony Eden (London)
(Copy)

DUBLIN, 29 January 1940

Dear Mr. Eden,

Although I am sure that Sir John Maffey has already given you a full report of my views in the case of the condemned men, Barnes and Richards, I feel, on account of its importance and its bearing on the relations between our two countries, that I should myself write to you about it.

I realise all the difficulties which the exercise of the prerogative in this case will present to your Government. I know that these men have been convicted of murder, in accordance with law, and that a considerable body of your public opinion may demand that the full penalty be exacted. I know, too, that at the present time, in the circumstances of war, your Government may think that it is necessary to be stern and feel that clemency may be misunderstood.

Nevertheless, I am convinced that it will be a mistake if you let these considerations prevail. There are, in my opinion, considerations of higher policy which dictate the opposite course. The history of the relations between our two countries has already been much stained with blood. Each succeeding generation of your countrymen have deplored the unwisdom of their predecessors and themselves fallen into the very errors they condemned. Ought you not to make sure that you avoid doing likewise, and should we not on both sides endeavour with all our strength to prevent the old round of violence and counter-violence beginning afresh. Our two Governments have achieved much towards putting the relations between the two countries on a level of decency. Is it not the best statesmanship to persevere resolutely in that course?

I believe that if your Government give this matter full consideration, they will agree. If these men are executed, the relations between our peoples will almost certainly deteriorate. It will matter little that Barnes and Richards have been found guilty of murder. With the background of our history, and the existence of partition, many will refuse to regard their action in that light. They will think only of the cause these men had it in mind to serve.

The moment Barnes and Richards are dead, they may well, in popular opinion, be enrolled in the long list of Irishmen who in varying conditions gave their lives in an effort to free their people, or to resist oppression. The execution of these men will give rise to new and bitter antagonisms between us which countries who see their profit in them will not hesitate to exploit. Is it wise, with eyes open, to permit this thing to happen?

Sincerely yours,
(Signed) EAMON DE VALERA

No. 117 NAI DFA 205/70

Minute from Frederick H. Boland to Joseph P. Walshe (Dublin) with later handwritten comment by Sheila G. Murphy (Dublin)
(205/70)

DUBLIN, 29 January 1940

When the German Minister was here on Friday, he said that he was afraid that the Vatican Broadcast accusing Germany of atrocities and religious persecution in Poland had done the German cause a great deal of harm in this country. He knew from experience how much anything in the nature of persecution of the Catholic Church was resented in Ireland. Both the Vatican report, and the other reports of German religious persecution in Poland which had appeared in the Press, were false, and had a definitely propagandist object. They had been strongly denied by the German Official News Agency, and the text of this denial had been sent by Dr. Petersen, the Press Attaché, to the newspapers here. He hoped very much that the denial would be published, and he thought this so important that he felt justified in asking the Department to speak to the newspapers or the Censor, with a view to ensuring that the German denial received due publicity. For this purpose, Herr Hempel gave me the text of the denial (copy attached).[1]

I told Herr Hempel that I had some doubts whether it would be possible to do what he asked. Our censorship was negative rather than positive. It could tell the

---

[1] Not printed.

papers what they must not print but I doubted whether it could tell the papers what to print. Quite apart from the question of legal powers, the Censor might very well feel that an approach to certain newspapers here with a suggestion that they should print a particular piece of news, even if the approach were made on an entirely informal basis, might expose him to the risk of serious criticism. Herr Hempel said that he appreciated these objections. He could very well see that there might be difficulty in the case of the 'Irish Times' and the 'Irish Independent' but he would be satisfied if the denial were printed by the 'Irish Press.'

I told Herr Hempel that I would put the matter before you.

[initialled] F.H.B.

A/Secy,
You will see from attached cutting of 27th January that the Irish Press published the German denial in full. They also gave on the 1st February a report of Dr. Seyss-Inquyart's speech. S.[heila] G. M.[urphy] 3/2/40

No. 118 NAI DFA 2006/39

Letter from Joseph P. Walshe to John W. Dulanty (London)
(Secret)

DUBLIN, 1 February 1940

Dear High Commissioner,
The Department of Defence ordered trench mortar ammunition from the firm of Brandt, Paris, in the earlier months of last year, and an advance payment of £21,000 was made in June. The total amount of the order is £72,270. The details are as follows:-
23,390 rounds of 81 mm. Brandt trench mortar ammunition at £1.17.0 per round;
700 rounds of 81 mm. Brandt trench mortar ammunition at £3.17.0 per round.
This ammunition was to be made up in 2,166 packages.

The French firm has been postponing the delivery of this ammunition, putting forward different pretexts. Our Minister in Paris intervened with the French Government for the purpose of expediting delivery, but so far without effect. It now transpires that the cause of the delay is anxiety on the part of the French Government lest the British Government should object to the completion of the transaction. Although normally we should of course profoundly object to these suspicions on the part of the French Government, war conditions oblige us to swallow the affront. In the circumstances, there seems to be no alternative to taking the realist view and to asking the Secretary of State for the Dominions to have instructions issued to the British Embassy in Paris for the purpose of conveying to the French Government that the British Government have no objection.

I should be glad to know the answer received to your request as soon as possible.

The Department of Defence are, of course, aware that there will be difficulties in relation to transport, but it will be time enough to raise that question when we know that there is no further obstacle to the release of the ammunition.

Yours sincerely,
[signed] J.P. WALSHE

No. 119 NAI DFA 2006/39

Handwritten minute from Joseph P. Walshe to John W. Dulanty (London) enclosing the text of a letter from Eamon de Valera to Neville Chamberlain

DUBLIN, 2 February 1940

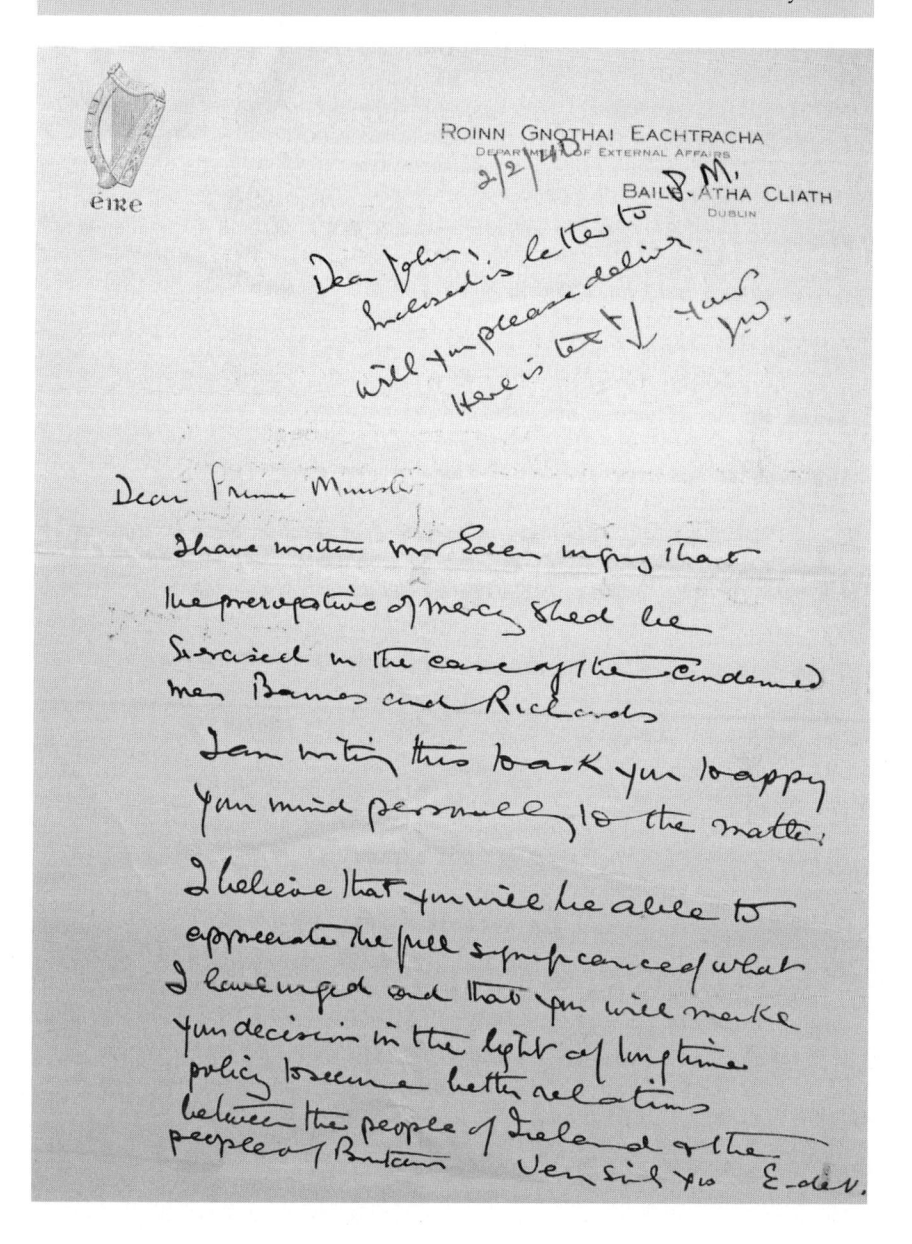

Dear John,

Enclosed is letter to P.M. Will you please deliver. Here is text of your yours.

Dear Prime Minister,

I have written Mr Eden urging that the prerogative of mercy should be exercised in the case of the condemned men Barnes and Richards.

I am writing this to ask you to apply your mind personally to the matter.

I believe that you will be able to appreciate the full significance of what I have urged and that you will make your decision in the light of long time policy to secure better relations between the people of Ireland & the people of Britain.

Very sincerely yours, E. de V.

No. 120 NAI DFA Secretary's Files S113

Letter from Eamon de Valera to Neville Chamberlain (London)
(Copy)

DUBLIN, 2 February 1940

Dear Prime Minister,

I have written Mr. Eden[1] urging that the prerogative of mercy should be exercised in the case of the condemned men, Barnes and Richards. I am writing this to ask you to apply your mind personally to the matter. I believe that you will be able to appreciate the full significance of what I have urged and that you will make your decision in the light of long-time policy to secure better relations between the people of Ireland and the people of Britain.

Very sincerely yours,
(Signed) EAMON DE VALERA

No. 121 NAI DFA Secretary's Files S113

Code telegram from the Irish Legation, Washington DC to the Department of External Affairs, Dublin
(No. 15) (Personal) (Copy)

WASHINGTON, 3 February 1940

Your despatch 11.[2] The State Department refused to intervene but accepted yesterday Friday statement from me for the President who is in Hyde Park.[3] Walker also contacted him. The British ambassador at Washington had no reply but assured me that his cable had gone to the highest authority.

No. 122 NAI DFA 2006/39

Letter from Eamon de Valera to Neville Chamberlain (London)
(Copy)

DUBLIN, 5 February 1940

Prime Minister

I have received your decision with sorrow and dismay. The reprieve of these men would be regarded as an act of generosity which would be a thousand times more valuable to Britain than anything that could possibly be gained by their death. The latter will be looked upon as an act fitting only too sadly into the historic background of our relations. Almost superhuman patience is required on both sides to exorcise feelings which the knowledge of centuries of wrongdoing have engendered. I hasten with a final entreaty that these executions be not permitted to take place.

EAMON DE VALERA

---

[1] See No. 116.
[2] See No. 112.
[3] President Roosevelt's birthplace, home and place of burial in Dutchess County, New York State.

No. 123 NAI DFA Secretary's Files S113

Confidential report from John W. Dulanty to Joseph P. Walshe (Dublin)
(No. 11) (Secret)

LONDON, 6 February 1940

I saw the Prime Minister on his return from France this evening

He was aware that I had had many conversations with Mr. Eden about Barnes and Richards and he had learned from Mr. Eden and from Sir John Simon that Mr. de Valera had said he would fly over from Dublin to London if it would have been of any avail.

I made no apology for appealing to him even at the eleventh hour to reverse the decision, the ill consequences of which would be so serious to both England and Ireland.

Mr. Chamberlain broke in and said that I need not go over the grounds that have already been covered. He felt sure he knew the arguments both for and against the suggested reprieve.

There was I suggested an aspect of the matter which was of great importance and had developed with rapidity in the last few days and that was the fact that the feeling of grave apprehension now embraced every section of opinion in Ireland. I referred to the Irish Times leader, part of which Mr. Walshe had given me over the telephone, and also the Evening Mail. I told him of the action of the Protestant Archbishop of Dublin, the Chief Rabbi, the large number of publicly elected representative bodies. All this on the Irish side. I then referred to the Manchester Guardian leader, to the appeal signed by H.W. Nevinson,[1] Professor Haldane,[2] D. N. Pritt[3] and others. I mentioned that Cardinal Hinsley[4] who had spoken in emphatic terms against the I.R.A. was at that moment writing a personal note to him, Mr. Chamberlain. I further told him that just before leaving to see him there came into my office Sir John Squire,[5] one of the greatest if not the greatest of the living English poets, to ask me whether there was anything he could do to prevent this awful calamity.

Mr. Chamberlain said he thought he was aware of all this. 'Certainly I recognise' he said 'that on this matter Ireland is speaking as one, which only increases our difficulties'. He said I must assure Mr. de Valera that they were almost as much worried about these sentences as he was. He thought there was malign fate opposing the desire for good relations between the two countries. The Irish Government certainly did not want this dreadful situation nor did they. He was sorry for Mr. de Valera and he was also rather sorry for himself. After going into some details of the horrors of the crime – mentioning for example that the young woman who was shortly to be married was so mutilated that she could only be identified by an engagement ring and part of a shoe – he mentioned that only the alertness of the police prevented many more lives being lost. There had now been hundreds of

---

[1] Henry W. Nevinson (1856-1941), journalist, author and social activist.
[2] Professor J.B.S. 'Jack' Haldane (1892-1964), a British geneticist; a Marxist and member of the Communist Party of Great Britain.
[3] Denis N. Pritt KC (1887-1972), British Labour MP for Hammersmith North.
[4] Arthur Hinsley (1865-1943), Catholic Archbishop of Westminster (1935-43).
[5] Sir John Collings Squire (1884-1958), editor and poet.

explosions, over ninety injuries and seven deaths. It was clearly the duty of any Government to protect the lives of its citizens but would I make clear to Mr. de Valera that they had not come to this decision lightly. They had taken the very unusual course of having the matter discussed at two meetings of the Cabinet, one of which was summoned to consider this and no other business. In addition there had been numerous conversations between individual Ministers. He, and he felt sure, his colleagues also would have been glad if they could have seen a way out but he felt that there would have been such a wave of indignation throughout England that they had no choice but to refuse a reprieve. Probably the relations between the two countries would suffer some deterioration. He hoped that might not be so and he hoped further that it would be only temporary. He begged me again to let Mr. de Valera know of his concern and to say that he was as deeply impressed as ever with the importance of improving Irish relations.

I said that was not the occasion for any contentious talk but he would remember that all through the 1938 conversations Mr. de Valera made it clear that so long as the cancer of the Northern trouble remained in our body politic there could be no immunity for either side from dangerous political conditions. Mr. Chamberlain, who looked tired after his long journey, said that he would have to talk about that when he was less exhausted.

[signed] J.W. DULANTY

No. 124 NAI DFA Secretary's Files S113

Note for file by Joseph P. Walshe (Dublin)
DUBLIN, 7 February 1940

Efforts to reprieve Barnes and Richards
Events of Tuesday, February 6th
The High Commissioner kept in touch with the Dominions Office throughout the day and spoke several times with Mr. Eden. The latter had at no time given Mr. Dulanty any hope of a reprieve, though he said that he was making every effort to secure it. The High Commissioner believed that Mr. Eden was genuinely worried about the situation. I telephoned to the High Commissioner in the early forenoon to inform him that the Taoiseach would be ready to fly to London if he thought that such a step would help the British Government to accede to our request. Mr. Eden thought that no change could be brought about by the Taoiseach's journey to London. Mr. Dulanty called by arrangement at Buckingham Palace about 11 o'clock for the purpose of asking the King to intervene. The King conveyed to him, through his Private Secretary,[1] that he would ask the Prime Minister to come to see him on his return from France in the afternoon to discuss the matter with him.[2] The High Commissioner was kept informed hour by hour of the development in the situation here, and he conveyed to the British Government the fullest information about the growing volume of appeals from all public bodies and all sections of the population. He also gave to the Dominions Office the text of a wire received by the Taoiseach from Tom Barry,[3] to the effect that if a delay of four days were granted,

---

[1] Alexander Hardinge (1894-1960), 2nd Baron Hardinge of Penshurst.
[2] See No. 123.
[3] Thomas Barry (1897-1980), IRA Flying Column leader in Cork during the Irish War of Independence.

he would go to the Home Secretary in London and produce evidence to prove that the condemned men were not guilty of the Coventry outrage. Mr. Sowby, the Warden of St. Columba's College, remained with us in the Department for the four hours phoning to influential people in England asking for their intercession. At his request, the Archbishop of Canterbury called on the Prime Minister at 5.30, and other influential people – amongst them the Dean of Westminster, Lord Sankey, and the Archbishop of York, intervened. The Taoiseach received Mr. Sowby at the end of his visit to the Department and thanked him for his zealous efforts, and expressed the view to Mr. Sowby that the intervention of the Archbishop of Canterbury was now the only hope of success. Mr. Sowby showed himself a true friend of peace and good relations with Great Britain, and his extraordinary anxiety and effective zeal in that cause deserve the greatest possible gratitude from the Government. The High Commissioner saw Cardinal Hinsley and asked him to use his good offices. The Cardinal wrote a letter to Mr. Chamberlain. Sir John Squire, the Literary Editor of the 'Times' and of the 'Statesman', got several of London's most prominent journalists to join with him in urging on the British Government the need of adopting a favourable attitude.

Towards 7 o'clock in the evening the High Commissioner saw Mr. Chamberlain[1] and received from him a message to the Taoiseach regretting that he had no choice in the matter, as considerations of overwhelming force prevented any alteration of the Government's decision not to grant a reprieve. He hoped, however, that good relations between the two countries would not be interrupted, or at least that they would not be interrupted for more than a short time. About 10 o'clock Mr. Antrobus, Secretary of the British Legation, phoned me a similar message for the Taoiseach from the Prime Minister. This message did not refer to any disturbance of good relations. On Monday evening the following message had been sent by Mr. Eden for the Taoiseach, through the Secretary of the British Legation:-

'Mr. de Valera's letter has been fully and sympathetically considered, and we entirely appreciate the spirit in which it was written. Nevertheless, after the fullest examination of all the facts and circumstances of the case, I regret to have to inform him that the conclusion has been reached that the law must be allowed to take its course.'

A letter confirming this message was received yesterday morning. The two men were executed at 9.15 this morning.

[initialled] J.P.W.

No. 125 NAI DFA Legal Adviser's Papers

Memorandum by Michael Rynne (Dublin)
(Secret)

DUBLIN, 7 February 1940

Some Queries and Theories on the Present Situation (7th February, 1940)
1. The first query which it seems well to set down for reply is this: Why did the British Government return the Irish ports in 1938?

In view of the indisputable fact that in British minds, Admiralty and otherwise,

---

[1] See No. 123.

the ports of Southern Ireland have always ranked as vital factors in British offensive and defensive naval strategy, the reply cannot be that the relevant treaty provisions were surrendered because the ports to which they referred had lost all importance for Great Britain. In 1938 the British Admiralty was preparing for a new offensive on the European trade-routes.

Following from this we may discount the theory that the ports were given back to us for 'keeps'. The question, therefore, resolves itself to 'why were the ports lent to us?'

There was no irresistible moral pressure brought to bear by the Irish Government in the matter and there was no adequate *quid pro quo* offered or accepted.

Nevertheless, one cannot be sure that the British action was simply 'a gesture of appeasement', 'a free gift to a free people'.

Even if we admit that some of the above elements entered into the decision of the British Government, we cannot pretend that their cumulative effect outweighed, in British minds, the vital interests of the British Empire.

It is submitted therefore, that the reasons why Ireland was allowed to become tenant-at-will of the treaty ports were as follows:

(a) the Treaty of 1921 had been all but repudiated by the Fianna Fáil Government. They could not have been trusted to honour their outworn 'obligations' to the extent of actually *protecting* British troops in their enjoyment of the ports in wartime. Yet, it was more than probable that those troops at such a time would be harried by disaffected Irish persons;

(b) In order to carry out their own protective measures with success, it would certainly be necessary for British garrisons at the ports to push into the hinterland to some extent.

Any such encroachments, to which even the doubtful treaty made no reference, express or implied, would seem certain to evoke protests from the Irish Government, which might be difficult to refute in a plausible way. Moreover, if the Southern Irelanders reacted badly and comforted the snipers, a large number of troops would be required to control the occupied areas.

Here it may be recalled that in 1938, the British Foreign Office was working hard to acquire allies and, particularly, to curry favour with the United States and, furthermore, that in 1938, the British War Office had not overcome the obstacles to conscription and that they expected a war in France which would have required the bulk of Britain's man-power.

(c) As a result of two Irish initiatives, the retention of the treaty rights was rendered more difficult, viz. (1) the fact that the Six County issue was loosely coupled with the issue of the ports, made the latter the lesser of two evils and harder to refuse, and (2) the fact that the Irish Government reiterated their resolve not to allow Ireland to be made a jumping-off ground for Britain's enemies, made the release of the ports easier to explain to uneducated public opinion in Great Britain. (Needless to remark the explanation could not be expected to satisfy the naval experts.) Supposing that in view of the two foregoing considerations, the return of the ports had been refused, the Irish Government would have been entirely freed from even the most theoretical duty to co-operate with the British garrisons to put down Irish extremists and they might, without any loss of face, decide not to carry out their more or less conditional pledge to repel Britain's enemies. In such a state of facts, any public opinion or popular sympathy which might survive the British world-censorship could not be other than unfavourable to Britain.

(d) By acceding to the Irish appeal to wipe out the Treaty clauses relating to the ports the British Government aimed at a number of miscellaneous objects viz.,
- (i) the postponement of the Six-County issue;
- (ii) the conclusion of a commercial agreement which would tend to throw back the Irish national economy to its pre-Fianna Fáil condition of dependence on Britain. (Also desirable as a wartime factor);
- (iii) the easier acceptance by Ireland of a tribute of £10,000,000 cash. (Useful for subsidising the arming of Czechs while retarding the development of Irish defence plans), and
- (iv) the excellent moral effect of the 'gesture' on the world at large and especially on Germany, the United States and the sceptical ally, France.

But these were only the minor motives which influenced the British.

(e) The main argument for giving the Irish Government the use of the harbours during peace-time was, undoubtedly, to be drawn from the improved prospects of occupying them efficiently in time of need.

Admitted that the ports can only be availed of to the fullest advantage when, either (1) backed 100% by a friendly Irish Government or (2) backed by the total occupation of Southern Ireland by a British Army of Occupation, unthreatened by a united Irish people. These alternatives were brought nearer by the concession of the ports. At the best, Ireland might have declared war on Britain's side and thus opened her strategic harbours to all allied men-of-war, at the worst, she might be argued to have betrayed the confidence reposed in her by Mr. Chamberlain and so to have rendered herself liable to the just use of force.

Either alternative would suit the military man, and perhaps the latter would be preferred by him to the former. In the one case the control of supplies, rolling-stock etc., necessary to the functioning of the ports, would have resided in a native Government, in the other, the country and all it contained would belong to the British forces for the duration. Only the civilian departments would be troubled by the forceful occupation of Ireland by their military friends. To them would fall the task of 'justifying' the move politically and silencing criticism abroad.

2. Our second question, therefore, must be this: Why, seeing that Ireland did not declare war on England's side, has no action yet been taken to regain the ports for Britain?

There are several answers to this query. They may be, however, condensed into two, viz. (1) there was no necessity to occupy the ports; (2) there was no suitable opportunity for doing so.

The fact that the war has so far been a winter campaign has driven enemy submarines into home waters. There was no need to patrol the Atlantic after the month of September, 1939. The fact that Scapa Flow, the Shetlands etc., were not rendered uncomfortable until recent months relieved the British Admiralty of the need to secure alternative deep sea harbours.

In parenthesis, let it be noted that the coming of Spring may intensify the submarine war off our coasts and the air war against the ordinary British naval bases within easy range of Germany.

There was no very good opportunity of securing our ports up to this, assuming that there was even a necessity for them from the Admiralty's technical standpoint.

Militarily speaking, the claim could not have been backed with force without diminishing to ridiculous proportions the available troops for France, where hostilities were vaguely expected and where French *mauvaise foi* had to be beguiled away.

There was absolutely no reasonable excuse for an invasion of Ireland whose Government had been studiously correct in regard to the war, the English bombings etc., and whose relations with the world at large had not so far become the plaything of German propaganda. The new-found unity of the Irish people on the neutrality issue must have astonished the British Government as much as it surprised many people at home. So long as the people were united on any large political issue, they could not be relied upon to split in case of a British invasion. The 'War Party' here had signally failed to absorb even the normal pro-British element. In short, it would have been a costly mistake to have attempted force against Ireland in the last few months, even had the necessity been there. How could Finland have been played up successfully in the American (British-bought) Press if Ireland had been similarly treated by a 'democratic' Britain? America may be secretly feared and despised but during the last few months, prior to the inauguration of 'Cash and Carry', it was necessary to woo her.

3. Our third question must inevitably be this: When will our ports be retaken by Great Britain?

The answer to this query can be 'Never' only in two cases viz. (1) if the war ends almost at once and (2) if we are able to preserve such unity among our people, under the present Government, that the planned invasion will still look too costly.

Apart from that, the answer must be: very soon now, as part of the Spring offensive or in a matter of months when the Irish situation has had time to 'develop' and the foreign publicity per Reuter has had time to take effect.

4. As a fourth question, in amplification of the foregoing, we may ask: How is the Irish situation going to so deteriorate as to enable the British to occupy the whole of Ireland in 1940?

In reply we may well assume that the deterioration has been already artificially put under way.

It is only too clear that the British Government's refusal to reprieve the Birmingham Irishmen[1] was based not on the facts of their case (no one believes that they were more than accomplices before a criminal accident) nor on the law (for, even according to English law their trial with the women prisoners was open to strong criticism) nor on public opinion (because, even in England there was an influential element in favour of reprieve and no blood-lust campaign in the Press).

Consequently, it must be assumed that the refusal to grant a reprieve was due to the policy of the Government which denied it. It is idle to argue that some of the British Cabinet were in favour of reprieve and it is not convincing to argue that one of them at least may have hoped that the executions would prove a deterrent to other wrongdoers (apart from the lessons of Irish history, there were bombings in England up to the day of the executions). The fact must be that 'Plan No. 2', by which all Ireland is to be brought under wartime control, has now been launched.

---

[1] See No. 124.

In time of war, military departments must always act on the assumption that hostilities will last for an indefinitely long period ahead, that no useful war measure, however difficult to carry out, should be postponed if it can be attempted at all; civilian departments, even while planning for post-war conditions, are compelled to recognise that so long as the war lasts, the soldiers must be allowed the decisive voice. If it should transpire, in connection with the Birmingham executions, that all the running was made by non-military members of the Government, that would not mean that the Admiralty and the War Office were opposed to a reprieve. Had they been so opposed (pointing out, perhaps, that the executions would render Ireland likely to prove troublesome to the successful progress of the war) they would have had to be heard and obeyed.

5. The final question for reply is, naturally, this: What can the Irish Government do to thwart Plan No. 2?

That will depend somewhat on what the British do, assuming that an endeavour is not made to forestall them. Probably the British hope to see the situation develop (with the active encouragement of their 'information' Bureau, Intelligence Service, etc.) as follows:

(a) Following Ash Wednesday's executions, a complete disintegration of the Fianna Fáil Government's support is looked for. Instead of containing a fairly solid centre of peace-loving 'neutrals' unsympathetic to Britain and Germany alike, plus the usual pro-British (but not active) Right Wing and pro-I.R.A. (but not active) Left Wing, it is hoped to see, at first, a breakup of the centre due to the majority going left.

(b) The next phase should be marked by a crescendo programme of outrages in England. At this stage it might be feasible to embarrass the Government by appealing to them publicly to co-operate in tracking down the criminals. A refusal would suit as well as the contrary. Any effort to elude the issue could be spread abroad as a national conspiracy against Britain which, since she gave Ireland back her ports, is fighting for democracy with one hand tied.

(c) The next move might be to deport the whole Irish male population of Great Britain (minus those in khaki) back to Ireland where they could be relied upon to make it still hotter for the Government.

(d) When all the powers of censorship and other emergency measures had ceased to check or conceal the discontent here, we might be faced with (i) a 'German Plot'[1] story such as was tried once before (ii) a threat to dock supplies owing to the losses of shipping off the Irish coasts.

(e) As soon as the Irish people seemed about to boil over, the Government might be asked for the use of at least one treaty harbour in the common interest. When they refused, supplies might drop somewhat while transport would not be regularly available for Irish cattle.

(f) In a reasonably short time it might be anticipated that the mass of the people would be ready for the coup d'etat which would 'justify' the reoccupation of Ireland.

---

[1] On the occasion of the so-called 'German Plot' of 1918 the British announced that they had evidence of collaboration between Sinn Féin and the German High Command. Many Sinn Féin leaders were arrested and imprisoned on the fabricated charge of treasonable activities with England's German enemies.

(g) The fact that all this unsettled state of affairs was ruining business in Ireland, terrifying many older people etc., would be all to the good inasmuch as it would tend to build up the nucleus of a pro-British party which would support even a puppet Government for the duration of the war, or of the puppet Government.

All this line of conjecture is very easy to arrive at and most people are already tightening their belts in anticipation. But need it come to pass? After all it is no more than the somewhat crude plan of British Government Departments responsible for the conduct of the war. Even if it turned out, in practice, to be a much subtler plan (e.g. if occupation were to be bracketed with an immediate measure of political unity with the North) it could not be necessarily forced on us.

We have, therefore, two courses open to us: (1) to hope that Plan No. 2 will be nipped in the bud by the British civilian Departments, that the whole thing will 'blow over', with the help of press censorship and the desire of so many citizens for a peaceful life, or, (2) to take it for granted that the Plan may be on its way and to prepare the world for our resistance to its consummation.

There can be no third alternative, such as that much-talked-of last resort of 'declaring the Republic' – if it ever comes to that, the Plan is as good a *fait accompli*. Personally, I feel that the situation might even yet be saved by the rapid defeat of Britain on sea and in the air. That is to say, that her prospects of victory in this round might appear so feeble in a few months that she may decide to seize on one of the many peace proposals and so postpone her designs on Europe for another decade or two.

But, seeing that States cannot be governed on the basis of miraculous aid, it would seem wisest to set about acting now as though Plan No. 2 had been put on foot.

This the Government can only do by explaining frankly to the people (i.e. the still unbroken centre block behind Fianna Fáil) what it may mean for them if they decide to give undue vent to their resentment of the Birmingham executions. Those that believe only that 'England's difficulty is Ireland's opportunity' (but fail to realise that the contrary is also the case) will scarcely listen to the facts. Their numbers need not, however, be too considerably augmented, if the whole truth be told.

The truth is this: The Birmingham executions doubtless represent the initiation of a vigorous campaign against the I.R.A. in Great Britain, but they stand for more than that.

In Ireland it is the Government which has just been flouted by the British Government. Why? Not because they supported the I.R.A. in Britain: they never condoned the bombings although they left nothing undone to save the lives of the condemned men. Surely, the slap in the face administered to the Irish Government and people by the British Cabinet can only be regarded as an attempt to spur them into revolt, perhaps even to drive them out of their neutrality into the arms of Britain's enemies who (like the rest of the world) are once more talking of Ireland as a 'problem' – 'a problem once again!' If that is so, and that *is* so, then it bodes no good for the Irish State, which has achieved such a measure of freedom that no foreigner may set foot on her soil without the people's permission.

The inviolability of Irish soil is as sacred to us as that of Finland is to the Finns. Our people, therefore, must not let themselves be provoked into such a condition of anti-British feeling, because of the way they and their Government have been spurned, as to appear to give encouragement to the few in Britain who have sinister intentions in our regard. Those few are mistaken if they think their plans will be facilitated by a disunited Irish people; they will be foiled by a united nation and by the use of force, if necessary.

Unless the foregoing issues are made clear at a very early stage it is hard to see how the Government can check an epidemic of rainbow-chasing during the next few weeks. If it were decided to face up to the menace at home in the way suggested, there is no doubt that it might be well to send out the same line, in diplomatic language, to America and elsewhere. In fact it might be best to open up the campaign abroad, before officially broaching it here. That is a question of tactics; the main thing is to unite the people for defence before they prepare for war and to prepare the world for another adventure in the tradition of perfidious Albion' and so render it next to impossible.

[initialled M.R.]

No. 126 NAI DFA 219/4

Extracts from a confidential report from William Warnock to Joseph P. Walshe (Dublin)
(43/33)

BERLIN, 8 February 1940

The execution of the two members of the I.R.A. in Birmingham yesterday is reported in the most prominent position in the leading German newspapers this morning, and was also given more space in the evening papers last night. It so happened that on the same day, Dr. Roos,[1] the leader of the Alsatian autonomists was executed in France, and this gave the German Press an excellent opportunity to expose the Western Powers' hypocrisy where the Freedom of small nations is concerned.

Early yesterday morning Dr. Wissmann of the Press Section of the Foreign Office phoned to tell me that he had just received the Havas report of the execution. He was very surprised, as it was expected in the Foreign Office that the British would relent at the last moment.

I was at an official reception for the Diplomatic Corps in the Japanese Embassy yesterday, and amazement at the British action was expressed on all sides, even by such cautious people as the Swiss and the Scandinavians. The Germans are astounded that the British should have voluntarily furnished them with such magnificent material for propaganda. Dr Wissmann told me during our telephone conversation that he would see to it that the affair got full publicity both in the press and over the wireless, and he was as good as his word.
[matter omitted]
The wireless reported the executions in the next news bulletin after they had taken place, and described them of yet another example of British oppression. A long comment was made in the news service in English.

---

[1] Dr Phillipe Roos was executed in Nancy, France, on 7 February 1940 having been found guilty of espionage.

I also heard the Italian news in English last evening. The executions were dealt with most unsympathetically from our point of view. The original explosion at Coventry was referred to as a 'dastardly explosion', and the speaker said that the men 'went to the scaffold' repentant.

[signed] W. WARNOCK

No. 127 NAI DFA Secretary's Files A20/3

> *Letter from Joseph P. Walshe to Juan Garcia Ontiveros (Dublin)*
> *(Confidential)*
>
> DUBLIN, 23 February 1940

Dear Señor Ontiveros,[1]

We understand from Mr. Kerney that the possibility of releasing all foreign prisoners other than criminals is now under examination by the Ministry of Foreign Affairs in Madrid. We are hopeful, therefore, that the case of Mr. Frank Ryan, against whom no criminal charge was made, will shortly be reviewed. It appears, however, that Mr. Kerney is somewhat apprehensive that his persistent representations for the release of Mr. Ryan are regarded in official circles in Spain as being inspired by motives of personal friendship rather than by instructions from the Irish Government. Mr. de Valera would accordingly be very grateful if you would be good enough to take an early opportunity of emphasising to your Government that in all his efforts on Mr. Ryan's behalf Mr. Kerney has acted and continues to act with the full approval and authority of the Irish Government.

Yours sincerely,
[stamped] (signed) J.P. WALSHE

No. 128 NAI DFA 219/49

> *Telegram from Joseph P. Walshe to John J. Hearne (Ottawa)*
> *(No. 13) (Personal) (Copy)*
>
> DUBLIN, 26 February 1940

Your letter 14/28 of 24th January.[2] An official statement out of the question. Privately you could explain neutrality is the natural and only attitude for Ireland with her history of persecution and economic impoverishment, loss of half her population through laisser faire policy etc. To go into the war would mean civil war. That is the universal view here. No need to apologise for our neutrality. The countries at war are fighting for their own immediate material interests. Spiritual evils cannot be cured by the supreme evil of war. All this will be admitted when the war is over as it was after the last war and Canada as well as other countries will admit that the Irish Government was right. For the present we have to be patient under adverse criticism. Even attempts to explain our neutrality publicly would cast some doubt on our conviction of its inherent necessity.

---

[1] See No. 113.
[2] See No. 111.

No. 129 UCDA P194/540

Confidential report from Michael MacWhite to Joseph P. Walshe (Dublin)
(Confidential) (Copy)

ROME, 27 February 1940

The series of explosions and bombings attributed to the Irish Republican Army, which have taken place in England during the past year appear to have alienated much of the sympathy that educated Europeans have invariably felt for Ireland. Honourable methods to achieve success in a just cause are always applauded, but when disfigured by crime and injury to innocent parties, they bring shame and confusion in their train and effectively undo the work they are expected to accomplish.

For weeks, at a stretch, the Italian press gave more than the usual space to I.R.A. activities which were invariably featured under the heading 'I Terroristi Irlandesi', 'The Irish Terrorists', not, as one may conclude, from the title, out of sympathy for Ireland, but rather out of enmity for England, which is not the same thing, and which is but a passing phase of present day politics. Anybody reading continental newspapers and glancing at these headlines from day to day would be led to believe that the Irish were a nation of terrorists whose standards of civilisation compare unfavourably with those of other European countries. The political background of the bombings is not widely known abroad and it inspires but little sympathy even, in the limited circles, where it is best understood.

The name Ireland had made for herself in the international field since her admission to the League of Nations, eighteen years ago, through the independent attitude of her representatives at world conferences, has all but vanished and to restore it in our time will be a difficult undertaking. The damage to our national prestige is incalculable.

In Vatican circles, too, these bombing activities have created considerable embarrassment. Ireland has, after Italy, the highest percentage of Catholics and according to Monsignor Tardini,[1] whom I met a few days ago, protestant Theologians and Divines cite Irish crime as an example of what may be expected in a country where the Catholic religion predominates. This explains, perhaps, why the official organ of the Vatican went to the trouble of telling the world that the Pope could not urge clemency for the two men executed at Birmingham in view of the fact that they had an impartial trial. Britain was, therefore, held up indirectly as a model of justice and fair dealing. Papal condemnation could not go much further. It is also likely to react unfavourably against Catholic priests of Irish origin as the question of the appointment of Bishops in countries like the United States or Canada presents itself. Vatican diplomacy is extremely subtle and sometimes exerts itself where least expected.

Another and more serious aspect of these I.R.A. bombings and the consequent loss of Irish prestige abroad would be keenly felt in case of any unexpected breach of our neutrality by any one of the belligerent powers. We would, unlike Finland, have but few friends to raise their voices on our behalf, as most people would be

---

[1] Monsignor Domenico Tardini (1888-1961), long-serving aide to Pope Pius XII in the Vatican State Secretariat; appointed Cardinal Secretary of State in 1958.

reluctant to plead the cause of a country that showed such a poor sense of its own responsibilities, for the disrepute affects the good name of the whole nation even though the organisation responsible for it may be able to boast of only a few hundred members.

No. 130 NAI CAB 2/3

> Extract from the minutes of a meeting of the Cabinet
> (G.C. 2/149) (Item 2) (S 10133)
>
> DUBLIN, 28 February 1940

New York World's Fair: Participation by Éire
It was decided that Éire should participate in the New York World's Fair, 1940, with a cultural exhibit only at an estimated cost of £5,500–£7,500.

No. 131 NAI DFA 219/4

> Confidential report from William Warnock to Joseph P. Walshe (Dublin)
> (43/33)
>
> BERLIN, 2 March 1940

The storm after the Altmark incident has now died down for the time being.[1] When the news first came through concerning the British attack on the Altmark in Norwegian territorial waters the indignation rose to fever pitch. In that the British had clearly violated Norwegian neutrality there was plenty of scope for the propagandists. At first it was maintained that the Altmark was an ordinary defenceless merchant ship, and no mention was made of her connection with the 'Graf von Spee'. Later she was described as a 'government ship' flying the service flag (not the navy flag).

I was speaking the other day to a neutral journalist who visited Jeseossingfjord a day or two after the incident. He said that the Captain first told him that they were unarmed, but afterwards remarked that they had two machine-guns which had been given to them by the 'Graf von Spee'. There were some bullet-holes in the vessel; it was impossible, however, to prove that they had been caused by firing from the British boarding-party.

The Norwegian attitude has displeased Germany. It is thought that protest to Great Britain should have been much more energetic. The last note from Dr Koht[2] is regarded as being almost apologetic in tone, when he admits that Norway may have made a mistake. Even supposing that Norway had no right to allow the Altmark cruise in her territorial waters, it was for Norway alone, and not for Great Britain, to decide whether Norwegian neutrality had been violated by the Altmark or not.

Neutral circles are, of course, very worried. It is felt that anything may happen from now on. The British have given a very bad example, and have furnished the Germans with a precedent for similar breaches of neutrality.

---

[1] The reference is to a naval confrontation during which British naval personnel boarded the *Altmark*, a German ship, in neutral Norwegian waters and freed British POWs onboard.
[2] Halvdan Koht (1873-1965), Norwegian Foreign Minister (1935-40).

The attitude of the Swiss press in the Altmark affair caused great anger in German official circles, in that the Gazette de Lausanne and some other papers are said to have condoned the British action.

Dr Goebbels addressed a warning to neutrals in a speech the other day. He said that while Germany had no intention of making demands on the neutrals like Mr Churchill had made, it was necessary that neutrality should be interpreted in its true meaning. Germany could not agree to a definition which confined itself to military matters, and omitted the political aspect. There should be no glaring distinction between the neutrality of a state and the neutrality of public opinion. It does not do for a government to declare its neutrality, and for the press to have freedom to abuse. To be neutral means to keep oneself out of the conflict in all its aspects.

The German railways have been under great strain for the past few months. The canals became frozen over just before Christmas, and they are not yet free. A considerable number of trains have had to be placed at the disposal of the armed forces, and passenger trains have been reduced to a bare minimum. The employees have to work long hours and the numerous accidents which have taken place are attributed to the fact that the men are overworked. Trains are also commandeered to carry coal to the cities, where the conditions were unbearable during the cold spell, which, by the way, has not altogether left us.

Very little railway material could be seized in the former Polish districts. The Poles kept withdrawing towards the east, and most of the Polish rolling stock which had not been destroyed during the German advance, was, at the end of the campaign, in the territory now under Russian control. The Russians have held onto it all even though they are re-laying the railway lines to suit their own gauge, which is wider than the internationally recognised 4 feet eight and a half inches.

Arrangements have been made to introduce more foreign labour than ever this year in order to meet present shortage. 50,000 Italian agricultural workers will be distributed over the country, and a large number of Polish labourers will be available this year. Czech technicians are a great help but for obvious reasons they are not allowed to work in the armament and allied industries. There are, I understand, almost 30,000 Slovak workers in Germany. I recently had an opportunity to discuss these problems with the Minister for Labour, Herr Seldte, and with Dr Syrop, the Secretary of State in the Ministry of Labour. Dr Syrop told me that the war had not created a new unemployment problem, as had happened in other countries, but rather the reverse. Certain industries were, of course, having a thin time, but the workers had been quickly absorbed into other branches. In order to offset the effects of mobilisation, the women and older men have had to be pressed into service. The unemployment figures are not published, but I understand from Dr Syrop that at the end of November there were in all greater Germany 100,000 unemployed, the most of whom were unemployable. The figure for February was 250,000 and the rise was explained by the fact that outdoor building work had to be curtailed owing to the severe cold. When one takes into account that the population of Germany is 80,000,000 these figures are negligible.

The British are claiming that one of their reconnaissance aircraft overflew Berlin the other night, and dropped leaflets. The report states that the pilot dropped rockets to light up the city. I find it very difficult indeed to believe this report. If leaflets had been dropped, I would have heard about it. As it is, nothing was known of the affair here until a denial was issued in the newspapers. The Poles issued statements in November to the effect that they have bombarded Berlin from the air.

People are saying that the war will start soon now. I myself consider it not impossible that the Germans will not after all take the offensive. They are confident that they can break through the Maginot Line, though, of course, with terrible loss, but why should they? Their opponents are powerless against them at the moment, and they are carrying on fairly well economically. The British blockade is ineffective in the east area from Saarbrücken to Vladivostok. And there does not seem to be any convincing proof that time is working against Germany.

[signed] W. WARNOCK

No. 132 NAI DFA 2006/39

Handwritten letter from Joseph P. Walshe to John W. Dulanty (London)
DUBLIN, 2 March 1940

Dear John,[1]

I enclose the cuttings promised on the phone i.e. 1) Gogarty's[2] Article in the 'Week', a weekly offshoot of the Herald – (see particularly last sentence): this is typical of other articles and lectures:- 2) series of articles by Douglas in the Washington Times Herald:- 3) Pender in W. Post of 5th Jan.

Our people here and in America are beginning to suspect that this is a B. campaign. In any case it is highly mischievous, and the British must at least take some responsibility for the stuff which they allow to go out from the London Correspondents of Am. Papers. We stop everything which might be injurious to the British. The continuation of the Unity move must be taken as inevitable. In yesterday's article Mrs. Long of the London Office of the Times tells America that the German Legation has the biggest staff of all the foreign missions in Dublin. This is such a palpable lie that it must have been told with a purpose. She has just been to Ireland and she knows damn well it is a lie. She says furthermore that the B. are at a greater disadvantage than in the last war in not having the ports, though she half admits that there are no secret refuelling stations.

The whole tone of the article is mischievous beyond description. There is nobody however in America who doesn't know that the significance of our ports and violation of our sovereignty would cause a revival of the conditions existing during the great war which allowed the existing of a sympathetic attitude towards G. submarines. The campaign is so madly conceived that the man or men responsible can only be described as worse enemies of the British than even the Germans.

It is said here and in America that Gogarty gets £100 a month from the British Council.

Yours
J.W.

---

[1] On 5 March 1940 Dulanty wrote to Anthony Eden conveying the substance of Walshe's letter to him and adding 'couldn't something be done to stop these articles which give trouble where none is wanted?' (NAI 2006/39).
[2] Oliver Joseph St John Gogarty (1878-1957), writer and surgeon.

No. 133 NAI DFA 219/22A

Extracts from the annual report on the work of the Irish Consulate General in New York and Consulates in Chicago and San Francisco for 1939-40
(108/12/40)

WASHINGTON, 6 March 1940

[matter omitted]
PROPOSED VISIT OF AN TAOISEACH TO THE U.S.
In co-operation with the National Reception Committee in New York, the Legation was engaged for several months in preparing for the visit of An Taoiseach. Reception Committees and other groups were formed in 27 cities in 19 States to handle the local details in preparation for Mr. de Valera's coming. The perfection of these arrangements entailed much correspondence at the Legation and necessitated several journeys by the Minister to New York and a visit to Chicago to consult with the committees. As a result of these preparations, everything was in readiness for Mr. de Valera's visit and it is safe to assume that his tour would have been a most successful one.

VISIT OF AN TÁNAISTE AND PARTY
An Tánaiste and his party on arriving at New York[1] were met by the Minister who attended with them at the official opening of the Irish Pavilions at the New York World's Fair. Later the party journeyed to Washington. An official dinner was tendered to them by the Minister, and an interview with the President of the United States was secured for An Tánaiste and Mr. John J. Hearne. The party, including the Minister, travelled on to Chicago and attended sessions of the Irish Race Congress which had arranged to convene in that city in anticipation of Mr. de Valera's visit.

[mater omitted]

U.S. NEUTRALITY ACT
The enactment of the U.S. Neutrality Act and the consequent inclusion of Ireland by the United States in a zone designated as 'combat area' received the serious attention of the Minister. Several visits were paid by him to the State Department to protest against Ireland's isolation and the loss sustained by her due to the stoppage of sailings of American ships to Irish ports. So far these protests have been unavailing.[2]

PAN AMERICAN AIRLINES AND AMERICAN EXPORT AIRLINES
Due to the prohibitions of the U.S. Neutrality Act, American trans-Atlantic air clippers have cancelled their sailings to Foynes and now make Lisbon their port of call. This is a great loss to the Irish Airport. The Minister has repeatedly endeavoured to get the State Department officials to consider the matter with a view to allowing trans-Atlantic planes to resume flights to Ireland. American Export Airlines is

---

[1] Seán T. O Ceallaigh arrived in New York on 12 May 1939, with a party that included John J. Hearne and Kathleen O'Connell, aboard the United States Steamship Lines SS *Washington*.
[2] See Nos 41, 45, 57, 69, 71 and 73.

endeavouring to secure a certificate of convenience and necessity from the Civil Aeronautics Authority to allow it to fly the Atlantic in competition with Pan-American Airlines. The Minister has had conferences with officials of both the above mentioned companies and has discussed with them matters affecting the interests of the Foynes airport and the airlines.

THE EXECUTION OF PETER BARNES & JAMES RICHARDS
Everything possible was done by the Minister in an endeavour to save the lives of these men. He solicited the aid of influential persons with a view to appealing to the President. We have been informed unofficially that the President intervened. The British Ambassador was approached and wired his Government that the execution of these men would be a grave mistake, but his intercession was unavailing.

PARTITION
During the course of the year material relating to the question of Partition has been supplied to several persons desiring to incorporate this information in articles for publication in magazines and periodicals. The Legation caused to be mailed 13,532 copies of the pamphlet entitled 'Unity of Ireland'. Copies of this booklet were mailed to the following: U.S. Governors of States and Territories; U.S. Senators and Representatives; newspapers represented in the Press Galleries of Congress; Catholic newspapers and magazines; High School libraries and public libraries, and to libraries of other classifications.

THE AMERICAN PRESS
During the year many articles on Ireland and news despatches of Irish happenings appeared in the American press. On the whole the tenor of the articles has been fairly favourable and the despatches accurate. On several occasions, however, it became necessary for the Minister to approach the editors of newspapers in Washington and New York and to register protests against anti-Irish articles appearing in their columns and to arrange to have replies addressed to these papers by friends of the Legation.
[matter omitted]

No. 134 NAI DFA Washington Embassy Confidential Reports 1940

Letter from Robert Brennan to Joseph P. Walshe (Dublin)
(108/13/40)

WASHINGTON, 7 March 1940

On Monday, February 26th, I gave a dinner party for Mr. David Gray, the newly appointed Minister to Ireland. Amongst the guests were Mr. Justice Douglas of the Supreme Court, Senator Murray of Montana, Representative Shanley of Connecticut, Mr. Thomas Burke, Chief of the Division of International Communications of the State Department, Mr. Garth Healy and their wives.

Mr. Gray told me that he was visiting the British Ambassador on the following day, and that he intended to impress on him the necessity of ending partition.

[stamped] (signed) ROBT. BRENNAN

No. 135 NAI DFA 219/8

> *Extract from a confidential report from Matthew Murphy*
> *to Joseph P. Walshe (Dublin)*
> *(10/M/40)*
>
> SAN FRANCISCO, 7 March 1940

I beg to report that in my minute No 9/M/40, dated the 6th March, 1940,[1] I mentioned that Mr. Wei Kuo Chiang,[2] son of Generalissimo Chiang Kai-shek,[3] was one of the guests at a musicale at our home.

    I had quite an interesting conversation with him after most of the guests had left. He was extremely cordial, and expressed his sincere appreciation of our hospitality. It was surprising his intimate knowledge of Irish history, and how closely he had followed Ireland's struggle for independence. Mr. Chiang also referred appreciatively to the fact that Mr. de Valera was the only one to make a stand at Geneva against the grabbing of Manchuria by Japan, and said it was a pity that the advice he gave at the time to the Assembly of the League of Nations was not heeded.

[matter omitted]

No. 136 NAI DFA Secretary's Files P15(i)

> *Letter from William J.B. Macaulay to Joseph P. Walshe (Dublin)*
>
> HOLY SEE, 8 March 1940

Dear Joe,

I have just returned from the Vatican after discussing the subject of Dublin. I gave them a memorandum on the lines of yours[4] with which they expressed pleasure and agreement. The need for a person of no ordinary attainments and character is realized as they realize the defects of the last incumbent, owing to ill health. It would be fatal at this stage for me to mention names but I find that Arthur Ryan of Belfast is very highly thought of.[5] I was told the Nuncio[6] was already interesting himself in finding the best man. I think that what he suggests will carry great weight, perhaps decisively so.[7]

Yours ever
[signed] W.J.B. MACAULAY

---

[1] Not printed.
[2] Wei Kuo Chiang (1916-97), officer in the German Army during the Spanish Civil War (1936-39) and during the early part of the Second World War.
[3] Chiang Kai-shek (1887-1975), Chinese Nationalist leader, President of Taiwan (1950-75).
[4] Not located.
[5] Father Arthur Haydn Ryan (1897-1982), academic, philosopher, member of the Senate of Queen's University, Belfast, and Pro-Chancellor of the University.
[6] Paschal Robinson (1870-1948), Apostolic Nuncio to Ireland (1929-48).
[7] Marginal note by Sheila Murphy: 'Secretary urged Mac on phone to expedite'.

No. 137 NAI DFA 219/4

> *Extracts from a confidential report from William Warnock to Joseph P. Walshe*
> *(Dublin)*
> *(43/33)*
>
> BERLIN, 16 March 1940

The conclusion of peace between Finland and Russia[1] formed the main item of news during the week. It was of great importance from the German point of view, not only economically, but also politically, as the Western Powers can be represented as having had a first-class diplomatic defeat. What surprised people here was that Monsieur Daladier did not make his notorious speech concerning the French expeditionary force until peace had almost been arranged. Mr. Chamberlain's declaration in the British House of Commons at a very late stage also caused some surprise, but I may say in all seriousness that speeches by British Ministers are now treated by the German press more as a joke than anything else, as they have so often been proved either equivocal or totally misinformed.

The Scandinavian countries, which had been receiving warnings for months past in the German press, are now praised for their wisdom in having avoided the transfer of Europe's major war to their territories.

It is said here that the French expeditionary force to Finland would have consisted of Poles and other refugees, and that it would have taken a considerable time before British volunteers could have been trained. The much publicised schemes of the Western Powers are thought to have been propaganda for home consumption rather than anything else.

[matter omitted]

Yesterday, the 15th March, was the anniversary of the incorporation of Bohemia and Moravia in the Reich as a Protectorate. Messages were exchanged between the Reichsprotector, Baron von Neurath,[2] and the Chancellor, and between the Czech President, Dr. Hacha,[3] and the Chancellor. I have unfortunately never had an opportunity to visit the Protectorate myself, but I hear that the general attitude of the population is one of sullen acceptance of the present state of affairs, and of thankfulness that they are not directly involved in the present war. All signs of the former Czech rule have completely disappeared in the Sudetenland.

Nothing much is known about Mr. Sumner Welles' discussions here, though it is said in diplomatic circles that Mr. Welles went away convinced of the Unity of Germany behind the present leadership.[4]

The visit of Herr von Ribbentrop to Rome is thought to have been – as much as anything else – a demonstration that the 'Berlin-Rome Axis' still exists. The Foreign

---

[1] The Russo-Finnish War of November 1939 to March 1940 saw initial Finnish successes give way to eventual Russian victory, with Finland ceding strategic territory to Russia through the 12 March 1939 Russo-Finnish Treaty signed in Moscow. When Germany attacked Russia in 1941 Finland declared war on Russia.

[2] Konstantin Freiherr von Neurath (1873-1956), German Minister for Foreign Affairs (1932-9), *Reichsprotektor* (Nazi-represenatative) to Bohemia and Moravia (1939-41).

[3] Emil Hacha (1872-1945), President of Czechoslovakia (1938-9), State President of the Protectorate of Bohemia and Moravia (1939-45).

[4] Benjamin Sumner Welles (1892-1961), United States Under-Secretary of State (1937-43).

Minister's audience with the Pope was reported in a few lines, and, in my own opinion, somewhat misleadingly. It is stated that Herr von Ribbentrop had 'Called' on His Holiness. The Nuncio said to me this morning that though he was unaware of the subjects of discussion he was very glad that the audience had been arranged. The German annexation of Bohemia and Moravia increased the Nuncio's work considerably, and he has now, in addition, the very difficult task of watching the rights of the Catholic Church in the occupied areas of Poland. The Polish hierarchy has now no channel of communication with Rome save through the Nunciature here.

Every few months a new rumour begins to circulate concerning the probable date of the end of the war. After the conclusion of peace in Finland some people suggested that perhaps the bigger war could be settled by negotiation, too; the ordinary people are being led to believe that in any case the war will be over by the autumn, even if a military decision is needed.

To-morrow our colony and some German friends will foregather here to celebrate St. Patrick's Day in our family circle. One of the advantages of our small size is that we all know one another very intimately. We shall miss the usual supply of shamrock, but that will not hinder our remembrances of home. In times like these St. Patrick's Day means more to us than ever.

[signed] W. WARNOCK

No. 138 NAI DT S11846A

Memorandum by John Leydon (Dublin)
(Most Secret)

DUBLIN, 19 March 1940

Trade with Great Britain
In the course of conferences and discussions which the secretaries of the Department of Supplies and the Department of Agriculture had with officers of various Ministries in London on 12th, 13th and 14th instant, it was evident that in considering the facilities which might be afforded to us in the matter of supplies of feeding stuffs, fertilisers, raw materials for industries, etc., the question of the extent to which such commodities would be utilised in the production of an exportable surplus of produce, etc., required in the United Kingdom was influencing the general policy in that connection.
2. The shipping position had now become so critical that, with a view to conserving space, the matter of giving preference to the importation of finished produce, such as beef, rather than feeding stuffs had to be considered and there was also the question of utilising in the United Kingdom itself the bulk of such feeding stuffs as it might be possible to import.
3. Certainly it would be exceedingly difficult for the British Government to grant facilities either as regards purchase, provision of foreign exchange or shipping which would result in the farmers of Éire being in a better position in regard to their raw materials generally than farmers in the United Kingdom. It is true that the British Government strongly desire a maximum production in these islands of the various essential food stuffs which are normally imported in large quantities but in the present emergency it is imperative that such production should be achieved mainly, if not wholly, by the use of home-grown foods.

4. There is the further important question of whether the prices obtainable in the United Kingdom for the various classes of our exportable produce would be at a level adequate to compensate our farmers for the cost of imported raw materials. Moreover, the British authorities are strongly opposed to agreeing to any facilities for the importation to Éire of raw materials for conversion into produce which may not in fact be urgently required by them.

5. The whole position in this connection is very obscure and it is most important that it should be examined immediately both in relation to price levels and to the quantities of our various agricultural products which the United Kingdom would be prepared to take from this country.

6. As a case in point, the present position in regard to bacon exports may be instanced. The price is satisfactory. Our quota was fixed at 40,000 cwts. per month but we now find we could export 55,000 cwts. per month after providing for our own needs. The Ministry of Food have, however, stated that they cannot possibly accept more than quota already fixed as they have very heavy stocks of bacon on hands which notwithstanding the increase in the ration is not moving into consumption rapidly enough to maintain stocks at the desired level having regard to storage space and the keeping quality of the commodity.

7. Butter might also be mentioned. The existing stocks in the United Kingdom amount to about 60,000 tons or, approximately, 2 months' supply at present rate of rationing. Having regard to the extent to which the use of margarine has been popularised and the rationing regulations, it is not at all clear to what extent the United Kingdom Authorities will arrange for the importation of butter in future. Whilst it is probable that they will raise no difficulty about taking our relatively small exportable surplus, there is every likelihood that the price which they will be prepared to pay will not be satisfactory.

8. The position appears to be that in order to decide what lines our agricultural production can most profitably follow, an understanding with the British Government is essential both as regards the quantities of various products they are prepared to take and the prices they are prepared to pay. Such an understanding entails also an understanding about the quantities of various feeding stuffs, fertilisers, etc. we are to import, and the shipping facilities to carry them. This indicates the necessity for a comprehensive agreement which, as it will involve major issues of policy, seems to require the intervention of Ministers.

No. 139 NAI DFA 2006/39

Confidential report from John W. Dulanty to Joseph P. Walshe (Dublin)
(No. 23) (Secret)

LONDON, 20 March 1940

In conversation with Mr. Eden today we were talking of the rapidity with which event followed upon event, and I said something about the tragedy of Finland having even now almost receded into the chill historic past, or some such words.

Mr. Eden said he was not so sure of that and in the gravest confidence told me, for the information of the Taoiseach, that the Finns had asked the British to leave all the munitions which they had sent to that country. Now the British say they could do very well with every ounce of war material which was not now being used. They had consulted their military experts and in the result they had reluctantly consented to the Finns retaining these munitions.

I asked did that mean that the Finns were apprehensive about the integrity of the Russians in implementing the terms of the armistice. Mr. Eden said he thought there was a good deal of that in the minds of the Finns, but again stressing the confidence he said that the Finnish trouble might resurrect itself.

No. 140 NAI DFA 218/55

Extract from a confidential report from William J.B. Macaulay to Joseph P. Walshe (Dublin) (MP 15/40) (Confidential)

HOLY SEE, 20 March 1940

[matter omitted]

Mr. Gray is going to spend five days in Paris and five days in London. He is especially anxious to convey to the British that with the continuation of partition it will be increasingly difficult for America to give fuller support to the Allies in view of opinion in America and the probability of groups in Congress making things difficult for the Administration so long as the Irish question remains unsolved. He came over on the ship with Duff Cooper[1] who promised to arrange interviews with Churchill inter alios. From what I could gather in our conversation President Roosevelt has instructed him personally to do all he can with the British and he saw Lord Lothian also on the matter whom he found helpful.

The Minister says he is anxious to get to know the members of the Government intimately but not to get involved in social activities. By this he means large parties etc. I liked him very much and am giving a dinner tomorrow night to which Mr. Taylor is coming since he has not yet met Mr. Gray.

No. 141 NAI DT S11846A

Memorandum on a Cabinet discussion by Maurice Moynihan (Dublin)

DUBLIN, 21 March 1940

Note: There was a general preliminary discussion at today's Govt. meeting of the question of trade discussions (to be conducted by Ministers) being opened with the British Government with a view to a comprehensive agreement. I was instructed that no note of the discussions was to be recorded in the minutes. No recommendation was before the Govt. and I was unaware of the existence of the attached memo now received from Mr Twomey.[2] The discussion was initiated by the Taoiseach.

I am informed by the Taoiseach that he has since decided that a despatch should be sent to the British Government suggesting the opening of negotiations.[3] Messrs.

---

[1] Alfred (Duff) Cooper (1890-1954), appointed First Lord of the Admiralty in 1937 but resigned in 1938 over the Munich agreement; Minister for Information (1940-1), Ambassador to France (1944-8).
[2] See No. 138.
[3] See No. 145.

Walshe (External Affairs), Leydon (Supplies) and Twomey (Agriculture) are aware of this decision and Mr. Walshe, in consultation with Messrs. Leydon and Twomey, has the draft text of the despatch in London.

No. 142 NAI DFA 218/55

> Extract from a confidential report from Michael MacWhite
> to Joseph P. Walshe (Dublin)
> (Confidential)
>
> ROME, 21 March 1940

Although audiences with the Pope are, as a rule, suspended during Holy Week, Mr. Gray hopes to be able to have a few minutes with him on Saturday when he proposes to consult him in regard to the elimination of the Boundary between Northern and Southern Ireland. During his stay in London he intends calling on the Secretary of the Dominions and other Cabinet Ministers with the same object in view. He hopes to be able to make an important contribution to the solution of the question and stated that President Roosevelt had this matter in his mind when nominating him to the Irish post.

No. 143 NAI DT S11846A

> Memorandum of a Cabinet discussion by Maurice Moynihan (Dublin)
>
> DUBLIN, 28 March 1940

At the meeting of the Government held on the 28th March, 1940, further consideration was given to the question of steps being taken with a view to trade conversations by Ministers with the British Government, and a draft despatch (attached)[1] prepared by the Department of External Affairs was read. The following decisions were taken:-

1. A report to be obtained from Mr. Dulanty, High Commissioner in London on any recent conversations he may have had with Messrs. Morrison[2] and Burgin.[3]
2. A report to be obtained on any discussions on trade matters which may recently have taken place between officials of the Departments concerned and Sir John Maffey, the British representative.
3. A memorandum or memoranda to be prepared at the instance of the Ministers for Supplies and Agriculture dealing with the trade problems which would come up for discussion and indicating solutions which would be satisfactory from the Irish point of view.
4. In the event of its being decided that Ministers should go to London for trade discussions, the Ministers to be selected for the purpose to be the Ministers for Supplies and Agriculture. These two Ministers will in the first instance conduct discussions of a general exploratory character and if necessary the question of the Taoiseach subsequently proceeding to London will be considered in due course.

---

[1] See No. 145.
[2] William 'Shakes' Morrison (1893-1961), Minister of Food (1939-40).
[3] Edward Leslie Burgin (1887-1945), Minster for Supplies (1939-40).

5. The draft despatch to be further examined from the point of view of considering whether it should be expanded so as to cover, for example, the question of supplies of essential raw materials.[1]

No. 144 NAI DT S11846A

Handwritten Memorandum from Joseph P. Walshe to Eamon de Valera (Dublin)
DUBLIN, 29 March 1940

The High Commissioner takes the view that a discussion between Ministers of the two countries should take place only if he has been able to ascertain that definite concessions could be obtained. At present he is not very hopeful i.e. and this is especially the case in regard to the butter situation. (The gap between the 126/per cwt. at which they can buy all the butter they want elsewhere and our 150/ being too wide to span.) The H.C. is arriving here on Monday morning and he can then inform you and the Ministers for Supplies, I&C and Agriculture of his recent conversations with British Ministers. These have been numerous, but the question of inter-Ministerial discussions has not been raised.

As soon as a decision has been taken by the Govt. we can put our case in detail to Maffey if you so desire. So far discussions with him have been of a general and preparatory character.

J.W. 29/3/40

No. 145 NAI DT S11846A

Draft despatch from Eamon de Valera to Anthony Eden (London)
DUBLIN, 29 March 1940

Sir,
1. In the course of recent discussions between officials of the two Governments, concerning our mutual trade position, it became apparent that something more than day to day arrangements of an administrative character might be required to meet the situation which has arisen out of the war. It appears to the Irish Government that the time has come for the Ministers concerned of both Governments to meet and review the situation as a whole, so that the Irish Government may be in a position to determine its policy as to the extent and nature of the productive activities in this country which might most usefully be continued or expanded to our mutual advantage. In this connection, the supply of raw materials, prices, and the shipping available for the transport of the former, would naturally arise for discussion.
2. I should be very glad to learn whether you share the opinion that such a review would serve a useful purpose.

---

[1] Marginal notes on this document state that items 1, 2 and 5 were to be conveyed to the Department of External Affairs, item 3 was to be conveyed to External Affairs, Agriculture, Supplies and Industry and Commerce and that item 4 was not to be communicated beyond the Department of the Taoiseach.

No. 146 NAI DT S11846A

Minute of a Cabinet discussion by Maurice Moynihan (Dublin)

DUBLIN, 29 March 1940

At the meeting of the Government held on the 29th instant the question of trade conversations by Ministers with the British Government was again discussed. The note of the discussion on the 28th instant[1] was read and approved and it was agreed that the decisions as recorded in that note should be conveyed to the Departments concerned with the exception of Paragraph 4.

Mr. Walshe's submission to the Minister for External Affairs, dated 29th instant, (attached),[2] was read and it was noted that a report from the High Commissioner in London on his recent conversations with British Ministers would be available when the High Commissioner comes to Dublin next week.

The revised draft despatch dated 29th instant (copy attached)[3] was also read and was provisionally approved subject to a reference being made in the despatch to the discussions which have already taken place with the British Ministries of Food, Supplies and Shipping and the Board of Trade.[4]

No. 147 NAI DFA 219/2A

Confidential report from Leopold H. Kerney to Joseph P. Walshe (Dublin)
(M. 19/4)

MADRID, 29 March 1940

Conversation with Foreign Minister

I took the opportunity of a conversation which I had with Colonel Beigbeder, chiefly with regard to Ryan, to tell him that I was a bit disappointed that the celebration of our National holiday had been given rather scanty notice in the press, and that I could not understand the attitude of the censor in this connection.

Some of the facts known to me (but which I did not disclose to him) were that one at least of the many photographers present on the occasion had sent photographs to all the papers, but that no photograph had been reproduced by any of them; that the Marques de Valdeiglesias[5] had sent a report to 'Ya' and 'A.B.C.', which was not published in the former and was very considerably cut down in the latter – the report itself, however, being much too long in my opinion; that reports were sent to 'Madrid' and 'Informaciones' by correspondents of these papers, but that the censor had prevented their publication.

The Minister explained that officials in the censorship office often acted stupidly and that the best way would always be to see him when we wanted anything published, and he would arrange everything – reports, photographs, cinema views and everything else; he would gladly take part in any ceremonies I might be organising, be present at any mass, or even go to Salamanca with me on any particular

---

[1] See No. 143.
[2] See No. 144.
[3] See No. 145.
[4] Marginal note by Moynihan: 'Substance conveyed to Mr. Walshe by telephone'.
[5] Alfredo Escobar y Ramírez (1858-1953) solicitor and journalist; managing director of *La Época* (1887-1953).

occasion, and have himself photographed 'arm in arm' with me, and I could count on his willing cooperation. He said the Italians always worked with him in this way, and that he himself made a point of arranging publicity in advance on all occasions; he was already making arrangements for photographs to be taken on the signing of the Italian treaty in a couple of days' time.

It was an opportune moment for referring to Partition; I told the Minister that I would gladly avail of his help in securing useful publicity at some later date; I gave him an outline of the position, which he listened to attentively; I explained that the Government's whole policy towards England was based on reason rather than force, and that an attitude of persuasiveness rather than hostility was the keynote of the Government's efforts to find a solution which was as much in England's interests as in ours. He told me that he would be accessible at all times whenever I wished to see him on this or other matters.

[signed] L.H. KERNEY

No. 148 NAI DT S11846A

Minute of a Cabinet discussion by Maurice Moynihan (Dublin)

DUBLIN, 4 April 1940

At the meeting of the Govt. held on the 3rd April, 1940, it was decided that Mr. Dulanty should make an oral communication to the British Government on the lines of the draft despatch dated the 29th March, 1940, (copy attached)[1] and that this procedure should be adopted in lieu of the issue of a despatch. The suggested Heads of Arrangement with the British Government circulated during the meeting by the Minister for Supplies were provisionally approved.[2]

No. 149 NAI DFA 219/7

Confidential report from Francis T. Cremins to Joseph P. Walshe (Dublin)
(S.Gen.1/1) (Confidential)

GENEVA, 10 April 1940

I have to forward, for the information of the Minister, the enclosed extracts from this morning's press[3] indicating the first reactions here to the invasion of Denmark and Norway by Germany.[4] The most profound interest is taken throughout this country regarding the new developments, and it will be seen that at Berne yesterday the members of the Conseil National manifested their lively interest as the news arrived. According to the note from Berne, the dominating impression in parliamentary circles was that the Reich had gained a point by its lightning stroke. The increasing tendency, on one side and the other, to disregard the rights of neutrals and the consequent danger to small peaceful States, was also remarked. Most of the comments, notably that from the 'Courier de Genève' do not hesitate

---

[1] See No. 145.
[2] Marginal note by Moynihan: 'Mr. Walshe, Dept. of External Affairs, informed on 3/4/40. Mr. Dulanty also informed by Taoiseach on the same date.'
[3] Not printed.
[4] Denmark and Norway were invaded by Germany on 9 April 1940.

to lay the responsibility on German shoulders, and to draw a clear distinction between action such as the laying of mines in territorial waters and the invasion of neutral countries, while several do not refrain from openly casting a gibe at the Danes for their passive acceptance of the situation. It is of course too early for the military writers to be other than guarded in their appreciation of the events. Col. Lecomte in 'La Suisse' thinks that if the allies succeeded in defeating the German navy, the position of German troops beyond the Skagerrak[1] might become precarious. He suggests however that the Germans may avoid a naval battle, contenting themselves with a defensive attitude behind their mines, hydroavions and submarines. This is not quite borne out by events so far, as there have already been some naval actions. Also that they may, notwithstanding their statements to the contrary, occupy Sweden also, thus turning the whole of Scandinavia into a theatre of war.

The Danish Minister here is so far completely cut off from his capital, and I understand that that applies to other Danish Ministers also, for instance to those in Rome and London, to whom he has been able to telephone. The new developments certainly do not take him by surprise. He was practically a fatalist in regard to the invasion of his country by Germany, as I indicated in a report about a year ago,[2] and he always maintained that, once invasion came, Denmark could only submit. I asked him a week ago if Denmark could, as in the last war, protest to the Germans that if they violated the country the allies would prevent the importation of oil cake and consequently there would be no cattle for the Reich. He replied in the negative. Denmark, he said, had in a large measure developed her own supplies of foodstuffs since 1919 in the struggle to attain a certain self-sufficiently. It is clear however that the loss of imported foodstuffs would be serious for Denmark and that great loss and reductions in cattle and dairy products must result. Meantime however the Germans would have the use of what was there, and they would no doubt endeavour to make up to some extent the shortage of foodstuffs, if possible from some other territories.

The Finnish Minister, with whom I have had a short conversation, thinks that it will not be an easy task for Germany to occupy Norway unless she is free to use the sea, as the principal communications in that country run from East to West and not from North to South. He mentioned that when he was Foreign Minister a couple of years ago he had proposed to Norway an improvement in the roads in the north making communications easier between the three countries, but Norway had refused on the ground that such an improvement might be regarded as a threat by Russia. Improved communications with Finland might have been useful to Norway in case help from Finland and Sweden were a probability, but their absence may render a little more difficult any possible moves against Norway or Sweden by the U.S.S.R.

As regards the Swiss here, I find that they have mixed feelings with regard to the invasion. There is naturally great sympathy with the Scandinavians as friends and fellow neutrals, but there is also a certain relief that the long expected opening up of the war in Spring should not have begun at either end of the Maginot line.

---

[1] The Skagerrak Strait runs between Sweden, Norway and Denmark connecting the Kattegat Strait, which leads to the Baltic Sea, with the North Sea.
[2] See DIFP V, No. 292.

At the same time there is general anxiety at the callous treatment to which neutral countries have been subjected, and the feeling is growing that the turn of Switzerland will come eventually. The Swiss continue, however, to feel fairly safe so long as Italy maintains her non-belligerency. Nevertheless, the possibility of a situation developing in the Balkans or in the near East somewhat analogous to that in Scandinavia is not absent from many minds, which increases the anxiety in view of its probable reactions on Italian policy. All accounts here agree that the Italian people do not desire war. It is freely stated in fact that many, especially in the north of Italy, are even hostile to Germany, but it is admitted that Mussolini remains firmly in the saddle, and that neither the popular feeling nor the influence of Ciano, Balbo, and others who are believed to be unfavourable to military action against the allies, nor even the influence of the Vatican, would prevent the position being worked up in order that the weight of Italy might if need be be thrown on the German side if at any time the allies found themselves in a disadvantageous position. Most people here consider that it would not be to Italy's advantage, no more than it would be to Russia's, to bring about a preponderating Germany. Nevertheless, the immediate claims of Italy are not against Germany but against Great Britain and France, and Mussolini is said to be determined to be in at the peace in order that he may regulate his position in the Mediterranean and his claims in Suez and North Africa, and in order that he may be in a position to impose his personality in the setting up of a new Europe. He would no doubt prefer to keep out of the war as long as possible in order to secure the balance of power as against weakened combatants. He may however find his plans precipitated by events arising out of the working of the blockade, and of the necessities of his partner in the axis. I received information very confidentially this afternoon from my Argentine colleague, who had it this morning from his Ambassador in Paris, that Mussolini is thought to be on the verge of taking a very grave decision indeed, a decision to throw Italy militarily on the German side. My informant added that the French Government are exceedingly worried about this position, and that they regard all hope of retaining Italy in a state of non-belligerency, or of attracting her to the side of the allies as being practically lost. My colleague is usually well-informed regarding events. If, however, there is a real success by the British in Norway, it might have, as one of its important by-products, the postponement of any precipitate action on the part of the Duce.

A few evenings ago I listened in private conversation to a discussion on the situation by the Press attaché of the Yugoslav delegation who had just returned from Belgrade. He seemed to me largely to be giving forth Yugoslav official views. Generally speaking, his line was that while admittedly the Germans had suffered greatly during the Winter, especially from cold, the Reich had now become militarily of such extra-ordinary power that she could not be beaten by the allies. He pointed out that there was no point at which the allies could strike at her effectively, and that the absence of a large coalition of small States acting with Britain and France, such as existed in the last war, might prove decisive. He said that he understood that these were also the Italian views and that Italian representatives abroad were propagating them. He discounted any idea of a break between the German people and the regime, stating that Hitler had succeeded in imposing on the Germans the view that 'the end of Hitler would be the end of Germany'. He regarded the Balkans as being in no danger of any immediate attack from any side, even from Russia. He was sure that the Balkan countries themselves would be against any attempt on the part of the allies to attack Germany through Roumania or elsewhere, and that Germany stood to gain more from Roumania at peace than from Roumania at war. He regarded Turkey as likely to remain neutral unless somebody else attacked a Balkan State. He is probably right in regard to the wishes of all those States, but he possibly did not attach sufficient importance to the incidence of the blockade – in the Balkans and the near East, as in Scandinavia – and to German and possibly Russian reactions. Moreover, if the information which I have mentioned above regarding Italy has foundation, his views regarding the unlikelihood of trouble in the Balkans or in the near East may be upset. His views regarding Italy were to the effect that Mussolini would remain loyal to Hitler, and that there was not the slightest possibility of detaching him from the German side. Italy, he said, was awaiting her chance to have her claims settled, and, in any case, Mussolini, from his earliest days, had looked forward to the downfall of the British Empire. The Duce was convinced that Germany would win, at least in the sense that she would retain her mastery in Eastern Europe, and he, as well as Hitler, believed that the French lacked stability and that they would eventually lose patience and agree to a plausible peace, with safeguards for Czech independence and the setting up of a restricted Poland. Further, Mussolini still adhered to the principles of his Four Power Pact.

As regards the suggestion that France might become unstable, there is no doubt some danger that a position of continued stalemate on the west might have a tendency to demoralise the French, but any opening up of the war in the north or the South-east would probably have the effect of dissipating this. In any case, the fear of Germany should go far to keep the French from losing confidence, and to maintain, or create, political stability.

The Attaché discussed the question of Italian preparedness and expressed the view that notwithstanding the improvement in the fortifications of Italy and in her armed forces during the past six months, she was not strong enough to wage war such as fully against Great Powers, although she would be effective in a restricted struggle in the Balkans. He did not believe that her entrance into the war was at all imminent, and he thought that Italy's plan, if she could succeed in carrying it out, was to bide her time as long as possible and see how the struggle developed. I asked what effect on Italy he thought an attack by Russia against Roumania would have, and he expressed the view that the U.S.S.R. would not attack Bessarabia, which might add Italy to the Roumanian side. This would not be a development agreeable to Germany.

As regards the situation on the West, I think that the view which prevails here at the moment, notwithstanding the sensational reports from America and elsewhere that immediate attacks by Germany against Holland and Belgium are in preparation, is that large-scale hostilities in the West are not imminent and that it will remain for some time, perhaps for months, a question of the accentuation of the blockade by the allies, with counter pressure on the neutrals by Germany, and any supporting or counteracting military action that the working of the blockade may bring. Greatly increased air and sea activity is also envisaged. It is a problem for the allies, in addition to restricting supplies to Germany, to force Germany to use what supplies she has. That is why they would probably be not at all averse from an extension of the conflict to some of the neutral countries close to Germany, if Germany decided to invade such countries. One of the great services rendered to the allies by the Finnish resistance was the use, and the waste, of war material of all sorts by Russia which could only be replaced from supplies which might otherwise have found their way to the Germans. The latter are of course at the moment so well provisioned in all sorts of materials that no blockade could have any early effect, but the moral effect should be crushing if it came home to the Germans that no matter what suffering they might be prepared to endure, the military and naval strength of the allies helped by the strangle-hold of the blockade would render their eventual defeat inevitable.

I should mention on that some friends of mine met at Easter at a Winter resort some German acquaintances who had come from Germany and the latter expressed to them the view that the Reich would find it difficult to sustain another Winter. On the other hand I met an Austrian not at all partial to Germany, who seemed well versed in the history of the war and the events which had led to it, and his view was that he was not at all sure that Germany could be beaten this time, and he thought that she would in any case succeed in retaining her mastery of Eastern Europe. An English writer whom I also met and who had just made a tour of the Balkans said that he could not see where the allies could make decisive contact with Germany outside the Siegfried line. The Balkans countries, he said, would be opposed to any extension of the conflict there, and he thought that Turkey would not at present be agreeable to opening the Straits to the allies.

It is I think the general opinion that such is the organisation in Germany that the blockade could not be made sufficiently effective to decide the issue, alone, and that it would require some great defeat, in addition, to affect seriously the German morale. The outcome of events in the north will be awaited anxiously by all neutral countries in proximity to the Reich. It will affect, and may possibly determine, their morale also.

[signed] F.T. CREMINS

No. 150 NAI DFA 2006/39

Confidential report from John W. Dulanty to Joseph P. Walshe (Dublin)
(No. 29) (Secret)

LONDON, 10 April 1940

Prior to my last visit to Dublin I mentioned to Mr. Eden on 29th March that the recent conversations on trade matters between the officials of our two Governments having proved inconclusive, I thought it possible that my Government might suggest a conference of Ministers of both countries for the purpose of seeing whether some comprehensive trade arrangement of mutual benefit might be achieved. Mr. Eden approved the suggestion.

On Friday last when I spoke to him again on the lines laid down by An Taoiseach he seemed somewhat less oncoming. He was not opposed to the suggested conference, indeed he would like it to take place, but he felt that he must as a first step consult his colleagues the Ministers for Food, Supply, and Shipping.[1]

---

[1] Respectively, Lord Woolton, Leslie Burgin and Robert Hudson.

He did not know what trade matters were involved and if they could do anything it would doubtless turn more on political considerations than on trade interests.

I have since spoken to the Minister for Food and Supply, both of whom welcomed the idea of a conference. Lord Woolton said that he had only that day taken office and it would clearly be necessary for him to make some examination of the questions involved, but apart from that he took the same line which his predecessor took with me, namely that our source of supply was far less precarious than others and that he would willingly take all he could from us provided that he could dispose of it with reasonable speed. Mr. Burgin, the Minister for Supply, not only expressed himself as supporting the idea of a conference but made certain suggestions which form the subject of a separate minute.[1]

Yesterday evening Mr. Eden told me that he had consulted Mr. Chamberlain who shared his view that whilst the idea of a conference was sound they ought to try and make sure that there was a reasonable chance of practical achievement thereat, and emphasising the undesirability for both sides of an inconclusive meeting. I pointed out that in the recent conversations between officials the principal questions had been explored and that in consequence there was practically no need for research or preparation of material since most of it was already in existence.

A meeting of the British Ministers concerned was called for today but I am informed that owing to the Scandinavian developments in the war situation it will not be possible to hold this meeting until next Friday. Thursday or Friday of next week (18th or 19th April) is probably the earliest date on which the conference could be convened.

No. 151 NAI DFA 219/7

*Extract from a confidential report from Francis T. Cremins
to Joseph P. Walshe (Dublin)
(S.Gen.1/1) (Confidential)*

GENEVA, 12 April 1940

[matter omitted]

The pro-German attitude of the Italian press and radio in connection with the attack on Norway and Denmark has been much commented upon in this country where it is a matter of extreme concern. As regards the radio, the Italian accounts were violently pro-German on the first day, but several persons remarked that it was slightly more 'nuanced' on the second day. The attitude of the Swiss press is wholeheartedly against the German action, and the German losses have been set out in large headlines. Amongst the public, I have so far detected little anxiety regarding the possibility of the early intervention of Italy in the war, to which I referred in my note of the 10th instant,[2] though British official circles are, I find, anxious in that regard. Everybody, however, is interested in the possibility of developments in the Balkans and the near East, and are speculating as to the attitude of Italy if trouble developed in those regions. There is also a growing fear that if Germany sustained a really serious check in Scandinavia, she might feel compelled to seek another

---

[1] Not printed.
[2] See No. 149.

victim in order to create a diversion for German opinion, and that that victim might be Switzerland 'in order that Italy might join in the war and take over the Tessin area.' The acquisition of the Tessin area in Italian Switzerland would certainly not be a sufficiently important bait with which to tempt Italy. Mussolini would I think enter against the allies if he judged that his entrance would be decisive. But, as Briquet says, Italy would not wish to join the losers, and that no doubt applies whether the losers were the Reich or the others. That is a reason why the first checks which the Germans have sustained in connection with their Scandinavian adventure might prevent Mussolini from taking precipitate action, and cause him to hold his hand until he saw how the Germans finally shaped there, provided of course that he had not committed himself irrevocably to something at the Brenner conversations.

The fear here that Switzerland might be a later victim does not at all mean that the Swiss do not hope for a German failure in Norway. The fact that the allies had at last shown themselves as being serious, and effective, in their help to a small State would greatly increase the morale of all those neutrals who feel themselves to be in danger and are, like Switzerland, ready, and well-prepared, to defend themselves.

There is somewhat less optimism here than existed up to a few days ago in regard to the question of hostilities on the West, chiefly owing to the news which is reaching from Holland and Belgium. M. Colijn's recent article, in which he suggested that small States, which found themselves in danger of attack, should seek allied help before the danger came, instead of waiting until it was too late, is much commented upon. I attach an extract,[1] though you probably have seen the article. Such a suggestion from M. Colijn is taken as an indication that he believes an early attack on Holland to be almost a certainty. One would imagine that the Germans would not so soon attack in the West, where so much time has been given for defensive preparation, but the misadventures of Germany in the sea operations off Norway suggest that Hitler is capable of serious misjudgments of the situation. He seems to have counted upon a complaisant Norway, which, with his seizure of Denmark and of so many vital points right around the Norwegian Coast, could be relied upon to secure him quickly the control of the country. With Norway secured, he could hope to deal at his ease with Sweden, and thus ensure continued and increased supplies of ore and other commodities, though the latter would have to travel by slower routes than before. At the same time he would have cut off very considerable supplies of foodstuffs and materials from Britain. He could then turn to Roumania for more foodstuffs, etc. and claim that his resistance to the blockade could be continued indefinitely. It would be an attractive programme, but his sea losses at the hands of Norway and the allies show that his first plans at any rate have largely miscarried. It remains to be seen how he will fare in the next few weeks in Norway and possibly Sweden, and whether he will be prepared deliberately to open up new fronts where the allies can make contact with him.

Needless to say, there is much speculation here as to whether the U.S.S.R. will intervene in Norway and Sweden in order to secure an Atlantic port and a share in Swedish iron. The intervention of the U.S.S.R. in the north might make allied intervention in the south-east of Europe inevitable. I have heard here in official British circles the fear expressed that Italy might at any time endeavour to occupy Salonika, a suggestion which I understand comes from Balkan sources. That would

---

[1] Not printed.

immediately involve Greece, and of course Turkey and the allies would hardly be slow to react. I am told that Yugoslavian policy is 'wobbly'. A serious check for Germany in Scandinavia might, however, for the moment at least, cause 'non-belligerents' to avoid adventures. I am told by a Frenchman here who has the reputation of being closely in touch with French Government circles, that if it came, the *military* people in France would view Italian intervention without too much anxiety. Italy might not of course, if not pressed by the French, interfere at first in the West, unless there was some sort of large-scale offensive in the West by Germany. She would in any case in all probability have her hands pretty full elsewhere.

In view of the uncertainty of the situation, it would be well if the Department could send me at once the instructions applicable to a time of crisis, which I asked for some time ago. (Your semi-official letter of the 27th October, 1939,[1] refers).

[signed] F.T. CREMINS

No. 152 NAI DFA Madrid Embassy 5/4

Letter from Joseph P. Walshe to Leopold H. Kerney (Madrid)
(Confidential)

DUBLIN, 12 April 1940

It is exceedingly difficult at this end to know precisely what kind of propaganda in relation to Partition would be allowed publicity in Spain and would be likely to win over influential opinion. I can quite imagine the Spanish Government, on account of its own difficulties with certain regions, being somewhat averse from tolerating what they would (unjustly) regard as propaganda of a similar type.[2] What the Taoiseach is above all anxious to do with regard to countries like Spain with numerous internal difficulties is to win over influential public opinion by a process of infiltration. An occasional article in an influential paper would, he believes, be more useful than hundreds of pamphlets and leaflets the fate of which we know from our own experience with regard to publications of other countries.[3] Moreover, anything like a campaign in a foreign country other than Great Britain or America would easily be resented by the authorities as an interference in their relations with Great Britain. I am sure you now know the editors of the principal papers in Madrid and have established friendly relations with them. Could you yourself not write occasional paragraphs or columns on the unity issue,[4] taking care to make them as international and as unlike the Basque parallel as possible?[5] I shall be very glad to hear from you what pamphlets or books we could supply you with in order to enable you to write articles of this type. They would no doubt be better received if they were interspersed with other articles on the cultural, historical and archaeological aspects of Ireland.

We are obtaining some copies of an article by Maurice Walsh in the 'Saturday Evening Post' which got tremendous publicity in America. No pamphlet or leaflet

---

[1] Not printed.
[2] Marginal note by Kerney: 'All wrong'.
[3] Marginal note by Kerney: 'Hundreds are not needed but information has to be given in Spanish, not English, and why not state our case in printed form?'.
[4] Marginal note by Kerney: 'Yes, but why not help me by preparation of a pamphlet? Is it too much trouble?'.
[5] Marginal note by Kerney: 'Does he take me for a fool?'.

of ours has ever been read in the United States by so many people. You will find it good material for your purpose.[1]

It would be very helpful to have from you at an early date a comprehensive appreciation of the possibilities of getting sympathy in Spain for the unity of Ireland, with details as to the personages most likely to be susceptible to Irish propaganda and the particular obstacles which such propaganda might be likely to meet in the minds of the ruling authorities.

Do you think that our insistence on the release of Frank Ryan has in any way lessened your influence in Government circles? I find that the Spanish Minister here[2] bristles up each time I mention the matter to him. I earnestly hope your splendid efforts on behalf of Ryan will soon succeed. The sooner he is released, the sooner we can have normal and more useful relations with the Spanish Government. I think your suggestion about bartering trade concessions for Frank Ryan's release or giving the slightest hint to the Spanish Government that you have such an idea in your mind would be thoroughly bad, and you should carefully avoid giving any such impression.[3] You can imagine the attitude of our Government towards any foreign representative who would offer a trade concession in similar circumstances.

I hope that you and Mrs. Kerney and the children are in good form, and that we shall see you all some time during the summer.

[signed] J.P. WALSHE

How is Spain likely to react if Germany's chances of winning are increased?[4]

No. 153 UCDA P194/540

> *Confidential report from Michael MacWhite to Joseph P. Walshe (Dublin)*
> *(Confidential)*
>
> ROME, 15 April 1940

Since the meeting at the Brenner Pass five weeks ago of Mussolini and Hitler the official attitude of Italy towards the belligerents seems to have undergone a fundamental change. From the outbreak of the war until the early days of March the Italian press was as neutral as any objective observer could desire. Official communications of the opposing forces were printed side by side with little or no editorial comment. Today the presentation of the news is no longer impartial. It is definitely pro German and anti Ally, so much so that one might be inclined to conclude that the country is being prepared for an eventual intervention on the side of Germany. So far, the general feeling has not been unfriendly to the Allies.

The Italian public were not altogether surprised by the sudden invasion of Denmark and Norway. The Italian press had previously emphasised that the Reich would take measures to offset in a sensational fashion the reinforcement of the blockade of the Norwegian coast by the English. Without exception it upheld German action in Scandinavia and had no word of sympathy for the victims.

---

[1] Marginal note by Kerney: 'In English, why not something in Spanish for Spain?'.
[2] Don Juan Garcia Ontiveros y Laplana.
[3] Marginal note by Kerney: 'See reply on Ryan file. JPW displays his ignorance of Spanish ways and his own weak attitude.'.
[4] Handwritten postscript by Walshe.

Suggestive newspaper headings appeared in different newspapers published in different parts of the country at the same time, such as 'Result of the violation of Norwegian neutrality by the British', 'Lightning reply to Franco-British provocation' and the 'Complete failure of the Anglo-French Fleet in its objective'. All press comments were to the effect that the action of the Reich was thoroughly justified being a case of legitimate defense.

In order to understand the Italian attitude on this subject it is well to recall that the Italian press has never protested against the torpedoing of neutral ships by German submarines. When Italian ships were sunk by German submarines or attacked by German airplanes, which was rare, the nationality of the aggressor was passed over in silence. In fact, one important Italian newspaper – 'The Telegrafo' – stated that it was well known to Italian seamen that all submarines and mines in the North Sea were not of German origin and insinuated thereby that Italian vessels were not all sunk by German mines.

In the case of the 'Altmark' the Allies held that once neutrality was violated it could not be integrally respected. The Italians, on the contrary, hold that Germany could not be reproached with the first violation of Norwegian neutrality of which the Allies alone were guilty. According to one Roman daily the laying of mines in Norwegian territorial waters was an act of war, equivalent to the seizure of the territory of a country that was outside the conflict.

After that any delay in taking counter measures would have compromised the German position. The Reich found itself, therefore automatically, under the obligation of occupying Denmark and Norway. Gayda went even so far as to suggest that the Allies intended occupying Denmark as well as Norway only that Germany, aware of their intentions, got there first.

There are other reasons for the anti British attitude of the Italian press. Gayda reproaches England with having always wished to impose her will on other countries by exercising an uncontested supremacy on the sea by which she forces the neutral states to participate in the blockade of one of the belligerents. It is this 'right of the neutrals' that Italy pretends to defend today.

It may thus be seen that the question of the blockade dominates the policy of Fascist Government. The refusal of the English to permit Italian ships to bring coal from Germany still rankles. The control to which Italian ships have to submit leaves a big mark on the Fascist escutcheon. It is humiliating for a proud nation and more than Fascism can afford. It is not, therefore, to be wondered that the Duce has given vent to his feelings. He may not be convinced, notwithstanding pretences to the contrary, of the final victory of the Reich in this conflict. The time may not be ripe for him to decide, but it is unlikely that he will find himself lined up with the losing side.

The 'Osservatore Romano', the circulation of which has risen considerably of late, takes a different attitude to that of the Italian press. In supporting the Allied cause it reminds its readers that sixty Norwegian ships have been sunk by submarines in which four hundred Norwegian sailors have perished. It finds nothing in the British mine laying to justify the occupation of Denmark and Norway by the Germans. The former was a purely naval measure, while the latter brought the conflict on the terrain of the violation of the neutrality of neutral territories themselves. The Vatican organ concludes by stating bluntly that 'the territorial neutrality of the two countries has been violated by the landing of German troops in Denmark and Norway'. The importance of this statement has been much commented upon here coming, as it does, from the highest moral authority in Christendom.

No. 154 NAI DFA 2006/39

Handwritten memorandum by Seán Nunan (London)

LONDON, 17 April 1940

Mr. Walshe telephoned regarding the attached cartoon in the 'Daily Mirror' of the 17th inst.[1] It has created a very bad impression in Ireland and he cannot imagine such an offensive and insulting cartoon being published without the consent of the British authorities. Such a cartoon would not be permitted with regard to Italy, Yugoslavia or other neutrals.

Without waiting for H. Cs. return, call up Stephenson[2] and inform him of our feeling on the matter.

Mr. Walshe said that such actions as this would make him inclined to consider ceasing cooperation with the British.

S. NUNAN

Spoke to Stephenson. He had not seen cartoon but would look into the matter. Expressed regret but said press is not censored.

No. 155 NAI DFA 219/22A

Extracts from the Berlin Legation annual report for 1939-40
(49/31)

BERLIN, 19 April 1940

(1) 1st April – 31st August 1939
[matter omitted]

B. German interest in Ireland
The campaign being carried on by the I.R.A. in England received much publicity in the German press, which had altered its previous policy of aiming at an Anglo-German rapprochement. Irish protests against Partition were frequently reported, so that even the man-in-the-street now knows that this problem exists in Anglo-Irish relations, even though his own ideas of the matter may be very vague.

Emphasis was laid on the fact that we recognised the Government of General Franco before Great Britain did so.

In a public reply on the 28th April 1939 to a letter received from President Roosevelt, who had asked him to define his attitude towards the independence of certain states, the Chancellor asked why Mr. Roosevelt should include Ireland on

---
[1] The cartoon, entitled 'Ireland for Ever', showed a blindfolded de Valera flanked by two blindfolded sentries oblivious to the Swastika-emblazoned 'Sword of Damocles' hanging over de Valera.
[2] John E. Stephenson, Assistant Under-Secretary, Dominions Office, who had responsibility for Irish affairs.

the list. He said that he had read statements by Mr. de Valera which seemed to indicate that Irish independence was threatened not by Germany, but by Great Britain.

Articles on Ireland began to appear more frequently than before in newspapers and periodicals, and books dealing with Ireland sold very well in the shops. The most important of these were:-

>   Robert Bauer:-   Irland, Insel der Heiligen und der Rebeller.
>   Bringmann:-   Gaschichte Irlande
>   Muller-Ross:-   Irland die andere Insel

and German translations of

>   Desmond Ryan:-   Eamon de Valera
>   Ernie O'Malley:-   On another man's wound.

The official German News Agency has a regular correspondent in Dublin since February 1939.[1]

Germany was represented at the European Boxing Championships held in Dublin, and secured one title. The German team was accompanied by journalists, who wrote very favourably of their reception in Ireland. One of them, who represented the official wireless service, spoke from Dublin over the German broadcasting system. A Military Jumping Team competed at the Dublin Horse Show.

A party of school-children from Dresden visited Ireland in August. The Irish side of the arrangements was looked after by Mr. C.L. Dillon, of the High School, Dublin, who, in co-operation with Dr. Thieme of Dresden, has been organising exchange visits for some years past. The Student-Exchange-Service sent five students to Ireland for the academic year 1938-39.

C. German-Irish Trade

The trade agreement concluded in November 1938 worked smoothly. It resembled that in force in the years immediately previous, with one important change, namely, that the various 'Reichsstellen' (State control offices) which purchased the entire amount of our agricultural exports to this country, sent a permanent representative of their own, Dr. Hobohm, to Dublin. All purchases for the Reichsstellen were made by this representative. In previous years agricultural products intended for Germany had been exported under the auspices of the Department of Agriculture, and delivery taken by the Reichsstellen at the German port of entry. The representative of the Irish Department of Agriculture at Bremen, Mr. O'Loan, was recalled, as, in view of the new arrangement, his services were no longer required there.

Live animals and agricultural products accounted for almost all our exports to Germany. The trade in feathers was maintained.

D. Consular Work of the Legation before the outbreak of war

The number of Irish citizens permanently resident in Germany is small, but, before the war, there were generally a few Irish students, though never very many, at German universities. 11 new passports were issued, and passports were renewed in four cases. One passport was made available for additional countries.

---

[1] Dr Karlheinz Petersen, the representative of the Deutsche Nachrichten Büro, later became Press Attaché at the German Legation in Dublin and was well known to Irish Military Intelligence (G2).

Visas for travel to Ireland were issued as follows:-

German citizens	273
American citizens	4
Polish citizen	1
Total	278

Notarial services were rendered on three occasions.
One citizen was repatriated.

E. Assistance given to Irish citizens to return home
A number of Irish citizens who came to Germany for holidays last summer took the wise precaution of sending their names and addresses to the Legation, as there was a constant fear that war might break out suddenly. Fortunately for non-combatants, particularly for neutrals like ourselves, the period of crisis before the catastrophe lasted for about a week, which gave sensible foreigners ample time to leave the country. While leaving the final decision to the individuals concerned, the Legation counselled all citizens who asked for its advice that they should leave the country unless they had some good reason for remaining. It was emphasised, however, that there was scarcely any possibility of Ireland's being involved in the war as a belligerent.

During the last week in August I took up residence in the Legation building. Telephone calls and telegrams came in at all hours of the day and night, and were dealt with promptly as they arrived. In some cases sums of money were lent to Irish people who were short of ready cash. The last of those who wished to return home, Mr. Michael O'Callaghan, of 18 Elgin Road, Ballsbridge, Dublin, left Berlin soon after the outbreak of war.

A special word of praise is due to Miss Walsh for her whole-hearted co-operation throughout that period of tense political excitement and correspondingly increased work for the Legation.

(2) 1st September 1939 – 31st March 1940
[matter omitted]
B. German Interest in Ireland
Our decision to remain neutral in the present conflict was given great publicity. Public interest increased, and articles on Ireland appeared even more frequently in the newspapers. Ireland became a favourite topic for lectures, and numerous requests for information were received at the Legation. Prominence is given to the activities of the I.R.A. The execution of Barnes and McCormick[1] in Birmingham was reported on the front pages of the newspapers, and was the subject of comment in leading articles.

Dr. Ludwig Muhlhausen, Professor Celtic at Berlin University, and Herr Joachim Gerstenberg, a well-known writer of travel-books, lectured in several important cities in Northern Germany under the auspices of 'Kraft durch Freude'.

Madame Maud Gonne MacBride's autobiography, 'Servant of the Queen', was translated into German, and had a large sale.

The German wireless stations inaugurated in December a weekly transmission of news in Irish, broadcast from Hamburg and Bremen. The speakers are Dr.

---

[1] James McCormick used the pseudonym 'James Richards'.

Muhlhausen and Dr. Hans Hartmann, who worked for some time in the Irish Folklore Institute under Professor Delargy.

The average German is at last beginning to see that the difference, politically and otherwise, between Ireland and Great Britain is something more than that between Baden and Wurtemburg, or between Prussia and Saxony, which was the nature of the analogy most people here would have drawn before the war.

One number of a series of propaganda booklets is devoted to 'England's rule by force in Ireland', and one section is given over to Ireland in a volume of facsimile reproductions from British and American sources, entitled 'Concerning English Humanity'.

Many people have expressed surprise that Ireland should not have warmly espoused the German cause from the start, though no statement of this kind has ever found its way into any public utterances. Various newspaper articles have suggested that our Government, in prohibiting the I.R.A., is – against its will – supporting Great Britain, and that the Taoiseach has been forced into a difficult position.

C. General work of the Legation

After the outbreak of war, the Legation was cut off for some weeks from direct connection with Ireland. Contact was maintained through the Irish Legation to the Holy See, which has been very helpful to this Legation on many occasions since September last. Direct telegraphic communication was restored in October. Postal communication never really ceased, but there were delays of over a month in the early stages of the war. The Legation mail was despatched through Rome until the end of December 1939, by which time direct connection had improved considerably.

Direct trading between Ireland and Germany ceased on the outbreak of war, and trade in general has come to a standstill since the introduction of the total blockade.

The most important part of the Legation's work in trade matters has been in connection with the German contraband control. Irish merchants were accustomed to buy large quantities of timber from Baltic and Scandinavian countries. Several ships bound for Ireland with cargoes of wood were brought into German ports for examination, and subjected to long delays. It was suggested that wood consigned to Ireland might be re-exported to Great Britain or Northern Ireland. Our Government gave explicit guarantees that this would not occur, but even this did not at first expedite matters, as the German authorities then suggested that the ships might be seized on the way by the British, and forced to discharge their cargo in an English port. Finally, after energetic protests to the Foreign Office the ships were released singly. The second was not released until definite confirmation had been received that the first had arrived safely in Ireland and so on, until eventually all the vessels were allowed to proceed.

As a result of representations made by the Legation, an alteration was made in the wavelength of the wireless station at Memel, which was interfering with the transmission of the medium-wave station at Athlone.[1]

---

[1] In 1939 the Radio Éireann station at Athlone, Co Westmeath, operated on 565 Kilohertz (Khz), while the station at Memel, now Klaipėda in Lithuania, operated on 564 Khz. Memel became part of the Third Reich on 22 March 1939 following the receipt of an ultimatum from Germany to Lithuania to cede the area to the Reich. In 1940 the Memel station moved frequency from 564 Khz to 1285 Khz.

At the request of the Foreign Office, the Legation agreed to deal with any matters affecting Ireland which might arise in the German occupied regions of the former Poland.

D. Consular Work of the Legation
A few persons of Irish origin who had previously held British passports applied for registration as Irish citizens, and several Irish citizens who had passports in the old form exchanged them for new passports. In all, 16 new passports were issued between 1st September 1939 and 31st March 1940. There were 4 passport renewals. Notarial acts were rendered in 7 cases.

8 visas were granted.

Enquiries were made concerning the whereabouts of Irish people in Poland.

3. Important questions still outstanding at the end of the financial year
(a) The German Government has not given a full report of the circumstances of the sinking of the S.S. 'Inverliffey' (Dept.'s reference 206/45).[1]
(b) The German Government has given no reply so far to our enquiry concerning the sinking of the S.S. 'Germaine' (Dept.'s reference 206/67).
(c) No arrangement has been made for the transfer of currency between Ireland and Germany. Germany is pressing in particular for the transfer of sums due in respect of contracts made before the outbreak of war.
(d) The question of the Legation premises had not been settled. The present lease expires at the end of this year.

4. Conclusion
The present state of war has broken off almost all connections between Ireland and Germany, and consequently the consular and trade work of the Legation has been considerably reduced, but the forty-odd Irish citizens living in Germany and in the German sphere of influence are continually turning to it for assistance and advice. The fact that the Legation still remained on after the outbreak of war was a clear demonstration to the German public, which had had only hazy ideas in the matter, that the Irish state has sovereign status, and can pursue its own foreign policy independently of that of any other country. It is of great historical and political significance that we are maintaining diplomatic relations with a country at war with Great Britain and the members of the British Commonwealth of Nations, and that our right to remain neutral is recognised and respected by both parties.

No political differences have arisen between ourselves and Germany, and the general attitude towards us is one of friendly interest.

[signed] W. Warnock

---

[1] See footnote 1, p. 48.

No. 156 NAI CAB 2/3

> Extract from the minutes of a meeting of the Cabinet
> (G.C. 2/163) (Item 1) (S. 11846)
>
> DUBLIN, 19 April 1940

Trade negotiations with the British Government

It was agreed that the Ministers for Agriculture and Supplies should go to London with a view to taking part in discussions on trade questions with British Ministers which are to commence during the week beginning 28th April, 1940.

No. 157 NAI DFA 219/4

> Extract from a confidential report from William Warnock
> to Joseph P. Walshe (Dublin)
> (43/33)
>
> BERLIN, 20 April 1940

Before sending you a report on the German invasion of Scandinavia a week ago, I had been waiting for the situation to become somewhat clearer.[1] So far, however, I have been waiting in vain. The Germans encountered no opposition worthy of note in Denmark, and have established themselves firmly in Southern Norway.

The German operations against these two countries came as a complete surprise to everybody. Not many days beforehand I had been in the Norwegian Legation, and the officers with whom I spoke were full of resentment against Great Britain, in view of demands by certain British politicians that the German trade with Narvik should be cut off at once, irrespective of Norway's rights as a neutral country.

[matter omitted]

No. 158 NAI DFA Secretary's Files A20/3

> Letter from Leopold H. Kerney to Joseph P. Walshe (Dublin)
> (Confidential)
>
> MADRID, 23 April 1940

Dear Mr. Walshe,

This is just to deal with the latter part of your confidential minute of 12th.[2]

I have reached the conclusion that there are occult influences working against Frank Ryan; I do not attach much importance, at least not at this late stage, to hostility originating in Ireland; that will not carry much weight at present; but I am struck now and again by some stray remarks in the course of conversations – insignificant when taken separately but which, when summed up, force me gradually to the conclusion that there is secret opposition from another country than Ireland. Whilst the attitude of the government as a whole is anything but pro-English, there are officials here and there, and not in Foreign Affairs alone, who are susceptible to English influence.

---

[1] On 9 April 1940 Germany invaded Denmark and Norway.
[2] See No. 152.

I have mentioned the name of Walter Meade[1] in some of my reports; he held the view two years ago that this was the position, and to-day he is absolutely emphatic on the point; he has been of great assistance to me, as you know. He distrusted completely Domingo de las Barcenas, who used to be Under-Secretary, who is now back in Berne as Minister (and who, incidentally, hates Beigbeder like poison); he held the same opinion of his son, Juan, who till a few days ago was Chief of Cabinet to Beigbeder, and who is a Stonyhurst[2] boy; another person in the background is Bolin (head of the Tourist Department), a very close friend of Franco, and who was sent by de la Cierva from London with an English aeroplane to the Canaries in July 1936 to take Franco to Morocco; Bolin used to be correspondent of the A.B.C. in London and I think it was in 1936 that he contributed to his paper an out-and-out anti-Irish article.

The Duchess of Tetuan is completely puzzled by the retention of Ryan, and thinks there is something 'louche' somewhere.

Peche, the new Under-Secretary, whom I saw on 20th April, dodged the issue when I tried to get him to make some statement which might show that he shared the belief of the Minister that prisoners would be released within 3 months; he told me other heads of Missions were also pressing for the release of their nationals and that the War Office was taking its time; but Meade knows for a positive fact that General Lopez Pinto (whom I convinced in Burgos) sent forward to the War Office a very favourable report ('informe'), that this 'informe' has been accepted and adopted at the War Office, and that it is recorded there about Ryan 'que no es culpable'. Meade used to be Aide-de-Camp to General Alonso Vega who is acting as Under-Secretary to the Minister for War; his information is first-hand. If Beigbeder is favourable, as I believe, and if his colleague at the War Office is favourable – well, there must be a nigger in the woodpile somewhere. I now aim at getting the Minister for War to take the initiative of mentioning the matter direct to Beigbeder – short-circuiting administrative intermediaries, who may act as a barrier.

There was a time when my interest in Frank Ryan aroused suspicion in some quarters here; I have lived that down; my relations with everybody at the Foreign Office, from the Minister down, are very smooth and friendly.

I am afraid that we must agree to differ about that suggestion of mine which strikes you as being so thoroughly bad; I think I know the Spaniards better than you do; the Americans mentioned cotton and the Spaniards gave way; the English would not sign a trade treaty without a promise of immediate release of Englishmen; forceful arguments are necessary at times, at least in Spain; I know my suggestion to be thoroughly good, but I defer of course to your view. Can you imagine a Government claiming a ransom of £5,000 in a case which is fresh in your memory? You cannot always compare one Government with another.

With kind regards,
Yours sincerely,
[signed] L.H. Kerney

---

[1] Walter Meade, the son of an Irish émigré to Spain, was General Eoin O'Duffy's driver and interpreter.
[2] Jesuit Catholic boarding school in Lancashire founded in 1593.

No. 159 NAI DFA 243/67

Memorandum from Michael Rynne to Timothy J. Horan (Dublin)
(243/67)

DUBLIN, 23 April 1940

Mr. Duff's minute of the 16th April,[1] forwarding a copy of his previous observations to Mr. Hearne (25th August 1938)[2] seems to have brought this file to life again.

From the practical point of view, however, it is obvious that the matter of 'refugees coming from Germany' no longer presents the problems which it did two years ago. And, from the 'policy' point of view, we must face the fact that the pre-war 'international co-operation' movement of the League of Nations is now as moribund as the League itself appears to have become. In other words, there is no international reason of policy compelling the Government to undertake new obligations vis-à-vis refugees and, clearly, no 'home pressure' upon them to concede further privileges to aliens during the existing war.

If it is felt that Mr. Duff's minute should get a reply, I think the Department of Justice will have to be asked quite definitely for the text of the various reservations which they may desire to have made. The same applies to the Department of Industry & Commerce, which will have to be approached before anything definite can be decided. Both Departments ought to be asked whether participation in the agreements will entail legislation or whether they are implementing, or will implement, their provisions under existing law (e.g., Aliens Act, 1935). If special legislation is essential, there would seem to be much likelihood of the Government postponing the whole matter for the present; if not, it seems questionable if participation in the agreements will serve any useful purpose beyond pleasing the League Secretariat – should that diminishing body be still interested in collecting signatures and ratifications for theoretical undertakings that date from the 'international co-operation' era.

As you are aware, we cannot finally embark on any international engagement involving legislation until that legislation has first been enacted. That is the settled rule in respect of all recent treaty-making in this, as in other, countries. In all the circumstances, it might be well to seek a positive direction from the Secretary at once before proceeding to press other Departments on this question.

[initialled] M.R.

No. 160 NAI DFA 2006/39

Confidential report from John W. Dulanty to Joseph P. Walshe (Dublin)
(No. 34) (Secret) (Copy)

LONDON, 26 April 1940

Further to my Secret minute No. 9 of 3rd February[3] enclosing a memorandum on the subject of the possibility of War refugees from Holland and Belgium, on several occasions the Duke of Devonshire and Mr. Stephenson have asked if we could give our views on the last two paragraphs of that memorandum.

---

[1] Not printed.
[2] Not printed.
[3] Not printed.

I told them that this even tentative inquiry presented difficulties for the Irish Government and asked whether the British Government did not now regard the contingency in question as of decreasing probability. They said it was impossible for anyone to give an opinion on the degree of probability but they felt it was of sufficient likelihood to make it incumbent on them to have some plan prepared. I next asked if they could let us have some indication of the type of preparations they were themselves making. In response they send the enclosed note[1] giving a general outline of their scheme and again say they would be grateful for an early expression of our Government's views as to whether they would be willing to assist on this problem should the necessity arise.[2]

No. 161 NAI DT S11846A

Minute and rough draft relating to the Terms of Reference of the British-Irish trade discussions by Maurice Moynihan (Dublin)

DUBLIN, 29 April 1940

NOTE:
The attached rough preliminary draft of Terms of Reference was prepared to-day on the instructions of the Taoiseach. The Taoiseach approved of its terms and consulted the Ministers for Supplies and Agriculture both of whom agreed. A copy of the document was handed by the Taoiseach to the Minister for Supplies with an intimation that it was to be regarded as constituting the Terms of Reference of the Irish delegation. A copy had previously been forwarded to the Minister for Agriculture.[3]

Rough Preliminary Draft
Trade Discussions with British Ministers
Terms of Reference

To discuss with members of the British Government the various points which have arisen in the course of recent trade discussions between officials of the two Governments, and, provided that arrangements satisfactory to the Irish Government can be made, to negotiate a trade agreement or trade agreements covering the following matters and any matters ancillary thereto:-

1. The disposal on the British market of Irish agricultural products.
2. Supplies of fertilisers, feeding stuffs and other products which form the raw materials of the agricultural industry.
3. Supplies of raw materials for our manufacturing industries.
4. Supplies of essential commodities, including manufactured goods, which we cannot produce ourselves.
5. Provision of foreign exchange.
6. Bulk purchases and chartering of freight.
7. Independent purchases and chartering of freight.

---

[1] Not printed.
[2] Marginal note by Dulanty's Secretary Ms Elizabeth 'Bessie' Foxe: 'Later: Several telephone conversations took place on above subject. B.F. 23/5'.
[3] Marginal note by Moynihan: 'Covering approval accorded by Govt. at meeting on 30/4/40'.

It is understood that no agreement will be entered into in respect of any matter comprised in the scope of the negotiations which would have the effect of prejudicing the position of this country as a neutral in the present European War or could reasonably be regarded by any of the belligerents as affording ground for an attack on this country.

No. 162 NAI DFA Madrid Embassy CON 4/7/22 No. 3

Handwritten minute by Leopold H. Kerney (Madrid)
MADRID, 29 April 1940

Frank Ryan

After visit by H. 'phoned Champourcin, who will communicate with Cuervo and ask latter to recommend, as he has done in other cases, that greatest consideration possible should be given compatible with regulations.

C. says his friend has been ordered to await detailed instructions before seeking interview. C. knows that any attempt to impose conditions may be fruitless.

No. 163 NAI DFA Madrid Embassy CON 4/7/22 No. 3

Handwritten notes by Leopold H. Kerney (Madrid)
MADRID, 30 April 1940

Frank Ryan

Champourcin says Spanish secret service has agreed to put forward request of G. colleagues; latter instructed to suggest visit by R. to G. or USA; told him G. inadvisable and out of question, but USA, perhaps. C. wants visit Burgos with friend after Tues 7/5, using my car.

No. 164 NAI DFA 205/4

Memorandum from Joseph P. Walshe to Eamon de Valera (Dublin)
LONDON, 30 April 1940

Note for the Minister's information[1]

(1) During the last three or four weeks it has been persistently rumoured that in the course of one of his talks, the German announcer known as 'Lord Haw-Haw'[2] made a statement to the effect that 'Ireland is at present a garden of roses, but she will very soon become a garden of tombstones if by trying to increase her exports of food to Britain, she involves herself in the war'.

(2) The Department has been unable to obtain any confirmation of this report. The various members of the Department listen very frequently to the broadcasts from Germany, and none of them has heard any recent unfriendly references to this

---

[1] This note was prepared in response to Deputy William Norton's Dáil question to de Valera of 30 April 1940. Deputy James Hickey (Labour) asked the question for Norton in Norton's absence (see Dáil Debates, vol. 79, col. 1945, 30 Apr. 1940).
[2] William Joyce 'Lord Haw-Haw' (1906-46), British Fascist who had grown up in Ireland and who made radio propaganda broadcasts to Britain from Germany from 1939 to 1945. Executed for treason in 1946.

country. On the receipt of the present question we asked the Legation at Berlin for particulars of any unfriendly references of which they had knowledge. Mr. Warnock has reported that neither he nor any of the other Irish people in Berlin know of any recent unfriendly references to Ireland on the German radio. The B.B.C. maintains a twenty-four-hour 'monitor' service which listens to and records all broadcasts of talks and news from Germany. They told the High Commissioner's Office that the only recent reference to Ireland of which they have record is the statement made on the 20th April in the course of a talk from the 'new British broadcasting station' (which is supposed to be in German territory), to the effect that 'Ireland will probably try to fill Denmark's place in the British market, but if she does, she will insist on getting a good price'.

(3) Although there is thus no official evidence to support the report of recent unfriendly references to Ireland in German broadcasts, it is of course not possible to state definitely that no such references were made. On the other hand, the possibility cannot be excluded that the reports now circulating are pure inventions put about by mischief-makers and circulated by people with no means of checking their accuracy. Last September Deputy P.S. Doyle[1] questioned the Taoiseach about a supposed reference in a German broadcast to 'Éire sheltering under Mr. Chamberlain's umbrella'. Mr. Doyle gave the time of the supposed broadcast and the name of the German station from which it was supposed to have been made. When we subsequently made enquiries in Berlin, the Germans flatly denied that any such reference had occurred in any of their broadcasts. They sent the German Minister in Dublin to the Department to repeat the denial. The report, which was very persistent, would appear to have been quite inaccurate.

(4) The draft reply refers Deputy Norton[2] to the reply made by the Taoiseach to Deputy Doyle last September, which seems to cover the ground very fully. But in view of the fact that we have recently been making representations to the British authorities about unfriendly references to this country in the British press,[3] it seems better that the remainder of the reply should discount the prevailing rumours rather than indicate any unwillingness to make representations to the German Government if the rumours were thought to be correct.

(5) The only foreign broadcasts which are systematically listened to and recorded by this Department are the Sunday evening broadcasts in Irish from Germany.

(6) If Deputy Norton challenges the reply, he might perhaps be told that the reply is as complete as it can be made on the information disclosed in his question, but that if he will furnish the Minister with full particulars of the unfriendly references he has in mind such further enquiries as are possible will be made.

---

[1] Peadar S. Doyle, Fine Gael TD for Dublin South-West.
[2] William Norton (1900-63), Leader of the Labour Party (1932-60).
[3] See Nos 132 and 154.

No. 165 UCDA P150/2571

Memorandum from Joseph P. Walshe to Eamon de Valera (Dublin)

LONDON, 1 May 1940

Discussions between United Kingdom and Éire Ministers

The attached report[1] of the first general meeting held yesterday evening, April 30th, will show the general attitude of the British in regard to trade concessions. Beyond Eden's remark about the fight being one for the freedom of the whole world and the reference in Hudson's[2] statement to trans-shipment there was nothing that could be said to relate to our neutrality. The atmosphere at the lunch in the Savoy and at the meeting in the Dominions Office was extremely friendly. I understand that the same is generally true of the meeting between our Ministers and the individual British Ministers at which special subjects are being discussed. The going is bound to be hard. They appear to be less keen to buy food than any other commodity. They could buy iron, copper, timber, etc. and almost at any price we wished to put on them. They cannot, they say, give us prices for agricultural products higher than those they give to their own farmers. The case is quite frankly stated at the general meeting by all the Ministers. Nothing further about trans-shipment has emerged at the time of writing (4.30 p.m.). Of course nothing will be done without reporting home for instructions.

A general desire to see the end of Partition was expressed by Eden to the Minister for Supplies.[3] Machtig, Deputy Secretary of the Dominions Office, expressed the same pious wish to me. Would you approve of my saying that they could at least hand over the Counties of Tyrone and Fermanagh at once as a gesture, and that we should accept them without prejudice to our claim to the union of the whole area within Ireland? I am quite sure nothing will come of it, but it is a pity to let them get away with the implication that *they* can do nothing. Even the British must admit that they haven't a shadow of a claim to Tyrone and Fermanagh.

There is very real pessimism about the present state of the war operations. The defeat in Norway[4] is regarded as a blow of the first magnitude, not merely to British naval power (which is primarily affected), but to the prestige of Great Britain all over the world. They don't know what to make of Italy's hostile manifestations,[5] as they cannot believe that she is prepared for war on a serious scale, but on the other hand they are not neglecting the necessary precautions. There is a feeling amounting to a conviction that Hitler will take over the whole Balkans and perhaps Holland and Belgium within the next few months, and the Allies have little or no hope of being able to stop him. They hope (why, I don't know) that Russia will not help Hitler and that Turkey will remain friendly. Next year, they say, with the machine they will then have at their disposal they will be able to undo all Hitler's conquests. One is bewildered to hear such optimism from sane men. I have formed the impression that the Government are too soft, too class-prejudiced (they are

---

[1] See No. 166.
[2] Sir Robert Hudson (1886-1957), Minster of Shipping (Apr.-May 1940).
[3] Seán Lemass.
[4] By 1 May British and French forces had begun to withdraw from Norway and German forces were consolidating their position across the country.
[5] See No. 167.

almost all of the wealthy Tory family type) to be able to win a war against men of steel like Hitler, Stalin and their followers. Another element of unwarranted optimism is that Japan will not go into the war against them. They seem to be entirely oblivious of their own reactions in the past to parallel world situations.

[initialled] J.P.W.

No. 166 UCDA P150/2571

> Minutes of British-Irish trade talks
> (Secret)
>
> LONDON, 1 May 1940

Discussions between United Kingdom and Éire Ministers

The first meeting between United Kingdom and Éire Ministers to discuss trade relations between the two countries was held in the Dominions Office at 4.30 p.m. on the 30th April 1940.[1]

MR. EDEN in opening the meeting expressed the pleasure felt by the United Kingdom representatives at the opportunity which these discussions gave them of welcoming the Éire Ministers and officials to London.

The meeting had arisen out of a suggestion from Éire that the detailed discussions of particular aspects of United Kingdom-Éire trade, which had so far been carried out on a basis of individual commodity, might now with profit to both countries be considered as a whole. The United Kingdom Government fully appreciated this view, and were equally anxious to explore the position in the hope of securing mutually satisfactory arrangements.

MR. EDEN suggested that as regards procedure the meeting then in progress should be devoted to a general exposition of the attitude of both Governments, and that various detailed subjects should then be further discussed at separate meetings between the Minister or Ministers directly concerned on both sides. As a result of such meetings, it should be possible to ascertain the points of agreement and the points, if any, on which differences of opinion still existed. A further general meeting could then be held to survey once again the whole field, in the light of these small discussions and, if possible, to secure a satisfactory general understanding.

On Mr. Eden's suggestion, it was agreed that the two secretaries who had been appointed, one from each side, should collaborate to produce an agreed minute of the meeting which would represent the substance of the discussion.

MR. EDEN then referred to the Anglo-Éire Trade Agreement of 1938,[2] which was the foundation of present-day trade relations between the two countries and which afforded a sure basis for the continuance of the development of their mutual complementary trading interests. The impact of the war had, however, had inevitable repercussions on these trading arrangements. In particular, the necessity which the United Kingdom Government had found of taking into their own hands the purchasing of all, or practically all, the main commodities which Éire could supply to the United Kingdom had brought about a situation in which further discussions between the two Governments could usefully be undertaken.

---

[1] Marginal note by Walshe: 'British Report of Meeting – It coincides with my recollection'.
[2] See DIFP V, No. 175.

The main items of imports from Éire to the United Kingdom were agricultural produce, particularly foodstuffs. The United Kingdom welcomed Éire as a source of supply of part of their essential requirements of foodstuffs. There were, however, certain general considerations governing the United Kingdom Government's purchasing policy which he would summarise.

(a) It was part of the United Kingdom Government's policy to encourage the development of agricultural production in the United Kingdom. This encouragement was directed to certain aspects of production not requiring the importation in excessive quantities of feeding stuffs and other material, since the provision of shipping and foreign exchange for such a purpose presented serious difficulty. It would, therefore, be impossible for the United Kingdom Government to take steps which could be represented as encouraging agricultural production in Éire in directions in which they were deliberately refraining from encouraging it in the United Kingdom.

(b) The price paid to the United Kingdom producer included a substantial sum paid by way of subsidy to encourage production, and this factor would have to be borne in mind in considering the price to be paid for Éire produce.

Apart from foodstuffs, the United Kingdom Government also welcomed Éire as a source of supply for other raw materials, both agricultural products and such materials as metallic scrap.

As regards the supplies required by Éire, the United Kingdom Government were willing to undertake, so far as reasonably practicable, to ensure the supply to Éire of the materials which she required to import from overseas. If these supplies were purchased through the United Kingdom, Éire would obtain the benefit of the reduction in price resulting from combining her requirements with the much greater requirements of the United Kingdom. She would also enjoy similar advantages resulting from the joint use of the shipping which can be secured by the United Kingdom. In return for the imports which Éire obtained from this co-operative buying and chartering, the United Kingdom felt that she should undertake to do all her buying and shipping of bulk commodities through the United Kingdom. In order to make the best and most economical use of the shipping facilities, it was clearly essential that programmes for imports should be worked out well in advance in consultation between the United Kingdom and Éire authorities.

As regards foreign exchange, the currency of Éire was linked to sterling, and Éire's requirements of foreign exchange, therefore, had a direct bearing upon the exchange position as between sterling and other currencies.

In conclusion, MR. EDEN stated that the United Kingdom Government regarded the present war as one being fought by them not only in their interests and those of their Allies, but in the interests of all those in the world to whom freedom and democracy were precious. They recognised, and indeed on their own principles were bound to recognise, that the attitude of the Government of Éire towards the war was a matter for the decision of the Government and people of Éire. They were anxious to maintain and promote good relations with Éire and the benefits of mutual trade between the two countries, but they must always bear in mind the paramount purpose of winning the war and of so arranging their policy as to consider always the interests both of themselves and of their Allies.

MR. LEMASS thanked Mr. Eden most cordially for the welcome extended to his colleagues and himself, and expressed the pleasure which the Éire Delegation in their turn felt at the fact that these discussions were talking place. MR. LEMASS also expressed the thanks of the Éire Government for the help and co-operation which had been extended to Éire in so many spheres by the United Kingdom authorities since the outbreak of the present war. Nevertheless, certain difficulties in the trade relations between the two countries had occurred, and it was with a view to clearing away these difficulties that the present talks had been suggested.

In the first place, Éire was anxious to determine what should be her policy in regard to agricultural production in the conditions created by the outbreak of war. The United Kingdom was the only possible outlet for Éire's exports of agricultural produce, and it was, therefore, of vital importance to Éire to know beforehand the quantities which it was possible for the United Kingdom to purchase of the various kinds of agricultural produce which Éire could export. It was also essential for Éire to know for the same purpose what quantities of feeding stuffs and fertilisers she could obtain to maintain her agricultural production.

The Éire Government fully recognised the advantages which resulted from the elimination of competition through the system of combined purchasing of commodities and joint chartering of shipping with United Kingdom Government Departments. Nevertheless, these arrangements had led to certain difficulties principally connected with the desire of the United Kingdom authorities in some cases to limit the quantities of material which Éire imported. Éire was prepared to accept certain limitations on her imports, but she felt it was necessary to reach an understanding as to the nature and degree of such limitations. She did not feel, for instance, that the same limitations on imports as was imposed in the United Kingdom should necessarily be applied to Éire, where conditions might be different. Similar considerations also applied to the chartering of shipping and the provision of industrial raw materials, all of which he hoped would be the subject of discussion.

DR. RYAN emphasised the difficulty of planning Éire's agricultural economy unless she knew beforehand what quantities of her production she could sell to the United Kingdom. He pointed out that agricultural production could not be expanded and contracted in a short space of time to the order of a rapidly varying market. Éire was, therefore, particularly anxious to know what market the United Kingdom could offer to the Éire farmer in present conditions, and then Éire would be able to estimate her requirements of imported feeding stuffs and fertilisers. It was only if the United Kingdom was able to supply the information desired that Éire farmers could receive proper advice from their Government as to the production policy which they should adopt.

Besides the question of the quantity of agricultural production which the United Kingdom could buy from Éire, there was the equally important question of the price which the United Kingdom would pay for it. The Éire farmer desired some long-term assurance on this point, particularly as since September, 1939, prices paid had frequently been unremunerative, to a large extent as a result of increasing costs of production in Éire and the increased cost of freight, especially on such things as feeding stuffs and fertilisers. Éire could not afford to increase subsidies to her farmers, and she must, therefore, look for a remunerative price in the United Kingdom market. Finally, Dr. Ryan mentioned that a reduction in the value of exports from Éire to the United Kingdom would, of course, mean a corresponding reduction in the value of Éire's imports from the United Kingdom.

MR. BURGIN stated that the United Kingdom already bought a great deal of Éire's production, but he and his officials at the Ministry of Supply would welcome further discussions on the quantities and prices of those commodities produced in Éire in which they were principally interested viz: hides, sheep and lambskins, wool, flax, iron and steel scrap and waste, non-ferrous scrap and waste, and timber. He felt that, provided the prices asked by Éire were reasonable, a mutually satisfactory agreement could be reached as regards these commodities. MR. BURGIN said that he would also welcome discussions as regards those commodities dealt with by the Ministry of Supply of which Éire was an importer, particularly phosphate rock and pyrites.

LORD WOOLTON said that he, like Mr. Burgin, was also a willing buyer from Éire, provided that the commodities concerned were offered at a reasonable price. He expected that there might be some difficulty over the question of price, and in this connexion he would like to emphasise that the United Kingdom authorities had to take into account not only the interests of the United Kingdom consumer, but also the difficulties of the United Kingdom farmer, which were very similar to those described by Dr. Ryan.

SIR REGINALD DORMAN-SMITH[1] supported Lord Woolton in his last point. He stated that, owing to the shortage of shipping, the United Kingdom Government had launched a ploughing up campaign with the object of making United Kingdom agriculture less dependent than had hitherto been the case on imported feeding stuffs and fertilisers. With the same object in view, the United Kingdom authorities were urging farmers to concentrate on cattle, as against pigs and poultry. He pointed out that it would, therefore, be impossible for the United Kingdom authorities to make an agreement with the Éire Government which would have the effect of encouraging in Éire, to a greater extent than in the United Kingdom, the kind of production which depended upon imported feeding stuffs and fertilisers. It would, therefore, be necessary to ask that the Éire authorities should in this matter accept equality of treatment with United Kingdom farmers.

SIR REGINALD DORMAN-SMITH also referred to the mutual interest of the United Kingdom and Éire in the supply of store cattle from Éire.

MR. HUDSON mentioned the desire of the Ministry of Shipping that Éire should continue to charter her ships through the United Kingdom, and that the two countries should co-ordinate their import programmes. He also stated that the Ministry of Shipping would like to discuss with Éire Ministers the possibility of making arrangements, in the event of an emergency, for transhipping commodities from ocean liners to coasting vessels in Éire ports;[2] other subjects which might profitably be discussed were the provision of storage for food and other commodities at Éire ports, and the repairing of merchant ships in Éire.

MR. McEWEN[3] stated that the interest of Scotland, like that of the Ministry of Agriculture, was to maintain the trade in store cattle between the two countries, and to see that the principle of equal hardship in the distribution of feeding stuffs and fertilisers was maintained as between farmers in Scotland and in Éire.

MR. LEMASS raised the question of the meaning of the phrase 'principle of equal hardship', to which reference had been made by several United Kingdom

---

[1] Sir Reginald Dorman-Smith (1899-1977), Minister of Agriculture (1939-40).
[2] Marginal note by Walshe: '"Harbours" was the word used'.
[3] John McEwen (1894-1962), Under-Secretary of State for Scotland (1939-40).

Ministers. He claimed that in some respects the hardships which had been inflicted on Éire by the present war were even greater than those which had been inflicted on the United Kingdom, and mentioned in this connection the unemployment situation in Éire. He considered, therefore, that it would not be fair to insist upon the application of equal hardship in every detail to Éire. Moreover, it had to be remembered that the Éire primary producer at the time of the outbreak of war was at a lower level of prosperity than the United Kingdom farmer, and allowances must be made to redress this position.

It was agreed that discussions between Mr. Lemass and Dr. Ryan and appropriate United Kingdom Ministers on detailed subjects should proceed without delay, and that a further general meeting should be arranged for the afternoon of Friday, the 3rd May, at 4.30 p.m.

No. 167 UCDA P194/540

Confidential report from Michael MacWhite to Joseph P. Walshe (Dublin)
(Confidential)

Rome, 2 May 1940

Since the outbreak of the present European conflict Italy has passed through many anxious moments when the country seemed to be on the brink of war. On none of these occasions, however, has the feeling been so intense as during the past week. Today, everybody is pessimistic and in diplomatic circles the worst is feared.

Last Friday, on winding up the session of the Fascist Chamber its President, Count Grandi,[1] a reputed moderate and former Ambassador to Great Britain, startled the public when he said 'The Fascist Empire is not and does not know how to be outside this conflict'. Then on Sunday night Signor Ansaldo, editor of the Foreign Minister's newspaper, 'Il Telegrafo', in a broadcast to the armed forces said 'We, Soldiers of Italy, give full honour to the valour of the allied forces, but we hope and trust that Germany will win. We are therefore awaiting orders. We are ready'.

Because of these declarations and the hostile attitude of the Italian press, the British, on Monday issued orders to their ships on the way to and from the Far East to keep outside Mediterranean waters and made provision, at the same time, for furnishing escorts to those ships already on the way between Gibraltar and Suez. The allied Fleets in the Mediterranean have been further reinforced and are believed to be in occupation of all the strategic points under their control in these waters. The personnel of the British and French Embassies have everything in readiness for a hurried departure.

The British Chargé d'Affaires[2] had an interview yesterday with Count Ciano, but the nature of their discussion has not transpired. The American Ambassador[3] also saw the Duce yesterday, because of the seriousness of the situation, but nothing has been disclosed as to the bearing of their conversation. Later in the evening I met at a party, a number of officials of the American Embassy together with their wives. They all seemed pessimistic and the women folk were apparently

---

[1] Count Dino Grandi (1895-1988), Italian Minister for Foreign Affairs (1929-32), President of the Chamber of Fasci and Corporations (1938-43).
[2] Sir Noel Hughes Havelock Charles.
[3] William Phillips (1878-1968), United States Ambassador to Italy (1936-41).

under the impression that orders would be forthcoming from Washington, at any moment, for them to return to the United States. One could only conclude that the impression left by the Duce on the Ambassador was responsible for their gloomy state of mind.

Despite these alarms, it does not seem that Italy is making any important military preparations. Only one class has recently been called to the colours which would bring the total under arms to about a million and a quarter men. The Italian air force, with about 3,000 planes, many of which are far from modern, is supposed to be on a war footing. The Italian navy is fully mobilised. This arm is particularly strong in submarines of which it has 113. Many of these are, however, of a low tonnage, but could be very effective at a radius of one hundred miles or so from their base.

Yesterday the Italian railway, postal, telegraph and radio services were put on a war footing. It would, therefore, appear that all the preliminary preparations have been made to permit Italy to change her policy from one of 'non-belligerency' to that of active participation on the side of her ally, or, to independent action against Yougoslavia, in the course of a couple of hours.

I am now satisfied that the Duce has made up his mind to enter the conflict on the side of Germany of whose eventual victory he seems to be convinced. It may be in a week or six weeks or even six months, but before taking that step Hitler must bring off some spectacular coup that would help the Italian public to make up its mind to back him to the limit. Had the invasion of Norway gone according to plan, Italy would probably have entered the conflict at once, and it is quite possible she will do so if the allied forces are ejected from Scandinavia. The anti British campaign in the Italian press has already convinced many Italians of the eventual defeat of the allies and the fact that the British forces in Norway are now fighting with their backs to the wall is being played for all it is worth.

No. 168 NAI DFA 219/4

Confidential report from William Warnock to Joseph P. Walshe (Dublin)
(43/33)

BERLIN, 4 May 1940

You will have seen in the press reference to the speech delivered in the Chancellery on Saturday afternoon by the Foreign Minister before the Diplomatic Corps and representatives of the foreign and home press. The invitations were issued suddenly on Friday evening. The entire Diplomatic Corps, from the Ambassadors down to the junior attachés, were invited.

The speech was intended to show that Great Britain had planned to land troops in Norway, and that the Norwegian Government would have connived at such action. British and French diplomatic and consular officials had been engaged for some time past in collecting information regarding Norwegian ports and aerodromes. An expedition was already on its way, but it was anticipated by the German Army and Navy. The British ships on the high seas turned back when the news of the German occupation of Denmark and the most important Norwegian ports became known.

After Herr von Ribbentrop's speech copies of a new White Book were distributed.

The book consists of facsimile reproductions of documents found in Norway, as follows:-
(1) Papers taken from British prisoners captured at Lillehammer. It is claimed that these papers show that a British force was on its way to Norway on the 6th and 7th April. Among the ships engaged in the operation was the cruiser 'Glasgow'.
(2) Copies in clear of telegrams sent by the British Consul at Narvik.
(3) A questionnaire sent by the Director of Intelligence at the British Admiralty to the British Consul at Narvik.
(4) Extracts from the papers of the French Naval Attaché in Oslo.
(5) Documents found in the Norwegian Ministry of Foreign Affairs.

The instructions issued to the 8th Battalion of the Sherwood Foresters on the 7th April would indicate that the battalion was on its way to Stavanger that day on board the cruiser 'Glasgow'. The 1st Battalion of the Leicester Regiment was to embark on the 7th April on the steamer 'Cyclops'. A captured diary has an entry under the 7th April: '10.00 hrs. Rosyth, on to H.M.S. Devonshire, to go to Stavanger'. In the German view, these papers refute completely British statements to the effect that the Allies at no time had any intention to occupy Norwegian Territory.

British and French agents had been making arrangements in Norway for some time beforehand. Former British naval officers were appointed as consular officials. They collected information concerning quays, docks, landing-places, etc. They endeavoured to conceal the real aim of their enquiries by mentioning the possibility of Britain's sending assistance for Finland. It appears from the reports of the French Naval Attaché at Oslo that even local military authorities were asked for information, from which the conclusion is drawn that the activities of these agents must have been known to the Norwegian Government – a further proof of unneutral behaviour on its part.

Documents found in the Norwegian Ministry of Foreign Affairs are reproduced to show that Mr. Koht, the Foreign Minister, was not in favour of taking any definite measures to resist a landing by Allied troops, should Britain and France propose to send assistance to Finland through Norway. In his opinion Norway should in such circumstances do no more than enter a formal protest.

The Norwegian Government must have been aware of the general nature of the Allies' intentions. On the 5th February the Norwegian Minister in London sent a confidential report of a meeting of Scandinavian press-men with Mr. Winston Churchill (See E. No. 4). Mr. Churchill is alleged to have declared openly that the aim of the British policy in Scandinavia was to bring Norway and Sweden into the war.

An introductory note to the White Book concludes as follows:- 'Although the Norwegian Government could thus be in no doubt as to England's real intentions, it allowed British espionage on Norwegian territory to continue further. Its whole conduct, as expressed in the anaemic protests against continued English violation of Norwegian territorial waters, amounted to a systematic favouring of antineutral intentions on the part of England. The then Norwegian Government thus knowingly advanced the plans of the Western Powers for the extension of the war, and ignored the vital interests of the Norwegian people'.

Both the speech and the White Book have made a profound impression on the German public, and the effect is increased by articles in the newspapers. German people are, in my experience, quite willing to place absolute faith in the utterances of their leaders, and never show much inclination to analyse or criticise them. At present they are in a very patriotic mood, and are cheerfully suffering discomforts in everyday life because they believe that they are fighting a just war – not one of their own choosing, but one which has been forced on them by the British, who grudge Germany a place in the sun. Great Britain with her vast empire, and enormous wealth, cannot bear to think that another country should prosper, for fear that she should lose her predominating position.

The news of the hasty retreat by the British from Southern Norway has, naturally, been received with great jubilation by the German press, and by the people, too. One is prompted to ask what has become of Mr. Churchill's boast that any German ship endeavouring to cross the Skagerrak would be sunk. The British wireless announced regularly every day last week that the German advance towards Dombaas in the Gudorandsdal was being checked, and that fresh British troops were arriving. At the beginning of the campaign it was reported that Bergen and Trondheim had been taken by British forces, and after this had been contradicted, it was announced that the Norwegians had re-conquered Narvik. The only people in ignorance of the Norwegian success were, said British propagandists, the Germans and the Italians. All this has made the Western Powers appear ridiculous in the eyes of the world, and their stock has sunk considerably. Acquaintances of mine from neutral countries are now, for the first time, expressing the opinion that Germany may win the war.

[signed] W. WARNOCK

No. 169 UCDA P150/2571

Report from Joseph P. Walshe to Eamon de Valera (Dublin)
(Most Secret)

LONDON, 6 May 1940

1. I saw Mr. Eden by appointment at 3 p.m. on Friday, 3rd May. The time had been arranged by Sir John Maffey but I asked the High Commissioner to accompany me. Mr. Eden received me in his usual very friendly way. I gave him your special good wishes and told him that you felt great satisfaction that our friendly relations had continued so successfully, notwithstanding all the difficulties created by the war.

2. I told him that you were particularly glad that you had been able to maintain your position of benevolent neutrality. The strict framework of neutrality had been maintained but Mr. Eden was fully aware that we were giving positive help in several ways. I then detailed to him the categories in which that help was being given. The list was quite an impressive one and he seemed to be getting the picture as a whole for the first time. I deliberately began in this way in order to let him see that his Government were very much in our debt.

3. I then went on to talk to him about the appearance of an anti-Irish article in the British press at almost regular fortnightly intervals and I gave him the News Review placard which was appearing all over London with the caption 'Nazi Activities in

Ireland'. I pointed out to him in detail how very serious to our good relations the continuance of such articles might prove. Quite a lot of our people were beginning to believe that there was some sinister purpose behind it. It was all very well for him and his officials to say to the High Commissioner and myself that the News Review and the other papers in which hostile articles had appeared were papers of no importance. He must remember that the worst prejudices were formed by the very people – the lower middle classes no doubt – who read these papers; such prejudices were bound to percolate upwards and eventually to influence the whole population against us. I had told Maffey before that I had a remote suspicion myself that these articles were encouraged by some branch of the Naval Intelligence. At any rate I succeeded in making Eden look quite worried and he expressed his determination to put an end to this type of article in the British press. At first apart from arguing the unimportance of the papers in which these articles were appearing, he hinted that their censorship had no real power to prevent the publication in the press of any particular type of article except it were of such a type as to provide information to the enemy. His argument is in effect contradicted by their own censorship regulations and I put it to Eden that if similar articles were being written against America, or Belgium or Holland they would very soon be stopped. The High Commissioner was rather opposed to my making a strong case in this matter on account of the relative unimportance of the press involved but I could not accept his view. His view was that to make too much of such matters might appear to Eden to be somewhat 'parochial'. I don't know whether you share that view but I feel myself that we must remain completely indifferent to what they may think of any particular protest. No doubt any interest of any member of the group of States with which they have special relations would appear to them to be of a relatively unimportant character and I can't feel that I have made a mistake in pressing for a real effort to put an end to anti-Irish articles. I intend to use every opportunity (as I already have done) with all the officials I meet to deplore such an interference with our good relations and to urge that appropriate measures should be taken.

4. I told Eden once more that any interference by them with our neutrality would be a disaster for them as well as for us. It would immediately turn against them the sympathy which had been evoked in their favour by the fact that they were opposed to a dictatorship which was largely anti-Christian in its outlook. Our neutrality should constitute for them a very real help in the United States where Irish opinion was free (because of what our neutrality symbolised) to follow its natural tendency to oppose anti-Christian forces. I did not however conceal from him that the establishment of close relations with Russia (however remote that might be) might make a very real change in the general Irish attitude towards the Allies. The leaders of Germany were indeed anti-Christian but a large section of the German people were good Catholics and good Protestants and might be trusted in the end to re-establish the prestige of Christianity in their own country, but Russia's atheism was aggressive and incurable. That country had moreover committed two acts of aggression which were just as bad as those committed by Germany. Eden said he really didn't believe that they would ever succeed in getting Russia on their side but at the same time he felt that they could not reject any help from that quarter.

5. I spoke to him about the impossible position in which their slowness in fulfilling our Army orders had placed us. Our Air Force might soon be grounded

through want of spare parts. Moreover, our aircraft were largely without the necessary machine guns and wireless equipment. Our coast patrols might soon become impossible and our Army would not have the essential aid of the Air Force in repelling possible attempts at landing from the sea or from the air. I told him that I intended, in conjunction with the High Commissioner, to visit the higher officials more immediately concerned with this question. Eden, while admitting that we should get spare parts and aeroplane equipment with all possible speed, said it was quite hopeless to expect more aeroplanes or more anti-aircraft guns. I had been more or less prepared for this attitude by Maffey in the course of a long conversation in the train between Liverpool and London. He said – and he was obviously repeating what he had been told by the military and naval people here – that he could not see what on earth we wanted to do with anti-aircraft guns, anti-tank guns, and similar equipment. There is not any doubt that we never should have asked for anti-tank guns because such a request was bound to make them suspicious and to extend their suspicions to all our demands. I thought it better to say to both Eden and Maffey that we were ready to discuss with the people concerned here what they really could give us outside the categories which they declared to be impossible to deliver now or within any reasonable period of time. I feel that we can get very soon Bren guns[1] and ammunition for them, aeroplane spare parts, and the necessary equipment in wireless and machine guns. They believe that this equipment would serve their interests as well as ours, and I don't believe it is of any use our trying to exert further pressure with regard to our general demands. If we do not concentrate on what they are ready to give us we might find ourselves in the position of getting nothing at all. It looks as if we might have to rely on Bren and other machine guns as our major defence weapon.

6. I tried to impress upon Eden the need for persuading his colleagues of the necessity of making trade concessions to us. The effect on public opinion would be considerable. He had plenty of political arguments to give his colleagues and they should be aware that the best propaganda the British could do in Ireland, which had a largely farming community, would be to give us better prices for our agricultural products.

7. I told him that you were constantly thinking of the unity of Ireland and that you earnestly hoped that he would give his serious attention to the restoration of the Six Counties. Although there was no time to receive any instruction from you on the particular point I did say that there was nothing on earth to prevent them handing over immediately Tyrone and Fermanagh as there could not be the slightest dispute as to what was the desire of the inhabitants. After all, they were fighting for small nations and public opinion could not oppose a measure which was so strictly in accordance with the ideals they were fighting for. Of course you do not renounce for a moment Ireland's claim to the whole excluded area but you could not see that there was any difficulty at all for them with regard to the two counties whatever internal political difficulties there might be with regard to the Six. Eden said it was not so easy as I thought and even the restoration of the two counties, would present serious difficulty. However, I think the raising of this question made

---

[1] The Bren gun was the main infantry light machine gun used by British forces during the Second World War. It remained in use late into the twentieth century in conflicts including the Falklands War and the First Gulf War. The weapon saw service with the Irish Defence Forces from the Second World War until the early 2000s.

him feel more acutely that they were illogical in making this exception to their general attitude and I feel that it had some effect in making him more determined to give us concessions on the trade side.

8. I learned from the Deputy Secretary of the Dominions Office[1] on Saturday afternoon, in the course of a drive into the country, that Maffey had been exceptionally helpful and that he kept impressing on all the Ministers concerned that it was a political necessity to make some real concessions to us on the trade side.

[initialled] J.P.W.

No. 170 NAI DFA Paris Embassy 19/34A

Extract from a confidential report from Seán Murphy to Joseph P. Walshe (Dublin)
(Copy)

PARIS, 11 May 1940

1. Belgium and Luxemburg both called on French aid yesterday. The general feeling is that the war proper has now begun. The press seems to be unanimous on that point and most of the papers have printed editorials to that effect. In so far as the military consequences of this latest development is concerned French opinion is very confident of the final result. A number of writers (de Kerillis, military correspondents of Le Jour, Petit Parisien, etc.) lay stress on the value of the Dutch and in particular the Belgian forces. The military correspondent of the Temps states that the Franco-British High Command has had prepared for a long time the system of defence of the area now invaded …
[matter omitted]
   On the whole it seems to be expected that the French front proper will, one way or another, become the field of big activities in the very near future.
[matter omitted]
4. There is little comment on the new Cabinet in London, opinion had, however, been somewhat prepared for Mr. Churchill's appointment as Prime Minister through Havas-Reuter dispatches yesterday as to the unwillingness of Labour to serve under Mr. Chamberlain and the possibility of either Lord Halifax or Mr. Churchill taking over. It is probable that Mr. Churchill's appointment will be favourably received by public opinion as he has acquired a reputation here for energy and wholeheartedness in the war against Germany.

No. 171 NAI DFA Holy See Embassy 14/9/1

Instructions from the Department of External Affairs to the Heads of Diplomatic Missions and other Offices abroad in the event of an emergency
(Secret)

DUBLIN, 11 May 1940

I. The following instructions are intended to cover the various sets of circumstances in which it may be found necessary for a Representative abroad to remove his Legation or Office from the capital of accredition at short notice. The instructions are intended primarily for the Principal Representative for the time being in

---

[1] Sir Eric Machtig.

Documents on Irish Foreign Policy, Volume VI, 1939–1941

the country concerned. Officers in charge of subsidiary posts (Consulates General, Consulates, etc.) should not act on the instructions without consultation with, and the approval of, the principal representative in the country in which they are stationed.

II. *In the case of a state of war arising between Ireland and the country of accreditation.*
(a) Appointment of neutral power to take charge of Irish interests
The Minister Plenipotentiary or other principal representative will be notified as early as possible of the existence of the state of war and of the name of the neutral power that will be requested to protect Irish nationals, property and interests. Unless there are special instructions to convey, this will be done by a telegram containing the word 'TONE' followed by the name of the neutral Government in clear. The Minister or other principal representative will at once notify the diplomatic representative of the neutral country named in the telegram that his Government are being asked by the Irish Government to charge themselves with the protection of Irish nationals, property and interests. He will request the diplomatic representative concerned to undertake these duties provisionally pending the formal assent of his Government, and express the hope that he will be prepared to take charge of any archives, Government property, etc. which it may be desired to entrust to his care.

(b) Notification to Government of accreditation
The Head of the Mission will next inform the Minister for Foreign Affairs or other appropriate Minister of the country of accreditation that he has received instructions to withdraw the Irish diplomatic mission and to request passports for himself, his family and his staff, including any consular staffs under his supervision. He will also indicate the Government that has been asked to take charge of Irish interests and add that, pending a definite arrangement, the protection of those interests has been confided provisionally to the diplomatic representative of that Government.

(c) Disposal of confidential papers, codes, etc.
Code and cipher books and all important confidential documents and files should be destroyed by fire *immediately it becomes apparent that the withdrawal of the mission is imminent*. A list of all the documents, etc. destroyed (which may take the form of suitable markings in the Register) should be brought away. In the case of confidential files, the list should contain, if possible, the reference number of any correspondence from the Department which may be on the file. Confidential papers should be regarded as including all papers on matters affecting the political relations between Ireland and other countries. The test to be applied in deciding what papers are to be regarded as confidential is, would the publication of the paper, or the knowledge of its contents by enemy country, embarrass the Government or endanger any public interest? The due destruction of confidential files and papers will be greatly facilitated if, as soon as even a remote possibility of withdrawal arises, an advance list of the documents, etc. that would require to be destroyed is prepared at once and the documents on the list kept segregated from the other papers in the office. Official seals, rubber stamps, etc. should be destroyed or defaced if they cannot be brought away. Particular care should be taken to destroy

by fire all passport blanks, consular stamps (unless they can be brought away), emergency certificate blanks, stamps for endorsing passports, and all other material normally used in the issue of passports and other documentary evidence of Irish nationality and identity.

(d) Termination of leases
If the office or residential accommodation provided for the Mission that is being withdrawn is rented by the State, notice of the termination of the lease or leases should be given in writing as soon as it is apparent that withdrawal is imminent, and arrangements should be made, to the extent that time allows, for the removal and storage of the State-owned furniture and effects.

(e) Disposal of non-confidential archives, office supplies, etc.
Non-confidential archives should be transferred to the neutral mission or Government that is being asked to take charge of Irish interests; but where the office occupied by the Mission that is being withdrawn is State-owned, such archives may be left on the premises. In such a case, the archives should be placed in presses or cupboards, which should be locked and sealed in the presence of a member of staff of the neutral mission. A protocol should be drawn up recording the fact that this has been done. If no neutral mission has been appointed to take charge of Irish interests, non-confidential archives, supplies, etc. should, so far as is possible, be destroyed.

(f) Accounts
The Mission's accounts should be brought up to date and a reconciliation account should be made out. (This emphasises the necessity of avoiding arrears of accounting work and of keeping the cash, stamp and other accounts written up to date).

The prepared current accounts and supporting vouchers and (if possible) consular stamps on hand should be brought away. If this proves impracticable, the accounts, etc. should be handed over to the diplomatic representative of the neutral Government that is being asked to take charge of Irish interests.

The cash in hand and to credit in the official account may be used for the issue of imprests to the head of the mission and the members of his staff who are Civil servants. A special effort should be made to arrange with the Bank for the transfer of any balance remaining, in United States dollars or some other free currency, to the account of the Department of External Affairs in the National City Bank, Dublin. Alternatively the Bank should be asked to issue a bank draft, payable to the Head of the Mission in United States dollars, or some other free currency, in some neutral country. If this is impracticable, the diplomatic representative of the neutral Government assuming the protection of Irish interests should be given the balance of the cash on hands and a cheque drawn in his favour to cover any credit balance in the official account.

The keys of State-owned office or residential premises should also be handed over to the neutral representative as soon as these premises have been finally evacuated and locked up.

A receipt should be obtained for everything that is transferred or handed over to the neutral diplomatic mission, and the receipts should be brought away.

If no neutral representative has been appointed and it is impossible to secure the transfer of surplus balances, a statement of the official account should be obtained from the Bank, and this statement, together with the accounts, vouchers, keys, etc. should be brought away.

(g) Functions of the Neutral Representative
It should be made clear to the neutral diplomatic representative that, in taking charge of the Irish interests, he does so on behalf of his own Government and not as acting Irish representative. It will therefore be necessary for him to account through his own Government and to use his own seals, stamps, etc. in respect of any consular service he may render on our behalf. It follows that any account books, cash in hand, seals and fee stamps that may be handed over to him are being left in his custody only, and should not be used by him.

(h) Staff
The appropriate notice of termination of appointment or payment in lieu of notice should be given to any locally recruited staff. It is possible that the neutral representative may ask that a member of the locally recruited staff be left on temporary duty to assist the work of transfer. The Minister or principal representative may agree to this at his discretion. Notifications should be issued to the appropriate authorities to terminate telephone, lighting, etc. services. In the case of State-owned premises, water, light, etc. should be turned off at the mains.

Having disposed of the foregoing and any other matters calling for his attention, the Head of the Mission, together with his family and his staff (other than any locally recruited staff) will proceed immediately to Headquarters. Should the likelihood of the withdrawal of any mission be foreseen sufficiently in advance, every effort will be made to provide the Head of the Mission in due time with any funds necessary to enable him to meet the travelling expenses. Alternatively, the American Express Company will be authorised to make suitable travel arrangements through their local offices, subject to reimbursement by the Department.

III. In case it becomes necessary owing to civil disorder, or air attack or invasion (i.e., in circumstances not involving a breach of relations between Ireland and the country of accredition) for the Mission to leave the capital of the country of accreditation and re-establish itself in a different, or some other part of the same, country

In the type of emergency contemplated under this heading, the following instructions will apply:

(a) Abandonment of capital of accreditation
The Minister or principal representative should not leave the capital of accreditation unless instructed by the Department to do so or, in the absence of instruction from the Department, unless the Government to which he is accredited and/or the diplomatic corps generally are leaving the capital.

(b) Disposal of confidential papers, codes, etc.
Unless their safe transit and subsequent safe custody can be assured, all ciphers and confidential documents and files should be destroyed in accordance with the

instructions contained in paragraph II (c) above. As it will be necessary, however, that the Minister or principal representative should continue to be able to communicate with the Department in a confidential code, the documents, etc. which constitute the machinery of the 'Personal Code' should not be destroyed without specific instructions from the Department. The consular seals and stamps, together with a supply of passport blanks, emergency certificate blanks and passport endorsement stamps, should be brought away. Surplus stocks of passport blanks, etc. may if necessary be destroyed, a proper record of the material destroyed being kept.

(c) Termination of leases
Leases should be terminated and arrangements made for the removal and storage of State property in accordance with the instructions contained in paragraph II (d) above.

(d) Disposal of non-confidential archives, office supplies, etc.
If the abandonment of the capital is caused by the actual or probable occupation of the capital by a country between which and Ireland a state of war exists, these should be destroyed. Otherwise, they should be placed in locked and sealed presses or cupboards and either left on the premises, if the premises are State-owned, or moved into storage with the official furniture and effects, if they are not.

(e) Accounts
The instructions contained in paragraph II (f) above should be followed *mutatis mutandis*. If the Minister or principal representative considers it desirable, however, the entire balance in the official account in the Bank may be withdrawn in cash and brought with him by the Representative for the maintenance of the mission in its new habitat pending the establishment of regular communications with the Department. Proper accounts will, of course, be kept.

(f) Staff
All locally recruited staff should be given notice or payment in lieu thereof. If the mission concerned has, however, only one shorthand-typist, and that one is locally recruited, the Minister or principal representative may, at his discretion, maintain her in the temporary employment of the mission if she is prepared to take up duty in the new quarters.

(g) Communication with the Department
The Minister or principal representative should inform the Department as soon as possible of the fact of his abandonment of the capital of accreditation and of the new address, telephone number, etc. of the Mission.

No. 172 NAI DFA Paris Embassy 19/34A

Extract from a confidential report from Seán Murphy to Joseph P. Walshe (Dublin)
(Copy)

PARIS, 14 May 1940

The tendency here, both in official and other circles, is to represent the new stage on which the war has entered as a result of the German invasion of Holland and Belgium, as not likely to give any definite result for some time. M. Frossard, Minister for Information, spoke on the radio at least twice in the last three days, and exhorted public opinion not to be expecting any rapid developments. The Military Correspondents all take the same view. They contend that the Allied plan of campaign involves preparations extending over several days, and that until these preparations are complete, Allied resistance to Germany cannot be expected to reach its maximum. On the whole they argue that the Belgian resistance is as effective as was to be expected, although they regret the fall of the fortress of Eben-Emael.[1] As far as the Dutch resistance is concerned, General Duval and the Paris Soir both point out that the traditional Dutch military tactics are to withdraw into the stretch of country between Haarlem, Utrecht and Rotterdam. Duval, in to-day's Journal says that 'the general progress of the Germans has only a relative and temporary substance. The battle is only beginning; it is clear that it will be hard and will require all our energy.' The military correspondent of to-day's Petit Parisien expresses more or less the same view. He lays particular stress on the success of a detachment of French tanks, which in the region of St. Trond were reported in last night's French war communiqué, to have counter attacked, and inflicted heavy losses on a German tank detachment. He states that this encounter proved the great superiority of the French tank material. The Journal and some others have suggested that the French should carry out reprisals for the bombardment by the Germans of French cities.

2. The military situation is naturally the dominating pre-occupation of the press at the moment. The 'Journal des Debats', however, had a leader on the changes in the French Cabinet. The paper more or less maintains its critical attitude towards the participation of the Socialists in the Government. It doubted whether 'the presence of two national Ministers will suffice to correct the notorious imperfections of the Cabinet' and held that it was 'with the idea of being useful, preventing bad decisions and urging good ones' that M. Marin[2] and M. Ybarnegaray[3] joined the Cabinet. On the other hand the Socialist Party Congress which met on the 12th inst. agreed to postpone all discussion of internal politics. It was thought that much might have been said both in regard to the responsibilities for M. Daladier's fall and participation in the Reynaud Cabinet.

---

[1] Belgian fortress on the Belgian-German border between Liège and Maastricht, near the Albert Canal. Built between 1931 and 1935 it was thought impregnable. On 10 May 1940 German paratroopers landed on the fortress with gliders and one day later, reinforced by German infantry, they captured the fortress.

[2] Louis Marin (1871-1960), academic and politician, joined Reynaud's cabinet on 10 May 1940.

[3] Michel Albert Jean Joseph Ybarnegaray (1883-1956), served as Minister of State in Reynaud's government from 10 May 1940.

The retirement of Mr. Chamberlain, and the arrival of Mr. Churchill as Prime Minister have not been extensively commented on. Bernus in the 'Journal des Debats' thinks that Mr. Churchill will be excellent, 'if – as there is reason to think, experience has added to his energy and spirit of initiative, an element of prudence or ponderation.' He thinks that history will do justice to Mr. Chamberlain's efforts for peace. This was also the view of Le Temps.
[matter omitted]

No. 173 NAI DFA 2006/39

> *Confidential report from John W. Dulanty to Joseph P. Walshe (Dublin)*
> *(No. 37) (Secret) (Copy)*
>
> LONDON, 14 May 1940

As I had made a courtesy call on Mr. Neville Chamberlain when he became Prime Minister three years ago I thought An Taoiseach would feel that it was fitting that I should make a similar call this afternoon on his leaving that Office.

He was in good spirits, apparently relieved more than depressed over the recent political crisis and its outcome, and certainly talked with unwonted freedom and candour.

Though but an incident in the war, Norway, he said, had been made the occasion for an outburst of discontent with the late Government on the part of the Opposition and certain newspapers. Some of the attacks had been made on him personally while others had taken the line that the blame was not so much on the Prime Minister himself as on those he had around him in the Cabinet. Though only a phase of a much bigger affair, Norway had proved a focus point and while people had said that if the time-table of the debate had been differently arranged – had Mr. Churchill spoken earlier instead of winding up the discussion a proper perspective would have been secured – he (Mr. Chamberlain) was clear that a new Government was essential.

Mr. Chamberlain referred to the infiltrations of treachery which the Germans had made in Norway. I mentioned that Dr. Koht, the Norwegian Foreign Minister, had said in a speech in London that whilst there had been a few instances of individual treachery he did not think that it had gone beyond that limited extent. Mr. Chamberlain said he had not seen Dr. Koht's statement but they, the British, knew there had been infiltration on a scale that had surprised even the most careful observer of conditions in Norway. 'If I were Mr. de Valera' Mr. Chamberlain continued 'I would keep the most meticulous watch on all the ports, communications, and wireless in his territory lest he wakes up one day and find the conditions of Norway repeated'. This was said by way of warning only and of course with no intention of influencing Mr. de Valera one way or the other, but after what he had seen abroad he was afraid almost anything might happen now in a neutral country. Two or three times in conversation to me he remarked that the attitude of neutrality had saved nobody. To Norway, to Belgium, and to Holland, they had offered advice and consultation, but so anxious were these people to preserve in the fullest sense their neutrality they had always refused – in fact what they had urged the British and the French Governments to do was to keep as far away from them as possible.

Mr. Chamberlain (as Mr. Eden had assured him already) said that the change of Government in Westminster involved no change at all in their attitude towards Mr. de Valera and his Government. Since he was talking with such candour I ventured the observation that although the present Prime Minister had shown an approach to the Irish question in his earlier years he had in more recent time taken a Diehard line. Mr. Chamberlain I thought looked doubtful of that suggestion. I referred therefore to Mr. Churchill's speeches opposing the Statute of Westminster, aimed openly and avowedly against us, and how in Parliament in opposition to the general wish of the Conservative party he had insisted on a division. I mentioned next the vigour with which he had attacked the restoration to us of our own ports on the 1938 Agreement.

Mr. Chamberlain said that he did not think there was any ground for apprehension. 'I have tried', he said, 'to do everything I could to improve the relations of the two countries and I am glad to hear what you told me Mr. de Valera had said at Galway on that subject.[1] Mr. Churchill has his own views which he is accustomed to state in rather strong terms but I think nevertheless there will not be any change in the attitude of this Government towards Éire. After all, I am a member of that Government,[2] and a fairly strong member, and I shall continue to do all I can to keep the two countries on the terms of good neighbours'. It was significant that he went so far as to speak of 'keeping a check on Mr. Churchill'.

I reminded Mr. Chamberlain of the Taoiseach's attitude on the Six County problem all through the 1938 conversations, and in so fateful a time for all European peoples how tragic it was that the Border question should still be allowed to embitter the relations of two peoples who ought to be in amity with each other.

Mr. Chamberlain said he knew how deeply Mr. de Valera felt on this point, and he could have wished that after the 1938 Agreement it had been possible for him to have done something, even if it were only in the way of a beginning, towards a solution: but Mr. de Valera no doubt for reasons sufficient to him had had to do things which had not helped him (Mr. Chamberlain) towards a settlement. (This I think referred to our beginning of the Anti-Partition campaign when he was about to have private conversations with Lord Craigavon).

About the sentiment of the Irish people he did not feel any serious doubt. He thought that the issue in Europe being what it was the Irish people could scarcely wish to see the Dictatorship school of political thought triumph. The British attitude towards us would remain unchanged provided we did nothing to provoke them. There was no such intention in our minds I said. And I asked what he meant by provocation. He said he was not thinking of any particular example but anything which disturbed their people or which looked to them like assistance to the Germans might well have serious repercussions over here. I rejoined that ever since the war began Mr. Eden had been perfectly satisfied as to the complete observance on our side of neutrality. To this Mr. Chamberlain immediately assented. And I went on to say that the benevolence of our neutrality was also clear to those concerned in Britain.

---

[1] On 12 May 1940, speaking at a political rally in Galway, de Valera spoke of the similar destiny and 'common interests' that existed between Britain and Ireland, though he regretted that the partition of Ireland remained a 'cause of difference' between both states. See Maurice Moynihan (ed.), *Speeches and Statements by Eamon de Valera 1917-73* (Dublin, 1980), pp 434-6.

[2] Chamberlain held the post of Lord President of the Council.

Mr. Chamberlain reverted to what he said about Norway and wished to make it clear that of course the Irish Government was perfectly free as to their course but he hoped I would not mind his repeating again that the attitude of neutrality had saved nobody.

He finished the conversation by asking me to give Mr. de Valera his warm personal remembrances and his hope that, however this ghastly struggle developed, the ideals of democratic Government, common as he thought to our two peoples, would in the end triumph.

No. 174 NAI DFA Washington Embassy Confidential Reports 1940

> *Confidential report from Robert Brennan to Joseph P. Walshe (Dublin)*
> *(108/41/40) (Copy)*
> WASHINGTON, 14 May 1940

The attack on Belgium and Holland and the swift advance of the German forces (unchecked at the moment of writing) has caused a profound effect here. Mr. Roosevelt's statement that public opinion in the United States was shocked and angered fairly expressed the situation. Mr. Hull, though he did not mention Germany, spoke of international anarchy which menaces the civilised existence of mankind. The isolationists are less outspoken than usual, and some of the best known columnists, notably Mark Sullivan (Republican) have come out boldly for intervention. A proposal that the Johnson Act forbidding loans to debtor nations be repealed met a downright isolationist statement from Senator Johnson, the author of the Act, but the Senator is being lambasted editorially in such organs as the New York Times and the New York Herald Tribune. The Times-Herald of Washington, formerly a Hearst paper and now independent, which hitherto has been isolationist has this to say of the President's recent statements: 'These, of course, are steps towards American intervention in Europe's latest war on the side of the Allies. Whether we shall ever arrive at actual Allied intervention is another question which only time can answer'. The Washington Evening Star of May 13th says 'It is time also to think seriously about other measures for our protection, such as the extension of even more substantial cooperation to Britain and France in whose battle against the spread of international gangsterism we have a very real and withal selfish interest.

Further indication of a change is the fact that a proposal to extend credit to the Allies has reached the floor of the House of Representatives. This week I have heard men, who might be described as old Tories, who hitherto were bitterly anti-Roosevelt, express the opinion that he should get a third term because they are convinced he would go into the war if re-elected.

Two factors, however, overshadow the situation. One is that because it is election year none of the leading politicians will, at this stage, advocate intervention for fear of antagonising a section of the electorate; the other is that it has been disclosed that America is wholly unprepared for war. The Fleet is stated to be excellent but it is only a one ocean Fleet. The Army is very small and is very inadequately equipped and manned, and compared with the European countries the Air Force is almost negligible. There seems to be general agreement that this state of affairs should be remedied right away.

[stamped] (signed ROBT. BRENNAN)

Documents on Irish Foreign Policy, Volume VI, 1939–1941

No. 175 NAI DFA Secretary's Files P3

Code telegram from the Department of External Affairs to William Warnock
(Berlin)
(No. 39) (Personal) (Copy)

Dublin, 15 May 1940

Speaking at Galway on 11th Taoiseach said of Holland and Belgium 'I think I would be unworthy of this small nation if I did not utter a protest against the cruel wrong that has been done them'. German Minister deprecated the statement particularly use of word 'protest'. He was told that statement was intended not as gratuitous judgment on rights and wrongs of German action but as assertion of a principle on which our own national security depends: Moral sympathy with Belgium and Holland would render violation of our neutrality less likely. The rest of speech contained categorical denial of rumours of deal with British about ports and strong re-affirmation of our neutrality and determination to resist attack from any quarter.

No. 176 UCDA P150/2548

Letter from Eamon de Valera to Neville Chamberlain (London)
(Copy)

Dublin, 15 May 1940

I hope you will not resent a personal note to tell you how much we have admired your dignity and patriotism in the recent events.

Those of us who understood the problems with which in recent years you were faced have no doubt that the courses which you took were the best available, and we are confident that in calmer times the importance of what you achieved will be appreciated by all your countrymen. I would like to testify that you did more than any former British Statesman to make a true friendship between the peoples of our two countries possible, and, if the task has not been completed, that it has not been for want of good will on your part.

I hope that you may still be able to work for, and that we may both be spared to see, the realization of our dream – to see our two peoples living side by side with a deep neighbourly sense of their value one to another, and with a friendship which will make possible wholehearted co-operation between them in all matters of common interest.

I know how the task of coping with the present difficulties must weigh upon you and your colleagues and I send you my most sincere good wishes.

Faithfully yours,
(signed) Eamon de Valera

P.S. This was written before the disquieting news of the surrender of Holland reached me.[1]

---

[1] Dutch forces surrendered on 14 May 1940.

No. 177 NAI DFA 219/6

> Code telegram from Michael MacWhite to the Department of External Affairs
> (Dublin)
> (No. 8) (Personal) (Copy)
>
> ROME, 15 May 1940

Situation here tense worse expected most diplomats hold aggressive steps unlikely unless Mussolini convinced collapse of Allies imminent. Students Scotch and English colleges leaving here to-morrow some Irish going with them. French embassy just now suspended transit visas until further notice.

No. 178 NAI DFA Holy See Embassy 14/5/1

> Extract from a confidential report from William J.B. Macaulay
> to Joseph P. Walshe (Dublin)
> (MP 23/40) (Confidential)
>
> ROME, 18 May 1940

Vatican circles are exceedingly pessimistic since the attack on Holland and Belgium and the success there to-date of the Germans. It is thought that a real break-through would bring Italy immediately in on Germany's side. What shape Italian intervention would take is hard to say but the Yugoslavs are very apprehensive that they would be the object and that the Hungarians would attack them simultaneously from the North. The seizure of Salonika by Italy is also suggested.

The English and Scottish Colleges have closed, all the students left yesterday. The North American college is closing in a few days. The Allied diplomats are ready to leave at a few hours notice and have burnt their archives.

I continue to be unconvinced that Italy will voluntarily enter a war for which she is really unprepared and the outcome of which is still in doubt. Despite the violence of the pro-German propaganda the people have no desire to go to war and their feeling would be manifested by serious internal disorder and widespread sabotage. One can conceive a civil war resulting, specially since it is said that in the North the people are very anti-German.

Italian intervention on the side of Germany, in addition to bringing the horrors of war to the country would, in the Vatican's opinion, entail serious consequences for the Church since German domination can be anticipated. Even now German power is evidenced by the prohibition of the sale of the Vatican paper and this by individuals in plain clothes against whom the Italian Police will take no action even when the most flagrant breaches of the peace are committed by these people under their eyes. Italians speaking English or French are beaten and the police move hastily away. A foreign priest was struck near St. Peter's on Friday for asking for the Osservatore, the attacker said he was acting under orders and defied a nearby Carabiniere to arrest him; the latter quickly walked off. The priest is Ecclesiastical Counsellor to a Legation but neither his diplomatic status nor his dress saved him. These acts of terrorism are widespread and are said to be instigated and financed by the German Propaganda Organisation.

No. 179 NAI DFA 219/4

Confidential report from William Warnock to Joseph P. Walshe (Dublin)
(43/33)

BERLIN, 18 May 1940

The German advance into Holland and Belgium took everybody by great surprise, even though there had been the suggestion from time to time that such might happen. The breaking of Dutch resistance after a few days adds, in the German view, another country to the list of victims of British and French promises, which now reads:- Abyssinia, Red Spain, Czecho-Slovakia, Poland, Finland, Norway, and Holland.

The general feeling is that the War has at last begun. It has always been said here that Germany will win, and that everything will be over by next autumn, and if the astounding successes of the German armies continue as at present (the news of the entry of German troops into Brussels came last night), it looks as if there may be something in this belief.

There is no hilarity, and there is much anxiety, but, naturally enough, pride and satisfaction are expressed on all sides. The man-in-the-street regrets the necessity for the invasion of Belgium and Holland (particularly the latter country). He has however, read in his newspapers that the Western Powers were planning to attack the Ruhr through the Low Countries, and consequently, in self-defence, the Fuhrer decided to anticipate them. In one week's fighting the following has been accomplished:

(1) The Dutch Army has capitulated. The flooding of the dykes, which was thought would work wonders of defence, presented no great obstacle to the German advance.

(2) The most modern of the Belgian forts and defences have been taken, and more than half of the country has been occupied.

(3) The Maginot-Line has been broken on a sixty-mile front, and its alleged impregnability shown to be a myth.

(4) The German Air Force has been proved to be an irresistible striking force, particularly in combination with tanks and armoured cars. The diving-bombers can silence even seemingly impregnable fortresses.

(5) Great Britain, the real enemy, is within easy striking distance, and her population, secure for hundreds of years, are in dread.

British air-raids on German territory have not caused much damage to military objectives, but the civil population has suffered. The Western Powers are endeavouring to distract attention from their failures by stories of German atrocities, which are usually old stories of the last war served up anew. It is strongly denied that German parachute-troops land in disguise, and the Supreme Command has issued a warning that severe reprisals will be taken if any parachutists are maltreated or wrongfully shot by enemy forces or by civilians.

The German forces are still smashing their way through Anglo-Belgo-French forces in Belgium and systematically breaking down all resistance, and I must say that even neutral circles here are expressing the view that Germany will win the war. But, even though events seem to be very much in favour of Germany at the moment, and the Allies have lost all the initiative, it is perhaps still too early to attempt to forecast the result.

Everybody is agreed on one thing:- that Germany will endeavour to get in a sharp blow on actual British territory, probably by intense air-raids, and maybe even with parachute troops. It is thought that this would have a shattering effect on the morale of the self-centred and self-satisfied British, who, secure on their island, have been free from foreign invasion for centuries, and have been able to regard Europe from a distance, and have one nation after another shed its blood for them. If any fighting had to be done, it was done on the Continent. But as the Fuhrer says, 'there are no longer any islands now!' The Germans, if successful, will by a mass combination of aeroplanes and submarines, isolate Great Britain completely.

The Taoiseach's reference in his speech at Galway to the invasion of Holland and Belgium was not reported, but his re-affirmation of our neutrality was given much publicity.[1] I gather from some remarks passed to me by a member of the Press Section of the Foreign Office that the Taoiseach's remarks on the invasion were not too well received. I may say by way of explanation that every German is convinced that the Fuhrer was right in anticipating an Allied attack through these countries, whose Governments had ill-concealed their enmity to Germany ever since the outbreak of war.

[signed] W. WARNOCK

No. 180 NAI DFA Paris Embassy 19/34A

Confidential report from Seán Murphy to Joseph P. Walshe (Dublin)
(Copy)

PARIS, 18 May 1940

There was a rather wide-spread feeling of depression on Thursday afternoon, following on a rumour, which has since been denied, to the effect that German armed columns had penetrated as far as Laon – which is about 100 kilometres south-west of the Belgian frontier and more or less in a direct line to Paris, from which it is distant about 130 kilometres. Although it was admitted that isolated German armed columns had penetrated deeply behind the allied lines, the feeling yesterday was much better. Judging, however, by the press comments this morning, the position is far from good in as far as concerns Franco-British resistance. The Maginot line proper ends at Montmédy which is situated along the Belgian frontier about 40 kilometres from its junction with that of Luxemburg. From Montmédy to the coast the fortifications have been described by one writer as constituting a reinforced field position. In Romier's view if the German drive between the Sambre and Rethel continues, the allied front in Belgium would be seriously threatened from the south. Duval, in his article, in the Journal seems doubtful of the possibility of a favourable result for the Franco-British forces from the battle in progress. His conclusion is 'I do not hope and no more do I fear, I even refuse to admit that the issue of the present battle should decide everything'. Gamelin,[2] on the other hand, in the 'ordre du jour' which he issued yesterday said that 'the fate

---

[1] See No. 175.
[2] General Maurice Gamelin (1872-1958), commander of French forces countering the German invasion of France in 1940. His plans, based on static defence, failed to halt the rapid German advance and he was removed from command on 18 May 1940 and succeeded by General Weygand.

of the fatherland, that of the allies, the destinies of the world depend on the battle in progress' and urged his troops 'if they cannot advance to die on their position rather than abandon a morsel of native soil entrusted to them'. Last evening's Paris-Soir indicated that the efforts of the French forces to block up the 'pockets' which the Germans have opened in their line have for object 'to substitute a continuous line to the mobility of the actions which are going on'. Almost certainly the French staff wants to convert 'the war of movement' which their communiqué of Thursday morning announced was developing into the 'war of position' which is the kind of warfare in anticipation of which the Maginot line and other fortifications were erected. This desire of the high command to 'fix the front and hold the enemy on more solid positions' was also mentioned by Duval in his article in the Journal des Debate last evening. One point which many commentators have mentioned as being in favour of the possibility of halting the German advance is that the further they advance and the greater the number of divisions engaged the more difficult it is to keep them fully supplied, particularly in petrol.

The public is being warned to give no credence to rumours which are not definitely confirmed. Such rumours were particularly alive on Thursday. M. Reynaud dealt with them to some extent before the Chamber on the 16th and over the radio on the same evening. He said, inter alia, that 'we shall be called on (in the future) to take measures which would have yesterday appeared revolutionary. Perhaps we shall have to change the methods and the men. For every failure, the punishment of death will come'. The phrase about changing the men caught the attention of some of the press. There has been a rumour which is unconfirmed that General Gamelin might be removed and replaced by perhaps Giraud[1] who has been in charge in Belgium. Up to the developments of last week, there was a certain amount of criticism of the tactics advocated by Gamelin who has apparently been completely in favour of staying on the defensive and awaiting an enemy attack which seems to have become replaced in fact by a war of movement. It has also been suggested that General Gamelin's possible successor might be General Weygand.

[stamped] (signed) Seán Murphy

No. 181 NAI DFA Washington Embassy Confidential Reports 1940

Confidential report from Robert Brennan to Joseph P. Walshe (Dublin) (108/42/40) (Copy)

Washington, 21 May 1940

The pace of the German Army's progress in Holland, Belgium and France, involving an immediate threat to France and England created a feeling of consternation here which amounted almost to hysteria. Most of the newspapers saw immediate disaster for England and the cry arose of what would happen America if the British Empire were destroyed. Two reporters whom I met on separate occasions on Friday, the 17th, asked me seriously if I did not think it would be America's turn next almost as if the Germans were already on their way.

---

[1] General Henri Giraud (1879-1949), commanded the 7th Army in the Netherlands in May 1940, subsequently held as a POW at Konigstein Castle, Dresden, until his escape in 1942. On the assassination of Admiral Darlan in December 1942 Giraud became de facto leader of the Free French though he was ultimately superseded by de Gaulle.

This mood was not helped by the feverish activity of the Administration. The President on Wednesday, the 15th of May, after a day long series of discussions with Army and Navy Chiefs and members of his Administration dramatically announced he would address a Joint Meeting of the Senate and House of Representatives on the following day. His speech was an appeal for a further billion dollars for defence, mainly aircraft, to meet a possible menace from overseas. His reception was tumultuous and it was obvious from the broadcast of the speech that his audience was in a very excited state. His proposals are being rushed through Congress at record speed.

The press was almost unanimous in backing up the President's stand. It was agreed on all sides that the President's demand for 50,000 planes as soon as possible, and 50,000 per year should be met. Walter Winchell[1] screamed over the radio on Sunday night that he had expert opinion that America would have only one year to prepare.

In the midst of all this clamour, men like General Hugh Johnson who state it would be foolish to build 50,000 planes as they would be out of date in a year, and Colonel Charles A. Lindbergh[2] who deplored the hysteria and said there was no danger for America except through the actions of the people who kept intervening in foreign affairs, seemed to be hardly heard in the general chorus of alarm. Incidentally many of the columnists came out openly for immediate active aid for the Allies.

No. 182 NAI DFA Secretary's Files A3

Minutes of meeting between representatives of the Government of Éire and representatives of the Dominions Office and Service Departments of the United Kingdom (Secret) (1st Meeting) (10/5/19) (Copy No. 2)

LONDON, 5.30 pm, 23 May 1940

THE FOLLOWING WERE PRESENT:-

United Kingdom
Sir Eric Machtig, Dominions Office
Mr. Stephenson, Dominions Office
Commander J. Creswell, Admiralty
Major G.D.G. Heyman, War Office
Squadron Leader R.E. de T. Vintras, Air Ministry

Éire
Mr. Walshe
Colonel Archer

SECRETARIAT:-
Major A.T. Cornwall-Jones

MUTUAL CO-OPERATION BETWEEN ÉIRE AND THE UNITED KINGDOM
SIR ERIC MACHTIG introduced MR. WALSHE and COLONEL ARCHER to the Service Representatives. He referred to the messages conveyed to the United

---

[1] Walter Winchell (1897-1972), American newspaper and radio commentator. Pro-Roosevelt and one of the first United States journalists to attack Hitler, his broadcasts were heard by an audience of over twenty million across America.

[2] Charles Lindbergh (1902-74), pioneering American aviator who became internationally famous as the first person to fly non-stop from west to east across the Atlantic Ocean. In the years before the United States entered the Second World War Lindbergh was a noted 'isolationist'.

Kingdom Government by Mr. de Valera. He understood the position to be as follows. Éire would fight if attacked by Germany and would call in the assistance of the United Kingdom the moment it became necessary. The political situation in Éire, however, was such that there could be no question of the Éire Government inviting in United Kingdom Troops before an actual German descent, and before fighting between the German and Éire forces had begun. If the United Kingdom forces arrived before such fighting had taken place, Mr. de Valera could not be responsible for the political consequences. If, on the other hand, fighting was in progress between Éire and German forces and the United Kingdom forces came in to help, Éire opinion would give whole-hearted support to British forces.

It was against this background that the meeting had to consider the problem of mutual co-operation.

MR. WALSHE agreed and said that as soon as it became apparent to the Irish people that an act of aggression had taken place against Ireland the whole attitude of the Irish people would change and they would gladly welcome support from British troops. Until the Irish people fully realised that the attack had come, however, the Irish Government could not call for British support.

The discussion first turned upon the question of the time at which the call for assistance should be given.

MAJOR HEYMAN pointed out that if assistance was to be effective it was essential that the request should be made at the moment the first German foot was placed upon Irish soil. If it was delayed and the Germans became established it would be all the more difficult to turn them out. He drew a parallel with the recent German invasion of Holland. The call for assistance in that case came too late. It was true that the Germans could not follow up a landing by seaborne troops in Éire with great mechanised columns. On the other hand, the landing might take the following form:-
(i) A considerable number of parachute troops might be dropped to begin with. It was difficult to say how many might be expected at any particular point but the Germans were known to have some 4,000-5,000 trained parachutists and a great many more might have received training in the recent operations.
(ii) These might be dropped in close proximity to the aerodrome or in suitable landing grounds for the purposes of capturing them.
(iii) It must be assumed that if parachute troops were to be dropped they would be followed up by a large number of carrier-borne troops. The Germans had 30 4-engine aircraft (Ju. 90's and FW.200's) the carrying capacity of each of which was 40. They also had 500 Ju. 52's each capable of carrying 15. These aircraft would be capable of carrying out probably two return flights in three days although most of them would have to refuel on Irish soil.
(iv) There might be a period of as much as a day or two between the landing of the parachute troops and the arrival of the troop carriers. Both would fly by night when interception by the fighter defence in the United Kingdom would be difficult.
(v) Recent experience indicated that troop carriers were extremely vulnerable at moment of landing which would probably be at dawn. The ideal therefore was to attack them as soon as they commenced to land. If there was any delay in calling for assistance a golden opportunity would be missed. Once established a force of this size would be extremely difficult to evict, and heavy bombing attacks which might cause civilian casualties would be necessary.

(vi) There was also a possibility that the enemy might land considerable numbers of men from submarines. It was possible that the Germans had as many as 100 submarines each capable of carrying 30 men.

COLONEL ARCHER appreciated that it was most desirable, if assistance was to be effective, that the call should be made at the earliest possible moment. He pointed out, however, that the political situation in Ireland was such that the Irish must take the first brunt of the attack. It would be quite impossible to call for assistance, even air assistance alone, until Irish public opinion had fully realised that the attack had taken place and that Irish troops were engaged. This realisation might be a matter only of hours, although it might, in the event, be a matter of a day or two. He asked whether it would be sufficient if the arrival of parachute troops were immediately made known and aircraft were detailed to stand by to await the call.

SQUADRON LEADER VINTRAS said that such warning would be better than nothing but it was most desirable that it should be accompanied with a definite request for assistance.

MR. WALSHE asked whether, if a warning were received of the landing of parachute troops in Éire, fighter aircraft could not intercept the subsequent flights of troop carriers. As he understood it the doctrine of hot pursuit in Irish territorial waters was already established. It seemed unlikely that there would be any objection to fighters pursuing enemy aircraft and attacking them in Ireland.

SQUADRON LEADER VINTRAS pointed out that interception could not be guaranteed, particularly during the hours of darkness when the troop carriers would probably pass our fighter defences. German aircraft could however be attacked on arrival if their probable destinations, as revealed by preparatory parachute landings, were known. The opportunity would be lost if no call for assistance had been made.

There was general agreement that the establishment of efficient and rapid communication between the Service Staffs in Ireland and the Service Staffs in the United Kingdom was of vital importance. At present no such arrangements existed. The perfecting of a first-class system of communications was therefore one of the first requirements in mutual co-operation.

The meeting then turned to consider, seriatim, certain precautionary measures which Service Departments suggested should be taken by the Government of Éire.

(1) That all shipping in and approaching ports should be searched with a view particularly to locating troops, munitions, refugees and suspicious characters.

COMMANDER CRESWELL pointed out that a landing by air alone would probably not be a threat of a decisive nature. The Navy would take all possible steps to prevent any reinforcements by sea. In the light of recent experience of German methods in Norway, it was vital that the Government of Éire should take all possible steps to scrutinise shipping, both in and approaching Irish ports.

COLONEL ARCHER said that measures to this effect were receiving urgent consideration when he left Éire.

After a short discussion, MR. WALSHE agreed that measures would be taken to tighten up precautions in this respect immediately.

(2) *That preparations should be made to prevent enemy landings at Aerodromes and Seaplane Bases, particularly Foynes, Baldonnell and Collinstown.*

COLONEL ARCHER outlined the measures which were in the process of being taken by the Irish Government to achieve this object. At Rineanna, for instance, the whole aerodrome was to be put out of commission except for a few small runways required for coastal reconnaissance aircraft. The aerodrome was being divided into sectors and staked and wired. Obstacles were being placed on the open runways when they were not in use and could be quickly moved into position in an emergency. Sandbagged M.G. positions were being erected round the ground and two armoured cars would patrol.

Similar measures were being taken at Baldonnell except that half of this aerodrome would be left open. At Collinstown two-thirds of the aerodrome was being put out of commission. In both cases piquets and machine gun posts were to be established and armoured cars would patrol.

It was not proposed to erect obstacles in Phoenix Park which was used by the public. Similarly the Curragh was being left open. In this area, however, there was a considerable reserve and no difficulty was anticipated in dealing with any German attempt to land. Three other smaller aerodromes in the vicinity of Dublin were being put out of commission. In regard to the aerodrome at Oranmore (near Galway) it was proposed to render this unserviceable by cratering.

He asked whether, in the event of the Germans landing on Gormanston[1] aerodrome the Navy would be able to render their position untenable by bombardment.

COMMANDER CRESWELL undertook to examine this question with the Naval Staff and provide Colonel Archer with a considered opinion. In discussion, there was general agreement that the above measures met the case. The following points, however, were made by the representatives of Service Departments:-

(i) German landings might take place on any open space, e.g. roads, golf courses, racecourses, parks, etc.

(ii) An immediate German object on landing would be to seize any stocks of oil in the vicinity. It was pointed out that arrangements might have been made with possible '5th Column' personnel in Éire, to have such stocks ready to hand on out of the way landing grounds. It was essential that arrangements should be made to destroy any stocks of oil in the vicinity of landing grounds, and that the closest investigation should be made with a view to detecting any concealed stocks.

(iii) In view of the vast number of points at which German landings might take place, the only possible method of dealing with the problem seemed to be by holding mobile troops at suitable focal points, ready to move at very short notice. The experience gained in recent preparations was at Colonel Archer's disposal.

COLONEL ARCHER explained that Irish troops had been organised in mobile columns to this very end. The limited amount of artillery available had been allotted to these columns. He was prepared to explain the details of the plans if so desired. He also took note of the necessity for making preparations for destroying

---

[1] Former Royal Flying Corps aerodrome (established in 1917) situated on the east coast of Ireland south of Drogheda, in Co Meath, taken over by the Irish Air Corps in 1922 and operational until 2002.

stocks of oil in the vicinity of landing grounds, and said he would be glad to have the results of the experience gained in recent preparations in the United Kingdom.

SQUADRON LEADER VINTRAS emphasized the necessity for dispersing aircraft on aerodromes. With regard to the question of placing landing grounds out of commission, he asked whether it might be possible to establish stocks of bombs and petrol at suitable landing grounds, for use by British Air Forces, if in the event, their assistance was required. Phoenix Park would probably not be suitable for this purpose.

COLONEL ARCHER asked Squadron Leader Vintras to let him know which particular aerodrome the Air Staff would like to use.

(3) *That preparations should be made to prevent the enemy seizing ports, particularly Shannon, Cork, Galway, Swilly and Berehaven.*
COLONEL ARCHER described the general plans for the defence of ports. In cases in which there was no Military forces at the port in question, defence was based upon mobile reserves.

COMMANDER CRESWELL asked whether there were any local anti-submarine defences at any of the ports. In particular if the British Navy were to be called in to assist the use of Berehaven and possibly Cork would be a necessity, and/or these local defences would be required.

COLONEL ARCHER said that the problem of the defence of ports was mainly a question of material and the availability of trained personnel.

COMMANDER CRESWELL undertook to examine the question of the provision of material in conjunction with the Naval Staff and inform Colonel Archer of the position.

(4) *That all possible measures should be taken against '5th Column' activities including the supervision of the German Legation and German firms.*
MAJOR HEYMAN stressed the vital importance of ensuring that the closest watch was kept upon all undesirable characters. While appreciating the impracticability of interning all such persons forthwith, he earnestly requested the Irish representatives to make all arrangements so that they could be interned at very short notice.

MR. WALSHE said that the Government of Éire were satisfied with the position as it now stood. If and when Éire were to become belligerent, there would be no difficulty in taking all necessary measures.

(5) *That a complete blackout should be organised forthwith throughout the whole of Éire.*
MR. WALSHE undertook to give this matter immediate consideration.

MAJOR HEYMAN then asked whether the Government of Éire were prepared to discuss detailed plans. The point was that if we were to be really prepared to meet a German attack, it was essential that ways and means should be discussed. This could be done with the greatest of secrecy if so desired. If it was agreed that this should be done, the War Office would be ready to start discussion in about three days' time.

MR. WALSHE and COLONEL ARCHER agreed that this was the essence of the problem. There was no use in talking generalities, the object must be to obtain the closest possible mutual co-operation.

MAJOR HEYMAN asked whether the detailed planning should be carried out in London or in Dublin. There might be certain advantages in their taking place in Dublin.

MR. WALSHE undertook to consider this point.

IT WAS AGREED:-
(a) That the representatives of the Government of Éire should give immediate consideration to the precautionary measures suggested by Service Departments, on the lines set out in the above record of discussion.
(b) That the immediate and most urgent problem was the establishment when the threat arises, of efficient and rapid communications between the Service Staffs in Éire and the United Kingdom. To this end expert advisers should be invited to meet Mr. Walshe and Colonel Archer the next morning and advise on the necessary steps that should be taken.
(c) That the representatives of the Government of Éire should be fully informed of the experience recently gained in respect of the following:-
    (i) The preparation of plans for defence against airborne and seaborne invasion.
    (ii) The methods adopted by the Germans in the employment of the '5th Column'.
    (iii) The methods employed by the Germans in carrying out parachute and troop-carrier attack.
    Advice on these subjects would be communicated to Mr. Walshe and Colonel Archer by Officers especially detailed by Service Departments.
(d) That detailed planning to ensure the closest of mutual co-operation should be considered as soon as possible in the greatest secrecy. In this connection, Mr. Walshe undertook to inform the Dominions Office whether it would be convenient that these conversations should take place in Dublin.
(e) To meet at 11.30 a.m. the next morning to consider further the problems in (b) and (c) above.[1]

No. 183 NAI DFA Secretary's Files A3

Minutes of meeting between representatives of the Government of Éire and representatives of the Dominions Office and Service Departments of the United Kingdom (Secret) (2nd Meeting) (10/5/19) (Copy No. 2)

LONDON, 11.30am, 24 May 1940

United Kingdom
Sir Eric Machtig, Dominions Office
Mr. Stephenson, Dominions Office
Commander J. Creswell, Admiralty
Major G.D.G. Heyman, War Office
Squadron Leader R.E. de T. Vintras, Air Ministry
Wing Commander Cadell, Air Ministry
Major Hoysted, War Office
Lt. Col. Clarke, War Office

Éire
Mr. Walshe
Colonel Archer

---

[1] See No. 183.

Secretariat:-
Major A.T. Cornwall-Jones

1. MINUTES OF THE PREVIOUS MEETING
THE MEETING considered the record of the previous meeting held on the afternoon of the 23rd May.[1]

A few amendments to the draft record were agreed.

MR. WALSHE signified his general approval to the record, reserving the right to make minor amendments after more careful scrutiny.

2. ITEMS OUTSTANDING FROM THE PREVIOUS MEETING
Arising from the discussion under Item 1 above the following points emerged:-

Possible location of stocks of bombs and petrol in Éire for use by the Royal Air Force
COLONEL ARCHER asked whether one aerodrome would be sufficient for R.A.F. purposes. He felt it would be a mistake to hold up the present work on landing grounds which was designed to prevent enemy landings.

SQUADRON LEADER VINTRAS said that this was a point which would require detailed examination. On the other hand, he agreed that it would be a great mistake to hold up any measures to deny the use of these aerodromes to the Germans, on this account.

Denial of the use of Gormanston aerodrome by naval bombardment
COMMANDER CRESWELL said that he had discussed this question with the Naval Staff. It transpired that ships would be unable to approach closer than 4,000 yards from the aerodrome. It was therefore impossible to guarantee that this aerodrome could be made untenable to the Germans by bombardment from the sea. He suggested that this aerodrome should be treated in the same way as other aerodromes.

Provision of material for port defences
COMMANDER CRESWELL referred to the question of anti-submarine booms and nets for the defence of Irish harbours. He had discussed this with the Naval Staff and regretted that at present no material was available for this purpose.

Subversive Activities in Éire
MAJOR HEYMAN said that he had been instructed to convey to Mr. Walshe the anxiety felt by the Director of Military Operations, War Office, in regard to the activities of the I.R.A. GENERAL DEWING[2] thought that the Germans might well decide to land a few troops to exploit the activities of the I.R.A. He thought perhaps this would cause grave concern to the Irish Government and he asked whether in these circumstances they would be likely to call for assistance.

MR. WALSHE said that the Government of Éire anticipated no difficulty in dealing with the I.R.A. In fact the outbreak of specific disturbances were the kind of opportunity which they were seeking in order to crush finally the organisation.

---

[1] See No. 182.
[2] Major-General Richard H. Dewing (1891-1981), Director of Military Operations, War Office (1939-40).

In any event they did not regard it as a serious threat and they did not anticipate having to call for any assistance from the United Kingdom.

Detailed Planning
COLONEL CLARKE put forward the proposals of the Director of Military Operations in the War Office, with regard to detailed planning in respect of the assistance to be provided by British land forces.

GENERAL DEWING considered that any assistance which might be required by the Government of Éire would come most speedily from Northern Ireland. This being so, he thought that the detailed planning involved should be carried out direct between the G.O.C., Northern Ireland and the Irish Military Authorities. It would be a waste of time to continue with these details now in London. Subject to Mr. Walshe's agreement, he, (Colonel Clarke) intended to fly to Northern Ireland the same afternoon and consult with General Huddleston.[1] In view of the urgency of the problem, he suggested that he should accompany staff officers from General Huddleston's Headquarters to Dublin the next day. He himself would then return to London and any steps required of the War Office could then be put in hand.

After a short discussion, it was agreed that Mr. Walshe and Colonel Archer should fly to Northern Ireland with Colonel Clarke and go from there to Dublin. Arrangements for a meeting the next day, or failing that, the day after, could be made after arrival in Éire. Before finally agreeing to a meeting in Dublin he would require to consult Mr. de Valera.

Identification Signals between port defences and British Naval vessels
COMMANDER CRESWELL suggested that a simple code should be devised so that coast and port defences in Éire would be able to recognise British ships if, in the event, they were to be called in to assist. He suggested that a two-letter signal might be devised, separate code letters being allotted for each day of a month.

COLONEL ARCHER undertook to consider this question and communicate a simple code to the Naval Staff through the Dominions Office.

Communication of recent experience gained by United Kingdom Staffs
COMMANDER CRESWELL handed to Colonel Archer a copy of the following documents:-
(a) Notes on Internal Security. (N.I.D. 2432/40 of the 20th May).
(b) Notes on the 5th Column menace, effect of German bombing at Antwerp, use of parachute troops in Holland and general lessons to be learned from the German attack on land. (N.I.D. 2475/40 of the 20th May).

3. POSSIBLE SEIZURE OF SHIP CONTAINING ARMS AND AMMUNITION
MAJOR HEYMAN said that the United Kingdom Government were interested in a rumour concerning a ship said to contain 200,000 mauser rifles and a considerable quantity of ammunition. It was alleged that this ship, whose name and flag were unknown, had sailed from America for Roumania, and for an unknown reason had arrived in a Dutch port immediately prior to the German invasion of

---

[1] General Sir Hubert Huddleston (1880-1950), GOC Northern Ireland, later Governor General of Sudan (1940-7).

Holland. The rumour, which it had so far been impossible to trace, now said that this ship was en route for an Irish port, also unspecified. The United Kingdom Government wished to suggest that this ship should be seized by the Irish Authorities. If they were agreeable, the United Kingdom would be glad to purchase both the rifles and the ammunition.

MR. WALSHE said that the rifles and ammunition might well come in very useful for arming the Irish population. He would, however, invite the Government of Éire to give urgent consideration to the question of seizing the ship if there was any truth in the rumour.

(At this stage the following left the meeting:- Mr. Walshe, Commander Creswell, Major Heyman, Squadron Leader Vintras, and Colonel Clarke.)

4. COMMUNICATIONS BETWEEN SERVICE STAFFS IN ÉIRE AND THE UNITED KINGDOM

THE MEETING next considered the question of the arrangement that should be made to ensure that, as soon as an emergency arose, there would be an efficient means of direct communication between the Irish Military Authorities and the United Kingdom Staffs.

It was considered that the problem was as follows:-
(a) In the first place, the quickest and most efficient means of communication was by cable (telephone and telegraph). It was essential that direct lines should be laid between Irish Military Headquarters and the War Office and the Air Ministry.
(b) It was quite possible, however, that these cables might be cut. Against this eventuality therefore it was essential that direct wireless communication should be prepared and held ready in reserve.

The question of cable communications and the installation of the necessary telephones was one for the Wireless Board. Major Hoysted explained that the War Office had not yet had time to consult this Board on the question.

The discussion then turned on the question of the establishment of direct wireless communications.

COLONEL ARCHER explained that there were two Military radio transmitting sets, one at Headquarters in Dublin and one at Air Force Headquarters at Baldonnell. The set at Dublin normally worked on a wave length of 857 metres, although it could work on 140-200 metres or 750-2,500 metres. Its range was from 600-1,000 miles, dependent upon atmospheric conditions. The set at Baldonnell was exactly the same but he was not aware of its normal frequency. Both sets were in operation at the present time. He pointed out that these sets were also used for internal communication, each Military station being equipped with a smaller wireless set.

WING COMMANDER CADELL said that the Wireless Board would almost certainly suggest that the wave length on which these sets were working at present would provide a certain beacon to approaching German aircraft. The first essential would probably therefore be to raise their frequencies.

COLONEL ARCHER asked whether these two stations could be linked up with similar stations in the United Kingdom immediately the emergency arose.

MAJOR HOYSTED pointed out that there would be certain difficulties which would first require to be examined. For instance, the normal procedure was for both ends of a terminal to be manned by personnel of the same Service. Otherwise difficulties would arise in respect of call signs and procedure. Moreover, the question of a code would have to be taken up.

SIR ERIC MACHTIG asked whether the arrangements for warning the Irish Authorities of the approach of aircraft were satisfactory.

It was understood that an arrangement existed by which red and yellow warnings in respect of enemy aircraft passing over the Midlands and the West Coast of the United Kingdom were passed automatically through normal Post Office Channels to the Government of Éire.

There was general agreement that the position in respect of the communication of warnings to the Government of Éire should be investigated with a view to ensuring that the Government of Éire was provided with the maximum possible warning.

IT WAS AGREED:-

(a) In view of the possibility that cable Communications might be cut, it was essential that direct wireless communication should be established between Service Staffs of the two countries.

(b) In order to put this into effect:-

(i) Colonel Archer undertook to investigate the possibility of allotting an existing Military W/T set in Éire to communicate direct with the United Kingdom. This investigation would be primarily directed to the possibility of raising the frequency at which the station was at present working, in order to avoid providing the Germans with a wireless beacon. He also undertook to consider the question of call signs, procedure and the use of a simple code, and to communicate the result of his enquiries to Wing Commander Cadell and Major Hoysted through the usual channels at the earliest possible moment.

(ii) Major Hoysted and Wing Commander Cadell undertook to investigate in conjunction with the Wireless Board, the possibility of providing a link in the United Kingdom.

(c) Meanwhile, until direct wireless communication could be prepared, it was accepted that the existing arrangements would stand.

(d) That the Secretary should consult the appropriate Departments with a view to ensuring that all possible information regarding the movements of enemy aircraft which might threaten Éire was passed on to the Irish Military Authorities.

(e) That the Secretary should consult the appropriate Department on the question of the preparation of a simple code, for use between the Service Staffs.

No. 184 NAI DFA Holy See Embassy 20/34

> Code telegram from the Department of External Affairs to William Warnock
> (Berlin) sent via the Holy See Legation
> (Copy)
>
> DUBLIN, 28 May 1940

All parties have promised Government closest cooperation in all measures taken for defence and security of country Mr. de Valera in Galway yesterday said 'there is a small group who appear to be meditating treason it does not matter what reason they may advance instead of following the footsteps of Pearse they will be execrated in Irish history for ever like Dermot McMurrough'[1] he asked the whole people to stand behind the Government in defence of the country should it be attacked. Repeat to Berlin.

No. 185 NAI DFA 219/4

> Confidential report from William Warnock to Joseph P. Walshe (Dublin)
> (43/33)
>
> BERLIN, 28 May 1940

The surrender of King Leopold of Belgium was announced this morning, little more than a fortnight after the commencement of the present campaign, and it may not be long now until the war is carried to Great Britain herself. Britain will be invaded for the first time since the expedition of William the Conqueror, and if events continue to develop as at present, it is not improbable that the German invader may come as a conqueror, too. The past few weeks have brought such a series of amazing surprises that it is well to consider them closely, even though the campaign is still in progress.

It is quite obvious that the Western Powers thought that their blockade would greatly weaken Germany, and that its effect would be so telling that military operations on a vast scale might not be necessary. The German pact with Russia, and the annihilation of Poland in less than three weeks, prevented the blockade from becoming a total one. All Northern and Eastern Europe remained open to Germany, and while some foodstuffs and raw materials were undoubtedly difficult to obtain, German energy and powers of organisation succeeded in overcoming almost all the difficulties immediately presenting themselves. Huge stores had been built up in recent years, and we were assured at the beginning of the war that Germany could hold out indefinitely. Agriculture has been so developed since 1933 that the country now produces about three-quarters of her food supply within her own borders; to this must be added the extensive agricultural districts in Poland which are also under German control, together with Denmark and Holland.

The failure of sanctions against Italy might have served as a lesson for the

---

[1] Dermot McMurrough (1110-71), King of Leinster, who, having been ousted by Tiernan O'Rourke, sought the assistance of King Henry II of England to regain his title and in doing so initiated the sequence of events which led to the Norman invasion of Ireland and Henry himself becoming Lord of Ireland. The Norman invasion of Ireland in 1169 is in nationalist Irish historiography portrayed as the beginning of English dominance in Ireland.

Western Powers, but they persisted with their ideas of an economic war. They thought that all they had to do was to remain on the defensive, and that after a while the civil population in Germany would be almost dead with hunger, the soldiers underfed, that there would be a scarcity of all necessities, no tyres for motor-cars or lorries, no petrol for tanks or aeroplanes, no cloth, and no metal for munitions or heavy industry. Even if this result could not be brought about within a few months, they hoped to accomplish it within a few years. The effect of hunger and privation would, it was thought, considerably lower German morale, and might, perhaps, even cause an inner revolution something like that of 1918.

I find that my colleagues from neutral countries are all astounded at the evident military unpreparedness of the Western Powers after nine months of war. The speed and thoroughness of the German advance must, undoubtedly, have knocked the Allies off their balance, but it was thought that they would surely recover themselves to some extent after a few days; instead of recovering themselves the only course left open to them has, apparently, been to retreat as fast as they can. Nobody would have believed – before the events took place – that it would be possible for Germany within the space of less than three weeks to over-run Holland and Belgium, and to break through the Maginot-Line and drive a corridor through Northern France to the sea, and thereby, by use of her enormous Air Force, to gain control of the English Channel. It is all very well for the British to say that the Germans are throwing men and machines into the fight regardless of cost – the most important point for consideration is that they are advancing and breaking all opposition at an incredible pace, and are at last in a position to set about the accomplishment of one of their most intense desires – a thrust at the heart of Britain. A total blockade of Great Britain by air is due to commence, and it is expected that submarines will also play their part.[1]

Where now, it is asked, are the gentlemen who went about telling the world that Germany was ripe for revolution, that the financial system was about to crash, that industry was on the point of bankruptcy, that German aeroplanes and munitions 'simply hadn't got the stuff', and who were prepared to rise to great heights of witticism at the expense of German substitute materials for rubber, wool, and the like? Tyres made of 'Buna'[2] have carried German troops to Boulogne and Calais, the alleged inferiority of their component parts has not prevented German aeroplanes from destroying the most heavily fortified positions of the enemy, nor from inflicting loss on the Allied navies, and even if the German tanks 'haven't got the stuff', the opposing anti-tank guns can do little against them.

British prestige has sunk very low, even amongst those of my acquaintances who are inclined to prefer Great Britain to Germany. The British Army is in danger of becoming a laughing stock, particularly since the debacle in Norway.[3] An American colleague told me the other day that the British troops who landed at

---

[1] This sentence has been highlighted by a reader in the left-hand margin.
[2] 'Buna' is a form of synthetic rubber.
[3] To counter the German invasion of Norway on 9 April 1940 British and French troops landed at Namsos, Harstad and Åndalsnes from 14 to 18 April. By the date of Warnock's despatch the combined force had suffered a series of defeats at German hands and, despite advancing on Narvik, had been forced into a series of evacuations. The Anglo-French force informed Norway of its plan to evacuate the country entirely on 1 June. By 10 June Norwegian forces had surrendered and the government of Norway was in exile in Britain. The campaign led directly to the resignation of Neville Chamberlain on 10 May 1940.

Åndalsnes had not more than their rifles for quite a while. They are accused of having caused wanton destruction in Belgium, not even sparing churches. No doubt the original purpose behind the destruction of bridges and the like was to delay the German advance, but many cases are cited where bridges and buildings were blown up ruthlessly without the slightest warning having been given to the civilian population living in the immediate vicinity.

British assistance to Holland appears to have been confined to the carrying-off of the Dutch gold reserve to London. For months they have been attempting to overcome the isolated German garrison at Narvik, and they do not seem to be any nearer success than when they started.

Here in Berlin the war still seems unreal at times, as we are so far away from the theatre of operations. We have had only two air-raid alarms, both of them in early September. The British raiders have not come any nearer than Hanover. Quite trustworthy reports reach me concerning the indiscriminate bombing carried out practically every night by the British over North-Western Germany. In some places as many as sixty civilians have been killed, but no damage at all done to military objectives.

In the Legation we are beginning to feel somewhat isolated, but we can still keep in touch as long as a connection remains through Rome. If Italy comes into the war, that link will go, and we may then be forced to fall back on telegraphic communication through the United States.

The German people are receiving the reports of the amazing military successes with a remarkable calm. They, too, are astounded; they simply cannot grasp the facts. One would have expected outbursts of jubilation, but life is very quiet. We have as yet no ideas of the losses on either side, though it is claimed that the German casualties are comparatively small.

[signed] W. WARNOCK

No. 186 NAI DFA Secretary's Files P3

Extract from a code telegram from William Warnock to Joseph P. Walshe (Dublin)
(No. 32) (Personal) (Copy)

BERLIN, 30 May 1940

I gather casually that recent utterances of members of Government have been received badly here but I understand protest not likely. [matter omitted]

No. 187 NAI DFA Paris Embassy 19/34A

Extract from a confidential report from Seán Murphy to Joseph P. Walshe (Dublin)
(Copy)

PARIS, 3 June 1940

The military correspondents of the Paris press insist on the splendid conduct of the troops both British and French who have been fighting their way to Dunkirk. Last night's official French communiqué, which is one of the longest issued since the beginning of the war stated that this retreat 'carried out by troops pressed from all sides, deprived of all rest for 20 days and suddenly left open on their left by the capitulation of King Leopold, will remain as an example of heroic tenacity in the

French and British armies'. It added 'France can be proud of the leaders and the soldiers of the heroic army of the North'. The communiqué also declared that as a result of the valour and energy displayed by the British and French troops, the territorial successes which the enemy has obtained have been bought at the cost of immense losses in human lives and material. A number of correspondents (e.g. Duval, the Temps correspondent, Fabry in the Matin) hold that the French material has been proved to be superior to the German and that the French troops have now learned how to deal with German armoured attacks. The same correspondents and others (e.g. in the Paris-Soir and in the Jour) contend that the German armament has been so much used up on the last three weeks that it is probable that there will be a respite in the fighting before Germany launches her next attack so as to give time for repairs to be effected and reinforcements to be carried out. Duval in support of this contention asserts that such a respite was necessary after the war in Poland which only lasted about the same length of time. As regards what the next German objective will be, practically none of the correspondents is definite. They all suggest that the Germans may either decide to attack the French troops in mass or to concentrate on England. An exception is the military correspondent of yesterday's Intransigeant who holds that the German threat of invading England is intended only to create confusion and to postpone the landing of British troops in France. He believes that the immediate German objective will be to get to Le Havre and Rouen so as to cut off petrol supplies and to cut off France from England.
[matter omitted]

No. 188 NAI DFA 219/5

Confidential letter from Colman O'Donovan to Joseph P. Walshe (Dublin)
(MP 25/40) (Confidential)

HOLY SEE, 3 June 1940

With reference to the question of the Dublin vacancy the Minister[1] had of his own accord impressed very strongly on the Holy Father that the present critical state of affairs had made it more than ever urgent that the appointment in question should be made. This in fact was the main purpose of the Audience. In these circumstances it is certain that any further pressure would give offence.

[signed] C.J. O'DONOVAN

No. 189 NAI DFA Washington Embassy Confidential Reports 1940

Extract from a confidential report from Robert Brennan to Joseph P. Walshe
(Dublin)
(108/50/40) (Copy)

WASHINGTON, 11 June 1940

The President's speech of June 10th, which is universally recognized here as making the United States a non-belligerent ally of Britain and France, culminated a week in which various progressive indications were shown bringing America closer to participation in the war. Amongst these might be mentioned the following:

---

[1] William J.B. Macaulay. Macaulay sailed for the United States immediately before Italy entered the Second World War (10 June 1940). He later submitted his resignation from the United States.

(1) There was increasing clamour on the part of the pro-ally press for Congress to extend to the allies all assistance short of war.
(2) New voices notably that of the important columnist Walter Lippman[1] were added to those who pleaded for a policy of peace and understanding with Japan – with the idea, of course, of releasing the fleet for service in the Atlantic.
(3) The New York Times headed a sudden cry which was heard on many sides for universal compulsory military training.
(4) Attorney General Jackson found a loophole in the law enabling America to sell the allies U.S. surplus stores of war munitions.
(5) The U.S. Navy permitted the transfer of fifty naval reserve planes to the allies by first trading them in to the manufacturers. This was supposed to be the beginning of a huge transfer of Army and Navy fliers to the allies. The isolationists objected to this but not very convincingly.
(6) The various armament appropriations were upped to close on five billion dollars.
(7) A second cruiser was sent to South America presumably to hunt for secret Nazi air bases, and it was reported that the U.S. was using pressure to compel some of the South American Governments to cancel the permits of German-owned air lines.
(8) Prominently displayed in the newspapers was an appeal by thirty lawyers, educators and professional men for a declaration of war on Germany.
(9) General Pershing[2] made a personal appeal for 'unlimited aid' for the allies.
(10) Senator Vandenberg[3] (Michigan) a Republican presidential candidate, publicly abandoned his policy of isolationism.
(11) The Committee on Defend America by Aiding the Allies headed by William Allen White[4] launched a nationwide publicity campaign with full page advertisements in the leading papers.
(12) There is not one friendly word for Italy in the American press. On the contrary, the papers vie with each other in hurling such terms as jackal, hyena, buzzard and vulture at Mussolini.
[matter omitted]

No. 190 NAI DFA 215/211

> *Draft letter from Joseph P. Walshe to John Leydon and R.C. Ferguson (Dublin)*
> *(215/211) (Secret)*
>
> DUBLIN, 12 June 1940

Dear Ferguson, Leydon,
I am sending you herewith copy of a minute which we have received from the High Commissioner's Office[5] regarding an enquiry from the British Ministry of

---

[1] Walter Lippman (1889-1974), American writer, journalist and political commentator.
[2] General John J. Pershing (1860-1948), led the United States Expeditionary Force to Europe during the First World War. Pershing was a noted advocate of aid to Britain during the Second World War.
[3] Arthur Vandenburg (1884-1951), Republican Senator for Michigan, who moved from isolationism to internationalism during the Second World War and was later to head the Senate Foreign Relations Committee.
[4] William Allen White (1868-1944), American newspaper editor, politician and author; invited by President Roosevelt to develop United States public opinion in favour of the Allies. White founded the Committee to Defend America by Aiding the Allies.
[5] Not printed.

Supply as to the engineering capacity available in this country for the manufacture of shell cases and fuses.

As you know, we have from the beginning set our face against the manufacture of armaments here, and I think a number of tentative proposals by Irish firms who were thinking of engaging in this type of work have already been turned down. I am by no means sure that this preliminary feeler from the British Ministry of Supply is not an indication that they themselves anticipate that we might see objection to the manufacture of shell cases and fuses here on grounds of policy.

We propose to ask the High Commissioner therefore to tell the British Ministry of Supply that he has ascertained that it is unlikely that engineering capacity would be available in this country for the manufacture of empty shell cases and fuses. I should be glad if you would let me know as soon as possible whether your Minister agrees.

Yours sincerely,
[stamped] (SIGNED) J.P. WALSHE

No. 191 NAI DFA Secretary's Files P3

Memorandum from Joseph P. Walshe to Eamon de Valera (Dublin)
(Copy)

DUBLIN, 17 June 1940

The German Minister called to see me today at 11 o'c. by appointment to make the following verbal communication.
1. The exclusive object of Germany's fight is Great Britain.
2. In pursuing this object there may be a possibility of her touching Irish interests.
3. Germany expects a real understanding of that position on the part of Ireland but without expecting Ireland to injure her neutrality.
4. The outcome of the struggle will be of definite importance for the definite fulfilment of Irish national aims.

In communicating the foregoing the German Minister said that he had of course kept his Government informed of the developments of events in Ireland, particularly since the Held affair.[1] He could not help noticing a certain deterioration in our neutrality attitude. The speeches made by Messrs. Dillon,[2] Mulcahy[3] and O'Higgins[4] pointed especially to Germany as the probable invader. He had noted Mr. Dillon's remark about some special knowledge which he said he possessed to

---

[1] In the course of a raid on the house of Stephen Carroll Held in Dublin on 23 May 1940 Gardaí found evidence of German-IRA co-operation including a parachute, a large sum of United States dollars, coded messages and evidence of 'Plan Kathleen', a projected German operation in Northern Ireland. The raid failed to capture German spy Herman Görtz who had been using Held's residence as a safe house.

[2] James Dillon (1902-86), TD for Monaghan (Fine Gael/Independent), leader of Fine Gael (1959-65); resigned from Fine Gael in 1942 over Ireland's wartime neutrality and urged that Ireland join the Allies.

[3] General Richard Mulcahy (1887-1971), Fine Gael TD for Dublin North-East; former Chief of Staff of the IRA, Commander in Chief of the National Army and Minister for Defence (1922-4); leader of Fine Gael (1944-59); Minister for Education (1948-51, 1954-7).

[4] Dr Thomas F. O'Higgins (1890-1953), Fine Gael TD for Laois-Offaly; brother of Kevin O'Higgins; founder member of the Army Comrades Association (the Blueshirts) in 1932; Minister for Defence (1948-51).

the effect that Germany was to be the invader. The Minister said he distinguished between the Taoiseach's remarks about Holland and Belgium which were based on the general principle that the territory of small nations must not be violated, and the definitely anti-German statements of the deputies mentioned.

The German Minister was very friendly. He said he understood perfectly the difficulties of our position. I explained to him that the measures taken by you were essential for establishment of the unity of the nation. You were desirous above all things to protect our people from the disastrous effects of the war being fought out in Ireland. You earnestly hoped that neither belligerent would violate our territory. Dr. Hempel said he felt sure such was not Germany's intention, but he could not ask his Government – as I had suggested – to make a statement saying they would not make use of Irish territory in their attack on England. That would be tantamount to a partial revealing of their plans to the enemy.

No. 192 NAI DFA Legal Adviser's Papers

Handwritten memorandum by Michael Rynne (Dublin)
DUBLIN, 17 June 1940

Appreciation of the Situation 17th June 1940

The surrender of the French forces today leaves Germany ready to enter *at once* on a new phase of the war.

There are no longer any 'Allies' and England must face alone three dangers:-
1. Invasion.
2. Blockade
3. Aerial Bombardment ('Reprisals')

2. Germany has never directly threatened to invade Britain. Britain has, however, been expecting and preparing against invasion for some time past. Roads from the coast are mined, barricades are everywhere in readiness. Munition factories are working night and day. Special fighter aircraft squadrons are in readiness. Such part of the fleet as is intact is standing to repel invaders. Food and other supplies are in stock and coming in rapidly. Internal communications so necessary to successful resistance at home are in almost normal working order. *Therefore, it would not perhaps be wise on Germany's part to attempt an immediate invasion of England.* That country must be, first of all, reduced and, if possible, demoralised and disorganised beyond hope of successfully dealing with invading forces.

3. The probabilities are consequently as follows:-
   (a) *Blockade* starting from tonight or tomorrow. That is, tonight or tomorrow the shipping of the world will be ordered off the English Channel, the Irish Sea, the North Sea and the Western Atlantic as far as the West of Ireland.
   (b) *Aerial Bombardment* starting from tomorrow on all English railway junctions, terminals and yards, on wartime and other factories, petrol storage reserves, dockyards, etc., etc. The fact that civilian lives will be lost in this campaign of demolition will be excused by the early publication of a 'List of Reprisals' by the German High Command.

4. After some weeks of the foregoing tactics, it will be less costly to attempt invasion. Possibly the threat thereof will suffice to bring about the resignation of Churchill and Co.

5. Assuming that the above outline of coming events materialises, *our problems will not include that of preparing to withstand German invaders*, but will embrace such matters as:-
   (a) the movements of Irish Shipping;
   (b) the continuance of essential imports;
   (c) the absorption of goods and produce not exportable by sea;
   (d) the internment of British troops should any cross our land frontier, or land from the air; the internment of German airmen making forced landings here;
   (e) the accommodation of refugees from Belfast and other Northern counties;
   (f) the readjustment of postal, or at least of telegraphic, communication abroad etc. etc.

6. The foregoing and other kindred problems will have to be given the immediate consideration of the appropriate Departments of State. As far as we are concerned, the main consideration will be to ensure that no decision now to be taken will be such as to compromise our neutrality.

It is submitted, as a matter of urgency, that we should press for an immediate prohibition on the putting to sea of all Irish-registered ships which find themselves in Irish ports at the commencement of the German blockade. It might be thought desirable (if safe) to indicate to shipping companies like the B&I that now is the time to transfer to the British flag. If not, they will simply have to remain in port just as American transatlantic shipping has had to do.

Another provision which we might now make would consist in putting all rail and road communications to Northern Ireland in such a state of defence as to be able, when the bombardment begins, to close down on them entirely. Otherwise, troop movements there are likely to overflow into our border towns to our great embarrassment. In case that should happen – despite any precautions which we may have taken – it would be, perhaps, advisable to have in readiness one or more camps capable of accommodating internees.

No. 193 TNA PREM 3/131/1

Note of a conversation between Eamon de Valera and Malcolm MacDonald
(Copy)

DUBLIN, 17 June 1940

I had a conversation extending over three and a half hours (in two sessions from 6 o'clock till 8, and from 10.15 till close on midnight) yesterday evening. He was in one way the old de Valera; his mind is still set in the same hard, confined mould as of yore. But in another way he appeared to have changed. He made no long speeches; the whole procedure was much more in the nature of a sustained conversation between two people than used sometimes to be the case. He seemed depressed and tired, and I felt that he had neither the mental nor the physical vigour that he possessed two years ago. He was, as always, very courteous and friendly throughout.

The following is the main substance of the conversation.

After some talk about the latest news from France, I said that I should like to let him know frankly the purpose of my visit. The war against Germany was beyond any doubt a struggle in defence of the freedom of every nation, great or small, in Europe. Éire's freedom could not be exempted. We in London felt that there was a strong possibility of an early German invasion of Éire. This might precede or be simultaneous with an attempt on the United Kingdom. A number of considerations led us to this definite conclusion. First, the Held papers, and other documents which had been discovered on members of the I.R.A. who had been arrested, as well as information which we got from other sources, indicated that there was a plan for the invasion of Ireland; secondly, the experience of Denmark, Norway, Holland and Belgium showed that the invasion of neutral countries was an accepted weapon which Germany had no hesitation in using in her attack upon her enemies; and thirdly, Éire would appear to be the next neutral country on the list now that Germany would fling her full weight against Great Britain. In order to prepare for such an event, his military people and ours had engaged in staff conversations.[1] We were grateful for the blessing which he had given to such conversations; at least he had been more prudent than the heads of some other neutral governments who had allowed no such prior planning. Nevertheless although the conversations had borne fruit in a military plan of action, we felt that merely having a carefully drawn plan in a pigeon-hole was not now enough. The experience of other neutral countries had shown that the Germans acted like a stroke of lightning. They were now in a position to strike swiftly at Ireland. They would have possession of the whole French coast, and would be able to send troops by motorboats and submarines to land on the Irish coast. Our Navy would be on the look-out for this armada, but unfortunately they had to operate from somewhat distant ports in the United Kingdom, they were denied use of the Irish ports, and therefore their patrol could not be as efficient as it should be. On a dark night, or in a fog, the enemy might well succeed in slipping through our patrol and landing troops at various places on Irish shores. At the same time, they would endeavour to land troops from the air. Ireland was an ideal country into which parachute troops could descend or upon which troop-carrying planes could land. Furthermore, these invaders by sea and air would receive very effective help from Fifth Columnists in Éire. There was a considerable number of German citizens at large there, and there were the members of the I.R.A. It would be comparatively simple for the Germans, owing to this combination of circumstances, to land several thousand troops in a night. Unless these could be mopped up within a few hours, they could establish themselves until reinforcements arrived, and within a very short time a number of military units might be advancing from strong positions in the country and achieving a veritable conquest. The Irish troops were not adequate to deal with them without assistance. That was the purpose of the plan drawn up by the military advisers of his Government and ours; it was proposed that our soldiers should come immediately from the north to aid in resisting the invader. But clearly one of the first objects of Fifth Columnists, parachute troops and German air raids in Ireland would be to destroy the railways and roads by which the reinforcements would come. The enemy were likely to carry out this plan with the same thoroughness, efficiency and speed that they had adopted in other neutral countries. So our reinforcements probably would not be able to arrive on the scene of action until too late. In fact, anyone who studied dispassionately the

---

[1] See Nos 182 and 183.

German tactics in Norway, Holland and Belgium must conclude that, unless we were more prepared than was the case to-day, Éire might be effectively overpowered, Dublin captured and an I.R.A government established within a few hours. So it was our deliberate opinion that the present plan was not enough.

The wisest course for Éire, in our view, would be the immediate abandonment of neutrality, and a joining with us in resistance to Germany so that from this moment onwards co-operation could be complete and we could put whatever naval and military forces were required at his disposal. I would not argue the case for that, because I presumed that nothing that I could say would influence Mr. de Valera in that direction; but I must say that we would strongly advise that course. We did not give this advice simply because it would help us; indeed, we gave it principally in the interests of Éire itself. We were quite capable of dealing with an invasion of Great Britain. It was true that the over-running of Éire would embarrass us, but it would not be decisive against us; it would only be decisive against Éire. But assuming that his Government would not at present abandon neutrality, was there nothing else that could be done to ensure that the military assistance which we could give to his forces was present, as seemed essential, at the moment that invasion began. Was it possible for his Government, with the support of the Opposition, to invite our ships now to use the Irish ports, and our soldiers to come down and guard strategic points. Surely some more or less legitimate excuse could be made for this. The universal experience of small neutral nations which had not taken proper precautions for instantaneous assistance from the Allies in the first hour of aggression must have impressed the Irish people. Our ships and troops would not be there for the purpose of taking offensive action from Irish waters or territory. They would simply be there to defend Irish neutrality, and would only act offensively if that neutrality were violated by Germany.

Mr. de Valera replied emphatically that there was no possibility of Éire abandoning her neutrality now. All parties in the State were agreed that they should maintain that as long as possible. With regard to my second proposal, he had already given it careful consideration. But he was inclined to the view that the Germans would not attack Éire. They would invade Ulster, probably acting in areas where there was a Nationalist majority. In that case they would try to make out that they had come to end partition in Ireland.

I replied that I did not think this would happen. Germany did not commit aggression by halves. She would be anxious to clean up the business in Ireland quickly, for time was of the essence of his programme. When Hitler attacked Norway he landed his troops simultaneously in half a dozen key places up the coast. He would probably act with the same thoroughness in the Twenty-six Counties as well as the Six Counties. It would be extremely unsafe to plan on any other assumption.

Mr. de Valera agreed that there was a real danger of this, and said that his chief difficulty was that his troops were not as fully equipped as he would like them to be. For a long time he had been begging us for equipment, but he had only been able to get a small part of what he wanted. He was not complaining; he realised that we had to equip ourselves and some of those countries on the Continent who were likely to receive Germany's first blows. He had then tried to get equipment from America, but failed. He had hoped that by now he would have 50,000 well armed soldiers. As it was, he thought he had only about half that force. Volunteers were coming in well; he could reach the 50,000 figure and later the 100,000 figure, if he could get the equipment. But at present he admitted that his forces were inadequately prepared. Nevertheless, they would resist a German invasion with all their strength. He thought his men would fight magnificently. The Germans would not find things easy, for the Irish were very skilful at guerrilla warfare; they were very good hedge fighters and would fight the invader from hedge to hedge.

I remarked that such tactics would not be any use against tanks. The Germans would very likely succeed in getting tanks across the sea. If any number of these got ashore they would race through the fields and the villages with impunity. That was why it was essential, if the German attempt were to be strangled at its birth, for our Navy to have the use of the ports. We could then patrol the coast much more efficiently, and check the arrival of any large force. At the same time our well equipped troops should be already waiting with the Irish troops on the shores to receive such invaders as got through.

Mr. de Valera repeated that he had given this most serious consideration. If there had been a United Ireland he might have been able to invite us in now. He wished that such a political change had been accomplished before the war. A United Ireland would have been a great strength to us. It is true that the country would (if he had had his way) have remained neutral at the outset of the war, but by now it might have been a belligerent. He merely told me this because it was his definite view that things would have been different if the country had been one. But he realised that facts were against the establishment of a United Ireland; he did not suggest that we could do anything now. Therefore he had to reckon with the state of his public opinion in the light of that. Many of his supporters were inclined to say that Ireland had already been invaded, by the British in the North. This feeling prejudiced many who would otherwise have been our friends. Nevertheless, there was a very strong feeling of national unity in Éire now; there was a firmer unity amongst people of all shades of opinion than had existed for many years; it was based upon a policy of maintaining neutrality and offering uncompromising resistance to any belligerent power who violated that neutrality. The best service that he could render to his country and to us was to maintain that unity against the day when Germany struck. He wanted to be able to resist with the full force of a united people behind him. If he now invited our ships into the ports or our troops into the country he would prejudice that unity. It would be said by many of his own people that he had taken the initiative in throwing in his lot with the Allies, that he had provoked any act of German aggression that followed. That would be a false step; it would divide his people. It would weaken resistance and increase the support which German invaders would afterwards get from Irishmen. He was ready to go as far as he could in co-operation with us at present, short of publicly compromising the country's neutrality. If the situation were left to develop so that Germany was clearly the aggressor, he could assure me that an almost completely united people would resist the invader. They would fight very fiercely.

I answered that if he had put this argument to me some months ago, I would have been inclined to agree that there was some force in it. I would perhaps have thought that he could wait safely for the Germans to strike before he called in the aid from us without which he could not hope to succeed. But recent experiences of the German technique altered the whole situation. In Norway, Holland and Belgium the German attack – both from without and from within – had been so instantaneous, thorough and cunning that it had in fact broken down the strong points of resistance before the Allies could effectively arrive upon the scene. It was obvious that the Germans had as complete a plan for Éire and that they would follow the same methods there. His people must realise this, and that it made all the difference. If they waited for the attack before calling in their friends, their friends would come too late. It was essential that the full weight of resistance that could be brought to bear should be ready awaiting the Germans in the territorial waters and on the shores of the island.

He replied that his people did not appreciate this. They knew too little of what had happened in the other small neutral countries. Their information service was not good. Moreover, so many Irishmen actually thought that the Germans would make them more free. Prejudice against Britain was still strong, it would still take a long time to remove such an old sentiment. Indeed, his countrymen would actually fight with greater zeal if we were the first to violate Éire's neutrality than they would if the Germans were the first aggressors. He was only able to keep national unity at its present unprecedented level by making it clear that the Government would resist whichever belligerent invaded the country.

I said that he wanted a United Ireland. That was out of the question now. But supposing we took a step towards creating official machinery for the discussion of common concerns? For instance, the present German threat was one to the whole island. Supposing that we were to establish a joint Defence Council, on which representatives of the North and of the South would sit and consult and take decisions together, that would be the first time for many years that any union between the Six Counties and the Twenty-Six Counties had been expressed. It might be only a first step, to be followed by others. If the habit of co-operation on matters of common concern were once established, it would be difficult afterwards to break it down. We would be prepared to establish a Joint Defence Council for the whole of Ireland straight away. No doubt its creation would be regarded with satisfaction by his supporters. It might enable the representatives of Éire, after discussion on that joint body to declare that the interests of the defence of Irish freedom required that British naval ships should be invited into the southern Irish ports.

He replied in the negative. His supporters would regard the creation of such a piece of machinery between neutral Éire and belligerent Ulster as itself prejudicing the former's neutrality. They would think it a provocation to Germany. They would argue that Germany, seeing Éire in consultation with her enemies and presumably planning to act against Germany, would have some justification in anticipating this situation by invading Éire. If he wished to maintain the national unity which he had spoken about, and which was all-important in case of an actual German invasion, he must not compromise his neutrality at the present moment in any way. He thought that the establishment of such a Defence Council would be necessary as soon as Éire and Ulster were fighting side by side in the war, though that situation would present certain difficulties between old enemies. Indeed, when that time came the wisest thing that we could do would be to make an immediate announcement that Ireland was not only one country united for the purposes of defence, but united also henceforth for the whole business of government.

I answered that such an announcement would be impossible. He must not expect anything of the kind. If he reflected for a moment, he would realise the damage it would do. A great majority of Ulstermen would object strongly. At the moment when we expected them to put up the firmest possible resistance to an invader, we should be announcing a policy which was deeply offensive to their strongest feelings. It would take the heart out of their resistance. I had not supposed that Mr. de Valera himself would wish us to do anything at that moment which would revive divisions amongst Irishmen and weaken the common resistance to the German enemy. So far as we were concerned, we would not think of doing it. The territory of Ulster was closest to Glasgow and the Clyde. We should not do anything which would weaken resistance there, and increase the chance of the Germans establishing themselves too close to one of our vital production areas.

Mr. de Valera agreed that it would be difficult to do this in the middle of war. We ought to have done it before the war.

I said that I would like to have some further comments on this question. It seemed to me that the best chance of Ireland eventually becoming united would be if the twenty-six counties came fully into the war. Both parts of Ireland would then be fighting side by side; their union would be sealed by comradeship in arms. It would be very difficult to bring that unity to a sudden end at the close of the war. I knew the temper of my generation in British politics. We should not give any encouragement after the war to the revival of old, barren controversies. But if Éire did not come into the war, the position would be different. If they showed they were not prepared to fight for the freedom of England, the United Kingdom and the other democratic countries of Europe – if they who had spoken so much about liberty now shrank from its defence in its supreme hour of danger, whilst Ulster fought fully for that defence – then the differences between the 26 and the 6 counties would certainly be aggravated and enlarged, and we politicians at Westminster who had gone through the fight would never agree to handing Ulster over to Éire against the former's will.

He replied that his countrymen would not believe that if they came into the war there would be a united Ireland at the end of it. On the contrary, they would feel that at the end we should say that Ulster must still maintain her independence of the rest of Ireland because she had entered the war at the very beginning, whilst Éire had come in late.

I said that it was no good speculating at length on what might or might not happen after the war. I had expressed the view of myself and my contemporaries. The one object on which we must all concentrate now was the actual, immediate urgent defence of Irish and well as British liberty. He and I must accept the facts as they were, and then see whether there was more that we could do on the basis of those facts to serve that common cause. The two basic facts between us seemed to be first, that Éire would not abandon her neutrality until she was attacked, and second, there would be no question of our declaring a united Ireland. Accepting that situation, what could be done? We urged strongly that in view of the lightning speed with which the Germans acted, Irish freedom could only be maintained if our Navy and our troops were allowed to use Irish ports and land. That was necessary to check the invader from without. But he said that was impossible. Would it be possible if troops other than those of the old British enemy came in – if French or Polish or Dominion troops were invited in by the Éire Government? Mr. de Valera answered in the negative. I said that there was still something else that could be done to improve the immediate prospect. German aggression did not proceed only by the importation of invaders from without. It was made doubly deadly by the co-operation of allies already within the territory of the victim. In the case of Éire these were the I.R.A. and resident Germans and Italians. These Fifth Columnists were an essential part of the German plan; their help as saboteurs and as assistants to troops landing by parachute or troop-carrying planes, could make all the difference between an immediate or a more protracted over-running of the country. If this enemy machine inside Éire could be smashed before the invasion began, the prospect of early German success would be greatly lessened. Would he therefore take the strongest possible action against the I.R.A.? Would he arrest and imprison all their leaders? Would he, moreover, intern suspect Germans and Italians? It seemed to us essential at this critical moment in his own self-defence.

He answered that as regards the I.R.A., this was no longer a large force, though he agreed that there was a wide 'fringe' to it. He could assure me that he had taken very severe action against it. He thought that all the leaders outside Dublin were under detention. The difficulty was the organisation in Dublin itself. The authorities could not lay their hands on all the leaders there. There was an underworld in Dublin into which these people disappeared. They simply could not be found. His Government took action against them whenever they got the slightest chance, but he had to confess that some of the Dublin leaders were still at large. As for the Germans and Italians, he could not intern them. That would be an un-neutral Act. But they were being carefully watched.

I answered that he surely had sufficient evidence on which to intern a good many Germans. The Held papers indicated what was afoot. I understood that several papers found on members of the I.R.A. had also indicated a plan for German action in Ireland. The experience of the other neutral victims of German aggression was strong circumstantial evidence that the German population in Ireland were prepared for the role of assistants to the invaders. In fact, it was clear that these people were parties to a conspiracy against Éire. He could get the support of his countrymen in taking the precaution now of locking them up.

He replied that this was not so. Held, for instance, had not been a German National, but a naturalised Irishman. The only evidence which had appeared in the various documents discovered had been evidence that they sought to establish the same sort of spy system which existed in other countries.

I replied that it seemed to me that the evidence was pretty strong. A parachute had been found in Held's house. It was known that a German had dropped in this parachute from a German aeroplane a few weeks ago. In fact, the Germans were definitely employing the same technique in Ireland as they employed elsewhere when they were contemplating invasion.

Mr. de Valera admitted that this case had shaken him considerably. But he did not think he had grounds, which would satisfy his public, on which to intern Germans. He could assure me, however, that they were all being closely watched. They would be arrested if there was any real reason for doing this. If a German invasion started, he thought they could round them up very quickly. Moreover, he did not think these people would really get much help from the Irish population. If German troops took the initiative in invading Ireland, national sentiment would respond swiftly, and the public generally would react strongly against any aiders or abettors of the foreign aggressor.

I repeated that we could only warn him in the plainest possible language that it looked to us as though Éire was likely to be overcome very swiftly.

Mr. de Valera asked whether I did not think that Hitler would leave Éire out of the picture. He had the whole of the coasts of Norway, Germany, Holland, Belgium and France from which to launch his attack on Britain. This surely gave him a sufficient jumping-off ground. It would be more difficult for him to reach and subdue Éire.

I said that I took the opposite view. If Hitler thought that he could defeat Great Britain he knew that it must be done in the next two months or so. After that he would have lost his chance. He must try within that time to destroy our production of aircraft and to cripple our overseas trade. It was true that he could act from the coasts which he possessed to the east and south of us. But his effort could not be fully mustered unless he could attack us also from the west. It might be that he would ***[1] our trade on the east and south coasts, but that would not break us if our western ports were still open. Hitler's motto was 'thorough'. It was an essential part of his plan to have a base in the west from which to complete the concentration of his attack upon us from all sides.

Mr. de Valera then asked whether I thought there was any prospect of the attack on us being postponed whilst Hitler made a move in the east of Europe. The latest advance of Russia might embarrass him.

I said that I thought Hitler would certainly not be drawn aside. He would have plenty of time to tear the Russian army to shreds later on; but he had very little time in which to accomplish our defeat. We were the only enemy that stood between him and his ambition to dominate Europe. If he did not beat us in the next two months, his ambition would be thwarted. He would certainly go all out for us at the earliest possible moment.

Mr. de Valera agreed that this was so, and asked whether there was any prospect of our settling this business by negotiating peace. Hitler had always said that he wanted us to remain in possession of our Empire. Would we on this basis agree to his having a predominant role in Eastern Europe?

I answered that there was no prospect whatever of this. We should regard a Europe under Hitler's domination as intolerable. There would be no freedom for anyone on the Continent, and there would be no security for our two islands. Hitler's word could not be trusted. He would only use the breathing-space given him to increase his forces still further, prior to a second attack upon us. Therefore we would continue to fight. We saw no reason why we should be defeated. Éire could be swiftly overrun by the German invader, but Great Britain could not. The position was quite different in our island. If some thousands of Germans landed in Éire, they could not, with Éire's present resources, be beaten back; but if a few thousand men landed in Britain, they would have a very hot reception. We admitted that, despite the patrol of our fleet, some thousands of men might slip through on a foggy night and land here and there on the shores of England. But within the first

---

[1] One word illegible.

few hours of daylight our air and land attacks on these troops would mop them up. We had the largest armed force in the United Kingdom that had ever been stationed there in our history. Our production of war material was increasing rapidly. Though our Air Force was smaller than that of Germany, the quality of our machines and our pilots were very superior to theirs. The evacuation of Dunkirk had proved that in a fairly confined space of sky our Air Force already had the mastery. Now that there was no need for a part of it to be dispersed over the battlefield in France, our Air Force could certainly keep the ceiling above England clear of any effective attacks by day. Our production of aircraft had doubled in the last few weeks. Both by the rate of our destruction of German craft and by the rate of production of our new craft we were gradually overhauling Germany's numerical superiority. Therefore we were confident that we could hold off any serious invasion during the next two or three months. By then American supplies of material would be reinforcing us very rapidly, and our blockade of Germany and Italy would be producing results. The large populations which Germany would be trying to hold down in Europe would be having a bad time. They would suffer both famine and oppression, and it might well be that the Nazi regime would crack.

Mr. de Valera agreed that there was a good hope of our doing this if the French Fleet were not surrendered to the enemy. But if Germany got control of that Fleet, he did not see how our blockade could succeed. He did not see how in those circumstances we would maintain our position in the Mediterranean. Germany and Italy would then possess a very powerful Fleet to do battle with ours.

I answered that this would undoubtedly greatly increase our difficulties. We must wait and see what did actually happen to the French Fleet. But even if it went to the enemy, that would not be decisive. Our air raids on Germany had already been extremely damaging to the enemy's supplies of oil and other material and stores. Our aerial bombardment of German territories would be intensified. At the same time we could still block up the two entrances to the Mediterranean and make our blockade effective. I had no doubt that America and the other neutral countries who share her disposition would put every difficulty in the way of supplies going to the two Dictators.

He asked whether Germany would not be able to destroy the factories producing our aircraft.

I answered that they would be able to do very little in daylight raids. Our fighters would do battle with the maximum of efficiency over our Island. When fighting in France they had never been certain where the enemy Air Force were in the skies. They had to go out and search for them. But over England our system of observation was so efficient that our fighter squadrons would always know exactly when and where the enemy were about to cross our coasts. The mastery that they had established over Dunkirk would be established over the whole of the United Kingdom. Germany's chance was to bomb our industrial centres by night. But for the next few weeks the nights would be short. And in any case, such damage as the enemy was able to inflict would be offset by the damage that we would inflict in turn by our raids over Germany. Thus, as between Germany and Italy and ourselves, it would be an eye for an eye and a tooth for a tooth. Our aeroplane production would no doubt suffer diminution, but so would theirs. Germany would get no supplies from outside, but we on the other hand would get increasing reinforcements of aeroplanes from Canada and the United States of America. Hitler could not bomb their factories.

Mr. de Valera was impressed by these facts, but nevertheless remained sceptical.

I said that if he were really filled with doubts as to our capacity to resist Hitler, then he ought not to hesitate a minute in coming to our aid. If our friends did not support us in time, and we were unluckily defeated, then Éire's liberty would unquestionably be extinguished.

He indicated that he was apprehensive of this, but repeated that at the present stage he could not go further than he had already gone in co-operating with us. He understood the arguments for meeting a German invasion of his country from the very first moment with a maximum of resistance. But for the reasons he had given he could not invite our forces to occupy his territory or his territorial waters in advance of a German attack. But he would ask us to do two things. First, we could immediately let him have further equipment for his own forces. He wanted anti-tank guns and machine guns, rifles and ammunition. Could we not let him have more of these? He felt that Dublin was very vulnerable to attack by tanks, if these should once be landed. He would like to have a ring of anti-tank guns around the city. Secondly, he would ask that we send our military help immediately that Germany attacked. The help that he would want most would be from our aeroplanes. It was true, as I had said, that parachutists and others might obstruct the railways and roads by which our troops were to come down from the North. But they could not impede the passage of our aeroplanes. He hoped that we would send a strong air force over as soon as he appealed to us.

I told him that I would report what he had said about the need for further equipment. But he must appreciate our position. Our Navy and our Air Force were very powerful. We also had more divisions of troops in the country than had ever been there. But some of these had lost a lot of their equipment in Belgium, and although our production was increasing so fast that their re-equipment was proceeding apace, we could do with all the anti-tank guns, machine guns, rifles and ammunition that we could produce for a long time to come. Moreover, we would have no inclination to send over equipment to Éire only to have it lost to the enemy. If we had confidence that Éire's resistance to the German invaders was going to be effective, we might send equipment. But the whole purport of my mission was to point out to him the reasons why we had not got that confidence, and to ask him in the interests of his own country to do what was necessary to correct the position. So far as our assisting him immediately after his appeal came to us was concerned, I could assure him that we should not hesitate a moment in sending our forces to help. But he could hardly rely on our Air Force to protect him in Dublin. We could not bomb Dublin without killing Irish civilians. I assumed that he did not want us to do that. If the defence of Dublin was to be made effective, he must let us protect his shores more efficiently than we could at present.

He urged again that we should let him have as much equipment as we could spare, and assured me that if and when the Germans invaded Éire his countrymen would resist that invasion with all their might, and that he would then take action against the German nationals who might help the enemy from within.

M.M.

Documents on Irish Foreign Policy, Volume VI, 1939–1941

No. 194 NAI DFA Paris Embassy 19/34A

Confidential report from Seán Murphy to Joseph P. Walshe (Dublin)
(Copy)

Ascain, 18 June 1940

1. Shortly after the outbreak of the war in September last, I received a letter from the French Protocol to the effect that among other possibilities considered by the military authorities was that of the departure from Paris of the President of the Republic in which case (so stated the note) 'a residence would be placed at the disposal of the Heads of Mission so that they might be able to continue to fulfil their functions with the aid of a reduced staff'. The note enquired what diplomatic staff and what personal staff I would wish to take in the event of such a possibility arising and the weight of the archives which I would desire to have moved. A reply was sent to this note at once.

2. I heard nothing further about the matter until, with the turn taken by the war in Belgium and Northern France, I thought it better to ascertain the exact arrangements contemplated, in the event of moving, both for accommodating the Legation and in providing transport for the staff and luggage. I first approached the Nuncio, as Dean of the Corps. He was under the impression that a special train would be provided for the transport of luggage and of members of the Corps other than Heads of Missions who, he believed, were expected to reach their future quarters in their own cars. He advised me, however, to address myself to the Protocol for all details. I, therefore, had an interview with the Chef du Protocole. From him I ascertained the name and situation of the Chateau in the Tours region allotted to us. Beyond that, he could furnish me with no particulars and suggested that the best thing for me to do would be to go and see the place. It was already clear, however, that there would be no special train and that the various missions would have to make their own arrangements for transport of staff and luggage. On the 29th May I went to visit the Chateau du Grand Boucher, Ballan Miré, Tours, where we were supposed to go. I called at the Préfecture at Tours to get particulars of what I should do to be able to see the house. The Préfet sent an Inspector to accompany me. The Chateau proved to be a three storey house standing in its own grounds with a court-yard, a garage and over the garage four small rooms. The house when we saw it consisted, apart from rather limited servants' quarters, of three rooms on the ground floor (dining room, salon and library) two large bed rooms each with a large bath room on the first floor and three rooms, two of which were arranged as bed rooms on the second floor. This was quite a different arrangement to that of the house when first inspected by the authorities and set aside for a Legation in April 1939. When we saw it the proprietor with a companion was living in it although he was absent at Paris that day. If the house were completely empty, it would have been possible, in case of necessity, to use it for the Legation as there would have been sufficient accommodation in the main building for myself and one or two members of the Legation staff and the annex over the garage could have been used as an office. It was clearly, however, quite out of the question to install a Legation in the building unless the proprietor were to leave it. When I got back to Paris, I informed the Chef du Protocole of the actual state of affairs and gave him my views as to the possibility of its being used by our Legation. As he was not

able to give me any information as to whether the owner would stay on, as I understood that the Government had not in fact requisitioned it and as it seemed abundantly clear that the proprietor had deliberately altered the house so as to prevent a Legation being installed in it, I decided that it would be rash to rely on it as a possible residence and that by far the wiser course would be to assume that we would have to make our own arrangements both in regard to our accommodation as well as in regard to our transport. The question of transport did not present any real difficulty as my car was capable of carrying all of the staff and the Secretary's car could carry such official luggage as we would require to bring with us. Events moved too rapidly, however, for me to be able to make arrangements in regard to accommodation.

3. Having to leave Paris to follow the Government became more and more a likelihood as time went on. All through the week ending on the 9th June it seemed inevitable that we would have to take this step. It was known on the other hand, because of the Government's decision announced after a council meeting at the end of May not to leave Paris except at the last possible moment, that one should be prepared to leave at very short notice. I had therefore made arrangements in so far as the official documents were concerned for our being able to leave within a very short time of receiving notice. Among other questions which were considered was that of leaving a member of the staff to look after the Legation and, in the event of no member of staff remaining, of leaving a concierge at the Legation. You will remember that I had discussed the former point with you during your visit to Paris in the middle of May. I felt that there was no point in any member of the staff remaining both because of the relatively unimportant nature of our interests in Paris and because no member of the staff had any locus standi vis-à-vis the French (or German) authorities except through the Foreign Office and by derivation from my position as representative accredited to the President of the Republic. As for leaving a concierge alone in the Legation, I decided against this course on the ground that I could not feel sure that the presence of a concierge, no matter how reliable, might not lead to some abuse and that, if a third party should forcibly enter the Legation, our position would be secure if all possible precautions to prevent such an event had been taken. I, therefore, paid off the concierge on the 10th June and, in accordance with the terms on which he was engaged in 1931, gave him a month's salary in lieu of notice. Before leaving Paris on the morning of the 11th I saw to it that all outside entrances to the Legation and Chancery were locked.

4. On the afternoon of Sunday the 9th June, the Nuncio visited the Ministry of Foreign Affairs to enquire as to the likelihood of the Corps having to leave Paris. Later in the evening the Nuncio conveyed unofficially to the Legation that it was probable that a decision that the Government should leave Paris would be taken within the next two days. On the morning of Monday 10th June we received a note from the Protocol advising us that, consequent on the Nuncio's visit, the Government 'saw no objection to our moving into the provinces'. We understood that the Nuncio intended to leave that day. I therefore made all arrangements for leaving early on the following morning. It was in these circumstances that I sent you my telegram No. 47.[1] That evening I called on the American Ambassador[2] to

---

[1] Not printed.
[2] William C. Bullitt (1891-1967), United States Ambassador to France (1936-40).

ascertain what course he proposed to follow and whether he had any information as to what the Missions of other neutral States were doing. He informed me that he was aware that all or practically all the Heads of Mission in Paris had either already left on the 10th or proposed to leave by the 11th. As far as he himself was concerned, he intended to remain in Paris because of the tradition in the American Service that the diplomatic representative in Paris remain there whatever should happen. Apparently this course was followed in 1870 and in 1914. I gathered from Mr. Bullitt that he had insisted on observing this tradition even in the face of a direct message from President Roosevelt which he had received the previous evening to the effect that he should leave Paris. Later the same evening I received a circular telegram from the Foreign Office to the effect that the Ministry was that day moving, leaving Paris 'to install itself in the provinces in proximity to the residence which had been allotted to the Legation' (sic).

5. I knew that Father Travers, Rector of the Irish College in Paris, was anxious to leave the city in the event of the French Government deciding to evacuate the capital. It was his intention in such an event to get to the House of his Order (Vincentian) at Rennes. As soon as our decision to leave had been taken, I communicated with him and offered, if he so desired, to take him with us to Tours where another House of the Order existed. He accepted this offer. On the following morning, therefore, we all assembled at the Legation i.e. the Secretary,[1] Mr. O'Byrne, Mme Froc, Miss Foley and Father Travers. We left the Legation for Tours at 8 a.m. An unusual and very dirty fog lay over Paris that morning whereas the weather up to then for a fortnight previously had been extremely fine with complete absence of cloud. This fog would appear to have been that which the official communiqué of the evening of the 11th alleged had been artificially created by the Germans with the object of crossing the Seine at various points west of Paris, the nearest of which was about 45 miles away. We understood that the roads leading out of Paris towards the south were likely to be heavily encumbered with traffic on account of the huge voluntary exodus of the civil population which was taking place. We, however, chose the direct road to Tours which runs through Versailles, Chartres, Chateaudun, Vendôme and Chateau Renault. The total distance from Paris to Tours by this route is 235 kilometres (somewhat under 150 miles). In normal circumstances, the journey would be performed in less than 3½ hours. As soon, however, as we had got to Garches, which is about 2½ miles out, we ran into a heavy line of traffic running in the same direction. The result was that it took us over an hour to reach Versailles, a distance generally covered in about twenty minutes. We reached Epernon, which is c.40 miles from Paris, at about 11 a.m. At this point we with the rest of the line of cars, were obliged by the military authorities to leave the main road for Chartres. Until we got as far as Gallardon, a distance from Epernon of 15 miles, our progress was relatively rapid. To cover this distance from Gallardon to Sours, however, (about 10 miles) it took us about three hours. This was by far the most unpleasant part of the journey as we were advancing by stages of only from 10 to 50 yards at a time and the day had become exceedingly hot. We reached Sours at about 2.30 p.m. On arriving here I decided to see the military authority to insist that, as we were on an official journey, we should be allowed to take the main road. This was conceded and

---

[1] Con Cremin.

we therefore went to Chartres (about 5 miles away) at a normal pace and from there by the main route to Chateaudun (about 27 miles) which we reached about 3.30 p.m. All the hotels and restaurants at Chateaudun were overflowing and short of food but we finally succeeded in getting something to eat. We left for Vendôme (25 miles away) by the main road, at about 4.30. On this stretch we did not encounter anything like the same volume of refugee traffic as on the whole journey so far as Sours. From Vendôme to Chateau Renault, a distance of over 15 miles, progress was relatively good for most of the way. We had a puncture however, some distance before Chateau Renault and immediately afterwards ran into a traffic block which it took us almost three quarters of an hour to clear. From Chateau Renault we took the reserved main road to Tours (20 miles away). It rained rather heavily on this stretch. We ultimately arrived at Tours towards 9 p.m.

6. I thought it best on arrival at Tours, before making any further arrangements, to call to see the Prefect and ascertain from him the exact position in regard to the Chateau allotted to us. He informed me at once that this chateau was no longer available as the owner had installed a large number of relatives. I gathered from him that the experience in regard to our chateau was not an isolated one and that the Nuncio and a few Ambassadors who had arrived the previous evening had had to spend the night in chairs in his house. He said that there was no room whatever available at Tours but asked his Chef de Cabinet to see what he could do for us. The latter went to great pains in the matter and ultimately succeeded in securing for us more or less by means of requisition, a total of three rooms in the Hotel de l'Univers, regarded as the best hotel in the town. We left the Prefecture for the hotel at about 9.30. Just as we left the anti-air-craft defences set up a strong barrage which continued more or less without interruption until towards 11 p.m. As the sky was overcast, it was impossible to see what was being fired at but the flames of the bursting shells were clearly visible. When we reached the hotel we found the place in a state of considerable chaos. I eventually succeeded in getting, in addition to the three rooms obtained for us by the Prefecture, another room for my chauffeur and his wife who had accompanied him from Paris. We had, therefore, a total of four rooms for eight people as Father Travers found it impossible to locate the House of his Order that night. On entering the hotel, I met M. Gaston Riou, Deputy and Vice President of the Chamber Foreign Affairs Commission. He advised me to go at once for dinner and offered to assist in obtaining it. The hotel management, however, said that it was no longer possible to serve dinner on account of the 'alerte'. They advised us to try a restaurant further down the street. We did so but were informed that 'not an egg remained'. We had, therefore, nothing to eat that night.

7. It was quite evident that Tours was in a complete state of chaos which was only likely to grow in subsequent days with the increasing influx of refugees on their way through to the south and of Government officials coming to be installed in the region. My experience had also convinced me that it would be quite useless to expect any assistance whatever in the matter of obtaining accommodation from the Protocol. At the same time so long as we were in a position to be in contact with the Government, there seemed no strong reason why we should be in very close proximity to them. I, therefore, decided to proceed towards the south in the

hope of obtaining accommodation, intending to go, if necessary, as far as Bordeaux. Poitiers, which represented our first stop and where we had lunch (it is about 65 miles from Tours) was completely full, both with refugees and the administration of the Belgian Government. Angoulême, the next stage of the journey (about an equal distance from Poitiers), was likewise completely full and there was nothing whatever to be had in the hotels. We, therefore, continued to Bordeaux which we reached on the evening of the 12th at about 8 p.m. I, at once, called at the Prefecture as offering our best hope of obtaining accommodation in Bordeaux if, as I thought would be the case, the hotels were full. I was unable to see the Prefect but had an interview with the Secretary General who, by a coincidence, happened to be the nephew of the Legation architect and was probably, therefore, better disposed towards us than might otherwise have been the case. He undertook to do what he could the following day to get us suitable accommodation. As regards accommodation that night, he said that the hotels were completely over-flowing but that he would see what he could manage in the way of rooms. He finally succeeded in securing for us a total of three rooms, one in the Hotel Continental and the others in the Hotel Terminus. The party was divided up between these hotels, myself, Mr. Cremin and Mr. O'Byrne staying in the one room in the Continental. The following morning I called, as arranged, at the Prefecture to have another interview with Mr. Ziwes. I was, however, quite unable to see him as he was in conference all morning. The explanation of the conference was that the Government had the previous night decided to move to Bordeaux. I tried on several occasions in the course of the day to see Mr. Ziwes but did not succeed in doing so until late in the afternoon when he told me that their arrangements had been completely upset by the sudden decision of the Government and intimated that there was little hope of any kind of suitable accommodation being placed at our disposal at least in the immediate future. This was my own judgment from the crowds which I could see in Bordeaux and from the developments which had taken place in the matter of hotel accommodation. Our hotel had that day been requisitioned for the Government and it was only by reason of the fact that our room was already regarded as requisitioned by the Prefecture for us that we were able to remain in it. Practically all other clients of the hotel were ordered to leave it in the course of the day. It has since been stated that by that date Bordeaux contained a population of three times as great as its normal population (about 250,000). As before leaving Paris the possibility of our having to go even further south had not been excluded, I had asked the Special Counsellor[1] who was leaving Paris for Ascain to look into the prospects of our obtaining accommodation in that region. It seemed unlikely that I could make any useful contact with the Foreign Office on the next day, Friday the 14th. I, therefore, paid a visit to Ascain which is about 120 miles south of Bordeaux. I found that Count O'Kelly had, in fact, been able to secure accommodation in Ascain itself for the whole party in the event of our requiring it and that he had also succeeded in finding rooms which could serve as an office. I, therefore, decided to move the whole party down to Ascain. I returned to Bordeaux the same evening and we left for Ascain at 3 p.m. on the following day (Saturday 15th June). I had spent the morning in Bordeaux in an effort to get in touch with the Ministry of Foreign

---

[1] Count Gerald O'Kelly de Gallagh.

Affairs but, though I ascertained where they were supposed to be, it proved impossible to find any member of the Ministry either there or elsewhere.

8. There are in all at least about 25 heads of missions in the Biarritz, St. Jean, Ascain area. In addition there is at Biarritz a considerable number of members of the staffs of other missions. From what I have since gathered from some of my colleagues it seems that my decision to push on in the first instance from Tours and in the second instance from Bordeaux was a wise one. Their experience in regard to the accommodation allotted to them at Tours was similar to mine and some of them have informed me that accommodation which was alleged to have been assigned to them near Bordeaux after the government decided to move there was not available. A number of the Missions which have remained in Bordeaux have, I understand, done so because of the facilities in the matter of personal and office accommodation offered by their Consulates in that city.

No. 195 NAI DFA Secretary's Files P15(i)

> *Code telegram from William J.B. Macaulay to*
> *the Department of External Affairs (Dublin)*
> *(No. 20) (Urgent) (Copy)*
>
> HOLY SEE, 19 June 1940

Saw Under-Secretary of State June 17th regarding Dublin urged insistently immediate appointment. He agreed with my remarks on leaving See vacant so long in such a critical time and said that he would make immediately urgent representations to Congregation.

No. 196 NAI DFA Secretary's Files A2

> *Memorandum from Joseph P. Walshe to Eamon de Valera*
>
> DUBLIN, 21 June 1940

Britain's Inevitable Defeat

Britain's defeat has been placed beyond all doubt. France has capitulated. The entire coastline of Europe from the Arctic to the Pyrenees is in the hands of the strongest power in the world which can call upon the industry and resources of all Europe and Asia in an unbroken geographical continuity as far as the Pacific Ocean. Neither time nor gold can beat Germany. It is frankly acknowledged in America that America must look to her own defences. She may be at War with Japan in a few short weeks. Senator Pittman,[1] Chairman of the Foreign Affairs Committee of the Senate, expressed the view yesterday to the Press that nothing that America could do could affect anything more than a delay in the final defeat.

England has the most concentrated industry and system of ports of any great power in the world. Her power of production would be wiped out in a few weeks of intensified bombing and her ports put out of action. Italian and German submarines acting in combination are strong enough to throw her merchant fleet into confusion. The German Air Force is acknowledged to have had an immense

---

[1] Key Pittman (1872-1940), Senator for Nevada, Chairman of the Senate Foreign Relations Committee (1933-40).

superiority in numbers even while France was in the War. Germany is foregoing the use of captured French planes against England. Britain has suffered a colossal military defeat and the bulk of her effective forces have been rendered useless for months to come by the loss of the greater part of her war material. All the smaller States in Europe on which she was relying for incidental support have grown cold and are abandoning her. Rumania is going Axis. Turkey has slipped out of her obligation to take action against Italy. Greece is having friendly talks with the Axis Powers. In Africa, Egypt refused active participation. South Africa is on the verge of Civil War because at least 50% of the population were opposed to participation and their numbers are now being rapidly added to by the clear evidence of England's approaching defeat. General Hertzog's return to power and South Africa's withdrawal from the War appear to be a certainty. In Asia Iraq is hesitating about further co-operation and is having consultations with Turkey and Egypt as well as the other Arab States. Japan is setting up an East Asia Monroe Doctrine and has begun an undeclared War against the British in Hong Kong. She is openly threatening an early move against French Indo-China and the Dutch East Indies.

No wonder the American radio is sending out rumours of pending peace negotiations through the British Ambassador in Madrid.[1] It is a fair deduction from the course of events that some members at least of the British Cabinet must be turning their thoughts to Peace.

No. 197 NAI DFA Paris Embassy 19/34A

> Confidential report from Seán Murphy to Joseph P. Walshe (Dublin)
> (Copy)
>
> Ascain, 21 June 1940

There can be little doubt that the decision of the Pétain[2] Government to seek the end of hostilities was dictated almost exclusively by military consideration. This emerges both from the speech of M. Baudoin, Minister for Foreign Affairs,[3] delivered over the radio on the same day as Maréchal Pétain forespoke (17th June), from the radio comment which since then has continuously laid stress on the military weakness of France and more particularly from Maréchal Pétain's second radio speech of the 20th. This latter speech can only be interpreted as being an effort to justify the decision taken and was probably delivered because of the existence of opposition to the decision reached. The importance attributed to military considerations alone in reaching this decision is also proved both by the composition of the Cabinet which only includes 7 politicians proper out of a total ministry of 16 in which there are 5 ministers whose career has been exclusively military (Maréchal Pétain, Général Weygand, General Colson, Admiral Darlan, Général Pugeol; it is also to be observed incidentally that national defence and war have for the first time for years been made two distinctive portfolios). The composition of the

---

[1] Sir Samuel Hoare, 1st Viscount Templewood (1880-1959), British Home Secretary (1937-9), Lord Privy Seal (1939-40), British Ambassador to Spain (1940-4).
[2] Marshal Philippe Pétain (1856-1951), Vichy France Chief of State (1940-4).
[3] Paul Baudoin (1894-1964), French Minister for Foreign Affairs (June to October 1940) who negotiated France's armistice with Germany.

delegation which is to receive the terms is also predominantly military (3 including the President out of 4 members).[1]

It was evident towards the end of last week that a way out of the situation by a cessation of resistance was being envisaged. The communiqué of the Cabinet meetings held towards the end of the week made mention of a new factor in connection with continued resistance, namely the nature of the American reply to Mr. Reynaud's appeal. Hitherto resistance had not been made as far as the public was informed dependent on any other consideration than the will of France to oppose the enemy to the end. The communiqué in question implied that if the American reply were considered unsatisfactory (apparently if the reply did not involve the entry of America to the war) France might be compelled to give up the struggle. At that stage there would seem to have been two main solutions – that which has been adopted or, and this would have been more consistent with what M. Reynaud had continuously said in his public pronouncements, the giving of authority to the military leaders to make the best arrangements they could in France by capitulation or otherwise combined with the departure of the Government from France either to North Africa as M. Reynaud had suggested in his first message to President Roosevelt on the 10th June or to some other place such as London. This latter solution would have been of the same kind as that taken by the Dutch Government and would have had the same objective, namely to preserve the French Empire for the conduct of the war and to preserve the fleet. Maréchal Pétain's decision would seem to have been based on the assumption that his offer coupled with the veneration attributed to his personality would have led to an immediate cessation of hostilities. It is probably subject to criticism in political quarters on the ground that the subsequent developments of the situation mean that the primary object which he could have effected has not been attained (as it seems likely that the hostilities will practically have been brought to an end by the occupation of the greater portion of France before agreement on the German terms is reached) and that it probably will involve the surrender of at least a portion of the French Empire and of the French fleet. It is not yet clear what conditions the Government will regard as acceptable. All Maréchal Pétain himself said was that he was asking the adversary 'whether he is prepared to seek with me as between soldiers after the struggle and in honour the means of putting an end to hostilities'. Maréchal Pétain's speech was, according to the radio, 'commented' that evening by M. Paul Baudoin, Minister for Foreign Affairs. In his speech, the latter said, inter alia, referring to Maréchal Pétain's reference to a cessation of hostilities in honour that 'the country is not disposed to accept dishonourable conditions, to abandon the spiritual liberty of her people, to betray the soul of France'. M. Peyrouton, Resident General in Tunis in a broadcast speech on Tuesday evening said inter alia 'honour remains, the Empire also: 60 million men, immense territory which our civilised genius brought out of long servitude'. It is difficult to see how the integrity of the Empire can be expected to continue considering that whether hostilities end or not before all France is occupied France will in effect have been decisively beaten in the war.

---

[1] On 22 June 1940 a delegation led by Marshal Pétain signed an armistice with Germany at Compiègne.

Documents on Irish Foreign Policy, Volume VI, 1939–1941

No. 198 TNA PREM 3/131/1

Note of conversations between Eamon de Valera and Malcolm MacDonald
(Copy)

DUBLIN, 23 June 1940

I have had two further long conversations with Mr. de Valera, on June 21st and 22nd. The following is their substance.

I told him that we had received his specific requests for military equipment. They were being examined in London, but I should like to make some preliminary comments. There were a few items in his list which we had already promised to supply, and we would do whatever we could to expedite the arrival of these. But the other requests were much more difficult. They were for material which we ourselves needed for our own troops in Britain. Bren Guns, anti-tank guns and rifles, rifles and ammunition were the very things of which we were short as a result of our losses in Belgium and France. We were producing them rapidly, but required as many as we could produce for the re-equipment of our trained divisions. Even so, we might release some of these weapons for his troops if we felt a reasonable confidence that the material would not fall into the hands of the enemy within a short time of a German invasion of Éire. We had had a rather bitter experience of losing valuable arms to the Germans, and were not minded to repeat it. At present neither our military advisers nor we felt any confidence at all about the position in Éire; on the contrary, we thought the danger of a quick success for a comparatively small invading force was so real that we would not, in present circumstances, contemplate letting him have valuable equipment. If we had a better assurance that Irish resistance to the enemy would be effective, then the situation would change. If our naval ships could use Southern Irish ports, and some of our troops and aeroplanes could be stationed forthwith on Éire's territory, and if he took greater precautions against the Fifth Column in his country, then we should feel that the chances of successful invasion were greatly reduced, and we should be ready to let him have additional arms for his troops to use in defence of the common cause.

He answered that this was impracticable. He had given much thought to these questions since our conversations the other day, and could only repeat that an invitation to British forces to enter Éire before any invasion started would be a fatal mistake. It would break that strong unity with which almost the entire population were at present prepared to resist a German invasion. Moreover, the situation might be even worse than that. The appearance of British forces in Éire would almost certainly be followed by the I.R.A. sniping at some of our troops. A most unhappy situation might grow from such an unfortunate beginning. He wondered why, if we were willing to send equipment with our troops into Éire, we were not willing to send the same equipment to arm his troops in the same place. He was not short of men, but only of equipment. He could raise plenty of troops, and they were as good fighters as ours. He could assure me that they would resist the invaders bitterly. He thought our policy very short-sighted. Éire was exposed to attack; it was a back-door through which the Germans might try to enter Britain, whilst they were at the same time trying to get through other doors on the shores of Britain itself. We ought not to keep all our guns to defend the British doors, but to send some to the back-door in Éire.

I replied that we were certainly concerned for the defence of the back-door. It could not be defended by infantry equipment alone. To secure it there should be a proper Naval patrol off the coasts, which meant our ships using Irish ports. That would secure that large numbers of the enemy invaders were drowned on the way over. As for the defence against those who succeeded in landing, we certainly did not under-estimate the fighting qualities of his men. They were very fine fighters indeed. But there was one important difference between his troops and ours. His were untrained, whilst ours were trained. The German invasion that we were talking about might happen any time now. There was not time to train troops in the use of equipment which many of them would never have seen before. That was why we wanted our troops with their own equipment to come into Éire.

He repeated that this would destroy the national unity which was all-important. He asked me whether we were partly reluctant to send equipment to Éire because we were afraid of Éire coming into the war against us. He said that if we made a mistake in this delicate situation, and ourselves committed an act of aggression against Éire, they would fight determinedly against us. But ruling out that possibility, were we afraid of the Irish helping the Germans?

I said that we had no mental reservation about that. We accepted that the great majority of his people would resist a German invasion, but we had to face the stern facts of German methods which had been employed with ruthless success in other neutral countries which had already been completely overwhelmed. The Germans could land troops by sea and by air without much difficulty in Éire, and there was a strong element of the Fifth Column inside the country already which would make their advance here at least as swift as it had been elsewhere. The reason why we would not provide equipment was that we were convinced that under present conditions that equipment would be quickly lost to the enemy.

Mr. de Valera said that the great majority of people in Éire desired very friendly relations with Britain. The agreement which we had reached with him two years ago had made a great difference. Certainly we had carried out our side of the bargain in the letter and the spirit. It was a pity that we were not able then to settle the only outstanding question, that of partition. If that had been possible, there might have been an alliance between the two countries by now. It was absurd for anyone to suppose that relations between the two countries should be anything but cordial. So far as the Irish were concerned, they were largely dependent upon Great Britain. This would be the case whether Britain won or lost the war. The destiny of Ireland must be closely linked with that of Britain. It was unthinkable that, so long as Britain did not interfere with Irish freedom, Ireland should give the slightest assistance to Britain's enemies. That was the general background to his whole view of the present situation. We ought not to have any qualms about his Government's intentions. He could not understand why we would not give them equipment with which they could hold up a German invasion for five hours instead of one, or perhaps for five days instead of one day, until our help could arrive. Coming in those circumstances, when the Irish had been attacked by the enemy and were putting up a stout resistance, the British would be welcomed by a united Irish people.

I said that I should like to repeat with greater emphasis something which I had said on the question of a United Ireland in our last talk. I had then told him that I thought the best chance of Ireland becoming united would be if Éire and Ulster were fighting side by side in the present war. It seemed to me that the co-operation and unity which would be established in war could not be broken when peace returned. In saying that the other day I had expressed my personal view, which I knew to be shared by my own generation in British politics. I could now tell him that this view was shared equally strongly by the War Cabinet in London. The Prime Minister himself, as well as Mr. Chamberlain and the others, had said that we should do nothing to discourage and everything that we could to encourage the unity of Ireland, so long as there was no coercion. The establishment of unity in war would almost certainly lead to the continuance of unity in peace. I therefore urged him to consider most seriously that by entering upon the war now he would not only be taking the most effective action in defence of the threatened freedom of Éire, but also the most effective action in the direction of union with the rest of Ireland.

He remarked that he by no means shared my view that the Germans would invade Éire. Such an invasion would not be easy, for it involved a long and difficult journey both by sea and by air from the French coast. Presumably the German ships and aircraft carrying troops would be subject to interference from our forces all the way. There was no need for Germany to take this risk in order to secure a fresh jumping-off ground for the attack on Britain. She already had far better bases on the continent from which to invade Britain.

I replied that no one could be dogmatic about this. I did not assert that a German invasion of Éire would positively take place. It might not. But the odds were in its favour. I then repeated the arguments which I had made in our earlier talk in support of the view that German thoroughness in seeking to bring the maximum of attack on Great Britain all at one time would lead them to Éire; and I added that no Government in this war could afford to leave anything to chance. Their plans and their preparations must be laid on the assumption that the worst would happen. The Government of Éire should make complete preparations on the assumption that their country was the next on the German list of victims.

Mr. de Valera agreed that this was the right course.

I then asked him whether there were any circumstances under which he would be prepared now, before a German invasion started, to invite our ships into his ports and our soldiers and aeroplanes into his territory, and to take vigorous action against the Fifth Column in his own country.

There followed a long discussion in which we examined three alternative possibilities. I made it plain throughout that my purpose was simply to explore the situation. The Government in London wished to have a clear picture of what was in his mind. The alternatives which we discussed were not proposals which I was making to him or which he was making to me. The British Government could consider what policy they wished to pursue in the light of his statement of his standpoint.

The three alternative courses, and the substance of the discussion which took place upon each, are as follows:-

I. That there should be a declaration of a United Ireland in principle, the constitutional and other practical details of the Union to be worked out in due course: Ulster to remain a belligerent, Éire to remain neutral at any rate for the time being: if both parties desired it, a Joint Defence Council to be set up at once; at the same time, in order to secure Éire's neutrality against violation by Germany, British naval ships to be allowed into Éire ports, British troops and aeroplanes to be stationed at certain agreed points in the territory, the British Government to provide additional equipment for Éire's forces, and the Éire Government to take effective action against the Fifth Column.

Mr. de Valera rejected this suggestion, saying emphatically that it was impossible for the two reasons which he had already stated in a similar connexion. First, the admission of British forces into the territory and territorial waters of Éire before a German invasion had started would be regarded by a large part of his own people as itself an abandonment of strict neutrality and a provocation of Germany. The result would be that national unity in the face of the German threat would be broken. Secondly, if British troops did come into Éire, there would be a grave danger of shots being fired at them by extremists and of most unfortunate skirmishes between the Irish and the British.

I asked him whether this was not only his own view, but also that of his Government.

He replied in the affirmative.

II. *That Éire and Ulster should be merged in a United Ireland, which should at once become neutral; its neutrality to be guaranteed by Great Britain and the United States of America; since Britain was a belligerent, its military and naval forces should not take any active part in guaranteeing that neutrality, but American ships should come into the Irish ports, and perhaps American troops into Ireland, to effect this guarantee.*

In proposing this, Mr. de Valera said that he was only expressing a personal view when he contemplated the possibility of American ships and troops being allowed to protect Ireland's neutrality. He thought that some of his colleagues might be critical of the proposal, since America had shown her partiality to the Allies and her hostility to Germany so strongly. He would have to consult his colleagues on the proposal, if there were any prospect of America agreeing to it.

He said that he had thought a great deal about his earlier conversation with me, and that the only way in which he thought we could overcome our mutual difficulties was by the establishment of a neutral United Ireland. He recognised the obstacles from our point of view, but urged the following arguments for his suggestion. It would have the effect of consolidating at once national unity in Ireland; there were plenty of people in Ulster who would favour the idea, and the majority there would only be a tiny minority of the whole population of the country. It would kill the I.R.A. organisation stone dead, for they lived only on partition nowadays. Moreover, the declaration of the neutrality of the whole of Ireland would mean that the entire island was denied to German action. Whilst Ulster was a belligerent, the Germans would be quite entitled to invade the Six Counties. The American guarantee should be an effective deterrent to the would-be German aggressors. If it did not prove a deterrent, then America would presumably be in the war on our side. That would be a very satisfactory result for us. Mr. de Valera added that he thought that the neutrality of a United Ireland might well be very short-lived; after a while Ireland might enter the war on our side.

I firmly rejected this suggestion, saying that it seemed to me entirely impracticable for four reasons. First, there was no prospect that the people of Ulster, who had been engaged in the war from its very beginning, would now agree to desert Great Britain at the moment when her situation was more perilous than it had been for a century. Even if for any reason they were reluctantly compelled to do this, the result would certainly not be that united national sentiment throughout Ireland which he had spoken about. The majority of the people in the North would feel deeply incensed, controversy on the issue of a United Ireland would be roused to its highest pitch, and the new State would be launched on its career under the worst possible circumstances. Secondly, we in Great Britain could not contemplate that Ulster should now become neutral. In the Six Counties some vital war production was proceeding, such as the shipbuilding in Belfast. We needed all the productive units that we had got; if some of these in Great Britain were temporarily knocked out as a result of air raids in the near future, the production going on in Ulster would become all the more important. No doubt in theory this could continue even if the Six Counties were neutral. But we could not count on that unless there was adequate defence for the shipbuilding yards and factories there. At present there were squadrons of our aeroplanes stationed nearby, there were anti-aircraft guns manned by trained crews, and there were considerable numbers of well-equipped British troops. These would all have to be withdrawn if Ulster became neutral, and the industrial establishments there would thus be undefended. Thirdly, Ulster was situated opposite some of our own important centres of production and trade, such as Glasgow and the Clyde. Whilst Ulster was a belligerent we could prevent its coasts from becoming lairs in which U-boats could hide. We had a constant patrol of reconnaissance aeroplanes flying over those waters protecting our shipping. But if Ulster became neutral, that reconnaissance work would have to cease. Fourthly, an American guarantee of Ireland's neutrality would be worthless if it were not implemented by the presence of American troops and ships, and I very much doubted whether the American Government would send those forces. Surely Germany had proved herself, even to those who had the most touching faith in her goodness, no respecter of neutrality. Whilst Ulster was a belligerent and we could keep troops, aeroplanes and ships there, we could offer a fair guarantee that the Germans could not establish themselves in the Six Counties; we were also somewhat more capable of coming to the immediate assistance of the Twenty-six Counties when their neutrality was violated. If our forces had to withdraw from Ulster, the net military result would be to expand the area of weakness on our western flank, and increase the size of the territory which Germany might successfully invade.

Mr. de Valera endeavoured to counter these arguments. He urged that his proposal really would make for greater popular unity in Ireland and for a much stronger resistance to the Germans when they landed. Our forces would still be only just across the water, and could come to the aid of Ireland almost as quickly as if they had been situated in Ulster itself. He added that he quite agreed that it would be a mistake for our aircraft and troops and trained anti-aircraft contingents to leave Ulster immediately on the declaration of neutrality. There would have to be a transition period, during which our troops were gradually being withdrawn and replaced by trained and equipped Irish forces. We ought to let them have equipment for this. If the Germans launched any attack whilst our troops were still in the Six Counties, making the excuse that their presence was a violation of the supposed neutrality, the whole of Ireland would treat that as a *casus belli*.

I maintained all my objections to the suggestion.

III. *That there should be a declaration of a United Ireland in principle, the practical details of the union to be worked out in due course: this united Ireland to become at once a belligerent on the side of the Allies.*
    I threw out this suggestion and invited Mr. de Valera's views upon it, in view of the fact that the present situation was a thoroughly dangerous one for Éire, that his country was likely to be dragged into the war under more unfavourable circumstances before long, and that the war in any case was one for Éire's freedom as well as everybody else's freedom, and that it was up to Éire to defend it. As there seemed to be insurmountable difficulties in the way of the two alternatives which we had already considered, was not this the only way out of Éire's difficulties?
    He answered that if there were not only a declaration of a United Ireland in principle, but also agreement upon its constitution, then the Government of Éire might agree to enter the war at once. He could not be certain about this. Perhaps the existing Government would not agree to it, and would be replaced by another Government which did. But the constitution of a United Ireland would have to be fixed first. As regards that, he thought it could be based upon the present constitution of Éire, which could be extended to cover the whole country. This would mean that its relation to the British Empire would be that of 'external association'; the King would continue to function as he did at present regarding all the external affairs of the State; he should not, for the present at any rate, be brought back any more prominently into the constitution, and Ireland should not be in the same position as the Dominions. Within this constitution, Ulster would enjoy a great deal of local autonomy in its own affairs. It would retain its Parliament to legislate on those affairs, and it would also send representatives to the Parliament of the United Ireland which would deal with all matters of common concern.
    I said that, quite apart from the over-riding difficulties connected with the proposal for a United Ireland, which we all knew, I saw two particular objections to his suggestion which made it impracticable. First, I saw no chance of a constitution being prepared and agreed as rapidly as the war situation required. We knew a great deal about constitution making in the British Commonwealth of Nations, and he too knew a bit about it from his experience in working out the constitution of Éire. These were matters which required somewhat protracted and careful conference between politicians, constitutional experts and others. It had taken him many months to prepare his own constitution. No doubt he would urge that this constitution really would do for a United Ireland, and that all that was needed was the immediate extension of its machinery over the whole Thirty-two Counties. But we could not hand that constitution to the people of Ulster and tell them to take it or leave it. There must be discussion, there must be give and take, otherwise there would be violent ill-will. This would require a considerable time, and there was no time for that if a German invasion was to be forestalled. Therefore, I suggested again that all that could be expected was a declaration of union in principle, and the immediate establishment of whatever machinery was immediately necessary to protect the vital interests of the new State born in the midst of a European war. A Joint Defence Council might be set up at once, and on this the beginnings of practical co-operation would be made. The second objection to his suggestion was even more formidable. He had said that on the conditions

that he had outlined the Government of Éire 'might' enter the war.

At this point he intervened to say that there would be a very big question mark after the 'might'.

I said that only made my point more important. We in London would not even consider the suggestion in return for a 'might'. We should not dream of spending time examining this proposal, nor of perhaps making approaches to the Ulster authorities, without a firm assurance that the Government of Éire would in fact on those conditions come into the war.

He replied that a mere declaration of union in principle would not be enough. His people would recognise the difficulties which would lie in the way of the working out of an agreed constitution, and they would suspect that there never would be an agreement, and that the declaration of principle would never be implemented. And even if we got agreement on a constitution he still could not go further than a 'might'.

I asked whether this would be not only his view but the view of the other members of his Government.

At first he said 'Yes', but then I thought he became rather uneasy. He said that he would cast his vote that way anyway, but that perhaps some of his colleagues would take a different view. He did not think they would. His, and he thought their chief reason for this attitude would be that their people were really almost completely unprepared for war. They had not a large equipped army, they had not guns to resist tanks and mechanised troops; Dublin was practically an undefended town; they had only a few anti-aircraft guns, there were not even any air raid shelters in the city and the people had not got gas masks. They would be mercilessly exposed to the horrors of modern war, and he and his colleagues could not have it on their consciences that in this state of affairs they had taken the initiative in an action which so exposed them.

I replied that we would not disagree with that general attitude. We would not wish the Government of Éire to declare war without proper defence precautions being taken. I was discussing a situation in which there was an agreement between them and us that they would enter the war. That would alter our whole attitude on the question of equipment. We could then presumably send our ships into their ports, and our troops and aeroplanes to join with the Irish soldiers in defending strategic points. We should feel that we had assurances then which would enable us to send such guns, rifles and ammunition, and such gas masks and other equipment for passive defence as was consistent with the proportionate defence of our own island. We should certainly see that they did not face the Germans unarmed.

He replied that the provision of so much equipment would take time.

I answered that it would not take nearly so long as the writing of a constitution for Ireland, which was what he contemplated doing before declaring war. We were facing a situation in which Éire's territory might be violated at any moment. It might be next week, or the week after. Germany was going to try to defeat Britain in the course of the next two months, and if Britain were defeated, Éire's freedom was lost.

But he only repeated his former argument with an emphasis which made me feel that one of the decisive factors in the whole situation is his country's nakedness of defence. He said that if they had proper defences for Dublin and equipment for their army the situation might have been very different. But as it was, some of his colleagues and advisers were almost in a state of panic. They had had a meeting of the Defence Council following my earlier conversation with him, when a review of the defence situation showed their dangerous condition. There was some talk which was thoroughly defeatist. But he himself was not so pessimistic as some others. If there were a German invasion they would put up a stout fight. They were already mining roads and bridges though they would have to be careful only to blow up those that might be useful to the enemy, whilst preserving those that might be useful to themselves and their friends. But, in the circumstances, he and his colleagues could not take a positive decision which exposed their people to war. If war were forced upon them, it would be another matter. He urged again that the best solution of our mutual difficulties was the creation of a United Ireland which should be neutral, at any rate until they were prepared to enter the war.

I answered again that this was out of the question.

He said that it would seem, then, that each of the three alternatives which we had discussed was impracticable for one reason or another. In those circumstances he would press us to let his troops have the equipment that he had asked for. He was particularly anxious for the material connected with 18 pounder guns, as he thought these would prove effective against tanks. He appealed strongly to us to give him as much as would enable them to keep the enemy in check until our forces could come to assist.

He said that he would report our conversation to his colleagues when he returned from a visit, which he had to set on that afternoon, to Galway. He understood that there was a certain pro-German element down there, and he was going to address himself to that audience.

We had some discussion which roamed over the field of the war in general. This followed the general lines of the talk on June 17th[1] and I need not repeat the detail here. But Mr. de Valera is evidently going to be influenced a good deal in his estimate of the war prospects by whatever is the fate of the French Fleet. If the French Fleet does not fall into Germany's hands, he holds the view that, provided we can withstand invasion in our island for the next two months, we shall defeat Hitler.

Finally, I said that I wished to press him further to take action against his Fifth Column. He had assured me that he was doing all he could to lock up I.R.A. leaders. But we attached importance also to German nationals being put under detention. Whenever I had raised this he had objected that to put them under lock and key would be regarded by his people as an unneutral act of provocation against Germany. I could see that this might be so if a hundred or so Germans were involved, though I still thought it a proper precaution in the light of what had happened in Norway, Holland and Belgium. But in any case, his objection did not really arise if he selected half-a-dozen of the most suspicious Germans and detained them. I had heard of a man called Becker,[2] and no doubt there were others who were under particular suspicion. Would he take action against them?

He said that he would certainly consider this. He thought that the Government

---

[1] See No. 193.
[2] Heinrich Becker, a German national, a folklorist and photographer, remained in Ireland after the outbreak of the war.

probably had power to do it under existing legislation and he would look into the matter.

M.M.

No. 199 NAI DFA Legal Adviser's Papers

Memorandum by Michael Rynne (Dublin)

DUBLIN, 24 June 1940

Appreciation of the Situation 24th June 1940
1. France and Germany appear to have made armistice terms extraordinarily satisfactory from the French point of view. Although France was beaten to the ropes, capitulated unconditionally, and helplessly allowed French soil to be almost completely overrun, the terms come to at Compiègne are vastly more reasonable than those which were imposed by the Allies in 1918 on a German Army still entrenched in France. Then it was the vanquished who withdrew and the victors who occupied by treaty German land which they could not invade by force. Now, the defeated French people will have the satisfaction of seeing their victors withdrawing out of a fertile part of France which they conquered only a few days ago.

Other vital conditions, regarding French naval and other Armaments, the French merchant fleet etc., are similarly better than even the most sanguine Frenchmen would have hoped for and, of course, compare very well indeed with the harsh terms of the 1918 truce.

2. Possibly the Italian Armistice terms may prove a disappointment, but probably they will not be allowed to impair the promising basis of a new Franco-German *rapprochement*.

3. Whether the creation of a puppet French Government in London, with its inherent threat of the *guerre à outrance*, assisted the French to obtain relatively good terms, is a point on which no one can speak with any certainty. Apart, however, from that hypothetical advantage, the Reynaud 'Committee' is clearly calculated to prove dangerous to the future welfare of the French people at home. If the Committee survives, it may well be used to justify an attempt to oust France from her Colonial possessions, to sink her returning fleet and to wage ruthless war on the 'rebellious' mother country.

4. If the foregoing gloomy forecast were to materialise there is but little doubt that the legitimate French Government would be compelled to range the country on the side of the 'Axis' in order to prevent France and her Empire from going down finally and completely with Great Britain.

5. From our point of view, it is to be hoped that the Reynaud Committee is merely a passing 'stunt' (such as was the fantastic plan of Franco-British Union according to which France was to be absorbed into the British Commonwealth of Nations). Should the new puppet regime be allowed to function with British financial and military support, we will be forced to take the view that Britain has ceased to bother about world-opinion.

The moment that Britain overtly betrays her former ally to the extent of driving her into the enemy camp, the United States of America, which is largely pro-French, will be split from top to bottom. Britain will thus have proved conclusively that she has ceased to care for American friendship, which admittedly has failed to help her in a practical sense up to now. But if Britain decides to flout American opinion instead of endeavouring to curry favour in the States, Ireland's position becomes much more precarious. This is the aspect of to-day's situation which we must prepare against.

6. Let us acknowledge that up to now, we have, for the best reasons in the world, been inclined to cry 'Wolf, wolf!'. The end has, no doubt, justified the means. We may even argue that a large amount of the evidence which seemed to point in a certain single direction is still uncontroverted. There is no conclusive evidence to prove that all our suspicions were based on a trumped-up case. But we must at this critical juncture take cognisance of a number of contrary indications which must be closely studied in connection with any obvious signs that Britain intends to break with the United States.

7. We must, in other words, visualise a position where a new threat (unlike the old, which was mainly under-sea and from the air) will take the form of land and sea invasion.

Against sea invasion we are helpless, that is to say, we do not have to fight. Sea invasion will draw air attack from the other belligerent and our main task in that event will be to take cover.

Land invasion, however, will compel us to act at once. If we do not do so, others will and the horrors of another civil war may add to the disaster.

Hence, we should take every possible preparatory step at once to diminish the risk of troops entering this country, at least from Northern Ireland.

It should not be impossible in a few days to mine all roads and railways leading to the Six Counties and to render much of the intervening country impassable. Apart from the danger of invasion (*and consequent fighting*) being made more remote in that way, the political reactions of such a determined step to secure Ireland's integrity would be good. Our potential invader would, at least, suspect we were in earnest and perhaps hesitate before risking our resistance.

No. 200 NAI DFA Legal Adviser's Papers

Memorandum by Michael Rynne (Dublin)
DUBLIN, 24 June 1940

Suggested Action in Intensified Emergency

It appears not unlikely that the emergency will, so far as this country is concerned, become greatly intensified during the next few weeks.

This is not to say that Ireland will necessarily become involved as a belligerent in the war.

The transfer of the war into Great Britain and Northern Ireland would suffice to create a new and much more serious state of affairs here with which the Government will be called upon to deal. Even if the preliminary stages of the hostilities against our near neighbours consist merely of blockade measures against them, our interests may suffer. In the event of the blockade being accompanied by an increased aerial bombardment of British objectives, Ireland's position will be still more serious. It will be gravely involved if and when an invasion of the 'United Kingdom' is attempted.

2. Certain necessary action to deal with an intensified emergency will immediately occur to the mind of anyone who gives the foregoing possibilities a moment's

thought. Many of the steps which will be necessary are, doubtless, having the attention of the Departments directly or exclusively concerned. Some of these steps, however, may have been overlooked or postponed although, in fact, extremely urgent.

3. In order to place such matters out of doubt, this Department which is mainly interested in the 'neutrality' aspects of the crisis now approaching, will have to raise a number of points for the observations of the various Departments. Eventually these points may have to be submitted to the Government for their decisions and, in some cases, for the making of new Emergency Powers Orders.

4. One of the chief questions which appears to require immediate consideration is that of closing our frontiers during the coming period of intensified emergency. This means the closing of both our land and sea frontiers. In regard to our land frontier, it is only too clear that unless we take early action to restrict immigration from the North, we may find ourselves quite unable to stem a flood of refugees from Northern Ireland when that territory falls victim to aerial bombardment or invasion. Such refugees would be largely destitute persons, undesirable aliens (Jews etc.) and possibly, would include members of the British Armed Forces. Our economic life, our public security and our neutrality would be, therefore, endangered by the continuation of the present system of an open land frontier. A cordon composed of military patrols, police, health officers, Customs officers etc. is, therefore, absolutely vital to protect this country from virtual 'invasion' from the Six Counties. That cordon ought to be formed and placed in readiness at once.

No one should be allowed to traverse the cordon in either direction except after personal identification (by the police) and when armed with a special permit (by the military).

The same applies, having regard to the somewhat different circumstances to travel to and from Ireland by sea. In that connection, we must have greatly increased preventive staffs at the recognised Eastern ports and constant patrols along the East coast, from Louth to Waterford.

5. Another point, which to some extent arises out of the foregoing, is that which relates to the landing in this country of members of the armed forces of the different belligerents. Whether these arrive over the Border, or by air, and sea, they should be interned until the end of the hostilities. This applies to land forces who may take refuge here having been routed in Ulster, to naval ratings shipwrecked on our shores and to airmen forced to land on our territory or waters by any reason. Consequently, preparations should be made to accommodate internees in camps established as far as possible from the war-zone.

6. The question of our cable and other communications abroad, especially with the Irish Legations in other countries and the question of contacting indirectly certain Legations during a time when they may find themselves directly cut off from Dublin are being considered in the Department. It is not necessary to advert in detail to these questions now.

7. The future movements of shipping, so far as we can control it, is of particular importance. It has formed the subject of semi-official discussions with the Department of Industry and Commerce (Transport and Marine Branch) and must be considered under three heads viz:-

(a) Irish shipping – should this be ordered to remain in port or to return to port for the duration?

(b) Atlantic shipping with cargoes for Ireland – should (and could) this be routed to West of Ireland harbours?

(c) Foreign shipping generally – can we prevent our Eastern ports and our territorial waters from becoming congested by British and other foreign ships during a time when British Western ports are in danger? In regard to all the above points Mr. Flynn (Transport and Marine Branch)[1] is inclined to agree with the view of this Department that merchant shipping of every nationality should be more strictly controlled by us, during a period of blockade warfare, insofar as we are able to exert any control at all. Thus, Mr. Flynn does not see any difficulty in retaining Irish ships in port, if the Government feel that by putting to sea, running the blockade and being sunk while flying the Irish flag, they would prove a source of embarrassment to the Government. The Minister for Industry and Commerce already possesses adequate powers over Irish shipping and it is thought that Irish shipowners would willingly obey the Minister's order to remain in safety. On the question of foreign ships destined for dangerous Irish ports, Mr. Flynn states that there should be no technical difficulty (so long as our wireless transmitters are working) in routeing such ships to Western ports. Doubtless in most cases the ships would take the advice passed to them.

With regard to the matter, however, of the overcrowding of our harbours and roadsteads by foreign shipping desirous of escaping destruction in the Irish Sea, Mr. Flynn pointed out that, unless we could use force to move on such shipping, it was unlikely to take to sea until all danger was past.

This problem is, consequently, one for the Department of Defence rather than for the Department of Industry & Commerce or the various peacetime Harbour Commissioners.

8. This Department must consider a number of emergency questions arising out of the gradual isolation of our diplomatic offices abroad. Probably the principal question of this kind relates to the financing of Legations which are no longer easily contacted from Dublin. We are discussing this point with the Department of Finance.

9. Finally, there are a number of minor considerations concerning which we in this Department have a view because of their bearing on Irish neutrality. Examples of these are the questions of blacking out (or lighting up) our territory during the war on England and the question of further restricting certain activities (e.g. civil flying over Ireland) which up to now have not been greatly interfered with.

These and other questions of a similar nature will have to be taken up without delay with the technical Departments concerned.

No. 201 NAI DFA Secretary's Files P7

Code telegram from the Department of External Affairs to
William J.B. Macaulay (Holy See)
(No. 22) (19/34) (Personal) (Copy)

DUBLIN, 25 June 1940

Your 22.[2] There is no reason whatever for anticipating a state of war between this country and Italy and you should do nothing to provoke the slightest suspicion

---

[1] T.J. Flynn, Transport and Marine Branch, Department of Industry and Commerce.
[2] Not printed.

that there is. We do not belong to the British Isles. If the impossible were to happen you would receive special instructions to do as you suggest.

No. 202 NAI DFA 219/49

> *Confidential report from John J. Hearne to Joseph P. Walshe (Dublin)*
> *(14/55)*
>
> OTTAWA, 26 June 1940

Views on the war situation are this week at the lowest level of depression yet reached. No one (i.e. no unofficial person) with whom I have spoken now sees any prospect of a long war – the long war which was to enable the Allied blockade to do its work and so bring final victory to Great Britain. The capitulation of France, although not unexpected, nevertheless, brought a realization of penultimate defeat. 'Peace this summer' was one comment made to me. 'I suppose we must just keep on', was another. 'Why can't it be fixed up now?' etc. etc. There were many comments of similar import. Resignation had taken the place of hope. 'It will be a long time before there is good news' Dr. Skelton said to me, rather dispiritedly, yesterday. I had a moment's conversation with Mr. King on the occasion – Friday last – of the arrival of the Earl of Athlone.[1] But he did not speak of the war.

The Prime Minister seems more weary than ever. One cannot but admire the brave smile on the grey, haggard face (as he greets everyone) and the obvious physical effort in the quick footsteps of the burdened statesman.

I have kept Dr. Skelton informed of the position in Ireland, as I know it, from your cables, the Taoiseach's recent speeches, and the speeches of Mr. Traynor (in the Dáil),[2] and Dr. Ryan (At New Ross).[3]

In a recent conversation which I had with Sir Gerald Campbell he spoke of the dissatisfaction he had heard expressed by Canadians with Mr. King's conduct of the war. He said that if Mr. King would 'make way for Ralston, something might be done'. Mr. David Meyer (who was also present) said that he too had heard the view expressed that Mr. King's tempo was too slow. I said nothing on this point although I know that Conservative circles in Ottawa are very critical of the Prime Minister. There is no doubt that the British are annoyed (the word 'annoyed' is mild) at Mr. King's caution. Mr. King's caution is not due to his sixty-five years (of age) or any lack of energy or conviction or zeal. It is evidence of his astuteness as a Canadian statesman who knows his people well.

Mr. Churchill's bitterness against the French has been the headline for many editorial attacks on Marshal Pétain, M. Laval[4] etc. Dr. Skelton has referred to Mr. Churchill's bitterness in conversations with me but not unkindly. The editorials are

---

[1] Major General Alexander Cambridge, 1st Earl of Athlone (1874-1957), Governor General of Canada (1940-6).
[2] Hearne may have been referring to Traynor's speeches during the passage of the Defence Forces (Temporary Provisions) Act by the Oireachtas in early June 1940.
[3] Speaking at New Ross on 6 June 1940 during an all-party meeting, Minster for Agriculture Jim Ryan told his audience that it was Ireland's 'obvious duty … to convince the belligerents that no small force will be permitted to gain a foothold in this country … we are united against all comers'.
[4] Pierre Laval (1883-1945), Prime Minister of France (July-Dec. 1940).

rather poor. Apart from them there is still but little jingoism. Ordinary Canadian people learn of events in Europe from day to day with heavy hearts and deep disappointment, but without exasperation. They can be extraordinarily detached and objective. Some, I know, take an objective view because they feel that it was the affair of both the British and the French Governments to have known beforehand where they were going when they went to war with Germany. Many more take an objective view because they regard the whole British Empire business as somebody else's business. They are able to reconcile a very realistic outlook upon the future of the Empire with a pathetically sincere devotion to colonial forms and British royal persons. The appointment of the Earl of Athlone as Governor General is welcomed by great numbers of Canadians who resented the lack of strain in the blood of the Tweedsmuirs.[1] It was nothing to them that the Tweedsmuirs were enobled more by nature than by patent and that they sought so splendidly to tone up the cultural life of the people. It matters almost everything to those of whom I write that Lord Athlone is the King's uncle and that the Princess Alice is the granddaughter of Queen Victoria. The Tweedsmuirs, moreover, had brought the office of King's representative nearer to the common people than any previous occupant of the position; but that again was felt to be wrong, the Governor General must, it was thought, be aloof from the people. I have heard even Irish Canadians say that there could never be a Canadian Governor General. And all this is talked about even while the war goes on as it does and its tide swirls around the steps of the English throne.

The suggested Canadian U.S.A. customs union would have been an impossible conception a few weeks ago. But with Canada's European markets dwindling the U.S.A. may have to stabilize the North American economy. Canada has sent trade representatives to South American countries.

The view is canvassed here that if Great Britain can hold out until the autumn the blockade will bring famine to Europe. The siege of England will result, in other words, in the siege of a starving Europe and by then the American and Canadian industrial machines will be supplying planes and tanks and guns and ships. It is felt that if the war party in the United States tried to get war declared now they would split the country. The United States is in fact in the war already as much as it can be now. And, if Britain holds out until November, a declaration of war by the United States would be the beginning of a new hope. But no one overlooks the possibility of a cessation of hostilities in the interval, or the entry of new factors which may complicate or confuse the situation more than ever.

[signed] JOHN J. HEARNE

---

[1] John Buchan, 1st Baron Tweedsmuir (1875-1940), Governor General of Canada (1935-40), Scottish novelist best known for *The Thirty-Nine Steps* (London, 1915).

No. 203 NAI CAB 2/3

> Extract from the minutes of a meeting of the Cabinet
> (G.C. 8/182)
>
> DUBLIN, 27 June 1940

COMMUNICATION FROM THE BRITISH GOVERNMENT
The Taoiseach informed the Government of the contents of a communication which had been conveyed to him on the 26th June, 1940, by an Envoy of the British Government. It was agreed that the proposals contained in the communication were not acceptable and that the views of the Government thereon should be communicated to the Envoy by the Taoiseach, accompanied by the Minister for Supplies[1] and the Minister for the Co-ordination of Defensive Measures.[2]

No. 204 NAI DT 2001/6/500

> Handwritten memorandum of a meeting of the Government by
> Maurice Moynihan (Dublin)
>
> DUBLIN, 27 June 1940

Meeting of the Government 27 June, 1940

Council Chamber
11 a.m. to 12.10 p.m.

Note: This record follows closely lines indicated by the Taoiseach personally
M.M. 23/7/40

Present
All members of the Government
In attendance

Parliamentary Secretary to the Taoiseach	Mr. Smith
Attorney General	Mr. Haugh[3]
Secretary to the Government	Mr. Moynihan

Communication from the British Government
The Taoiseach informed the Government of the contents of a communication which had been conveyed to him on the 26th June, 1940, by Mr. Malcolm MacDonald on behalf of the British Government. He said he had informed Mr. MacDonald that he was satisfied that the proposals contained in the communication could not be accepted, but that he would submit them to the Government.

The view which had been expressed to Mr. MacDonald by the Taoiseach was confirmed.

The Taoiseach said that Mr. MacDonald had suggested that some members of the Government might like to ask him questions about the matter whilst he was in

---

[1] Seán Lemass.
[2] Frank Aiken.
[3] Kevin Haugh (1902-69), Attorney General (1940-2).

Dublin. Arrangements were being made for a luncheon at which Mr. MacDonald would be a guest and the Taoiseach thought it would be well if one or two members of the Government, in addition to himself, were present at the luncheon, when he would inform Mr. MacDonald of the Government's decision. He was of opinion that there would be an advantage in Mr. MacDonald meeting members of the Government in addition to himself. He proposed, in this connection, the Ministers for Supplies and Co-ordination of Defensive Measures. This was agreed to.

No. 205 NAI DFA Secretary's Files P4

Confidential report from John J. Hearne to Joseph P. Walshe (Dublin)
(14/56)

OTTAWA, 27 June 1940

More and more, interest is manifested in the Irish situation. More and more people ask me what the future will bring. Will Germany invade Ireland, North and South? Can the Irish armed forces deal with the invasion, if it takes place? Would the Irish Government invite the British to help them? How great is the likelihood of considerable Irish assistance to German invaders? What is the strength of the I.R.A.? Would the Irish people passively resist, or would they simply accept a German occupation of the country? Would the situation be a repetition of (1) 'Denmark'? or (2) 'Norway'?

No one asks whether we anticipate an attempted rush in by British forces to forestall a German attempt at invasion. But the Montreal 'Gazette' has a bad article (from our point of view) on that. It is with the cuttings in this bag.

The newspapers are fuller than usual of Irish news, including the statements of the Reverend Mr. Little M.P.[1]

I confine myself in conversation to the careful texts of the speeches of the Taoiseach and Ministers. I have also quoted the broadcast speech of Dr. O'Higgins T.D.[2] (which was given great prominence in B.B.C. shortwave broadcasts to North America) and the speech of the Bishop of Galway at Gort.[3]

If you think it advisable to add to the clear and balanced statements of Ministers (in so difficult a situation) I would be very grateful for your official or personal views as to the possibilities and probabilities and certainties of the near future, for my own information, or for such use as you consider I might make of it in any contingency you would specify. But I understand that course may not commend itself to you in all the circumstances.

[signed] JOHN J. HEARNE

---

[1] Reverend James Little (1869-1946), Unionist MP for Down at Westminster (1939-46).
[2] In a radio broadcast on 16 June 1940 Dr T.F. O'Higgins TD said that the people of Ireland could put aside civil war differences and 'face an invader with confidence in their army and trust in themselves' and called on men to join the Defence Forces or the Local Security Force (*Irish Times*, 17 June 1940).
[3] Michael Browne (1895-1980), Bishop of Galway (1937-76), told a congregation at St Colman's Church, Gort, that 'to invade a peaceful country like Ireland was not lawful war, but murder, and those who assisted it in any way were guilty of the crime of murder before God. Not even the pretext of solving partition or securing unity would justify the crime of any Irishman in assisting any foreign power to invade his own land.'

No. 206 NAI DFA Paris Embassy 19/34A

Extract from a confidential report from Seán Murphy to Joseph P. Walshe (Dublin)
(Copy)

Ascain, 28 June 1940

[matter omitted]

In so far as concerns General de Gaulle,[1] no formal statement has, as far as I am aware, been made in regard to his activities, apart from a declaration made over the Radio on the 18th June. A decree putting him on the retired list as Colonel, was taken by the Government on the 23rd inst., and on the same date he was charged in court martial for desertion. The text of the radio statement and the newspaper reports of the subsequent action taken in respect of him, are contained on the attached sheet marked A.[2]

Apart from the specific replies to Mr. Churchill's allegations, a tendency is noticeable in the official comments to diminish the importance of the assistance which France received in prosecuting the war from Great Britain. Marshal Pétain in his second speech last week said in dealing with the reasons which had involved the French Government's seeking terms, that whereas in 1918 there were 85 British divisions in France, there were only 10 divisions present in May, 1940. M. Ybarnegaray in his speech to the ex-combatants on the 25th inst. stated that France had been 'betrayed by one ally' (Belgium) 'and abandoned by another'. M. Jean Prouvost[3] in his statement to the American press referred to the fact that successive French Governments had since the outbreak of war, called the attention of the British Government to the difficulty of keeping Frenchmen of 48 years of age mobilised, while classes over the age of 28 were not mobilised in Great Britain. He also referred to the fact that 26 British divisions should have come to France at the outbreak of war. Marshal Pétain in his speech on the 25th inst., referring to the battle of Flanders and the presence of English and French divisions, said simply 'these latter' (i.e. the French) 'fought bravely'.

PS. Since the above was written, I have seen the text of an official statement issued by the Government Information Service at Bordeaux in regard to the position of General de Gaulle and other Frenchmen abroad who set themselves up in opposition to the French Government. The text of this statement is contained on the attached sheet marked B.[4] This statement seems not to have been reproduced in the majority of the press.

---

[1] General Charles de Gaulle (1890-1970), appointed Under Secretary of State for National Defence and War by Reynaud (6 June 1940) and placed in charge of Anglo-French military co-ordination. Opposed France's surrender to Germany and on 16 June 1940 proposed a political union between France and Britain to last for the duration of the war. Fled France on 17 June 1940 and established and later led the Free French Forces (1940-4). De Gaulle's radio appeal of 18 June called on the French people to resist the occupation of France and work against the Vichy government. Became Prime Minister of the French Provisional Government (1944-6), Prime Minister of France (1958-9), President of France (1959-69).

[2] Not printed.

[3] Jean Prouvost (1885-1978), French newspaper publisher, Minister for Information (June-July 1940).

[4] Not printed.

No. 207 NAI DFA Secretary's Files P13

Memorandum of talks between Eamon de Valera and Malcolm MacDonald by Joseph P. Walshe (Dublin)
(Copy No. 1)

DUBLIN, 28 June 1940

Résumé of Talks between the Taoiseach and Mr. Malcolm MacDonald

Mr. Malcolm MacDonald came to Dublin on Monday, 17th June. He told the Taoiseach that the purpose of his visit was to make clear the conviction of the British Government that a German invasion of this country was imminent. This belief was founded on
(a) the Held case;
(b) a story told by Dutch officers that they had seen a plan for the invasion of Ireland;
(c) what had happened elsewhere;
(d) Fifth Column activities, which they think are more dangerous than we believe.

Mr. MacDonald urged the Taoiseach to establish relations with Craigavon. Neutrality had saved nobody, and the sooner the Taoiseach and Craigavon got together, the sooner it would be possible to form a Joint Defence Council.

The Taoiseach replied that he appreciated the warnings of the British Government, that we were taking every possible means to protect ourselves against the invaders. On the other hand, we were very severely handicapped by the lack of war material, which, notwithstanding repeated requests, the British were still withholding from us. The Taoiseach added that the unity of Ireland was an essential and primary condition for the adequate defence of Ireland. The whole of Ireland as a neutral State would be in a position to present a united front to any invader. The Taoiseach further suggested that the whole of Ireland should be immediately established as a neutral State guaranteed by the United States of America.

Mr. MacDonald opposed to these suggestions the usual difficulties concerning the intransigence of Lord Craigavon and his followers and the reactions which would be provoked in England by bringing pressure to bear on the Six Counties.

Mr. MacDonald returned to Dublin on Friday, 21st June, saw the Taoiseach that afternoon and the following day. He came back to point out again the imminence of our danger and again mentioned the old reasons for the view that an invasion was certain. Everything would be all right if the Belfast and Dublin Governments could be brought together, but pressure on the Belfast Government would spoil the efficiency of that part of the United Kingdom as a participant in the war. The Taoiseach emphasised very strongly the comparatively defenceless position in which we had been left by the reluctance of the British to give us arms and munitions. Mr. MacDonald thought that the Germans had already captured enough of British war material and they did not intend to let them do it again. Giving war material to Dublin in present circumstances would mean its eventual capture by the Germans who were certain to invade Ireland. The only way to meet that difficulty was to agree now to allow the British and naval forces to co-operate with the Irish forces in the defence of the whole of Ireland.

Mr. MacDonald returned again on the evening of Wednesday, 26th June. He saw the Taoiseach that evening; and the following day at lunch he met the

Taoiseach, the Minister for Supplies and the Minister for the Co-ordination of Defensive Measures. In the course of the meeting with the Taoiseach on Wednesday evening, he handed to the Taoiseach a document containing the following:-

'The Government of the United Kingdom makes the following proposals for the consideration of the Government of Ireland:-

1) the United Kingdom would make a declaration forthwith accepting the principle of a united Ireland;

2) a joint Committee of representatives of the Éire and Northern Ireland Governments to be set up immediately to work out practical details of the 'Union of Ireland', the United Kingdom Government to give such assistance as might be desired;

3) a joint Defence Council of Éire and Northern Ireland to be set up immediately;

4) Éire to enter the war on the side of the United Kingdom and her allies forthwith, and, for the purposes of the defence of Éire, the Government of Éire to invite British naval vessels to have the use of ports in Éire and British troops and aeroplanes to co-operate with the Éire forces and to be stationed in such positions in Éire as may be agreed between the two Governments;

5) the Government of Éire to intern all German and Italian aliens in the country and to take further steps to put an end to Fifth Column activities;

6) the United Kingdom Government to provide at once military equipment for the Éire Government.

A list of military equipment attached.'

The Taoiseach told Mr. MacDonald that a declaration by the British Government of the principle of a united Ireland was of no use. He could not enter into serious discussions on any basis except the immediate establishment of a united neutral Ireland. Moreover, the Taoiseach made it clear to Mr. MacDonald that Ireland belonged to the Irish people, and Great Britain had no right of any kind to attempt to barter the unity of the Irish nation for the blood of her people. Ireland's unity and complete independence would come some day. The Government would defend the country against invasion, but they would not purchase unity by an act which would bring civil war and disaster to the people and would in all probability put an end to the independence we now enjoyed.

Mr. MacDonald appeared to be very depressed by the Taoiseach's reply to his proposals, but he assured Mr. de Valera that he would secure an amendment of the proposals which would be an advance towards the establishment in fact and immediately of an independent united Ireland. The Taoiseach agreed to wait for the amendment, but he warned Mr. MacDonald that he could not accept anything less than a completely independent neutral State for the whole of Ireland, the Parliament of which could alone determine the issue of war and peace in relation to our country.

No. 208 NAI DFA Secretary's Files P13

> *Memorandum from Joseph P. Walshe to Eamon de Valera (Dublin)*
> *(Copy No. 1)*
>
> DUBLIN, 1 July 1940

The British proposals for a united Ireland can be summarised as follows:-
1) The British Government would give a solemn undertaking that the Union of Ireland would become an accomplished fact at an *early date*. There would be no turning back from that declaration.
2) A joint body of the Belfast and Dublin Governments would meet at once to work out the constitution and practical details of the Union of Ireland. The United Kingdom Government would give whatever assistance might be desired towards the work of this body. The purpose of the work would be to establish at as early a date as possible the whole machinery of government of the Union.
3) The two Parliaments might even get together at once for the purpose of legislating for the whole of Ireland in regard to matters of common concern. This combined legislation would not prejudice the form of the constitution of the Union.
4) The condition that Ireland should forthwith enter into the war on the side of the United Kingdom and her Allies is the sole hypothesis on which the foregoing proposals are made. The fact that our entry into the war, instead of taking place through a formal declaration of war (the only way which would be appropriate to our independent status), would be realised by our allowing British forces into our territory, does not affect the issue.
5) The Joint Council of Defence appears to be part of the hypothesis of our entry into the war.

Comments on the Foregoing
Mr. Chamberlain's letter,[1] according to a statement made to me by Mr. Antrobus[2] of the British Legation here on Saturday morning, 29th June, proceeded from the labours of two different Committees sitting most of the day on Friday. No doubt, representatives of the Committee of Imperial Defence, of the Foreign Office and of the Dominions Office were the chief members of the Committee.

There is not any guarantee that, having accepted the very vague and half-boiled proposal for a Union of Ireland, the Northern Government would be under any obligation to accept our view as to what that Union should be. The Northern Government would, of course, desire the assistance of the British Government on the Joint Committee, and we might take it for granted that the complete absence of any previous guarantee of the status of the Union as a whole would lead to the establishment of a new State which would be far less independent than Éire. In any case, if the British succeeded in getting us to join the war as mercenaries, whether at a joint meeting of the two Parliaments or prior to it, they would naturally postpone any further developments concerning the Union until the war was over. The truly appalling situation in which they now find themselves, fighting alone against the might of Germany, would be quite a sufficient excuse before the

---
[1] Not printed.
[2] Maurice E. Antrobus, Principal Secretary, British Representative's Office, Dublin (1939-41).

world for concentrating exclusively on the defence of these islands against Germany.

Mr. Chamberlain's penultimate paragraph makes it clear beyond doubt that the British would not proceed with the suggestion for the establishment of the Union of Ireland if there were any possibility of the Six County area being withdrawn from its present state of belligerency. There is a clear warning in Mr. Chamberlain's last paragraph not to play with the idea that we can have any kind of constitutional unity without having beforehand committed ourselves to entry into the war.

The German Minister's statement to you on Saturday morning that Germany had a specific interest in the disposal of the Six Counties as being part of the State with which she was at war is true in international law, and the Germans have a certain basis for holding the view that we cannot now withdraw the territory of the Six Counties from the belligerent area without consultation with the German Government. Furthermore, it is a tenable proposition that negotiations undertaken with the British for the absorption of the Six Counties into a united Ireland with the intention, on either the British or the Irish side, of bringing a united Ireland into the war, constitutes a breach of neutrality.

Unless we make the clearest possible statement declaring that the policy of the Irish Government is and will remain that of strict neutrality, whether for the 26 Counties or for the whole of Ireland (should there be a united Ireland), until invaded by one or the other of the belligerents, the danger of an invasion by Germany will continue to exist. It is not sufficient to say that we want a Parliament for the whole of Ireland which will include amongst its rights that of going into the war. Such a statement only sows suspicion in the minds of the Germans and of our own people, and makes the latter believe that we might possibly accept entry into a war, which, so far, is none of our concern, as the price of our neutrality. Neutrality has given the people more faith in what the Government has achieved for the independence of this country than any other act of theirs. They regard it as a sign and symbol of our independence, and, if it goes, they will believe – and rightly – that our independence has gone with it.

No. 209 NAI DFA Secretary's Files A2

Memorandum by Joseph P. Walshe to Eamon de Valera (Dublin)
(Most Secret)

DUBLIN, 1 July 1940

Weekend Developments in the War Situation

The hourly increasing gravity of the war situation and its implications for us can be seen in the events of the weekend, which are briefly as follows:-

1. The Open Breach between France and England. The British have allowed General de Gaulle, an Under Secretary of State in charge of military operations in the Reynaud Cabinet, to set himself up in Great Britain as head of a National Committee for France. General de Gaulle, in a broadcast statement last night, makes it clear that his Committee does not regard Marshal Pétain's Government as the legal and established Government of France. He has been cashiered by Gen.

Weygand, Minister for Defence, and ordered to return at once to France. Churchill made a statement yesterday expressing the grief and amazement of the British Government at the acceptance by the 'French Government at Bordeaux' of the armistice terms. He said that such an acceptance meant that the soil of France and the resources of the French Empire and the French Government would be used against France's ally with the approval of the Bordeaux Government. In an official statement issued from London, described on the radio as 'official comment', Pétain's Government is accused of having submitted to the shame of handing over territory and material for war against the ally with whom France has a solemn agreement not to conclude a separate peace.

Last night on the French radio, Marshal Pétain answered the British. He said that Churchill was a judge of the interests of his own country, but he could not be a judge of the interest of France. France's honour was in the keeping of France and her flag was without a stain. No one could divide France at the moment when her country was suffering. The French people, he said, were showing a greater spirit in their defeat than if they had given in to 'vain and illusory suggestions'.

It is quite clear from Pétain's statement that he and his colleagues rejected Britain's suggestion for a Franco-British union and a sharing of all resources because they were fully convinced that a British defeat was inevitable.

2. The German terms, as published by the British exclusively, while severe enough on the military side, provide for the continuation of the French Government's jurisdiction over the whole of France. The Navy, except so much of it as is required for the defence of the French overseas empire, is to be disarmed. No part of it is to be used for the prosecution of the war against Britain except those units necessary for coast-watching and minesweeping.

3. The Japanese Government have ———[1] up their forces to the close neighbourhood of British territory at Hong Kong, and Japanese Committees in Tokyo are sending messages of congratulations to the German and Italian Governments.

Russia has officially denied that she is concentrating any forces against Germany.

The taking over of the Baltic States is, no doubt, in accordance with her original pact with Germany, which must include a reversion to the 1914 position, and perhaps also an Atlantic port in Northern Norway as well as freedom of action towards India and the Persian Gulf. There cannot be any reasonable doubt that the partition of Asia between Japan and Russia, with formidable concessions to Germany and Italy, has been decided upon in detail.

The King of Egypt, following the resignation of Ali Maher Pasha's Government, is having long discussions with the British Ambassador in Cairo, clearly resisting the latter's attempt to bring Egypt into the war. The Arab States are discussing with Turkey the future position of the Middle East.

Roumania has created a Totalitarian State, with King Carol as the principal leader, and a pro-Axis policy has been outlined. Bulgaria is leaning more and more towards Germany. The Press of Greece and Yugoslavia has gone pro-Axis, and Russia has declared on the Moscow Radio that she has no intention of resuming 'the Imperialistic policy of Pan-Slavism'; therefore, she is not going to interfere on the side of the Slav States in the Balkans.

---

[1] Word missing in original typescript.

It does not seem that there is a single organised State left in Europe or Asia which is not ready to profit by what they regard to be the impending downfall of Britain.

In America, President Roosevelt seems to have overreached himself. He has infuriated the Republican Party by the appointment of Stimson[1] and Knox,[2] and Isolationism, which up to now was held by nebulous and scattered groups, is likely to become the fixed policy of the Republican Party.

4. Anglo-Irish Position. The British weekend Sunday Press takes a very serious view of the situation.

There is an interesting article by Major Fielding Elliott[3] in the 'Sunday Express'. It was clearly released or sponsored by the British Government in order to show the people how dangerous the situation is and perhaps to prepare their minds for peace. He declares that the task of the Navy is more difficult than it has ever had to face before. Germany can blockade the Straits of Dover so that no merchant vessel can pass up that way. From Norway, she can prevent entrance into the North Sea. The greater part of British shipping will have to use west coast ports, principally Bristol, Liverpool and Glasgow. The approach between Land's End and Ireland will be far more dangerously covered by German aircraft operating from Brittany, than the North Channel between Northern Ireland and Scotland. 'Both of these channels will see a tremendous congestion of shipping in conditions which will be ideal for the operation of submarines as far as the location of targets is concerned.' 'Even an attack on Éire is not to be discarded. At the tip of Brittany, the Germans would be under 300 miles from the south coast of Éire'. In this connection, it is interesting to note a statement made by Admiral Luetzow[4] on the German radio last night in the 11.15 p.m. talk. He said that the east and south coasts of England were already almost useless, and that Germany would very soon put the west coast into a similar position by operating with her aeroplanes and U-boats (plus the Italian U-boats) against Britain in the Irish Sea.

Hilaire Belloc,[5] in the 'Sunday Times' on the 'Pros and Cons of Invasion', having mentioned the possibility of aid coming from the Soviets or from the United States, went on to say 'there are other indeterminates (including Ireland) upon which we cannot yet pronounce, but which might in a moment change the whole situation'.

The weekend British Press is remarkably quiet in our regard. The articles in the 'Daily Mail' and the 'Evening Standard' of Friday (the latter clearly officially inspired) seemed to presage a fierce campaign over the weekend. It may be that our protest (made on Friday) has been effective. We cannot, however, exclude the hypothesis that the Press campaign to bring us in through fear on the side of Britain has been given up in favour of direct and immediate measures to be taken without warning.

The High Commissioner saw Lord Caldecote yesterday. The latter was exceedingly distressed. He was unshaven. He and his colleagues had been up during the

---

[1] Henry L. Stimson (1867-1950), United States Secretary of War (1940-45).
[2] Frank Knox (1874-1944), United States Secretary of the Navy (1940-4).
[3] Major George Fielding Elliot (1894-1971), journalist, military and naval correspondent and news analyst for CBS, also a prolific writer of short stories.
[4] Vice Admiral Luetzow (1881-1964), German radio commentator on naval matters, attached to the staff of the Commander-in-Chief of the Kriegsmarine (1939-45).
[5] Hilaire Belloc (1870-1953), French-born Catholic writer who later became a British subject; a prolific commentator and writer during the first half of the twentieth century.

whole of the previous night waiting for the Armistice terms. He described the late, but especially the present, French Government as 'rapscallions', who had no sense of honour or right dealing. They had made the position of the British Ambassador impossible by refusing to keep him *au courant* or give him information. Caldecote believed that they were all right as they had the Fleet, etc., but God help us. At lunch yesterday, Dulanty met Chamberlain's Private Secretary,[1] who said to him 'You are going to have a terrible time, you will all be murdered.'

In connection with the British description of the present French Government, it is interesting to recall that Pétain and Weygand are, and have been, very distinguished French Catholics held in the highest esteem. They belong to the French traditionalists who take the view that France has been brought to the present pass by the corruption of Freemason and pseudo-Democratic Governments, especially that of the Front Populaire.[2] We may, therefore, expect to see developing in France very soon an anti-Semite and anti-Freemason campaign. Indeed, although the French are not likely to be so ruthless as the Germans, a movement towards Totalitarianism must be regarded as a probability of the immediate future. The probability has been increased by the foolish policy of Britain in ignoring the movement towards the Right in France and Spain and in supporting elements who did not represent the fundamental traditions of the people. Britain's final folly was committed during the weekend, when Churchill, by his accusations and his support of de Gaulle, threw France into the Totalitarian bloc and made England's defeat inevitable.

No. 210 NAI DFA Legal Adviser's Papers

> *Letter from Michael Rynne to Joseph P. Walshe (Dublin)*
> *(Secret) (Copy No. 5)*
>
> DUBLIN, 1 July 1940

The 'Region of War' Theory and the Cession of Northern Ireland
The question put to me can be phrased in two ways, viz.,
1) Would the Irish Government be entitled to claim to remain neutral in the present war while negotiating bilaterally with Great Britain for the immediate cession to Ireland of the Six Counties, or
2) Is Germany, as a belligerent in the present war, entitled to assert a vital interest in the territory of Northern Ireland sufficient to justify her in regarding Anglo-Irish negotiations for the cession of that territory during the war as an unfriendly act on Ireland's part? How would an Anglo-Irish arrangement to 'neutralise' the ceded territory affect Germany's rights, if at all?

2. It does not matter very much which of the above forms of the question at issue is taken as the basis of this note. The second approach, which starts out from Germany's pretensions, brings us, however, more quickly to the point. For the question before us involves, not merely the duties of a neutral, but also the rights of a belligerent.

3. We must first distinguish generally between the respective interests of Great Britain, Ireland and Germany at the present time in the territory known as

---
[1] Possibly John Colville or Douglas Alexander.
[2] The alliance of left-wing movements and parties that formed the government of France from 1936 to 1938.

'Northern Ireland'. We have to admit that only Great Britain and Germany have any real rights in the Six Counties. Ireland has no legal claim whatever, and nothing at all that resembles a right in law. Thus, while both the belligerent Powers may lawfully insist upon world-recognition for their individual pretensions in respect of the Six Counties, Ireland's demand for the cession of all or any of those Counties is not cognisable by the law of nations.

4. The *ad misericordiam* aspect of our claim for Irish unity is something we have grown accustomed to during seventeen years of peace. In that long period the fact that we had no legal foundation for our claim was of little or no consequence. Owing, however, to the new European situation which has endowed a Central European Power with a definite interest recognised by international law in Northern Ireland, our position as a mere moral 'claimant' becomes both difficult and dangerous.

5. The basis of Germany's present interest in the fate of the Six Counties depends mainly on the international law theory of the 'Region of War'. This must be distinguished from the theory of the 'Theatre of War', a theory which would not apply to Northern Ireland at the moment, although it might do so in the near future. According to Oppenheim,[1] Region of War is 'that part of the surface of the earth in which the belligerents may prepare and execute hostilities against each other'. So, for instance, as Oppenheim points out, during the War of 1914-18, 'Australia, Canada, India and so on, were included with the British Islands in region of war'. Clearly, then, Region of War is always potentially Theatre of War, and this is true even where a neutral State has been suddenly transformed into a region of war, as in the recent case of Norway after the laying of mines by Britain in Norwegian territorial waters. The least of belligerent rights in a region of war is that of occupation with a view to treating it as theatre of war.

6. Germany may allege, without fear of contradiction, that Northern Ireland is a part of the surface of the earth in which she is entitled to prepare hostilities against Great Britain. The question arises as to whether she could maintain her claim if the Irish and British Governments were simultaneously to declare that the Six Counties had been excluded from the region of war through neutralisation. Oppenheim and other writers have written several pages on this kind of action in time of war. From all these text books one point of essential importance arises. It is this:– *A region of war can be neutralised only by means of a special treaty concluded between all the interested belligerents.*

7. Consequently, it would not be within the competence of the Irish and British Governments to abstract Northern Ireland at this stage from the region of war. The British gesture would fail for being unilateral; Irish concurrence therein would be judged absolutely null and void as being no more than an expression of opinion of an outside neutral State in a matter at issue between belligerents.

8. From all this it follows that the only means of rendering the Six Counties neutral now would be to secure agreement to that effect between Great Britain and Germany. Mere cession of the territory to this neutral State could not possibly separate the North from the region of war and would soon come to be considered a vitiation of Southern neutrality.

---

[1] Lassa Oppenheim (1858-1919), Whewell Professor of International Law, University of Cambridge (1908-1919); wrote the introduction to the first edition of *Satow's Guide to Diplomatic Practice* (1917).

9. I have not gone into other aspects of Germany's likely objections to Anglo-Irish negotiations about the North at present, because I am convinced that the foregoing in itself is uncontrovertible and final. You can, however, easily imagine some minor repercussions on German interests that a cession of British territory to a third party would occasion at this critical juncture. Should Germany win the war – as she confidently expects to – every inch of British soil would be regarded by her as her lawful prize. Apart from the remote possibility that she may wish to garrison Northern Ireland herself as a permanent means of subjecting England, there is the practical certainty that Germany will want to control all England's financial, economic and territorial assets until she has recouped her own outlay on the war. If neutral States were to be allowed to aid and abet Britain to unload her assets at this stage, Germany might find that, at the end of all the Reich's sacrifices in blood and treasure, her debtor could plead *nulla bona*. No neutral State dare lend itself to such a perilous transaction, even without intent to defraud. Otherwise, why should the British Empire not be at once transferred to the United States of America for safety? But it is not difficult to anticipate where the war would be carried by Germany if such an event were to take place.

No. 211 NAI DFA Washington Embassy Confidential Reports 1940

Confidential report from Robert Brennan to Joseph P. Walshe (Dublin)
(108/56/40) (Copy)

WASHINGTON, 3 July 1940

The general view here is that England has now little or no chance of avoiding defeat, and that while helping her with supplies as long as she holds out, America should concentrate on home defense. There is a faint hope that the Russian activity (which consists of grabbing contiguous countries, a policy which in this case finds no word of condemnation here because it is supposed to weaken Germany's position) may delay the attack on England, and enable her to stave off defeat until the winter when the chances might be more equal.

(A hundred times during the past week I have been asked why we should not in time call England to our assistance to stave off a possible invasion. When I try to give the reasons the questioners look as if they would like to shrug impatiently and turn away).

The American Fleet sailed from Hawaii last week presumably bound for the Atlantic. Key Pittman, the Chairman of the Foreign Affairs Committee of the Senate, who often talks out of turn, suggested that the British Government should give up the fight since they have no chance, and later stated that the British Fleet was going to join the U.S. fleet in the Atlantic. Three days later the U.S. Fleet returned to Hawaii, and the Fleet Commander announced that he had been engaged in a routine war game. It was noted, however, that in the meantime the high officials of the Japanese Government had come out for a Monroe policy for Eastern Asia.

[stamped] (signed) ROBT. BRENNAN

Documents on Irish Foreign Policy, Volume VI, 1939–1941

No. 212 NAI DFA Secretary's Files P3

> *Code telegram from Joseph P. Walshe to William Warnock (Berlin)*
> *(No. 32) (No. 61) (Personal) (Copy)*
>
> DUBLIN, 4 July 1940

Your 40.[1] Irish Government determined to maintain and defend neutrality. There is no justification for allegations in yesterday's German Press and wireless that neutrality is not being strictly observed. There is no question of making any agreement which would involve departure from neutrality. The reports referred to are part of campaign designed to force Ireland out of neutrality. Government determined to maintain neutrality even in face of offers of concessions on unity question. We will immediately resist any violation of the neutrality of our territory or territorial waters. Keep us informed by wire.

No. 213 UCDA P150/2548

> *Letter from Eamon de Valera to Neville Chamberlain (London)*
> *(Copy)*
>
> DUBLIN, 4 July 1940

The memorandum handed to me by Mr. MacDonald,[2] and your letter of June 29th,[3] have been considered by my Government.

We are unable to accept the plan outlined, which we note is purely tentative and has not been submitted to Lord Craigavon and his colleagues.

The plan would involve our entry into the war. That is a course for which we could not accept responsibility. Our people would be quite unprepared for it, and Dáil Éireann would certainly reject it.

We are, of course, aware that the policy of neutrality has its dangers, but, on the other hand, departure from it would involve us in dangers greater still.

The plan would commit us definitely to an immediate abandonment of our neutrality. On the other hand, it gives no guarantee that in the end we would have a united Ireland, unless indeed concessions were made to Lord Craigavon opposed to the sentiments and aspirations of the great majority of the Irish people.

Our present Constitution represents the limit to which we believe our people are prepared to go to meet the sentiments of the Northern Unionists, but, on the plan proposed, Lord Craigavon and his colleagues could at any stage render the whole project nugatory and prevent the desired unification by demanding concessions to which the majority of the people could not agree. By such methods unity was prevented in the past, and it is obvious that under the plan outlined they could be used again. The only way in which the unity which is so needed can in our view be secured is, as I explained to Mr. MacDonald, by the immediate establishment of a single sovereign all-Ireland Parliament, free to decide all matters of national policy, internal and external – the Government which it would elect being responsible for taking the most effective measures for national defence.

---

[1] Not printed.
[2] Not printed, but see No. 208.
[3] Not printed, but see No. 208.

It was in this connection that I suggested as a line to be explored the possibility of creating such a parliament by the entry into the parliament here of the present representatives in the parliament at Belfast.

I regret that my proposal that the unity of Ireland should be established on the basis of the whole country becoming neutral is unacceptable to your government. On the basis of unity and neutrality we could mobilise the whole of the manpower of this country for the national defence. That, with the high morale which could thus be secured and the support of the Irish race throughout the world, would constitute the most effective bulwark against attack, and would provide the surest guarantee against any part of our territory being used as a base for operations against Britain.

The course suggested in your plan could only lead to internal weakness and eventual frustration.

Yours sincerely,
(Signed) EAMON DE VALERA

No. 214 NAI DFA Secretary's Files P14

Telegram from the Department of External Affairs to all missions aboard
(Personal) (Copy)

DUBLIN, 5 July 1940

Obtain widest possible publicity for statement in immediately preceding cablegram.[1] Following to guide you in your attitude when expressing your views to authorities and other influential people.

Recent Press reports concerning our vulnerability and likelihood of defence agreement between ourselves and British are part of a campaign designed to force us into the war.

Government determined to maintain neutrality even in face of offers of concessions on Partition problem. Departure from neutrality would break the unprecedented national unity achieved on basis of that policy. We shall of course resist invasion from any quarter.

Supposed dangers of neutrality far less than dangers of any policy likely to lead to our involvement in war. Latter would entail internal division and disaster and make us cockpit of final struggle.

Reference to Ireland in Churchill's speech yesterday[2] may have conveyed suggestion to some people that there is secret collaboration between the two Governments. All such suggestions should be met with the emphatic statement that neutrality is the fixed policy of the Government and the unanimous desire of the people and that the Government is resolved to maintain country's neutrality in all circumstances.

---

[1] Not printed, but see No. 212.
[2] In a speech to the House of Commons on 4 July 1940 on the fate of the French naval fleet Churchill stated that Britain was 'making every preparation to repel assaults, whether directed at Great Britain or Ireland'.

Documents on Irish Foreign Policy, Volume VI, 1939–1941

No. 215 NAI DFA Secretary's Files P13

Confidential report from John W. Dulanty to Joseph P. Walshe (Dublin)
(No. 41) (Secret)

LONDON, 5 July 1940[1]

1. This evening I handed to Mr. Chamberlain An Taoiseach's letter of the 4th July.[2] After reading it twice over he remarked that its terms were not unexpected.
2. Mr. de Valera, he suggested, was probably insisting on uncompromising neutrality because he expected that the British would be beaten. I said I had not heard Mr. de Valera express any such view. 'He thinks that nevertheless' rejoined Mr. Chamberlain 'because he said so to Mr. MacDonald'.
3. All the same he was not sorry that he had made the effort and sent Mr. MacDonald over. It was, unfortunately, not his only unsuccessful effort, especially on this question of neutrality so tragically ignored by the Germans in other countries.
4. I said, as Mr. MacDonald had doubtless reported, our policy of neutrality was that of our three political parties and had the universal approval of our people. No Government in Ireland would last twenty-four hours if it abandoned neutrality.
5. Mr. Chamberlain feared that on our side there was an ineradicable suspicion which defeated the attempts of himself and others in trying to establish better relations between the two peoples.
6. I reminded him of the grounds we had for suspicion. Leaving out of account the past centuries of misrule acknowledged by their own historians it was within the living memory of even young Irishmen today that we had been shamefully let down in the Home Rule Act of 1914 and in the dismal business of the Boundary. It was not the fault of our statesmen that they had to step warily and with more caution than their European contemporaries.
7. Notwithstanding that, however, neither Mr. Eden, Mr. MacDonald, Lord Caldecote, or any other of his colleagues who were informed of our proceedings entertained the least doubt of the amply benevolent character of our neutrality. To which statement he gave a cordial assent.

'I do not criticise' he said. 'Mr. de Valera is of course completely within his right to decide whichever way he and his Cabinet think fit. But I do reflect that in beginning these conversations I was thinking of you as well as of ourselves. In the mind of the Germans our two countries will assuredly be regarded as one front. I am afraid Mr. de Valera is missing a great opportunity.' With respect I invited him to consider whether they were not missing an even greater opportunity.

8. I mentioned the apprehension in the minds of some of our people that the British might try to take our ports and land troops on our territory without invitation from our Government. It was vital that the British should realise that any such attempt our people would fight resolutely inch by inch, Mr. Chamberlain strongly repudiated any such intention exclaiming with heat, and in language he rarely uses 'Good God, haven't we enough trouble already?' To my suggestion that in view of the spate of articles about us in the British press it would be a good thing to allay apprehensions which, according to him, were groundless, he said that I could certainly

---

[1] Marginal note by Walshe: 'Sent from H.C.'s office on 9th July received here on 10th July. J.P.W. 10/7/40'.
[2] See No. 213.

inform Mr. de Valera that his position and, he felt sure, of his colleagues, was that they had no intention of entering Éire uninvited.

9. There was a pause at this point and I thought the interview was at an end when in earnest tones Mr. Chamberlain said 'There is one question I would like to ask you. It is this. If the Germans came into Éire would Mr. de Valera fight them?' Without hesitation I said An Taoiseach would fight, and referred to his unequivocal statements long before the war that he would not allow our territory to be made the base of attack on Britain, and, further, his repeated statements during the war that he would resist invasion from whichever quarter it came. Mr. Chamberlain said he was glad to know that we would fight if attacked.

He concluded by saying he supposed we must continue on our present lines and hope for the best.

[signed] J. W. DULANTY

No. 216 NAI DFA Secretary's Files P3

Memorandum by Joseph P. Walshe

DUBLIN, 6 July 1940

The German Minister called today to make the following communication.

He said that he had a telegram from Woermann[1] instructing him to inform the Government –

1) That British Press reports quoting German papers as having warned Ireland of her dangerous position were pure inventions. No such statements had appeared in the German Press.
2) That the Irish Government should have no doubt about Germany's attitude and feelings with regard to Ireland.
3) That Germany had only one aim with regard to Ireland in the present war – that she should maintain her neutrality. Germany did not intend to violate Irish neutrality.
4) That it was senseless to talk about a Fifth Column in Ireland. It was non-existent.

I thanked the German Minister for his communication, and told him that I would convey it to my Minister, and I took the opportunity to urge upon him once more how disastrous it would be for Germany's relations with the United States if his Government acted against his (Dr. Hempel's) advice and that of his Foreign Office.

No. 217 NAI DFA Secretary's Files P13

Confidential report from John W. Dulanty to Joseph P. Walshe (Dublin)
(No. 42) (Secret)

LONDON, 8 July 1940[2]

1. I learned from Mr. Malcolm MacDonald today that his colleagues were not surprised at An Taoiseach's reply to Mr. Chamberlain's memorandum and letter of

---

[1] Dr Ernst Woermann, Under-Secretary of State, German Foreign Ministry.
[2] Marginal note by Walshe: 'Sent from H.C.'s office on 9th July received here on 10th July. J.P.W. 10/7/40'.

29th June.[1] In the War Cabinet the Prime Minister and Mr. Greenwood[2] felt that the odds were against the acceptance of the proposal but the Cabinet as a whole thought that it was an effort worth making.

2. He had not reported on his return that An Taoiseach thought the British would be beaten. But he had said that after discussions of some length on the ultimate issue of the war his own clear impression was that Mr. de Valera had been progressively doubtful of the British being victorious. On each of his visits An Taoiseach and he had discussed this question and he felt An Taoiseach was more doubtful on the occasion of his third visit than he was when he, Mr. MacDonald, first crossed to Dublin.

3. I mentioned to Mr. MacDonald the grave danger of any suggestion of their coming into any part of our territory without the direct invitation of our Government. Mr. MacDonald, with what appeared to be genuine conviction, assured me there was no such intention. He was, however, against any public statement to that effect at present. That was his personal view only – he had not discussed the point with his colleagues.

4. In speaking about the possibility of an invasion by the Germans of both England and Ireland he said they could land forces so much more easily on our shores than on the English. I made the obvious point that the Germans would now have far less distance to traverse to attack England than they would have to attack us. Why did he think they would land more easily on our shores? His reply was that their Navy had a very strong defence in every port and around the coast and even if on a foggy night a few German ships managed to land troops the British military dispositions were such as to wipe them out immediately. In the case of air attack they were confident that the Germans would get far more than they gave. But there was no naval defence in the normal sense in our ports. The British naval guard would be much more out to sea and could not be so concentrated as it was around the British coast with the result that there would be more gaps through which German ships might slip to our shores. If a landing followed he doubted whether we had sufficient military strength to stand up against strong well-organised German forces. This he thought was also An Taoiseach's view.

5. Mr. MacDonald said his own view was that the result would be achieved in the air. When the real bombing began it was possible that the enemy's air force and their own would almost cancel out, but the enemy would then be at the end of his resources or at any rate not able to replace his losses as speedily as the British could. There was an impressive increase in aeroplanes and munitions production in Britain and in addition there was the immense help coming (a) from America in planes and (b) from Canada in trained airmen. I asked if he would be good enough to give me information about the American assistance. He said that the American production at the beginning had been slow. A few months ago they were only getting about 200 planes a month. Despite the action of Mr. Henry Ford,[3] they were now getting upwards of 500 a month and before long the American export would

---

[1] See No. 213.

[2] Arthur Greenwood (1880-1954), deputy leader of the British Labour Party (1935-45), Minister without Portfolio in the War Cabinet (1940-2).

[3] Henry Ford (1863-1947), founder of the Ford motor company and of modern assembly lines. Ford disliked Roosevelt and did not approve of United States involvement in the Second World War.

be 1,000 aeroplanes a month. He thought the enemy would suffer from a shortage of materials – already the Italians were feeling this in their shipbuilding. The blockade would be particularly effective in respect of food and coal. I suggested that the history of the blockade in the last war when Germany had so many enemies at her gate was not convincing as a war measure in the present conflict when Germany had now only England to fight. I thought that it had been recognised by experts that it was impossible to starve Germany. Mr. MacDonald said there might be something in my contention, but that you couldn't get output on the requisite scale and at top speed from men who were only half nourished. He and his colleagues were firm in their belief that if they could hold out for another six or eight weeks victory would be with them.

[signed] J.W. DULANTY

No. 218 NAI DFA Paris Embassy 19/34A

Confidential report from Seán Murphy to Joseph P. Walshe (Dublin)
(Copy)

LA BOURBOULE, 8 July 1940

1. The result of the war seems to be accepted without active discontent. The public has already been informed by Marshal Pétain that France was beaten because of her unpreparedness, and the lack of British support. It is being exhorted both by the press and public men to look only to the future and see that the mistakes and lack of cohesion and organisation which led to failure in this case, do not recur.

2. It seems to be assumed in public quarters that France's destiny, not only in the remote, but in the immediate future, lies in her own hands, and that if the population will work hard, increase in numbers, be disciplined, and (in the words of Marshal Pétain) not allow 'the spirit of enjoyment to triumph over that of sacrifice' France will again become a big power. Most of the press seems to imply that France may become a great power in a very short time. M. Baudoin, the Foreign Minister, in one of his declarations to the press, seems to draw a parallel between the present position of France and her position in 1815, and to imply that her immediate future, internationally, may follow similar lines to those on which she developed in the years following 1815. At least one newspaper (Paris-Soir) had developed this thesis and informed the public that the France which was completely beaten militarily in 1814, became the arbiter of Europe at the Congress of Vienna the following year. A parallel seems also to be made with France's history after 1870. It is not impossible that this process may even be extended in the minds of some to the German recovery after 1918.

3. There is a distinct possibility of the French Government and public cherishing illusions as to France's future, both from drawing inexact historical parallels, and attributing the French defeat wholly or partially to wrong motives. There is no doubt that France's defeat is in a large measure due to the rot which seems to have pervaded all French life for years past. From a demographic viewpoint France has been in a precarious position for many years, without any real effort having been made to mend it. Her public life has of course been characterised by an astounding instability in Governments which have risen and fallen for all sorts of internal reasons, questions frequently of a most unimportant kind. Deputies and Governments

have, in the absence (or rather non-exercise) of the dissolution weapon, felt completely immune, during the term of the legislature, from the verdict of their constituents and have only rarely been guided exclusively by the general interests of the country. The history of the present legislature, up to the outbreak of war, was one of a continuous displacement of the reins of Government from the Socialist Left, which undoubtedly was the representative majority, to the Centre and Right with Daladier. The French Parliament was in fact behaving up to the war, almost as if France existed in a vacuum with no possibility of disturbing influence from outside. The public administration must have been one of the most inefficient in the world, as far as getting work done was concerned. The war only brought into relief the defects of the system. Most people believed that while the Civil Administration might be (and was admittedly) inefficient, an Army with the traditions behind it which the French Army has, could not but be of the first class both in planning, organisation and equipment. This does not seem to be the case. M. Reynaud's statement in the Chamber in May that France 'expected a classic war' (and this after the experience of Poland and Norway) shows the deficiencies on the intelligence or strategic side. The French General Staff seemed to be aware neither of the size or number of the German tanks and armoured divisions. The Corap[1] Army which was sent to hold the bend of the Meuse was according to M. Reynaud's statement completely disorganised. I have been told on reliable authority that the French Government two years ago bought the licence of a cannon for 50 million francs, and then only manufactured 12. I have also been told by an eye-witness that the guns used by at least some of the soldiers, were the actual guns (i.e. not only the same model) as those used in 1914-18 war. Finally I was informed from two different sources that American 'planes which arrived in France months ago were never unpacked. The relative lack of men in France is intelligible considering her population. It is amazing, however, that a wealthy country like France and a country which has, nominally at any rate, spent much money on armaments since the last war, should have been defective in material as Marshal Pétain said was the case. The Maginot line on which much was spent and in which so much reliance was placed was, of course, eventually turned by the Germans and captured with little effort, the French having already withdrawn their troops from some portions of it. The failure to prolong this line to the coast seems inexplicable in the light of events. Presumably the French General Staff thought it advantageous for them to have an open frontier in which they believed they would eventually beat their opponents. Certainly the General impression in Paris when the Germans entered Holland and Belgium and 'the attack which had been awaited since October' (Gamelin's 'ordre du jour' of 10th May) was that it was only now a matter of a short time until France would be victorious.

The French Army having proved as inferior as it did, it is not surprising that France was beaten. The inferiority of the French Army (apart from numbers) was a direct product of the prevailing state of French public life and the French philosophical conception of what made life worth while. As already mentioned, Marshal Pétain has informed the French people of this fact. His words may, however, be lost sight of, or there may be a tendency to attribute what has happened to other

---

[1] The reference is to the Ninth French Army, commanded by General André Georges Corap, which defended the River Meuse in 1940.

causes and to nourish false hopes. Already the public is probably beginning to think, because of the official emphasis which is being laid on the point, that the British failure to send sufficient troops or the fact that British Foreign policy controlled that of France, means that, after all, the blame cannot be put wholly on the French system. Both the above causes contributed to France's present plight. It is a question, however, whether the subordination of French foreign policy to that of Great Britain was really as important as it is being represented in so far as France's going to war with Germany is concerned. French policy for at least a hundred years and perhaps for three hundred (since Westphalia)[1] seems to have been based on the fear of Germany (or Prussia) as a danger to her existence. A fact which is indisputable is that most Frenchmen believe that France lost a golden opportunity of crushing a Germany regarded as dangerous to herself in March 1936.[2] The belief that Germany did represent a danger to France seems to have been strengthened and to have become almost universal after the German occupation of Czechoslovakia. So far from holding that in allying herself with England, France was being led into a path which her interest said she should not follow, one had the general impression that it was France which sought the English alliance. In the result this was mistaken policy. In the absence of the result it would have been difficult to prove it. The practical side of this question is that the conclusion drawn may lead Frenchmen to think that their reliance on Great Britain was responsible for their defeat, and that their general lack of organisation was to that extent not to blame.

5.[3] The tendency to draw parallels from the past is capable of creating illusions as to France's future status, and seems to be already having this effect. The parallel with 1815 would seem to be based on one fundamental error, in that the position accorded to France in the following years was a function of the principle of the balance of power in Europe. The principle of the balance of power in Europe seems to have been mainly a British pre-occupation for the reason that England was not herself interested in expansion in Europe, and only desired that no Continental power should be so strong as to threaten the security of Great Britain, while she was busy developing her interests in other parts of the world.

6. If Great Britain should be defeated in this war, there would seem to be no reason why Germany should be anxious to apply the same principle. As for the parallel with the 1870 defeat, the conditions here too may be quite different. France recovered from the 1870 defeat sufficiently to be able, with her ally, to defeat Germany in the 1914-18 war, because once the peace treaty of 1871 was signed, Germany did not actively and directly interfere with developments in France – to such an extent that Bismarck more or less directly encouraged French colonial development, and a consequent increase in the wealth and man power of which

---

[1] The Peace of Westphalia, 1648, refers to a set of treaties that ended the Thirty Years' War and Eighty Years' War and resolved the structure of the European states' system until the nineteenth century. The resulting 'Westphalian System' used to describe post-1648 international relations was based on stability preserved by the balance of power, international law and diplomacy.

[2] On 7 March 1936 German forces occupied the demilitarised zone in the Rhineland. Britain and France did not oppose the move. Germany's armed forces were judged, even by Hitler, to be weak in 1936 and in retrospect it seemed that London and Paris could have thwarted Germany's expansionist foreign policy by a decisive military response to the remilitarisation.

[3] There is no section numbered 4 in this document.

France disposed. It is possible that Germany, if victorious, will draw a lesson both from the French experience after 1870, and to a greater extent, her own experience after 1918, so as to prevent France being in a position for a long time to come to threaten the conquest of Germany.

7. One of the strongest themes of all French thought and writings on international affairs since Germany began to grow in strength during the last 7 years, has been that France made a great mistake in not taking measures of a permanent kind after the Versailles treaty, to see that Germany should not again rise to a position of such strength as to be able to threaten France. French writers have always asserted that this would have been done (by the permanent occupation of the left bank of the Rhine, as suggested by Foch,[1] and other measures of a like kind) but for British opposition again inspired by her desire to maintain the balance of power. Practically all that was written since the war began on the terms to be accorded to Germany in the post-war period, and on the assumption of a German defeat, went at least the length of insisting on possession of the left bank of the Rhine, and in many cases went further in the direction of advocating the breaking up into small states of the German Reich.

8. It is difficult to see how in the event of final victory, Germany will not impose conditions on France, and provide for their observance, which will keep France harmless. Official utterances do not, however, seem to betray a consciousness of this likelihood, and speak of the future of France as if it is something which depends exclusively on the French people and Government, untroubled by any outside interference.

No. 219 NAI DFA Washington Embassy Confidential Reports 1940

> Extract from a confidential report from Robert Brennan to Joseph P. Walshe
> (Dublin)
> (108/60/40)
>
> WASHINGTON, 9 July 1940

The general opinion here is that the Nazis will invade England and defeat her. This is regretted on all sides as a major disaster for Europe, for the democratic form of Government and for civilization. There is a constant speculation as to what is to happen the British Fleet, and a real fear for America if it should fall into German hands. Realization that America can do little or nothing to stave off this catastrophe is causing tremendous anguish.

Under the circumstances it is natural that the public mind should be tremendously interested in the question of defense. This atmosphere is reflected in Congress where appropriations for defense are passed in bewildering succession of larger and larger estimates.
[matter omitted]

---

[1] Marshal Ferdinand Foch (1851-1929), French general, Supreme Commander, Allied Forces, Europe (1918); accepted Germany's surrender in 1918; Marshal of France (1918).

No. 220 NAI DFA Paris Embassy 19/34A

> *Confidential report from Seán Murphy to Joseph P. Walshe (Dublin)*
> *(P.19/34A) (Copy)*
>
> Vichy, 10 July 1940

I gave you a short summary in my telegram No 68[1] of some of the most important statements on French foreign policy contained in the declaration made to the press on the 4th inst. by the French Minister of Foreign Affairs in connection with the Mers-el-Kebir incident.[2] The following is the full text of the passages in question of M. Baudouin's declaration:

'French foreign policy has for years past been dictated by the desire to do nothing which could disassociate us from the foreign policy of Great Britain. The policy of sanctions which separated us from Italy is due solely to this anxiety; the same way our policy vis-à-vis Central Europe and Germany. The negotiations which led to the Munich agreement were carried on personally by Mr. Chamberlain; we entered into war against Germany in the wake of England who first declared war ... these facts (the attack on the French vessels at Mers-el-Kebir and the blocking of French war vessels in Alexandria) cannot fail to exercise a profound influence on the reaction of our policy. Our relations with England pass on to a new plane. We had this morning sorrowfully to take the decision to break diplomatic relations with a country responsible for the blood of our sailors ... To this unconsidered act of hostility the French Government did not reply by an act of hostility. It remains calm, attentive to the development of a situation which it did not wish, only anxious to defend by the means which rest to it and by a new policy which it will feel called upon to adopt, the honour and the interest of France'.

M. Baudouin said also in the course of his declarations that for the previous six days England had no diplomatic representation in France although 'on several occasions I asked our Chargé d'Affaires in London[3] to intervene with the British Government to get it to re-establish direct contact with the French Government'.

The whole press followed the Government's lead in condemning in unmeasured terms the British attack on Mers-el-Kebir. Incidentally the French Government ordered certain air squadrons in North Africa to attack in Gibraltar the British units which had bombarded the fleet at Mers-el-Kebir. This action was likewise applauded by the press. Apart from the characterisation of the incident the French press was at one in regarding the British action as an enormous psychological blunder. Many organs (Figaro, Le Temps, etc.) attributed the British action to bad advice on the part of French men in London. Mr. Churchill was also represented as being the prime instigator. The only exception I saw in the press to the general violent outcry raised against Great Britain was an article in the Jour by Fernand-Laurent in which, while he deplored what had happened, he urged that the strong ties which had united Great Britain and France for so many years should not be

---

[1] Not printed.
[2] The Royal Navy destroyed the French fleet at anchor at the French Algerian port town of Mers-el-Kebir near the port of Oran on 3 July 1940. The British were concerned that France's main warships would fall into German hands after the signing of the armistice between France and Germany on 25 June 1940. The incident is also referred to as the Oran affair.
[3] Marquis de Castellane, French Chargé d'Affaires in London (1940).

forgotten and that no precipitated action should be taken. He expressed the hope that what had happened would not mean an irremediable breach of Franco-British good understanding. Some local newspaper went so far as to suggest that French foreign policy should make a complete volt-face. The Figaro said that the action freed France from a 'moral load' put upon her by the armistice; as a result of the armistice France was in a position of a flock of sheep without guidance, being driven from one side to another; her sentiments called her towards Great Britain, but necessity pulled her away, the Mers-el-Kebir incident 'has restored liberty to French diplomacy'. The Temps which treated Franco-British relations in a number of successive articles started off immediately after the incident by asking as a question to be put seriously whether war was likely to come about between Great Britain and France. Developing the theme of Mr. Baudouin's speech as to the subordination of France to British foreign policy the Temps said 'for the last 20 years Great Britain, while favouring the rise of Germany so as to prevent a development of France, who was however in no way a menace, always prevented any rapprochement between Paris and Berlin as well as any intimacy between our country and Italy. At the time of the Abyssinian conquest we stifled one of the strongest currents of our public opinion to apply to Italy the sanctions wanted by England. In Central Europe our policy has been modelled on that of Great Britain. It was Mr. Chamberlain who conducted the negotiations of Munich. It was England who, after having inspired this policy of conciliation decided us suddenly to change our attitude and to enter into war with Germany.' The Temps adds that 'it was France which supported the total weight of land hostilities'. The article continues 'let us not reproach England with the incoherence of her guiding principles and do not let us reproach her either for having by pressure or persuasion decided us to follow her like a shadow in her capricious and dangerous promenades ... let us particularly know how to draw a profitable lesson from our maladresses and misfortunes. Let not our future resemble our past. Let our diplomacy become at last free. Let it not be any longer the instrument either of hollow ideologies or of foreign schemes. France only became a great nation in the course of centuries only thanks to the independence of her external policy.'

I have been informed that Mr. Churchill's speech in the House of Commons in justification of the Mers-el-Kebir action was much more full than reported in the French press and in particular that the British squadron offered a third alternative to the French Admiral (namely to go to one of the French possessions such as the Martinique) besides the two published in the French press and official communiqués (either to join the British fleet or to scuttle his ships). The only reference I have seen to the third alternative in the French press was contained in a leading article in Le Temps of the 8th inst. which mentioned the matter incidentally in saying that 'the English suggestion to send the French ships to the Martinique – a suggestion which if it had been accepted would have constituted a violation of the armistice – would not have offered any guarantee for our fleet and would only have underlined the suspect nature of the English manoeuvre'.

The French Government and press have treated this incident as a gratuitous and unjustified action on the part of the British Government and in so far as the reason given by London for undertaking it is concerned (i.e. lack of confidence in the German undertaking not to use the French fleet against England) as an insult to French honour. Both the Minister for Foreign Affairs and the Admiralty and other official sources have asserted emphatically that the French Plenipotentiaries who signed the armistice had expressed instructions to break off negotiations if the Germans insisted on the unconditional surrender of the French fleet and that the British Government was aware of this fact. The feeling provocated against Great Britain has been enhanced by the insistence with which official quarters and the press have blamed the failure of full British support on land for France's defeat. The political writer of the Action Française considers that British history itself will pass a very severe judgment on the British action. He thinks that 'England committed an act of inexcusable violence and traitory' and that the British Admiralty 'satisfied its passion and followed a long tradition in endeavouring by every possible means to destroy a navy of which it is jealous and which it fears'.

The anti-British theme in regard to foreign policy was developed both by M. Laval and M. Georges Bonnet (Minister for Foreign Affairs from April 1938 to end September 1939) at one of the informal sessions of the Chamber last week. M. Laval was reported to have emphasized the extent to which during his administration of the Quai d'Orsay in 1935-36 he endeavoured to free French foreign policy from its subordination to that of England. M. Bonnet pointed out (this was alleged at the time both by the German and Italian news agencies) that he had accepted the Italian offer of mediation of the 2nd September without insisting on the withdrawal of the German troops from Poland but that 'his efforts were frustrated by the British and Polish intransigence'.

No. 221 NAI DFA Secretary's Files A2

> *Memorandum by Joseph P. Walshe to Eamon de Valera (Dublin)*
> *(Copy)*
>
> DUBLIN, 11 July 1940

1. Neutrality was not entered upon for the purpose of being used as a bargaining factor. It represented, and does represent, the fundamental attitude of the entire people. It is just as much a part of the national position as the desire to remain Irish, and we can no more abandon it than we can renounce everything that constitutes our national distinctiveness. If either party invades us, we are then going to fight to defend our integral national life against an enemy who wishes to destroy its essential character in time of war. In defending our neutrality against an invader by force of arms, we are not giving it up – quite the contrary.

Clearly, Belgium, Holland, Norway and Denmark had the same conception of neutrality. They had to run the risk of avoiding military alliances with neighbouring Great Powers as an attempt to safeguard their ultimate national existence. An alliance with either Great Power, in their view, would only have brought earlier disaster upon them. Neutrality kept three of the small States concerned out of the last war. The fact that Germany regarded their territories as essential to her for waging the war against England and France does not necessarily mean that they are to be incorporated ultimately into the German State. Their neutrality at least has given them a right to the sympathy and good will of all other peoples in their eventual effort to regain their independence. A military alliance would not only have lost them that sympathy, but would have caused the world to say that they deserved the fate of the Power with which they had cast their lot.

2. Notwithstanding the hostile attitude of a section of the American Press which supports England so long, and just so long, as they think her financial power has a chance of continuing, the vast body of the American people whose good will we retain while we remain neutral can be a powerful – even a determining – factor in the restoration of our independence should we lose it during the war as a result of defending our neutrality.

If, on the other hand, we ally ourselves with England, that good will will disappear and we shall be classed once more as part of England deserving whatever fate may befall her in defeat. Whatever the ups and downs of world fortunes may be, the eventual good will of America is essential to Germany if her European order is to be a success. Our sheet anchor is in the common people of the United States. The hopes and fears of Germany's future are linked up with her future relations with America, and that is our hope, whether of avoiding a German invasion altogether or of eventually getting back our independence if invaded by Germany during the war.

3. The detailed practical reasons for not abandoning our neutrality are related to the foregoing general considerations. If England is victorious, our relations with her must return to normal. Even States at war with each other resume normal relations in due course. Our attitude towards England is more than benevolent. A few years of unjustifiable resentment might follow her victory – but what is that to the deservedly complete loss of our independence which would follow a German victory if we make ourselves one with England now. It might even suit Germany to be able to treat Ireland as part of England and to subject us to perpetual occupation and absorption. We can at least do what we can to save our people from that fate, and what we can do is to refuse to give Germany the right of conquest by accepting our reabsorption in the United Kingdom, for that is the meaning of establishing a military unit between ourselves and Great Britain.

4. Let us beware also of a very vital factor in the British agitation for a military alliance. It is beyond belief that a great many of Britain's public men do not recognise the grave danger of defeat in which she now stands. Many of them must be thinking of possible peace terms. If Ireland becomes a unit with Great Britain, it is entirely probable that the two countries would be treated as such by Germany, and the losses, financial, economic, etc., would be spread over both territories. Ireland would not be given separate privileges. Instead of playing our natural role as a separate State with an important position as the outpost of Europe towards America, and being treated with favour by the dominant State of Europe naturally desirous of keeping us strong in population and prosperity vis-à-vis England, we should be turned into a barren German fortress. It is natural that England should not cease – even in her present desperate straits – to adhere to the policy of having a weak country on her western flank. Some day she might hope to take back the fortress, but she could never again defeat an Ireland with a strong and prosperous population. A strong Ireland would be a gain to the European continent. To all true Britishers it would constitute a weakening of Britain. That has been an elementary fact of British policy for centuries, and it was last formulated in Churchill's book on the Great War.[1]

5. To abandon our neutrality is therefore to accept Britain's conception of our place in the world. It would be a clear indication that, at the very crisis of our national

---

[1] Winston Churchill, *The World Crisis, 1911-1918* (London, 1923).

life, we had not yet grasped the elementary truths of world politics, and we should deserve the consequences of our fatal ignorance.

6. England is already conquered. That is also an elementary fact for everyone who has not allowed himself to be overcome by Britain's belief in her permanent invincibility. The moment Germany and Russia (even without Italy and Japan) proposed to act together against England, her fate was sealed. To the sane looker-on, Chamberlain's announcement of England's declaration of war on Germany in his radio talk on 3rd September, 1939, sounded the death knell of the British Empire. She went into the war on a broken diplomatic front and no fleet, no financial power, could save her from a combination stretching from France to the Pacific. Now, she has suffered the greatest defeat in her military history in the Battle of Flanders. Driven out of Norway, Belgium, Holland and France, she is a relatively small, densely populated, industrial island beleaguered by an air force which is at least five times as strong in numbers as hers. America's delivery of planes does not exceed 500 a month, and, with increasing tension in the Far East and America's ingrained fear of Japan, this number is likely to decrease. The argument that American aid to England is the best way to beat Germany who is only a potential enemy will have little or no force with the American people when Japan begins to take over the white man's possessions in East Asia – an event that will in all probability coincide with the later phases of Germany's attack on Britain.

The admitted superiority of the British fighter plane is wholly exaggerated by the manner in which the British Press and radio feature individual combats. There is no guarantee that the qualitative superiority of the fighter plane will last. Germany's resources for the rapid manufacture of new planes have enormously increased with the acquisition of France's industrial plant, and her easy access to the ore mines of France and Spain. Russia, too, under the guidance of German experts who are known to be in Russia since the beginning of the war, must already be in a position to produce planes and other weapons for Germany.

The Norway expedition, and the failure of the Fleet to operate with any real success in narrow waters against aircraft and submarines, is a sufficient indication that the Fleet cannot save England from invasion against a Power with a larger air force and a considerable submarine fleet. In the end, the real invasion must take place over narrow waters, and the Channel provides the passage.

7. The addition of France as a passive enemy is already producing its effects in America, where sympathy has slackened since the Oran affair. The French Canadians are sullenly resentful. In matters of this kind, sentiment is slow to gain the upper hand of reason, but it invariably does in the long run. Italy's submarine and air fleet are admitted to be relatively efficient. They will at least be a powerful aid to Germany in completing the defeat of Britain. Spain is on the verge of joining the Axis. Her non-belligerency officially declared was a warning to Great Britain that she would come into the war at the appropriate moment. Gibraltar and the _____[1] as well as Ceuta,[2] will be in Germany's power. Italy and Spain have shown themselves willing instruments of Germany. France may become so through England's blunders. The situation is, therefore, entirely different from that of the

---

[1] There is what appears to be a deliberate gap in the original text at this point; an unknown number of words have been left out.
[2] Ceuta is a Spanish enclave in northern Morocco.

Napoleonic period when States submitted only unwillingly to him. Poland, the Low Countries and Norway will bow to fate when they see Britain abandoned by all her former adherents, and Germany will have willing or half-willing populations to aid her in her schemes for a new Europe.

8. To conclude, the possibility of a German invasion which does exist gives no excuse for abandoning our neutrality. As I have suggested, it makes the maintenance of that policy all the more essential. A neutral State has a better chance of resurrection in the final settlement, and, in our particular position, departure from neutrality would be attended by many other evils, as already explained. But we should not take a German invasion as a certainty. Militarily, it is a hazardous venture. It would mean establishing relatively small forces isolated from their base by a distance of 300 miles. It would mean incurring the risk of a major defeat and the loss of transports at sea. Germany's lightning progress is being helped by the prestige already won, and she cannot want to run the risk of a severe blow to it in the course of what could only be a subsidiary operation. The mere landing of troops from planes could not be expected to effect a permanent hold without advancing troops in the rere (which happened in all the attacks on the small Continental Powers). Our Army, at least with the help of the British Army, could quickly bring such attempts to nought.

Moreover, Germany does not want to alienate the entire public opinion of America. She knows that the Irish, Germans and Italians form a very powerful group there, with Irish influence paramount. She knows how grievous a moral loss she would suffer if she attacked Ireland, which is not – as were the other States attacked – in the way of her advance to England. It would be an enormous underestimate of Hitler's ambitions to believe that he is not determined to win the good opinion of America for his real aim in the building of a new Europe under German leadership.

9. The arguments relating to our internal situation are too obvious to need formulation. Dissension, demoralisation, and the final moral and material defeat of the nation, is a brief summary of the consequences.

Some priests who have no world Church outlook and overcome by hatred for the passing phenomenon of Nazism, say we are bound to join the fight against Germany. The Pope does not seem to share that view.

No. 222 NAI DFA Secretary's Files P2

> *Code telegram from Joseph P. Walshe to Robert Brennan (Washington)*
> *(No. 85) (Personal) (Most Secret) (Copy)*
>
> DUBLIN, 11 July 1940

Your telegrams 107 and 108.[1] This démarche certain to be most helpful in keeping out neighbour though in light of past history danger of sinister action direct or following air attack faked to appear as if coming from other belligerent by no means out of question. Could you get secret approach made to other Ambassador by influential Senators urging the unwisdom especially from point of view of Irish American public opinion of using Ireland as base against England. German

---

[1] Neither telegram printed.

Minister here has urged this point with his Government but not doubt strong argument from Ambassador would have great weight. The lull in fight is giving opportunity to anti-Irish Press in Britain and America to try to weaken the morale of our people. It is unfortunately true that each side has an interest in inducing the other to invade first. The situation at the moment therefore requires the greatest care and watchfulness. So long as both sides keep out the Taoiseach is determined to maintain our neutrality at all costs.

No. 223 NAI DFA 205/4

Code telegram from the Department of External Affairs to William Warnock (Berlin) (via Geneva)
(No. 43) (No. 69) (Personal)

DUBLIN, 13 July 1940

Your 41.[1] Swiss correspondents of English newspapers reported 3rd July that Deutsche Allgemeine Zeitung accused Ireland of not realising that by offering shelter to the British Merchant Navy in their ports they are encroaching on strict neutrality. Please telegraph translation of passage referred to.

Same correspondents reported on same date that German Press (names of papers not given) charged Ireland with not observing neutrality and gave following quotation 'Sooner or later Germany may have to act in consequence, as in the case of other small European neutrals.' Examine papers carefully for this quotation and any such charges. Cable result.

No. 224 NAI DFA Secretary's Files P12/1

Code telegram from Seán Murphy to the Department of External Affairs (Dublin)
(No. 73) (Personal) (Copy)

VICHY, 15 July 1940

Saw Charles Roux, Secretary General of the Foreign Office, last night Friday at his request. He wanted to explain to me, for the information of the Irish Government, that reasons given by the British Government for the attack on Fleet at Oran were completely untenable. He said the French Government and people regarded the attack as a dastardly act of aggression and cruelty. British were kept informed during the negotiations for armistice. They were aware armistice terms could in no circumstances contemplate handing over of French Fleet to Germany. The Germans did not seek this because they knew it would end negotiations which Germans were anxious to bring to a conclusion. The terms of armistice were of course dictated by Germany and it was only natural that they would require disarmament of Fleet excepting ships required for protection of French Colonial Possessions. The Fleet was to disarm under supervision of Armistice Commission but ships were to remain property of France under the control of French naval guard on board each ship. The proposals made by British Admiral could not be accepted because any one of them involved breaches of armistice terms. The result would be complete occupation of France by Germany. French vessels at Oran were

---

[1] Not printed.

in process of disarmament. They were anchored with their furnaces completely extinct. They had no reason to believe that these ships could be used against them. In the view of the French, British action which cost lives of 1,200 Frenchmen was an act of brutality. The further action of bombing and machine-gunning the ships resulting in 250 dead was unprecedented in naval history. He felt Franco-British relations will be embittered for years to come. He was anxious that Irish Government should know French point of view as until the last few days this had not been broadcast and their news agencies' messages were being held up by the British.

I made no comment upon this statement. I merely asked what he thought to be the reason for British action. He said he was sure Churchill and Admiralty were chiefly responsible. The latter were enraged at not getting the French Fleet which would have been of great assistance to them. He commented very unfavourably on the British Army's part in the war and said that even the Navy had not done as well as the French Navy. I promised to transmit the statement by telegram.

With regard to Franco-British relations in general, Press and Government here are doing everything possible to belittle part of England in the war. This with a view to ingratiating themselves with Germans though, apparently, with little success. The French attitude can only be explained by the belief that Germany will win. I understand this is the view of Pétain. One gets the impression that the resurrection of France is hoped for from new constitution, but one cannot help feeling that neither the Government nor the people fully appreciate serious situation of France. This is the view of members of diplomatic corps to whom I have spoken. The behaviour at National Assembly would not lead one to think that there are any fundamental changes of attitude on the part ———[1] representatives. The fact that 80 members voted against Constitutional changes may be indication of further difficulties when Constitution is submitted to people for ratification, a condition demanded by representatives of ex-soldiers.

No. 225 NAI DFA Secretary's Files A2

> *Memorandum by Joseph P. Walshe to Eamon de Valera (Dublin)*
> *(Most Secret) (Copy No. 2)*
>
> DUBLIN, 15 July 1940

The International Situation and Our Critical Position in Relation to It

The British daily Press departed from its threatening attitude about the middle of last week, and the 'Times' on Saturday admitted that 'Éire enjoys geographical advantages denied to Norway, Holland and Belgium', adding 'if help were needed to meet a German invasion, it would be neither belated nor ineffective'.

But the 'Economist' and the 'Tablet', amongst the weekly reviews, kept up the hostile campaign. The bad equipment of our Army is stressed.

In the course of a letter to the 'Scotsman' a week ago, Berriedale Keith said 'It is patent that Éire is utterly unable to defend her neutrality by her own resources, which are negligible against modern methods of war … I trust it has been made clear to Mr. de Valera that, if he fails to secure the neutrality of Éire in fact, the British forces will be used forthwith for that end. This country is no longer prepared

---

[1] There is what appears to be a deliberate gap in the original text at this point; an unknown number of words have been left out.

to acquiesce in inaction in face of imminent perils, and Éire is under the clearest obligation forthwith to concert effective measures of defence with Britain. If she fails to do so, our right to act is beyond doubt.'

Our alleged deficiency of arms has been the usual theme in the British campaign against us. It has been the strongest argument in favour of our accepting the presence of the British Army.

On Friday, the 'New York Post' published an article from Ludwig Lore[1] in which the writer stated that Churchill should use towards Ireland the firmness which he displayed towards the French Fleet at Oran. John Steele, in a message to Mutuals, told American radio listeners that the position could be regarded as being similar to that in which Long Island was three-quarters a free nation and one quarter American. In such circumstances, said Steele, America would know what to do.

But the most serious indication of Britain's real intentions towards us is a commentary in a Secret document containing an analysis of foreign broadcasts normally circulated to Government Departments in England and to us through the High Commissioner. In the confusion and lack of cohesion which exists in British Departments, the following comment escaped the notice of the officials who usually transmit such documents to our Government:-

Defence of Éire

This question has been dealt with by American broadcasters from London. Fred Bate (N.B.C) is the only one who has given comment by describing Lord Craigavon's proposal as 'peremptory and one-sided – scarcely meriting the term offer'. If the views of one leading commentator – Major Elliott – may be taken as typical, it would appear that America's enthusiastic response to any positive act on the part of Britain would even extend to an occupation of Éire. Discussing the danger from Hitler, Major Elliott said:-

'The (Irish) Government is carrying on with outworn conceptions of being protected by its neutrality .... It remains to be seen if the British Government will take vigorous steps to overcome that point of view while there is still time, if there is time.'

In considering the implications of this comment, we must remember that the B.B.C. is now controlled by the Ministry for Information, and its statements and comments, public or secret, represent the views of that Ministry.

During the weekend, the Press Association has informed the world that an agreement had been entered into between the Irish and British Governments to provide for the entry of British troops into Éire in the event of a German invasion of this country.

Notwithstanding all the assurances of the British Representative here that the British Government was playing a straight game with us, and that he was relying on us for any information which might be useful to the British in the event of a German invasion of this country, the Assistant Deputy Adjutant General of the 53rd Division,[2] now stationed in Ulster, was captured on Friday in the course of

---

[1] Ludwig Lore, American Marxist writer who edited the Communist Labor Party of America (CLP) publication *Class Struggle* in the 1920s and later the *New York Volkzseitung*.
[2] Major E.Y. Byass, arrested with his wife by gardaí at Mullingar, Co Westmeath, in July 1940 and found to have military maps and plans in his possession.

carrying out military espionage activities. The papers discovered on his person fully confirm that his mission was officially sanctioned.

Mr. Craig,[1] of the British Legation here, told me yesterday morning that a Swiss Military Intelligence Officer had informed the British Intelligence that the Germans were about to violate the neutrality of Ireland and Iceland on 15th July. In subsequent conversation, he urged that I should advocate the suppression of all motor traffic. The suggestion is interesting in view of the fact that the British Press has been seizing upon statements recently made by our Ministers to exaggerate them and to create a panic in this country.

American public opinion seems to me to be the only effective weapon left to us against an early occupation by the British Army as soon as British political intrigues prove unsuccessful. It will be necessary to repeat to the American people that Irish neutrality is so fundamental a part of the Irish national position that to fail to defend it against all comers would involve the loss of our independence. It must be shown to the American people that neutrality is not a mere bargaining factor or a military expedient of the moment. No doubt, we have also to tell the American people, in view of British statements, that we are ready to accept any help against invasion by either belligerent.

A further statement by you to the American people seems to be an urgent necessity. The British are now using against us all the tricks and wiles which they commonly use against small peoples. We must, therefore, make use of our fullest resources where our people are strongest.

As each day goes by, the situation of Britain grows more serious, and no doubt the British threat to us will, up to a point, increase in gravity. The weekend Press is at last admitting the futility of hoping for a break between Russia and Germany, and the immediate danger of a complete collapse of Britain's position in the Middle East. Britain's promise to Japan to close the Burma road to further supplies for Chungking is provoking adverse comments in America. We know from our own sources that the British are finding it daily more difficult to obtain supplies from the United States, and an early complete stoppage is to be expected since the Army appears to have obtained the final say in the matter. The Certificate of the Chief of Staff that supplies of any kind are not essential for America's defence needs is now necessary before any export of arms can take place. I have instructed our Minister in the United States to bring further pressure to bear on the British Embassy, through the means available to him, so that the British Government may become eventually persuaded that anti-Irish propaganda in America, as well as any attempt to re-occupy this country, would in the end deprive them of their only remaining hope – the support of the United States.

In view of recent events, it is safer for us to make the assumption that the further and extraordinary means of communication being requested of us by the British are intended, not to meet the eventuality of a German invasion, but to facilitate the British Army in its task of re-occupation.

[initialled] J.P.W.

---

[1] James D. Craig, Assistant Secretary, British Representative's Office, Dublin (1939-45).

No. 226 NAI DFA Secretary's Files A3

> Letter from Colonel Liam Archer to Joseph P. Walshe (Dublin)
> (G2/X/0321) (Secret)
>
> DUBLIN, 15 July 1940

Dear Joe,
Re attached, the following message was sent by radio in clear at 4.42 a.m. on 3.7.'40:
'To
O.C. Cheroot.
O.C. Ballina.
The following message received from Duty Officer, D.O.D. at 03.25 hours. Garda H.Q. reported that the R.U.C. at Newry reported they had information that the invasion of Éire was to take place tonight or early this morning. Invasion likely to take place from the air with a probable attack on the North.
Orderly Officer
Mona'.

'Cheroot' is a code address for 'Finner Camp'[1] and 'Mona' is a code address for Command Headquarters in Athlone.

It is apparent that the above message is that which was intercepted by the British Government station, and that the complete message was not intercepted.

This is understandable as the radius of action of the Athlone station would not be sufficient to give good reception in England. You will note that the portion of our message which stated the origin of our information is omitted from the message sent to you.

I am enquiring into the cipher which followed this message.

There is one important discrepancy, and that is that the British message was intercepted at 5.30 a.m., whilst the original was sent at 4.42 a.m. It would be as well to ask on what frequency was the message intercepted, because the possibility exists it may have been relayed by some illicit station.

Yours sincerely,
[signed] L. ARCHER

No. 227 UCDA P150/2571

> Letter from Joseph P. Walshe to Eamon de Valera (Dublin)
> (Most Secret) (Copy No. 1)
>
> DUBLIN, 15 July 1940

Interview with Sir John Maffey, 4.30 p.m., Monday, July 15th, 1940

The British Representative called to see me at 4.30 (as arranged at his request) last evening. He was accompanied by Mr. Price,[2] his Military Adviser. The latter remained only five minutes while Maffey was talking on his first point.

The following is a brief summary of the conversation:-
1. I have already informed you about the suggested visit of Harrison.

---

[1] Irish Defence Forces camp on the shores of Donegal Bay near Ballyshannon.
[2] Major M.H. Pryce, Military Attaché, British Representative's Office, Dublin (1940-2).

2. I spoke at length to Maffey about the anti-Irish propaganda in the British Press up to Wednesday of last week, and its continuance in the American Press in the form of despatches or radio broadcasts from London. I referred in particular to the Press Association message about a supposed military pact between us, and to the pernicious messages from John Steele and Ludwig Lore. Maffey was at first inclined to repeat the arguments with which British Ministers reply to the High Commissioner when he protests against anti-Irish articles in the British press, but, in the end, he admitted that the British Ministry of Information must have been doing things without consulting the Dominions Office. When I referred to a paragraph in an official analysis of foreign broadcasts, which he himself had already read, he further admitted that the stupidity of some people in the Ministry of Information was bad enough to lead them into doing propaganda in America which any ordinary intelligent person would regard as being very much of the boomerang type.

3. I then expressed my great regret at the discovery we had recently made relating to a highly placed officer in the 53rd Division, and I emphasised that such an incident was bound, like the activities of the Ministry for Information, to provoke the deepest suspicion between the two peoples. I reminded him of the assurance he had so frequently given me that he was master of the situation on the British side as far as the channel of communication between the two countries was concerned. He seemed to be genuinely horrified at the espionage episode, and he did not express any desire for the early release of the officer concerned. It may be significant that Maffey asked me not to tell his military aides about this matter.

4. I then went on to speak of Tegart's[1] visits. I told him once more of the expressions he had been known to use and of his efforts to persuade 'deputies' of the folly of our neutrality. I said that the frequency of Tegart's visits, the extreme facility with which he was allowed to pass to and fro (in contrast to the great difficulties experienced by other travellers the legitimacy of whose business was more apparent), and the persistence with which he adhered to a course in which he, as an individual, could have only a passing interest, were giving grounds for the suspicion that he was being used by the Ministry of Information. I then told Maffey that such efforts on the part of Tegart or any other 'agent', if continued, would render his position here as the Official Representative of Great Britain quite impossible. Certain people, not members of the Government, were already beginning to suspect a serious intention on the part of his Government to interfere in our internal affairs. I knew perfectly well that he, Maffey, knew our history well enough to realise that such methods were foredoomed to failure. And I did not merely mean that the efforts themselves would be unsuccessful; the very fact of their being made would render fruitless all the splendid work he had done to establish the relations between the two countries on a basis of real friendship and understanding. At this, Maffey turned to me quite earnestly and said that he was in a real difficulty about these 'agents'. He would be very grateful to me if I instructed Dulanty to go to Caldecote and tell him not to

---

[1] Sir Charles Tegart was a native of Derry, educated at Trinity College Dublin, and a prominent senior member of the Indian police service (1901-36); served on the Council of India (1931-37); organised the Palestine Police Service (1937). On retirement he worked in Ireland for British intelligence, returning with stories of U-boat incursions and IRA preparations for a German invasion.

send Tegart or any other 'agent' here in future, that they were doing nothing but harm, etc. He begged me not to mention his name in this connection, as he felt his position would not allow him to object to such missions. I was naturally amazed at this sudden complete avowal of the truth. It quite clearly arose from his conviction, however belated, that a very grave error of judgment had been made.

[signed] J.P. WALSHE

No. 228 NAI DFA Secretary's Files P2

> Code telegram from the Department of External Affairs
> to Robert Brennan (Washington)
> (No. 92) (Personal) (Most Secret) (Copy)
>
> DUBLIN, 16 July 1940

Your telegram 124.[1] For your information and background. There is no pact. For a long time, as you will have seen from the Taoiseach's statements in the Dáil, it has been understood that, if we were attacked in overwhelming force by an enemy of Britain we would, if necessary, accept her aid. In recent months talks have taken place between officials about this possibility. We adopted the attitude that, if there was a Germany invasion, we would defend our neutrality, and any entry of British troops without an express invitation would be regarded as a counter invasion. British gave explicit assurance that they would not come unless and until invited. That was the comprehensive position until the recent offer to establish a committee of representatives of our Government and that of Northern Ireland to consider with Britain the future constitution of a United Ireland.[2]

In return for this promise, we were at once to go into the war with Britain. Taoiseach's answer was that we wanted the whole of Ireland as an independent neutral united country whose Parliament could come to any decisions it liked about the defence of the country. Since the refusal, British propaganda in Britain up to last Wednesday, and still apparently in America has been directed to forcing us to accept the presence of British military now.

The Government believe that the only safeguard of our ultimate independence is to keep our neutrality, even if a German invasion were certain. A British invasion is still a possibility. John Steele is closely in touch with Ministry for Information and his statement was almost certainly inspired.

You must, therefore, continue your efforts with Senators. Further friendly pressure on British is essential. Friendly pressure on German Embassy also essential.

Saturday's 'London Times' leader goes back on former affirmations about our danger and says our geographical situation altogether different from that of other neutral countries invaded and British aid was immediately available. It expresses disappointment at our attitude.

---

[1] Not printed.
[2] See No. 208.

Documents on Irish Foreign Policy, Volume VI, 1939–1941

No. 229 NAI DFA 2006/39

Letter from Joseph P. Walshe to John W. Dulanty (London)
(Secret)

DUBLIN, 17 July 1940

Dear High Commissioner,
You should, immediately on receipt of this instruction, make representations to Lord Caldecote textually as follows:-
'Certain persons have of late made rather frequent visits to Ireland. These visits did not seem to be connected with any normal business transaction which might explain their frequency. On the other hand, well founded rumours have reached the Government that these persons have been talking to Deputies and other Irish citizens in a manner likely to be detrimental to the interests and general well-being of the Irish State. The visits have given the definite impression that there was interference in the internal affairs of our country. The fact that these persons had been invariably in London immediately before the visits to Dublin has given rise to the suspicion that they were acting with, or on behalf of, some British political group.

The Irish Government would be very glad to obtain the help of the Secretary of State for Dominion Affairs in putting an end to further visits of this character, whoever the persons concerned may be. The Government were particularly perturbed that the visits of the persons whose activities have been noted coincided with a campaign in the Press of Great Britain and in a section of the American Press directed against the policy of the Irish Government, which is based on the fundamental and universal desire of the Irish people. The Minister for External Affairs would be very grateful to the Secretary of State for Dominion Affairs for his aid in eliminating, as far as his resources enable him to do so, activities which cannot but end in a serious breach of the real friendship and goodwill which exists between our two peoples. The Secretary of State will realise as strongly as the Irish Government how quickly the excellent work of the British Representative in Ireland could be brought to nought by well-meaning busybodies who are ignorant both of the history of Ireland and of the abiding determination of its people to work out their own destiny.'

Yours sincerely,
[signed] J.P. WALSHE

No. 230 NAI DFA Secretary's Files P3

Memorandum by Joseph P. Walshe (Dublin)
(Most Secret)

DUBLIN, 18 July 1940

Dr. Hempel called to see me today, and remained for over two and a half hours. The main object of his visit was to emphasise Germany's intention not to violate our neutrality, and, above all, not to invade Ireland. He said that, at the time he last saw the Taoiseach, he had not been free to speak as clearly as he was now. He could now speak quite definitely and reaffirm in the strongest way the attitude just described. He felt, during his talk with the Taoiseach, that there was still in the Taoiseach's mind an element of suspicion with regard to Germany's intentions. He was most anxious at the time of the conversation to dissipate these suspicions.

I suggested to Dr. Hempel that it was natural that the Taoiseach should still be suspicious at the time of the conversation to which he referred, as he (Dr. Hempel) had said that, notwithstanding his conviction that there would be no attack on our neutrality, he could not say so openly and explicitly for strategic reasons. I was very glad that he had given us the new assurances on 6th July,[1] and again today, which contained no reservations whatever. He must always remember that the Held case gave the very gravest occasion for suspecting Germany's intentions about this country.

Dr. Hempel's reaction to my mention of the Held case was what it always has been – that, whatever the truth may have been, it was an extremely unfortunate incident for the relations between the two countries. But, whatever about the past and whatever suspicions had been created, he was now able to affirm without reservations (on account of the definiteness of his last instructions) that our neutrality would continue to be respected by Germany so long as we did not tolerate any violation of it by the other belligerent. Incidentally, he would like to remind me that there was a great deal of anti-Irish propaganda in the British Press, and in that section of the Press in America which was controlled by Britain; whilst in Germany, neither on the radio nor in the Press, was there anything but a friendly attitude towards this country. It was unfortunate that a certain number of people who were known to be friendly to Germany had been imprisoned in this country.

I replied to this last remark that the people he referred to were not in prison because they were friends of Germany, but because – even before the war began – they had been plotting to overthrow the existing State set up by the majority of the Irish people. It was, of course, natural that any group plotting to overthrow the State would be ready to seek the help of an external Power, and, in putting these men in prison, the Government was only carrying out its primary duty of defending the State which was the only bulwark between the people and chaos. Dr. Hempel would realise that there was no country in which the defence of the fabric of the State against internal enemies was so well understood as in Germany.

Dr. Hempel left expressing the hope that nothing would occur on the German or the Irish side in future which would interfere with our good relations, and he urged me to keep our Chargé d'Affaires in Berlin[2] as fully informed as possible of the Government's firmness in the matter of neutrality.

[initialled] J.P.W.

---

[1] See No. 216.
[2] William Warnock.

Documents on Irish Foreign Policy, Volume VI, 1939–1941

No. 231 NAI DFA Secretary's Files P3

> Code telegram from William Warnock (via Geneva)
> to the Department of External Affairs (Dublin)
> (No. 46) (Personal)
>
> BERLIN, 20 July 1940

My telegram 42.[1] Under Secretary of State states German Minister at Dublin has been instructed to convey German attitude to you.[2] He informs me that Germany wishes that we maintain our strict neutrality and that we may count with absolute certainty on no violation by Germany though increased naval operations may unavoidably affect us adversely.

No. 232 NAI DFA Secretary's Files P3

> Code telegram from the Department of External Affairs (via Geneva)
> to William Warnock (Berlin)
> (No. 47) (No. 74) (Personal) (Copy)
>
> DUBLIN, 20 July 1940

Your 46.[3] Position now regarded as quite satisfactory. Fears of German invasion no longer seriously entertained. Inform Woermann and thank him for communication. Continue to emphasise determination to remain neutral, taking the line that we regard our neutrality not as bargaining factor but as essential expression of our national independence.

Current reports in American Press alleging Anglo-Irish defence agreement and inciting Britain to show Oran spirit in dealings with us are part of campaign referred to in my 61.[4] Recent reinforcement of British troops in Six Counties is regarded here as due to British fear of German invasion of Ireland. British attack now considered unlikely but will be strongly resisted if made.

My 70.[5] Thank Woermann for action in Smith case.

No. 233 NAI DFA Secretary's Files 12/1

> Code telegram from the Department of External Affairs
> to Michael MacWhite (Rome)
> (No. 32) (Personal) (Copy)
>
> DUBLIN, 20 July 1940

Please wire report on present attitude of Vatican towards totalitarian States and Pétain as shown in Osservatore Romano, Vatican broadcasts and comment in Vatican circles.

---

[1] Not printed.
[2] See No. 230.
[3] See No. 231.
[4] See No. 212.
[5] Not printed.

No. 234 NAI DFA Secretary's Files P2

> Code telegram from Joseph Walshe to Robert Brennan (Washington)
> (No. 97) (Personal) (Most Secret) (Copy)
>
> DUBLIN, 21 July 1940

Footnote to your reply in 'Chicago News' shows that something further must be done to prevent papers of such standing publishing lying reports against us. Kirkpatrick[1] and Cowles[2] reported to be in this country again. Could you ask friends in New York, Chicago and San Francisco to form small strong committees to watch Press and Radio which are apparently so bad that Ministry of Information officials London are advising their Government that America is ready to accept British reoccupation of Ireland. They feel fortified by statements on radio of Major Elliott and Lynton Wells of C.B.S., as well as John Steele and Vincent Sheehan.[3] (Foregoing information is, of course, strictly confidential). Could you inspire all Irish papers to launch campaign against pro-British American journalists who are misleading American public about Ireland and preparing opinion for a British invasion of Ireland. Suggest as feature comparison of 'London Times' article my telegram 94,[4] with recent despatches of Cowles, Kirkpatrick and company.

You should try to get our neutrality explained in Irish and friendly American Press as follows.

'Neutrality is of the very essence of Irish independence. It is based on the fundamental and universal will of our people, so much so that no Government could depart from it without at once being overthrown. It was not adopted as a bargaining factor but as the fullest expression of our independence in time of war. We are determined to defend it against all invaders to the bitter end. The hostile attitude of certain Americans to Ireland is completely opposed to American statements about small nations and self determination. Ireland is fully alive to her real position in the Europe of today. The Government is in a better position than any Americans to decide the policy which is most likely to save the independence of the nation and the lives of the people from destruction. By her seven hundred years of resistance to the invasion of a Great Power, she has done more than any other nation to keep alive in the world the principles of liberty and justice on which the American Republic was founded. Her neutrality is a manifestation of her continued resolution to save the remnant of our race from destruction.'

Please let us know what, if any, defence is being made of our position by Irish Americans.

---

[1] Possibly Sir Ivone Kirkpatrick (1897-1964), British diplomat; Director, Foreign Division, British Ministry of Information (1940-1); later served as Permanent Under-Secretary at the Foreign Office (1953-7).

[2] Possibly a reference to United States newspaper publisher Gardner Cowles Sr (1861-1946) or, more likely, to his son Gardner 'Mike' Cowles Jr (1903-85), also a newspaper publisher and editor.

[3] Vincent Sheehan, war correspondent of the *Herald Tribune*, made famous through his reporting during the Spanish Civil War and on whose 1935 memoir *Personal History* Alfred Hitchcock's 1940 film 'Foreign Correspondent' was based.

[4] Not printed.

No. 235 NAI DFA Secretary's Files P4

> Code telegram from Joseph P. Walshe to John J. Hearne (Ottawa)
> (No. 46) (Personal) (Most Secret) (Copy)
>
> DUBLIN, 21 July 1940

Your despatch 14/56 of 27th June.[1] Continue to emphasise strongly our determination to remain neutral, taking line that we regard our neutrality not as a bargaining factor, or as a cloak to be taken off if there is some advantage to be gained by so doing, but as an essential expression of our national independence.

For your information, we have sound evidence for regarding German invasion as very improbable. Report referred to in your 39[2] is part of campaign mentioned in my 41[3] which still continues and is doing considerable harm to relations between the two countries.

Many American syndicated Press reports with Dublin date lines are not sent from Dublin and are grossly misleading. Recent reinforcement of British troops in Six Counties probably due to British fear of German invasion of Ireland. British attack on us is considered unlikely here, but will be strenuously resisted if made.

You should see and be guided by Taoiseach's interview published in 'New York Times' of 6th July.[4] Speeches of Opposition leaders not reliable guide.

Public opinion here accepts probability of British defeat.

No. 236 NAI DFA Paris Embassy 12/1

> Code telegram from Joseph P. Walshe to Seán Murphy (Vichy)
> (No. 98) (Personal) (Copy)
>
> DUBLIN, 22 July 1940

Your 73[5] and 85.[6] You should keep in close touch with Nuncio who is more likely to know real views of French Right than other diplomats. From all our sources of information, belief is general, even in countries friendly to England such as America and Portugal, that Britain has lost the war and at the very most could only achieve a stalemate which might leave her part of her Empire, but it is recognised everywhere that she has no hope of regaining her influence in Europe.

We feel the greatest sympathy with France in her difficulties and have so informed French Minister. The sympathy of the whole country is with Pétain. You should adopt same attitude towards Leroux and other officials. It is felt here that our destiny henceforth will be cast with that of the Continental Catholic nations. At this present stage it is to be expected that France should have internal difficulties. The results of the Front Populaire regime which destroyed France cannot disappear

---

[1] Not printed.
[2] Not printed.
[3] Not printed.
[4] On 5 July 1940 de Valera told Harold Denny of the *New York Times* that 'come what may, Éire is determined to preserve her neutrality and stay out of the war if humanly possible'. If invaded, Ireland would resist 'and it does not matter what nation invades her'. De Valera explained that letting in one country would provoke the other, and said that Ireland's only hope was to maintain its 'strict neutrality'.
[5] See No. 224.
[6] Not printed.

overnight. We want to be kept informed as exactly as possible of every development. Please always give sources of your information. As you are no doubt aware, Vatican shows greatest sympathy towards new regime in France.

No. 237 NAI DFA Secretary's Files P2

> *Code telegram from Robert Brennan to the Department of External Affairs (Dublin)*
> *(No. 142) (Personal) (Most Secret) (Copy)*
>
> WASHINGTON, 23 July 1940

Your telegram 97.[1] Shall carry out instructions but please realise atmosphere: outside of few informed Irish, everyone here from highest administration to man in the street considers that we are foolish not to invite British aid and that England shows great forbearance in not securing weak flank by reoccupation: all arguments to contrary such as you use received with shrug. Even well-wishers like Senator O'Mahoney[2] take this view: this derives not so much from propaganda as from fear that Britain will collapse and Fleet pass to Germany thereby creating immediate vital threat to America.

No. 238 NAI DFA Secretary's Files P12/14/1

> *Confidential report from John W. Dulanty to Joseph P. Walshe (Dublin)*
> *(No. 47) (Secret)*
>
> LONDON, 23 July 1940

I asked to see Lord Caldecote today so that I might inform him of my conversation last Saturday afternoon with Lord Woolton.[3] Before I began, however, Lord Caldecote, who is normally imperturbable, expressed himself strongly on the representations I had made to Lord Woolton. He read parts of the letter which that gentleman had written to the Chancellor of the Exchequer,[4] quoting from it the actual words I had used about the suspicions entertained in Ireland as to British War policy in relation to us. Lord Caldecote implored me not to talk like this. It did no good to our case and it did not help him in his advocacy on our behalf. To suggest that they had been deliberately and of set purpose dilatory on the trade negotiations was ludicrous. There were many Departments to be consulted, they were housed up and down the provinces, they were all overworked, and it was not reasonable to expect that decisions on complicated questions could be reached today, when they were living from crisis to crisis, as quickly as in normal times.

I repeated the case I had made to Lord Woolton and said no fair-minded man could resist the conclusion that all these weeks and weeks of delay justified our doubts and misgivings. For my part I found the explanations offered most unconvincing.

He went on to say that they were no more responsible for the recent newspaper articles than we were. On the contrary it was a matter of annoyance to them. We knew that both he and Mr. MacDonald had raised the question at the War Cabinet.

---

[1] See No. 234.
[2] Joseph C. O'Mahoney (1884-1962), Democratic Senator for Wyoming (1934-53, 1954-61).
[3] Frederick James Marquis, 1st Earl of Woolton (1883-1964), British Minister for Food (1940-43); appointed by Chamberlain and retained by Churchill.
[4] Sir Kingsley Wood (1881-1943), Chancellor of the Exchequer (1940-3).

We must have seen how the Minister of Information had tried without the least success to tighten the censorship. As a result of his representations Mr. Duff Cooper had personally seen the Lobby correspondents and the Chief Press Censor had seen the other newspaper men and asked them to 'let-up' on the question of Ireland.

It was distressing to him to find these suspicions, which were entirely groundless, still prevailing. What could they do to allay these suspicions, what could they do to remove them?

I suggested they could do two things – they could reach an immediate decision on the proposed Trade Agreement, and they could give us further help about munitions. He said he would make it his business to see that something definite was done one way or the other on the trade question. About munitions, he reminded me that he had already stated that he was pressing the War Office, which pressure he would continue to exercise.

I asked when he could give me something definite on the munitions question. His reply was 'Give me forty-eight hours'.

Lord Caldecote was then called away to the War Cabinet.

[signed] J.W. DULANTY

No. 239 NAI DFA 2006/39

Draft of a confidential report from John W. Dulanty to Joseph P. Walshe (Dublin)[1]
(Copy)

LONDON, 23 July 1940

You will recall that when I was in Dublin last month I reported that on the 21st June Lord Caldecote had told me that there was no intention on the part of the British Government to land troops in Éire without an invitation from the Irish Government.

Subsequently to that conversation a widespread campaign had been sustained in the London and Provincial newspapers, articles had appeared in a section of the American press and talks had been broadcast from the United Kingdom to America – all directed against the policy of the Irish Government and suggesting or implying that the time had come for the British Government to take steps to occupy our territory.

When at my request Lord Caldecote saw me today I referred again to the above-mentioned campaign and said an inevitable consequence had been a deterioration in the general attitude of the Irish people. Clearly these doubts and misgivings were not calculated to promote the understanding between the two countries which my Government desired.

Lord Caldecote said he had no hesitation in giving an assurance that there was no intention in the mind of the British Government to take any military or naval action in our territory unless and until they were formally asked to do so by the Irish Government. Mr. de Valera would, however, understand that in a War

---

[1] It is not clear that this document was sent to Dublin. It has been included here because it provides a succinct summary of some of the key points in British-Irish relations over the previous months. For the origins and purpose of this document see No. 243.

future such as that which confronted them, so full of uncertainties and wholly incalculable factors, it would not be possible for the British Government to give today a guarantee that in no circumstances would they refrain from entering Éire uninvitedly.

But it was a statement of solid fact, he continued, to say as he had said before that it was absolutely no part of their policy to go into Éire unless the Irish Government invited them.

No. 240 NAI DFA 2006/39

Confidential report from John W. Dulanty to Joseph P. Walshe (Dublin)
(No. 48) (Secret) (Copy)

LONDON, 24 July 1940

After leaving Lord Caldecote yesterday I spoke to Sir Eric Machtig and expressed surprise that the action of the British Government in mining the Irish Sea could have been taken without prior consultation with the Irish Government. He said the first intimation the Dominions Office received from the Admiralty was yesterday afternoon when the order to lay the mines had already been given.

He spoke to me on much the same lines as did Lord Caldecote about my conversation on Saturday last with Lord Woolton. He urged that the delay in reaching a Trade Agreement had noting sinister about it and enlarged on the difficulty of paying us a higher price for butter than they could pay Australia or New Zealand.

I pointed out that the discussion on that phase of the question had been concluded weeks ago as was shown by their own alternative proposal in respect of help over our fertiliser imports. That proposal, he knew, we had found unacceptable and I had understood some time ago that they were investigating the question of an arrangement on cattle. Surely he could see that, making full allowance for any Departmental discussions, the delay in reaching a decision was altogether unjustifiable. He admitted the delay but did not agree that it was unjustifiable. The collapse of the French had altered the position considerably and if we had made the agreement on the lines originally intended it would look unreal in the light of the present War situation. Then there were the MacDonald conversations – if we had seen our way to accept their proposals obviously the British position on our trade matters would have been importantly different *which confirmed my personal suspicions mentioned some time back.*[1]

On the question of the supply of arms, Sir Eric Machtig emphasised that we did not appreciate the immense difficulties with which they were faced. The losses of munitions in France were staggering. As a matter to be treated with the greatest secrecy he could assure me that until quite recently only one Division of their troops in England had been equipped. Lord Caldecote had visited the New Zealand troops the previous day – a contingent of between 6,000 and 7,000 men – and the Commanding Office was complaining bitterly that not 25 per cent of them were anything like properly armed. The War Office view which the Dominions Office were resisting was that if a German attack on Ireland began it would be

---

[1] The portion of the sentence in italics was inserted by Dulanty by hand.

something really portentous and on such a scale that our own Irish forces, or even much bigger forces would be overcome in no time. When they, the War Office, were so short of rifles, anti-aircraft guns etc. couldn't we see what a battle it was to get anything out of them. Notwithstanding that, however, Lord Caldecote was continuously trying to get some further ammunitions for us.

No. 241 NAI DFA 2006/39

Confidential report from John W. Dulanty to Joseph P. Walshe (Dublin)
(No. 45) (Secret) (Copy)

LONDON, 25 July 1940

On the long outstanding question of the proposed comprehensive agreement to govern the trading relations between ourselves and the British, I have repeatedly pressed for a decision with the senior officials concerned, Mr. Lloyd, Assistant Secretary, Ministry of Food; Mr. Jenkins, Assistant Secretary, Ministry of Shipping, and Sir William Brown, Permanent Secretary of the Board of Trade; Sir Quintin Hill, Financial Secretary, Ministry of Food; Sir Henry French, Permanent Secretary, Ministry of Food; and Viscount Caldecote. The latter told me that he had written to Lord Woolton who had replied with assurances that there was no delay.

Getting no satisfaction I saw Lord Woolton at his Office on Saturday afternoon last. I represented to him the great dissatisfaction of my Government at the unjustifiable delay on the part of the British. It seemed open to the interpretation that the British knew we had no other market and they were therefore adopting tactics of dilatoriness, not to say discourtesy. If our supplies were of any importance to them this unexplained delay was the right way to dry up the sources of that supply. The drop in price was already operating against us in lambs and live pigs.

Lord Woolton laughed at my remark about discourtesy.

I told him there was soreness throughout our agricultural community and there was also an increasing deterioration in the feelings of our people towards Britain. There had been a sustained campaign in the British press against our neutrality, coinciding with an unfriendly attitude in a section of the American press and, in various broadcasts from London by American commentators, implying that the British should invade our shores. It was not to be wondered at if the doubt existed in Ireland that these simultaneous activities were merely fortuitous and in no way inspired. It would be far better to give a decision, even if it were a refusal to meet our difficulties, than for the British to pursue this policy of delay.

Lord Woolton said he was a businessman and not a politician. He was responsible to Parliament and the British people for buying food supplies on a business basis. He was not in favour of our Ministers crossing over to London at the end of April last because he felt that he was not in a position to assist them. If the market proved advantageous to us he was willing and ready to pay, but if in other commodities as for example butter the market was against us, he was sorry that he could not alter his position as a buyer. If he did he would have the High Commissioners of New Zealand and Australia pressing immediately for the same favourable consideration he had shown the Irish. If, for political considerations, the War Cabinet thought fit to arrange special terms for the Irish, he had no objection. He said that he had been impressed by what I had said and he would go to the Chancellor of the Exchequer and suggest that since he (Lord Woolton) could not depart from his 'market' attitude the Chancellor should consider making a grant to maintain supplies from Éire.

I said that it would be impossible at any time, but more particularly now for the Irish Government to accept what really amounted to a direct subsidy.

I had understood from discussions with other Departments that an arrangement with regard to cattle – which contained no competitive element – was a feasible plan. Lord Woolton did not agree but said he would look further into it.

No. 242 NAI DFA 226/43

Code telegram from Francis T. Cremins to the Department of External Affairs (Dublin) (No. 52) (Personal) (Copy)

GENEVA, 26 July 1940

Comment as follows made to me regarding telegram from Secretary General:

Resignation of complex history, finally the result of French instruction. They wish to remain in the League but desire Avenol to resign. The higher officials now number four, including Lester and three in charge of technical Departments. There was difference on policy recently between Avenol and senior colleagues. Latter wished to avoid political complication. Mr. Lester prefers to go but urged from many sides to remain. Probably eight technical officials going to U.S.A. soon. I suggest a reply acknowledging receipt and expressing regret at notification of resignation.

No. 243 NAI DFA Secretary's Files P5

Confidential report from John W. Dulanty to Joseph P. Walshe (Dublin) (No. 49) (Secret)

LONDON, 27 July 1940

As I have already informed you, in the conversations I have had with him during the past few weeks Lord Caldecote has emphatically repudiated any suggestion of an intention on the part of the British Government to invade our territory unless and until they had received a formal request for help from the Irish Government.[1]

In one of these conversations on the 21st June I told Lord Caldecote that I thought his statement was of such high importance that, in the interests of both Governments, it should be made publicly. He replied as I informed you already at the time that it was the fact and as far as he was concerned there was no reason why it should not be said, though he doubted whether it could, as yet, be said publicly.

On the 23rd July I told Lord Caldecote that on the occasion of a recent visit to Dublin I had informed my Government of his statement that no British entry into our territory was contemplated and I suggested that I should forward to Dublin a

---

[1] See No. 239.

note of what he had said to me, but in order to ensure complete accuracy of statement I would like to show him beforehand what I proposed to report. Lord Caldecote, after some discussion, said he would not mind looking at any draft I cared to show him.

Last evening I left with him the enclosed draft[1] but as he was overdue at another meeting I arranged to see him again this morning.

Today Lord Caldecote said that he fully accepted my account of our conversations: he had nothing to withdraw but he could not give his imprimatur to the draft without consulting his colleagues. What he had said represented his opinion but he could not say it was an authoritative statement of his Government. He believed we would fight the Germans if they attacked us and he believed that we would ask the British for assistance if we needed it but he did not think it advisable to go to the Cabinet to get their consent to his approving the enclosed draft. He thought the wisest course was to let matters rest as they were at the moment. Our affairs, he thought, were going fairly satisfactorily – which remark had reference I think to his efforts to secure a trade agreement and to obtain further supplies of munitions. My impression is that Lord Caldecote is convinced that the British Government have no idea of going into Éire without invitation. He feels that it would at present be better not to go to the British Cabinet on the question. Reading between the lines I suspect that he is apprehensive that a request to the Cabinet at this point of time might evoke difficulties with some of the die-hard school which he wishes to avoid.

[signed] J.W. DULANTY

No. 244 NAI DFA Paris Embassy 12/1

Code telegram from Seán Murphy to Joseph P. Walshe (Dublin)
(No. 104) (Personal) (Copy)

VICHY, 28 July 1940

Paid courtesy visit to Foreign Minister yesterday evening. I found him friendly. I took the opportunity of expressing to him the sentiments mentioned in your telegram 98.[2] He said that he never doubted Ireland's sympathy and was very grateful for my message which he would not fail to give to the Marshal who would much appreciate it. He asked me whether Ireland remains neutral and I replied that was the intention of the Government and unanimous wish of the whole people. I asked whether he knew how the war was going between England and Germany. He replied that he knew there were unofficial conversations taking place between England and Germany with a view to settlement. The Germans would have nothing to do with Churchill or the British Government, although he believed that some members of the Government were anxious for a settlement. I then asked him if he had hopes of the Government's return to Paris in the near future. He said that unfortunately they were having great difficulty on this matter. The Germans, in view of the continuance of the war with England, were being difficult. He hoped they would succeed in returning to Paris soon as Government away from Paris was almost impossible. He himself would be prepared to put up with almost any

[1] See No. 239.
[2] See No. 236.

inconvenience if they could get back to Paris. When I was leaving him he said that he would always be pleased to see me and to give me information regarding the situation in France.

The newspapers today state that all railway and postal communication between occupied and non-occupied territory is temporarily suspended.

No. 245 NAI DFA Secretary's Files A2

> *Letter from Joseph P. Walshe to Eamon de Valera (Dublin)*
> *(Most Secret)*
>
> DUBLIN, 29 July 1940

I asked Sir John Maffey to come to me at 12 o'clock today for the purpose of conveying your decision to him concerning the condition which was attached to the delivery of the new military equipment. I told him that you had examined the suggestion that a certain number of men should come over with the anti-aircraft guns, and that it could not be accepted. We had always expected to be able to secure a greater number of this type of gun as he knew from the orders we had placed with his Government, and the Army had in consequence trained several crews. At the present moment, we had crews sufficient to man three times the number of guns the British were at present ready to give us. I told him that you were grateful for the efforts he had made to secure the fulfilment of this part of our order, and you were sorry that a condition was attached which made it impossible for you to take delivery. The refusal on our part should not be taken in any way as an indication that the work he had done in connection with our general orders for equipment was not fully appreciated.

Sir John Maffey said that he was very sorry that you had persisted so much in regarding the 'offer' as a condition. I reminded him that, in talking to me the other day from his home, he had said most emphatically that the acceptance of the crews was a condition *sine qua non*. He replied that his people were only anxious to be helpful, and they felt that, in the course of the weeks during which these crews would be with us, they could, if an emergency arose, man the guns and the Bren carriers[1] for us. It was very regrettable, Sir John Maffey said, that we could not honestly cooperate in matters like this. Of course, he understood that there were political considerations, and he believed that they were a more important ground for our refusal. I acknowledged that there were serious political considerations connected with our neutrality, and he was already aware what serious misconstructions the British Press had shown itself capable of in matters relating to our neutrality.

I told Sir John Maffey that the Bren gun carriers would not present any difficulty to our Army. The competent officers concerned did not see how they would be so very different from other fighting vehicles. However, in this matter, while the same objection held in regard to a crew or crews, we were ready to accept the services of one or two men in a civilian capacity if the British technicians thought it really necessary.

Sir John Maffey said he would report immediately to his people, and he hoped that, notwithstanding our attitude which, after all, he personally understood, he

---

[1] A fast, lightly armed vehicle used to carry infantry, specifically those armed with the Bren light machine gun.

would succeed in getting the War Office to fulfil the order.

In the course of this conversation, Sir John Maffey mentioned that the American Minister had remarked to him how wrong our ideas were on the American Press. Mr. Gray had said that we had some ridiculous idea that a part of their Press was British-inspired because it took an anti-Irish line. I replied that Mr. Gray was wrong in thinking that we thought the Press in question was British-inspired because anti-Irish. We knew it from the fact that the anti-Irish messages appearing in a section of the American Press came from London and we knew that all messages going out from London were censored in the Ministry of Information. Our opinion, therefore, was not formed on some pet conception of British perfidy, but on sound fact. And, as I had already said on several occasions, we were aware that the Ministry of Information contained an element in it which did not conceal very anti-Irish prejudices.

[initialled] J.P.W. 30/7/40

Sir John Maffey informed me today that the Supplies were being given unconditionally. He saw the Taoiseach and informed him in a similar sense.[1]

[initialled] J.P.W. 31/7/40 Wednesday

No. 246 NAI DFA Madrid Embassy CON 4/7/22 No. 4

Confidential report from Leopold H. Kerney to Joseph P. Walshe (Dublin)
(M. 10/11) (Confidential)

MADRID, 29 July 1940

I paid my last visit to Ryan on Saturday evening 12th July, and handed him his sister's letter sent by you on 18th June as well as two parcels of books.

Knowing what was in the wind, I wished to have a serious talk with him on matters which we had not previously breached, and which it had always been my intention to discuss with him whenever he should be relieved of his shackles; as I could no longer count on giving him the hospitality of the Legation, I had to make this special visit.

It was of course understood all along that your efforts and mine to secure his liberty were not associated with any desire to impose conditions of any kind on him, but it was desirable that I should make it clear to him that our genuine concern for him as an Irish prisoner in a foreign land did not relieve us of responsibility of taking certain precautions, after his liberty had been secured, so that no harm might result from any failure on our part to observe his future movements and associations.

And so our conversation, in the usual frank and friendly manner, concerned itself with whips, scorpions &c. I pointed out to him all the dangers of the present situation, as I saw it, and, whilst agreeing with him that morally there could be no objection to using certain remedies, I got him to agree with me that sometimes a remedy can be more annihilating than the disease. He said that he had no intention of relying on information which might be given to him from other than Irish sources, and that he was really in the dark at the moment; he asked me where were

---

[1] Handwritten insertion by Walshe.

Seán MacBride[1] and Moss Twomey,[2] but I knew nothing about them; he told me that news had reached him that Seán Russell[3] had left the U.S.A. for Germany in May, and that the I.R.A. had tried to prevent his journey thither, that Russell had been expelled in 1937 from the I.R.A., and that he himself (Ryan) had previously left that organisation, although this did not mean that he would keep aloof from his former friends. I warned him against allowing himself to be drawn into any action likely to lead to the shedding of blood in Ireland; I told him that I knew he would allow himself to be shot before doing anything dishonourable, but, as mistaken judgment on his part might have deplorable consequences, he should think twice before doing anything; I reminded him how he had been utterly wrong in his judgment of the Spanish situation, and, that if the side for which he fought had won, that victory would have gone far towards making the realisation of his present hopes impossible.

He said that, if he got to Ireland, he would go to thank Mr. de Valera for all that had been done on his behalf, but that, having done so, he would retain his right to oppose the policy of the Government; I told him that nobody would object to that attitude, but that it might be my duty to suggest that his movements in Ireland should be watched so that any opposition of a violent nature could be countered.

Ryan was suspicious of the Government's attitude in the present upheaval and was inclined to think that there might be certain secret commitments; I could only assure him that, so far as I was aware, there was no justification for these suspicions, that I believed we would defend our neutrality at all costs, against the first intruder certainly, and quite possibly against the second as well; any Irishman helping one or the other would re-kindle civil war in Ireland.

When we finished our conversations, I told Ryan, in the same friendly spirit, that, apart from the satisfaction of succeeding in an almost impossible task, I had many selfish reasons for being glad to get rid of him, as he had taken up a great deal of my time, given me a lot of worry and caused me no little expense, whilst the almost impassable road from Burgos to the prison had certainly shortened the life of my car. I gave him one final assurance and that was that I would see to it that the final chapter was not going to be – 'Shot whilst attempting to escape', or, at least, that, in such an unlikely event, it would not be a case of 'Spurles versenkt'.[4] I accomplished that promise, as you know, at a cost of 1,500 pesetas (petrol is 5 pesetas per litre) of which amount I would like to claim a refund whenever circumstances permit.

On 17th July, believing Ryan to be still in prison, I sent six tins of condensed milk, using a certain address in Burgos for the purpose, and the same day I wrote a line of encouragement, though I was becoming concerned myself, as I was completely in the dark and new complications seemed to have arisen.

On 24th July, I sent him a prepaid wire asking him to let me know whether he needed 150 or only 100 pesetas at the end of the month, and also to send me by letter a list of necessary foodstuffs; the wire served its purpose; I got no reply.

---

[1] Seán MacBride (1904-88), Chief-of-Staff of the IRA (1936), founded Clann na Poblachta (1946), Minister for External Affairs (1948-51); practised at the Irish Bar during the Second World War, where he defended a number of IRA members brought before the courts.
[2] Maurice Twomey (1887-1978), Chief-of-Staff of the IRA (1927-36); Adjutant General, IRA (1938-9).
[3] Seán Russell (1893-1940), Chief of Staff of the IRA (1938-9).
[4] Literally 'sunk without trace'.

I am of opinion that it would be useless for me to attempt to obtain any more information about Ryan through official channels, and I do not expect to hear anything from any other source, at least for weeks to come.

No. 247 NAI DFA Secretary's Files P48A

Letter from Joseph P. Walshe to David Gray (Dublin)
(Copy)

DUBLIN, 31 July 1940

Dear David,
Thanks very much for your very helpful letter of July 25th ...

I read your memorandum with great interest indeed. Perhaps it would be better to postpone any discussion of it until we meet next week. I should, however, like to say this much. There's not any question of American newspapers taking orders from any Government or in any way changing their attitude towards the world situation. We only ask those of them who have shown themselves particularly hostile to Ireland – such as the 'San Francisco Chronicle' – to remember that neutrality is of the very essence of Irish independence at this stage of our history. And, if we do not act as certain American papers wish us to act, it is not through any sense of perversity or any failure to see where our interests lie. It is simply because of our conviction, founded on a profound knowledge of our own people, that the action in question would put an end for ever to the existence of an ordered Irish State. It does happen to be the case, almost by a miracle of history, that our neutrality, though for very different reasons, suits both sides in the present conflict. The extent to which we blame the British for matter appearing in American papers is limited by our precise knowledge as to the source and to the failure of the Ministry of Information to keep a guiding hand on those journalists in London whose superficial knowledge of international affairs leads them into the grossest errors concerning this country. John Steele's parallel between Ireland and Long Island is a perfect example of 'intelligent journalism'. However, we can talk plenty next week.

Yours sincerely,
J.P. WALSHE

No. 248 NAI DFA 219/3

Extract from a confidential report from Robert Brennan to Joseph P. Walshe
(Dublin)
(219/3)

WASHINGTON, 1 August 1940

The delay in Hitler's projected invasion of England is raising hopes here that the British will be able to withstand the shock and may not be defeated after all. The consequence, as Anne O'Hare McCormick[1] points out in her article in the New York Times of July 29th, is a decided step up in the desire to help the British in every possible way. Further, it encourages the idea that the war may be a long one

---

[1] Anne O'Hare McCormick (1889-1954), English born American journalist who worked as a foreign affairs correspondent for the *New York Times*; the first woman to win a Pulitzer prize (1937).

and, therefore, that American aid in output of planes and munitions may contribute to the ultimate defeat of Germany. The cutting of the U.S. supplies of oil and scrap metal, though primarily aimed at Japan, is also considered a help to England by depriving Germany of supplies through Spain.

The extension of the British blockade to include Spain and Portugal, though it adversely affects American trade interests, was received here not merely with equanimity but almost with applause.
[matter omitted]

No. 249 NAI DFA Secretary's Files A3

Department of External Affairs memorandum of a meeting between Eamon de Valera, Sir John Maffey and General Harrison

DUBLIN, 2 August 1940

The Taoiseach received Sir John Maffey and General Harrison (late Governor of the Channel Islands) at 4 o'c. today.

After a long general chat General Harrison explained his role. If ever their help was required and asked for it would be necessary to have somebody who knew our country and the people with whom their Army might have to work. He had been appointed as Chief Liaison Officer. There were many matters which would in any emergency call for action by him. We might want artillery support, or tank support, at this point or that. The British might want transport or certain supplies. Or it might be a question of commandeering for billeting etc. In any event a liaison staff of a dozen or so (a few officers, a few clerks and a few signallers) would be of the greatest help in smoothing out difficulties and preventing confusion. General Harrison would also be responsible for suggesting that in this case the Irish officer, in another the British officer, should take command.

The Taoiseach said that he would see the General again with the Minister for the Co-ordination of Defensive Measures and the Minister for Defence.[1]

The general line taken by General Harrison might apply to the easy going wars of the Indian frontier.

In reply to a question whether an attack by Germany was more likely in the North General Harrison emphatically agreed, though he thought Donegal was a good point from which to attack the Six Counties. He thought furthermore that an effective attack on Ireland could not be made unless and until the British fleet had been put out of action.

---

[1] See No. 252.

No. 250 NAI DFA Secretary's Files P3

> Code telegram from the Department of External Affairs (through Geneva)
> to William Warnock (Berlin)
> (No. 61) (Personal) (No. 93) (Personal) (Copy)
>
> DUBLIN, 2 August 1940

Please address a note in following terms to Foreign Office:
Begins.
'1. At 3.45 p.m. Irish Summer Time, on the 1st August, the Irish-registered vessel S.S. 'Kerry Head' was attacked by an aircraft bearing German markings at a point 1½ miles south of Sovereign Island at the entrance to Oyster Haven, Co. Cork. The vessel was on a journey from Swansea to Limerick with a cargo of coal. The S.S. 'Kerry Head', which is owned and managed by Mr. William Talbot Herriott of Limerick and is registered at the port of Tralee, was flying the Irish colours and had the Irish flag painted conspicuously on both sides of her bridge.
2. The aircraft directed several bombs against the S.S. 'Kerry Head', one of which fell 10 feet from her starboard side. The vessel suffered certain damage, including the putting out of action of her steering gear.
3. The Irish Government enters a formal protest against this occurrence, and reserves the right to claim full compensation for the damaged caused.'
Message ends.
In presenting Note, you should add verbally that point of attack is within Irish territorial waters, that owner of boat is own insurer and loss is serious for him, and that, while we are anxious to avoid difficulties, this incident which was witnessed by civilians from the shore is rather too flagrant to be passed over. We hope that German authorities will keep their aircraft away from this part of the world and so prevent such incidents in future.

No. 251 NAI DFA 2006/39

> Confidential report from John W. Dulanty to Joseph P. Walshe (Dublin)
> (No. 50) (Secret) (Copy)
>
> LONDON, 5 August 1940

You may recall that I reported over the telephone recently a conversation I had had on the 26th July with Mr. W.P. Crozier, Editor in Chief of 'The Manchester Guardian', in which I deplored the wholly unjustifiable campaign of the British press against our country. When he expressed his belief that there had been no direction or secret inspiration by the British Government I showed scepticism saying that these ignorant and unbridled expressions of opinion had been so widespread and so sustained that it was hard to believe that they were not inspired. He then said he would consult a press colleague, whose name he did not give but who, Mr. Crozier said, enjoyed in a special sense the confidence of the Government here. He has done this and his letter marked Private, of 2nd August – of which a copy is enclosed[1] – is the result.

The closing sentence of Mr. Crozier's letter refers to my asking whether a suggestion might not have been put quietly to the 'Lobby' correspondents – as distinct from a Press Conference.

---

[1] Not printed.

No. 252 UCDA P150/2599

> *Handwritten memorandum by Frank Aiken (Dublin) of a meeting with
> Eamon de Valera, Sir John Maffey and General Harrison*
>
> DUBLIN, 6 August 1940

On Friday 2nd Aug. 1940 the Taoiseach received Sir John Maffey and Gen. Harrison. The Ministers for Co-ordination and for Defence were present.[1]

Gen. H. said that his job would be to act as liaison officer in the event of our calling for British assistance. In order to fulfil this task efficiently he wished to make personal contact with the people he might have to work with here. He stressed the importance of getting to know members of the G.H.Q. staff.

The T.[aoiseach] indicated the neutral attitude of our people and pointed out that it would be impossible to have anything like staff talks. He wished to examine the possibility of arranging that Gen. H. should meet one or two members of G.H.Q. for the purpose of getting personally acquainted.

In reply to the Minister for Co-ord. Gen. H. said that in the event of British troops being invited to come to our assistance it would be advisable if we should have about twenty five officers to assign as liaison officers to the H.Q. of the British force and to the staffs of the various units making up this force. Billeting and other arrangements with the public would have to be made through the Irish Liaison Officers.

The T. pointed out the necessity for supplies of arms and Gen. H. said that he felt it to be one of his primary functions to insure that the Irish Army would be as well equipped as possible and that he had already pointed out the importance of this to his own people. He would continue to press for additional supplies of airplanes, anti-aircraft guns, and anti tank guns, machine guns etc.

The T. and the two ministers stressed the importance of getting supplies quickly.

[initialled] F.A.

No. 253 NAI DFA Paris Embassy 19/34

> *Telegram from the Department of External Affairs to Seán Murphy (Paris)
> (No. 121) (Copy)*
>
> DUBLIN, 8 August 1940

London Daily Mail publishes today despatch from Harold Cardozo[2] from Vichy stating that it is believed in Vichy that Germany about to make dual attack Ireland south-east England. Can you find any confirmation of this so far as Ireland is concerned.

---

[1] See No. 249.
[2] Harold G. Cardozo, a journalist with the *Daily Mail* best known for his travels with Franco and the Nationalist forces during the Spanish civil war.

Documents on Irish Foreign Policy, Volume VI, 1939–1941

No. 254 NAI DFA Paris Embassy 19/34

Extract from a confidential report from Seán Murphy to Joseph P. Walshe (Dublin)
(P.19/34A) (Copy)

VICHY, 8 August 1940

[matter omitted]
On the whole it would seem to be safe to say that France will be quite prepared to collaborate closely with Germany in the economic system, which she intends to apply to Europe if she should have final victory in the War. On the other hand while there is undoubtedly a tendency to introduce a system modelled on German lines in political as other matters, there seems to be, judging by M. Baudouin's statements as well as by press comment, the desire that the changes to be made in that direction should not be completely imitative, but should be conditioned by the special characteristics of the French race. In the press Morass[1] has already on several occasions come out against the tendency of some writers (in particular Déat)[2] to adopt German solutions completely, and the Temps has had articles suggesting that France should be inspired in the changes to be made by the good elements of all her past history, including that of the Third Republic.

No. 255 NAI DFA Madrid Embassy 34/1A

Letter from Patrick J. O'Byrne to Seán Murphy (Vichy)
(M. 10/11)

MADRID, 8 August 1940

I have to state for your information that an enquiry has been made here on behalf of a Mr. Samuel Beckett, who is at present residing at the Villa St. Georges, 135 Bd. de la Plage, Arcachon, Gironde, who is without funds and has no means, apparently, of having funds transmitted to him from Dublin.

Having discussed the matter with the person[3] who called here on Mr. Beckett's behalf, it was decided to request Mr. Beckett's brother at Dublin to lodge with the Department of External Affairs the sum of £100, all of, or a portion of, which might be cabled to you for Mr. Beckett's account. The following telegram was therefore despatched from the Legation yesterday:

'Frank Beckett, 6 Clare Street, Dublin.
Please lodge with the Department of External Affairs £100 for transmission your brother care of Irish Legation France.
Legirlanda'

It is believed that if and when he receives the money Mr. Beckett will decide to leave France for home via Portugal. The question as to whether all or only a

---

[1] Probably Charles Maurras (1868-1952), leader of the Action Française.
[2] Marcel Déat (1894-1955), French neo-socialist and writer who founded the *Rassemblement National Populaire* (RNP) during the Vichy regime; became Minister of Labour and National Solidarity in 1944.
[3] Marginal insertion by O'Byrne: 'The person who called here was Mr Reavy, British Institute. P.J. O'B'. 'Mr Reavy' was George Reavy, a friend of Beckett whom he had first met in Paris in 1930.

portion of the amount requested should be sent to France in Francs will presumably be decided by Mr. Frank Beckett in consultation with the Department.

[initialled] P.J.O'B

No. 256 NAI DFA Secretary's Files P3

Memorandum by Joseph P. Walshe (Dublin)
(Most Secret)

DUBLIN, 9 August 1940

Have We a Guarantee against Invasion from the German Government?
The position is as follows:-

The German Minister informed the Minister for External Affairs on 17th June[1] that the exclusive object of Germany's attack was Great Britain. He thought, in the pursuit of that object, there might be a possibility of Ireland's interests being affected. The German Minister could not give any details about the manner in which our interests were to be affected.

On 6th July, the German Minister, on instructions from his Government, informed me[2] –

1) That the British Press reports quoting German papers as having warned Ireland of her dangerous position were pure inventions. No such statements had appeared in the German Press.
(We have independent confirmation of this statement.)
2) That the Irish Government should have no doubt about Germany's attitude with regard to Ireland.
3) That Germany had only one aim with regard to Ireland in the present war, namely, that she should maintain her neutrality. Germany did not intend to attack Irish neutrality.

The German Minister called on Thursday, 18th July,[3] for the purpose of reaffirming Germany's intention not to violate our neutrality, and, above all, not to invade Ireland. He said that he wished to give these assurances without any reservations whatsoever. His instructions had the full authority of the German Minister for Foreign Affairs. His Government desired to eliminate any suspicions with regard to Germany's intentions which the Irish Government might have entertained.

The German Government's anxiety to give us assurances against an invasion by the German Army was dictated not merely by the questions put to the German Minister by the Department, but also by the reiterated statements in British and American Press and radio about Germany's intentions with regard to this country.

Owing to the imminence of the blitzkrieg, I expressed the hope to the German Minister yesterday morning (8th August) that the assurances his Government had given to us would be fulfilled to the letter. He replied that he had no doubt whatever that this would be the case.

---

[1] See No. 191.
[2] See No. 216.
[3] See No. 230.

Documents on Irish Foreign Policy, Volume VI, 1939–1941

No. 257 NAI DFA Secretary's Files P3

Memorandum by Joseph P. Walshe on a meeting with Edouard Hempel (Dublin)
(Secret)

DUBLIN, 9 August 1940

The German Minister called to see me this morning. He was with me only for a quarter of an hour, as I had to sandwich his suddenly announced visit between two other appointments. His main purpose was to hand me a letter which he had received from an anonymous person in Belfast and which had all the appearance of being a trap laid for him.

I have since given this letter to the Chief of Military Intelligence.[1]

As the blitzkrieg was very much in the papers and on the radio, I remarked to Dr. Hempel that, as things were now beginning to look really lively, I hoped that our country would not suffer any serious inconvenience. He assured me that he felt the most absolute confidence in the assurances he had received from his Government, and which he had given to me on more than one occasion, to the effect that the German Government had no intention whatever of invading this country. Moreover, he could say that the instructions conveyed to him concerning this matter had come from Herr von Ribbentrop himself.

No. 258 NAI DFA Secretary's Files P5

Memorandum by Joseph P. Walshe (Dublin)

DUBLIN, 9 August 1940

Has Britain guaranteed not to invade us?

The position is as follows:-

Acting on instructions, the High Commissioner called on Lord Caldecote on 23rd July,[2] to protest against the widespread campaign in the London and Provincial newspapers directed against the policy of neutrality of the Irish Government and suggesting the time had come for the British Government to take steps to occupy our territory. Doubts and misgivings had been caused which would have to be cleared up if the good understanding between the two countries were to continue. Lord Caldecote told the High Commissioner that he had no hesitation in giving an assurance that there was no intention in the mind of the British Government to take any military or naval action in our territory, unless and until they were formally asked to do so by the Irish Government. Mr. de Valera would, however, understand that, in a war future such as that which confronted them, so full of uncertainties and wholly incalculable factors, it would not be possible for the British Government to give today a guarantee that in no circumstances would they refrain from entering Ireland without an invitation. It was however no part of their policy to go into Éire unless the Irish Government invited them.

In order to consolidate the position, if possible, the High Commissioner was instructed to show to Lord Caldecote his report of the foregoing interview, and to ask him whether he fully accepted the High Commissioner's account of the

---

[1] Colonel Liam Archer.
[2] See Nos 239, 240 and 243.

conversation. Lord Caldecote looked at the report. He said he did accept the account of the conversation, he had nothing to withdraw; but, on the other hand, he could not give his imprimatur to the draft without consulting his colleagues. What he had said represented his opinion, but he could not say it was an authoritative statement of his Government. He did not think it advisable to go to the Cabinet to get their consent to his approving the draft report. He thought the wisest course was to let matters rest as they were at the moment.

That is how the matter stands to date.

No. 259 NAI DFA 2006/39

Confidential report from John W. Dulanty to Joseph P. Walshe (Dublin)
(No. 51) (Secret) (Copy)

LONDON, 9 August 1940

As already reported orally, on the 18th July I read to Lord Caldecote your Secret minute to me of the preceding day[1] and gave him a verbatim copy of the representations contained therein.

On reading the words 'certain persons' Lord Caldecote said 'What is the meaning of this? I know of only one person. I suppose this refers to Tegart'. I agreed and said I thought there were others. He said that he could assure me the Government had no part in Sir Charles Tegart's visit. I got the impression that he attached no importance to it.[2]

He was not aware of the visits of journalists nor did he understand how, under existing regulations, they had been able to obtain permits to leave this country. He appreciated the objections to these visits and would do what he could with the Permit authorities to prevent further visits in future. I spoke to Lord Caldecote on the 6th instant and asked him how the matter now stood. He told me that he had taken the matter up with the Permit authorities and he thought they were now firmly refusing permits to anyone outside the limited categories of persons entitled to travel.

On the reference in your minute about the campaign in the British press he repeated his former statements to me that he had tried to get these articles stopped. He had that evening spoken to the Minister for Information who told him that he had seen the Lobby Correspondents of the preceding night and had asked them to 'let up' on Ireland. A similar request would be made to the press people generally. Lord Caldecote said that whilst he hoped for a good response on the part of the Press he thought it was too much to hope that there would not be some 'black sheep'. I suggested that it would have been better to have stopped these ignorant and misleading statements earlier. Lord Caldecote doubted whether it could have been done. In the absence of any real power any attempt on his part to stop the articles when they were, so to speak, in the full spate, would have provoked an outcry from the Press which would have made matters much worse.

---

[1] See No. 229.
[2] This sentence is a handwritten insertion by Dulanty.

Documents on Irish Foreign Policy, Volume VI, 1939-1941

No. 260 NAI DFA Secretary's Files P5

Extract from a letter from Robert Brennan to Joseph Scott[1] (Los Angeles)
(Personal) (Copy)

WASHINGTON, 12 August 1940

[matter omitted]

The policy of neutrality, as you know, was decided on by the Government as the only policy which was feasible and advisable in the interests of the country, and of the ultimate unity and independence of the nation. It is supported by the three major parties and possibly by 95% of the people. It is not a bargaining point. Similarly, Ireland's claim to the restoration of the six counties is a simple national right, and no one has such a claim as to demand a price for granting it. Even if the British Government had offered an immediate end of partition, which they did not, any question relating to the continuance or otherwise of neutrality would have to be decided by the Parliament of the whole of Ireland.

I know that you are aware that this is the situation. I am glad to say that the Chief is delighted with the work you are doing.

No. 261 NAI DFA 205/55

Memorandum from Frank Gallagher to Eamon de Valera
and Joseph P. Walshe (Dublin)

DUBLIN, 12 August 1940

Suggestions re News Bulletin for Shortwave transmission in Morse

1. The value of such transmissions depends on up-to-date contents. As News that would be internationally interesting would not justify anything like a long bulletin (there would hardly be three minutes of such news a day), it might be best to have the transmission reduced to five minutes daily or to have it twice a week for ten or fifteen minutes.
2. Into such a transmission a good deal of disguised propaganda could be inserted in the form of quotation from leading articles, semi-official comment on home or foreign events and in times of crisis, statements by Ministers.
3. The bulletin should contain also, in particular, replies to U.S. mis-representation – our Minister in Washington would wire, say, what the 'New York Times' said and the answering comment would go out in the Bulletin within a few hours of the misstatement, if necessary.
4. A section of the Bulletin could be devoted to statements of fact in reply to whatever the current misrepresentation was as, for instance, that the Germany Legation has a staff of six, that no submarines can come to our shores without being observed, etc.
5. It should be an essential part of the scheme that our Legations and Consulates everywhere abroad notify beforehand as many newspapers and political people as possible of the hours of transmission and keep reminding them of it.

---

[1] Joseph Scott (1867-1958), prominent Los Angeles attorney and strong supporter of Irish nationalism; President of the American Congress for the Unity and Independence of Ireland and founder of the American League for an Undivided Ireland (1947).

6. The Transmission could be kept semi-official by calling it a Newsagency.
7. If the right man could be found, such a feature as a military correspondent who would give an intelligent comment on the latest war news would help to establish the transmissions among intelligent listeners.
8. It would also help if External Affairs could now and then (as frequently as possible) give little bits of international news not generally known which would be published either as news or used as the basis of comment. This would give the transmissions a standing with listeners who themselves were well-informed and so help in getting accepted the purely Irish part of the transmissions.
9. It would be better to have no transmissions at all rather than anything immature or not completely informed and moderately stated.
10. A sample of what the Bulletin might contain is added:

Dublin – It is stated officially to-day that the number of Irishmen who have now answered the call for recruits is just over the 170,000. This is in addition to the highly trained Standing Army, the Reserve and the Volunteer Force. Including the armed section of the Local Security Force it means that the Irish Government has now its military forces over 150,000 and in its Observer Patrols over 50,000 others. On a population basis this means that of the male population between the ages of 18 and 64 one in every four is in the Defence forces.

Dublin – In connection with the reports published here of the Havana Conference, in which strong German populations in the South Americas were mentioned, it is stated that the total German population here is 326, of whom 170 are refugees and 134 women. The staffs of the Legations, including Consular officials, are:

United States	...	9
Great Britain	...	9
Germany	...	6
France	...	6
Italy	...	5

No. 262 NAI DFA 205/55

Extracts from a memorandum from Frank Gallagher to Eamon de Valera (Dublin)
DUBLIN, 12 August 1940

Submitted to An Taoiseach Concerning the Establishment of a Regular High Speed Morse Wireless Receiving and Transmitting Station

General

Apart from steamships and Air Mails, the only means of communication between Ireland and the rest of the world are via Great Britain; there is a Cable to Newfoundland passing through Valentia, but this Cable is controlled by Great Britain. The result of this position is that Ireland is now completely cut off from the whole of Europe and can only communicate with America by the good will of Great Britain.

It can, I think, be stated definitely that Ireland is the only country in Europe which has no independent means of communication. All the other European countries have, in addition to their telegraphic and cable lines, regular wireless communication systems which leave them independent of their neighbours.

The lack of proper wireless receiving and transmitting facilities here is one of the factors which prevents the direct receipt and despatch of news to and from Ireland. The bulk of news from Ireland has to be sent to London from where, after being sub-edited, it is sent to the Rugby Wireless transmitter; from there it is sent by high speed Morse to various parts of the world. The bulk of the news reaching Ireland is likewise received by wireless in Rugby and sub-edited in London before it reaches Ireland.

It is now generally recognised that wireless high speed Morse is the most satisfactory method of transmitting news and this method is now in general use, both in Europe and America. All the big newsagencies which have offices in London transmit and receive the bulk of their news by this method from Rugby. The Rugby Transmitter itself is operated by the British Post Office.

If an Irish wireless transmitting and receiving station were established, it would be possible to get away from the present news distribution system. It would certainly facilitate at some future stage the establishment of an official Irish newagency.

Under present conditions, it is very likely that some of the big American and Continental newsagencies would operate from Ireland instead of England if proper facilities were made available.

I have dwelt on the advantages of an Irish wireless transmitting station from the news point of view because this is a question with which I am familiar. There are, however, other considerations which are, perhaps, even more important from a Governmental and business point of view. For instance, communication difficulties between External Affairs and Irish diplomatic Representatives abroad could be maintained even in time of stress, when they become more important. Financial and business dealings could, likewise, be carried on even when cable and telegraphic communications are interrupted. Such a transmitter could also be used for internal communications by Government Services and also for communications between Ireland and Great Britain in the event of the cables breaking down.
[matter omitted]

Urgency.
If this scheme is to be adopted, there are a number of reasons which favour its being put into operation with the least possible delay.

The first of these is the necessity for independent means of communication with the outside world in the present situation. Another reason is that the present war situation would favour the use of the proposed transmitter by newsagencies. If the war situation develops on British soil, it is quite possible that Ireland would find itself completely cut off from America and Europe.

No. 263 NAI DFA Paris Embassy 19/34

> *Telegram from the Department of External Affairs to Seán Murphy (Vichy)*
> *(No. 134) (Personal)*
> DUBLIN, 15 August 1940

Your very interesting reports June 18th[1] June 21st[2] June 27th June 28th[3] from ASCAIN received today: hope you have kept and continue to keep full records of events even though communications with department so difficult.

No. 264 UCDA P150/2571

> *Cover letter and memorandum by Joseph P. Walshe on The German Note (Dublin)*
> DUBLIN, 19 August 1940

The attached Note was handed to me by the German Minister at 4.45 p.m. on Saturday, 17th August.[4]

The position, as clarified in a conversation with the German Minister, can be stated briefly as follows:-

1) The German Government, having established a total blockade of Britain, will endeavour by every means at its disposal, to sink all cargoes going into and departing from British ports.
2) The German Government suggest to the Irish Government that the latter should take steps to prevent Irish ships and Irish citizens from incurring the risks involved in running the blockade.
3) The German Government are ready to instruct their naval and air forces to refrain from attacking ships sailing under the Irish flag (and this includes neutral ships under the Irish flag carrying Irish cargo), provided
    a) that the Irish Government give a guarantee that the said ships are not carrying cargoes to England and are not carrying from Ireland to other countries merchandise of English origin (i.e., goods already imported from England into Ireland); and
    b) that the Irish Government give due notice to the German Government of the times of sailing of these ships and the route to be followed.
4) The net effect in our B. trade in practice would be that, while Irish ships, or neutral ships under Irish colours, could fetch cargoes from England, Irish cargoes going to that country would have to be sent in British bottoms.

MEMORANDUM

1. The German Note raises two separate problems. First, there is the question of the effect of the German blockade measures on traffic between this country and Great Britain, and secondly, there is the German offer to make an arrangement with us whereby ships coming to this country with vitally essential supplies would be exempt from attack.

---

[1] See No. 194.
[2] See No. 197.
[3] See No. 206.
[4] Not printed.

2. So far as traffic between this country and Great Britain is concerned, the following considerations must be borne in mind:-
(a) The danger of German attacks on shipping must not be underrated. So far as ships sailing to and from this country are concerned, the activity of the last three days has already belied the British attitude that the German declaration was merely a bluff and that it would make no difference in the situation existing before it was made. The new total blockade may be intended merely as a temporary diversion but, as long as it lasts, it is likely to make itself felt.
(b) Assuming the danger to shipping and passengers to be a real one, the immediate question is what action should be taken to safeguard or protect Irish citizens and ships against the risks, and to prevent serious trouble arising between this country and Germany. The German suggestion, made in the official statement declaring the blockade, is that we should prohibit our citizens and ships from entering the war zone. We would say that that would be unneutral and would be tantamount to doing the work of Germany's blockade for her. The Germans would reply that, in taking such action, we would be doing no more than countries like the United States and the Argentine have already done, at great economic loss to themselves, in the interests of their neutrality. A serious point for us, however, is that the British would almost certainly resent this or any other similar action on our part implying recognition of the effectiveness or legitimacy of the German blockade.
(c) Assuming that Irish citizens and ships are to continue free to enter the blockade zone, there remains the question of what other official action might be taken to minimise the risk of loss of life and property and to guard against the charge of timidity in the assertion of our neutral rights. Over 75% of the passenger traffic between Britain and Ireland is carried by the L.M.S.[1] boats which are of British registry. Only about 10% of traffic is carried in Irish ships. So far as the question of the safety of our citizens is concerned, there would probably be no serious difficulty, even from the British side, about the issue of an official statement to the effect that 'Owing to the present risks, Irish citizens are strongly advised to avoid travelling by sea if they can do so without serious disadvantage or inconvenience.' If necessary, an exit permit system restricting travel could be instituted. But that would involve increased expenditure to the Exchequer and additional inconvenience to travellers.
(d) There remains the question of Irish ships. Here the position turns very largely on the question of the legality of the German blockade. On account of the novelty of blockade by air and for other reasons, a positive statement with regard to the legality or otherwise of the German measures is hardly practicable; but so far as the precedents go, there is a good deal more to be said in favour of the legality of the blockade than against it. If the German blockade is not illegal, any action by the Government in the direction of arming Irish vessels to enable them to force the blockade, or to combat the blockade measures, could be regarded as an act of war by Germany. The position would be the same if Irish ships were to be escorted by Irish naval units with instructions to resist the blockade measures. Whatever the legal position may be, however, politically an official attitude of defiance and resistance to the German blockade measures,

---

[1] The London Midland and Scottish railway company.

would be liable to maximise the political repercussions of such incidents as did occur and to lead to a severe strain on our relations with Germany. There does not seem to be any ideal course. It might help if the Department of Industry and Commerce were to discuss the matter with the strictly Irish companies on the basis that measures of armed protection are not practicable in the case of neutral ships. In somewhat similar circumstances, other neutral governments kept their ships in port. Serious as the loss would be, if the proportion of sinkings became very high, our shipping companies might want to take similar action on their own initiative.

(e) There remains only the question whether, and if so in what form, we should make a formal protest to the German Government with regard to the application of the blockade measures to Irish citizens and ships. Our reply to the German Note would, of course, draw attention to the vital importance of trade with Britain to our national economy, and to the resentment likely to be felt by Irish people all over the world if Irish citizens and trade are seen to suffer the consequences of a conflict in which this country is not involved. But it is not easy to see on what we could base a formal diplomatic protest in the ordinary sense. As has been said above, there is more to be said in favour of the legality of the German measure than against it. We could also urge the German authorities in verbal representations to exercise discretion and forbearance in the case of ships of Irish registry. But here we would be likely to be met with the argument that the legality of the German blockade depends on its universality, and the German Government could not discriminate in our favour without leaving themselves open to challenge by other States.

3. The second part of the German Note contains an offer to exempt from the blockade measures ships flying the Irish flag coming to this country with vitally essential supplies. The offer is subject to the conditions that each ship should be notified individually and should follow any sailing instructions the Germans may give, and that the Irish Government should give an undertaking not to allow supplies so imported to be re-exported or trans-shipped from this country. The German Note apparently contemplates a more or less formal agreement on these general lines. The German Minister has been authorised to enter into negotiations about this agreement and is anxious to get a reply on this part of the Note as quickly as possible. No doubt, the Germans have an eye to the propaganda value of an agreement with us. On the other hand, the spirit in which the proposal is put forward by the Germans is not such that we can afford simply to ignore it.

4. The following considerations arise with regard to this German offer:-

a) On prestige and other grounds, the British reaction to any such agreement between us and Germany at this stage would, of course, be very bad – and, of course, we are dependent on the British for shipping, foreign exchange, supplies and so on. The British reaction would be particularly bad at the moment because they are about to approach us with a proposal that we should facilitate them by doing the very thing against which the Germans ask for a guarantee, i.e., by allowing British cargoes to be trans-shipped in our ports. It is barely possible that, in certain circumstances, the British might be brought to see certain material advantages for themselves in an arrangement of the kind proposed between ourselves and Germany. That might be the case, for example, if the arrangement guaranteed our imports of feeding stuffs and enabled us to increase the proportion of finished live stock which we send to Britain. The likelihood is, however, that the Germans would take care to define the term 'vitally essential supplies' in such a way as to make anything like this impossible.

b) On the other hand, we must allow for the possibility of the war continuing for a considerable time and the German blockade proving effective. The consequences for us might be wholesale industrial unemployment and serious reduction of our live stock population and agricultural production. It was precisely consequences of this type which, both in the last and in the present war, forced States like Holland, Switzerland, Denmark, etc., to make agreements with Britain of the kind which Germany is now proposing to us. We have, of course, useful stocks on which we could rely. But, in the situation in which we are now placed, such stocks as we have are a vital guarantee of our independence vis-à-vis Britain. According as our stocks were depleted, we would become more dependent on her, and, if she is at the same time feeling the effects of the blockade herself, she will not be able to give us much and what she has available to give will be more likely to be accompanied by political conditions. Furthermore, if, owing to the German blockade, internal conditions here become bad, firms are closed down and unemployment increases, public opinion will find it increasingly hard to understand why advantage is not taken of the German offer. Therefore, although there are strong reasons against making any formal agreement with Germany now, there are almost equally strong reasons for trying to keep open the possibility of making an arrangement on the lines suggested at a later stage if it should become really necessary to do so.

c) We could put our disinclination to enter into any agreement on the ground that it could be held not to be strictly neutral. We could support this by pointing to the German attitude to the War Trade Agreements concluded by Britain with Holland, Denmark, Belgium, etc., both in the last and in the present war. The Germans would, no doubt, counter this by saying that, what they objected to in the British War Trade Agreements with the Border neutrals was that the Border neutrals concerned were the normal channel for the passage of essential overseas supplies to Germany which the Agreements were intended to cut off. The British could not challenge the proposed arrangement between Ireland and Germany on the same ground.

d) The legality of German measures against cargoes coming to this country from overseas is much more doubtful than the legality of their action against trade between this country and Britain. Once again, however, the Germans would be able to point to lengthy and inconclusive diplomatic correspondence during the last war in which they would be able to find a colour of legal justification for their action. The trouble is that the sinking of cargoes coming to Ireland in Irish ships from countries other than Britain will be capable of being quoted in the British Press as instances of German violation of our neutrality. We shall have to take every such case up with the German Government to avoid the charge of allowing our neutrality to become a dead letter.

e) Our attitude to the German offer to grant immunity to cargoes coming to this country might be based on the following principles:-

i) The making of anything like a formal agreement is out of the question in present circumstances. An effort might be made to get the German Minister here to see this point of view and recommend it to his authorities.

ii) We should avoid entering into any obligation vis-a-vis Germany on the question of re-export or trans-shipment, but we could point out to the German Minister that, as a matter of policy, there has been no re-export or trans-shipment from this country since the beginning of the year, and that there is no intention of altering this position. The object would be to get the German Government to accept a statement somewhat on these lines in a Note as a satisfactory substitute for the guarantee for which they ask.

iii) The German Minister would be told verbally that, owing to practical difficulties connected with insurance and the fact that most of our overseas cargoes are carried in neutral vessels of other than Irish registry, we are not in a position at the moment to put forward concrete suggestions for any general arrangement such as the German Government suggests, but that we are looking into the possibility of making, in an emergency, practical arrangements of a kind which would enable us to put forward suggestions, and we will communicate with him later. The general idea would be not to reject the German offer out of hand and to keep it open for the present.

iv) We would tell the German Minister that, in our view, the sinking of cargoes coming to this country from countries other than Britain in Irish or neutral vessels would be contrary to international law and would give us a right to compensation which we would assert and claim in every case.

No. 265 UCDA P150/2571

Letter from Joseph P. Walshe to Eamon de Valera (Dublin)
(Secret)

DUBLIN, 19 August 1940

Following your instructions, I asked the Secretaries of the Departments of Supplies, Agriculture and Industry and Commerce to meet and discuss the contents of the attached German Note[1] concerning the total blockade of England. After a long discussion, we reached the following general conclusions:-

1) No matter what agreement were made with the Germans, they could not guarantee us safety against the mines with which the Irish Sea is now apparently infested.

2) If we made an agreement with the Germans and gave them a guarantee that we should not export merchandise in our ships to England, the British would probably retaliate either by decreasing the supplies now being received from them or by preventing neutral ships under their control from carrying our cargoes from distant countries; or they might use both these weapons together.

3) The continuation of our normal trade with Great Britain being of vital importance to our people, as a Government we could not agree to stop exports of our own volition. If our export trade becomes impossible through the physical destruction of our ships, that is another matter.

---

[1] Not printed, but see No. 264.

4) The Government, therefore, would appear to take the proper course if they refrain from taking any measures which would constitute an interference with normal commercial arrangements for the conduct of our export trade.

5) The loss of our ships through the total blockade, once it becomes effective all round, leaves us no legitimate case for complaint against the German Government. Since the beginning of the war up to now, the Germans had not actively interfered with our normal British trade.

6) For the moment at any rate, it would be better not to make any public statement, which would be an exceedingly difficult document to formulate without giving offence to one side or the other.

7) If the blockade of Britain in the Irish Sea becomes really intense, it is probable that the vessels on the Irish Register which do not belong to Irish owners will seek permission to transfer to the British Register. So long as they sail under the Irish flag, we cannot allow them to go in a British convoy or to carry guns.

Meanwhile, if you agree, I shall inform the German Minister of our general attitude, and will endeavour to secure some amelioration of the situation.

Of course, the real danger of the new German measure is that it gives the British a further opportunity of trying to bring us into the war on their side. In exactly similar circumstances, they exercised considerable pressure on Belgium and Holland.

No. 266 NAI DFA 2006/39

Confidential report from John W. Dulanty to Joseph P. Walshe (Dublin)
(No. 52) (Secret) (Copy)

LONDON, 19 August 1940

As already reported orally, Lord Caldecote told me on the 15th August that the recent big air raids on Britain certainly marked Germany's intention to force the issue.[1]

There was, thus far, no depression in either the War Cabinet or among the Chiefs of Staff – the latter in fact, after studying the results of the recent air attacks, had feelings of increased confidence. It was, of course, possible that the Germans had some weapon or form of surprise attack unknown to them but if they had no more to face in the future than the attacks they had encountered thus far the present attitude of the British experts was that there was little or no cause for worry.

The Spitfire,[2] whose fighting superiority and manoeuvrability Lord Caldecote thought was established, had given them a great deal of trouble in the experimental stages. For over a year they had had one disappointment after another in the machine trials. Their engineers and designers however persevered and today there was no doubt that they had a first class machine. I inquired as to the possibility of the Germans being able to build Spitfires – using one they had captured as a model.

---

[1] The second week of August 1940 saw an increase in the severity of German air raids directed against infrastructure and airfields in England.

[2] The design of the Supermarine Spitfire fighter was accepted by the Air Ministry in 1935. The first prototype flew in 1936 and by the outbreak of war in 1939 nine RAF squadrons were flying the aircraft. By the outbreak of the 'Battle of Britain' in the summer of 1940 nineteen RAF Fighter Command Squadrons were equipped with Spitfires.

Lord Caldecote said the Germans might build one or two as models but from his experience as Minister for Co-Ordination of Defence he estimated it would take at least a year to produce this type of aeroplane on the big scale necessary for war purposes.

It had been remarkable he thought that they had as yet suffered so little from the extensive raids. There had been no interference at all with munitions supply nor, the frequency of the attacks notwithstanding, had any port been out of action.

He dealt at some length with an inquiry I ventured as to whether the losses of German planes reported by the British were completely accurate, assuring me that the figures given by the Air Ministry were always based on fact and were nearly always underestimated. They had never even considered any suggestion of adjusting reports of German [origin] on their own losses to meet apprehension on the part of the British public.

On the question of the new social order which it is suggested is to emerge after the war, Lord Caldecote said there had been no discussion at the Cabinet. They were all so preoccupied with winning the war that no one had time to think out plans for a new world order. As far as Britain is concerned I said it would probably follow the lines already well marked in their history of trial and error and slow growth, rather than on organised scientifically worked out plan. He was confident that the new order, whatever shape it took, would be worked out in the way I had suggested.

Dr. James Hallon, the Warden of Toynbee Hall, with close associations with the Archbishop of Canterbury (President of Toynbee Hall) and with the British Labour Party took precisely the same line saying that the problems had got no further than elementary discussions from the intellectuals and the social reformers.

Professor V.G.S Adams, Warden of All Souls College, Oxford, who is connected with the intellectual left wing life of Oxford and elsewhere told me today that whilst a number of people were thinking about the new order it was necessarily in the most general terms at present, seeking for example some short cut with the problem of unemployment which must of course be of great urgency the minute the war finished. The recent raids on Britain he thought had increased rather than diminished the determination of the citizens to fight to a finish.

I reminded Lord Caldecote of the suggestions made by Dr. Salazar, President of the Republic of Portugal, that some really dependable estimate of the strength of the German war forces should be attempted and enquired whether the position was any clearer than a few weeks ago. Lord Caldecote said that estimates of this kind were, as we all know, based upon reports from Secret Service officers. He was frankly sceptical about those Secret Service reports. They generally represented a small fragment of wheat in an immense amount of chaff. He thought some of the rumours about Germany's strength or lack of strength were put about by busybodies who had no information and who were really defeatist at heart. He said that the Daily Mirror was not merely an enemy of the Government, which circumstance could not of course perturb him, but he was beginning to think was an enemy of the country.

Documents on Irish Foreign Policy, Volume VI, 1939–1941

No. 267 NAI DFA 2006/39

> *Confidential report from John W. Dulanty to Joseph P. Walshe (Dublin)*
> *(No. 53) (Secret) (Copy)*
>
> LONDON, 19 August 1940

Sir Arthur Street, Permanent Secretary of the Air Ministry, lunched with me a few days ago when I asked him about the recent big raids of German aeroplanes over England.

He said every Air Ministry communiqué went out over his signature and their reports of their own and German air losses could be relied on absolutely. Their experts summarised the reports for the War Cabinet under three headings:-
1. Losses proved beyond doubt.
2. Probable losses but not of unassailable proof.
3. Damaged planes.

They reported only the first category. The second, if included, would often send up the figures by fifty per cent. For that reason they think their reports of German losses are considerably understated. The Prime Minister was most emphatic in his direction that the completest accuracy should be observed in the reports whether or not they were favourable to the British. He would be glad at any time to investigate any instance I could give him of seeming inaccuracy in any of these reports.

The loss of a plane was of course serious enough, and the loss of a plane and a pilot was far more serious. Until the recent big fights the British pilots saved from destroyed aeroplanes were about two in every ten. During this week when there had been bigger raids than ever the losses of their pilots were only about half what they had been before. So far, Sir Arthur Street said, the German tactics in the air had worked out precisely as the Air Ministry's experts had predicted – but he felt sure that this war needed more than ever new strategy, new inventions, and new weapons. Up to now the Germans in their recent fights in England had not shown anything with which the British were not equal to cope.

No. 268 NAI DFA Washington Embassy Confidential Reports 1940

> *Confidential report from Robert Brennan to Joseph P. Walshe (Dublin)*
> *(108/78/40)*
>
> WASHINGTON, 20 August 1940

Contrary to expectations Mr. John Cudahy, Ambassador to Belgium, was not rebuked by President Roosevelt for his injudicious London interview in which he praised the conduct of German soldiers in Belgium, and called for American food supplies to avert famine there. On emerging from his interview with President Roosevelt, Mr. Cudahy said he was authorized to state he had not been rebuked and that he did not intend to resign. Later his interview with Undersecretary of State Sumner Welles was described as cordial although Mr. Welles had previously issued a statement which was a sharp reprimand to the Ambassador. Opinion here is that this denouement had nothing to do with the case, but that it had a great deal to do with the coming Presidential election, and with the vote in Wisconsin, Mr. Cudahy's native State. An incident which may have helped also was the demonstration in Mr. Cudahy's favour when he landed at La Guardia airport from Europe. A crowd estimated at 1,000 assembled at the airport and give Mr. Cudahy an enthusiastic cheer very much to his surprise. The demonstration had been very hastily organized by Mr. Martin Conboy[1] and Mr. J.C. Walsh.[2]

No. 269 NAI DFA 205/4

Confidential report from William Warnock to Joseph P. Walshe (Dublin)
(76/30) (205/4)

BERLIN, 20 August 1940

After the entry of Italy into the war, and the collapse of France soon afterwards, I suspended sending press reviews as, firstly, it was doubtful if postal connections with Ireland could be maintained at all, and secondly, weekly reports would be of little interest in view of the long period between the occurrence of events mentioned and the probable time of arrival of mail in Ireland. Events move so quickly that it is well-nigh impossible to determine which happenings are really of permanent importance.

One thing may be said quite definitely concerning the attitude of the German press; and that is: the tone used in reference to Ireland has never been inimical, and it has often been very friendly. I know from my personal acquaintance with members of the Foreign Office that official circles are anxious to avoid incidents which would displease us. Certain utterances by Irish political leaders have been resented by the Foreign Office, but, although the matter was raised with you through the German Minister in Dublin, no mention was made of them in the German press. This is all the more interesting when one recalls that any remark savouring of unfriendliness towards Germany made by – say – a Swiss or Swedish politician or newspaper calls forth a stern rebuke in the German press at once.

I have already reported to you by telegraph regarding the attention given to Ireland in the Press at the beginning of July, when it was reported in British and some American newspapers that Great Britain was endeavouring to come to some agreement with us which would enable her to gain the use of our territory and ports for her own defence.[3] In this case the German press confined itself entirely to reports which had come to the United States from Great Britain. The version given over the British wireless (I have not seen any British newspapers for some months past) of what was alleged to have appeared in the German press was quite misleading – and inaccurate. The press campaign for the violation of our neutrality seems to have been started by the British themselves.

Much attention is paid abroad to the leading articles in the 'Berliner Boersen-Zeitung', which is often said to be the mouthpiece of the Foreign Office. I doubt whether under existing circumstances any one newspaper is favoured by official circles more than another; they are all subject to the same control. Be that as it may, it is of interest to note that while the Diplomatic Correspondent of this newspaper, Dr. Karl Megerle, has told his readers on a few occasions that Great Britain was

---

[1] Martin Conboy, District Attorney for the Southern District of New York (1933-35) and prominent Irish-American.
[2] Secretary to Martin Conboy.
[3] See Nos 212, 214, 216, 223, 231 and 232.

seeking an opportunity to occupy strategic points in Ireland, he has never thrown any doubts on the sincerity of our Government, nor has he ever questioned our attitude in any private conversations which I have had with him.

Since the beginning of July Ireland has not occupied much space in the German press. The matters which have since received most publicity have been, apart from the Chancellor's peace offer before the Reichstag, the complete collapse in France ensuing on military defeat, and articles on inner conditions in Great Britain intended to show the social inequalities existing under the liberal capitalist system, nothing more than a desperate effort on the part of a comparatively small number of people to maintain their wealth and the influence which it brings with it.

In view of the amazing run of German successes there is practically no need for me to portray current feeling here. Everyone is proud. The prohibition on dancing at present in force helps to preserve the general calm atmosphere. There is, in fact, a certain dignity in the attitude of the population as a whole. Things are going well with the man-in-the-street. The summer has brought abundant food, and a surprisingly large number of people managed to get away for short holidays.

[signed] W. WARNOCK

No. 270 NAI DFA Secretary's Files A2

Memorandum from Joseph P. Walshe to Eamon de Valera (Dublin)
(Secret)
DUBLIN, 21 August 1940

The High Commissioner 'phoned me about 10.15 last night to say that he had been requested by Lord Beaverbrook[1] to go to his house at 10.30. He asked Beaverbrook if he would be good enough to tell him the object of his request. Beaverbrook replied that he was going to ask him whether it would be possible for the Irish Government to give facilities in Ireland for the training of civilian pilots.

The High Commissioner then 'phoned Lord Caldecote and asked him whether there was any connection between Beaverbrook's request and the delay which had taken place in a final decision regarding the price of our cattle. Caldecote said there was not, but he gave the High Commissioner the impression that the British were going to ask us for facilities for transshipment.

When I told the High Commissioner that he should oppose both suggestions at once and make it clear that, in his view, the Government could not accept them, he replied that, when the Ministers were in London in early May, they gave him and the British the impression that something could be done about the facilities for transshipment. I warned him that, whatever the Ministers might have said in early May, the situation with regard to our neutrality had become very much more serious since then and he would have to show in his attitude that it would be exceedingly difficult for his Government to accept these proposals.

[initialled] J.P.W.

The invite to Lord B. was later postponed until 4.30 p.m. today. J.P.W[2]

---

[1] Sir Max Aitken, Lord Beaverbrook (1879-1964), Minister for Aircraft Production (1940-1).
[2] Handwritten insertion.

No. 271 NAI DT S11846

> *Confidential report from John W. Dulanty to Joseph P. Walshe (Dublin)*
> *(No. 54) (Secret) (Copy)*
>
> LONDON, 23 August 1940

Confirming my telephone conversation, I had a meeting to-day at his Office with Sir William Brown who was accompanied by Mr. Stephenson of the Dominions Office, and Mr. Willis who recently returned from the Ministry of Supply to the Board of Trade.

Sir William Brown said that he had hoped to be able to have given me a draft of the proposed trade agreement. Unfortunately it had not been possible to do this, one reason being that whilst his Committee was engaged on framing the draft the Cabinet were considering a modification of cattle prices which would have affected the terms of the proposed agreement.

There had been on his Committee considerable argument about the cattle prices. He, together with Mr. Stephenson, and the representative of the British Ministry of Agriculture had had to do stout battle all the time against the representatives of the Treasury and the Ministry of Food. The Ministry of Agriculture, being the producer, was all out for as good a price as it could get from the Ministry of Food. The latter were, as might be expected, always trying to buy at the lowest possible price, and in this they had the unremitting support of the Treasury.

They had, however, decided – as Lord Caldecote had already informed me – to meet us on cattle prices in such a way as to pay us the current price plus the sum of half a million pounds per annum.

They felt that it would be advisable for us to set up an Export Board to whom the British would pay the half million pounds and to whom our Government would give directions as to its distribution. Sir William Brown then passed to what he described as the provisional tentative arrangements which we had made, subject absolutely to a comprehensive agreement being accepted by both sides. These provisional arrangements included joint chartering, bulk purchasing, war insurance arrangements and so on. To these they would propose to add the granting of facilities by our Government to the British in transhipment in our territorial waters of cargoes from big vessels to small. This was intended, as we knew, to help to relieve the congestion in the British deep water ports.

He next mentioned Supply questions such as flax, where the prices he thought were settled already; pit props where the prices were to be agreed, and said that they were anxious to secure an agreement about wool prices with us at the earliest possible moment. His information was that we were sending smallish consignments at low prices which were interfering with their price structure, and the Board of Trade had been asked by the Ministry of Supply to prohibit all wool imports and thus end the disturbance to their price structure. On the schedule of agricultural produce such as bacon, eggs, cheese etc., their proposals would be much on the line already discussed with us.

After expressing disappointment that we were still without even a draft of the agreement I said I thought we could finish the discussion there and then if this suggestion of transhipment were to be pressed. They would remember that when the Ministers were over here Mr. Lemass said quite definitely that it was a question which would have to be reserved, and referred to the importance of the Governments being completely excluded from any such proposal. I did not at that stage propose to offer any observations on the other matters which it was proposed to put into the agreement because I felt sure my Government would not look at any document asking for the transhipment facilities mentioned.

Sir William Brown said I might take it that if the transhipment point were to be abandoned there would be no agreement.

At this point Mr. Stephenson asked if he might say something 'off the record.' He said that his Minister had met with considerable opposition from his colleagues in the Cabinet on the proposed agreement and he knew that Lord Caldecote had secured the Cabinet sanction by presenting what he described as a list of 'colossal benefits' which would accrue to the British if this agreement were approved. At the head of this list of colossal benefits, said Mr. Stephenson, they had put this question of transhipment. And he said that just as I was emphatic about the exclusion of the transhipment arrangement, he, with Sir William Brown, was equally emphatic that the whole proposals would fall to the ground if the transhipment request were refused.

They urged that the proposal was for a contingency which they hoped might not arise. It was navigationally impossible to carry out this transhipment except in sheltered water. They had already experimented with parts of the Bristol Channel but had not succeeded. Sir William Brown said that the contingency was now more remote than it was in April. I asked him what he meant by this. He said that in April they had thought that their western ports would be very much more severely damaged by air attack than had proved to be the case. If the future held nothing worse for them in this regard than what they had already experienced the necessity for implementing that part of the agreement would most likely never arise. Transhipment would be purely a commercial transaction and the executive arrangements would be made between the shipping companies concerned.

If the business were so entirely commercial I enquired why they wished to include in an agreement between Governments a matter which if it arose would on their own showing be clearly one not for Governments but for shipping firms. What did they mean by the expression 'facilities' they suggested we should provide? Sir William Brown replied that facilities would be more a matter of goodwill than of executive action. Government action would really be inaction. But it might be that Local Authorities near the sheltered waters in question would approach our Government representing the risk to their area of the proposed transhipping and if our Government could soothe these Authorities he did not think any more could be asked of us.

Sir William Brown said that it was not the intention to publish the agreement as a whole: certain parts of it might have to be announced for trade requirements but there would be no publication of the part referring to transhipment. I said that suggestion made the proposal less acceptable – if that were possible.

Finally, I pressed Sir William Brown strongly to let me have a document for submission to my Government setting out exactly what they had in mind. He said he would do his best to let me have such a document to-morrow (Saturday).

No. 272 NAI DFA Secretary's Files P3

Telegram from William Warnock (via Geneva)
to the Department of External Affairs (Dublin)
(No. 55S) (Personal) (Copy)

BERLIN, 23 August 1940

Your telegram 93.[1] Under-Secretary of State W.[oermann] asked me to call; informed me inquiries have shown S.S. Kerry Head was in fact bombed by German aircraft. He stated he had been authorised to express regret of German Government formally.

No. 273 NAI DFA Secretary's Files P12/1

Telegram from Seán Murphy to Department of External Affairs (Dublin)
(No. 152) (Personal) (Copy)

VICHY, 23 August 1940

After some difficulty and delay succeeded in obtaining permission from German authorities to go to Paris. Cremin and I left here Saturday and returned yesterday Thursday. I saw Father Travers, priest at Avenue Hoche, Father Griffin, Sister Olive and Community. All were safe and well. I saw some of the Irish colony. The majority of them though born in Ireland hold British passports and are now very anxious to obtain Irish passports. Although they are not likely to be interned they have to report daily. I took applications for passports and registration and promised to issue passports valid for one year renewable gratis when registration effected. The majority are living on small savings and will soon be destitute. In most cases relatives in Ireland will not be able to assist; others have no relatives there. Stock of passports exhausted. I consequently propose to have document printed here which will state that it is exchangeable for normal national passport as soon as circumstances permit.

Father Monahan interned at Bordeaux because holder of British passport. Have made representations to German authorities stating that he is Irish and that I am prepared to give him an Irish passport. The Germans, however, do not consider us as having any locus standi vis-a-vis them and anything they may do is an act of grace. Have asked for permission for Cremin to go to Hendaye[2] but as yet have no reply.

No. 274 NAI DFA 219/2A

Confidential report from John W. Dulanty to Joseph P. Walshe (Dublin)
(No. 55) (Secret) (Copy)

LONDON, 24 August 1940

Adverting to recent telephone conversations with the Secretary of the Department, one of the chief impressions of the general situation here is the absence of any

---

[1] See No. 250.
[2] Hendaye, the most south-westerly town in France, is situated on the River Bidassoa, which marks the Franco-Spanish border.

serious war nervousness. So ordinary does the conduct of life – work and recreation – appear that no one would conclude that a war of the magnitude of the present conflict is hourly continuing. From the windows of this Office during the last few air raid warnings one saw people going about their business normally and even leisurely.[1] At the big drapers' store opposite women were looking in the shop windows as though nothing was happening. It is of course true that no serious raids have taken place in London but even in Essex, where my son works, and where raids are frequent, the people appear to have great composure. The rationing of food appears to be satisfactory; the public have now got quite accustomed to the black-out, and during this morning at 9 o'clock when an air raid warning was sounded, the movement and transport of people proceeding to their work went on much as usual.

The general political situation appears to be that the Government's popularity is not as great as was the case a few weeks ago. I meet with expressions of considerable dissatisfaction about Mr. Duff Cooper and it is thought that before long he will be moved, though not out of the Cabinet. On the other hand the appreciation of Lord Beaverbrook's successful drive in increasing armaments is very general.

Mr. Neville Chamberlain's Private Secretary told me a day or two ago that his Chief had made a successful recovery. In view, however, of the fact that the operation was in connection with an intestinal stoppage of a rather unusual kind it may be that, at his age, Mr. Chamberlain will hardly be able to take the active part he has taken hitherto. He is not I think a man to leave the Cabinet but health considerations might compel this, and if he did go there would inevitably be a big reconstruction of the Cabinet.

The view in the City – a potent factor in these matters – is that even yet the Government are not putting anything like the requisite energy into their task. Munitions in practically every direction are not being produced according to the existing capacity of the country. Lord Beaverbrook succeeded in finding idle capacity and putting that capacity on a twenty-four hour time table for aircraft, and it is said that the same thrust should be shown in other quarters.

Allowing for the terrific losses just before Dunkirk there is a good deal of uneasiness here that, notwithstanding what Mr. Churchill said recently, the equipment of the army in England is still a long way below what it should be. Further, the training being given to the men in many instances is said to be not only inadequate but out of date.

Of the nine millions per day reported being spent on the war effort there was at least a wastage of 25 per cent. From my own recollection of the last war I would think this estimate reasonably correct.[2]

The present basis of the Excess Profits Tax the City argue will prove to be a mistaken policy since it will not only lead to excessive extravagance but tend to lessen the necessary control essential to obtaining the best results for output. On a matter of this kind the view of the City must of course be taken with reserve, but there is no doubt about their feeling that hasty, not to say panic, legislation is affecting efficiency. I think they are right.[3]

[signed] J.W. Dulanty

---

[1] The office of the Irish High Commission was on Regent Street in London.
[2] From 1917 to 1918 Dulanty served as Principal Assistant Secretary in the British Ministry of Munitions.
[3] The final sentence is a handwritten addition by Dulanty.

1940

No. 275 NAI DFA 244/8C

> *Telegram from Leopold H. Kerney to the Department of External Affairs (Dublin)*
> *(No. 51) (Personal) (Copy)*
>
> MADRID, 24 August 1940

Your 58.[1] Travelling East has reached destination foreshadowed in my telegram No. 34[2] precise whereabouts not ascertainable here. I suggest advising Brennan though I consider assumed name and passport not unlikely. No objection here to information leaking out but please note only knowledge I am supposed to have is that he escaped with help of American friends and I understand any official enquiry would be answered accordingly. I suggest deferring official enquiry until rumour affords pretext.

No. 276 NAI DFA Secretary's Files P3

> *Code telegram from the Department of External Affairs (via Geneva) to*
> *William Warnock (Berlin)*
> *(No. 111S) (Personal) (Copy)*
>
> DUBLIN, 26 August 1940

Between 2 and 3 this afternoon an aircraft identity not yet definitely established but reported to be German dropped bombs near Waterford Harbour and Bannow Bay at Campile, Ballymitty, Duncormick and other places. Details not yet available.[3] Occurrence probably due to mistake, but please inform German authorities at once, ask them to have German airmen specially warned against danger of such mistakes and say if German nationality of plane is established we shall, of course, have to make a protest and claim compensation. Some bombs did not explode and are in hands of military.

No. 277 NAI DFA Secretary's Files A20/4

> *Confidential report from Leopold H. Kerney to Joseph P. Walshe (Dublin)*
> *(M. 10/11) (Secret)*
>
> MADRID, 26 August 1940

Frank Ryan

My only justification for not giving you a full and detailed report immediately and for notifying the main facts in veiled language was the desire not to compromise or expose to possibly serious danger a friend (whom I shall refer to as Mr. B.)[4] without whose help I would probably have achieved no success, and also out of consideration for Ryan's own chances of getting clear of new friends and old enemies.

---

[1] Not printed.
[2] Not printed.
[3] The aircraft were in fact German, two Heinkel-111 medium bombers; they were identified as such by the Irish Defence Forces as they passed into Irish airspace. In the attack at Campile three young women were killed.
[4] Marginal note: 'B = Champourcin'.

Mr. B. now assures me that he fears no danger from Spaniards, is indifferent to any British action and only wishes not to be compromised with his German friends; on the other hand Ryan is in the U.S.A. I can now write more freely, with the knowledge that, if my report were to be read by those for whom it is not intended, no evil could result therefrom, the only risk being that, if it were to fall into German hands, Mr. B. might incur their pleasure.

Mr. B. was in the Spanish Secret Service during the civil war and formed close contacts with the German intelligence service; he is on friendly terms with certain Germans in Madrid;[1] being aware of my concern for Ryan and having helped us in many efforts, he suggested some time ago that the Gestapo[2] might serve to secure Ryan's liberation. About the middle of May (see my report 23rd May)[3] I decided to fall in with this suggestion; I was beginning to doubt the likelihood of my direct petition to the War Office meeting with success; all our other appeals had met with a deaf ear; for some unaccountable reason, Franco himself was the stumbling bloc, and it appeared likely that Ryan's imprisonment would last as long as his own life or that of the regime itself.

Mr. B. spoke to his friends here and told them casually of Ryan's case in which he was taking a professional interest; in other conversations he aroused their interest in Ryan and convinced them that, if he was kept in prison after all Americans and British had been liberated, it was because the British Intelligence Service had been active; he induced them to take up the case; this they agreed to do, laying down the condition that I was to know nothing of their intervention; there has been no communication direct or indirect, between me and the Gestapo, and, as far as latter organisation is concerned, the only information given to me by my professional adviser (Mr. B.) is that Ryan has reached the U.S.A., having succeeded in effecting his escape with the help of American friends. The facts are as follows:

June 11 B's friends were pursuing the matter actively and with continued interest; they were following it up daily with Generals Martinez Campo and Vigón (in charge of the Spanish Secret Service), and would employ direct contact with Franco if present channels failed.

June 27 As there were no developments, I requested B. to press his friends to use 'direct contact' in question.

June 30 I learned that it was General Vigón who had been informed that Franco had a personal interest in Ryan, and it was suggested to me (but this was only a suggestion and nothing more) that there might be some personal bargain with the English at the back of it. The 'direct contact' was about to be resorted to, as the Spanish Secret Service had not succeeded in obtaining satisfaction for their German colleagues.

July 1 The 'direct contact' (a German) saw Franco this day; Franco believed the matter could be arranged and told him to come back in a couple of days.

July 3 Franco was again seen and this time said definitely 'yes'; he was giving instructions to Finat, Chief of Police. (Finat owes his position to Serrano Suñer, whose secretary he formerly was.)

July 4 Finat telephoned Burgos to obtain information ('antecedentes')[4] of Ryan's case, for identification purposes, but without success.

---

[1] This sentence to this point has been highlighted in the left-hand margin.
[2] Kerney may have meant the Abwehr, the German intelligence service. The Gestapo was the name applied to the German secret police.
[3] Not printed.
[4] 'Historical records'.

July 5 B. saw Finat and showed him a copy of Ryan's sentence, from which he took extracts; Finat said that the only legal way of securing the liberation of Ryan was by means of a pardon ('indulto'); his orders were to hasten the pardon ('activar el indulto'). This meant that he would take up with the War Office, where the ground had already been completely prepared by me, and gave me the hope that the 'indulto' would be notified to me, through regular channels, in due course.

July 9th I learned that Finat had taken the necessary steps with the War Office, and also that he had made the statement that 'it was incredible that Ryan should have been kept prisoner, although English, Canadians and Americans had been released'.

July 12 B. saw Finat and was told that Franco found it impossible for him to sign the 'indulto', but had given orders for Ryan's 'escape' to be officially organised as a solution; he would be put into France and the Director of the Prison would be ordered to report that he had escaped. I saw Ryan the same evening in Burgos as reported at the time.[1]

July 15 Some hitch seems to have occurred.

July 23 Still no news, but B. had been congratulated by some German friends a couple of days previously on his success; they turned the conversation when they saw he was surprised; B. also told me that there appeared to be an impression amongst his friends that I was 'pro British Empire', and this might account for great caution.

Wed. July 24[2] Thinking Ryan might have already 'escaped', I sent him a pre-paid wire but got no reply; at 6 p.m. B. got in touch with me and told me that all was arranged; I gave him 1,500 pesetas on account of expenses, as he was carrying out his promise to me to be an eyewitness; he was borrowing a Packard car and petrol alone would cost that amount – 1,000 km using 30 litres per 100 km at 5 pesetas per litre.

Thursday July 25th At 9 a.m. a trunk call from B. reported simply that 'everything had gone off satisfactorily'.

At 2 a.m. on that date B. stopped his car on the roadside a short distance away from the prison. Half an hour later two cars drove past; in the first were Finat's secretary and a German; in the second there were two armed uniformed Falangistas, members of Serrano Suñer's personal bodyguard. About 20 minutes after entering the prison, they emerged with Ryan; this additional passenger was seen to be in one of the two cars as they again passed in front of the stationery car. B.'s larger car then returned to Burgos and, getting ahead of the others, reached Irun about 7.30 a.m.; B. left his car in the town, and proceeded on foot to the international bridge; about 8.30 a.m. the two cars arrived at the bridge, papers were quickly produced and the barrier lifted almost at once, but B. saw Ryan in his car and Ryan gave a quick glance showing he recognised B., but without betraying the fact to those beside him (B. had already seen Ryan on one occasion in prison).

At 3.30 p.m. the same day in San Sebastian B. was handed by his German friend, who had accompanied Ryan in one car, a letter addressed to him by Ryan and headed 'Saint Jean de Luz 25th July 1940'; before the letter was left with B., however, the part showing the place and date was cut away with a scissors; this

---

[1] See No. 246.
[2] This paragraph has been highlighted in the left-hand margin by a line in blue pencil.

was a letter of thanks, saying that everything had gone off without a hitch, that he was not returning immediately to Ireland but was going on a journey that would take some weeks; B. suggested to me that his destination might be the U.S.A. via Siberia, and I presumed that there were some grounds for his making the suggestion.[1]

I heard nothing further until the night of 22nd August when B. told me that Ryan had now reached the U.S.A. and B.'s German friends had agreed to his informing me that Ryan had escaped with American help; they assured him that Finat would give this explanation if he were to be questioned; above all there must be no knowledge of German participation in the 'escape'.

In view of Ryan's letter of 25th July, there is no reason for doubting the truth of the statement that he was in the U.S.A. by 22nd August. Is he there under an assumed name? Does he hold a false passport – British, American or Irish? If he entered the country illegally, will he be deported? Is it possible for him to remain in the U.S.A., even under an assumed name, without the fact becoming known?

Before the Gestapo in Madrid busied itself on Ryan's behalf, they referred the matter to Berlin and got a prompt reply to go ahead; they must have known a good deal about Ryan in Berlin; if certain Irish elements in the U.S.A. or elsewhere had been in contact with Berlin and had been anxious to secure Ryan's liberty instruction would have been given from Berlin in the first place and the initiative would not have been taken in Madrid.

It is worth noting that Franco was unable to give any definite assurance on 1st July; he had, apparently, to consult with somebody else and, as a result of this consultation, he was able to give his consent two days later; I think he may have talked the matter over with his brother-in-law Serrano Suñer, in the interval; then, instead of instructing the Minster for Foreign Affairs, who had so often brought the matter to his notice previously, he instructed the Chief of Police, Serrano Suñer's protégé. It is strange that, whereas on July 5 Finat made it known that his orders were to hasten the conclusion of formalities for the granting of a pardon, by July 12th Franco found himself unable to give his signature to the pardon; what had happened during these seven days? Had Franco at some earlier date given a formal promise, in return for some consideration, never to release Ryan? Did he think on July 3 that the bargain might have been forgotten with the passage of time? Did some other secret service find out, say at the War Office, what was about to take place? Is this why the signature had to be withheld?

It also has to be noted that Franco rejected all Irish appeals in favour of Ryan, even when precedents had been created by the release of others; if he had granted a pardon, Ryan would have remained under Irish control and supervision; he authorised and ordered a very unusual procedure, as a concession to Germany and not as a concession to Ireland; he authorised the placing of this alleged dangerous Communist at Germany's disposal – a gesture which could conceivably have unpleasant consequences for the Irish government, and therefore anything but a friendly gesture towards Ireland.

---

[1] A subsequent account, based on Kerney family sources, explains that Kerney personally observed the handover from a further vehicle parked at a distance from the border (see www.leopoldhkerney.com (accessed 12 June 2008))

It is natural enough that relations between the German and Spanish intelligence services should be very close; there are apparently certain services which the Head of the State is ready to render to Germans even if this means exposing himself to reproaches from other friends.

If Frank Ryan is alive and at liberty today, we have no reason to thank the Spanish Government, and the result has been secured in spite of opposition from the highest quarter.

[signed] L.H. KERNEY

P.S.[1] B. has been referred to in different reports of mine; see that of 23rd December 1939 re Frank Ryan; 1st and 2nd paragraphs.[2]

No. 278 NAI DFA Paris Embassy 19/34

Confidential report from Seán Murphy to Joseph P. Walshe (Dublin)
(Copy)

VICHY, 27 August 1940

I have already stated in a telegram[3] that I visited Paris accompanied by Mr. Cremin on the 17th inst. After being turned back from the line of demarcation two weeks previously I had asked Count O'Kelly who has been in Paris since the end of July, to apply for a permit to enable me to make the journey. The arrangements were made with the German authorities at Moulins on the 16th. We were therefore able to effect the trip without any difficulty. The distance to Paris is about 350 kilometres (220 miles). There is little sign along the road of extensive havoc wrought by the war. Apart from some partially broken bridges and rather extensive damage (caused I think by the German attack of the 3rd June) to the aerodrome at Orly, about six miles south of Paris, I noticed nothing in particular. There are German troops, however, stationed in all the villages and on the upward journey we were stopped on a number of occasions, while soldiers examined the outside of the car. About 30 kilometres before Paris, we were held up by the final German control station which after examining our papers allowed us through with little delay. The actual entry to Paris is not easy as most of the gates are blocked up by sandbags – only three or four on the outskirts being left free. On arrival in the city I went to see the Legation and found everything just as I had left it, the flag which we had hoisted on the morning of our departure being still flying. Count O'Kelly had received the visit of a number of persons of Irish birth in, and around Paris, who were anxious to obtain Irish papers so as to avoid difficulties with the German authorities. All these people were told to come to the Legation on the Monday and Tuesday following. Some of them only wanted advice. The required particulars were taken from those who asked for Irish passports. Their cases are dealt with in separate minutes.[4]

2. On Sunday morning I called on Fr. O'Grady, Fr. Travers and Fr. Griffin, as well as Monsignor Bertoli, Secretary of the Nunciature who had remained in Paris, and

---

[1] This postscript has been highlighted in the left-hand margin by a line in blue pencil.
[2] See No. 99.
[3] See No. 273.
[4] Not printed, but see also No. 298.

for whom I had correspondence from the Nuncio. I invited all four as well as Fr. O'Farrell – the only other member at present of the clergy of Avenue Hoche to lunch on Monday. Fr. Griffin was unable to accept as he was going on retreat that evening. The other four accepted and seemed to enjoy the lunch which was attended also by Count O'Kelly and Mr. Cremin. The four Irish priests are all in excellent form. Fr. O'Grady must, I think, have had a considerable amount of worry since the occupation of Paris, as his Congregation has very seriously dwindled and on the other hand, he has had a number of visits from the German authorities who have sealed up a number of rooms in the Presbytery. You are probably aware that this church is under the joint protection of the British and American Embassies. It is however as you know generally considered to be an English Church. He informed me that the Germans had said that they intended to return to examine the contents of the rooms which they had sealed. So far they had not done so, and he told me that the Catholic Chaplain-General of the German forces who is quartered in the Park Monceau hotel in the same street, and says Mass regularly in the church had undertaken to intervene on his behalf. I believe that the Spanish church in Paris was sealed in a similar manner, but that on a protest from the Embassy the seals were removed. Neither Fr. O'Grady nor Fr. O'Farrell has been personally molested although Fr. O'Grady holds a British passport. This passport is now expired, and as he is a citizen under the 1922 Constitution he could obtain an Irish one. He said however, that he would prefer not to do so, at least for the time being as the fact of his holding a British passport enables him to get funds from members of his Congregation from the American Embassy (as representing British interests), whereas this recourse would be closed to him if he held an Irish passport.

3. On Tuesday I and Mr. Cremin lunched with Fr. Travers at the Irish College. Up to then the College had not received any visit from the German authorities. One room of it has been for some time past and still is used by officials of the Defense Passive. By a coincidence while we were talking after lunch, the German officer came along to inspect the building which he understood was empty, with a view to installing some of his men there. I was therefore able to explain to him directly that it was the property of the Irish Bishops and used by them for lodging Ecclesiastical students at present on holiday. Later I gave Fr. Travers a signed document to be put on the door in Irish, French and German to the effect that the property belongs to the Irish Bishops and is used for ecclesiastical studies.

4. I mentioned in a previous minute that I understand that the German authorities had carried out considerable perquisitions in ecclesiastical establishments – my information on this point came from the Nunciature. Mgr Bertoli when I was in Paris told me that shortly after their arrival the Germans went to the Archbishopric and examined carefully everything they found there. After a few days the Cardinal-Archbishop of Paris who only took up his functions towards the end of May, was completely confined to his room to the extent of his being unable to say Mass. Latterly, however, the German treatment of the Archbishop and Archbishopric has been less severe, and he is able to carry on his activities more or less normally. Mgr. Bertoli's opinion is that the search conducted by the Germans is directed to finding proofs for their suspicion of political action injurious to them on the part of Cardinal Verdier, against whom he says they are inspired by an extreme hatred. They consider that during his missions abroad to countries like Czecho-Slovakia,

Austria and Hungary, he carried on a political propaganda opposed to Germany. They apparently also suspected the church in France of having assisted Jews and political émigrés, and suspect political connivance between them. Apart from the Archbishopric one or two other ecclesiastical institutions of an international character have also been searched and are at present under seal. Mgr. Bertoli confirmed also that the Germans have on one or two occasions already held non-Catholic ceremonies in some churches including the Madeleine. According to the Nuncio a similar service was held in Notre Dame.

5. As far as the superficial aspect of Paris under German occupation is concerned the most striking feature is by far its relative emptiness. The 1936 census gave Paris proper a total population of 2,829,776 inhabitants. I do not know the total exodus from Paris in the days immediately preceding the German entry. On the 7th July the Paris population according to a census taken on that date was 1,056,000, which meant that about 1,800,000 persons were absent. On the 12th August another census gave the figure of 1,403,000 as the then population of the city, which represents approximately about half the normal total population. Apart from the Champs Elysées the streets on the whole, when we were there, had a very empty air. This is probably due to some extent at least to the fact that a great number of business houses even belonging to people who had returned have not yet re-opened, and that the economic life of the city is undoubtedly still only in process of resuming. In the Champs Elysées one sees large numbers of German soldiers and Officers. Practically all the cars circulating in the city are German cars or cars requisitioned by the German authorities. Private traffic is completely suspended. The only other vehicles which circulate are those engaged in bringing provisions etc. A large number of the first-class hotels have been taken over by the Germans – those already requisitioned by the French Government and a number of others – Georges V, Prince de Galles, Crillion, Meurice, Majestic, Grand Hotel, Claridge, Napoleon, Raphael, Continental, Ritz. German administrations are installed in some of these Hotels, such as the Crillon and the Majestic, and also in a few French Ministries; the Ministry of the Marine is used for the German Admiralty, the Palais Bourbon is used for the issue of certain kinds of permits; the Ministry of War is taken over and many of the others are closed. The Elysée has not been taken over. The rumours which circulated here from time to time both in regard to the taking over by the occupying authority of certain houses and flats, and the transport to Paris of large numbers of German families, are, if not entirely false, very exaggerated. I was able to see for myself that the houses in the Avenue Foch, which belong to the Rothschilds were not taken over. There are not a great number of German women to be seen, and I understand that those that are there, are, firstly, those belonging to the Red Cross and other units, and secondly those serving as typists. The Officers serving in Paris are not for the most part accompanied by their wives. M. Abetz[1] is installed in the German Embassy. His wife is apparently French. The black-out at night is at least as full as prior to the German occupation. A considerable number of military convoys pass through the city. As far as I could observe the

---

[1] Otto Abetz (1903-58), German Ambassador to Vichy France (Nov. 1940-July 1944). Though assigned to the German embassy in Paris in 1940 and appointed in November Abetz was never formally accredited owing to the fact that a formal peace treaty between Germany and France was never signed.

German military individually do not interfere at all with the population, and their conduct is not in any way truculent. Food supplies are better in Paris than here in Vichy. The restaurants offer a much greater choice of food and seem to do a thriving business. The restrictions on circulation are of course a result of the lack of abundant supplies of petrol. Up to the middle of August each diplomatic mission was entitled to a certain quantity of petrol per month – 800 litres per Embassy – and 500 litres per Legation. The system changed while we were there and I understand that the new system has not yet been fully arranged. The time at Paris is, of course, one hour in advance of that in the unoccupied zone as Central European time is observed.

6. As far as I can gather there is only a small section of the French Administrations installed in the city. Mgr. Bertoli told me that the Minister for Finance and the Minister of Communications who had gone to Paris with the intention of remaining there had been invited by the Germans to leave. What is certain is that they are not at Paris now. It seems that the French administration is the executive authority for all measures relating to the Government of Paris and matters arising therefrom. I think, however, that all measures in this connection are either decided by the Germans or at least have to be approved by them. The French press consists of three or four dailies, the main one being the Matin. The Matin is published only at Paris and not at all in the free zone. Its owner who was always regarded as being primarily anti-Russian and incidentally rather pro-German, chose that course. There is also a Paris edition of Paris-Soir, which however, in its previous form appears in the free zone. In addition there is a newspaper called 'La France au travail', and another called 'Les Dernieres Nouvelles de Paris'. Finally there are a few weeklies including one called 'Au Pilori' which is mainly anti-Semitic and is, I understand, the revival of a newspaper on similar lines which appeared at the end of the last century at the time of the Dreyfus case.[1] All the French newspapers published adopt the German point of view, and are frequently at the least sceptical of the prospects of success of the French Government. They are critical of the sincerity or effectiveness of the measures taken by the Government to alter political morals and to bring those responsible for France's defeat to book.

No. 279 NAI DFA 244/8C

Letter from Joseph P. Walshe to Eilís Ryan[2] (Dublin)
(244/BB) (Strictly Confidential) (Copy)

DUBLIN, 27 August 1940

Dear Miss Ryan,

I should be glad if you would come to see me on your return to Dublin. We have been informed by Mr. Kerney that your brother has been 'unofficially' released. He wrote to Mr. Kerney from St. Jean de Luz on the 25th July thanking him for all his attention and kindness, and explaining that he did not intend to return direct to Ireland. Since then Mr. Kerney has heard that he has reached the United States. He

---

[1] The Dreyfus case caused a political scandal with anti-Semitic overtones that divided France from the 1890s to the early 1900s. It involved the wrongful conviction for treason, in 1894, of a Jewish army Captain, Alfred Dreyfus (1859-1935).
[2] Sister of Frank Ryan.

does not know his address but understands that he will communicate direct with you.

I should explain that Mr. Kerney has not been informed officially of the release. He has been given to understand that your brother escaped with the help of American friends, but there is no doubt that the Spanish Authorities connived at the 'escape'. We cannot, therefore, make any official announcement, and I should be glad if you would keep the information in this letter strictly confidential until I have had an opportunity of talking to you about it. There is, of course, no objection to informing your parents confidentially.

Yours sincerely,
[stamped] signed J.P. WALSHE

No. 280 NAI DFA Secretary's Files P3

*Code telegram from the Department of External Affairs
to William Warnock (Berlin)
(No. 114S) (Personal) (Copy)*

DUBLIN, 28 August 1940

My 111.[1] Plane now definitely identified as German by witnesses and unexploded bombs. Coroner's inquest found plane was German. There is no reasonable doubt. Three girls were killed several persons suffered minor injuries creamery at Campile was destroyed and other private property was damaged. Please make formal protest reserving rights to full compensation. Public opinion here regards occurrence as unfortunate mistake but newspapers in Britain and America reported it as something more sinister. In view of this publicity particularly New York Times leader of 28th we consider it in mutual interest that we should be in a position to publish at earliest possible moment communiqué stating German Government on evidence available admit possibility of error having occurred and express regret and sympathy with relatives of victims. Statement should also indicate German readiness to compensate damage and loss. Endeavour to arrange this.

Concerning blockade we are wiring you to-day. Urge on Foreign Office strongly the view that for the present the less publicity there is about our position in relation to the blockade the better. The German semi-official statements made on this matter so far have served only to foster newspaper propaganda against us in America.

No. 281 NAI DFA Secretary's Files P12/1

*Code telegram from the Department of External Affairs to Seán Murphy (Vichy)
(No. 164) (Personal) (Copy)*

DUBLIN, 29 August 1940

Your 152.[2] Very glad you succeeded in getting to Paris. Are Legation premises and contents intact? How many Irish citizens approximately will need help. Approve issue of substitute documents. Would it help if we asked German Government to

---

[1] See No. 276.
[2] See No. 273.

give you special facilities to deal with our citizens in occupied area. Please let me know before you leave for Paris again. Have many inquiries for you to make there. Your 168[1] just received. Family very well still in Bettystown. Cremin family also well.

No. 282 NAI DFA Secretary's Files A3

Memorandum by Joseph P. Walshe on the response of British troops in Northern Ireland to a German invasion of Ireland

DUBLIN, 30 August 1940

If Germany invaded Ireland what steps would the British troops in the Six Counties be likely to take?
1) Their Air Force would attack the Germans. Consequently, they would take aerodromes in the neighbourhood of Dublin, establish depots there, as well as service units. It is very likely that the men and materials for this purpose are now in Newry ready for immediate transfer to the Dublin area.
2) No doubt the British are most afraid of a German invasion through Donegal, and they must have made preparations to advance immediately to Lough Swilly from Derry. Donegal would be overrun at once by the British troops now stationed in Derry. Our troops in Donegal would, in those circumstances, be faced with the immediate problem of the attitude to be taken towards the British troops.
3) If the Germans invaded us first, and we had to request the aid of the British, we should have to inform them before they actually crossed into our territory of our plans for the demolition of bridges, etc. This would be done through Liaison Officers who would also be responsible in such circumstances for the requisitioning of billets for the invited troops. The Liaison Officers would also inform the invited troops of the medical arrangements, hospitalisation of wounded men, etc.
4) Supplies for the invited troops would come to Dublin by rail, whereas the troops themselves would come by road. The Liaison Officers would have to know all about rolling-stock facilities. We should have to allow the invited troops to make a general base in or near Dublin for all kinds of supplies of clothing, munitions, etc. Dublin, being a port, provides the obvious site for such a supply base.

No. 283 NAI DFA Secretary's Files P20

Telegram from the Department of External Affairs (in three parts via Geneva) to William Warnock (Berlin)
(No. 71, No. 73, No. 74)[2] (Personal) (Copy)

DUBLIN, 30 August 1940

On 17th August German Minister presented a note regarding blockade.[3] It suggested Government action to prevent Irish citizens and ships entering danger areas and said German Government was prepared to exempt from blockade ships flying

---

[1] Not printed.
[2] This telegram was sent in three separate transmissions; for the sake of clarity it is reproduced here as one document.
[3] See Nos 264 and 265.

Irish flag carrying essential supplies to us on condition of guarantee against transshipment. Hempel was authorised to negotiate special agreement on latter lines and strongly urged early reply.

As we have explained to Hempel, we appreciate regard for our interests implied in offer of special agreement, but even from the strictly practical point of view difficulties connected with insurance, the possibility of chartering neutral shipping prepared to fly Irish flag and other matters make immediate reply impossible. From the political point of view we must have regard to the conformity of any special agreement with our strict neutrality and to the possible use against us of German official statements about Holland and Belgium's attitude to British blockade such as those of 6th December, 29th February and 1st March. As regards transshipment, we do not allow it and there is no intention of changing this policy.

Government are much concerned at prospect of disturbance of Cross-Channel trade. In so far as legality of German measures is doubtful, we must reserve all our rights. Practically measures will hit us more than Britain because our exports to Britain are only 2½% of her imports but are 85% of our export trade and therefore of vital importance to us. Politically attacks on our trade will have bad repercussions internally and externally. These and other considerations make it likely that Germany would lose more than she would gain by attacks on Cross-Channel trade. We strongly urge therefore that our trade with Britain be exempt from blockade measures. The L.M.S. mail-boat is a case in point. It is of British registry but vast bulk of passengers are Irish. Use your knowledge of what the effect would be on public opinion here to impress on German authorities that particularly as mail boat carries only passengers and mails, to attack it, even though it is a British ship, would be a major blunder. The Rosslare-Fishguard boat also British has already been machine gunned twice. Perhaps the most immediate question however is that of German attacks on Irish registered ships. We are anxious in interest of our neutrality and relations with Germany that German forces should be given orders not to make specific attacks on ships flying Irish flag, including those engaged in Cross-Channel trade. As we have explained to Hempel this course is strongly commended by following considerations.

One. Our exports are a small fraction of British imports and an even smaller fraction of British imports are carried in Irish ships. For the first seven months of this year the figures are 2½% and ½% respectively. We are giving details of these figures to Hempel. For Germany the material interest involved is infinitesimal.

Two. Political repercussions of frequent attacks on Irish ships would be deplorable. Though other losses would be suppressed attacks on Irish ships would be headlined in British and American newspapers as violations of our neutrality. Irish opinion in America and elsewhere abroad would be dismayed. Propaganda against our neutrality would be given a powerful weapon. The political and propagandist disadvantages from Germany's point of view would be out of proportion to any material result achieved.

Three. Bad prices and smaller purchases are likely to cause reduction of certain exports particularly store cattle in near future. Farmers will suffer. Absence of attacks on Irish ships would lessen risk of blockade being regarded by public opinion here as responsible for hardships due to other causes.

Four. We have striven to keep our export trade on normal peace-time lines. We do not allow transshipment or re-export or acceptance of abnormal war contracts. Irish ships are not armed and do not sail in convoy. This policy calls for some reciprocity on German side. It will be difficult to maintain if even Irish exports in Irish vessels are attacked.

We have only 10 vessels over 1,000 tons of which 8 are less than 1,500 tons and one of the remaining two is a passenger ship. Of the ten, four are mainly in Spanish and other trade outside Irish Sea. We appreciate German Government cannot guarantee against mines and damage by raids on British ports. But we do expect that they will abstain from directly attacking Irish ships at sea by air or submarine. We would agree that there should be no disclosure of any kind about the exemption and that it should not be abused by increases in frequency of sailings, etc.

Please see Woermann at once and speak to him on lines of foregoing.

No. 284 NAI DFA 221/147

*Code telegram from the Department of External Affairs
to Robert Brennan (Washington)
(No. 131) (Personal) (Copy)*

DUBLIN, 30 August 1940

View generally held here that Wexford bombing due to navigational error on part of pilot. Conclusions of press leaders referred to in your 195 and 199[1] are completely unwarranted. Similar violation of neutrality with loss of life occurred in Denmark in September and in Switzerland in June former by British latter by French. We are seeking apology and reparation from German Government. Better avoid making statement for present.

No. 285 NAI DFA Washington Embassy Confidential Reports 1940

*Confidential report from Robert Brennan to Joseph P. Walshe (Dublin)
(108/84/40) (Copy)*

WASHINGTON, 3 September 1940

Apart from the Conscription Bill and the huge votes for armaments now totalling eighteen billion dollars, there is ample evidence that the United States is working up a war spirit. A mediocre song entitled 'God Bless America' written two years ago by Irving Berlin,[2] has been adopted as the campaign song by both the Republican and Democratic parties. One hears it everywhere, in theatres, cafes, on the radio and in the street. Miniature American flags appear on all sides, in shop windows, on bicycles, automobiles, etc. The stores are full of toys and ornaments worked in the national colors, red, white and blue, and they seem to be very popular. One gets the impression that very little would be needed to send the people in thousands parading in the streets in war processions.

Judging by the press and radio the feeling in favour of England and against Germany is growing by leaps and bounds.

[stamped] (Signed) ROBT. BRENNAN

---

[1] Neither telegram printed.
[2] Irving Berlin (1888-1989), Russian-born naturalised American composer and lyricist. 'God Bless America' was written originally by Berlin in 1918 and was revised by him in 1938. The song is at times considered the unofficial anthem of the United States of America.

No. 286 NAI DFA 221/147

*Code telegram from the Department of External Affairs
to William Warnock (Berlin)
(No. 134) (Personal) (Copy)*

DUBLIN, 5 September 1940

Essential urge German Government to complete investigations re Campile. All arguments are in favour of liquidating incident with all possible speed. Apology for Kerry Head produced excellent effect. You should emphasize again absence of any reasonable doubt of plane's nationality.

No. 287 NAI DFA Secretary's Files 12/3

*Code telegram from William Warnock (via Geneva) to
the Department of External Affairs (Dublin)
(No. 60S) (Personal) (Copy)*

BERLIN, 5 September 1940

Your 129[1] material effect Berlin slight, Carpentry Department of Zagret Cable Company damaged; some damage to private property in City; ——[2] civilians killed. A few bombs fell near Legation. More damage Western Germany but, owing to excellent organisation, quickly repaired. In Hamburg and Bremen slight damage to industries in spite of frequent Air Raids. Planes remain very high. Fair proportion of bombs do not explode. General moral effect small apart from that caused by loss of sleep. The remarkable German successes this year have made people so confident that nothing short of major set-back could undermine morale at the present time.

General opinion if war not over in about a month it will probably continue Winter. There is always hope that Hitler will once more spring brilliant surprise.

No. 288 NAI DFA Secretary's Files 12/1

*Code telegram from the Department of External Affairs (via Geneva)
to William Warnock (Berlin)
(No. 136S) (Secret) (Personal) (Copy)*

DUBLIN, 6 September 1940

Minister in Vichy recently visited Paris with permission of German Authorities.[3] He found that many Irish citizens there will soon require financial assistance. Majority of them hold British passports but Murphy is trying to arrange exchange for Irish. There are many of our citizens scattered throughout occupied territory but since cutting of communications between two areas it is very difficult for him to obtain information about them or even when located to give them financial or other assistance. It would be very helpful if German Government would give

---

[1] Not printed.
[2] No number is given in the document.
[3] See No. 278.

special facilities to Murphy or Cremin to visit occupied territory in the interests of Irish citizens. As things stand, German Authorities do not consider him as having any locus standi in that area. For instance, he is unable to do anything officially for Father Monahan, Passionist, interned in Bordeaux because holder of British passport. Murphy has made unofficial representations for release explaining that he is prepared to issue Irish passport.

Will you please put above considerations before Foreign Office and endeavour secure facilities for Murphy to look after Irish citizens in occupied territory.

No. 289 NAI DFA Legal Adviser's Papers

Extracts from a memorandum by Michael Rynne on Transhipment
DUBLIN, 6 September 1940

1. Transhipment consists in the re-export of goods imported by a neutral State to a belligerent State. One may distinguish between transhipment via searoutes and overland transportation.
[matter omitted]
3. The question naturally arises, therefore, whether, in view of the common fate which appears to await all classes of neutral export trade, a neutral State should not freely indulge in transhipment.
4. If that question were to be answered without reference to any particular state of facts, it could clearly be replied to affirmatively.

As far as Ireland is concerned, however, the problem is not so simple. We, in this country, have to bear in mind the history of our export trade since this war began and to take note of the following points:-
  (1) Our export trade since the war began has been, as always, mainly directed to one of the belligerents only;
  (2) It has been a 'contraband' trade, according to the German list of the 12th September 1939, and, as such, liable to penal measures, according to the German Prize Law of the 3rd September 1939;
  (3) Our export trade was, however, recognised by the German Government, through the German Minister at Dublin, early in the war, as vital to this country whose neutrality Germany desired to see maintained;
  (4) Irish export trade to Britain has been, notwithstanding the lack of any supporting principle of international or German national law, regarded by Germany as falling into a special class which it has been found convenient to describe as 'normal trade;'
  (5) Germany has so far made no deliberate attack on Irish 'normal trade';
  (6) Transhipment and the export to Britain of contraband articles and materials manufactured, or capable of being manufactured here, but not normally exported have not been so far indulged in;
  (7) Since the 17th August 1940, Germany has declared a total blockade of Britain, and has accordingly withdrawn her promise to respect our normal export trade. The German Government have, however, as an exceptional measure offered to respect our import trade on certain conditions, one of which is that we do not tranship imported goods to Britain.

5. The foregoing historical summary would not be complete without reference to the fact that, so far, no advantage has been taken of the recent German offer to negotiate in regard to our future import trade. On the contrary, we have instructed the Chargé d'Affaires at Berlin to impress on the German Government this country's strong desire for the uninterrupted continuance of her normal export trade with Britain.[1]

Incidentally, however, Mr. Warnock is instructed to emphasise to the German Government that the Irish Government has not hitherto permitted and does not, in the future, intend to permit the transhipment of foreign-produced goods to England.

6. The position is, therefore, that, at this moment, the fate of our whole normal export trade with Britain is in the balance. Likewise, of course, that of our import trade in feeding-stuffs and raw materials.

During recent weeks shipments of cattle to England have not been attacked by German forces but of this immunity there is, as yet, no guarantee.

[matter omitted]

8. On the assumption that a transhipment policy were to be adopted at this stage we may, however, anticipate the following reactions on the part of Germany:
   (1) during this transition-period, when nothing has been finally decided about our export trade, which is, however, carrying on as usual to date, the Germans might be expected to deliberately attack that trade on the grounds that the boats were transhipping. The 'normal trade' theory would vanish overnight;
   (2) one of the important conditions attached to the German offer to respect our vital import trade would disappear and the offer would doubtless be withdrawn.

Our own reactions to the foregoing would necessarily take the form of endeavouring to protect our vital trade in every way possible.

Thus, we should probably have to arm our ships and accept British convoys. These steps would entail:
   (1) the treatment of armed Irish registered ships (where owned in Britain) as part of the British fighting forces;
   (2) the treatment of all incoming and outgoing ships in British convoy as enemy vessels to be sunk at sight;
   (3) the loss of our neutrality in the event of British convoys or merchant vessels of any nationality being attacked in our waters. (Even the 'hovering' of British destroyers outside our waters would be a breach of Ireland's neutrality.)

9. In view of the appalling chaos which transhipment activities would bring about in our normally peaceful trade with other countries, there would seem to be grave reasons for not allowing such activities on any account.

Add to that the incalculable disasters which might result on Irish lives and property by drawing the belligerents towards our side of the Irish Sea and Channel, and we are compelled to recognise that the arguments are altogether in favour of maintaining the *status quo* as far as lies in our power. The fact that we are prepared

---

[1] See Nos 283 and 291.

to risk Irish-registered ships, Irish seamen and Irish f.[ree] o.[n] b.[oard] cargoes in order to maintain our normal trade with Britain ought to sufficiently prove our readiness to oblige our best customer, without his requiring us to give free rein to activities likely to culminate in the destruction of all trade between these islands.

[initialled] M.R.

No. 290 NAI DFA Madrid Embassy CON 4/7/22 No. 4

Handwritten notes by Leopold H. Kerney (Madrid)

MADRID, 10 September 1940

10.30 p.m.	'phoned Champ. re O'Reilly cable, and reply thereto; said would call next day, afternoon or evg. to discuss matters.
11.45 p.m.	He 'phoned me to say had G. friend in office just as I 'phoned; that a letter was on the way to me by 'Clipper'[1] written in R's peculiar style, and this would make everything clear and open in a few days' time; meanwhile better wait; Ch. had seen copy of letter.
8 p.m.	Saw Ch. told him of my cable and reply to, also re N.Y. Said if I saw friend latter was instructed what to say. Told him why I cd. not approach friend direct; had not told his friends that I was seeking news, and they were puzzled at this; told him to say he had now given me information.

No. 291 NAI DFA Secretary's Files P20

Memorandum by Frederick H. Boland for Frank Aiken on the German Note
(Secret)

DUBLIN, 11 September 1940

1. On the 17th August, the German Minister in Dublin presented a Note officially notifying us that the seas around England would in future be a centre of warlike operations at sea and in the air.[2] The Note suggested that citizens and Irish ships should not travel in the endangered areas, and went on to say that the German Government wished to facilitate shipments of essential supplies to Ireland and that the German Minister was authorised to negotiate an arrangement with us with regard to the conditions under which this could be assured.

2. On the 30th August, the Chargé d'Affaires at Berlin was instructed to make representations to the German Foreign Office to the effect that the Irish Government were much concerned at this development.[3] We were particularly ~~disturbed~~ concerned at the prospect of our Cross-Channel trade being disturbed. We referred to the doubt as to the legality of the proposed German measures and said that we reserved all our rights. The disturbance of Cross-Channel trade would affect us more than it would affect England because our exports to Britain are only 2½% of her imports, but are 85% of our total exports. Attacks on our trade would have bad

---

[1] A reference to the Pan-American Airlines transatlantic flying boat service that had begun operations in the late 1930s.
[2] See Nos 264 and 265.
[3] See No. 283.

repercussions internally and externally. We were particularly anxious about attacks on Irish-registered ships. We had very few ships and the political reactions of attacks on ships flying the Irish flag would be out of all proportion to the material interest involved. We expected that Germany would refrain from directly attacking Irish ships at sea by air or submarine. What was true about Irish ships was also true about the L.M.S. Mail Boat, which was a British-registered ship. It carried only passengers and mail, and a large number of passengers were Irish. To sink it would be a major blunder.

3. We have not yet received the German reply to these representations. In the meantime, however, the German Minister has been instructed to explain to us that Ireland was included in the danger area only as a matter of absolute military necessity, and that the German Government were anxious to minimize the effects so far as we are concerned.

No. 292 NAI DFA Paris Embassy 12/1

Code telegram from William Warnock (via Geneva) to Joseph P. Walshe (Dublin)
(No. 61S) (Personal) (Copy)

BERLIN, 11 September 1940

Your 136.[1] German Army strongly opposed diplomats travelling to and from occupied territory. All small countries in the same position. Foreign Office suggests application to military authorities demarcation line. Application possible Berlin, but would require long notice and details precise date and purpose.

No. 293 NAI DFA 221/147

Code telegram from William Warnock (via Geneva) to Joseph P. Walshe (Dublin)
(No. 62S) (Personal) (Copy)

BERLIN, 14 September 1940

Your 134.[2] Enquiries of German Air Force do not give any reason to believe that German aeroplane was over Irish territory and dropped bombs 26th August. It appears, however, from information received from German Minister at Dublin that bombs dropped in Campile bore German markings. In the circumstances, it is possible that bombs were dropped by German aeroplane owing to bad visibility that day; pilot might have been wrongfully under the impression that he was over the West Coast of England. Accordingly Under Secretary of State Woermann authorized to express regret of German Government for incident. He requests that regret(s) also be conveyed to relatives. Compensation will be paid, method to be discussed later. German Government request they be consulted as to text of any communiqué to be issued.

Woermann emphasized that this attitude shows great consideration and is concession on their part.

---

[1] See No. 288.
[2] See Nos 276, 280 and 286.

No. 294 NAI DT S11846

Extract from a memorandum from James J. McElligott to Maurice Moynihan
(Dublin)

DUBLIN, 19 September 1940

Observations on the Heads of Proposed Agreement with Great Britain[1]
[matter omitted]
GENERAL CONSIDERATIONS

17. It is important to consider the consequences which might follow from failure to make a Trade Agreement with Great Britain particularly if the British Government went so far as to withdraw existing trading facilities outwards and inwards.

18. In 1936 home production of all goods valued exclusive of duties was £105,000,000 for the making of which there were imported materials the c.i.f.[2] value of which was £23,500,000, or about one-fourth of the value of production. Exports of domestic produce amounted to £21,000,000, or about one-fifth of the value of production. Imports ready for use were estimated at £16,000,000. Total visible imports are, accordingly, more than one-third of the home production. Impressive as are these figures of external trade in relation to production, they are not a complete index of the importance of such trade because a large part of this country's production could not be carried on at all without certain imports which, at normal times, might constitute only a small proportion by value of output; and in order to purchase such essential imports without making inroads into investments abroad, it is necessary to maintain visible exports.

19. In 1938, Great Britain and Northern Ireland took over £22 millions worth of Irish exports, or 92.6% of the whole, while all other countries in the world purchased less than £2 millions worth, of which about £1¼ million went to countries in Europe now shut off from trading with us. The only countries remaining with which it is conceivable that any trade could be done are the U.S.A., Canada, and some of the South American countries. Exports to all non-European countries amounted in 1938 to only £431,000. The prospect of increasing trade with any or all of these countries to such an extent as to replace in any important degree exports to Great Britain and Northern Ireland is hardly conceivable in present abnormal conditions. The type of Irish goods for which there is a demand overseas and for which an increased demand might make itself felt under favourable conditions, does not include appreciable quantities of this country's major exports of which cattle are by far the most important. A close examination of the possibility of increasing exports to these and other countries was made during the last seven years or so but at no point was there any indication that such a trade could in any conceivable circumstances be fostered. The position would appear to be that, so far as Irish domestic exports are concerned, there is, in reality, no alternative market on any scale even in normal times except Great Britain and Northern Ireland.

---

[1] This memorandum was prepared by an informal committee of the Secretaries of the Departments of Agriculture, Supplies, Industry and Commerce, External Affairs and Finance.
[2] 'Cost, insurance and freight'.

20. Owing to increased freight and insurance charges since the outbreak of war and the high U.S.A. tariff, there is no doubt that even under the most favourable conditions imaginable at the present time a transfer of markets to the United States for a substantial part of our exports would result in a catastrophic fall in prices. There seems to be no ground for believing that such a transfer is practicable at all.

21. In 1938, 50.5% of this country's imports originated in Great Britain and Northern Ireland, and of the rest about 17% came from European countries with which trade has practically been stopped by the war. Of the remaining imports the bulk is made up of cereals, feeding stuffs, timber and oil, which still come from the overseas countries which formerly supplied them. The greater part of our imports which normally came from Great Britain, Northern Ireland or certain European countries were made up of a certain proportion of finished goods but a still larger proportion of raw and semi-manufactured materials for home industry. The continuance of a supply of industrial materials is almost as vital to the economic life of the country as is the assurance of a market for domestic exports as almost every branch of industrial production is absolutely dependent to a major degree on a continuance of imports.

22. Apart from substantially increased cost, the principal difficulty in the way of switching over the purchases of raw and semi-manufactured materials for industry to Canada or the U.S.A. is that the quantities required by our industries are comparatively small. This constitutes a difficulty in respect of shipping and times of arrival even if the problem of financing larger scale purchases in order to obviate this difficulty could be solved. Further, want of knowledge of sources of supply and of American standards of quality, etc., would be embarrassing and involve delay. If it became necessary to obtain essential imports from the U.S.A. in substitution for those formerly obtained from the United Kingdom and other European countries in which there could be no increased demand for our visible exports, it would be necessary (in the absence of our existing facilities for obtaining foreign exchange) to consider how such imports could be paid for by our invisible exports, by liquidation of our external assets or by the raising of dollar credits or loans. In present circumstances it would be impossible without the cooperation of the U.K. Government to dispose of any substantial part of our sterling holdings for dollars or other non-sterling currencies. The prospect of raising a dollar loan would also be remote.

23. Income from investments in the non-sterling bloc of countries (which include Canada) was in the neighbourhood of £500,000 per annum (before the war), so that our holdings in these countries may be set at about £10 millions pre-war. The value of these holdings is now probably much reduced, as is the volume of emigrants' remittances from the United States, which formerly amounted to £2¼ millions per annum. The marked depreciation of the £ sterling (and hence in the Irish £) and the increased transport charges from overseas to this country would result in a substantial increase in the c.i.f. prices which we are at present paying for our raw materials. The liquidation of our external non-sterling assets would entail a considerable loss on the pre-war value of these assets and there would, presumably, be considerable difficulty in the way of the Government's acquiring them from private holders. The proceeds would barely, if at all, pay for one year's imports.

24. On purely economic grounds there is, therefore, an unanswerable case for making every effort possible to accept such terms of any draft Agreement as are

reasonable and do not endanger this country's neutrality. The terms of the draft put forward by the British Government have the attraction of preserving and, possibly, improving existing trading, shipping and financial relations. The unsatisfactory prices proposed for agricultural produce could be the subject of negotiations and might later be improved. Certain other details, e.g. the provision of shipping, the level of freights for overseas imports, facilities for insurance of cargoes and ships through the British War Risks Office and the provision of foreign exchange for our reasonable requirements also require further negotiation and clearer statement in the draft. Most of these matters could probably be settled as a result of negotiation on, at least, a fairly satisfactory basis.

TRANSHIPMENT FACILITIES

25. The outstanding difficulty would appear to be in respect of the transhipment facilities which are asked for by the British Government. In the course of a visit to the Secretary, Department of External Affairs, on 2nd November last,[1] the German Minister made it plain that the development of a re-export and transhipment trade in our ports would be regarded as altering the character of our neutrality. He asked for an assurance that such a trade would not be allowed to grow up. No such assurance was given, but as a matter of internal policy steps were taken to check the development of the traffic. The provision of facilities would not constitute a breach of any established rule of international law. But no doubt such a development would have a very adverse effect on our relations with Germany. If Irish ports became unloading centres for ocean-borne cargoes intended for Britain, there is danger that German bombing and mine-laying activity would be extended to our coast and territorial waters. If such danger materialized, the British might take advantage of it to station naval units for defence in our ports. We are at present making an effort to secure that Irish ships and Irish trade with Britain will enjoy some measure of immunity from German blockade measures. Any hope there may be of achieving this object, now or in the future, would probably disappear if we were at this stage to allow our ports and waters to be used from the transhipment of British cargoes.

26. If the facilities were to be of advantage to Great Britain, the operation would become, no doubt, large-scale and the question might arise for the British Government whether, in fact, such transhipment facilities in Dublin, Cork or elsewhere would be safer or more immune from attack than port facilities in their own country.

27. Apart from the attitude of the German Government towards this country, it would seem almost certain that the arrival in Irish waters of large convoys and the transhipment of cargo from the vessels in these convoys on a large scale would lead to immediate attack by the German Forces on those vessels whether in our waters or not. In these circumstances, it would appear best, if and when actual negotiations open on the basis of the draft proposed, to postpone, if possible, discussion on the subject of transhipment facilities, and when the matter is raised to endeavour to persuade the British authorities to drop their request on the ground that it would provide no advantages from their point of view commensurate with the risks involved to us. According to the High Commissioner's reports, however, the British authorities are likely to regard the proposed transhipment facilities as an essential part of any agreement.

[1] McElligott may have been referring to the events covered in No. 65 above.

28. Apart from the danger of attack on British ships in Irish waters, there would appear to be definite economic advantage for this country if transhipment facilities were possible. Depending on the volume of trade handled by way of transhipment, there would be greatly increased employment of dock and allied labour and, in addition, if it were decided to rail goods from any of these ports to an eastern port for re-export, there might be increased traffic by rail.

No. 295 NAI DT S11846A

Letter from Frederick H. Boland to Kathleen O'Connell (Dublin)[1]
(Secret)

DUBLIN, 19 September 1940

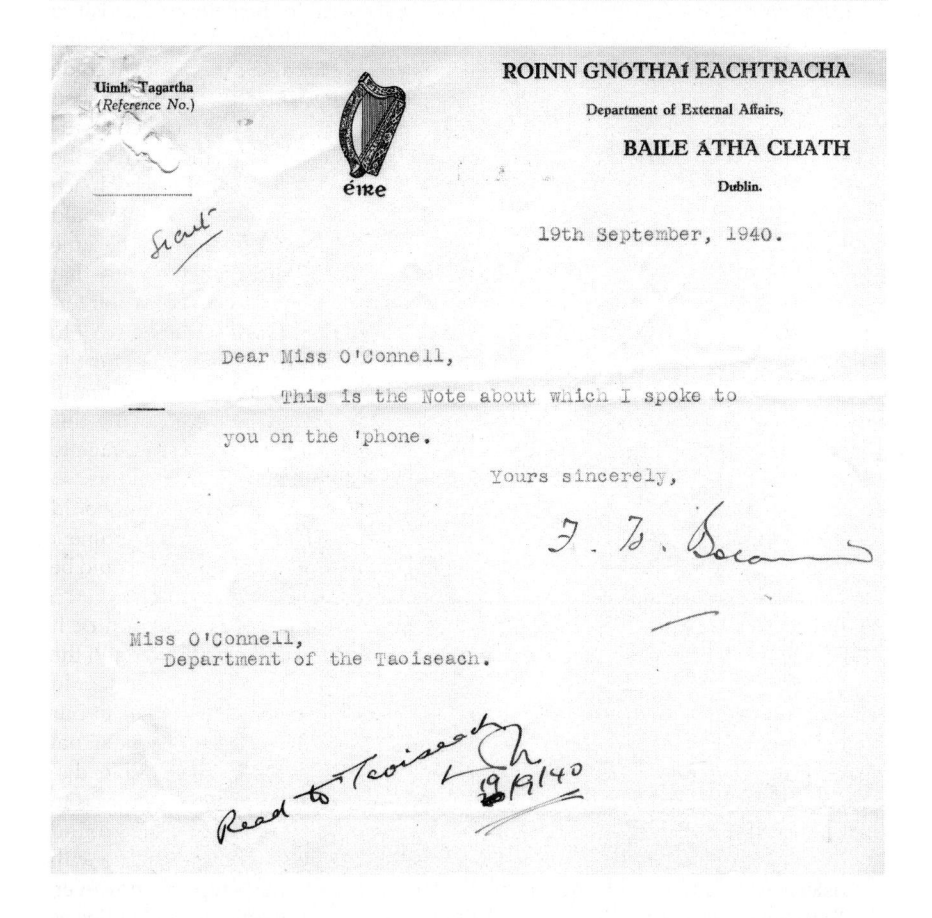

Dear Miss O'Connell,

This is the Note about which I spoke to you on the 'phone.

Yours sincerely,
F. H. Boland

Miss O'Connell,
Department of the Taoiseach.

---

[1] Covering note attached to No. 296.

No. 296 NAI DFA Secretary's Files P25

Note and cover letter from Frederick H. Boland to H.C. Brady[1] (Dublin)

DUBLIN, 19 September 1940

Dear Mr Brady,
I told Mr Aiken that I would send him a Note on the Memorandum which has been circulated to the Government about the proposed trade agreement with Britain. A copy of the Note is attached.

Yours sincerely,
[initialled] F.H. B.

The Proposed Arrangement with Britain

1. The memorandum circulated to the Government[2] proceeds to a large extent on the assumption that the conclusion of a trade agreement with Britain will assure us the advantages stipulated for in the agreement. That assumption is not necessarily sound. The British have had already to reduce their purchases of cattle and sheep from this country, owing to the interruption of transport, distribution, and other facilities. That a similar measure has been imposed on their own producers indicates that the British action is the result of sheer physical necessity. Though one cannot be sure how things will develop in Britain, the likelihood is that, for some time at least, they will become worse rather than better. That being so, allowance must be made for the possibility that even if we made a trade agreement, physical conditions might develop in such a way as to render it wholly or largely inoperative. If, in order to get the agreement, we had had to make concessions, we might then be in the position of suffering all the disadvantages of the arrangement without reaping its advantages.

2. In the course of the discussions which preceded the drafting of the memorandum, apprehension was expressed lest our failure to conclude a trade agreement with Britain would result in strained relations, and in the withdrawal of some or all of the facilities which we at present enjoy in connection with foreign exchange, shipping, supplies, etc. From the External Affairs point of view, there is no reason to think that our failure to conclude an agreement would *of itself* evoke any strong political reaction. The position is rather that if, for any reason, the British Government wished to exercise pressure on us, they will find means of doing so, even if we conclude this agreement. The mere fact of their failure to negotiate an agreement on the lines suggested would only cause the British to adopt an unfriendly attitude to us if they regarded the transhipment and other facilities which they would get under the agreement as being of such importance from their point of view as to be worth the risk of a serious quarrel between the two countries.

3. The memorandum circulated to the Government throws out the suggestion that if, and when, negotiations are begun, we should try to get agreement on our demands with regard to prices, etc., and postpone discussion on the question of transhipment in the hope that, when it came to consider transhipment, we would

---

[1] Private Secretary to the Minister for Defence.
[2] See No. 294.

be able to persuade the British to drop their request. From the information available to the Department of External Affairs, there is little, if any, chance of such an endeavour succeeding. One of the points strongly made by the British representatives when they handed Mr. Dulanty the proposals was that, from the British point of view, the proposed transhipment and storage facilities were an integral and essential part of any agreement and that, in fact, 'without transhipment, there can be no agreement.'

4. This being so, the position would appear to be that, unless we are prepared to meet the British on the question of transhipment, any negotiations initiated on the basis of the present proposals would be doomed to failure. Even giving full weight to the importance of a satisfactory agreement to our economic situation it would seem better, on the whole, that there should be no formal negotiations at all than that negotiations should be initiated which were certain to break down.

5. Recent developments have, no doubt, increased the British Government's interest in the question of transhipment facilities in our ports and waters. Within the last few days, the Germans have shown some tendency to extend their continuous bombing of British port facilities in the Thames Estuary, the Bristol Channel and the Mersey, to the Clyde and Belfast Lough. There can be no reasonable doubt, having regard to the prevailing circumstances, that the grant of transhipment facilities to British shipping in our ports and harbours would bring the War to our shores.

No. 297 NAI DFA 244/8C

Code telegram from the Department of External Affairs to Leopold H. Kerney (Madrid) (No. 72) (Personal) (Copy)

DUBLIN, 19 September 1940

Now that you have personal code please wire full report on Ryan case.

No. 298 NAI DFA Paris Embassy P33/13

Letter from Count Gerald O'Kelly de Gallagh to Seán Murphy (Vichy)

PARIS, 20 September 1940

My dear Seán,

I enclose herewith another batch of documents as follows:

1) - From Miss Kathleen RABBETTE, 11 rue St. Dominique, PARIS – her expired passport together with application for new one. She asks also that a wire be sent to her mother, as follows:
   'RABBETTE, College Road, Galway – Kathleen well – anxious news of family.'
2) - From Miss TWOHIG a letter to Madame de Ansaldo, at the Spanish Embassy.
3) - From the Rev. J.S. DUNLOP of Institut Missionnaire St. Augustin, Lormoy, Monthléry, S.&.O. – his expired British passport, together with application forms for Irish passport and two photographs. Father Dunlop has sent the sum of 288 francs which I am holding to the credit of the Legation.

4) - From J.H. KELVEY, Chief Officer S.S. [City of] Limerick,[1] at the present interned at the Camp de St. Avén prés Vannes. I have taken the matter up with the German Embassy and hope to get Kelvey and his five mates liberated in due course. But I would very much like to know what action to take if and when they are freed. They will presumably have no means of support.

5) - From the Rev. B. THORPE, Fenioux, Déux Sèvres, a letter together with passport application forms and photographs. In the letter he alludes to a p.o. for 291,80 frs. It has not so far arrived, but it may turn up. I am acknowledging the letter and stating that I have forwarded it to you.

6) - From Miss Grace BROWNE, 66 Rue de la Bastille, NANTES, a letter with text of wire which she asks to have sent to her family. I am acknowledging the letter.

7) - From Madame M.C. BONSCASSE, 14 Bd. Gouvion St Cyr, PARIS 17ème a letter replying to yours of the 12th and asking that a message be sent to her people in Ireland. She also asks about the possibility of going to Ireland. I have not replied to the letter.

8) - From Mr. B. GOTTSCHALK, 82 Rue Boileau, BORDEAUX, and addressed to the Consul-General de Belfast. I have not replied.

9) - Copy of the certificate I gave John O'SULLIVAN.

10) - Copy of my letter (of the 18th inst)[2] with enclosure, to the German Embassy, giving particulars asked for in a circular letter.

11) - Copy of a letter I addressed to REVILLOD of the Préfecture de Police and which speaks for itself.

12) - From Mrs. GRIERSON, letter to you together with letters destined for Mrs. WALLER and Mr. JOYNT.

13) - From the Comte FITZGERALD a letter to you. I have not replied.

14) - From the German Embassy a letter enclosing laisser-passer application form and presumably intended for you to sign and return.

The Guaranty Trust have telephoned to the effect that the money held for the Legation by the Credit Lyonnais at Tours has been refunded to the Legation a/c in Paris.

I understand from the German Embassy that arrangements are being made for the diplomatic correspondence between Vichy and Paris to be transmitted through the French Mission in Paris. As soon as I learn that the system is in operation, I will let you know, though you will probably be au courant yourself before I will be.

I have just had a visit from Monsieur GUYOT (Lord Granard's[3] agent) accompanied by the Marquis de St Sauveur, to inform me that, though the boxes at Lamorlaye were restored to them, the dwelling house was being kept by the German military Authorities. I am taking the matter up with the German Embassy on principle, though I don't expect much satisfaction. The Military seem to do what they please.

---

[1] Despite being painted with Irish markings, the *City of Limerick* was bombed and sunk by German aircraft seven hundred miles west of Ushant in the Bay of Biscay on 15 July 1940. Two crew members were killed and the survivors were interned in France.

[2] Not printed.

[3] Sir Arthur Patrick Hastings Forbes, 9th Earl of Granard (1913-90), served with the RAF as air adviser to the Minister of State for the Middle East during the Second World War.

Mr. Samuel BECKETT: 6 Rue des Favorites, PARIS 15ème, has just called. He is without news of his family and is anxious that a wire be sent to his brother, Mr. Frank BECKETT, 6 Clare St., DUBLIN, stating that he (Samuel) is back in Paris and asking for news of the family. He also asks that his brother Frank should arrange for his monthly allowance of Livre 20 – hitherto paid through the Société Générale – to be paid through the Department of External Affairs and the Legation.[1]

Yours ever
[handwritten] G. O'KELLY DE GALLAGH

21.IX.40
15) Letter from Guarantee Trust just arrived. I phoned up and told them to comply with your instructions.
16) Letter from Sister Marie Monique Malone. I have not replied.

No. 299 NAI DFA Secretary's Files 12/1

Code telegram from Seán Murphy to the Department of External Affairs (Dublin)
(No. 218) (Personal) (Copy)

VICHY, 23 September 1940

Severe food restrictions which come into force at noon to-day received by public with resignation. Severity is attributed to requisitioning on large scale by German Authorities and to fact that free zone is poorest in food. The continuance of two zones causing considerable unemployment and lack of all communication great discontent and difficulty for French Government as the population of the occupied territory regards itself as abandoned by the French Government. The Government is very discouraged by the result of effort and possibility of resignation in the fairly near future cannot be excluded. It is alleged German Authorities are fostering discontent against French Government. General impression is that French Government is being hampered and is unable to cope with existing situation. Public opinion and sections of official opinion have become recently at least anti-German. My telegram 200[2] based on general rumour of co-operation involving occupation by Germans of all frontiers.

No. 300 NAI CAB 2/3

Minutes of a meeting of the Cabinet
(G.C. 2/204) (Item 1) (S. 11846)

DUBLIN, 24 September 1940

DRAFT TRADE AGREEMENT WITH GREAT BRITAIN
Consideration was given to a memorandum, dated 19th September, 1940, entitled 'Observations on the Heads of Proposed Agreement with Great Britain' submitted by the Department of Finance.[3]

---

[1] See No. 255.
[2] Not printed.
[3] See No. 294.

It was agreed that the proposed Trade Agreement is not acceptable and it was decided that a draft communication to the British Government should be prepared accordingly by the Department of External Affairs in consultation with the other Departments concerned intimating that the request for transhipment facilities cannot be entertained and making observations where appropriate on other matters referred to in the proposed Agreement.

No. 301 NAI DFA Secretary's Files P15(i)

> Code telegram from Colman O'Donovan to
> the Department of External Affairs (Dublin)
> (No. 61) (Personal) (Handwritten copy by Sheila Murphy)
>
> HOLY SEE, 25 September 1940[1]

Following is confidential and urgent for Walshe:-
In view of rumours from two Vatican sources concerning Galway and Dublin saw substitute this morning and pressed for pre-publication information as a ——[2] and very special case. Holy Father at this season is available to Heads of Missions desiring audiences and substitute thought that I should make this request of him. Please cable at once if you desire me to ask for audience and instruct me what to say. It would be desirable also to let me have information regarding general situation in Ireland and position regarding Minister as I am likely to be questioned as to both.

No. 302 NAI DFA 221/147

> Code telegram from the Department of External Affairs to
> William Warnock (Berlin)
> (No. 164) (Personal) (Copy)
>
> DUBLIN, 26 September 1940

At their request made on 23rd instant we have shown German Legation material evidence of German responsibility including pieces of bomb bearing impressed German crests and other markings, contents of unexploded bomb clearly of German origin and statements of witnesses who saw German markings and identified the two planes from blank outlines as Heinkel III K. Hempel commented on fact that one of cartridges of unexploded bomb was of French manufacture but appeared otherwise satisfied.[3]

Legation's request may be occasioned by story in a pamphlet circulated by I.R.A. that Campile bombing was a deliberate British plot, or Hempel may have heard some opinion expressed by individuals with no knowledge of circumstances. There is no evidence whatever for this theory. Both the inquest and the subsequent military investigation establish beyond reasonable doubt explanation in communiqué that bombs were dropped by German machines

---

[1] This document is dated by its received date because there is no indication of its date of despatch.
[2] Word missing in original.
[3] This was later identified as Irish Defence Forces ordnance of French origin. See No. 305.

in mistake. Vast majority of people held this view and German denial would be severe shock to confidence in German good faith. For obvious reasons, French cartridge is against British plot theory rather than otherwise.

We sincerely hope, therefore, that Germans won't depart from original decision on strength of a completely uninformed and unsubstantiated theory. The rumour is also in circulation that Germans bombed Wexford deliberately to intimidate creamery exporters. A German denial would dispose of this malicious rumour and confound those such as Stephen King-Hall[1] who have quoted this and other recent incidents as evidence of growing difficulties between Ireland and Germany. The Government, with all its means of judging what is most in interest of mutual relations, is convinced that agreed communiqué is best solution and is most anxious that it should be published as soon as possible.

Please see W.[oermann] at once, ask how matter stands, if he refers to new difficulties, speak on these lines and urge early issue of communiqué. If W. refers to British plot theory, remind him that wholly uninformed and irresponsible rumours nearly caused difficulty in our relations before. An I.R.A. broadcast from Belfast was source of misunderstanding referred to in your 25/39 of 30th December.[2]

No. 303 NAI DFA Secretary's Files P4

Handwritten letter from John J. Hearne to Joseph P. Walshe (Dublin)
OTTAWA, 26 September 1940

My dear Joe,

I send you a copy of Skelton's letter to me enclosing a copy of MacKenzie King's telegram of the 16th June.[3]

I need hardly tell you that when I read the text of the telegram I was dumbfounded. If you were to regard the whole business as an indication of the failure of our work here so far, I could not complain. But I am hoping you will prefer to regard it as an indication of the gravity of our task.

It is, of course, possible to explain the telegram on one or more of many grounds. The explanation given by Skelton may be the right one, that the Prime Minister did it off his own bat. I know that he is flushed with victory since the general election and that both the election and his conversations with Roosevelt have given him a 'leadership' complex. He may have been put up to it by the British Government. (I do not believe that they know nothing in London about a message sent in D.O. cipher.) Or he may have wanted to place himself on record in Canada in the sense of the telegram at the particular time.

Your delay in sending an official reply was, I submit, the best possible initial answer to the preposterous document itself. The fact, moreover, that Ireland has not been invaded in the interval falsifies the view that 'ruthless fury' would immediately be 'concentrated' upon us.

---

[1] Sir William Stephen King-Hall (1893-1966), British journalist, politician and playwright; served in the Ministry of Aircraft Production during the Second World War; National Labour/Independent MP for Ormskirk (1939-45).
[2] Not printed.
[3] Not printed.

In my recent report[1] I said that there was no reason why Skelton should have explained his not having told me about the telegram. But, nevertheless, as our personal relations are excellent, I confess I am at a loss to know why he didn't mention the telegram to me – not even on the 9th July – until I asked him to show it to me when conveying your apology for the delay in replying. I have, of course, shown no annoyance or disappointment. But I feel pretty cheap. He did, however, assume that I knew about it on the 9th July. Well, that's that.

We are all well. I hope the strain of events has not been too severe on you. Things are getting a bit difficult here between the French Minister and 'Ottawa society'. In addition French Canadians are getting restive about all the English children coming out, they don't want a new English colonization. The Dakar affair[2] and the bombings of Gibraltar have made the position of the French legation more difficult still.

What next? Hambro made a speech at Winnipeg last week to the effect that the next German objective is Iceland.

As ever,
JOHN

No. 304 NAI DFA Secretary's Files P15(i)

*Telegram from the Department of External Affairs
to Colman O'Donovan (Holy See)
(No. 55) (Personal) (Copy)*

DUBLIN, 26 September 1940

Your 61.[3] You should follow advice of Substitute and ask for audience when you could sympathise on behalf of Government with Holy Father on the difficulties for the Holy See brought about by the war.

You could inform him of the Government's unshakeable resolve to maintain the neutrality of Ireland to the end. Then you should add that the early filling of the See of Dublin would give the Government great satisfaction and that of course the Government would be grateful to know from the Holy Father who has been appointed. You could say Macaulay asked to return to Rome at once.

No. 305 NAI DFA 221/147

*Code telegram from the Department of External Affairs to
William Warnock (Berlin)
(No. 166) (221/139) (Personal) (Copy)*

DUBLIN, 27 September 1940

My 164.[4] Further investigation following conference with German Minister on 23rd instant has disclosed most regrettable and embarrassing error on part of

---

[1] It is unclear exactly what report Hearne is referring to.
[2] On 23 September 1940 British forces attempted to capture the port of Dakar in French West Africa. The intention was to install de Gaulle's Free French forces in place of those of Vichy France. The operation was unsuccessful.
[3] See No. 301.
[4] See No. 302.

our military authorities. The French cartridge picked up on site and included among exhibits is of trench mortar type. It was not (and technically could not have been) part of aerial bomb but is identical with cartridges used in Stokes Brandt mortars which are part of regulation equipment of our infantry units some of which were on exercises at Campile two days before bombing. Mortars and ammunition were supplied to us by Messrs. Edgar Brandt of Paris and we have shown German Minister cartridges from our stock identical in every respect including the serial number on cardboard cap to the cartridge picked up at Campile. Only explanation of so inconceivable a mistake is that in the desire to get fullest evidence to German Minister as quickly as possible, he was sent details of all the articles picked up in the area before the aerial bombing experts here had concluded their examination of them. Once they came to examine the things in detail, the mistake was obvious.

Please express apologies to W.[oermann] who will probable have heard from Legation here. We appreciate reluctance of German authorities to release communiqué in view of the cartridge but now that it has been explained we hope for reasons in my 164 that communiqué may issue at once.

No. 306 NAI DFA Secretary's Files P15(i)

> *Code telegram from Colman O'Donovan to*
> *the Department of External Affairs (Dublin)*
> *(No. 64) (Personal) (Handwritten copy by Sheila Murphy)*
> HOLY SEE, 30 September 1940

Your tel 55.[1] Substitute has spoken to Holy Father who has heard nothing yet. This means that appointment has not yet been made. The Holy Father is asking to have the matter expedited and will have the name communicated to me. My audience will be early in the week.

The Minister tells me he has re-offered his resignation as he cannot return and in any case intends to resign at end of December. It may assist your consideration of situation to know that many people here including substitute have expressed the hope that I will be appointed to succeed.

No. 307 NAI DFA Secretary's Files P15(i)

> *Code telegram from Colman O'Donovan to*
> *the Department of External Affairs (Dublin)*
> *(No. 65) (Personal) (Copy)*
> HOLY SEE, 4 October 1940

Your telegram 55.[2] At Audience this morning Holy Father promised attention should be given matter when Cardinal Rossi returns to Rome towards the end of month. Imparts special Blessing to Government and people.

---

[1] See No. 304.
[2] See No. 304.

No. 308 NAI DFA 219/2A

Confidential report from John W. Dulanty to Joseph P. Walshe (Dublin)
(No.57) (Secret)

LONDON, 5 October 1940

Whilst the British press and wireless give a passable account of the German air raids on London their reporting is necessarily restricted.[1] The following supplementary notes may be of interest.

The targets at which the German airmen have aimed in the London areas have been

I. Communications (especially Main Line Railways)
II. Power Stations
III. The weakening of public morale

On I they have been only partially successful, yet the destruction of houses, craters in roads which one sees within a few yards of the railways suggest that this particular attack has not been 'blind shooting'.

Similarly on II the bombs have dropped near but not near enough – except in the case of the Battersea Power Station which was hit but was not put out of action. Canon W. Wood (my parish priest) has his Presbytery between two targets of this character – one a municipal power station and the other a commercial trading undertaking. He and his three curates spend their nights at casualty stations – where a few nights ago they had to deal with eighty-five dead, mostly Irish, taken from an underground shelter, the entrance to which had received a direct hit from a high explosive bomb.

But the distribution of the damage leads one to think that the Germans have been keener on the disorganisation of the ordinary day to day life of the people than on a strategic plan of concentration on key military objectives. This view is supported by their increased use of parachute mines which cause wide havoc and dislocation. They cannot be aimed at a particular point, their blast force exceeds that of a 500 kilogramme High Explosive bomb and one detonation alone has demolished one hundred and fifteen houses. The same purpose of terrorisation of the civilian population is seen in the delayed action bombs which mean that the local authorities must order hundreds of people out of their as yet untouched homes at a moment's notice.

The question of public shelters appears to be beset with difficulties. I expect to complete my inquiries in a few days when I will send a further report. Meanwhile here are official figures given with every entreaty for secrecy about direct hits on public shelters:-

LONDON
September 11 to 19	4,191	Seriously Wounded
	976	Killed
September 19 to 26	2,200	Seriously Wounded
	1,300	Killed

---

[1] The German 'Blitz' on London lasted from 7 September 1940 to 10 May 1941.

PROVINCES

September 11 to 19	4,051	Seriously Wounded
	988	Killed
September 19 to 26	3,060	Seriously Wounded
	1,593	Killed

These figures have not been made known outside the British War Cabinet and I was *urged to limit the knowledge of them to An Taoiseach and to you*.[1]

The British say that war production, public utility services have suffered no serious interference. Delay would of course happen whilst a delayed action bomb was removed but their authoritative statement is that production of essentials has not been delayed beyond one per cent.

The British press is eloquent upon the 'chin-up' attitude of the people. My own observation confirms this. I go night and morning on a twenty-five mile railway journey. Normally in a carriage which takes five passengers on each side we travel with seven on each side and six people standing in the middle of the carriage. In the ordinary way the journey takes forty minutes. It is fortunate if the same journey is achieved in three hours. Tired, hungry and worried, the people show miraculous calm – cheerful acceptance of things which they are powerless to alter. In the morning journeys you can see listlessness and weariness borne of sleepless nights but you hear no 'grousing'. Whether this will continue in the winter and possible epidemics of influenza remains to be seen. As yet, the food distribution is good, there are no queues, and leaving out of account the East End, which is horror piled on horror, the social system appears to work more or less normally.

The military and naval plans appear to have worked out well. But the plans for the civilians, particularly the East End, have been tragically lacking. It is a commonplace to say that administration of any sort is as much a matter of imagination as of regulation. Unfortunately regulation has been the dominant note, with the result that warring local authorities with no central over-riding power have 'dillied and dallied' where action super-urgent and instantaneous was needed. In this indescribable misery the Irish in the East End have depended on their priests. Aldermen, councillors, and social workers, who have no understanding of and therefore no sympathy for the Catholic religion have been lyrical in their praise to me of the young Irish priests who have worked so assiduously in the East End without any regard to the denomination aspect.

Some of the military experts say that this indiscriminate bombing is a sheer waste of effort on the part of the Germans. When you ask them for their reasons they reply that Hitler schemed to fill all the main lines of traffic, road and rail, with fugitives from the eight millions of Londoners. Militarily they think this is a hopeless plan. Their army they say is mechanised beyond the dreams of 1918, their country is as well-roaded, if not better, than any similar territory in Europe and the Germans may as well wait for the crack of doom as to wait for the repetition in Britain of the 1940 confusion of Belgium and North Eastern France.

[signed] J.W. DULANTY

---

[1] The portion in italics has been underlined in pen by Walshe. Marginal note by Walshe: 'H.C. told me at 4.30 today that these figures were total casualties – although the B had given them to him as exclusively shelter casualties. J.P.W.'

Documents on Irish Foreign Policy, Volume VI, 1939–1941

No. 309 NAI DFA 221/147

Statement by the Department of External Affairs on the Campile bombing
(Copy)

DUBLIN, 8 October 1940

In connection with the aerial bombing in County Wexford on the 26th August the Chargé d'Affaires in Berlin has been informed by the German Foreign Office that although the inquiries made by the German authorities provided no ground for believing that the bombs were dropped by a German aircraft, the German Government – in view of the evidence furnished by the Irish Government with regard to the markings on the bombs and because of their desire to act in the spirit of their friendly relations with Ireland – are prepared to admit the possibility that the bombs were dropped by a German aircraft the pilot of which had lost his way owing to bad visibility.[1]

On this basis, the German Foreign Office expressed to the Chargé d'Affaires the regret of the German Government at the occurrence and their sincere sympathy with those who had suffered. The Foreign Office also expressed the willingness of the German Government, subject to agreement as to method, to pay compensation for the loss and damage sustained.

No. 310 NAI DFA 217/39

Memorandum by the Department of External Affairs for Eamon de Valera
on the establishment of an Irish Legation in Berne[2]
(Copy)

DUBLIN, undated, but October 1940

1. Last year the Swiss Government raised its Consulate General in Dublin to the status of a Legation and sent us a diplomatic representative with the rank of Chargé d'Affaires. I need not say that the Government welcomed this step very warmly. In return it is now proposed to establish an Irish Legation in Berne and to accredit an Irish Chargé d'Affaires to the Swiss Government. The present estimate makes the necessary provision for this.

2. It is very appropriate and desirable particularly at the present time that we should have direct diplomatic relations with the Swiss Confederation. Switzerland occupies a very central position in Europe. The great continental systems of communication traverse her territory and the main European cultures meet in her population. The national character and traditions of her people give her a position of leadership among the small nations of the world. Switzerland is the seat of the International Red Cross Committee and of other international organisations of which this country is a member. Even in times of peace there is always a considerable number of our citizens in Switzerland

---

[1] Visibility on the day in question was in fact very good, with only light cloud.
[2] The text of this document is close, but not identical, to the remarks on the same subject by de Valera in Dáil Éireann on 8 October 1940 (*Dáil Debates*, vol. 81; cols 61-2). The original of document 310 is undated. It has been printed at this point in DIFP VI so that it appears immediately before document 311 dealing with Cremins' presentation of his credentials in Berne.

either as visitors or as residents for health and other reasons. The new office in Berne will thus not only give Irish citizens on the Continent a further centre to which they can look for help and protection but it will serve as a further link between this country and the life of the Continent at this very difficult juncture of our history.

3. It is not proposed to continue the present office in Geneva once the Legation in Berne has been established. Even in the past very few countries maintained representatives of diplomatic rank in both Berne and Geneva, and in the present circumstances the office in Geneva is difficult to justify. The cost of the new office in Berne will be covered to a large extent, if not entirely, by the saving on Geneva so that the present proposal will represent little if any increase in the annual Vote for External Affairs.

No. 311 NAI DFA 217/39

Confidential report from Francis T. Cremins to Joseph P. Walshe (Dublin)
(X.163) (217/39)

GENEVA, 11 October 1940

I have to state, for the information of the Minister, that on the 10th October, 1940, as notified to you by telegraph, I presented my Letter of Credence, as Chargé d'Affaires of Ireland, to M. Pilet-Golaz,[1] President of the Swiss Confederation, Head of the Federal Political Department. M. Pilet-Golaz received me in his capacity as Head of the Federal Political Department in his *cabinet de travail* at the *Département Politique*. I attach copy of a note which I received from the *Département* confirming the arrangements for the presentation.

M. Pilet-Golaz received me very cordially. I handed him the letter, which I had closed in accordance with what I was informed was the usual custom. He did not open the letter while I was there, but handed it to M. de Grenus,[2] who was present, saying, 'We can look at the document later'. He then asked me to sit down and began to talk about Ireland, touching on many aspects of our affairs, our neutrality, trade, horses, population, etc., and on general matters. He expressed no views on the present international situation but he seemed to think that Ireland, and the same applied to Switzerland, had a measure of safety in not being rich in raw materials such as iron and oil. The interview lasted half an hour. When I was leaving, he expressed his pleasure that Berne would have an Irish representative, and he assured me that I would get every help from the various departments in the fulfilment of my mission, while, as for himself, he would be most happy to receive me at any time I thought that personal conversations would be helpful for the solution of any question that might be under discussion between our two countries.

I attach also copy of a note[3] which I received from M. de Grenus relating to the leaving of cards on the Federal Councillors. I learn from the recently

---

[1] Maurice Pilet-Golaz (1889-1958), member of the Swiss Federal Council (1928-44) and President of the Swiss Confederation (1940).
[2] Edmund de Grenus, Swiss Federal Political Department.
[3] Not printed.

appointed Chargé d'Affaires of Colombia that he was informed by the Secretary of the Nunciature, Mgr. Sensi, whom he saw in the absence of the Nuncio, that it is usual for Chargé d'Affaires to pay personal calls also on the Federal Councillors at their offices, though this did not seem to be the view of the Political Department. He paid brief calls accordingly. I will ascertain exactly what should be done before taking action.

[signed] F.T. CREMINS

No. 312 NAI DFA 2006/39

Letter from Joseph P. Walshe to John W. Dulanty (London)
(Secret)

DUBLIN, 17 October 1940

You will remember that arrangements were made in September, 1939, for the supply of certain meteorological reports by the British Meteorological Office. There has, of course, been a considerable reduction in the number of broadcast reports since the war began, and, in order to enable our Meteorological Service to prepare even sketchy charts upon which to base the forecasts supplied to the Defence Forces, it is essential that we should now receive additional reports from the material available to the British Office.

A statement setting out our present requirements is enclosed.[1] This question of securing additional information arose when the trans-Atlantic flights were resumed this year. The British Meteorological representatives showed, in discussion, the greatest reluctance to give us any further information, but eventually agreed to supply it. Since the flights started, therefore, we have received the information set out in the enclosed statement, or as much of it as was available at any particular time.

The Department of Industry and Commerce were under the impression that, once the principle had been accepted, the supply of this more extensive set of data would be continued irrespective of whether trans-Atlantic flights were in progress or not, but they now understand, semi-officially, that the British Meteorological Office regard the arrangement for the supply of these reports as terminating automatically with the cessation of trans-Atlantic flights.

As these data are of the utmost importance in forecasting for the Defence Forces, we should be glad if you would approach the Dominions Office urgently with a request that the information in the enclosed statement be supplied to us *as a regular routine*.

In the discussions in London on 26th April, 1939, regarding the supply of meteorological information in war, the British undertook to make available to us all the material they had, on the basis of reciprocity. In the Memorandum dated 25th August, 1939, informing the British Government of the Irish Government's decision to continue, in the event of war, the supply to them of reports from Irish observing stations, the reciprocity aspect was again referred to.[2]

---

[1] Not printed.
[2] Not printed.

We have kept our part of this bargain very thoroughly. Our routine observations have gone to them regularly, and, when telegraphic communications have been bad, the Meteorological authorities have gone to the trouble of repeating the reports by telephone direct to the British Meteorological Office in order to ensure that they got through; furthermore, we have sent them any other information available to us whenever they required it. In addition, although the point was not specifically referred to in the agreement, the authorities here have taken very special precautions to ensure that the British material should not, in any circumstances, fall into the hands of unauthorised persons. We feel entitled, therefore, to expect the British Meteorological authorities to adhere without demur to the arrangement for the exchange of information.

[signed] J.P. WALSHE

No. 313 NAI DFA Secretary's Files A2

Letter from Joseph P. Walshe to Eamon de Valera (Dublin)
(Secret)

DUBLIN, 18 October 1940

Sir John Maffey came to see me today, by arrangement, at 11.15 a.m. When we had spoken about British refugees (concerning whom he is to write immediately) and a few other less important matters, he referred once more to the question of the boom. I asked him how it was that neither Harrison nor Godfrey[1] had spoken about the boom. Harrison at least, who spoke in so much detail about the nature of our defences, would have felt bound to speak about it if it had been mentioned to him as an urgent matter. Maffey replied that he had no doubt that the question was still and would remain a very live one. How could we expect the British Fleet to give us serious help, when requested by us in the event of a German invasion, if we did not provide some harbour with the protection required by them. He thought we had over-stressed our political difficulties in this matter. Our arguments appeared trivial to the British Government, on account of the extreme importance of close co-operation if Ireland were to be invaded. Anyhow, we could use the boom to prevent British ships coming in if we thought fit to do so, and, that being the position, Maffey did not see why the political difficulties could be regarded by us as serious.

I told him that the size of the boom and the number of men and ships required to put it up were difficulties not easy to overcome either vis-à-vis our own people or vis-à-vis the Germans whose planes must now be in a position to survey our territorial waters even when flying outside them.

Maffey went on to urge that the acceptance of the boom – and he was ready to tell his people to erect it with as little ostentation as possible – was a means of establishing greater confidence between us.

Having dismissed the boom question, much to my surprise he reverted to our difficulties of July last. He asked me if I had ever believed a British re-occupation of this country possible. I said that at one time I felt quite sure it was going to take place, and anybody who had as much evidence as I had would

---

[1] Admiral John H. Godfrey (1888-1971), Director of Admiralty Intelligence (1939-42).

have come to the same conclusion. The sustained campaign – specifically in favour of re-occupation – in Great Britain and America, the Tegart mission, and the positive statements made to us by people closely connected with the British Army, made it impossible for my Minister not to entertain serious suspicions about British intentions. He would remember that I said all that to him in July, and I had not changed my view since. The events, and the order in which they occurred, seemed to furnish greater proof of the intention to re-occupy each time I went back over them.

He than asked me if I thought he was implicated. I replied that I had not excluded that possibility, but I also made allowance for the possibility of his Government keeping him in the dark about a project with which he was not in agreement. This reply seemed to disconcert him somewhat, and he assured me in most earnest fashion that, if at any time he thought that such a project was seriously entertained, he would at once have resigned his position as British Representative here.

I insisted that the British Government, either through Dulanty or through him (Maffey), had not taken much pains to eliminate our suspicions during the bad period. In fact, to this day we had never received any explanation of the military movements in the Six-County area during the first week of July. Maffey replied to this point by saying that he himself, although he had asked for the explanation at my instance, had never been given any; but he presumed it was some foolish alarm which the military people did not want to acknowledge.

He then came to the real purpose of his reference to the re-occupation issue. He said he thought, in order to remove any suspicions which might still linger, especially about his personal connivance, that he should explain what really happened at the time and what was, in his view, the source of all the trouble. There had been serious and prolonged discussions between the politicians and the Army on the issue of the British troops entering our territory. The military pressed very strongly for a decision allowing them to enter our territory, without an invitation from the Irish Government, at the moment of the German attack. The political considerations had prevailed and the Army had to acquiesce, and, in his (Maffey's) view, there was no possibility whatever of the British forces coming in here without the existence of an interval, or a 'hiatus', as he called it, between the beginning of a German attack and your formal invitation given personally through the United Kingdom representative.

I assured Maffey that you would be very glad to hear what he had said about the whole incident, as it would to a very considerable degree explain the rumours which were reaching us during that period. I said it was very frank of him to give me this information, and he could take it that my suspicions were now dissipated. However, in order to provide for possible difficulties in the future, I thought it better to say that we could not expect that the British Army authorities had given up their point of view; on the contrary, we must expect them to press that point of view more and more strongly as the German menace of an invasion of Britain increased.

He again emphasised that the political decision was final. Irish matters were the most delicate that the British Government had to deal with. They had to consider, not merely the degree to which Irish feeling in Britain would be moved by the occupation of this country, but they had to consider above all the feelings of the United States and the disastrous repercussions which would inevitably be caused over there.

I asked him what he thought generally of the possibility of an invasion of this country by Germany, and particularly of the case made for such an invasion by Godfrey and Harrison. Personally, I said, I did not think that the arguments were convincing. The Germans would expose themselves to almost certain defeat, and it was incredible that they could maintain themselves in this country and operate against Britain or British commerce without a safe line of communication with their bases. If ever the invasion were to take place, it could only be a successful operation carried out in conjunction with the invasion of Great Britain.

Maffey agreed with this point of view, and said that he was not convinced, but, on the other hand, the British Army had to provide for every contingency and they were naturally anxious to secure the fullest co-operation from us.

No. 314 NAI DFA 226/1

Memorandum by Michael Rynne concerning Ireland's membership of the League of Nations

DUBLIN, 21 October 1940

1. Owing to the disastrous effects that the war has had on the organisation and activities of the League of Nations, it is becoming clearly desirable to review with the Minister the question of Ireland's continued League Membership. It is hoped that the following observations may assist in such a review and, to some extent, serve as the basis of an explanatory memorandum for the Government should that be considered necessary at a later stage.

2. At the present moment the Department is confronted with this question, namely, (1) whether to prepare, at once, for submission to the Dáil early next year an estimate to cover our League contribution and connected expenditure for 1941-42, or (2) whether, when paying over our 1940 contribution in a few weeks' time, to take that opportunity to announce Ireland's withdrawal from her League Membership.

3. If the first-indicated course is to be adopted, a convincing case will have to be got ready for the Minister who may find next year, that, (contrary to other years), the onus will rest upon him to satisfy the House and the country that positive benefits may be anticipated to accrue from membership of a diminished League of Nations, which will cost the State funds over £15,000 per annum.

4. If, on the other hand, it is decided to give notice of withdrawal, a number of points will arise for immediate consideration, for example, (1) the question whether we are going to recognise the 'two year's notice of withdrawal' rule to the extent of continuing to pay our League contributions until 1943, and (2) the question of what action, if any, is going to be taken about Mr. Lester who has been released from the Department to act as Secretary General of the League.

These are the two most difficult points involved, but there would doubtless be others.

5. Arguments for remaining in the League of Nations will not be easy to invent. Generally speaking our case will have to depend on an appeal to the old argument that any change is bad, if there are not strong positive reasons for it, and that no policy which has worked over a period should be dropped in a hurry.

A case might also be made for the League on the ground that it is the only body which still purports to aim at international cooperation in a world at war. In the event of peace, a body such as the League of Nations might well be required to deal with post-war problems of all kinds, mainly at first, problems of a humanitarian kind, and the existing League's chance of becoming that body will to some extent depend on the present solidarity of its neutral Members.

It is scarcely necessary to point out that this is really a debating argument for, unless there is British victory in the European hostilities and a Japanese defeat in the Far East, the League is doomed whatever its few remaining Members may or may not do just now. However, there are a number of Deputies (e.g. Deputy J.M. O'Sullivan)[1] in Dáil Éireann who may be expected to support an Estimate for a further £15,000 for the League on the basis of merely plausible arguments. Moreover, the fact that the League may have been entirely removed to the United States of America by next Spring, instead of discouraging the small pro-League element in the Dáil, will probably be welcomed by them as a further reason for continuing Ireland's membership.

There is no need therefore, to despair of a certain measure of support, at least in Dáil Éireann, for another League of Nations Vote next year. Whether the country will preserve its usual apathy in regard to the League, in view of the notoriously distressful conditions of that institution at present, is a question which cannot be answered hypothetically at this date. The most important aspect of the matter from the Government's point of view will doubtless lie, not in the immediate measure of support which they might secure for Ireland's continued League Membership from the Dáil and the people, but rather in their judgment of what is best in the long run for the country.

6. Taking all the known facts into consideration, it would seem to be most in the country's interest that no further contribution be made to the League after the £15,000 for the current year has been paid next month.

The Minister has already been furnished with the facts (in connection with a recent Parliamentary question) and it is, therefore, only necessary to resume very briefly the main points of note, viz.:-

(a) In 1923, when Ireland was admitted to the League of Nations, there were already over 50 other members. A few years later there were over 60 members. Now there are about 30 effective members.

(b) In the pre-war League all the Great Powers (except the U.S.A.) were members from time to time. There were never less than three Great Powers at any time. Now only one Great Power (Britain) definitely belongs to the League. Russia was debarred from Membership at the end of 1939 and France, having

---

[1] Professor John Marcus O'Sullivan (1891-1948), Fine Gael TD for Kerry North (1937-43), Minister for Education (1926-32); a member of Ireland's delegation to the League of Nations in 1924, 1928, 1929 and 1930. See biographical details in DIFP III, p. xxvi.

caused Mr. Avenol to resign, has shown no interest in the League since the Franco-German Armistice.

(c) Formerly, practically all the European States belonged to the League and their influence there far outweighed that of the non-European Members. Now only about eight European countries (including Ireland) make any pretence of remaining in the League. Important States such as Sweden and Spain which are still independent and could, if they wished, continue to frequent Geneva are notably absent and likely to remain so. The League consists mainly of a proportion of the Latin American countries, the British Empire and about ten so-called 'States' inhabited by coloured peoples in various remote parts of the world.

(d) Apart from its composition, the work of the League also shows a sharp decline.

Political activities have completely ceased and since the futile League Assembly on the subject of Russia's aggression in Finland, no attempt whatever has been made by the League to intervene in political questions. The humanitarian and social work of the League is now never heard of. War conditions in many countries have created tremendous tasks for international organisations, such as the Geneva Red Cross Society and religious or charitable bodies with branches in various places. The League of Nations has taken no part in such activities.

On the Administrative, Economic and financial sides, the League's work (or the work of the League and the I.L.O. together) still proceeds, but only on a scale so reduced as to be utterly negligible in comparison with former years.

(e) Owing to the great lengths to which it has been necessary to push the economy campaign, the League Secretariat has been reduced to a small fraction of its normal complement.

Although it still includes an expensive high political direction (Mr. Lester's immediate entourage) which does not function at all, the Secretariat as a whole consists of only about 150 permanent officials. There are, it is understood, some 40 temporary clerks, messengers, gardeners etc. still on the payroll and the I.L.O. still pays about 100 persons in various grades of whom three-fourths are in America. That is to say, the combined contributions of some thirty countries are now devoted to maintaining a skeleton staff, comparable in size to that of our Stationery Office. The League costs £300,000 yearly, the Stationery Office £195,000.

7. On the basis of the foregoing facts, it is submitted that the case to be made for our continued contributions to the League is not a good one and that our withdrawal from membership, after payment of our current £15,000, might be the best course to adopt. From the purely financial standpoint, it would seem that we are being asked to pay roughly the same amount every year for a service which is progressively declining in value and, in view of the present policy of transferring the League and I.L.O. to dollar countries, there is but slight hope of any reduction in the size of our League of Nations Vote.

From the political point of view, our continued Membership of the present League would seem to offer none of the advantages which we once associated therewith. On the contrary, there would appear to be a certain element of danger involved from the standpoint of Ireland's neutrality in remaining associated with a body which is clearly intended to be used by Britain to foster an Anglo-American alliance against Germany and other former League Members. Taking a still longer view, we may anticipate that a certain stigma will be regarded as attaching to League Membership in the event of a German victory. Such membership would in that event serve as a handicap rather than as an advantage. In other words, while leaving the League now would give offence to no other friendly State, remaining too long in the League might injure the good relations of Ireland with many of the principal European countries and perhaps debar her from participating in any new League which may evolve out of the present war.

[initialled] M.R.

No. 315 NAI DFA 233/40

Code telegram from Seán Murphy to the Department of External Affairs (Dublin)
(No. 291) (Personal) (Copy)

VICHY, 22 October 1940

Your telegram 241[1] delivered yesterday Monday. Cypher in question together with all other codes and cyphers except the Government Telegraph Code 1933 were destroyed 16th May on receipt of instructions from the D Ext Affairs for destruction of all secret documents. In addition our file(s) together with British Black List were destroyed.

No. 316 UCDA P150/2601

Letter from Eamon de Valera to Lord Cranborne (London)
(Copy)

DUBLIN, 23 October 1940

Dear Lord Cranborne,

I want to thank you for the kind personal note you sent me on your taking over at the Dominions Office.

I assure you that I also shall do everything possible to maintain friendly relations between our two countries. This war unfortunately coming on the unsettled problem of partition has I fear given a set back to the rapid improvement which was taking place. I hope it will be a temporary set back only and that when it is overcome progress even more rapid than before will be made.

I would like to express to you my sincere sympathy with your people in their present sufferings.

Very sincerely yours,
EAMON DE VALERA

---

[1] Not printed.

No. 317 NAI DFA Secretary's Files P22

Letter from Joseph P. Walshe to Maurice Moynihan (Dublin)
(Copy)

DUBLIN, 25 October 1940

I am directed by the Minister for External Affairs to refer to your minutes (S.12096) of the 19th and 30th September,[1] relating to the measures which would have to be taken by the Government in the event of either belligerent making an attack on this country. The first task of this Department, on the occurrence of such an emergency, would be to make a protest to the Government of the country concerned and to inform the Governments of neutral countries, especially that of the United States, that our neutrality had been violated. The Government of the other belligerent Power would also be informed, and, if our Government so decides, would be requested for aid against the invader. This first essential step recalls the necessity of maintaining our communications with the outside world. This is especially true of the radio station at Ballygirreen through which all our official communications to America are now routed, but it might be well to consider whether special statements should be broadcast over the Athlone medium and short waves in order to secure as wide a publicity as possible for our protest against the invader. I understand that a provisional decision has been reached to render the Athlone station useless immediately the arrival of an invader has been signalled. It would, I think, be well worth while considering some modification of this decision. I think we should run the risk of an enemy eventually seizing Athlone in order that we may retain it for a sufficiently long time to launch our protest to the world and to give to our own people whatever instructions the Government desires to give them. Its value to the enemy would be trivial, while to us – for those first hours at any rate – it would be a vital necessity. Moreover, we must assume that the station will be required by our civil authorities on the cessation of hostilities. The two likely invaders are in a position to provide themselves with a powerful station at any time after a successful invasion of this country. Whatever we destroy we have to re-make ourselves, and I understand that, if Athlone is destroyed, it would take us years to restore it.

No matter what decision is ultimately taken about the transfer of the central Government, the principal staff of this Department should remain in the capital in order to provide a channel for dealing with the invader when he arrives there and to do everything possible to lessen the harshness of the measures which he may wish to impose on the people. In any case, the Department must remain with the Representatives of foreign Governments, and no purpose would be served by allowing these latter to leave the capital.

[stamped] (Signed) J.P. WALSHE
Rúnaí

---

[1] Neither document printed.

No. 318 NAI DFA 2006/39

> *Confidential report from John W. Dulanty to Joseph P. Walshe (Dublin)*
> *(No.58) (Secret) (Copy)*
>
> LONDON, 25 October 1940

I learned from a well-informed friend that the danger of an invasion of Britain is regarded as remote. As a factor in the development of the war he thinks it now almost negligible. A neutral Ambassador in London told him that Goering recently urged a colleague of his – the Ambassador's – not to refer to the invasion when speaking to the Fuehrer. Their failure to invade Britain was a constant grief to him. They were bothered about the Fuehrer's health and they didn't want him to be aggravated by any reference to the invasion.

Notwithstanding what the newspapers might say he felt confident that America would not enter the war. This view was strongly held by the American Ambassador who is now on his way to Washington.

On the question of the defence against German air raids my friend said that from the reports of the experts the British Cabinet felt that they were now in a strong position about the daylight raids – 'Although an occasional raider may get through, in the daytime fighting we have the Germans whacked'. A deafening explosion and huge columns of smoke about 100 yards from this office (12.00 noon today) with women falling in Piccadilly from fright, no warning until 12.05, suggest that my friend was indulging in undue optimism in his use of the world 'Whacked'.[1]

The night raids presented of course a difficult problem, but the latest types of Spitfires, Hurricanes,[2] and Defiants[3] would be much more effective. The guns on the Spitfire and the Hurricane are in the forepart of the machine and can only fire frontwards. The Defiants have their guns in the tail and cannot therefore fire frontwards but the gun is movable and can fire backwards in rather more than a semi-circle from left to right, and, what is very important, can fire upwards or downwards. Their principal hope however is in the important technical developments for detection of enemy planes. This is done by radio projection. If the projection reaches nothing no indication is made on the dial in front of the pilot but if it does reach an aeroplane it returns to the pilot making a luminous spot about the size of a pocket watch on the dial in front of him. This is a definite location of the plane and the pilot is then able to follow it however dark the night and fight his adversary. I asked what would happen if this detector located a friendly instead of an enemy plane. The answer was that it shows a different kind of luminous sport on the pilot's dial. They were getting these radio detectors into their planes as quickly as possible and in a few months time they hope to have most of their planes so equipped. At present the radio projector was bringing down on an average an

---

[1] Handwritten sentence inserted in the margin by Dulanty.
[2] Hawker Hurricane, a British fighter aircraft, which entered service in 1937, and which was the workhorse of the RAF during the Battle of Britain.
[3] Boulton-Paul Defiant, a British fighter-bomber aircraft used as an interceptor in the early years of the Second World War. The sole-armament of a rear turret was found to be a considerable drawback.

enemy plane once a week. By the turn of the year they hoped to see that number greatly increased. This week a British plane – Defiant – was able by its radio apparatus to detect a German bomber, followed it for 150 miles and by shooting from below brought it down near Liverpool.

These developments were the result of several years research and were only now coming to fruition. Had the fall of France taken place six or nine months later than it had the history of aerial warfare for the British would have been very different, and far more favourable for them. They had, he thought, not done badly but a good deal of their night fighting had been worse than looking for a needle in a haystack. They are now confident that before long they will have the mastery in night fighting.

I reminded my friend of the fecundity of resource which the German scientists had shown in the last war – was it not likely that they were developing these highly technical devices? He thought not. From their experience in night flying over Germany they thought that the Germans had not even started on the problem of night interception by scientific measure. A German plane could start from Dieppe and be over London in twenty minutes. A British plane had to travel over an immense part of German territory before raiding their targets and the losses in the night trips were very small indeed.

There were however other ways in which the Germans were much better than the British. I asked him for an example. He said that their rubber boats were far ahead of anything the British had. When a German airman bales out of his machine over the sea he has attached to his back not only a parachute but a folded rubber boat. The latter on impact in the sea by some chemical action immediately opens and the pilot is comfortably seated in a boat which will stand even rough seas. It is painted yellow, the best colour for detection from the air, and in addition it emits a vapour. The colour of the boat and the vapour enable a German airman to see his colleague in the water with ease.

My friend said that it would probably sound monotonous to the uninformed listener to hear of repeated visits by the British air force to comparatively unknown places in Germany. Our tactics he said are to pick the eyes out of German industry. We went recently to the biggest ball-bearing producing centre in all Germany and the photographs show that we put it completely out of action.

On the point of avoiding hitting civilians the photographs of Hamburg revealed that whilst the residential parts were practically intact, save for one small bit, there was scarcely a brick left standing on a brick of the warehouses at the docks.

I asked him about the economic position of this country. He said he thought the picture given by Maynard Keynes[1] in a recent broadcast and recent articles was painted in much too optimistic a colour.

He was called away suddenly to a meeting and I had not the opportunity to ask him about the Mediterranean which of course again looks as though it might be the decisive theatre of the war.

---

[1] John Maynard Keynes (1883-1946), British economist, author *The General theory of employment, interest and money* (1936) and a founder of modern macroeconomics.

Documents on Irish Foreign Policy, Volume VI, 1939–1941

No. 319 NAI DFA Secretary's Files P12/3

Telegram from the Department of External Affairs to William Warnock (Berlin)
(No. 200) (Personal) (Copy)

DUBLIN, 1 November 1940

Your telegraphic reports are far too infrequent. We should have reports several times each week on such matters as material and moral effect of British raids, food and other conditions in Germany, and reactions of people with whom you come into touch towards current developments such as trend of American foreign policy, Spanish failure to enter war, Italian invasion of Greece, and progress of attack on Britain. You should of course report at once all press or other references to Ireland and whenever you visit Foreign Office or have talks with other officials you should report conversations including incidental comments on Irish affairs which cast light on general attitude towards this country. When you are instructed to make representations, you should report when you have made them and how they were received even if no immediate reply is given. We should also like to have regular news of such members of the Irish Colony as Francis Stuart[1] and Bewley. Have you any indication that Seán Russell or Frank Ryan have been in Germany?

No. 320 NAI DFA Secretary's Files P12/4

Telegram from the Department of External Affairs to Leopold Kerney (Madrid)
(No. 100) (Personal) (Copy)

DUBLIN, 5 November 1940

Your 104.[2] You should be careful to avoid anything which could be interpreted as demonstration against Spanish Government. Expulsion is sufficiently explained by third charge.[3] We cannot afford risk of even minor quarrels with Foreign Governments unless on matters directly concerning our own interests.

No. 321 NAI DFA Secretary's Files P2

Telegram from William Warnock to Joseph P. Walshe (Dublin)
(No. 74S) (Personal) (Sent via Geneva) (Copy)

BERLIN, 5 November 1940

Your 200.[4] I regret eye trouble forced me to restrict telegrams to the minimum in the last week(s). Coding and Decoding involve long strain on the eyes.

---

[1] Francis Stuart (1902-2000), Irish writer domiciled in Germany during the Second World War. Stuart broadcast to Ireland via the Redaktion-Irland service and had links with the IRA and German intelligence. He kept in touch with Frank Ryan until the latter's death in 1944.

[2] Not printed.

[3] The Comte Charles de Romrée de Vichenet, the Belgian Ambassador to Spain, had been expelled on the official pretext of his 'personal attitude', though the expulsion of the entire staff of the Belgian embassy suggested other motives, Kerney suggesting that the expulsion was inspired and 'possibly foreshadows' the expulsion of the Polish Ambassador. Kerney, with the American, British and French ambassadors and other diplomatic representatives, saw the Ambassador off from Madrid.

[4] See No. 319.

Material effect of air raids on Berlin small but there is certain moral effect from loss of sleep and because the people were given to understand it would be impossible for British aircraft to attack Berlin. Evacuation of children encouraged but on voluntary basis. So far air raids on too small a scale to have a decisive effect. Air raids in the West more often and possibly more effective. Damage to Hamburg slight except in the residential quarters; oil tanks hit but are empty. British aircraft often deceived by dummy factories and fires started by Germans themselves.

Food rations higher than at beginning of war.

People disappointed that high hopes of victory this autumn not fulfilled but do not doubt ultimate result. It is thought United States may enter in Spring; some surprised that Spain will not participate but not in official circles who appreciate Spanish economic position. Comment upon Greece reserved except to point out that it is a mere tool for Great Britain.

According to reports attacks on London and South East Coast have devastating results. Public now finding it difficult to understand if reports are correct how it is London population still holding out.

No. 322 NAI DFA Secretary's Files P20

Code telegram from William Warnock to Joseph P. Walshe (Dublin)
(No. 75S) (Personal) (Copy)

BERLIN, 6 November 1940

Your telegram 121.[1] Blockade. Foreign Office states they have already conveyed to you through German Minister, Dublin, they find it difficult to exempt our trade with Great Britain.[2] Ruter and others inform me in private conversations that they have given the matter serious consideration. So far as I can see, Naval authorities cannot see way to excluding Ireland. Foreign Office still open to proposals on our trade with countries other than Great Britain.

No. 323 NAI DFA Secretary's Files P15(i)

Telegram from Colman O'Donovan to the Department of External Affairs (Dublin)
(No. 88) (Personal) (Copy)

HOLY SEE, 7 November 1940

My 86.[3] An official in the Secretariat of State told me privately today (Thursday) that he had heard X. had been appointed, but all I could get from Tardini was that he hoped to have information for me within a few days. He made, however, reference to X. which I took to be a deliberate hint.[4]

---

[1] Not printed.
[2] See No. 264.
[3] Not printed.
[4] Marginal note by Sheila Murphy: 'In personal letter to Secretary X stated to be Fr McQuaid CSSp. (Blackrock Coll.)'.

Documents on Irish Foreign Policy, Volume VI, 1939–1941

No. 324 NAI DFA Secretary's Files P2

Telegram from Joseph P. Walshe to Robert Brennan (Washington)
(No. 170) (Personal) (Copy)

DUBLIN, 7 November 1940

Your 249 and 250 received.[1]

The British press following Prime Minister's statement on Tuesday 5th[2] has started a campaign for the occupation of the ports. No doubt the campaign is organised and will be carried on also in America.

You should see some of our good friends, explain seriousness of position and get them use their influence against it. Government determined to resist to bitter end.

There is of course danger that American administration ignorant of real feeling here may encourage campaign or even join in official pressure here. You should do everything possible to make known to them that the people will defend neutrality to death no matter who violates it because they regard neutrality in this world struggle for power as the fundamental condition of their survival as a nation.

On the British argument any great power should be allowed to use the ports of any small nation which is protected or dominated by its fleet if these ports happen to facilitate her war operations. You should most strongly emphasize that from the British point of view any such campaign seriously pursued would be disastrous. Our relations have greatly improved in recent months and Churchill's speech is regarded here as another bad blunder.

Continue to keep us closely informed.

No. 325 NAI DFA Secretary's Files P2

Telegram from Eamon de Valera to the delegates of the conference of the American Association for the Recognition of an Independent Irish Republic (New York)

DUBLIN, 8 November 1940

Greetings to delegates. In view of new menace request your members and all friends of Ireland to organise and put Ireland's case, including Partition, and the condition of the Nationalist minority in the partitioned area clearly before American public. To force into this war a people relatively defenceless against air attack would be an inhuman outrage. The Irish people have a right to keep out of it as Americans have and we shall defend that right to the utmost. Beware false parallels. Ireland belongs to the Irish people and our territory cannot be lent or leased to any belligerent for war purposes without involving us in the war.

---

[1] Neither document printed.
[2] On 5 November Churchill told the House of Commons that the lack of the Irish ports was 'a most heavy and grievous burden', and continued that it was 'a plain statement of an unpleasant fact designed to serve as a warning that it may not be possible to let matters rest as they are'.

No. 326 NAI DFA Washington Embassy File 61

Telegram from Robert Brennan to John J. Hearne (Ottawa)[1]
(Copy)

WASHINGTON, 9 November 1940

At the outbreak of the war the Irish Government in accordance with previously stated policy declared Ireland's neutrality. This policy was supported by all parties in the Dáil and by the entire press of the country.

Britain did not question Ireland's right to declare this policy and no attempt was made to interfere with it. The policy of neutrality has been scrupulously observed. The Government established a costly Coast Watching Service to see that none of the warring powers should take advantage of it. In order to defend Ireland's independence and safeguard its neutrality the Government raised the armed forces to 200,000 men all volunteers. A similar force in the United States in proportion to population would be eight million men.

The friendly feeling between the British and Irish peoples which had arisen after the settlement of 1938 was steadily increasing in spite of the fact that the last remaining grievance of the Irish people that of Partition had not been remedied.

On November 5th the British Prime Minister in the course of a speech in the House of Commons said that Britain's deprivation of the use of Irish ports as naval and air bases was a serious handicap in fighting the war being waged on British shipping. This was followed by a chorus of demands in the British Parliament and in the British press for the return of these ports to England and this campaign found an echo in the American press. Press statements emanating from London asserted that the goodwill of the President of the United States might be enlisted to induce the Irish Government to concede the use of the ports by Britain.

In the view of the Irish Government cession or lease of the ports would be a breach of neutrality which would bring Ireland into the war contrary to the declared policy of the Government and the wishes of 99% of the people.

Mr. de Valera asserted on the 7th November[2] that Ireland would resist by force any attempt to occupy the ports or to impair Ireland's sovereignty by any of the belligerents. That is the determination of the government and of the people. Under no circumstances will this policy be departed from.

The Government and people of Ireland are in hopes that America the cradle and home of democracy will realise the justice of Ireland's attitude in thus seeking to preserve its independence its peace and its democratic institutions.

---

[1] This is a copy of a statement given to Under-Secretary of State, Sumner Welles, by Brennan. It was transmitted to Hearne for his information.
[2] On 7 November de Valera made a statement in Dáil Éireann in response to Churchill, concluding that 'we shall defend our rights in regard to these ports against whoever shall attack them, as we shall defend our rights in regard to every other part of our territory'. See Maurice Moynihan (ed.), *Speeches and Statements by Eamon de Valera 1917-73* (Dublin, 1980), pp 449-52.

No. 327 NAI DFA Secretary's Files A8

Memorandum by Colonel Liam Archer
of a discussion with Joseph P. Walshe (Dublin)

DUBLIN, 9 November 1940

1. I have reason to believe that a diplomatic offensive is being launched by England in America on the following lines:
    (a) Bases in S. Ireland are essential to England to combat the submarine menace.
    (b) Mr. de Valera won't give these without a lot of fuss and trouble.
    (c) The U.S. could get them easily.
    (d) By amendment of the Neutrality Act S. Ireland can be declared outside the combat zone and traffic in 'non-contraband' carried on between the U.S. and Ireland in U.S. bottoms as well as British.
    (e) Owing to German attacks such traffic must be given protection and should be convoyed by U.S. Navy outside the combat zone, i.e. to and from Ireland. U.S. Navy to get the necessary terminal facilities in S.W. Ireland for this convoy protection.
2. It is expected in well informed circles that Pres. Roosevelt's policy will be one of gradual but persistent increase in the amount and nature of support to England leading to the participation of the U.S. Navy (and Naval Air Service) in the protection to Trade Routes in the Western Approaches; that his policy does not contemplate the employment of the U.S. Army in Europe or even a declaration of war by U.S. The onus to be on Germany of attacking U.S. convoys or declaring war on account of U.S. activities. The U.S. battle fleet is expected to remain in the Pacific and the naval activities in the Atlantic to be undertaken by the light forces and the U.S. naval air service. The question of European bases for this service thus arises as does the A.A. and ground protection of them.
3. Parallel with the U.S. Canadian Defence talks Washington and London are exchanging information on Atlantic and Pacific defence questions.

No. 328 NAI DFA Secretary's Files P15(i)

Telegram from Joseph P. Walshe to Colman O'Donovan (Holy See)
(No. 71) (Personal) (Copy)

DUBLIN, 11 November 1940

Your 92.[1] News officially confirmed by Nuncio. You should take very early opportunity of informing Holy Father through Secretary of State of pleasure of Government at appointment.

---

[1] Not printed, but see No. 323.

No. 329 NAI DFA Secretary's Files P53

> *Telegram from Robert Brennan to Joseph P. Walshe (Dublin)*
> *(No. 285) (Copy)*
> WASHINGTON, 11 November 1940

I saw Under Secretary, gave him copy of Chief's speech and statement of position; he said it was very clear from both that Ireland could have no other policy and that Ireland's peace was asset to Britain and any clash between two countries would be disastrous for both: he assured me no approach had been made from Britain: asked if it were desirable I should see President he said there was no need because he would immediately put position before him fully.

No. 330 NAI DFA Secretary's Files P14

> *Telegram from the Department of External Affairs to the Irish Legations at Ottawa,*
> *Geneva, Rome, Madrid, Vichy*
> *(Nos 66, 107, 72, 105, 350) (Personal)*
> DUBLIN, 12 November 1940

British demands for ports have not yet gone beyond parliamentary and press campaign. Taoiseach's reply to Churchill represents universal will of people. Ports will not be yielded except to overwhelming force. Full text of Taoiseach's statement will be broadcast short wave Wednesday 8.45 p.m. G.M.T.

To Rome: Inform other Legation.

No. 331 NAI DFA Secretary's Files P48A

> *Letter from Joseph P. Walshe to David Gray (Dublin)*
> DUBLIN, 12 November 1940

Dear David,

I was glad to receive your letter of November 11th, enclosing what you describe as a rough memorandum of your impressions of our after-lunch talk last Thursday. I am glad you so describe it, because, following our agreement to be completely frank with each other, I feel at liberty to describe your memorandum as a little post-impressionist, if not verging on the futurist. Of course, I may be wrong and I may have imbibed over-freely of the excellent wines which you gave us at lunch. If that is so, I was, of course, capable of saying anything, even the exact contrary of what I would wish to say in my sober moments. In any case, my dear David, I do not think an after-lunch conversation of that casual character merited being immortalised in a memorandum, and, if you don't mind, I should much prefer to see the memorandum destroyed than to attempt to make any serious effort to correct your impressions of what I said.

Of course, we can have a serious discussion on the same subject any time you wish, either here or in the Legation, but I should like beforehand to have a chat with my Minister on the net issues, so that I could convey to you the official view. My personal views on matters of such extreme gravity are of no import whatever, except perhaps for idle speculative discussion of the semi-bibulous character which one usually indulges in after a pleasant meal.

However, even in this short note, it might be just as well, in the nature of a preface to our next discussion, to cast a cursory glance over your memorandum and to make a remark here and there about its contents as the need strikes me. Of course, I accept your judgments on American public opinion, but I wonder are you absolutely correct in assuming that the country which more than all others has preached the right of self-determination would be impatient with us for exercising the essential sovereign right to remain out of the war. In the case of Ireland, which has won its independence, an essential condition of continued existence as a nation is abstention from participation in world conflicts. I quite understand the very laudable motives for which the majority of the English people are fighting this war, but we must look outside immediate causes and motives when taking our stand in face of such a cataclysm. The present war seems to me to be part of the natural process of world evolution towards a system of confederations of States. Germany and England are mere playthings of destiny serving an ultimate purpose to which their peoples are blind. The entry of Ireland into the war, viewed in this background, would be no decisive factor as far as the future of the world is concerned, but it would most decidedly put an end immediately or in the near future to the independence and cultural existence of the Irish people. I have always been a believer in some such system of federation as the British Commonwealth of Nations, but I always felt that it was incomplete and unstable so long as it remained in its present scattered form. That is why I frequently spoke to my English colleagues and to permanent Civil Servants in the other States concerned of the need for broadening the basis of the Commonwealth. I thought, and I still think, that the entry therein of the Scandinavian States and of the United States of America is an essential condition of permanence Indeed, I doubt very much whether it is possible for Ireland and Britain alone of the States of Europe to enter into a lasting compact of federation with the United States and the present Dominions. Ireland and Britain must take several States of Europe with them into the new combination, or enter into a new European federation.

You will find very few people in Ireland to accept wholeheartedly the view that the British Fleet is protecting us from potential enemies. We have no doubt that such was not the position until we obtained our relative freedom in 1922, and Mr. Churchill's speech makes us wonder whether it would not be wiser to wait a long time before being quite certain that the Fleet acts in our regard in a purely protective role. As I have said, I do not wish to contradict your impressions of what I said to you, but it would be so contrary to my knowledge of Irish history to say that the Irish people were grateful for the protection of the British Fleet that I hardly think I can have said it.

But now we come to the most important point. You make me say that I had little doubt that there would be no difficulty about arranging for the lease of ports and air facilities to the United States should she become a belligerent. I do not think I was anything like so definite, but in any case I can make myself clear now. If America came into the war and the federation I speak of (i.e., the U.S.A., Great Britain, Ireland and the Dominions, to begin with) were already in being, we should in that framework most certainly have to give very serious consideration to the request of the United States for facilities here while endeavouring at the same time to maintain the neutrality which our people will continue to desire. The formation of this Anglo-Irish-American federal group pre-supposes a guarantee by America and Britain of the continued independence of a united Ireland. That is a very different situation and a very different attitude from being ready to hand over our ports to the United States at the present moment merely for the asking. When America has become – as she is rapidly becoming – the dominating Power in the world, we shall feel a very real security as far as our independence is concerned, and we should, of course, be ready to agree to a mutual granting of defence facilities to common citizenship and to many other things in order to be part of the system the working out of which she would in the ultimate analysis be able to control.

In any case, let us have another talk together before your talk with the Taoiseach. That would perhaps be the best way to get our ideas clear on this whole very important issue.

No. 332 NAI DFA Secretary's Files P12/1

> *Code telegram from Joseph P. Walshe to Seán Murphy (Vichy)*
> *(No. 349) (Personal) (Copy)*
> DUBLIN, 12 November 1940

Have had no telegraphic reports from you recently. You should report on situation at least once a week and as frequently as there is anything special to report. Press reports show considerable and very important diplomatic activities in France. Apart from telegraphic reports you should keep whole situation from day to day written up to forward when occasion arises. Families in great form.

No. 333 NAI DFA Secretary's Files P20

> *Code telegram from Joseph P. Walshe to William Warnock (Berlin)*
> *(No. 217) (Personal) (Copy)*
> DUBLIN, 13 November 1940

Your 75 re Blockade.[1] Do you think we could construe reply as indicating that though German authorities can not formally commit themselves they are disposed to give effect to our representations in practice.

No. 334 NAI DFA Secretary's Files A2

> *Memorandum by Joseph P. Walshe of a meeting with Sir John Maffey*
> DUBLIN, 13 November 1940

Sir John Maffey called to see me this morning at his suggestion. He had been in London for four or five days, and I was rather surprised that he had deferred

---

[1] See No. 322.

a call so long, as he had returned on Saturday, 9th. However, the delay can no doubt be explained by Mr. Churchill's speech on Tuesday, 5th, and the Taoiseach's reply on 7th.

He began by talking generally about the effect of the bombing in London. To the casual visitor, there was little trace of serious damage. He stayed at the Wyndham Club. His breakfast, lunch and dinner were served as usual. He could go out and take a taxi where he liked. All this independently of the fact that the raids were frequent and the German bombers could be heard occasionally overhead. He had not been to the East End, but he knew that there at least the damage was pretty serious.

I asked him what he thought about the Molotov visit to Berlin. He said he thought it very serious, though he personally always felt opposed to any kind of British alliance with Russia, as it could bring no real advantage to their cause.

After a few general remarks of no particular importance about the world situation, he went on to the purpose of his call. He stated that he found the Dominions Office worried about Churchill's statement. They had known nothing beforehand about it, and, of course, the statement was typically Churchillian. Nevertheless, he must say, in defence of Churchill, that he merely expressed regret at the loss of the ports, and, of course, as far as Churchill was concerned, there was no question of any threat to seize the ports. I remarked at this point that the Taoiseach would not have made his statement if Churchill's speech had not been followed by several speeches in the House of Commons dotting the is and crossing the ts of what the Prime Minister had said, and leading our people to believe that there was a serious threat involved. The situation became worse when there was a general Press chorus the following day on a still higher pitch, and this spread to the United States.

Maffey said that, of course, as he had said before, the Press will say what they want to say, just as Members of Parliament will, and we should attach official significance only to what was said by the Prime Minister himself. He regretted the whole matter and hoped it had now blown over.

His purpose in going to the other side was mainly to discuss the trade agreement. Of course, he had not found the atmosphere too good on account of the Prime Minister's statement, but he did succeed in persuading them that the trans-shipment condition was unwisely included in the draft agreement, that naturally the Irish Government felt it might be a means of dragging us into the war. In fact, he said, he had pressed that point so strongly that they had agreed to drop it. The Dominions Office were now examining our memorandum on the proposals, the matter would, of course, have to go to the Cabinet, and he hoped we should get a reply fairly soon. On the other hand, he had no hope for an increase in prices, whatever chance we might have of getting some contribution analogous to the £500,000 already discussed.

While he was in London, Maffey had discussed with the Dominions Office the difficulties in which he was frequently placed by British journalists coming to Dublin and publishing in the London papers articles injurious to the good relations between the two countries. He suggested that he should have a Press Attaché here, and he asked me if there was any objection. I told him that, as it was quite a normal thing for Legations in every country to have a Press Attaché, we did not wish to raise any objection. On the contrary, if the Press Attaché was going to help him to keep unfriendly articles out of the British Press, as I am sure he would, we should be very glad to see him here. I had, of course, in mind, the difficulty of objecting to the presence of a Press Attaché in the British Legation so long as there was a Press Attaché in the German Legation. The request was a perfectly fair one, and we can make a strong case with Maffey when the British Press goes wrong. It is, of course, quite clear that the Press Attaché will try to influence our Press to insert more British propaganda, but that is a situation we shall have to face.

At the end, Maffey once more expressed his desire to have the Taoiseach for lunch, and I said that perhaps now, as the country was more organised, the Taoiseach was subject to less pressure and would be able to go. He suggested lunch for 25th (Monday) or 28th (Thursday), and I told him that I would convey the invitation to the Taoiseach.

No. 335 NAI DFA Secretary's Files A4

Code telegram from John J. Hearne to Joseph P. Walshe (Dublin)
(No. 68) (Personal) (Copy)
OTTAWA, 14 November 1940

Very ugly anti-Irish campaign appears to be starting in Canadian newspapers. Mentioned it to Skelton in conversation today Wednesday. Also stated to him that reply to my telegram 67[1] was really contained in speech November 7th. He said he thought speech very clear statement. Skelton was not present during my conversation with Prime Minister last evening.

No. 336 NAI DFA 217/39

Letter from Francis T. Cremins to Seán Lester (Geneva)
(X.163) (Copy)
GENEVA, 14 November 1940

Sir,
I have the honour to inform you, on behalf of my Government, that I have been appointed Chargé d'Affaires of Ireland in the Swiss Confederation, and that my appointment as Permanent Delegate accredited to the League of Nations now ceases.

It is the intention, however, that I should remain the channel for communications between the Government of Ireland and all International Organisations in Switzerland. Accordingly, I will be grateful if, as from the 19th November, 1940, all documents and communications relating to the League of Nations which have hitherto been sent to me here by the Secretariat are forwarded to me addressed as follows:-

---

[1] Not printed.

Mr. F.T. Cremins,
   Chargé d'Affaires,
      Legation d'Irlande,
         24, Beatusstrasse,
            Berne.

On taking my departure, I would like to say how much I appreciate the cordial and happy relations which have always existed between the Secretariat of the League and the Irish Delegation. In the long period during which I have acted as Permanent Delegate, I have received from the Secretariat nothing but the most valuable assistance in my work, the most friendly co-operation and the greatest courtesy. For that, I desire to express my sincere appreciation and gratitude.

I have the honour to be,
Sir,
Yours faithfully,
[Stamped] F.T. CREMINS

No. 337 NAI DFA Madrid Embassy 27/4

Telegram from the Department of External Affairs to Leopold H. Kerney (Madrid)
(No. 106) (Personal)

DUBLIN, 16 November 1940

My telegram 105.[1] Press campaign has almost ceased in USA and is dying down in England we feel for the moment at least threat is receding

No. 338 NAI DFA Secretary's Files P20

Code telegram from William Warnock to Joseph P. Walshe (Dublin)
(No. 86) (Copy)

BERLIN, 16 November 1940

Your tel. 217.[2] Whilst I feel convinced of German goodwill towards us and of their reluctance to inconvenience us it would be a mistake for us to be too sanguine in view of technical difficulties in exempting us and importance of blocking British food supplies.

No. 339 NAI DFA Secretary's Files P12/7

Code telegram from Joseph P. Walshe to Francis T. Cremins (Berne)
(No. 111) (Personal) (Copy)

DUBLIN, 18 November 1940

You should send regular telegraphic reports on general outlook as seen from your post including reports on your conversations with Swiss Ministers and officials and general impression in Switzerland on progress and probable out-

---

[1] See No. 330.
[2] See No. 333.

come of war. In particular, report fully all infringements of Swiss neutrality by air or otherwise stating actions taken by Swiss Government and reply made by offending belligerent. Wire short summary of measures taken in connection with flights over Switzerland at night.

No. 340 NAI DFA Secretary's Files P2

> Code telegram from Joseph P. Walshe to Robert Brennan (Washington)
> (No. 177) (Personal) (Copy)
>
> DUBLIN, 18 November 1940

Your 268.[1] You should contact prominent individual or two amongst the sixty and suggest that answer be sent to Monitor[2] pointing out that granting of ports to England involves Ireland in the war and entails temporary if not ultimate loss of independence. For Ireland choice is between neutrality and loss of independence. The un-American character of this pressure on Ireland should be stressed as also the defenceless position of Ireland in the immediate war area compared with the position of America with all her defence resources three thousand miles away. Who are the two Bishops? Perhaps you should contact them both.

No. 341 NAI DFA Secretary's Files P12/1

> Code telegram from Seán Murphy to Joseph P. Walshe (Dublin)
> (No. 336) (Personal) (Copy)
>
> VICHY, 18 November 1940

Your telegram 349.[3] Regret was unable to give you some advance information as to recent meetings and conversations between France and Germany. These meetings and conversations came as a complete surprise to all here, including members of Government who were unaware of first meeting until after it had taken place and of second until it was in progress. I knew from wireless that you were aware of these meetings, and I considered it was needless expense to telegraph when I was unable to add anything to what you already knew.

The greatest secrecy was observed regarding these meetings, and matters discussed were only given in broadest outlines. Secrecy is supposed to be one of Laval's characteristics. The policy of collaboration was received here by public with mixed feelings, and even more so in occupied territories. Laval is universally unpopular and distrusted, and public are afraid he may lead Marshal into an impasse from which he cannot retreat. Laval is avowedly anti-British and pro-German. It is known here that several prominent Frenchmen not associated with politics have represented to Marshal that Laval's presence in Government is very badly looked upon and that it is injurious to Marshal's prestige and influence. It is generally said there is a considerable difference of opinion between Marshal and Laval on policy of collaboration. The Marshal is

---
[1] Not printed.
[2] *The Christian Science Monitor* newspaper.
[3] See No. 332.

not prepared to _____[1] in a policy directed against England, whereas Laval wants to go 100 per cent in collaboration with Germany. It is true that any _____[2] collaboration between two countries must be indirectly against England, but difference of opinion is appreciable.

It is commonly believed that conversations have had a setback owing to capture of Gabon by de Gaulle and British. The German reaction is that, if France cannot defend her colonies, Germany and Italy must take steps to do so.

Public opinion in both zones is uneasy because conversations are not giving some tangible result. Students' demonstration in Paris recently resulted in University being closed by Germans, and Rector and Secretary-General removed from office by French Government. The food situation in both zones, but particularly in occupied territory, becoming more difficult.

There is, of course, strong Press campaign here controlled by Laval in favour of policy of collaboration as only solution for France, but as it is known to be made by him, it has suspects. There is great activity on part of Laval, who is constantly going to and fro to Paris, but it is generally believed no great advance is being made. It is known that French made certain proposal tenor of which is said to be only known to Pétain and Laval, to which Germans have replied. The conversations are continuing on basis of German reply.

Apart from this event, there has been nothing important since my last telegraphed report. There are hosts of rumours which everyone hears sooner or later and which have to be sifted carefully to ascertain whether they have any basis of truth. Vichy is a town of rumours of all kinds.

I would have sent telegraphic reports of my impressions of the situation here were it not for fact that I understood from your telegram 98[3] that you only wanted reports which could be supported by some authoritative source and that you were generally better informed on situation here from elsewhere than I could inform you, which is[4] correct. If, however, you desire me to give you my impression of the situation here, I shall do so as often as there is anything of importance to report. I am, of course, keeping record of important internal and external questions as they arise.

No. 342 NAI DFA Secretary's Files P2

> *Code telegram from Robert Brennan to Joseph P. Walshe (Dublin)*
> *(No. 273) (Personal) (Copy)*
> WASHINGTON, 19 November 1940

For your information, description of present conflict in your telegram 170[5] 'Struggle of world power' I cannot use here. It would be fiercely resented because they hold it is a fight for decency, democracy, civilisation, Christianity, etc., against power of evil.

---

[1] Text missing in original.
[2] Text missing in original.
[3] See No. 236.
[4] An insertion mark has been placed here in the text in pen, but no word has been inserted.
[5] See No. 324.

Your despatch 177[1] 'choice is between neutrality and independence'. This is dangerous argument, because there is a come-back, already voiced in some letters, that America would guarantee ultimate restoration of independence.

Best line, I find, is to point out that England's friends are doing her ill-service in encouraging her in course which, if pursued, will only increase her difficulties. Please remember cry is getting louder each day that American interests are vitally concerned and that defeat of England means disintegration of America and disaster for United States.

Following message has been received from Dr. Sheehy[2] today – 'Tell de Valera his friends will not let him down, but as Americans we shall oppose Hitlerism to _____ death'.[3]

No. 343 NAI DFA Secretary's Files P2

> Code telegram from Joseph P. Walshe to Robert Brennan (Washington)
> (No. 180) (Personal) (Copy)
> DUBLIN, 21 November 1940

Your 273.[4] Thanks your comments. You are of course quite right to adapt language to local needs. Is the view you attribute to Americans about identification of interests with Britain universal? As there is a real possibility of a British defeat there must be some Americans who see that and who do not accept such a complete identity of interests? What is the dominating racial element in favour of participation in the war? What is the reaction to the rapprochement between Russia and Axis? Is there not strong Russophile element in America?

No. 344 NAI DFA Secretary's Files P4

> Letter from John J. Hearne to Joseph P. Walshe (Dublin)
> (85/2)
> OTTAWA, 22 November 1940

I have the honour to report as follows:-

On Tuesday afternoon the 12th November Mr. Hanson,[5] Leader of the Opposition speaking in the House of Commons, raised the question of the ports. As I knew that Mr. King was to speak that evening after Mr. Hanson, I got in touch, as soon as I could, with Dr. Skelton. Dr. Skelton said he had not heard that the question had been raised by Mr. Hanson. He had, he said, just

---

[1] See No. 340.
[2] Dr Maurice S. Sheehy, head of the Department of Religious Education, Catholic University of America, known for his anti-Nazi views. In November 1940 Sheehy had written to the British Ambassador in Washington urging that Ireland should not be forced to give up her neutrality and suggesting that Churchill's 5 November statement on the ports was ill-advised.
[3] Text missing in original.
[4] See No. 342.
[5] Richard Hanson (1879-1948), interim leader of the Canadian Conservative Party (1940-1) and Leader of the Opposition (1940-3) (party leader Arthur Meighen did not have a seat in parliament).

seen one of Mr. King's private secretaries and the private secretary had not mentioned it. He did not think Mr. King would make any reference to the matter in his speech. Dr. Skelton was sure there was no reference to it in the prepared speech. (I confirm that that was so, as later that night, I saw the prepared text and the official reporters report of additional remarks made on points raised in the debate.) 'He may put the matter off in some way with a very few words', Dr. Skelton added; 'I don't think he will discuss it'.

When Mr. King concluded his speech (Mr. Conway and I were in our places in the Speakers gallery) we went to the Official Reporters' office to get the exact text of the reference to Mr. Hanson's remarks. The Official Reporters' note had gone to the private secretary's office for checking and we accordingly went there and saw the text. As we were going home we met Mr. King in a corridor outside his office. He was with some others. He immediately hailed us with the words 'Oh, Mr. Hearne, I wanted to see you'. He then brought me to his Office.

After asking me whether I had been in the House during the debate the Prime Minister said that he would like Mr. de Valera to know from him that the question of the ports had been raised in the House. It would be gratifying to him (the P.M.) if he could be of any help in the matter. He said that he knew our attitude. He knew (he said) that if we gave the ports to one of the belligerents we would involve ourselves with the other and have the country bombed and wrecked. But he nevertheless felt that as the question had been raised Mr. de Valera should know from him (he repeated this) and, if he could help, it would be very gratifying to him. He himself would not wish to put the question of a lease of the ports (to the Canadian Government) to Mr. de Valera; and if it would embarrass Mr. de Valera in any way and if he were assured beforehand that the question could not be entertained, he would not put it at all. But he might be pressed in the course of the debate to do something about the matter as it had been put up to him and if he were pressed, he would not like it to be said he had done nothing whatever about it. He would like to be able to say he had been in touch with Mr. de Valera.

I asked Mr. King if he had read the Taoiseach's speech of the 7th November (which I had sent to Dr. Skelton on receipt of the text from Mr. Brennan). He said he had read it and added that he understood the situation very well. He made no further comment on the speech. I said that I thought the answer to any message to Mr. de Valera was contained in that speech. I emphasised that the question was not whether the ports could be leased to one of the belligerents rather than another; the speech expressly referred to all the belligerents and the real issue involved in the ports question was the maintenance of our neutrality. I said that I saw no prospect of a fundamental change of national policy at this stage. I stated that there was no *possible* Irish Government that could go behind the people's manifest will in this matter. The nation was not divided on it; we had, in fact, never secured so complete a national unity on any other policy. I referred to a speech made by Mr. Cosgrave sometime ago where he said that the Government should not take too much credit to itself for having kept the country out of the war; it was the people themselves that had made the decision. (I did not purport to give Mr. Cosgrave's exact words: but I remember the speech.) Mr. King's eyes opened wide at the mention of Mr. Cosgrave's name. (Mr. Cosgrave's portrait is in his study.) He seemed genuinely surprised that Mr. Cosgrave should have spoken thus. I may say that I had spoken often to Dr. Skelton of the attitude of all our political parties to the war. Looking back upon Mr. King's surprise at my mention of Mr. Cosgrave I would now attribute it to the fact that he had read the New York Times report that Opposition and Labour Parties in the Dáil were 'gloomy and preoccupied' during the Taoiseach's speech of the 7th November. I may be wrong in this; but Dr. Skelton made a definite point of the report to me when I brought him the substance of the relevant portion of your cable No. 67 of the 16th November[1] on Monday morning the 18th November. There seems to be an impression that the gloom and preoccupation indicated the beginnings of a difference of opinion between the Government (Mr. de Valera in particular) and the parties referred to. My own interpretation has been that the whole House was impressed by, and shared, the preoccupation of the Taoiseach himself, and of his words, with the possible consequences of the British press campaign which had followed Mr. Churchill's speech. Be that as it may, I emphasised to Mr. King that even the 'Irish Times' newspaper was against our entry into the war from the very beginning: and so on.

The Prime Minister was very easy in his manner; he avowed to, or professed, a full understanding of our position. I must do him the justice of recording that he gave me the impression that he knew the answer to any message he would send to the Taoiseach, but that he wanted to be able to save himself the embarrassment – in Parliament – of having failed to do anything about an appeal made to him by the House of Commons, that is, should Mr. Hanson's speech be followed by a number of others in the same sense. He wanted to be able to say to the House: 'I have done as the House desired'.

Mr. King is not regarded as a great leader, but he *is* regarded as one of the most astute politicians in Canadian political history. I cannot, therefore, discount the likelihood of his having wanted to send a message to Mr. de Valera at this stage in the war for the sole purpose of putting himself on record – although ostensibly off the record – in the sense of my cable to you – the words of which he practically dictated. I wrote them down as he spoke.

It was towards midnight when I left Mr. King. Mr. Conway and I sent cable No. 67 by about 3 a.m. on the 13th November.

Next morning I spoke to Dr. Skelton about my interview with Mr. King. He had not yet seen Mr. King and apparently had no knowledge of my interview with him on the previous night. I told him about it and gave him the sense of my cable. His only comment was that he would have liked me to have asked you to allow Mr. King to refer (in the House) to his telegram of the 16th June.[2] I said that Mr. King had not mentioned that, and that his anxiety appeared to be confined to the reply he would have to give in Parliament to Mr. Hanson's appeal especially if there were others along the same lines. Dr.

---

[1] Not printed.
[2] Not printed. In his telegram to de Valera the Canadian Prime Minister warned of the imminent dangers facing Ireland; in particular the likelihood of a German invasion. MacKenzie King appealed to de Valera and to the Prime Minister of Northern Ireland, Lord Craigavon (to whom he sent a similar telegram), to 'meet and work out a basis upon which united and effective resistance could be offered in the event of invasion or attack' (NAI DFA P4).

Skelton accepted that, but felt that we might have to cable again about the telegram of the 16th June.

I had no doubt as to what your reply to my cable would be. Although I knew it was my duty to send the cable when the Prime Minister had requested it, I keenly felt the affront of the whole business and the futility and silliness of the suggestion to lease our ports to the *Canadian* Government. Apart from that, Mr. Conway kept on emphasising to me the excellent point that the proposal was based on the assumption that our neutrality policy was primarily anti-British. I hoped that you would send me in addition to your reply, an official – or personal – reprimand for not having kept the Canadian Government better informed of our position. I would gladly have shown it to Dr. Skelton as he knows how frequently I have summarised our national attitude and policy for him following the instructions you have sent me from time to time. It would have been a rebuke to *him*, chiefly. They should certainly not have tried this on. But perhaps on the whole it was as well they did. Your message may have stopped a ramp at the very beginning. Anyway the Prime Minister is not, so far, being pressed in a spate of speeches in Parliament to take the matter of the ports up with the Taoiseach. The Orangemen's spokesman T.J. Church M.P. of Toronto (the gentleman who objected to my going to Toronto early on this year) confined his remarks to praise of Ulster's war effort.

On Monday the 18th November I delivered your message to Dr. Skelton and left him a copy of the words of the cable (copy herewith).[1] He simply smiled and said that was what he had expected! He had previously said as much. No doubt you will ask, then why did they ask you to send the message at all? I refrained from asking that question myself.

Dr. Skelton asked me whether your words 'it would be extremely awkward if the Prime Minister said he was in touch with the Taoiseach' referred to the Prime Minister's cable of the 16th June. I said that I thought you clearly did not want any public statement at all by Mr. King to the effect that he had been in touch with Mr. de Valera either in June or recently. I added that your reply to Mr. King's message on the ports applied a fortiori to his message of the 16th June. I suggested that the message of the 16th June was practically telling the Irish people to give up their neutrality. (He seemed to think that was a bald way of putting it.) He said that he would talk to the Prime Minister about the question of sending you another cable asking whether he might refer publicly to the fact that he was in touch in June. I said that I thought it would be a mistake to send another message asking you that, as you clearly wanted no public reference at all to either of Mr. King's messages. We agreed that I should not ask you then but should simply report to you that I had delivered your reply to Dr. Skelton and that he said he would pass it on at once to the Prime Minister. I have so far heard nothing more about the matter and have not enquired.

In the course of the conversation just referred to, Dr. Skelton quoted the Dublin press message that the Opposition and Labour Parties were 'gloomy

---

[1] Not printed. The telegram (No. 67, Estero to Ottawa (NAI DFA P4)) pointed out that while de Valera was 'most friendly' towards Canada, 'Canadian critics do not realise Ireland's right to independence and to the absolute ownership of her own territory'.

and preoccupied' during or at the end of the Taoiseach's speech of the 7th November. He made quite a point of it. I think they have some idea here that men like Deputy Dillon (and certainly Senator MacDermot)[1] would go into the war if they held office and that there is the possibility of a Government alternative to the Taoiseach's which would hand over the ports. I pointed out to Dr. Skelton the falsity and danger of that line of thinking. I said that it was a complete mis-reading of the situation to think that any Irish public man could stand a moment's chance of election on a policy of going into the war or handing over the ports.

[signed] JOHN J. HEARNE

No. 345 NAI DFA Secretary's Files P12/1

> *Code telegram from Joseph P. Walshe to Seán Murphy (Vichy)*
> *(No. 391) (Personal) (Copy)*
> DUBLIN, 25 November 1940

Your 336.[2] It would be interesting to learn Nuncio's view of present situation. How is country receiving Catholic and national trend of Pétain Government activities? Have they not secured sufficient support to be independent of unpopularity of even important Minister? What are Laval's constructive plans for the future? What classes of people are against him? Is not some form of future collaboration with Germany accepted as inevitable? What particular political act has made Laval unpopular? What is view of ordinary people about de Gaulle?

No. 346 NAI DFA Secretary's Files P53

> *Code telegram from Joseph P. Walshe to Robert Brennan (Washington)*
> *(No. 187) (Copy)*
> DUBLIN, 26 November 1940

Your 258.[3] American Minister reported to Taoiseach Friday last substance of statement of Under Secretary to you on November 9. Statement much less favourable than your report. Under Secretary reported as saying we were endangering our own position by holding back ports which were apparently essential for British success. Although no approach made to American Government by British he felt obliged to express his views to you because they were the same as those of most Americans.

For your information Gray thinks on exclusively British lines and believes the Germans are really going to invade America. Taoiseach left him without any doubt whatever that we had no intention of giving the ports to anybody.

---

[1] Frank MacDermot (1896-1975), politician (National Centre Party and Fine Gael), Senator (1937-42); a prominent critic of Irish neutrality.
[2] See No. 341.
[3] See No. 329.

Documents on Irish Foreign Policy, Volume VI, 1939–1941

No. 347 NAI DFA 2006/39

> *Confidential report from John W. Dulanty to Joseph P. Walshe (Dublin)*
> *(No. 63) (Secret) (Copy)*
> LONDON, 26 November 1940

I asked Lord Cranborne yesterday whether the British had any information about the meetings between M. Molotov and Herr Hitler and other German leaders. He said beyond a number of conflicting reports which cancelled each other out they had heard nothing really reliable. The Russians, as everybody knew, were most illusive and deliberately enigmatic. No one could tell from day to day what their objectives, immediate or ultimate, were. His own view was that they would keep out of the conflict as long as possible, though in a world of such unpredictable and critical events they might be compelled to join in the struggle later.

Whether the position in Albania was due to the superiority of Greek strategy or to the extremely poor fighting quality of the Italians he did not know. Certainly the Greeks had done amazingly well and the British were easier in their minds now about both Greece and Egypt. The Germans were of course past masters in the art of developing high tension war nerves but he thought the Yugoslavs would resist domination either from them or the Italians. The Turks would fight if Bulgaria were induced to attack Greece but whether they would fight because of a passage of troops through Yugoslavia he was not sure.

So far, Lord Cranborne gives one the impression of great caution, possibly due to a sense of having to learn his job as a new member of the Cabinet. Certainly he is less communicative than certain of his predecessors. This view is shared by other High Commissioners.

No. 348 NAI DFA 226/1A

> *Memorandum from Frederick H. Boland to Joseph P. Walshe (Dublin) on*
> *Ireland's contribution to the League of Nations*
> DUBLIN, 26 November 1940

1. We must now take a decision as to:- (a) Whether our contribution to the League of Nations for the year 1940 – amounting to over £15,000 – should be paid at all and (b) what, if any, provision we should make in the estimates for 1941/42 for the payment of a contribution to the League of Nations in respect of the year 1941.
2. The League budget for 1940 was duly voted. When we were asked by the League last May when we would pay our subscription, we said we hoped to do so in September. Since May, however, the League has completely foundered. Part of it is now in the United States; another section is in Geneva, and the most recent information we have about a further section, comprising some of the principal officials of the Secretariat, is that it is stranded between Switzerland and Portugal, unable either to get back to Switzerland or go forward to the United States. We have ceased to receive any evidence that the League is able to do more than publish from time to time a few statistical

publications. The last return of contributions which we have received – dated 31st March, 1940 – shows that at that date only one State had paid its contribution for 1940 in full and only four had made part payments.

3. Under these circumstances, it is difficult to see how we could justify paying over more than £15,000 of the public money to the League. It would be virtually impossible to answer the argument that, as most of the activities for which the budget for 1940 was voted, had been abandoned, we had no right to pay over our full contribution. It might be said, of course, that as the budget for 1940 was duly adopted and voted, we are under some legal obligation to make the payment. It is unlikely that anybody would raise the legal question when the whole basis of the League itself has obviously broken down, but, in view of this element in the case and the possibility of our having to make the payment at a later stage, it would be well, I think, if we decided to withhold payment, to secure the concurrence of the Department of Finance beforehand.

4. The second question is that of the provision, if any, to be made for a contribution to the League of Nations in the estimates for the year 1941/42. Provision for our contribution to the League of Nations has hitherto always been made by means of a special Vote separate from that for the Department of External Affairs.

5. A provision for a normal contribution seems to be quite out of the question because the Supervisory Committee of the League has apparently been unable to meet and, therefore, no League budget for the year 1941 has been drawn up or agreed to. That being so the only alternatives before us seem to be either to make no provision at all or to make a merely token provision of £10. To my mind the former course is the only one we can reasonably take. The appropriate League regulations provide that the budget estimates, once drawn up by the Secretary-General, must be examined by the Supervisory Commission appointed by the Assembly and, after examination by the Commission, circulated to all the members of the League, together with the Commission's report, not less than three months before the Meeting of the Assembly. They must then be discussed by the Finance Committee of the Assembly and adopted by the Assembly unanimously before they have any binding force. None of this procedure has been complied with, and the possibility of following it in present circumstances is practically nil. The fact that there is no proper League budget for 1941, therefore, would be a completely satisfactory reason for our not making any provision for League contributions in our 1941/42 estimates.

6. If, on the other hand, the Minister felt that not to make any provision at all for the League in the estimates would have the character of a positive political act and expose the Government to the criticism that it was taking the initiative in abandoning the League and setting a bad example to other small States, our proper course would be to make a token provision of £10, as evidence of our willingness to make whatever provision we were bound to make as a member of the League but of our inability to assess the amount of our contribution owing to the breakdown of the League budgetary machine.

7. The simplest course seems to be not to make any provision for the League in the 1941/42 estimates.

[initialled] F.H.B.

Documents on Irish Foreign Policy, Volume VI, 1939–1941

No. 349 NAI DFA Paris Embassy 49/16

Letter from Seán Murphy to James Joyce (St-Gérand-le-Puy)
(Copy)

VICHY, 26 November 1940

Dear Mr. Joyce,

I was both surprised and disappointed to receive a note (of which I enclose a copy herewith)[1] from the German Embassy through Count O'KELLY, to the effect that your daughter's[2] journey to Switzerland cannot take place.

I do not know why this decision has been reached unless it is because, as it may be possible to infer from the note, she is the holder of a British passport. I had gathered as I told you at the time from the informal talk which I had with a member of the Embassy during my visit to Paris in August last that her journey would not give rise to any difficulty in spite of her holding a British passport. I may add, however, that there is no doubt that since the month of September, the German authorities have become more strict in regard to the travelling of foreigners.

No. 350 NAI DFA 2006/39

Confidential report from John W. Dulanty to Joseph P. Walshe (Dublin)
(No. 64) (Secret) (Copy)

LONDON, 27 November 1940

Although in his public statements about the war prospects the British Prime Minister is naturally very guarded I hear that his private opinion is that, whilst they have of course not won, they have, to use his own words, 'turned the corner'.

Professor F.A. Lindemann,[3] F.R.S., a Physicist of European reputation, is an intimate friend of Mr. Churchill. His scientific forecasts are said to have been exceptionally accurate, particularly about the German air position and air warfare generally. Referring to An Taoiseach's Dáil speech he said to a friend of mine recently 'What made the Irish Prime Minister fly off the handle about Churchill's reference to the Irish ports'? I mention this remark because his very close association with Churchill lends a possible significance to it.

No. 351 NAI DFA 2006/39

Confidential report from John W. Dulanty to Joseph P. Walshe (Dublin)
(No. 65) (Secret) (Copy)

LONDON, 27 November 1940

I have taken up with the British Authorities the questions raised in your minute of 17th October[4] about the discontinuance of the supply of certain

---

[1] Not printed.
[2] Lucia Joyce (1907-82), daughter of James Joyce and Nora Barnacle.
[3] Frederick Alexander 'the Prof' Lindemann (1886-1957), 1st Viscount Cherwell, English physicist; scientific adviser to the British government and confidant of Winston Churchill; Paymaster-General (1942-5, 1951-3).
[4] See No. 312.

meteorological reports which were furnished during the currency of the recent series of Transatlantic flights.

The position as it is understood by the British appears to be that our Government were approached in November 1938, as to the making of arrangements for the mutual exchange of reports between our Meteorological Services and the United Kingdom in time of war, and it was suggested that our Government would wish to consider the nature of the meteorological reports which they would require in those circumstances. In our reply of the 28th August, 1939, we stated that we were prepared, in the event of war, to continue the existing arrangement under which observations made at weather reporting stations in Ireland were furnished to the United Kingdom Meteorological Office on the understanding that meteorological reports and forecasts would continue to be furnished by the latter to us. In September 1939 the Officer in Charge of the Meteorological Station at Foynes asked for information from certain stations and arrangements were made to supply, as from the 15th September, the information asked for by the authorities at Foynes, and this information has continued to be supplied regularly since that date up to the present time, with the exception of the Belgian and French reports which, of course, are no longer available. In the circumstances, the United Kingdom Meteorological Office feel that so long as they go on supplying the information asked for in September 1939, in so far as it is available, they are fulfilling their part of the reciprocity arrangements.

The British Meteorological Office also point out that at the present time they receive from us reports from five stations and one auxiliary station, wind reports from two stations and no upper air temperatures. On their side they supply reports from sixteen stations, upper wind reports from five stations and send upper air temperatures twice daily. In the circumstances they feel that they have very adequately fulfilled the undertaking as to reciprocity.

They realise, of course, that certain additional reports over and above those set out in September 1939 were made available during the period of the recent Trans-Atlantic flights. These reports were, however, supplied in special circumstances which cease to operate during the winter months, and they understand that there are certain difficulties about continuing to supply them now that the flights have ceased. Nevertheless, the best way of approaching the difficulty seems to be for discussion of the requirements of the Meteorological Service to take place direct between the representatives of the two Meteorological Offices concerned. As you doubtless know, early in the year, semi-official arrangements were made for the Director of the Éire Meteorological Service[1] to come and discuss meteorological questions, including his requirements as to reports, with the Director of the British Meteorological Office. The proposed visit was postponed but the British still think that the best method of tackling the present problem, at least initially, is for these direct discussions between the two Services to take place.

I should be glad to know if this suggestion is acceptable.

---

[1] Austen H. Nagle (1903-95), Director of the Irish Meteorological Service (1936-48).

No. 352 NAI DFA Secretary's Files P22

Letter from Joseph P. Walshe to Seán Moynihan (Dublin)
(Secret)

DUBLIN, 27 November 1940

Dear Ó Muimhneacháin,

We have given careful consideration to the questions put to us in your confidential letter E.109/55/40 of the 5th November.[1] Though naturally much would depend on the circumstances, the answers to your queries, so far as this Department is concerned, seem to me to be as follows:-

(a) If the Central Government continues to function from Dublin, part of the country being cut off by hostilities, we will probably require to maintain all our existing services. This will be so even if Dublin is subject to bombardment, involving dislocation of transport, etc.

(b) If the Central Government has to be transferred to a provincial centre, we would require to maintain, and transfer to the centre in question, the following minimum staff:- One Secretary, one Assistant Secretary, one Legal Adviser, two Assistant Principal Officers, two Cadets, one Accountant, one Archivist, five Clerical Officers, three Typists.

We would require to bring typewriters, the departmental seals, supplies necessary in connection with the issue of passports, etc. I suppose the papers we would require would fill six or eight large steel boxes.

I have made these particulars as specific as possible but, naturally, they would be subject to some variation according to circumstances.

It is very important that, in any arrangements which may be contemplated for the transfer of the Central Government from Dublin to a provincial centre, due provision should be made for the transfer at the same time of the Diplomatic Corps. Both from the practical and the prestige point of view it is essential that the Diplomatic Corps should remain with the Government and international practice places the duty of making suitable arrangements for the transfer of the Diplomatic Corps in such a case on the Government concerned.

Yours sincerely,
[signed] J.P. WALSHE

No. 353 NAI DFA Washington Embassy 1940 Reports

Confidential report from Robert Brennan to Joseph P. Walshe (Dublin)
(108/107/40) (Copy)

WASHINGTON, 28 November 1940

For the first time last week some of the advocates of aid to Britain came out openly for war, the most notably being Prof. William M. Agar of Columbia University. The William Allen White Committee to defend America by aiding the Allies stated 'we may have to change the Neutrality Act to allow these products (planes and guns) to go to Britain in American ships. We may have to become a non-belligerent instead of a neutral ... it can be argued that we

---

[1] Not printed.

should go into this war at once'. The Gallup Poll, however reported that on the question whether the U.S. should give all aid to Britain, even if it involved America in war, the percentage had dropped from 52 in September to 50 today.

Lord Lothian on returning from England last Saturday told reporters that Britain wanted ships, planes and munitions, and that she would soon need financial aid. On Monday he had a long interview with President Roosevelt, but said he had not discussed finances. Between the two events there had been an immediate adverse reaction on this question. Senator Johnson promised 'one hell of a battle' if any attempt was made to repeal the Johnson Act. The AP issued a report that members of the Administration unnamed thought the appeal for financial aid was premature, and quoted figures showing that Britain still held assets totalling nine billion dollars in the United States, Canada, and South America. Senator Nye tabled a notice to move for an investigation of British assets in the United States. When the Foreign Relations Committee of the Senate met, however, it decided to postpone all consideration of this matter until the new Congress convenes on Jan. 3rd.

President Roosevelt at his press conference Saturday, the 23rd, surprised reporters by sternly stating that Britain was getting all the aid America could give at present, and that the amount of munitions and planes could not be doubled over-night by merely giving orders.

There are signs that the President is facing a tough session. Though he affected to be unconcerned, there is no doubt he was disappointed when the house last week decided against adjournment, the vote being carried by 191 to 148, the majority consisting of a combination of Republicans and bolting Democrats. Similarly this week the Senate passed the Walter Logan Bill in the face of a threat by Majority Leader Barkley that the President would veto it. The Bill seeks to curb by allowing appeals to the courts the activities of such federal agencies as the National Labor Relations Board. Both of these actions are taken as reverses for the Administration and an indication that they will have to go slow particularly in the matter of new foreign commitments.

It may be the case that Ambassador Kennedy's[1] disclosures are having an effect. He appears to be talking quite freely along the lines of the interview reported in the Boston Globe, and afterwards repudiated by him. For instance this week the Washington Merry-Go-Round reports him as telling a group in Hollywood that England though fighting heroically was virtually defeated, and that the U.S. should limit its aid to what was necessary to gain time to rearm. Alf. Landon, the defeated Republican Presidential candidate in 1936 joined those who maintain aid to Britain should be limited because of the fear of involvement in war. He strongly opposed any easing of the Neutrality Act.

Whatever the reason for the change, there is one, though it is slight at present. The isolationists in the House and Senate are talking more freely than

---

[1] Joseph P. Kennedy (1888-1969), United States Ambassador to Britain (1938-40). On 10 November 1940 Kennedy said to the *Boston Globe*: 'Democracy is finished in England. It may be here'. He later said to Louis M. Lyons of the *Boston Globe*: 'The whole reason for aiding England is to give us time ... as long as she is in there, we have time to prepare. It isn't that [Britain is] fighting for democracy. That's bunk. She's fighting for self-preservation.' Kennedy submitted his resignation in October 1940, but it was not accepted until February 1941.

they have been in months, and the columnists and news commentators are becoming more outspoken on the matter of Britain's slender chances. The Gallup Poll, however, shows that those who believe England will win jumped from 32% in June to 63% today.

The NY Times Washington correspondent, Frank R. Kelley, stated on Tuesday that Lord Lothian brought back a memorandum to the effect that Britain wanted immediately from the U.S. 100 destroyers, 3 battleships and 6 cruisers. Lord Lothian promptly and emphatically denied this.

Despatches from London in the past few days painted a gloomy picture. Drew Middleton, the well-known correspondent of AP, writing from London described the present as the darkest hour of the war for Great Britain. He ridiculed the statements that the night bombers are not damaging production plants, dwelt on the seriousness of the shipping losses, and said that Britain was nearing the end of its financial tether. This despatch which, of course, passed the censor, said that the censor was behaving as did the French censor before the collapse of France.

Another gloomy despatch which appeared at the same time was a report of the broadcast by Mr. Ronald H. Cross, the British Minister for Shipping. He said that the resources of the Empire were not sufficient to make good the losses of ships at sea. William H. Stoneman, Chief of the London Bureau of the Chicago Daily News, back from England told a New York audience that Britain could not win unless America went to war and put war industries here on a twenty-four hour basis.

Albert Warner, the Washington news commentator for the Columbia Broadcasting Company, said over the radio that some leaders in Washington believed that London reports were allowed out so as to impress America with Britain's dire needs. If that is so, it shows a very bad sense of psychology. If people here get the impression that England's plight is so bad that there is little chance for her, the reaction could probably be serious from the point of view of extended aid.

No. 354 NAI DFA Secretary's Files P12/1

> Code telegram from Joseph P. Walshe to Seán Murphy (Vichy)
> (No. 401) (Personal) (Copy)
>
> DUBLIN, 28 November 1940

Your 355.[1] It is better keep on insisting on need for [your] visit to Paris giving reasons. Have you any idea of ground of objection to you or to Switzerland? Are Americans allowed to go? Cannot understand hesitation if no guarantee or conditions. Please send details of your case and we shall appeal to Berlin again.

---

[1] Not printed.

No. 355 NAI DFA 226/1A

Minute by Joseph P. Walshe on Ireland's contribution to the League of Nations
Dublin, 30 November 1940

I talked it over with the Minister.[1] He feels we might have to use the device of the token vote in order to avoid accusation of deserting League. He agrees that our general attitude towards the League and its offshoots should be that of negative benevolence.

[initialled] J.W.

No. 356 NAI DFA Secretary's Files P12/1

Code telegram from Seán Murphy to Joseph P. Walshe (Dublin)
(No. 372) (Personal) (Copy)
Vichy, 1 December 1940

Your telegram 391.[2] Had a talk with Nuncio yesterday. He thinks public opinion in free zone has hardened against policy of collaboration, for the following reasons. Firstly, because of feeling created by expulsions from Lorraine, secondly disappointment at lack of results from meeting and thirdly Greek success. He thinks Marshal's prestige is very high and that internal policy is gaining ground, but that there is still considerable opposition. The majority in occupied territory very opposed to collaboration and strongly pro Britain. The Government can, of course, carry out its policy without popular support, as it is all-powerful.

Laval has not disclosed any plans. The Nuncio had not heard of any. All classes of community dislike and distrust Laval; reason given for unpopularity is that he is opportunist and has made great fortune from politics. Neither reason seems sufficient in France. The fact of unpopularity is beyond doubt. Majority does not accept collaboration as inevitable and sincerely hope it will not become so. The attitude is influenced by continuance of war which French hope will not end favourably for Germany.

De Gaulle has little personal support: what he represents has considerable support in occupied territory. The students' demonstrations at Paris were in his favour. I am sending full report on situation by courier and hope it will arrive by middle of December.

---

[1] See No. 348.
[2] See No. 345.

No. 357 NAI DFA Secretary's Files P2

> *Code telegram from Joseph P. Walshe to Robert Brennan (Washington)*
> *(No. 189) (Personal) (Copy)*
>
> DUBLIN, 2 December 1940

Your 289.[1] Everything possible should be done to prevent project maturing. Press campaign for occupation of ports becoming more pointed. Essential to keep our friends in America in touch with seriousness of position and the evil consequences which would follow any attempt to seize the ports. You should especially stress the inevitability of bloodshed and most bitter struggle, as entire people behind Government.

No. 358 NAI DFA Secretary's Files P12/1

> *Confidential report from Seán Murphy to Joseph P. Walshe (Dublin)*
> *(P48/18) (P48/15) (P48/14)*
>
> VICHY, 3 December 1940

With reference to my telegram No. 372[2] I am taking the opportunity of a friend who is going to London to send you a more detailed report on the situation here.

I gather from your telegrams No. 98[3] and 391[4] that you have formed a definite opinion on the situation with which the views expressed in my reports are not in harmony. I have always endeavoured to give you the facts of the situation as I see it objectively and without prejudice and it is consequently somewhat disheartening to receive telegrams of the kind to which I have referred, which seem to suggest that I am drawing on my imagination. Whatever may be your other sources of information I think my reports are entitled to be taken on their face value until at least they are shown to be incorrect.

In order to properly appreciate the situation here one has to remember that France has received a knock out blow and has only recently recovered consciousness. At first the only desire of the French people was to find someone to blame for their defeat other than themselves. They very naturally came to the conclusion that it was due to lack of British support. In this view they were greatly assisted in the official statements made and by the incident of MERS EL KEBIR. Their great desire was that the war should end quickly so that they could return to more or less normal existence. Being very egotistical they could not see how the British could resist the German attack longer than they had. However, as the war went on and the end had no appearance of arriving they began to look for other reasons for their defeat. They gradually came to the conclusion that they were mainly responsible themselves. With the growth of this point of view they became less and less anti-British until now the majority even in this zone are hoping for a British victory.

[1] Not printed.
[2] See No. 356.
[3] See No. 236.
[4] See No. 345.

The grant of full powers to Marshal PETAIN and the suspension of the parliamentary system was generally accepted for want of a better solution of the existing difficulty. It might be said that at the moment the new regime had what we understand as popular support. The fact, however, that the majority of the National Assembly were in favour of the grant of full powers to the Marshal, with the authority to frame a new Constitution, does not necessarily mean that the same majority is in favour of his use of the full powers. The Marshal is, of course, a dictator in the fullest sense of the word. Full powers are invested in him personally and he has of course the means to enforce his policy. I am not suggesting that the policy has not support. What I do suggest is that it has not popular support as we understand that term. This state of things is not unnatural when one considers the various laws which have been decreed since he took power. The wholesale dismissal of prefects and sub-prefects, the removal of primary and secondary school-teachers, on a large scale, the dissolution of municipal councils are not acts which one can expect to be popular. The deputies and senators continue to draw their parliamentary salaries. They are still a sphere of political influence in their various circumscriptions and have not abandoned hope of returning to their former activity. In addition the South of France which forms a good part of the free zone, has always been, and I understand still is, very 'Red'. All these facts, together with the disbandment of free masons, and the law against the Jews explains why the present regime has not the popular support. A very considerable number of people have been effected directly or indirectly by these measures and in nearly all cases the groups affected had heretofore very considerable influence.

The PETAIN Government has, of course, the support of the Church, not because its policy is Catholic, for it is up to date only incidentally so, but because it is conservative and less anti-clerical than those which preceded it. The suppression of free masonry was purely a political act. The abolition of the law prohibiting teaching by Catholic congregations was merely removing a legal disability rather than creating a new situation of fact. It was really more an act of non anti-clericalism than of positive Catholicism.

I have already reported on the unpopularity of LAVAL,[1] and have given the reasons for such unpopularity which I have said do not seem sufficient. There is no doubt that he is generally unpopular, even amongst his colleagues in the present Government. I think there can be no doubt that if the Marshal were to die in the morning, LAVAL would not be accepted as his successor. In my opinion, which is I think fairly general, the present regime will last as long as the Marshal lasts.

With regard to the question of collaboration with Germany, as I have said in my telegram the French public do not consider it inevitable and they very much hope that circumstances will not make it inevitable. At the beginning they were prepared for a form of collaboration in the hope that it might assist the internal situation. They had great hopes after the meeting of MONTOIRE[2]

---

[1] See No. 356.
[2] Hitler and Pétain met at Montoire-sur-le-Loir on 24 October 1940; the meeting, arranged when Laval and Hitler met at the same location on 22 October, marked the start of organised French collaboration with Nazi Germany.

that good results would follow almost at once. If this had happened, I don't think there is any doubt that it would have had a considerable effect on public opinion, at least in this zone. They were led to believe by statements made by LAVAL and by official press releases that the results of the meeting would bring about the release of a great number of prisoners, almost at once, facilities of transport, a betterment of the economic conditions in both zones, and a considerable reduction in the costs of occupation, which at present is 400,000,000 francs per day. In all these things they have been disappointed and to make matters worse 70,000 French from LORRAINE have been expelled and have had to seek refuge in the free zone which is already greatly strained from the economic point of view. All this has not been helpful to the PETAIN regime and has if possible increased LAVAL's unpopularity as he is the author of collaboration.

With regard to the occupied zone, I understand that at the beginning the population took the occupation very calmly and were even prepared to be friendly with the Germans. After some time, when German regulations and restrictions of various sorts were put into force, the opinion began to change. They began to see that the Germans were going to make them feel their defeat and humiliate them as much as possible. The opinion now is, I understand from those I have met from Paris, very strongly pro-British and somewhat critical of the Government here whom they regard as having somewhat abandoned them. They are very strongly opposed to any policy of collaboration, because they believe from experience that it will bring them nowhere with the Germans. DE GAULLE has considerable support in the occupied zone and particularly in Paris. Here, again it is what he stands for that finds support and not himself, personally. I understand that there is great unemployment in the occupied zone and although the Government is doing what it can, it is unable to make much impression on the situation. Also the food situation is very serious, and there is great lack of coal for heating and cooking. This situation is aggravated by the fact that the Germans are sending considerable quantities of food to Germany and are of course requisitioning large quantities for the Army of occupation. One can well imagine in these circumstances that a policy of collaboration would not find much support. It may, of course, eventually have to come but the French are anxious to put off the evil day as long as possible. In a word the general attitude is one of expectancy.

I hope that I have succeeded in covering all the points of interest and in making more clear the facts of the situation here. I should be glad if you will let me know if you desire me to report from time to time by telegraph on the situation here.

[signed] Seán Murphy

No. 359 NAI DFA Secretary's Files P2

> Code telegram from Joseph P. Walshe to Robert Brennan (Washington)
> (No. 193) (Personal) (Copy)
>
> DUBLIN, 4 December 1940

Your 285.[1] When the American Minister was giving the Taoiseach the alleged account of what Under Secretary said to you, he said he had received instructions to do so. He prefaced his statement by saying that Americans could be cruel if their interests were affected and Ireland should expect little or no sympathy if the British took their ports. He added that, in any case, America herself was coming into the war in a short time, and then Ireland would have to give the ports to America. Gray is very imprudent. He repeats these views publicly in the diplomatic corps and amongst his ascendancy friends and has told them that he had been instructed to give the message in question to the Taoiseach. Since this attitude may give the impression here that America wants the British to seize our ports, it might be well to visit Under Secretary once more, tell him that Taoiseach naturally disturbed at tone of message, and unable to understand discrepancy between what Under Secretary said to you and account given in instruction (if it was an instruction). Gray left text of report as sent to him. Text given in immediately following telegram.[2]

No. 360 NAI DFA Madrid Embassy 10/11 Pt 4

> Telegram from Leopold H. Kerney to Joseph P. Walshe (Dublin)
> (No. 120) (Personal) (Copy)
>
> MADRID, 5 December 1940

Mrs Clissmann[3] Copenhagen writes November 21 'I have seen someone who has many many reasons to be thankful to you and who asked to be remembered to you'. This can only refer to Ryan.

No. 361 NAI DFA Secretary's Files P2

> Code telegram from Joseph P. Walshe to Robert Brennan (Washington)
> (No. 196) (Personal) (Copy)
>
> DUBLIN, 5 December 1940

Your 294.[4] Same interviews being published in Socialist review 'Forward'.[5] We have text. His argument easy for friends to refute. If Britain seizes our ports

---

[1] See No. 329.
[2] Not printed.
[3] Elizabeth 'Budge' Clissmann, née Mulcahy, wife of Helmut Clissmann, representative of the Deutscher Akademischer Austauschdienst (German Academic Exchange Service) in Dublin who developed connections with the IRA in the late 1930s for the German intelligence services. Helmut and Budge Clissmann were close friends of Kerney.
[4] Not printed.
[5] In an article written for circulation by United Press, the writer and dramatist George Bernard Shaw urged Churchill to occupy the Irish ports.

merely because useful to win war, she follows example of her enemies and destroys whole moral basis of her case. Ireland's only hope of survival is to fight against any country that invades her territory. Ports alone in modern conditions useless, seizure means reoccupation of whole territory. British planes would not gain more than ten or fifteen minutes by being based here instead of in Six Counties. Almost all sinkings by planes and submarines take place between one hundred and six hundred miles from north-west. We believe British agitation based on desire to find scapegoat, but composition of Cabinet makes situation uncertain and dangerous. Minister very pleased your splendid help.

No. 362 NAI DFA Secretary's Files P2

Code telegram from Robert Brennan to Joseph P. Walshe (Dublin)
(No. 296) (Personal) (Copy)

WASHINGTON, 6 December 1940

Your 196.[1] British Ambassador at Washington told me all traffic was diverted to Northern route because they do not have Cobh and Berehaven. This makes convoy easier target because one line is more vulnerable than two. Is it not the case that time would be required to fit these places for destroyers, protective guns, etc., that Germans could break up such preparations, and that supplies would have to be brought in through supply lines easy to attack? Any argument on these lines extremely useful.

No. 363 NAI DFA Secretary's Files P12/1

Telegram from the Department of External Affairs to William Warnock (Berlin)
(No. 241) (Personal) (Copy)

DUBLIN, 7 December 1940

Your 61.[2] Several weeks ago Murphy applied to German military authorities for permission to visit Paris in order to deal with questions regarding Irish citizens and to obtain some things from Legation including winter clothing.[3] After several reminders permission has been refused, no reason being given. Murphy cannot understand this as several of his colleagues have been allowed to visit Paris in the last couple of months – some more than once – including Yugoslav and Finnish Ministers.

Please see Under-Secretary of State W. and urge him to obtain sanction for visit. You should say that we cannot understand discrimination against Ireland.

---

[1] See No. 361.
[2] See No. 292.
[3] See No. 354.

No. 364 NAI DFA Secretary's Files P2

> *Code telegram from Joseph P. Walshe to Robert Brennan (Washington)*
> *(No. 197) (Personal) (Copy)*
> DUBLIN, 9 December 1940

Your 296.[1] Route was selected because of proximity of German bases to southern route. Your assertion in 2nd part of telegram undoubtedly true but it would perhaps be better to stick to fundamental fact that any attempt to seize our ports would be act of aggression which would be resisted to bitter end. Britain has no more right to our ports than Italians to Greek ports. Government's supreme duty is to keep our people out of war because war means our destruction as a nation. The seizure or handing over of ports means instant involvement. No people in the world has shown more definitely its desire to remain at peace. Would Americans talk about going into war themselves if they knew that their destruction would follow? Judging from your cuttings the best argument is that the people will resist to the last man.

No. 365 NAI DFA Secretary's Files P53

> *Code telegram from Robert Brennan to Joseph P. Walshe (Dublin)*
> *(No. 305) (Personal) (Copy)*
> WASHINGTON, 10 December 1940

Your telegram 193.[2] I saw Under Secretary of State. He said Minister had got things mixed. He had not said to me many of the things stated. What happened was that, subsequent to my interview, he had seen President, who decided to let you know what was opinion here and instructed Minister accordingly something as follows:-

They were anxious to do everything possible to prevent British defeat, and one factor was they should have use of ports. They had in mind that, if Germany won, there would be end of freedom and democracy in Ireland.

He was sorry for misunderstanding. He said Minister had no right to say that America would enter war. He added their naval experts considered greatest danger to Britain's prospects at present was destruction of shipping and that everything should be done to equip them to meet menace. He said President had said he would like to see me on whole question when he returns.

I pointed out cession or leasing would invite destruction, that that was a certainty, whereas alternative was only a possibility and that we would stick to decision to defend against all.

---

[1] See No. 362.
[2] See No. 359.

No. 366 NAI DFA Secretary's Files P2

Code telegram from Joseph P. Walshe to Robert Brennan (Washington)
(No. 213) (Personal) (Copy)

DUBLIN, 12 December 1940

Your 305.[1] If you see President and if he says we ought hand over ports, following line will suggest itself to you. Handing over equivalent in immediate and ultimate consequences to entering war. The Irish Government are determined not to expose people of this small nation to horrors and destruction of being made a cockpit between two great Powers. The entire people behind the Government in their determination. If the British seized the ports, there would be widespread bloodshed. Army and menfolk as well as women would resist to the last against the violation of our territory. Does President realise Ireland belongs exclusively to the Irish people. Britain had no more right to our ports than she had to Calais and Boulogne far more vital to her security. If one nation can seize or demand territory of another because of geographical propinquity the whole basis of international order disappears. Would President enter war if he was quite certain that his people and their homes, their national treasures, would be wiped out in a few hours? Democracy and freedom are only benefits if a people sufficiently alive to enjoy them, and, when we are told that we must be sacrificed in order to save these benefits for Britain, we feel very much like what the President would feel when faced with the same issue. Yielding the ports to force or peacefully means certain and immediate destruction for us. We have no certitude that we are going to lose freedom if Britain is beaten and there is not even a probability of our destruction if we keep out of the war. Americans must realise Ireland still suffering from long struggle for freedom for her own people. Her very national existence is precarious and involvement in this war would bring it to an end.

No. 367 NAI DFA Secretary's Files A20/4

Letter from Colonel Liam Archer to Joseph P. Walshe (Dublin)
(G2/0257) (Secret)

DUBLIN, 12 December 1940

Dear Joe,
Further to recent correspondence regarding Frank Ryan, I now append copy of the text of the telegram from O'Reilly, New York, to O'Reilly, 82 Ballymun Road, Dublin, which Major Bryan[2] communicated to your Department by telephone; it reads as follows:

'Handed in 7/12/1940. New York. O'Reilly, 82 Ballymun Road, Dublin. Please inform O'Donnells and friends Frank safe Lisbon. Wishes no further enquiries made about him for present. O'Reilly.'

---

[1] See No. 365.
[2] Major (later Colonel) Dan Bryan (1900-85), Deputy Director of Military Intelligence (1938-41), Chief Staff Officer and Director of Military Intelligence (1941-52), Commandant of the Military College (1952-5).

I also append an extract from a letter addressed by J. Nolan, 9 Marlboro' Place, Dublin, (a leading member of the Communist Party in Ireland) to J. Prendergast, 58 Theobalds Road, London, W.C. which reads as follows:

'About Frank, I expect now that you have some news, you'll hear the rest'.

It is now evident that the mystery surrounding Frank Ryan's whereabouts has been cleared up in so far as his immediate political friends are concerned.

With regard to Mr. Kerney's telegram,[1] I am in a position to say that Clissmann met Frank Ryan in Dublin in 1936 and was seen occasionally in his company. Furthermore, Clissmann's wife was known to have political leanings similar to those of Frank Ryan, consequently it is not at all unlikely that the Clissmanns would help Ryan through their German friends and it is conceivable that he was both at Lisbon and Copenhagen. An alternative theory might be that his American friends were deliberately misled by being advised that Ryan was at Lisbon, which is in a neutral country, in order to cloak his transfer to Copenhagen, at present under German control.

Yours sincerely,
[signed] L. ARCHER

No. 368 NAI DFA Secretary's Files P12/7

Telegram from Francis T. Cremins to Joseph P. Walshe (Dublin)
(No. 112) (Personal)

BERNE, 13 December 1940

Contact with all colleagues. Visited already Nuncio, new French Ambassador, Italian, Spanish, British, American, German, Argentine, Hungarian, Chinese, Japanese Ministers.

Nuncio expressed highest understanding and appreciation of Taoiseach's ports statement.[2] Thinks, as outside observer, attack on the ports improbable owing to reaction of United States, Dominions.

The Italian Minister expressed most cordial friendship of Italy for Ireland.

Spanish Minister stated Spain's need of speedy peace, economic position very bad owing to cost of civil war and blockade. Expressed the view that, on the whole, Ireland safe from attack.

The French Ambassador considers war may go on almost indefinitely if Britain holds out till Spring; thinks Italy blundered by attacking Greece, and attacked without German consent; thinks ebullition at present between Italian Army and party of Germans; diversion Gibraltar possible, but he thinks not, as Spain morally and economically too weak to be pushed too far; thinks Irish neutrality safe, at any rate for the present.

U.S. Minister is of opinion Germany will make strong bid to finish war quickly.

The Hungarian says Germany adverse to conflict with Balkans and Italian setback will prolong general war.

---

[1] See No. 360.
[2] See No. 324.

German Minister remarked, re Irish neutrality, matter of life or death for Ireland, not to depart from it.

All gave me very friendly welcome and displayed interest in policy and conditions in Ireland.

A Central European view is that the war will not end without a clash between Germany and Russia, easy victory over France not suiting latter's policy of promoting general exhaustion. Moreover Ukraine question not settled finally.

I find that people generally consider danger to Ireland comes from one side or the other according to their own predilections.

I have met no one who expects war to end quickly. Position of Great Britain regarded as serious but her power of resistance remains great.

No. 369 NAI DFA Secretary's Files P12/3

Code telegram from William Warnock to Joseph P. Walshe (Dublin)
(No. 95S) (Personal) (Sent via Berne)

BERLIN, 15 December 1940

New York reports on London visit of Northern Ireland Prime Minister[1] quoted in the Press. Reports allege that Churchill discussed the question of Irish ports; it is also suggested this will be discussed at forthcoming secret session of Parliament on shipping.

Great success claimed in recent raids on Birmingham, Bristol, Sheffield. There is disappointment at war not yet concluded, but this does not mean discontent.

Small staff of this Legation is often commented on in view of the fact that people here consider that it is our most important representation at present, particularly as so much of interest happens here. Tendency of other missions is to increase staff. Foregoing also mentioned to me in private conversation by Foreign Office officials.

No. 370 NAI DFA Secretary's Files A2

Memorandum by Joseph P. Walshe of meeting with Sir John Maffey (Dublin)

DUBLIN, 17 December 1940

Sir John Maffey called to see me this morning. He explained that he had been to London recently, but that any rumours to the effect that he had had any discussions with Andrews[2] were untrue. On the way back from London, he did in effect meet Mr. Andrews in the train, and they had a general chat. He had never met Andrews before.

He spoke about the Trade Agreement and the inevitable slowness involved in coming to any conclusion when conditions were changing from day to day.

I spoke to him about the present Press campaign about the Irish ports. He said that he had spoken strongly to Duff Cooper and Cranborne, and they

---

[1] John Miller Andrews.
[2] John Miller Andrews, Prime Minister of Northern Ireland.

assured him that they were doing everything possible to damp it down. We must, on the other hand, remember that their shipping losses were bound to cause a good deal of adverse comment in the Press, and, in the present condition of their censorship, they could not do more than modify the more violent types of publicity.

I reminded him that the campaign was going on in America and was being fed from London by material similar to that published in the British Press.

He did not believe anybody was contemplating the possibility of seizing our ports. He knew Churchill was temperamental, but, of course, Churchill might not continue in power. At the present moment, he was on top of the wave, but, when the war became less critical, changes were likely.

I referred to a conversation I had last evening with Capt. Shaw (Irish Convention, 1917),[1] and to Shaw's opinion about the possibility of Bevan[2] taking Churchill's place. He said he hoped very much that Shaw was right, because he believed that a Labour man of Bevan's type was more likely to take the long view about Ireland and to avoid any action which might be permanently detrimental to the good relations between the two peoples.

Maffey told me that the agreement about the navicert had been concluded with Ferguson.[3]

No. 371 NAI DFA Secretary's Files P2

Code telegram from Robert Brennan to Joseph P. Walshe (Dublin)
(No. 320) (Personal) (Copy)

WASHINGTON, 18 December 1940

Most people here, when position is explained, realise our case, but that impact of war fever is steadily rising here is obvious from attitude of man in the street. The following is typical. Last night, at school function, I was introduced to a man whose mother is from Kerry. He said 'When we go into war in a month or two, you will have to yield the ports to a joint British-American demand; if not, we will go in and take them, and, if you resist, so much the worse for you.' I gave all the arguments in vain. His reply was 'Your attitude is jeopardising American interests'. I said talk of that kind only encourages Britain to a course which would merely increase her difficulties because we will fight.

---

[1] The Irish Convention to which all Irish political parties were invited sat in Dublin from July 1917 to March 1918 in an unsuccessful attempt to agree on a method of introducing domestic self-government for Ireland.

[2] Aneurin Bevan (1897-1960), British Labour politician who was one of the main opponents of the wartime British coalition government led by Churchill; later Minister for Health (1945-51).

[3] Postscript handwritten by Walshe on 19 December 1940.

No. 372 NAI DFA Secretary's Files A21

Facsimile reproduction of a memorandum from Edouard Hempel to Joseph P. Walshe (Dublin) with marginal notes by Walshe

DUBLIN, 19 December 1940

Deutsche Gesandtschaft
Dublin.

PRO MEMORIA

<u>Aeroplane</u>: Junkers 52 Civil Aeroplane Matriculation No. D-AGAK

Lufthansa Crew Three: Naumann, Mitschur, Amthlett
Passengers Four
Arrival: Airport of Limerick 21st December, 1940, at daybreak.

It is requested

1.) to grant permission to land for aeroplane passengers and crew,
2.) to give assistance for wireless navigation (Peilhilfe) and on special request to get in touch with the aeroplane to secure its arrival (in Flugsicherungsverkehr treten),
3.) to give wireless frequencies and call-signals (Rufzeichen),
4.) to grant permission to enter Irish territory for passengers and crew.

Dublin, December 19th, 1940.

Deutsche Gesandtschaft Dublin.

PRO MEMORIA

Additional Personnel for the German Legation

Legationssekretär Böhme-Fettelbach und
Frau Böhme-Fettelbach,
Konsul Fiedler,
Konsulatssekretär Hartmann.

Dublin, December 19th, 1940.

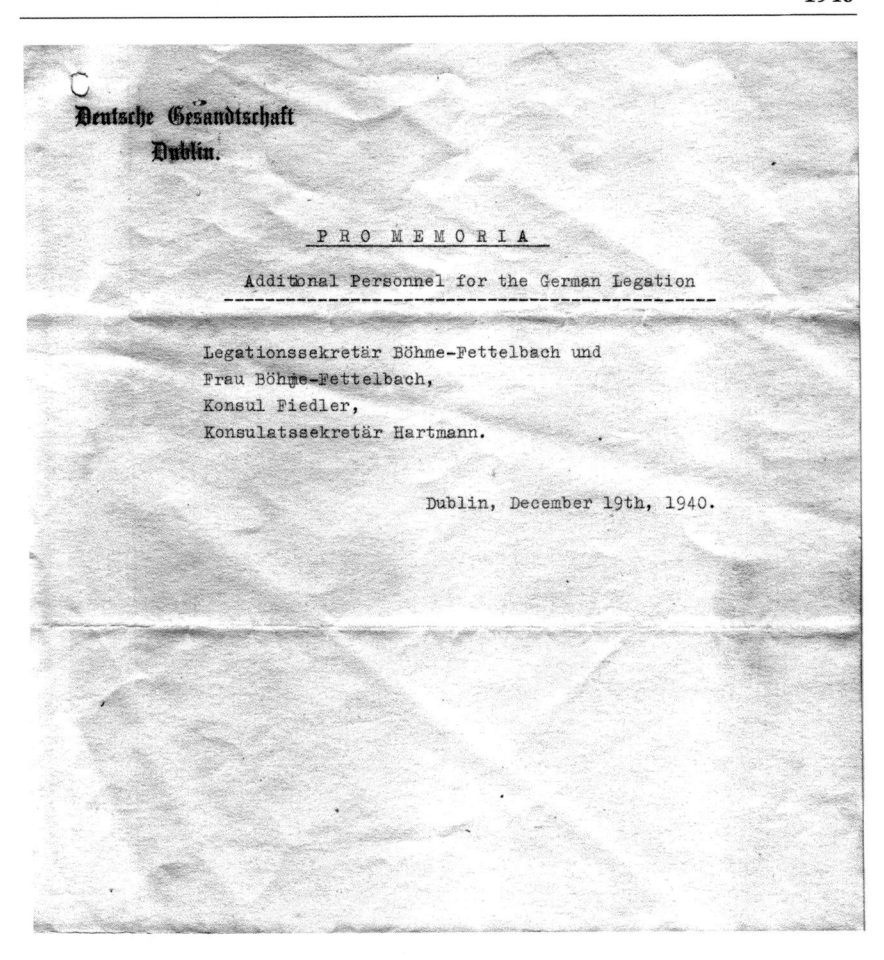

No. 373 NAI DFA Secretary's Files A21

Code telegram from Frederick H. Boland to William Warnock (Berlin)
(No. 254) (Personal)
DUBLIN, 10.45 pm, 19 December 1940

See Woermann immediately. Explain that reasons which will be obvious to you why request made by Hempel today concerning staff of German Legation here is politically impossible from our point of view. It would add enormously to our difficulties. Proposal might be revived at another time but quite impracticable at the moment.

No. 374 NAI DFA Secretary's Files A21

> *Extract from code telegram from William Warnock to Joseph P. Walshe (Dublin)*
> *(No. 100S) (Personal) (Copy) (Sent via Berne)*
> BERLIN, 11.00 pm, 24 December 1940

Your telegram 254.[1] Under Secretary of State had not been dealing with this matter personally. He was surprised that we would have objections. As you did not state nature of request I was somewhat at a disadvantage at first but was able to explain matters.

No. 375 NAI DFA Secretary's Files P12/3

> *Extract from code telegram from William Warnock to Joseph P. Walshe (Dublin)*
> *(No. 100S) (Personal) (Copy) (Sent via Berne)*
> BERLIN, 24 December 1940

Recent air raids on Berlin caused no damage to buildings. Tramways and underground railways in two shopping centres temporarily interrupted, but quickly repaired.

No. 376 NAI DFA Secretary's Files P22

> *Memorandum from Michael Rynne to Joseph P. Walshe (Dublin)*
> *(Secret)*
> DUBLIN, 30 December 1940

The memorandum required from this Department by the Cabinet Committee on Emergency Problems is to refer in particular to plans for propaganda abroad in the event of war.
2. Obviously, such plans will involve arrangements for framing and distributing an official protest against the aggressor whose attack on our neutrality has brought Ireland into war.
3. Protests of the kind are essentially 'propaganda' and provided that their relatively less important diplomatic and historical aspects are not entirely ignored, they ought to be drafted and distributed in whatever manner seems most likely to ensure that none of their propaganda value is lost.
4. Protests need not be confined to a detailed summary, addressed to the aggressor state, of the events leading up to the aggression. They may also take the form of notes addressed to all the world and especially to those friendly states with which the victimised state preserves its diplomatic relations. Such notes, as a rule, merely set out the fact that the aggression has taken place and that the victimised state intends to defend its liberty while relying on all possible support and sympathy from other neutral or allied states.
5. Clearly the type of protest which is directed in the first instance to the aggressor state must be mainly a diplomatic-historical document in content and nature. It cannot therefore be drafted until all the events to which it must

---

[1] See No. 373.

relate have actually taken place.

Although a protest of this kind would, of course, be eventually transmitted abroad to friendly states, it would not seem likely to play a very important part in the plans for foreign propaganda regarding which the Cabinet Committee desires our observations. At best, the detailed protest which will have to be despatched in the first instance to the aggressor of Ireland's neutrality would constitute a belated form of propaganda, of interest mainly to those educated foreigners willing and capable of studying a fairly lengthy document.

6. The second type of protest, that is, the message to the world at large, asserting this country's innocence of unneutral conduct and her determination to resist aggression, might, however, be drafted now in its main outlines.

The value of such a protest as propaganda depends largely on its immediate release to the news distributing agencies of the world. The less detail it contains the more likely it is to be read or listened to by a wide public.

7. In informing the Department of the Taoiseach in the foregoing sense, we might, if you agree, submit for the consideration of the Cabinet Committee, a draft protest (of the second kind) to fit any eventuality, with a request for approval to instruct our representatives abroad of its terms at once. I attach a draft in general terms such as were adopted in recent months by some of the countries which suffered foreign invasion.[1]

8. Another medium of 'protest-propaganda' appears to lie in the proclamation or official communiqué which the Government (Head of State as a rule) of an invaded country issues to its own people. These declarations generally resumé the most recent facts of the military and diplomatic situation, protest emphatically against unwarranted aggression and call upon all citizens to rally to the flag.

The wording of documents of this kind are nearly always directed to impress foreign opinion as well as that of the people at home. Queen Wilhemina's proclamation to her people on the occasion of the invasion of Holland had all the appearance of being drafted largely for foreign consumption (e.g. the 'flaming protest' reference).

9. Unless and until an invasion has taken place there would not seem to be any use trying to frame an appropriate proclamation to the Irish people. No doubt, if a proclamation were to be drafted now or later, this Department would be consulted as to its terms.

[initialled] M.R.

---

[1] Not printed.

1941

No. 377 NAI DFA Secretary's Files P4

> *Code telegram from Joseph P. Walshe to John J. Hearne (Ottawa)*
> *(No. 1) (Personal) (Copy)*
>
> DUBLIN, 1 January 1941

Your 90.[1] Appreciate difficulty of dealing direct with such resolutions. Best way to get Irish-Canadians of standing to show that, apart from decision of Irish people to keep out of war, cession of ports would mean immediate destruction of our completely undefended centres of population.

Small nations like Ireland do not and cannot assume role of defenders of just causes except their own. No answer to say Britain would defend us since she can't save her own towns.

Existence of our own people comes before all other considerations. What choice would Canadians make if participation involved them in immediate and terrible destruction.

Moreover, Ireland has been decimated and impoverished by wars and retains only the last remnant of her people and national heritage; another war would make national survival impossible. Some Canadians may say that will be position if Germany wins, but no Government has right to court certain destruction for the people; they have to take the only chance of survival and that is to stay out.

Of course, the real national arguments are much stronger but your friends cannot use them.

No. 378 NAI DFA 221/147A

> *Telegram from Joseph P. Walshe to William Warnock (Berlin)*
> *(No. 4) (Personal) (Copy)*
>
> DUBLIN, 2 January 1941

Aircraft dropped incendiary and explosive bombs with German markings at Curragh[2] this morning between six and seven. About same time bombs dropped in Terenure[3] and in Borris Co. Carlow. Three people killed in Borris and seven injured in Terenure. Bombs dropped 9.45 last evening at Drogheda. About five planes in all took part. Presumption is all were German. Investigations proceeding.

---

[1] Not printed.
[2] The Curragh, Co Kildare, close to the Defence Forces Eastern Command headquarters.
[3] A suburb in the south of Dublin city.

You should immediately make vigorous protest in regard to Curragh bombing and point out once more detrimental effect of such incidents on relations between two countries and urge that instructions be issued at once that Irish territory is not in any circumstances to be overflown.

No. 379 NAI DFA Secretary's Files A21

Memorandum by the Department of External Affairs on the German request to provide extra staff for the German Legation in Dublin
(Copy No. 2) (Secret)

DUBLIN, 3 January 1941

At 5 p.m. on 19th December, the German Minister asked to see Mr. Walshe urgently. He arrived a quarter of an hour later and told Mr. Walshe that he had a wire from Berlin saying that three additional officials had been appointed to the staff of the German Legation in Dublin and they would arrive at the Limerick airport (sic) by a Luft Hansa civil plane at daybreak, on 21st December. Mr. Hempel handed in an official Note[1] making a formal request for permission for the new officials and the crew of the aircraft to enter Éire and for particulars of the call sign and wavelength of the Shannon wireless station, which Herr Hempel wished to wire to Berlin at once. Copy of this Note, together with a list of the names of the new officials, is attached hereto.

2. Mr. Walshe told Herr Hempel that the proposed increase in the staff of the Legation would occasion us political embarrassment at the present time, and he felt sure that the proposal was the work of some official in Berlin who did not possess that keen appreciation of the situation here which Herr Woermann and the other senior officials of the German Foreign Office had always shown. He would wire Mr. Warnock at once and instruct him to tell the Foreign Office that the proposed arrangement was politically impossible from our point of view.[2] In the meantime, he was going to see the Taoiseach and he would mention the matter to him at once.

3. After Mr. Walshe's departure, Herr Hempel remained with Mr. Boland, and the Secretary of the German Legation, Herr Thomsen, arrived and handed Herr Hempel the text of the Berlin telegram which apparently had not been fully decoded when Herr Hempel left the Legation. On reading the text, Herr Hempel asked with great insistence that we should not wire Mr. Warnock, that we should deal with the matter through him, and that, pending consideration of the general question, the airport should be cleared 'in order to save time' and we should let him have at once the call sign and wavelength of the airport wireless station.

4. On Mr. Walshe's return from the Taoiseach about 7.30 p.m., a wire was sent to Mr. Warnock telling him to see the Under Secretary of State and tell him that the proposed arrangement was impossible from our point of view, that it might be reviewed at a later time, but that, for the moment, it was out of the question.[3]

---

[1] See No. 372.
[2] See No. 373.
[3] See No. 373.

5. On the morning of the 20th December, Herr Hempel called again on Mr. Walshe. He argued with considerable emphasis that the German Government had the technical right to increase the staff of its Legation here if it wished to do so, and that for us to refuse to allow them to exercise that right would be a serious matter. He referred at one point to the possibility of a breach of diplomatic relations.

Mr. Walshe told Herr Hempel that we did not deny the technical right, our attitude was, not that the right did not exist, but that its exercise in present circumstances would occasion us serious political embarrassment. We were entitled to expect that the German Government would have regard to our interests in the matter, and therefore we had told Mr. Warnock to ask the Foreign Office in Berlin to withdraw the request.

Herr Hempel promised to wire Berlin and put the considerations advanced by Mr. Walshe before his Government, but he urged again that, pending some decision, the airport at Rynanna[1] should be cleared and he should be given the call sign and wavelength of the Shannon station.

6. On the same day, Mr. Walshe saw the Minister for Coordination and the Minister for Defence and informed them of the development. He had already mentioned the matter to Mr. Aiken on the previous evening.

7. Nothing further was heard of the matter until the morning of the 26th December, when Herr Hempel came to see Mr. Walshe and told him that he had received a wire from Berlin the previous evening to the effect that, as the German request represented no more than the exercise of a right which they undoubtedly possessed, there was no room for discussion.

Mr. Walshe re-emphasised the considerations which made the request impossible and unreasonable from our point of view. He pointed out that it would furnish propaganda against Irish neutrality, which Germany had professed herself so anxious to see maintained, with a strong weapon and would aggravate the delicate situation created by the American and British Press campaign about our ports. The matter was put to us on the basis of the German Government's right to increase the staff of its Legation if it wished to do, but even Herr Hempel himself would not pretend that the present staff of the Legation was inadequate. Germany had thus no apparent interest in the matter commensurate with the political embarrassment which the proposed arrangement would create for us, and, in the circumstances, we could only regard the German persistence in the request as most unreasonable. He hoped it would not be necessary for us to return a positive refusal, and he would therefore ask Herr Hempel himself to urge his Government again to withdraw the proposal. If he was not prepared to do this, it was perhaps better that he should see the Taoiseach.

Herr Hempel said that he hesitated to ask for an interview with the Taoiseach about what was really a routine administrative matter, and for him to do so would perhaps give the request an aspect of political importance which it had not got. However, he would consider the matter.

8. During this interview, Herr Hempel made it quite clear again that, in fact, the request was being treated by his Government as a matter of very

---

[1] Rineanna (Rynanna), the original name for Shannon airport.

considerable importance. He referred again to the possibility of 'serious consequences' following if the request were refused, but, when Mr. Walshe told him that for Germany to break off relations with us over what Herr Hempel himself had characterised as a routine administrative matter would expose the German Government to ridicule throughout the world, Herr Hempel at once said he had no instructions to say that the refusal of the request would mean the breaking-off of relations. In fact, when he referred to the possibility of 'serious consequences' following a refusal of the request, he was voicing merely a personal impression. He had no instructions whatever on the point.

9. Throughout the interview Herr Hempel seemed to be at some pains to remove any unfavourable impression created by the insistent and somewhat menacing tone in which he had put forward the matter at earlier interviews.

10. On the morning of the 27th December, Herr Hempel called again on Mr. Walshe and said he would like to see the Taoiseach. Much of the ground covered at earlier interviews was traversed, and once again Herr Hempel seemed in a calmer and more resigned frame of mind.

11. Herr Hempel saw the Taoiseach on 28th December. The Taoiseach told him he would like the request withdrawn, but he indicated that, if the request were persisted in, it would be refused.

12. In the course of an informal conversation on 29th December, Herr Hempel told Mr. Boland that he had reported these conversations to Berlin; he was very worried as to what the reactions would be, but he thought it possible that, as an alternative, the German Government might instruct him to visit Berlin. He hoped there would be no difficulty if he were so instructed. He would leave his wife and children here.

No. 380 NAI DFA 221/147A

Memorandum by Joseph P. Walshe on the dropping of bombs on Irish territory by German aircraft
(Secret)

DUBLIN, 3 January 1941

I saw the German Minister at 12.45 today by appointment. I told him that the series of bombings which had occurred during the last two days was causing the greatest perturbation to the Government and amongst our people. No doubt, the bombings were due to carelessness on the part of the German aviators, but, if they continued, both the Government and the people would be obliged to conclude that they were due to a deliberate policy on the part of the German Government. He would realise how detrimental these incidents would be to our relations with Germany. Apart from the natural indignation of the people, the German Government could not fail to recognise the propaganda value of such incidents to their enemies.

The German Minister suggested that they might have been British planes.

I replied that we had fragments of bombs with German markings from some of the places bombed, and we felt sure that the whole series of bombings was carried out by German planes. He must remember that there were a great many Irishmen in the British Air Force, whether born in this country or of Irish parents, and it would be quite impossible for the British authorities to give an order for the bombing of any part of Ireland without it coming to the knowledge of some Irishman in the British Forces. He could realise what a serious effect that would produce on morale and discipline. I urged the German Minister to tell his Government in the most serious fashion that all flights over Ireland should be strictly forbidden. We had already given instructions to our Chargé d'Affaires in Berlin,[1] but we relied on him, on account of his special knowledge of conditions here and of our relations with Great Britain and the United States, to convince his Government of the gravity from every point of view of these incidents.

The Minister said he would wire immediately.

[initialled] J.P.W.

No. 381 NAI DFA 221/147A

Telegram from Joseph P. Walshe to William Warnock (Berlin)
(No. 6) (Personal) (Copy)
DUBLIN, 6.30 pm, 3 January 1941

My telegram No. 4.[2] Three bombs were dropped at 7.45 p.m. last night near Ballymurrin, Co. Wexford, and two at 3.55 a.m. this morning in Donore Avenue, South Circular Road.[3] Some houses demolished and several people injured.

Bomb fragments found at Duleek and Julianstown, Co. Louth, have also been identified as German. Investigation of bombings at other places, including those bombed last night, is proceeding. The evidence found at Duleek, Julianstown and the Curragh, coupled with the fact that the bombings at these places coincided with a German raid on Merseyside, and those last night with a raid on Cardiff, makes it only too clear that German planes are responsible. You must therefore make an energetic protest at once at continued violation of our air-space in breach of assurance given to you on 4th December (your 92).[4] We expect an early apology, which we would wish to publish on receipt, and we must of course hold German Government liable for damage caused. For the moment, however, the most important thing is that there should be no recurrence. Strongly urge that measures should be taken immediately to ensure this. Any idea that the German bombs were dropped by British planes is untenable, if for no other reason than that the consequences of discovery if planes were shot down would be too great.

Now ascertained bombs at Borris, Co. Carlow, which caused three deaths, also of German origin.

---

[1] See Nos 378 and 381.
[2] See No. 378.
[3] Donore Avenue runs off South Circular Road in Dublin city.
[4] Not printed.

No. 382 NAI DFA 221/147A

Memorandum by Joseph P. Walshe on the dropping of bombs on Irish territory by German aircraft
(Secret)

DUBLIN, 4 January 1941

The German Minister called to see me at 12.45 p.m. today. He was still very disturbed in manner as a result of the bombings. He said he naturally understood the indignation and feelings of the Government and our population at what had happened, but, at the same time, he wished to protest in a friendly way at the attitude taken up by the three Dublin papers in their leading articles of this morning. He said it was unfair – especially of the 'Irish Press', which must be regarded as voicing in some way the views of the Government – to imply that the bombings were deliberate. The chief offending sentence was the following:-

'It is hardly conceivable, therefore, that any experienced airmen could mistake our soil for belligerent territory.'

The Minister went on to say that the 'Irish Times' was very much worse, but he recognised that the organ was not controlled by the Government.

I explained to the German Minister that we had nothing to do with the writing of the leader in the 'Irish Press'. If we had, it would not be done in quite the same way, but he must remember that there was very considerable indignation, both in the Government and amongst our population, and, the newspapers had to reflect in some way the general feeling. After all, as nobody wished to put an end to these incidents more than he himself, he should be rather glad that the Press expressed itself so freely. He should inform his Government that the Press was only a mild reflection of what the people felt, and he should again urge them to give the strictest instructions to the German aviators in no circumstances to fly over Irish territory. That was the only way to make certain of avoiding further trouble.

[initialled] J.P.W.

No. 383 NAI DFA Holy See Embassy P4/1

Telegram from the Department of External Affairs to Colman O'Donovan (Holy See)
(No. 3) (Personal)

DUBLIN, 6 January 1941

With reference to my telegram no. 2[1] bombings on the night of 1st and 2nd coincided with German raids on Merseyside and those on the night of 2nd and 3rd with raids on Cardiff and other parts of British West Coast. The bombings have caused local uneasiness here but informed opinion regards them as unintentional and on a par with admitted British bombings of Malmo and Helsingborg in Sweden and Zurich Basle and other Swiss cities. The intentional German bombing of Ireland at the present stage obviously most unlikely.

---

[1] Not printed.

Associated Press reports of broadcast by Columbia and National networks that foreign planes flew over Dublin in daylight yesterday and that the expulsion of the German Minister is under consideration are pure fabrications. We hope that early German apology and admission of liability will dispose of the matter.

Accident explanation attributes happenings variously to icing up difficult navigation and scattering of German raiders by British night fighters. Please inform other Legation[1] for personal and confidential information.

No. 384 NAI DFA Secretary's Files A21

Memorandum by Joseph P. Walshe on Berlin's request to provide extra staff for the German Legation in Dublin[2]
(Secret)

DUBLIN, 6 January 1941

The German Minister called to see me today at 12 noon, in connection with the request made by him before Christmas for sanction for the landing in Ireland of a plane carrying new personnel.[3] He told me that he had received instructions from his Government to inform the Irish Government that, in response to Mr. de Valera's personal request and the considerations advanced by him to the German Minister, the German Government had decided to withdraw their request. They adopted this attitude in spite of their difficulty in understanding why a matter of such ordinary routine should have such consequences. On the other hand, their acceptance of the situation in relation to the means of locomotion to be used did not change either the necessity for providing the required staff for the Legation or the intention of the German Government to provide them. The German Government are, therefore, examining at the moment the possibility of setting free German officials in the American Continent who would be suitable and of sending them to Ireland by the ordinary means of transport. The German Minister was given a specific instruction to enquire whether the Irish Government would raise any obstacles to the arrival of the new personnel in this fashion. He was instructed, furthermore, to ask for an immediate answer.

I told him that I should have to talk to my Minister before giving him a reply, but might it not be just as well to inform his Government now that the ordinary means of travelling to Ireland from the American Continent was by the Pan-American passenger line to Lisbon and thence to England by British plane.

[initialled] J.P.W.

---

[1] The Irish Legation to the Quirinal.
[2] A copy of this document in the de Valera papers at UCDA (P150/2571) includes the note: 'Read for Gov[ernment] and agreed to raise no obstacle in accord with last para[graph]'.
[3] See Nos 372, 373, 374 and 379.

No. 385 NAI DFA Madrid Embassy 34/1A

Letter from Seán Murphy to Leopold H. Kerney (Madrid)
(P2/112) (P1/9(1))

VICHY, 6 January 1941

I have the honour to refer to your letter M34/1A of the 17th ult.[1] in which you were so good as to transmit me certain information received from the British Vice-Consul in San Sebastian concerning the treatment of Irish citizens in German occupied territory. This information is in general incorrect in so far as concerns occupied France, in that holders of Irish passports are generally speaking not interned. It is a fact that, at first, some holders of Irish passports were interned but in every case which came to our notice, the person concerned was released on our making representations to the German authorities. It is probable that a number of citizens who hold British passports have been interned and it is certain that there is a large number of Irish persons, capable of acquiring citizenship by registration, in concentration camps. The German authorities have, however, agreed that in all cases where an internee was born in Ireland and where we are prepared to issue a passport (pending registration), release will be effected. They are more reserved in regard to persons claiming citizenship on the basis of the birth of a parent in Ireland. Their practice, however, seems liable to variation depending on the official looking after these matters, and it is possible that as a result of recent changes in their staff, persons born in Ireland and holding British passports, but who only left Ireland after 1923 (i.e. at a time when they could have obtained Irish passports) will not be released.

[signed] SEÁN MURPHY

No. 386 NAI DFA Secretary's Files P2

Code telegram from Robert Brennan to Joseph P. Walshe (Dublin)
(No. 9) (Personal)

WASHINGTON, 6 January 1941

Arthur Krock[2] had me to lunch. He said President's speech places America in war, but declaration may not come for some months unless Germany wishes it sooner. He says United States will draw out if England collapses within that period. President is considering sending food ships to Ireland but he will ask for *quid pro quo*.

He asked if Ireland would give use of ports to (a) Britain, (b) America under an American guarantee of Irish independence and unity (or federation) after war. He said it might be made to appear that, by refusing, Ireland was taking a stand against whole English-speaking world, North America, South America, Scandinavia, Belgium, Poland, etc.

I said I believed Ireland would stick to her neutrality whatever offers were made, and that an American guarantee would not save her from being

---
[1] Not printed.
[2] Arthur Krock (1886-1974), journalist, Washington correspondent and Bureau Chief of the *New York Times*; four-time winner of the Pulitzer Prize.

bombed. I asked how guarantee would be implemented if, after war, America had again become isolationist, or a new administration refused to be bound by undertaking, and I recalled Wilson.

He said there seemed to be no reply. He had expected to have a more complete proposal in writing, but it had not arrived. He asked if Chief would invite Ambassador Kennedy to discuss food situation, realising, however, that other matters would also be discussed.

I said I was sure Chief would like to forestall any mistake United States Administration might make and so might like to see Kennedy. He asked what outstanding American had confidence of Irish Government, and I said Conboy.

He said that he had discussed this matter with President, Secretary of State, British Chargé d'Affaires and Kennedy, and that latter is quite ready to go to Ireland. He is to give me something more on the matter in a day or two.

I had almost similar representations made to me on Saturday from more obscure sources.

No. 387 NAI DFA Paris Embassy 49/16

Letter with enclosure from Francis T. Cremins to Seán Murphy (Vichy)
(254/4)

BERNE, 7 January 1941

I have to refer to the case of Miss Lucia Joyce, a patient in a clinic in occupied France, and to forward herewith, for your information, copy of a reply which I have received from the Irish Chargé d'Affaires at Berlin to whom I had sent particulars of the case at the request of Mr. James Joyce, father of Miss Joyce.[1]

Mr. Warnock tells me further in a semi-official note that he could not without special instructions normally make any enquiries regarding this case, as you act for the whole of France, occupied as well as unoccupied.

I have informed Mr. Joyce of the substance of Mr. Warnock's reply. He said that he would await a reply from the American Embassy at Berlin, which was endeavouring to do something, and if the reply were unfavourable he would get in touch with you on the question of an Irish passport.

I have had a few cases at Geneva in which some Irish persons in Switzerland with British passports desired to obtain Irish passports. I submitted the cases to the Department and the passports were sent to me. I have just now received passports for this Legation, but I suppose from what Mr. Warnock tells me that I should continue to ask the Department for instructions. If you have any information on this point I would be glad to receive it.

[signed] F.T. CREMINS
Chargé d'Affaires

Enclosure

With reference to your minute of the 23rd December[2] regarding Miss Lucia Joyce, a patient at a clinic in occupied France, I beg to enquire whether Miss

---

[1] See No. 349.
[2] Not printed.

Joyce is an Irish citizen within the meaning of the Irish Nationality and Citizenship Act, 1935.

There appears to have been considerable difficulty in France in cases where persons of Irish origin hold British passports. I have been instructed by the Department to take no action towards assisting such people without prior reference to Dublin.

I suggest that Mr. James Joyce be asked to supply definite information concerning his daughter's citizenship, and that if she is entitled to Irish citizenship, her case be referred to the Department for instructions.

(Sd.) W. WARNOCK
Geschäftsträger a.i.

No. 388 NAI DFA Secretary's Files P12/1

> *Code telegram from Joseph P. Walshe to Seán Murphy (Vichy)*
> *(No. 27) (Personal)*
>
> DUBLIN, 7 January 1941

Your written report 3rd December received.[1] Most interesting and useful. As requested in my telegram 349[2] you should send similar weekly reports by telegram.

No criticism intended in our telegrams 98[3] and 391.[4] You have evidently misunderstood our desire to know Vatican attitude. It is of course of utmost importance for us to know Vatican views at all stages of situation especially owing to character of Pétain Government. The questions in our tel. 391 were put for purpose of obtaining more detailed information on the matters treated by you and were not in any way intended as criticism of the objectivity of your reports. Questions may often be necessary in order to elucidate special points.

Chief thing to keep in mind is that very frequent reports from you are an essential factor in our day to day judgment of a situation which affects the vital interests of our own State.

No. 389 NAI DFA 221/147A

> *Memorandum by Joseph P. Walshe on the dropping of bombs on Irish territory*
> *by German aircraft*
> *(Copy)*
>
> DUBLIN, 7 January 1941

The German Minister informed me at 12.45 today that he had received a communication from his Government in reference to our Chargé d'Affaires' protest to his Government concerning the bombings in Ireland and the statement alleged to have been made to the Press by the Foreign Office spokesman on Saturday, 4th January.[5]

---

[1] See No. 358.
[2] See No. 332.
[3] See No. 236
[4] See No. 345.
[5] See Nos 378, 380, 381, 382 and 383.

With regard to the Press statement, the Foreign Office spokesman had not said what was attributed to him by the Associated Press, viz., the bombings were done either by the British or were imaginary. What he had said, in effect, was that it would be unproper to publish the views of the German Government before a communication were made to the Irish Government.

On the 6th January, the same question was put at the Foreign Office conference, and the reply was given that nothing could be said before the Irish Minister had had time to explain matters fully.

To his protest about the bombings, Warnock had received the reply that the German Government had ordered an enquiry, which was not yet finished, but so far the result was negative. In case the enquiry should alter the situation, the German Government would not refuse to express regret and give compensation. At the same time, the German Government mentioned to Warnock the effect of the assumption of the Irish papers as to Germany's guilt on British propaganda and on the American Press which made the Irish references the basis of their attacks on Germany. The Minister went on to say that the German Government would be glad if the Irish Government would give facilities for examining the material pieces of evidence, i.e., the bomb splinters. The German Government further said to Mr. Warnock, according to the German Minister, that British implication should not be excluded.

[initialled] J.P.W.

No. 390 NAI DFA Secretary's Files A21

Memorandum by Joseph P. Walshe on Berlin's request to provide extra staff for the German Legation in Dublin

DUBLIN, 7 January 1941

I asked the German Minister to call to see me today at 1.45 in order to convey to him the Taoiseach's reply to the request that, if the new German personnel were sent from the Continent of America by the ordinary ways of travel, no objection would be made to their arrival.[1]

On the Taoiseach's instructions, I informed the German Minister that no objection would be made to the arrival of the said officials if they came by ordinary ways of travel.

[initialled] J.P.W.

No. 391 NAI DFA 221/147A

Code telegram from William Warnock to Joseph P. Walshe (Dublin) (No. 2S) (Personal) (Copy) (Sent via Berne)

BERLIN, 7 January 1941

Your telegram 4[2] and subsequent correspondence arrived with some delay. Your telegram 7 arrived January 6th.[3]

---

[1] See No. 384.
[2] See No. 378.
[3] Not printed.

Under Secretary of State on leave. I have seen his deputy, Minister Plenipotentiary von Rintelen, head of Political Department.[1]

I protested as instructed and asked that measures should be taken to prevent recurrence.

He informed me German authorities had already begun enquiries. Preliminary examination concerning night January 1st–January 2nd not yet completed. Enquiries about night January 2nd–January 3rd so far negative. He stated if their investigations show German aircraft had been concerned, they would not hesitate to apologise and pay compensation. He added it is difficult to judge matter from Berlin, and he requested any available evidence be shown to German Minister or that photographs be sent to me. As was to be expected, he mentioned possibility of British provocation.

Continuation to follow.[2]

No. 392 NAI DFA Secretary's Files P14

> *Code telegram from Colman O'Donovan to Joseph P. Walshe (Dublin)*
> *(No. 2) (Personal)*
> HOLY SEE, 9 January 1941

The following headings long article 'Giornale d'Italia' yesterday:
'Under British Yoke – Ireland Awaits Movement of Redemption – Eminent Irish Prelate Speaks to 'Giornale d'Italia' about Martyrdom of his Country during Eight Centuries of Slavery'.

I know privately that interview was given by Rector of Irish College,[3] and I am today endeavouring to have some ecclesiastical restraint put on him at this end. I have many times warned the Rector that, if he felt that he must play a part in our international affairs, he should base himself on the public statements of Taoiseach, but he is recognised to be a man of intelligence and rabidly anti-British.

I suggest someone in authority over him at home be informed and urged to warn him to attend to his own business.

The following is text of concluding paragraph of interview:-
'If England attacks our neutrality in any way, at that very moment will break out most atrocious civil war. We may even be starved, as they try to do, but national sentiment will triumph over everything and general up-rising of spirit will put an end to centuries-old iniquity.'

The Minister at Quirinal wishes to be associated with this démarche. The Irish College is alone in its attitude and interview is deplored by other Irish institutions.

---

[1] Emil von Rintelen (1897-1981).
[2] It is unclear what communication this sentence refers to.
[3] Mgr Denis McDaid, Rector of the Irish College in Rome (1939-51).

No. 393 NAI DFA Secretary's Files P12/1

> Code telegram from Seán Murphy to Joseph P. Walshe (Dublin)
> (No. 24) (Personal)
>
> VICHY, 13 January 1941

Thanks for your telegram 27.[1] I realise questions may be necessary for various reasons. It was not the fact, it was the way in which the questions were put which led me to misunderstand the position.

I am in constant contact with the Nuncio. His views regarding situation here may not necessarily be those of the Vatican. Further views that Nuncio expressed to me may not be exactly those he gives to the Vatican.

Consider weekly telegraphic reports might often be sheer waste of money for lack of news. Will send reports whenever matters of interest to report.

No. 394 NAI DFA Paris Embassy 49/16

> Letter from Seán Murphy to Francis T. Cremins (Berne)
> (P2/112) (P33/14)
>
> VICHY, 13 January 1941

I have the honour to refer to your minute of the 7th inst. with the enclosure thereto concerning Miss Lucia Joyce and to inform you that I have already had occasion to deal with this case.[2]

In July last Mr. James JOYCE called to see me here in connection with his daughter whom he was anxious to have removed to Switzerland. As she holds a British passport I informed Mr. JOYCE that I could not officially intervene on her behalf, having no 'locus standi' in the matter. I undertook, however, during a visit which I proposed to make to Paris in August to raise the matter unofficially if a suitable occasion presented itself and in particular to endeavour to ascertain whether there would be any objection to Miss JOYCE'S leaving France in view of the fact that she was seriously ill. She suffers from a mental disease known as 'Hyperthuria' which apparently sometimes reduces her to a serious and dangerous condition. I did in fact visit Paris in August and found an opportunity of mentioning the case to a member of the German Embassy. He gave it as his personal opinion that no difficulty would be put in the way of Miss Joyce's journey on the part of the occupying authority. He asked, however, that a note on the case be submitted so as to elicit a definite reply. This was in fact done. I did not either in my conversation or in the note conceal the fact that Miss Joyce held a British passport although I did explain that she was in a position, if she so desired, to apply for and probably obtain Irish nationality. On my return to Vichy I informed Mr. JOYCE that I gathered from the conversation I had had with a member of the Embassy in Paris that there would be no obstacle put in the way of his daughter's going to Switzerland. In November, however, I received a note from the German authorities to the effect that a journey to Switzerland by Miss Joyce who holds

---

[1] See No. 388.
[2] See No. 387.

a British passport could not take place. The contents of this note I communicated in due course to Mr. JOYCE. He later asked me whether I thought there was anything further I could do in the matter. I said I did not think there was in view of the contents of the German note. He then enquired whether it would be well to have his daughter obtain an Irish passport. I told him she was perfectly entitled to claim citizenship by registration and that, if she should apply for registration, I would be prepared to issue her a passport valid for one year pending the decision of the Minister for Justice on her application. I added, however, that, in view of the fact that the Germans had already considered her case and, therefore, knew she had a British passport, it was quite possible that her holding an Irish passport, issued subsequently might not weigh with them in securing her permission to leave and that her applying for one at that stage might only be regarded by them as a ruse. I suggested that in all the circumstances the best thing to do might be for him to endeavour to get his daughter out of France through the good offices of the American Foreign Service, encharged with British interests. I understood from Mr. Joyce, before he finally left for Switzerland, that he intended to try this course.

In view of the history of this case I would suggest that you inform Mr. Joyce that if he wants to use the good offices of our service for securing permission for his daughter to leave France, he should continue to address himself to this Legation. I may state that I was surprised to learn that he had approached you independently on that subject, especially as he does not seem to have informed you of what he knew of my efforts in this respect already. I should stress that I have told him repeatedly that I had no official standing for intervening in this case as long as his daughter held a British passport. On the first occasion in which he raised the matter (in July) I clearly implied to him, without actually suggesting that she should do so, that by far the best way to handle the matter in my opinion would be for his daughter to take out an Irish passport. If he had decided on this course in the first instance, I have no doubt that she would have been allowed to undertake the journey to Switzerland long since. He, however, showed no inclination to follow it at the time. I may add that he has never suggested applying for an Irish passport for himself and that his son[1] also holds a British passport although at one time, when it looked as if he might be refused a French exit visa for that reason (being of military age), he did enquire about the procedure for getting an Irish one. He did not, however, pursue the matter, presumably because he was able to get an exit visa on his British passport.

If Miss Joyce should apply for citizenship I shall, of course, consider the case of the issue to her of an Irish passport on its merits. I do not think, however, that there is any further action of any nature which can be taken by us on her behalf as long as she holds, a British one.

---

[1] Giorgio Joyce (1905-76).

Documents on Irish Foreign Policy, Volume VI, 1939–1941

No. 395 NAI DFA 205/84

> Letter from Frederick H. Boland to Thomas J. Coyne (Dublin)
> (Copy)
> DUBLIN, 13 January 1941

Dear Tommy,[1]

I am sorry that I have not been able to write you before now, as I promised, about the Italian Minister's[2] representations with regard to the Press.

As I told you, the Italian Minister has been assailing us, ever since the outbreak of the War in Greece, about the way in which news of the Italian military campaigns is presented in the daily newspapers, particularly in the Irish Press. We have not given him much satisfaction. We told him that in our view there was nothing in our papers to which anyone could point as departing from the general duty of objectivity and impartiality. We made the suggestion (for which I think there is a good deal of ground) that what he was really complaining about was the fact that the news of Italian defeats was printed at all! When he referred once or twice to the failure of the newspapers here to publish certain Italian statements or official commentaries, we said we felt quite certain that the papers make impartial use of any Italian news they receive, and that any suggestion that there was power to tell the papers what they must print, as opposed to what they must not print on censorship grounds, was quite unwarranted.

When the Italian Minister last spoke to me about this matter, however, I pointed out to him that he had always discussed it in the terms of the widest generalities and that he had never yet given us a concrete example of what he was complaining about. He undertook to repair this omission and he has now sent me a bundle of newspapers marked to illustrate his points. From this material, the substance of the Italian complaint appears to be:-

(a) That the newspapers, and the 'Irish Press' more than the other papers, take their headlines *exclusively* from the British and Greek official communiqués and Press despatches presenting their statements as *facts*. The statements made in the Italian communiqués are usually referred to only in minor column cross-headings and are described as 'claims'.

(b) On occasion, the papers make scare headlines of mere phrases in British Press despatches which are wounding to Italy and tend to magnify, and give an exaggerated idea of, Italian reverses.

  The principal example of this is the headline 'Flower of Italy's Army Scattered' in the 'Irish Press' of the 29th November.

(c) That in the papers, and once again in the 'Irish Press' more than others, the British and Greek news is always put at the head of the column and the Italian version is placed at the very end of the news under some such heading as 'Italian communiqué', 'Italian claims', etc. Even when the Italian communiqué reported relatively major developments – and, according to the Italian Minister, the campaign in Greece was not always

---

[1] Marginal note by Boland: 'Copy with encl.[osure] sent to Mr. F. Gallagher for personal information. F.B. 14/1'.

[2] Vincenzo Berardis (born 1889), Counsellor, Italian Embassy, Moscow (1933-8); Minister to Dublin (1938-44).

one-sided – no prominence whatever was given to the Italian official report. For example, on the 29th November an Italian communiqué referring to the local Italian successes was printed in the 'London Times' but not in the 'Irish Press'.

The points, and a number of others as well, are referred to in the attached copy of an 'aide-memoire' left with us by the Italian Minister since we last spoke.[1]

As you will see, the complaint does not come to very much. It amounts to little more than saying that the newspapers publish the Press Association report as they get it; and it, of course, tends to minimise and discount the Italian version.

Still, I thought you had better know of Berardis' representations. We don't intend to approach you officially about the matter because there doesn't seem to us to be any real substance in the complaint; but at the same time, from the point of view of avoiding friction and keeping our Italian friend in an amenable frame of mind, if you do find it desirable and practicable to take any action on the representations we shall be just as glad!

[stamped] (signed F.H. BOLAND)

No. 396 NAI DFA 205/4

Code telegram from the Department of External Affairs
to William Warnock (Berlin)
(No. 21) (Personal) (Copy)

DUBLIN, 16 January 1941

Several German and German-controlled stations have recently broadcast quotations from Swedish Press saying that Germany is determined to counter intended British invasion of Ireland by action similar to that taken in Belgium and Norway. Statements to this effect were broadcast from Bremen in English at 12.30 p.m. on 9th instant, and from Breslau at 23.30 on 8th instant. A broadcast from Brussels on 8th inst. devoted great attention to British military preparations in Six Counties.

From our point of view, such broadcasts, however well intentioned, do more harm than good. They are used by British and American propaganda as proof of German intention to invade us, and this exercises unsettling effect on people here and Irish-American opinion. Please express these views in proper quarters with a view to discouraging any similar references to Ireland in future.

No. 397 NAI DFA Secretary's Files P22

Memorandum from Joseph P. Walshe to General Peadar MacMahon (Dublin)
(P22) (Secret)

DUBLIN, 16 January 1941

I am directed by the Minister for External Affairs to refer to your minute (S/255) of the 11th January,[2] relative to the decision of the Cabinet Committee

---
[1] Not printed.
[2] Not printed.

on Emergency Problems in regard to certain 'forms of notification' affecting your Department.[1]

I am to state that the list of matters requiring notifications appended to your minute has been examined in this Department which offers the following observations for your Minister's consideration.

In the first place, it is suggested generally that, as all the notifications indicated in your list will require to be addressed to countries with which normal postal communication no longer exists, both secrecy and expedition demand that they should be conveyed by code telegram to the appropriate diplomatic representatives abroad. In order to guard against the possibility of this country's telegraphic channels being suspended or terminated at the outbreak of hostilities, it is strongly urged that all the notifications to be formally made by Irish representatives to foreign Governments in a certain eventuality should be wired to the former as soon as may be possible. The representatives concerned would be relied upon to fill in such missing details as cannot be furnished prior to the actual occurrence of the eventuality.

If this general suggestion commends itself to the Minister for Defence and is subsequently approved by the Cabinet Committee, no need will arise for complete drafts of the proposed notifications. Each representative abroad will submit the substance of the notification to be made by him in the diplomatic form which he usually adopts when addressing the Government to which he is accredited. In most cases, he will merely have to draw up a suitable covering letter with which he will forward the material (Regulations, Emergency Powers Orders, Army Orders etc.) supplied by the Department of Defence.

It is observed that your Department intend to forward in a short time, for the approval of the Minister for External Affairs, draft regulations which are being made, for the purpose of implementing the Prisoners of War Convention, 1929. When these are finally settled, it is thought that they might be wired textually to the Chargé d'Affaires at Berne for communication to the Geneva Red Cross authorities when the need arises.

With regard to the question of the uniform to be worn, (and the organisation as a whole) of the Local Defence Force, similar action could be taken, although it is felt that the better course might be to first publish a list of the distinguishing badges etc. in one definitely official document which could be made directly available at once to all potential enemies.

The foregoing remarks apply to 'Notifications' Nos. 2, 4 and 5 on your list. Of the two outstanding items, the first (No.1) is being dealt with as described below while notification No. 3 pursuant to Article 10 of the Red Cross Convention, 1929, is being made immediately as a peacetime measure in accordance with your Department's suggestion.

The first notification mentioned in your list will require a relatively elaborate draft to be submitted, when ready, to the Cabinet Committee. It is proposed that it should take the form of a Note relating the circumstances of an attack on Irish territory, and asserting Ireland's constant adherence to strict neutrality and the intention of her people to resist the aggressor.[2] It will

---

[1] See also No. 376.
[2] See No. 409.

probably conclude with an appeal for neutral sympathy and support.

The Minister is advised that the legal effect of such a Note as is being prepared, will be to render unnecessary any more specifically technical notification under Article 2 of the Hague Convention relative to the Opening of Hostilities.

No. 398 NAI DFA Secretary's Files P48/A

> *Memorandum by Joseph P. Walshe*
> *(Secret) (Copy)*
>
> Dublin, 17 January 1941

Mr Gray's Memorandum[1]: Notes Thereon

1. The use of the expression 'diverging sympathies' in the introductory note is likely to give rise to a misunderstanding.
2. The reference to Ireland of the American President in his recent speech was clearly intended as an appeal to our people to go into the war on the side of the British, and it should be regarded as a much graver international offence than our telling the American people that we were seriously in need of defensive weapons. (Beginning of page 3).
3. It is impossible to imagine that there should be impatience with discussions of the Irish question, seeing that at the present moment in America it is regarded as almost a crime to put American interests before European interests. Some of the American papers (e.g., the 'Boston Post' and the 'Boston Globe') complain that America was being forced by propaganda to put British interests before American. (End of page 3).
4. Mr. Gray's assertion that American influence could not be expected to support any Irish demand which could be construed as inimical to the success of the Allies seems to assume that the Allies are fighting for something else besides small nations and international justice, which, after all, could be the only secure basis for the sacrifices which the American people are about to be asked to make.
5. Mr. Gray said that, if it could be shown beyond reasonable doubt that the survival of Britain and of Ireland depended on the use of our ports, America would not criticise their seizure by Great Britain. It would be a pity to let him away with the hypothesis that there might be such an essential inter-relation. It has been very frequently said in Britain that what the British wanted was more destroyers, and Colonel Knox said a few days ago that America could not give Britain more destroyers without seriously affecting the efficiency of the Fleet. So it would appear that America is not ready to sacrifice even a part of her Fleet efficiency for what she asks us to make incalculable sacrifices.[2] Moreover, everybody knows that destroyers on the high seas are far less vulnerable targets than port installations. Neither can it ever be said that the eight or ten hours difference in distance to the scene of operations of the U-boats would be sufficient to constitute

---

[1] Marginal note in unknown hand: 'with Taoiseach'.
[2] This sentence is reproduced as found.

a decisive factor. And, if it is a decisive factor, then it is only one of several. With the adequate help of the American Fleet, Britain might be able to take back the Western French ports. Or, again, if the Americans would hand over to Great Britain the effective control of a large number of their aeroplane and munitions factories, they would provide England with something which is a more obviously decisive factor than would be the shelter of a few Irish ports. One of the things which is maintaining the anti-Irish campaign in America is the easy assumption that the possession of a few Irish ports would in itself win the war for the British. The sacrifices which are still open to America to make before she reaches the magnitude of those involved for us in the handing over of the ports are enormous, and we are getting tired of America's vicarious heroism at our expense. Mr. Stimson spoke on 16th January about a possible invasion of America from the air, and the need of being ready for it. If one member of the American Cabinet is so terrified of Germany as to believe that she can carry out an invasion at 3,000 miles distance the Cabinet as a whole will understand our hesitation in opening ourselves to bombardment by the same Fleet since we are only a few hundred miles from its bases. It is hard to bring home to the American mind the kind of silly demand they are making on us, but let us suppose that America was definitely decided not to go into the war and England had acquired Japan as an ally, would America hand over to Japan the ports of New York, Philadelphia and Baltimore in order to make sure that the Germans would be beaten in the Atlantic. If and when the Germans had wiped out these ports from the air, the Americans would begin to taste, relatively speaking, what our losses would be within twenty-four hours.

6. There is not any doubt that, if the neutral countries now occupied by Germany had allied themselves with Germany's enemy, their case for freedom in a European system would not be recognised by Germany after the war, and it is doubtful if it would be taken up by the other countries of the world in face of a victorious Germany. Even if our people did not want to be neutral, it would be the duty of any Irish Government to avoid going into the war until it had absolute certainty that Great Britain was going to win. If Great Britain lost the war and Ireland had joined her side, while England, as a great country, would remain at least relatively free, Ireland in those circumstances would certainly be held by Germany. And, again, the world would say 'The devil mend her, why did she join with the British'. Our only chance of survival and of having a case before Germany and the world for keeping our freedom in the event of a German victory is to stay out of the war. Mr. Gray knows perfectly well that, if he or the members of his Government were in charge of Ireland's destiny at this precise moment in history, they would be absolutely obliged to follow the policy of neutrality, at least until that moment when a defeat of Germany became a certainty.

7. Mr. Gray unfortunately does not accept the normal situation that an Irish statesman or an ordinary Irish citizen can be simply pro-Irish: he must be anti-British or pro-German. As Prof. O'Rahilly[1] says in this week's

---

[1] Professor Alfred O'Rahilly (1884-1969), Registrar (1920-43) and President (1943-54) of University College Cork.

'Standard', in reply to Bernard Shaw,[1] 'there are too many people who regard Irishmen in general as a sort of inferior brand of Englishman, but Englishman all the same'.

[initialled] J.P.W.

No. 399 NAI DFA Secretary's Files P12/1

Code telegram from Seán Murphy to Joseph P. Walshe (Dublin)
(No. 38) (Personal)
VICHY, 20 January 1941

Laval-Pétain reconciliation surprising and not inherent in what was understood to be taking place over the past three weeks. It was generally believed his return was demanded by the Germans (see my telegram 408)[2] but that Pétain conceded on that point. On the other hand, departure of certain Ministers opposed to Laval (see my telegram 395)[3] was considered likely so as to give the Germans partial satisfaction. This will probably now happen, principal Minister involved being Alibert[4] and probably Peyrouton,[5] Minister of the Interior. There is little doubt that Laval's return to favour is due to German pressure. It will probably lead to toning-down in very violent anti-Government campaign carried on latterly by Déat and others in Paris Press, and it may mean more practical turn being given to collaboration about which Government was considered to be observing recently reticent attitude following on British successes in North Africa and consequent increased importance in Mediterranean of French Fleet.

No. 400 NAI DFA Paris Embassy 49/16

Handwritten letter from Francis T. Cremins to Seán Murphy (Vichy)
BERNE, 20 January 1941

I have to thank you for your minute of 13th January, 1941 (P.2/112 / P.33/14)[6] relative to the case of Miss Joyce. I presume that you have since learned that Mr. James Joyce died on the night of the 12th January after a couple of days illness. I do not know if Mrs. Joyce, or his son, will now pursue the question of getting Miss Joyce out of France, but if any further approach to me is made, I will inform them as you suggest, that they should continue to address themselves in the matter to you. That was in fact his intention, as he told me, when I spoke to him on the telephone after hearing from Mr. Warnock, that he had received the necessary forms from you. He said that he would if necessary raise the matter of the Irish passport if efforts which were being made by someone in the American Embassy in Berlin failed to produce results.

---

[1] George Bernard Shaw (1856-1950), Irish playwright, novelist and winner of the Nobel Prize for Literature (1925). Though born in Ireland, Shaw lived in England from the age of twenty.
[2] Not printed.
[3] Not printed.
[4] Raphaël Alibert (1887-1963), Minister of Justice (1940-1).
[5] Marcel Peyrouton (1887-1983).
[6] See No. 394.

I see now that I should have sent on his request to you. He *had* explained to me all that you had done for him, expressing his gratitude for it in unmeasured terms, and had informed me that you had secured the permission in August which was only cancelled in Nov. before he was in a position to avail himself of it, the delay on his part being due to delay in obtaining the necessary entry permit for Switzerland. He enclosed me a note giving all the details regarding his daughter and asked me to send it to our Chargé d'Affaires in Berlin, as he thought that that would help the efforts which were being made. It was a useless move as our Chargé d'Affaires could not take any action, but that did not occur to me at that time. I took it that the matter was simply at a new stage.

In view of what Mr. Warnock said, I have raised the question with the Dept. as to whether I have authority to supply Irish passports in lieu of British ones without reference to the Dept., as I have now several such applications from Irish persons in Switzerland, one of whom states that she may have to return to France. For their information, I gave the Dept. a brief account of the Miss Joyce case (as it was that which raised the issue in my mind) in explaining how I had been in touch with Mr. Joyce.[1] They wired to me for details regarding his death. These latter I gave in a telegram, followed by a minute.

I note in particular the last paragraph of your minute. If Mrs. Joyce, or Mr. Joyce, Jnr., writes to me in the matter I will pass on the communication at once to you and inform them that I have done so.

Mr. Joyce had informed me also that the Swiss entry permit would expire on the 31st December, but that he had no doubt that he would be able to secure an extension.

F.T. Cremins
Ch. d'Affaires

No. 401 NAI DFA P22

Memorandum by Frederick H. Boland on matters arising in the event of Ireland becoming involved in hostilities

Dublin, 21 January 1941

1. On the 18th January, the Secretary discussed with the Taoiseach the various questions which would arise in the event of this country's being invaded and becoming involved in the War. The Assistant Secretary[2] was present.
2. The Taoiseach approved the proposal that instructions should issue at once to the missions abroad telling them, in the event of an invasion, to present a formal note of protest to the Governments to which they are accredited. The Taoiseach approved the draft text of the proposed note (marked A opposite)[3] and the draft text of the proposed instructions (marked B opposite).[4]
3. The Secretary suggested to the Taoiseach that, in the event of our being invaded, a formal declaration of war against the invader would not be necessary.

[1] See No. 387.
[2] Frederick H. Boland.
[3] See No. 409.
[4] Not printed.

If there were a formal declaration of war, it would be necessary to notify it to the foreign countries with which we are in diplomatic relations; but international law did not require a formal declaration of war in the case of resistance to an unprovoked attack. The resistance itself was sufficient. The Taoiseach said that he personally accepted this view and didn't think a formal declaration of war would be necessary, but he thought the point was one which might be discussed at the Defence Conference[1] and he asked Mr. Walshe to bring it to Mr. Aiken's notice for this purpose.

4. The Secretary also raised the point whether, in the event of an invasion by Germany, we should break off diplomatic relations with Italy and/or declare war against that country. He said that, in his view, we should avoid taking these steps if at all possible. The Taoiseach said that he agreed with this view but he thought that this point also might be raised at the Defence Conference.

5. Mr. Walshe told the Taoiseach that the question would also arise what action, including necessary measures of restraint we should take against the diplomatic representative of the invading country, his staff and their families. Probably the best course would be to quarter the entire staff of the mission or missions concerned together in a hotel or suitable residential premises pending the making of arrangements for their repatriation. To leave them in their Legation or ordinary residence, would involve the risk of secret means of communication being used. On the other hand, the Legation and its office and residential premises would pass at once into the hands of the 'neutral' power and, therefore, to search or occupy them might lead us into diplomatic complications. Mr. Walshe suggested that the steps to be taken in connection with this particular matter should be discussed, and agreed upon in advance, between this Department and the Department of Defence. The Taoiseach approved of this proposal.

6. Mr. Walshe told the Taoiseach that, in the event of invasion, it would be necessary to ask some neutral power to take charge of Irish interests in the invading country, and in any other country with which we might be involved in war as a result of the invasion. Such an appointment was necessary, not only to ensure protection of the interests of our nationals, supervision of their conditions of internment, etc., but to make possible the formal communications under the provisions of the Red Cross and Hague Convention which one belligerent had to make to another on the outbreak of hostilities. Mr. Walshe proposed that we should sound the United States authorities as to whether they would be prepared to take charge of Irish interests in Berlin and, if necessary, in Rome. If the United States themselves became involved in war, the next best choice would probably be Spain. The Taoiseach agreed that the United States Government should be approached informally as proposed. The question of the protection of Irish interests in the United Kingdom if Britain were the invading power was left over for a later decision.

7. Mr. Walshe explained to the Taoiseach that, when Finland, Norway, Denmark, Holland, Belgium and France had been invaded, all the assets of those countries in the United States, including their current accounts in

---

[1] An inter-party conference of leading members of all parties in the Dáil which held meetings during the 'Emergency' to discuss matters relating to national defence and security.

American banks, had been 'frozen' by executive orders made by President Roosevelt. The effect of this action was that the assets in question could not be touched or used at all, so that the countries concerned had been virtually left without the foreign assets necessary for the support of their diplomatic missions in the United States and elsewhere; for the conduct of essential propaganda work and the purchase of vital supplies. We understood that the Dutch Government had successfully anticipated this action by the President of the United States by giving beforehand a contingent power of attorney to their Minister in Washington. Mr. Walshe suggested that we should consider similar action and that, for this purpose, the matter should be discussed between this Department and the Department of Finance. The Taoiseach agreed.

[initialled] F.B.

No. 402 NAI DT S12078

Memorandum by the Department of the Taoiseach on matters requiring immediate action should Ireland become involved in hostilities

DUBLIN, 22 January 1941

Matters in regard to which immediate action would have to be taken by Ministers in the event of this country becoming involved in hostilities.

1. *TAOISEACH*
   (a) Issue of Directions under Emergency Powers (No. 48) Order, 1940 (Regional Commissioners).
   (b) Broadcast to the People.
   (c) Summoning of Dáil and Seanad.
2. *EXTERNAL AFFAIRS*
   (a) Protest to Government of country concerned in attack.
   (b) Notification to Governments of neutral countries of violation of neutrality of this country.
   (c) Request for aid against an invader.
   (d) Notification to the enemy of (1) Voluntary Aid Societies authorised to give assistance to the medical Services of the Defence Forces (2) Military and marine titles and ranks (3) Uniform worn by L.D.F.
   (e) Notification to the Swiss Federal Council of regulations governing custody, discipline, etc. of prisoners of war.
3. *SUPPLIES*
   (a) Issue of instructions to Regional Commissioners to proceed to their regions.
4. *FINANCE*
   (a) Proclamation of Bank Holidays.
   (b) Closing of Stock Exchanges.
   (c) Transfer and allocation of Civil Service Staffs (if necessary).
   (d) Suspension of payments to enemy country.
5. *LOCAL GOVERNMENT & PUBLIC HEALTH*
   (a) Issue of instructions to Local Bodies and their staffs regarding their relations with an invader.

6. *CO-ORDINATION OF DEFENSIVE MEASURES (OR PARLIAMENTARY SECRETARY TO THE MINISTER FOR DEFENCE)*
    (a) Order under Section 27 of the Air Raid Precautions Act, 1939, empowering any local authority to take possession of premises for use for A.R.P. purposes.
    (b) Order under Section 57 of the Air Raid Precautions Act, 1939, empowering the Commissioners of Public Works to take possession of premises for use for State purposes.
    (c) Order under Emergency Powers Order, 1939, providing for continuous black-out.
    (d) Authorisations under Section 45 of the Emergency Powers Order, 1939, enabling rescue and demolition work and contamination measures to be carried out.
7. *POSTS & TELEGRAPHS*
    (a) Instructions to Area Officers to proceed to their districts.
8. *DEFENCE, INDUSTRY & COMMERCE, EDUCATION, JUSTICE, LANDS, AGRICULTURE.*
    Nil.

Note: Items 1(a), 1(b), 1(c), 2(a), 2(b), 2(c) and 5(a) will first be considered by the Government.

No. 403 NAI DFA Washington Embassy File 119

> *Code telegram from Joseph P. Walshe to Robert Brennan (Washington)*
> *(No. 20) (Personal) (Copy)*
>
> DUBLIN, 22 January 1941

The American Minister, at the request of the Minister for Finance, has enquired of State Department whether Irish Government would have goodwill of American Government in raising a loan in United States naming National City Bank. Please tell State Department you have received this information from your Government, and say your Government would like to obtain a loan in America, preferably from American Government, to amount of about fifty million dollars to be used as credit in U.S. for purchase of supplies and ships.

Explore also possibility of getting supplies and shipping on basis of lend lease system for above purposes, including defence, but make absolutely certain no implication of belligerency involved.

No. 404 NAI DFA Washington Embassy File xiii

> *Letter from Robert Brennan to Joseph P. Walshe (Dublin)*
> *(Copy)*
>
> WASHINGTON, 23 January 1941

It is difficult to write reports when one knows that it will be weeks before they are read and that the events with which they deal will then have been long out of date.

At the moment of writing it would appear that the Lend-Lease Bill will be passed by the first of March, probably with some amendments. After that it will be a matter for Germany to decide when and if the 'short of war' line has been passed. In other words, the Administration will adopt progressively forward steps in aiding Britain leaving it to Germany to say if and when America is at war.

Restraining factors in the matter of declaring war are not so much whether Britain can hold out as, firstly, whether a possible conflict with Japan could be decided favourably in time to enable the American Fleet to be diverted to the Atlantic and, secondly, the doubt about some South American countries notably the Argentine. It is felt that if Britain fell these countries might want to resume trade with Europe.

There is thus a dilemma. A declaration of war on the part of the U.S. would possibly line-up all the South American countries with similar declarations. But the U.S. would then face a long drawn out struggle in the Pacific with the Japanese Navy refusing to come out and fight and, meanwhile, a possible German success with capture of all or portion of the British Fleet would at once pose a serious problem in the Atlantic. On the other hand if war is not declared and Britain should fall Hemisphere solidarity would be at once threatened by the desire of the South American countries to resume trade with Europe.

No. 405 NAI DFA 218/25

> *Code telegram from Joseph P. Walshe to Seán Murphy (Vichy)*
> *(No. 95) (Personal) (Copy)*
>
> Dublin, 23 January 1941

As you know French Government have decided to economize in matter of Commercial Attachés and Lestocquoy[1] has received preliminary notice through his Minister. Could you suggest to French Government that Irish Government think it pity that this excellent official with nine years experience in Ireland highly esteemed by everybody and an ardent supporter of Pétain ideals should be taken away at a time when his intimate knowledge of Irish agricultural and commercial conditions can be of such service in preparing for closer economic cooperation after war. He is only person in Legation who takes serious interest in this country or in his work. Lestocquoy would be extremely grateful to you for a good word. The actual regulation leaves French Government considerable latitude and they could leave him here without departing from it.

---

[1] Eugène Lestocquoy, French Commercial Attaché to Ireland (1932-48).

No. 406 NAI DFA Paris Embassy Miscellaneous Papers, Box 40

Facsimile reproduction of a letter from Samuel Beckett to Count Gerald O'Kelly de Gallagh (Paris)

PARIS, 23 January 1941

6 Rue des Favorites
Paris 15me

23/1/41

Dear Count O'Kelly

Thank you for your letter.

I should be glad if you could arrange for a telegram to be sent to my brother (Frank Beckett, 6 Clare Street, Dublin), simply to the effect that I keep very well and want for nothing. The expense of telegram could be deducted from my next instalment, unless you prefer that I pay it to you now.

I enclose receipt for mandat received this morning.

Yours sincerely

Samuel Beckett

(Samuel Beckett)

© The Estate of Samuel Beckett

No. 407 NAI DFA Secretary's Files P12/8

> Code telegram from Joseph P. Walshe to Michael MacWhite (Rome)
> (P30) (No. 20) (Personal) (Copy)
>
> DUBLIN, 24 January 1941

Your reports on Italian situation are too infrequent. You should make a practice of wiring once a week a brief commentary covering such matters as food and supply position, reaction of public opinion to principal military and other events of the week, state of public morale, changes in Government and army command, newspaper and private comment and feeling regarding Ireland, etc. Should like to learn from you at once general impression in Rome as to future of war in view of North African campaign and American policy.

No. 408 NAI DFA P22

> Memorandum on questions affecting the Department of External Affairs which would arise in the event of an invasion of Ireland, with covering note from Frederick H. Boland to Maurice Moynihan (Dublin)
>
> DUBLIN, 28 January 1941

With reference to your minutes S.12223 of the 9th and 14th January,[1] I am directed by the Minister for External Affairs to forward herewith a note of a number of questions affecting this Department which would arise in the event of an attack on this country.

With regard to the documents referred to in your minute of the 9th January, I am to invite attention to paragraph 3 of the memorandum. The matter referred to in you minute of the 14th January is dealt with in paragraph 4 of the memorandum.

[stamped] (signed) F.H. BOLAND

Note of questions affecting the Department of External Affairs which would arise in the event of an invasion.

1. *Declaration of war on the aggressor.*
In the event of resistance to unprovoked aggression, a formal declaration of war by the invaded country is neither usual nor required by international law. In the event of this country being attacked therefore, a formal declaration of war by the Government would not be necessary and, as it would tend to obscure the defensive character of the Government's action, it were better avoided. When on the eve of the invasions of Greece and Belgium, the Italian and German Ministers respectively presented notes containing demands to the Foreign Ministers concerned, the reply made in each case was that the note was regarded as a declaration of war. A similar course might be adopted here according to the circumstances.

2. *Declaration of war on Italy in the event of invasion by Germany.*
If we are invaded by Germany, the question of our relations with Italy will at

---

[1] Neither document printed.

once arise. Particularly having regard to the large number of Irish citizens in ecclesiastical colleges and religious communities in Italian territory, it is proposed that there should not be an immediate rupture of relations with, or declaration of war on, Italy. Such action can be taken later if circumstances render it necessary, but the question of complying with Article 28 of the Constitution may then arise. It will be remembered that Greece did not declare war on Germany when she was invaded by Italy and is still in diplomatic relations with the former country.

3. *Notifications and protests to foreign powers.*
The Minister for External Affairs proposes to issue instructions at once to the representatives abroad to ensure that, in the event of invasion, a note in the terms of the enclosed text[1] will be presented at once to all the friendly governments with whom we are in diplomatic relations. A protest in diplomatic form to the Government of the invading power would not be usual or desirable.

4. *Requests for aid from foreign powers.*
The procedure with regard to any request for aid the Government might decide to make in the event of invasion has, in part, been settled already. It is considered preferable to leave such measures as have not already been decided upon to be determined in the light of the prevailing circumstances.

5. *Diplomatic representation in belligerent capitals.*
In the event of war, it is usual for each belligerent to entrust the interests of its nationals in the territory of the other to the care of a 'neutral power'. Formal communications on such matters as the observance of the Red Cross Conventions, the Hague Conventions on the rules of land warfare, etc., are made through the 'neutral power'. The Minister at Washington has been instructed to ask the United States Government in confidence whether in the event of war they would be willing to take charge of Irish interests in Germany, and, if necessary, Italy.

6. *Repatriation, etc. of diplomatic staffs.*
The Minister for External Affairs is anxious that the measures to be taken in the event of invasion to restrict the movements, etc. of the diplomatic representative of the invading country, his staff and their families should be discussed and settled in detail beforehand. He is accordingly arranging for an early discussion of the matter between representatives of the Departments of External Affairs, Justice, and Defence.

7. *Activity of Irish diplomatic missions abroad.*
The Irish diplomatic missions abroad will have instructions to regard their primary task under the new circumstances as one of propaganda. They will work to foster sympathy and counter the propaganda broadcast by the invader in defence of his action. A major role in this work will be played by the Legation in Washington, and, if communications are cut off, the Washington Legation

---

[1] See No. 409.

will act as the co-ordinating agency for all the offices abroad. The question of ensuring that any Irish assets and bank balances in the United States will not be 'frozen' by the Executive Order, which it is the practice of the United States Government to make in respect of invaded countries, is under discussion between the Departments of External Affairs and Finance.

8. *Formal notifications to the enemy Government.*
The Minister at Washington and the Chargé d'Affaires at Berne are being given instructions to ensure that, in the event of invasion, the notifications listed in paragraphs 2, 4 and 5 of the enclosure to the Department of Defence minute S.255 of the 11th January[1] will be made at once. They are respectively certain notifications required by the Prisoners of War Convention 1929, the Red Cross Convention 1929 and the Hague Convention of 1907. The Swiss Government has already been informed that the Irish Red Cross Society is the sole authorised Society so far as Ireland is concerned for the purposes of Article 10 of the Red Cross Convention of 1929.

The following matters will also arise in the event of invasion but may have been already dealt with:-

1. *Appointment of Custodian of Enemy Property.*
In the event of invasion all or many of the nationals of the invading country resident here would presumably be interned at once and would no longer be able to look after their businesses. International practice requires that in such a case due provision should be made to safeguard the interests and property of the enemy aliens. In our case this would best be done by appointing a 'Custodian of Enemy Property' to take over the necessary work. The Custodian could be a firm of Accountants working on a fee basis but legislation would be required to empower and indemnify them.

2. *Seizures of ships in the event of invasion.*
In the event of our being invaded or becoming involved in war, the ships in our harbours registered in enemy or enemy occupied territory would become properly seizable.

No. 409 NAI DFA Secretary's Files P22

Draft by Michael Rynne of the note to be sent to foreign governments in the event of an invasion of Ireland
DUBLIN, **undated, but January 1941**

Draft Note to Foreign Governments
1. Despite Ireland's loyal adherence to a policy of strict neutrality in the tragic conflict which has ravaged Europe for so long, and, notwithstanding the sincere desire of the Irish people all over the world to keep their country at peace with all men and nations, the Irish Government have to announce

---

[1] Not printed.

that (insert nationality) forces attacked Irish territory at (add available details of time and place).
2. The Irish Government and people are determined to resist the unwarrantable aggression which has been committed against them and to defend, with God's help, their ancient sovereignty and the measure of independence their fathers so hardly won.
3. *(If the attacking country is Britain):-*
With the sympathy and support of other freedom-loving nations, and of the millions of the Irish race abroad, Ireland faces this new threat to her existence with the determination not to rest until freedom and peace have been restored to the Motherland.
(If the attacking country is any country other than Britain):-
With the sympathy and support of other freedom-loving nations, and of the millions of the Irish race abroad, Ireland faces this threat to her national existence with the determination not to rest until freedom and peace have been restored to the Motherland.

No. 410 NAI DFA Secretary's Files P2

Code telegram from Joseph P. Walshe to Robert Brennan (Washington)
(No. 23) (Personal) (Copy)

DUBLIN, 28 January 1941

Your 34.[1] Transhipment would violate neutrality. Has been constant subject of difficulty with British but demands so far successfully resisted.

No. 411 NAI DFA Secretary's Files P12/8

Code telegram from Michael MacWhite to Joseph P. Walshe (Dublin)
(No. 13Z) (Personal) (Copy)

ROME, 29 January 1941

Official Italian feeling towards Ireland has become more friendly, particularly since our attitude was clarified November 7th. Political importance of the Irish in America also seems to be appreciated, and their opposition to Administration policy has not escaped attention. Italian newspapers are very friendly and exploit every criticism of our attitude to Britain's disadvantage.

No. 412 NAI DFA Washington Embassy File xiii

Code telegram from Robert Brennan to Joseph P. Walshe (Dublin)
(No. 36) (Personal)

WASHINGTON, 30 January 1941

Your 19.[2] Reply is vague: the U.S. is anxious to help but no definite commitment can be made in view of possibility of changed relations of countries concerned.

---

[1] Not printed.
[2] Not printed.

No. 413 NAI DFA Washington Embassy File xiii

> Code telegram from Robert Brennan to Joseph P. Walshe (Dublin)
> (No. 37) (Personal)
> WASHINGTON, 30 January 1941

Your 20.[1] Replies are vague as follows:
1   There is no objection to raising loan on open market
2   Any application to export import bank will be considered on its merits having in mind purpose of credits: if such purpose does not conflict with policy of U.S. in aiding Britain it probably will be favourably considered
3   Question re lend lease plan cannot be answered because plan has not yet been passed on by Congress and in any case selection of countries to benefit from plan will rest in discretion of President.
See telegram immediately following.[2]

No. 414 NAI DFA Washington Embassy File xiii

> Code telegram from Robert Brennan to Joseph P. Walshe (Dublin)
> (No. 38) (Personal)
> WASHINGTON, 30 January 1941

My 36[3] and 37.[4] It was Berle I saw: usually friendly he was almost caustic on matter of lend lease and made it clear without saying so we will not benefit unless we fall in line: it is obvious administration considers we are not playing game and will give us no facilities they can reasonably withhold: their attitude is England must win whoever suffers: they could not make good case for refusing credits for food and fertilisers but they will not sanction munitions: I suggest I should approach Export Import bank for loan for food fertilisers and ships but we will not get ships if England wants them.

No. 415 NAI DFA 221/147A

> Code telegram from William Warnock to Joseph P. Walshe (Dublin)
> (No. 12S) (Personal) (Copy) (Sent via Berne)
> BERLIN, 30 January 1941

Your 26.[5] Under Secretary of State informed me this morning sense of reply which German Minister has been instructed to convey to you. I understand from him that, in view of friendly relations, they are anxious to have matter cleared up, but wish to have available evidence examined by German experts. They appear to be definitely of opinion that German aircraft not responsible for bombing on January 2nd–January 3rd, and in general they do not regard our evidence as conclusive proof.

---

[1] See No. 403.
[2] See No. 414.
[3] See No. 412.
[4] See No. 413.
[5] Not printed.

No. 416 NAI DFA 221/147A

Memorandum by Joseph P. Walshe on the dropping of bombs on Irish territory by German aircraft
(Copy)

DUBLIN, 30 January 1941

The German reply to our protests against the bombings of the 2nd and 3rd January
The German Minister called to-day for the purpose of handing me the German reply in the above matter in the form of an *aide-mémoire*. He told me that notwithstanding the description which he had sent his Government of the bomb fragments shown to him, his Government regarded it as essential for further investigation to have the fragments examined by experts. When the German Minister said this, I naturally felt that a new attempt was being made to get some kind of messenger from Germany to this country. I asked him whether one of the airmen in the Curragh would not be sufficiently expert to explain all the technical details to his Government by telegram.[1] The Minister replied that there was no technical expert amongst the airmen. They knew nothing about the bombs except what was involved in the external handling of them. His government could not reach any conclusion as to whether or not the bombs had been dropped by the crew mentioned in the *aide-mémoire* nor could they do so until they knew the exact composition of the bombs. From the description received they had to come to the conclusion that the bombs were partly of German and partly of non-German origin. This made it all the more necessary to have expert examination of the fragments. I explained to the Minister that we could not send the fragments to Germany. Our bags took at least two months to reach Berlin, and, he could imagine what might happen on the way to a bag with such obviously suspicious contents. Neither could I see how it would be possible for experts from Germany to come to this country without causing all kinds of difficulties to arise. I urged upon the Minister that he should suggest to his Government to put all the necessary questions in detail to him and that we should get our experts to answer them. We should be very glad to leave him the bomb fragments and photographs with all the details his Government required. As a matter of fact, the Secretary of the Legation had received all the information during his discussion with our Army experts before the minister's communication to Berlin.

Dr. Hempel insisted that there could be no satisfactory conclusion to the affair until the fragments had been examined by the experts of his Government.

I suggested to Dr. Hempel that, quite independently of the ultimate findings, it was advisable to secure the agreement of his Government to some sort of interim public announcement. The feelings of our people would be allayed when they saw that the German Government had made the serious admission of the presence of the plane on the night of 1-2 January, especially when it was accompanied by an assurance that investigations would be continued. I asked him, furthermore, to point out to his Government that the evidence of a crew

---

[1] A number of Luftwaffe personnel were by this stage of the war interned in the military camp at the Curragh, Co Kildare, their aircraft having crash-landed on Irish territory.

which had lost its way after a bombing expedition could not be completely trusted. Their bombing racks might have got loose and the bombs might have been dropped without the crew being aware of it in the noise and confusion. The lights the crew saw were clearly those of Dublin, and, as there was only one plane over Dublin that night, the bombs must have come from the German plane.

[initialled] J.P.W.

No. 417 NAI DFA Secretary's Files P12/14/1

> *Confidential report from John W. Dulanty to Joseph P. Walshe (Dublin)*
> *(No. 1) (Secret)*
>
> LONDON, 30 January 1941

1. I took a well informed friend to dinner last night when we had a fairly lengthy conversation. I said that recent events suggested, to put it no higher, that the attitude of the British toward us had undergone a change for the worse. From our recent experience in connection with shipping, petrol, dollar facilities, and navicerts, it would appear that whilst the British were ready to accept our help in a variety of ways they now showed no inclination to reciprocate. Indeed it looked as though they had adopted a policy, if not of active opposition, of indifferentism. I went into some detail quoting incidents under each of the various headings, stressing that of the dollar question, where we were not dependent upon understandings but British Treasury letters in black and white.

2. He said I was absolutely wrong. Taking first the question of shipping, the British were in the position that while the Germans have now 2,000 miles of coast line, and an increasing fleet of submarines with a far longer reach than in 1914-18 they (the British) had, even with the American lendings, a destroyer strength materially below that of 1917-18. The War Cabinet were of opinion that whoever was running the German submarine campaign was very good at his job. On my remarking that their shipping losses within the last few weeks showed a decline he said there were not today so many ships afloat but the really big feature of the problem was that the Admiralty were seizing every vessel on which they could lay hands for transport of troops and supplies – the variety, bulk, and weight of the latter being immense. Obviously if they could wind up their battle with the Italians it would be a most potent factor in the evolution of the war and for that reason the Government had given the Admiralty super-priority in shipping.

3. They were hoping that they would get some help from America. Whilst the shipping pool there was not entirely dried up there were not today many ships available. If an American shipowner sells a ship which involves transfer of flag he has to give an undertaking that he will replace the tonnage which he has sold. Some American shipowners were not ready to give this undertaking but those who were so willing sold their ships at a price which naturally reflected this undertaking. Yet even at soaring prices the British were most anxious to buy and he doubted whether their buyers would let any opportunity slip to get vessels.

4. Their dollar position he described as extremely worrying. They were trying all the time to keep a small reserve but they were very apprehensive about the future. They had requisitioned all dollar securities in this country. They had used their gold reserve and they did not feel that they could go and throw themselves on the mercy of the Americans – though if the situation did not improve they might have to do that.

5. The truth was that they had seriously interfered with the national economy of many countries not in the war at all. The Willingdon[1] Mission to South America was of course meant to maintain their South American trade connections but it was also meant as a point of equal importance to act as a soothing of the South American States for the interference which arose from (a) the deliberate policy of blockade and (b) the facts of the war apart from the blockade. It seemed to him that we, like these far-away countries, had inevitably come into the arena of the war and its unavoidable interference.

6. Whilst no one could foretell the course the war might take he thought that they had not seen the full force of the German submarines but would soon be subjected to an even more intensive campaign. When the weather improved their experts thought there would be aerial bombardment of Britain on a far bigger scale than heretofore. These two war processes would be followed by an attempt at invasion. Napoleon waited for years at Boulogne saying that he could see a hundred ways of getting into England but not one way to get out. He cared for his soldiers. Hitler had no such feeling. His army was now the biggest the world had ever known and the loss of half a million or even more men would not deter him.

7. He knew the Prime Minister's mind and I could tell my Government that the British had never taken any step for the purpose of embarrassing us. Thus as in certain ways 'the fell clutch of circumstance' caught us so it caught them. They were carrying the strain of the biggest war in history and the measures they adopted had one object, and one object only, the defeat of their enemy.

8. I said it was unfortunate to find so many people in this country who still looked upon Ireland in much the same way as diehards of pre-1914 did. If we were not 'lesser breeds without the law' as the old Jingoes declared, many people, including some young lions of Fleet Street, regarded us as though we were their property. My friend said this was partially true. Only a few days ago he had been discussing our position with three Back Benchers who seemed to think that Mr. de Valera ought to bring the Irish people into the war. 'I told them', he said, 'that without going back to Cromwell the history of the relations between the two countries in our own time made it impossible for Mr. de Valera or anyone else who was at the head of the Irish Government to abandon neutrality'.

9. I referred, as I had done in a previous conversation with him, to Mr. Churchill's reference to the ports. He again said that he thought that statement in Parliament was unfortunate. In passing I may mention that I put the same point to Mr. W.P. Crozier, the Editor of the 'Manchester Guardian', who took

---

[1] Freeman Freeman-Thomas, 1st Marquess of Willingdon (1866-1941), Governor General of Canada (1926-31), Viceroy of India (1931-6).

exactly the same view as my friend adding that the same opinion had been expressed to him by several people here in London. I could not obviously very well ask him who the people were but as I know he is in personal touch with people of political importance here it is reasonable to assume that it was people of that type who expressed the opinion.

10. My friend having said that there were frequent differences of opinion between the British and the Dominions I thought it well to talk to the High Commissioners for South Africa, New Zealand and Australia.

11. Mr. Waterson[1] told me that the 30,000 tons of shipping for their fruit trade which had been agreed upon between the British and his Government at the beginning of the war was reduced not long ago to 10,000 tons of shipping. On his making representations he secured an increase from 10 to 20,000 tons. Within a week of that arrangement being made and without any reference to him Lord Woolton made an announcement which meant they were refused the 20,000 tons. In consequence of this the South African Government had to take over all the fruit and with heavy subsidies were now having it canned for export when ships might be available. Their dollar position was not unsatisfactory. They had always had a big transatlantic trade and they had an ample gold reserve. Their petrol, which came from Persia, did not present any serious difficulty.

12. The British Government, Mr. Jordan[2] informed me, had entered into a formal contract with New Zealand to take 140,000 tons of meat each year. They had taken about one-third of this purchase but were unable to move the remainder owing to shortage of ships. The New Zealand Government had taken the line that this was unquestionably a breach of contract and were pressing to be allowed some advance on the meat purchased but not removed from New Zealand. Thus far they have not succeeded in obtaining any such advance. Notwithstanding the fact that they had requisitioned all their dollar credits they were short of dollars for some time now. They had been unable to buy anything from America, notably Virginia tobacco. They had fortunately laid in big stores of petrol and fertilising materials but their petrol ration was below the standard obtaining in Britain.

13. He, in common with other High Commissioners, complained about the lack of information from the British. At their daily meetings with Lord Cranborne they were given information which invariably was in the newspapers the following day. He had however stressed for some information about the publication of war aims. A Cabinet Committee representing all the political parties had sat for some weeks and had produced a somewhat idealistic picture of a brave new world. The theme of social justice including the abolition of unemployment, and the unqualified recognition of the principle that the employee was to be every bit as important as the employer, loomed largely in this new picture. Mr. Jordan with his strong Labour sympathies enquired whether preparatory steps were now being taken to enable effect to be given to this report when the time came. He gathered that no such steps were being taken and when he asked if he might refer to it in a public speech he had to make at

[1] Sidney Frank Waterson (1896-1976), South African High Commissioner in London (1939-42).
[2] William Joseph Jordan (1879-1959), New Zealand High Commissioner in London (1935-51).

Durham a few days ago he was told that no reference of any kind should be made to the report at present.

14. Mr. Bruce[1] had had the same story to tell. He said they also had a contract with the British Government, theirs being for a quarter of a million tons of meat per year. Here again the British had taken part of their purchase but had said they were unable to remove the rest and admitted a breach of contract. Fifteen ships normally under service between Australia and Great Britain had been withdrawn, with the result that their canned food and their wine industries had been 'completely torpedoed'. This blow had fallen on a Government in Australia which had really no working majority and had caused a state of mind which it was no exaggeration to describe as hysterical. He had made appeals to the British Ministers concerned and had seen the Prime Minister. All he got was regrets but no ships. Their wheat position was no better. A large part of their crop they used to sell in the North Pacific. Here again the necessary ships were to seek. He had himself chartered three Greek vessels but had been told by the British that he could not have them. They were very badly off for dollars. They were ready and willing to buy aeroplanes from America but they had no dollars nor could they get help from the British. Like New Zealand they had put in a big reserve of petrol but they were now on a very low ration and were worried about their future.

15.[2] The breaches of food contracts should be put in juxtaposition with the widening acute shortage of food supplies in this country – the present meat ration, even when it is obtainable, being clearly inadequate.

16. The office staff having gone I have just time to get this note away for the train. On Monday I will send a further note.

[signed] J.W. DULANTY

---

[1] Stanley M. Bruce (1883-1967), Australian High Commissioner in London (1935-45).
[2] Points 15 and 16 handwritten by Dulanty.

Appendix 1
Destruction of files and documents dating from 1938 to 1940 by the Department of External Affairs

On 25 May 1940 Eamon de Valera ordered that files and documents that the Department of External Affairs feared would fall into German hands in the event of a German invasion of Ireland be 'confidentially destroyed' by officials in the Department of External Affairs. The files known to have been destroyed came from the 100-Series and 200-Series general registry files and the entries relating to these files in the departmental file registers were marked with 'CD 25/5/40' against their record. Details of these 'confidentially destroyed' files are given below. The files represent only a small portion of the 100-series and 200-series. There are also large gaps in the 100-series due to files migrating to the subsequent 200-series and from the 200-series into the later 300-series. It is clear from the titles and chronological scope of the destroyed files that they often contained extremely important material and material which is irreplaceable for the historian of Irish foreign policy.

Of these files the most significant are the confidential report files:

1	119/1	Confidential reports from Berlin	14 Jan. 1937-7 Dec. 1938
2	119/2	Confidential reports from Rome	12 Jan. 1937-30 Dec. 1938
3	119/5	Confidential reports from San Francisco	4 Jan. 1937-20 Dec. 1938
4	119/7	Confidential reports from Washington	12 July 1937-3 Jan. 1939
5	119/8	Confidential reports from Paris	18 July 1938-12 Jan. 1939
6	119/8A	Confidential reports from Paris	18 July 1938-12 Jan. 1939
7	119/10	Confidential reports from Geneva	4 Feb. 1937-28 June 1938
8	119/17	Confidential reports from St Jean de Luz	21 Aug. 1937-28 Nov. 1938
9	219/1	Confidential reports from Paris	1939

In many cases it has been possible to locate copies of the documents destroyed in the 'Embassies Series' records for the relevant Legation or in personal papers, but the destruction of the Irish Legation in Berlin during an Allied air raid in November 1943 and the previous destruction in May 1940 of confidential reports from Berlin for 1937 and 1938 has left a large gap in the material reproduced in this volume relating to Irish reporting on events in Germany during the war years. In an effort to partially overcome the loss of the material in file 119/1, section four below reproduces, as taken from the register of correspondence for file 119/1, the topics and subjects of confidential reports from Charles Bewley in Berlin for 1937 and 1938.

It seems likely that considerable portions of what are now known as the Secretary's 'S' Series files were also destroyed in 1940. At the time these files were known as 'Secret' files and were kept in the custody of the Secretary of the Department of External Affairs and the Private Secretary to the Secretary.

Documents on Irish Foreign Policy, Volume VI, 1939–1941

The appendix below is divided into four sections:
1. 100-Series (Sections 101-147). List of files destroyed on 25 May 1940.
2. 200-Series (Sections 201-247). List of files destroyed on 25 May 1940.
3. Other collections of files known to have been destroyed in whole or in part.
4. Titles/Subjects of confidential reports by Charles Bewley contained in 100-Series file 119/1 and destroyed on 25 May 1940.

1   100-Series (Sections 101-147). List of files destroyed on 25 May 1940

1	101/64	Issue of British nationality certificates	1937-8
2	101/228	Proposed legislation dealing with public display or interference with foreign national flags	1938
3	101/324	Polish citizenship laws	1938
4	102/16	Non-recognition of Saorstát Éireann (SÉ) passports by British Consuls abroad	1937
5	102/19	Visa fees and regulations for aliens visiting Irish Free State (IFS)	unknown
6	102/30	Passports withheld for travel to Russia	1937
7	102/31	British suspect – Index list	1937
8	102/31A	British suspect – Index list	1937
9	102/31B	British suspect – Index list	1938-9
10	102/39	IFS citizens desiring British passports	1937-9
11	102/42	Passport and visa fees: Special list 1925-31	1925-31
12	102/55	Prolongation of stay in IFS of certain German nationals	1937-8
13	102/104	SÉ nationals in Germany and German nationals in SÉ	1937-8
14	102/129	Permission for Herr Klaus, German National to remain in SÉ	1937
15	102/205	Case of Abdul Hadi Bey: Palestinian national	1937
16	102/302	Visas: Ireland and Germany/Austria	1938
17	102/302A	Visas: Ireland and Germany/Austria	1938
18	102/302B	Visas: Ireland and Germany/Austria	1938
19	102/408	Case of individuals who arrived at Baldonnell from Austria	1938-9
20	102/427	Permission for German student to attend school in Waterford	1938
21	102/572	Naturalisation of German nationals as Irish citizens	1938-9
22	102/657	Visa to Dr Stefan Lendt	1939
23	105/3	Coronation of King George VI	1937
24	105/5	Coronation of King George VI	1937
25	105/17	Coronation of King George VI	1937
26	105/18	Germany's claim to Colonies	1937
27	105/27	Co-ordination of policy re exhibitions limited to members of the Commonwealth	1937

Destruction of files and documents dating from 1938 to 1940

28	105/79	Visit to Paris of George VI	1938
29	105/83	Arrest and imprisonment of Eamon Donnelly	1938
30	106/13	Hydrographical services in SÉ	1937
31	106/19	Lands occupied by British forces in Ned's fort and vicinity	1937
32	106/20	Norwegian territorial waters	1937
33	106/22	Submarine cables in Cork harbour	1937
34	106/31	Inspection visit by British to SÉ coastal defences	1937
35	106/42	Repairs: Fort Carlisle	1937
36	106/48	Defence of Merchant Shipping	1938
37	106/49	Visit of foreign war vessels and aircraft to British ports	1938
38	111/3	Purchase of ammunition, guns etc from Britain	1937
39	111/4	London Naval Treaty: 1930	1937
40	111/6	Disarmament (Geneva)	1937-8
41	111/18	Small arms factory	1937
42	111/35	Torpedo aircraft	1938
43	115/100	Aircraft factory	1937
44	115/430	Aircraft fuel oil production	1938
45	115/460	Alleged campaign by Jews in Ireland to boycott German goods	11 Apr. 1938
46	116/95	Request for Foreign Office publication dealing with privilege of documents	May 1937
47	117/60	Irish-German political relations	5 Oct. 1938-12 Dec. 1938
48	119/1	Confidential reports from Berlin	14 Jan. 1937-7 Dec.1938
49	119/2	Confidential reports from Rome	12 Jan. 1937-30 Dec. 1938
50	119/5	Confidential reports from San Francisco	4 Jan. 1937-20 Dec. 1938
51	119/7	Confidential reports from Washington	12 July 1937-3 Jan. 1939
52	119/8	Confidential reports from Paris	18 July 1938-12 Jan. 1939
53	119/8A	Confidential reports from Paris	18 July 1938-12 Jan. 1939
54	119/10	Confidential reports from Geneva	4 Feb. 1937-28 June 1938
55	119/17	Confidential reports from St Jean de Luz	21 Aug. 1937-28 Nov. 1938
56	119/38	Bewley interview	17 Mar. 1937
57	119/41	British Consular instructions	20 Sept. 1937-12 Nov. 1937

Documents on Irish Foreign Policy, Volume VI, 1939–1941

58	119/47	Report on work of Berlin Legation 1937-38	4 Apr. 1938
59	119/52	Confidential reports from Rome (Quirinale)	16 May 1938-19 Dec. 1938
60	119/59	Paris: Belgian Foreign policy	20 Oct. 1938-10 Jan. 1939
61	121/20	German overflights of Irish territory	29 Jan. 1937-5 May 1937
62	121/35	Irish Army officers attendance at RAF courses	19 Mar. 1937-30 Apr. 1937
63	121/36	Lufthansa facilities in SÉ for transatlantic flight	1937
64	121/39	Permission for Zeppelin overflights	Mar. 1937
65	121/75	Experimental German transatlantic flights	15 July 1937-12 Nov. 1937
66	121/180	Interdepartmental Committee on Air Raid precautions	Oct. 1938-July 1939
67	121/189	Permission for George Charles Avon to enlist in RAF	Dec. 1938
68	124/64	Re-occupation of the Rhineland	July-Dec. 1937
69	127/66	Blockade of Germany during 1914-18 War	13 July 1937
70	127/140	Agreements between Hungary and the Little Entente	24 Aug. 1938
71	127/145	Irish Friends of the Spanish republic: non-intervention	19 Oct. 1938
72	127/147	Germany's claim to Colonies	25 Oct. 1938
73	130/7	London: Electric Power invention of A. J. Haldane	17 Feb. 1937-18 Mar. 1937
74	134/48	Communication from Mr Richard Monahan MD, Switzerland	10 Sept. 1937
75	134/58	Political situation in Germany (1938)	Feb. 1938
76	135/21	Important public functions in UK: measures to prevent landings of undesirable aliens	1937
77	138/50	Position of the Church in Germany	1937
78	138/221	Position of Dr Mahr, National Museum, in connection with his membership of the Nazi Party	Aug. 1938
79	141/14	General O'Duffy's Irish Brigade for Spain and other volunteers from Ireland	1937-8
80	141/70	Desertion of Private R. Stringer from Irish Army and charge for wearing British uniform	1938
81	141/71	Private Looby, Irish Army Reservist, application for enlistment in RAF	1938
82	141/74	Particulars of service of Private Thomas Franklin in Irish Army	1938

Destruction of files and documents dating from 1938 to 1940

83	141/94	Enquiry of Commander K. Mitchell MVO re posts for ex RN officers in Irish services	Aug.-Nov. 1938
84	141/99	M. Hayes, RAF, position in event of war	1938
85	141/112	Communication re National Defence and Recruiting	Oct. 1938
86	144/7	Resolutions for release of Irish political prisoners in SÉ	1937-8
87	144/41	Enquiry re John Scanlon, former Flight Sergeant RAF	July 1938
88	144/49	Application of Civic Guard for post in Palestine Police	1938

2 200-Series (Sections 201-247). List of files destroyed on 25 May 1940

1	202/12	Permits for admission of German and Austrian nationals to Ireland
2	202/13	Issue of visas for Ireland by British consuls
3	202/19	British suspect list
4	202/19A	British suspect list
5	202/19B	British suspect list
6	202/50	Issue of passports by British representatives in countries where there are Irish representatives
7	202/71	Theft of passports from the Imperial Iranian Legation at Berlin
8	202/75	Siemens Ireland Ltd, employment of aliens
9	202/77	Copies of visas for the United Kingdom issued by British passport control officers, Paris, to Germans who will probably visit Ireland
10	202/89	Ernest Klaar: suspect false visa application
11	202/93	Mutual abolition of visas, agreement with Czechoslovakia
12	202/111	Palestinian visa regulations (original file destroyed)
13	202/118	Procedures regulating visas for alien refugees in Ireland who wish to proceed to Britain and dominions or colonies
14	202/135	Visa certificates of origin for Turkey
15	202/136	Passport visa requirements of foreign countries
16	202/149	Alien refugees: channel of enquiry
17	202/156	Iraqi visa and passport requirements
18	202/199	Helmut Joseph, visa application
19	202/53	Facilities for renewal of passports of Irish citizens
20	202/311	Alleged unauthorised issue of passports to persons desirous of leaving Germany
21	202/408	Alois Ludwig Rutter and Bertha Rutter, visa application
22	202/550	Transjordan nationals: visas and passports for Transjordan
23	202/709	Aliens employed by Irish Sugar Company
24	202/842	Reciprocal check between British and Irish authorities on the issue of visas to aliens
25	205/4	Press comments in Germany on Irish affairs

Documents on Irish Foreign Policy, Volume VI, 1939–1941

26	205/12	Messages of greeting to King George (first part confidentially destroyed)
27	205/77	Alleged meeting of protest of Irish republicans at Hotel Seville in New York, July 1935, against policy of government of Éire
28	206/39	Seaplane floats observed by SS *Hibernia* off Kish lightship
29	206/42	Fisheries vessel *Fort Rannoch*
30	206/59	Supply of Admiralty charts
31	206/61	Transfer to German ownership of MV *Sophia*
32	207/60	German-Romanian commercial agreement
33	208/76	Deportation from Ireland of Germans (some papers destroyed)
34	211/1A	Brandt mortar and ammunition, importation from France
35	214/8	Information re Irish affairs in German press
36	216/24	British government war establishment. Publications from Dept of Defence
37	218/31	Position of former consul and staff of Czechoslovak consulate in Dublin
38	219/1	Confidential Reports, Paris, 1939
39	219/1A	Anglo-American luncheon, Paris
40	219/1B	Germany's peace proposals
41	220/8	Customs facilities for Czechoslovak consul (papers prior to 25 May 1940 destroyed)
42	220/75	Entry duty free for Czechoslovak consul (papers prior to 25 May 1940 destroyed)
43	227/22	European situation: temporary file (first part confidentially destroyed)
44	232/77	International tobacco congress under auspices of International Federation of Technical Agriculturalists
45	233/13	Transfer of wireless stations from British to Irish government
46	241/1	Facilities in connection with visits of Irish Army officers to British Admiralty
47	241/8	Visits of officers of Dept of Defence to London in connection with purchase of gas masks and ARP equipment
48	241/18	Purchase of stores by Dept of Defence from British War Office
49	241/37	Course for gas detection officers
50	241/71	Direct correspondence on technical matters between Dept of Defence and Woolwich Inspection Officers
51	241/91	Position of civil servants and employees of local authorities who wish to join the Irish Defence Forces and also Reserves in the British Army
52	241/99	Visit of Irish Army officers to War Office
53	241/120	Enquiry by Commanding Officer Irish Guards re Michael McArdle

Destruction of files and documents dating from 1938 to 1940

3 **Other collections of files known to have been destroyed in whole or in part**
1 S Series Secretary's Files (an unknown quantity of these files was destroyed)
2 Berlin Legation (RAF raid, Nov. 1943)
3 London High Commissioner's Office (shredding in the 1950s due to water damage)
4 Washington Legation (unknown reason)
5 Geneva Office (some confidential files for 1939-40 destroyed by Frank Cremins)

4 **Titles/Subjects of confidential reports by Charles Bewley contained on file 119/1 and destroyed on 25 May 1940**

Headquarters file reference	Date	Berlin Reference	Subject/Title
119/1	14 Jan. 1937	43/33	German troops in Spanish Morocco
119/1	26 Jan. 1937	43/33	Political report – European Situation
119/1	5 Feb. 1937	43/33	Reminders re letters of 14th and 26th January
119/1	8 Feb. 1937	43/33	Position of Ambassador von Ribbentrop
119/1	15 Feb. 1937	43/33	Reminder re letters of 26th January and 5th February – instructions re SÉ govt's position vis-à-vis Spanish Civil War
119/1	5 Mar. 1937	43/33	Instructions re SÉ govt's position vis-à-vis the Spanish Civil War
119/1	5 Mar. 1937	43/33	German claim for colonies
119/1	14 Apr. 1937	43/33	Relations between German govt and Catholic Church
119/1	25 May 1937	43/33	New govt in Valencia: English proposals for truce in Spain
119/1	4 June 1937	43/33	Germany's attitude to UK and France in connection with Spain
119/1	18 June 1937	43/33	Coronation picture shown under patronage of Ambassador of Great Britain and Ireland
119/1	23 June 1937	43/33	General political report
119/1	7 July 1937	43/33	Question of colonies and raw materials
119/1	23 Aug. 1937	43/33	Expulsion of an English journalist Mr Ebbuth from Germany
119/1	16 Sept. 1937	43/33	German Policy: Nuremberg Parteitag
119/1	20 Sept. 1937	43/33	General European situation
119/1	8 Oct. 1937	43/33	Reference to colonial question in Hitler's speech at harvest thanksgiving
119/1	11 Oct. 1937	43/33	Results of visit of Mussolini to Berlin: summing up of 'BZ am Mittag'
119/1	28 Oct. 1937	43/33	Political report

Documents on Irish Foreign Policy, Volume VI, 1939–1941

119/1	15 Nov. 1937	43/33	Adhesion of Italy to German-Japanese pact
119/1	13 Dec. 1937	43/33	Relations between Germany, Italy and Japan
119/1	31 Jan. 1938	43/33	Visit of Yugoslav Minister President Stojadanovic to Germany
119/1	7 Feb. 1938	43/33	Changes in German Army command, Govt and Diplomatic corps
119/1	14 Feb. 1938	43/33	Reports in Foreign Press re 'crisis' in Germany
119/1	21 Feb. 1938	43/33	Chancellor's Reichstag speech, Feb. '38
119/1	11 Mar. 1938	43/33	Announcement of plebiscite in Austria
119/1	14 Mar. 1938	43/33	Austria – intervention by Germany
119/1	18 Mar. 1938	43/33	Austria – report re
119/1	1 Apr. 1938	43/33	Austria – report re
119/1	13 Apr. 1938	43/33	Austria – report re result of plebiscite
119/1	25 Apr. 1938	43/33	Successful termination of English-Italian negotiations
119/1	3 May 1938	43/33	German–Czechoslovakia situation
119/1	1 June 1938	43/33	German–Czechoslovakia situation report re
119/1	2 June 1938	43/33	German–Czechoslovakia situation report re
119/1	28 June 1938	43/33	International situation
119/1	9 July 1938	43/33	German minority in Czechoslovakia – copy of 'Volkabund'
119/1	29 July 1938	43/33	Position of the Sudeten Germans
119/1	14 Sept. 1938	43/33	Check of false news disseminated by press: mention of Taoiseach
119/1	22 Sept. 1938	43/33	Article entitled 'Hitler's Germany provides work for them'
119/1	28 Sept. 1938	25/32	*City of Limerick* not landing its cargo at Bremen
119/1	12 Oct. 1938		Anti-Jewish feeling in Czechoslovakia
119/1	27 Oct. 1938	10/34.	Regulations governing admission of Jews into Germany
119/1	18 Nov. 1938	76/36	Anti-British article in Borsen-Zeitung ref Black and Tan period in Ireland
119/1	30 Nov. 1938	13/38	German press on British atrocities in Palestine
119/1	7 Dec. 1938	Confid.	re dinner to Mr Pirow – report re
119/1	1 Feb. 1939	43/33	Hitler's speech in the Reichstag 30 Jan. 1937
119/1	1 Mar. 1939	43/33	General political report

Appendix 2

Months of the year in Irish and English

Irish   *English*

Irish	English
Eanair	January
Feabhra	February
Márta	March
Aibreán	April
Bealtaine	May
Meitheamh	June
Iúil	July
Lúnasa	August
Meán Fómhair	September
Deireadh Fómhair	October
Samhain	November
Mí na Nollag	December

Appendix 3

Glossary of Irish words and phrases

This list was compiled with the help of the Royal Irish Academy's Foclóir na nua-Ghaeilge project. Details of the editorial conventions on the reproduction of Irish language material are given in the introduction

Aire	Minister
Aire Lán-Chómhachtach	Minister Plenipotentiary
Ard-Fheis	Convention
A chara	Dear Sir/Madam (literally: Friend)
A chara dhílis	Dear Sir/Madam (literally: Dear friend)
a.s. Rúnaí (ar son Rúnaí)	p.p. Secretary
Do chara/Mise, do Chara	Yours sincerely (literally: Your friend)
Dáil	the Lower House of the Irish parliament
A dhíl/A dhílis	Dear (salutation)
Garda Síochána	Police (literally: Guardians of the Peace)
Le mór mheas/le meas mór	With much respect
Is Mise, le meas/Mise, le meas	With respect
Príomh-Aturnae	Attorney General
Rúnaí/Rúnaidhe	Secretary
Saorstát	Free State
Saorstát Éireann/An Saorstát	Irish Free State
Sinn Féin	Sinn Féin (political party) (literally: ourselves)
Teachta Dála (TD)	Dáil deputy
Uachtarán	President

Appendix 4
List of Irish Missions Abroad: 1939-1941

Britain (opened 1922)
Occupant	*Post*	*Dates*
John W. Dulanty	High Commissioner	1930-49

League of Nations (opened 1923, closed 1940)
Occupant	*Post*	*Dates*
Francis T. Cremins	Permanent Delegate to the League of Nations	1934-40

United States of America
Washington DC (opened 1924)
Occupant	*Post*	*Dates*
Robert Brennan	Minister Plenipotentiary and Envoy Extraordinary	1938-47

Boston (opened 1929)
Occupant	*Post*	*Dates*
Percy Galwey-Foley	Consul-General	1929-43

New York (opened 1930)
Occupant	*Post*	*Dates*
Leo T. McCauley	Consul General	1934-46

San Francisco (opened 1933)
Occupant	*Post*	*Dates*
Matthew Murphy	Consul General	1933-47

Chicago (opened 1934)
Occupant	*Post*	*Dates*
Daniel McGrath	Consul-General	1934-42

France (opened 1929)
Occupant	*Post*	*Dates*
Seán Murphy	Minister Plenipotentiary and Envoy Extraordinary	1938-50

Holy See (opened 1929)
Occupant	*Post*	*Dates*
William J.B. Macaulay	Minister Plenipotentiary and Envoy Extraordinary	1934-40
Thomas J. Kiernan	Minister Plenipotentiary and Envoy Extraordinary	1941-46

Documents on Irish Foreign Policy, Volume VI, 1939–1941

Germany (opened 1929)

Occupant	Post	Dates
William Warnock	Chargé d'Affaires ad-interim	1939-43

Belgium (opened 1931)[1]

Occupant	Post	Dates
Seán Murphy	Minister	1938-50

Spain (opened 1935)

Occupant	Post	Dates
Leopold H. Kerney	Minister Plenipotentiary and Envoy Extraordinary	1935-46

Italy (opened 1938)

Occupant	Post	Dates
Michael MacWhite	Minister Plenipotentiary and Envoy Extraordinary	1938-50

Canada (opened 1939)

Occupant	Post	Dates
John J. Hearne	High Commissioner	1939-49

Switzerland (opened 1940)

Occupant	Post	Dates
Francis T. Cremins	Chargé d'Affaires	1940-49

---

[1] From 1931 the Minister to France also held the non-resident appointment of Minister to Belgium. A resident Minister to Belgium was appointed in December 1949, William P. Fay taking up the appointment in 1950.

Appendix 5
Calendars for years 1939, 1940 and 1941

1939

January
S	M	Tu	W	Th	F	S
1	2	3	4	5	6	7
8	9	10	11	12	13	14
15	16	17	18	19	20	21
22	23	24	25	26	27	28
29	30	31				

February
S	M	Tu	W	Th	F	S
			1	2	3	4
5	6	7	8	9	10	11
12	13	14	15	16	17	18
19	20	21	22	23	24	25
26	27	28				

March
S	M	Tu	W	Th	F	S
			1	2	3	4
5	6	7	8	9	10	11
12	13	14	15	16	17	18
19	20	21	22	23	24	25
26	27	28	29	30	31	

April
S	M	Tu	W	Th	F	S
						1
2	3	4	5	6	7	8
9	10	11	12	13	14	15
16	17	18	19	20	21	22
23	24	25	26	27	28	29
30						

May
S	M	Tu	W	Th	F	S
	1	2	3	4	5	6
7	8	9	10	11	12	13
14	15	16	17	18	19	20
21	22	23	24	25	26	27
28	29	30	31			

June
S	M	Tu	W	Th	F	S
				1	2	3
4	5	6	7	8	9	10
11	12	13	14	15	16	17
18	19	20	21	22	23	24
25	26	27	28	29	30	

July
S	M	Tu	W	Th	F	S
						1
2	3	4	5	6	7	8
9	10	11	12	13	14	15
16	17	18	19	20	21	22
23	24	25	26	27	28	29
30	31					

August
S	M	Tu	W	Th	F	S
		1	2	3	4	5
6	7	8	9	10	11	12
13	14	15	16	17	18	19
20	21	22	23	24	25	26
27	28	29	30	31		

September
S	M	Tu	W	Th	F	S
					1	2
3	4	5	6	7	8	9
10	11	12	13	14	15	16
17	18	19	20	21	22	23
24	25	26	27	28	29	30

October
S	M	Tu	W	Th	F	S
1	2	3	4	5	6	7
8	9	10	11	12	13	14
15	16	17	18	19	20	21
22	23	24	25	26	27	28
29	30	31				

November
S	M	Tu	W	Th	F	S
			1	2	3	4
5	6	7	8	9	10	11
12	13	14	15	16	17	18
19	20	21	22	23	24	25
26	27	28	29	30		

December
S	M	Tu	W	Th	F	S
					1	2
3	4	5	6	7	8	9
10	11	12	13	14	15	16
17	18	19	20	21	22	23
24	25	26	27	28	29	30
31						

1940

January
S	M	Tu	W	Th	F	S
	1	2	3	4	5	6
7	8	9	10	11	12	13
14	15	16	17	18	19	20
21	22	23	24	25	26	27
28	29	30	31			

February
S	M	Tu	W	Th	F	S
				1	2	3
4	5	6	7	8	9	10
11	12	13	14	15	16	17
18	19	20	21	22	23	24
25	26	27	28	29		

March
S	M	Tu	W	Th	F	S
					1	2
3	4	5	6	7	8	9
10	11	12	13	14	15	16
17	18	19	20	21	22	23
24	25	26	27	28	29	30
31						

April
S	M	Tu	W	Th	F	S
	1	2	3	4	5	6
7	8	9	10	11	12	13
14	15	16	17	18	19	20
21	22	23	24	25	26	27
28	29	30				

May
S	M	Tu	W	Th	F	S
			1	2	3	4
5	6	7	8	9	10	11
12	13	14	15	16	17	18
19	20	21	22	23	24	25
26	27	28	29	30	31	

June
S	M	Tu	W	Th	F	S
						1
2	3	4	5	6	7	8
9	10	11	12	13	14	15
16	17	18	19	20	21	22
23	24	25	26	27	28	29
30						

July
S	M	Tu	W	Th	F	S
	1	2	3	4	5	6
7	8	9	10	11	12	13
14	15	16	17	18	19	20
21	22	23	24	25	26	27
28	29	30	31			

August
S	M	Tu	W	Th	F	S
				1	2	3
4	5	6	7	8	9	10
11	12	13	14	15	16	17
18	19	20	21	22	23	24
25	26	27	28	29	30	31

September
S	M	Tu	W	Th	F	S
1	2	3	4	5	6	7
8	9	10	11	12	13	14
15	16	17	18	19	20	21
22	23	24	25	26	27	28
29	30					

October
S	M	Tu	W	Th	F	S
		1	2	3	4	5
6	7	8	9	10	11	12
13	14	15	16	17	18	19
20	21	22	23	24	25	26
27	28	29	30	31		

November
S	M	Tu	W	Th	F	S
					1	2
3	4	5	6	7	8	9
10	11	12	13	14	15	16
17	18	19	20	21	22	23
24	25	26	27	28	29	30

December
S	M	Tu	W	Th	F	S
1	2	3	4	5	6	7
8	9	10	11	12	13	14
15	16	17	18	19	20	21
22	23	24	25	26	27	28
29	30	31				

1941

January
```
S   M   Tu  W   Th  F   S
            1   2   3   4
5   6   7   8   9   10  11
12  13  14  15  16  17  18
19  20  21  22  23  24  25
26  27  28  29  30  31
```

February
```
S   M   Tu  W   Th  F   S
                        1
2   3   4   5   6   7   8
9   10  11  12  13  14  15
16  17  18  19  20  21  22
23  24  25  26  27  28
```

March
```
S   M   Tu  W   Th  F   S
                        1
2   3   4   5   6   7   8
9   10  11  12  13  14  15
16  17  18  19  20  21  22
23  24  25  26  27  28  29
30  31
```

April
```
S   M   Tu  W   Th  F   S
    1   2   3   4   5
6   7   8   9   10  11  12
13  14  15  16  17  18  19
20  21  22  23  24  25  26
27  28  29  30
```

May
```
S   M   Tu  W   Th  F   S
                1   2   3
4   5   6   7   8   9   10
11  12  13  14  15  16  17
18  19  20  21  22  23  24
25  26  27  28  29  30  31
```

June
```
S   M   Tu  W   Th  F   S
1   2   3   4   5   6   7
8   9   10  11  12  13  14
15  16  17  18  19  20  21
22  23  24  25  26  27  28
29  30
```

July
```
S   M   Tu  W   Th  F   S
    1   2   3   4   5
6   7   8   9   10  11  12
13  14  15  16  17  18  19
20  21  22  23  24  25  26
27  28  29  30  31
```

August
```
S   M   Tu  W   Th  F   S
                        1   2
3   4   5   6   7   8   9
10  11  12  13  14  15  16
17  18  19  20  21  22  23
24  25  26  27  28  29  30
31
```

September
```
S   M   Tu  W   Th  F   S
    1   2   3   4   5   6
7   8   9   10  11  12  13
14  15  16  17  18  19  20
21  22  23  24  25  26  27
28  29  30
```

October
```
S   M   Tu  W   Th  F   S
            1   2   3   4
5   6   7   8   9   10  11
12  13  14  15  16  17  18
19  20  21  22  23  24  25
26  27  28  29  30  31
```

November
```
S   M   Tu  W   Th  F   S
                        1
2   3   4   5   6   7   8
9   10  11  12  13  14  15
16  17  18  19  20  21  22
23  24  25  26  27  28  29
30
```

December
```
S   M   Tu  W   Th  F   S
    1   2   3   4   5   6
7   8   9   10  11  12  13
14  15  16  17  18  19  20
21  22  23  24  25  26  27
28  29  30  31
```

Index

This volume is indexed by page number and should be used in conjunction with the list of documents reproduced (pp xxxiv-lv). The term 'Anglo-Irish', though now superseded by 'British-Irish', has been used in this volume.

A
ABC, 170, 187
Abetz, Otto, 345
Abwehr, 340n
Abyssinia, 74, 214, 288
Action Française, 289, 318n
Adams, Professor V.G.S., 331
Admiralty, British, 43, 46, 48, 153, 289, 454
  Bremen statement, 117
  Irish Sea mined, 307
  liaison sought, 44–5
  Oran affair, 294
  and Treaty ports, 149–52
advertising, 29
Africa, 250
Agar, Professor William M., 404
agriculture, 196, 227, 358
  Anglo-Irish talks, 194, 195, 202, 308–9
  bacon exports, 166
Agriculture, Department of, 165, 168, 356n, 445
  exports to Germany, 182
  and German blockade, 329–30
Agriculture, Ministry of, UK, 169, 186, 189, 335
Aiken, Frank, Minister for Co-ordination of Defensive Measures, 266, 267, 270, 315, 360, 424
  Boland memo on German Note, 354–5
  invasion contingencies, 443
  memo on British Army liaison meeting, 317
Air Ministry, UK, 225, 330n, 331, 332
Air Raid Precautions Act, 1939, 445
air raids, 11, 206–7, 338, 445
  on Britain, 228, 233, 242, 361, 406, 416, 455
  blitz, 319, 320, 368–9, 380–1, 390
  plans for, 215
  on Germany, 39–40, 214, 229, 242, 351, 381, 383, 420
  shelters, 368–9

air warfare, 46, 226. *see also* Luftwaffe; Royal Air Force
  defences against, 220–1
  forced landings, 72
  Irish airspace restrictions, 23–4
  overflights, 3, 44–5
  protection of aerodromes, 220–1, 223
  radio projectors, 380–1
  repatriations, 51
  shipping attacked, 73
aircraft, 50, 57, 338
  British production, 242–3, 282
  for coast watching, 44
  German landing request, *418–19, 419–20*
  Irish shortages, 16–17, 201–2
  pilot training, 334
  transatlantic, 136, 161–2, 372–3, 403
  from USA, 231, 291, 405, 440
Aircraft Production, Ministry of, 365n
Aitken, Sir Max (Lord Beaverbrook), 334, 338
Albania, 400
Albert Canal, 208n
Alexander, Douglas, 275n
Alexandria, 93, 287
Algeria, 287n, 394
Alibert, Raphaël, 441
Aliens Act, 1935, 188
All Souls College, Oxford, 331
Altmark incident, 158–9, 180
American Association for the Recognition of the Irish Republic (AARIR), 108n
  de Valera telegram to, 384
American Congress for the Unity and Independence of Ireland, 322
American Embassy, Berlin, 430, 441
American Embassy, Berne, 415
American Embassy, Paris, 246, 344
American Embassy, Rome, 197–8
American Export Airlines, 161–2
American Express Company, 206

475

American Foreign Service, 435
American League for an Undivided
    Ireland, 322
American Legation, Dublin
    Gray-Walshe talk, 387–9
Amsterdam, 71
Åndalsnes, 228n, 229
Anderson, Sir John, 1st Viscount
    Waverly, 120
Andrews, John Miller, 416
Anglo-Egyptian Treaty of Alliance,
    1936, 18n
Anglo-French-Turkish Agreement, 74,
    76
Anglo-Irish relations, 34, 279, 299, 300,
    304, 378. *see also* Anglo-Irish trade;
    Treaty ports
    British Army liaison talks, 315
    British invasion possible, 234, 261,
        296, 299, 303
    denied, 305–7, 309–10
    guarantee against, 320–1
    Maffey disclaimer, 373–5
    British press on Ireland, 72, 274–5,
        280–1, 294–7, 299, 301, 305–6, 308,
        311, 316, 320–1, 416–17, 455
    co-operation proposals, 217–26,
        266–7, 271–2, 278–9, 280–1
    rejection, 281–3
    de Valera-MacDonald talks, 234–44,
        252–60, 269–70
    diplomatic representation, 12
    German invasion possible, 269–70,
        294–6, 448–50, 451
    German reports on, 333–4
    Ireland seeks munitions, 144
    Irish diplomatic representation,
        15–16, 35–6, 61, 71, 119, 132, 133
    Maffey, 37
    title of, 42, 43, 45–7
    Irish neutrality, 18–20, 33–4, 53, 293,
        365
    Irish territorial waters, 23–4
    IRA bombing campaign, 89, 119–21,
        127–8, 152, 157–8, 181
    IRA executions, 140–1, 142–3, 154,
        155–6
        de Valera appeal, *145*, 146
        reasons for, 152–3
    McDaid interview, 433
    offers on NI, 275–7
    pressure on neutrality, 289–92

use of Foynes, 50
Walshe visits Eden, 15–20
Anglo-Irish trade, 1. *see also*
    transhipment
    discussions, 167–70
    Eden talks, 202–3
    essential supplies, 47–8
    and German blockade, 325–30,
        348–50
    German suspicion on, 93
    Germany and Irish re-exports, 184
    memo on, 165–6
    talks, 175–6, 186, 192–3, 305–6,
        308–10, 335–6, 356–9, 416
        Boland on, 360–1
        draft agreement, 363–4, 390
        minutes of, 193–7
        Terms of Reference, 189–90
Anglo-Irish Trade Agreement, 1938, 193
Anglo-Irish Treaty, 1921, 150
Angoulême, 248
Ankara pact, 74n
Anschluss, Austria, 22, 97
Anthropological Expedition, Harvard,
    110
anti-aircraft guns, 44, 256, 258, 311
anti-Comintern pact, 75
anti-Partition campaign, 17, 121–2,
    148, 181, 272–7, 378
    Chamberlain on, 210
    and Eden, 19, 202–3
    effects on neutrality, 86
    Gray supports, 167, 168
    sidelined, 101
    in Spain, 171, 178–9
    and trade talks, 192
    and Treaty ports, 150–1
    in USA, 141, 162, 322, 384
anti-Semitism, 67, 104, 133
    France, 275, 346, 409
Antrobus, Maurice E., 149, 271
Antwerp, 101, 224
Arcachon, Gironde, 318
Archer, Colonel Liam, 72, 320
    Irish co-operation talks, 217–26
    letters to Walshe, 297, 414–15
    memo of Walshe conversation, 386
Arensberg, Conrad M., 110n
Argentine, 62, 68, 173, 326, 446
Argentine Embassy, Berne, 415
Ark Royal, HMS, 73
Armistice Day, 1939, 88

Index

arms. *see* munitions
Army Comrades Association (Blueshirts), 232n
Ascain, 325
  evacuation to, 248–9
Associated Press (AP), 92, 94, 405, 428, 432
Athenia (liner), 97
Athlone, Co Westmeath, 184
  army HQ, 297
  broadcasting, 11, 379
  short-wave station, 78
Athlone, Major General Alexander C., 1st Earl of, 264, 265
Atlantic theatre, 151, 386
Au Pilori, 346
Australia, 20, 88, 142, 276, 307, 308–9, 456
  British trade, 457
Austria, 6, 32, 175, 345
  Anschluss, 22, 97
  South Tyrol, 135
Avenol, Joseph, 62n, 309, 377
Avro Anson monoplane, 16

B
Baden, 184
Balbo, Italo, 75, 173
Balby, Léon, 9
Baldonnell aerodrome, 220, 225
Balfour, Captain Harold, 89
Balkan States, 32, 76, 77, 176, 177, 400, 415
  Italian interest in, 113
  safety of, 173–4, 175, 192
Ballygireen radio station, Co Clare, 379
Ballymitty, Co Wexford, 339
Ballymurrin, Co Wexford, 426
Ballyshannon, Co Donegal, 297n
Baltic States, 9, 57, 60, 273
  and Germany, 97, 134
  and League of Nations, 108, 118
  and Russia, 70, 87–8, 105–6
  timber exports, 93, 184
Baltimore, 440
Baltimore Sun, 100
Baltrusaitis, Jurgis, 70n
Banco Hispano Americano, Madrid, 79, 80
Bannow Bay, Co Wexford, 339
Bantry, Co Cork, 101

Barcelona, 123
Barnes, Peter, 119–21, 140–1, 152–3
  de Valera appeal, 142–3, *145*, 146
  execution, 162, 183
    effects of, 154, 155–6
  reprieve efforts, 146–9
  sentence, 127–8
Barry, Thomas, 148
Basel, 22, 427
Basque region, 178
Basutoland, 20n
Bate, Fred, 295
Battersea Power Station, London, 368
'Battle of Britain', 330n, 380n
Baudoin, Paul, 250, 251, 283, 318
  Oran affair, 287, 288
Bauer, Robert, 182
Bay of Biscay, 56, 362n
BBC, 191, 267, 295
Beaverbrook, Lord, 334, 338
Bechuanaland Protectorate, 20n
Becker, Heinrich, 259
Beckett, Frank, 318–19, 363
Beckett, Samuel, 318–19, 363
  letter to O'Kelly (facsimile), 447
Beigbeder Atienza, Juan, 26–7, 98, 99, 124–5, 170–1, 187
Belfast, 234, 320, 362, 365
Belfast Lough, 361
Belgian Embassy, Madrid, 382n
Belgium, 11, 89, 94, 241, 259, 268, 294, 429
  and blockades, 349
  embassy expelled from Spain, 382n
  French aid sought, 203
  government in exile, 248
  invasion of, 208, 211, 214, 216, 235–6, 244, 284, 330, 369, 437, 443–4
    British losses, 229, 252, 291
    de Valera on, 212, 233
    expected, 88, 174, 177, 192
    German reaction, 214
    Note, 448
    speed of, 228, 238
    surrender, 227
  Irish diplomatic relations, 132
  and League of Nations, 118
  meteorological reports, 403
  mobilisation, 54–5
  neutrality, 9, 30, 49, 51, 54, 55, 201, 209, 289–90
  refugees, 188–9

US aid sought, 332
War Trade Agreements, 328
Belgrade, 173
Belloc, Hilaire, 274
Beneš, Edvard, 83
Berardis, Vincenzo, 436–7
Berehaven, Co Cork, 45, 59, 221, 412.
    see also Treaty ports
    strategic importance of, 56–8
Bergen, 200
Berle, Adolf Augustus, 92, 452
Berlin, 66, 113, 115, 453
    air raids, 229, 351, 383, 420
    blackout, 25
    British women arrested, 104
    Christmas, 1939, 129–31
    German administration, 288, 342, 355, 406, 423, 424, 425
    Irish colony, 382
    living conditions, 26, 106, 134
    Molotov visit, 390, 400
Berlin, Irving, 350
Berlin Legation, 5–6, 84–5, 354, 382, 416, 442, 443. *see also* Warnock, William
    air-raid shelter, 25
    communication with, 227, 229
    food shortages, 134
    German bombs dropped in Ireland, 370, 453
    German-Irish relations, 67–8, 71, 76, 141–2, 191
    report, 1939-40, 181–5
    St Patrick's Day, 165
    tenancy, 68, 185
Berlin University, 183
Berliner Börsen-Zeitung, 333–4
Berne, 88, 171, 187, 438
    Cremins in, 371–2, 391–2
    Legation proposed, 370–1
Berne Legation, 371–2, 450
Berriedale-Keith, Professor Arthur, 20
Bertoli, Monsignor, 343–4, 346
Bessarabia, 88, 174
Bettystown, Co Meath, 348
Beurgerbrau bomb, 89
Bevan, Aneurin, 417
Bewley, Charles, 67, 382
B&I Line, 234
Biarritz, 249
Bidassoa, river, 337n

Bird, Major General Sir Wilkinson D., 58, 59
Birmingham, 416
    Barnes and Richards trial, 127–8
    executions, 155–6, 157
Bismarck, Otto von, 285
blackouts, 21, 221, 263, 338
    Germany, 25, 40, 78, 130
    invasion contingencies, 445
Blackrock College, 383n
Blitz, 215, 319, 320, 368–9, 380–1, 390
blockades. *see* Britain: German blockade of
Bloom, Sol, 13
Board of Trade, UK, 46, 170, 308, 335
Bohemia, 97, 164, 165
Boland, Frederick H., 423, 425
    correspondence
        Brady, 360–1
        Coyne, 436–7
        Kerney, 24
        MacWhite, 114–15, 119
        O'Connell (facsimile), *359*
        Warnock, 13–14, 41, 67–8, 68–9, 71, 76–7
    memos by
        to Aiken, 354–5
        invasion contingencies, 442–4
        to Walshe, 131–2, 400–1
    minutes from
        broadcasts, 71
        to Sheila Murphy, 80–1
        to Walshe, 143–4
    note on DEA memo, 448
Bolin, Luis, 187
Bonnet, Georges-Étienne, 70, 289
Bordeaux, 248–9, 268, 273, 337, 352, 362
Borris, Co Carlow, bombed, 422, 426
Boston, 108–10
Boston College, 110
Boston Globe, 405, 439
Boston Post, 439
Boulogne, 228, 414, 455
Boulton-Paul Defiant aircraft, 380, 381
Boycott, A.G., 58
Brady, H.C.
    note from Boland, 360–1
Brandt munitions firm, 144, 367
Bratislava, 81
Bremen, 182, 437
    air raids, 351
    broadcasts, 183–4

Index

Bremen (liner), 117
Bren carriers, 311
Bren guns, 202, 252
Brennan, Robert, 339, 396
 aide mémoire to Hull, 74
 correspondence
  Scott, 322
  Walshe, 91–2, 162, 445–6
 reports to Walshe, 10–11, 12, 13, 103, 125, 211, 216–17, 332–3
  Boston visit, 108–10
  British prospects, 277, 286, 314–15
  lack of communication, 34–5
  US attitudes to war, 20, 230–1, 350, 404–6
  US-Japan relations, 99–100
 telegrams
  DEA, 299, 305, 350
  Hearne, 385
  Walshe, 60, 62, 94, 95, 292–3, 387, 395, 412, 451
  anti-Irish propaganda, 303
  Gray, 399
  Irish neutrality, 394–5, 429–30
  Treaty ports, 384, 393, 408, 411–12, 413–14, 417
  US loan, 445, 451–2
Brenner Pass meeting, 177, 179
Breslau, 437
Brest, 58
Bristol, 274, 416
Bristol Channel, 336, 361
Britain, 10, 20, 24, 25, 65, 87, 94, 97, 126, 130, 388. *see also* Anglo-Irish relations; anti-Partition campaign; Treaty ports
 and conscription, 112
 First World War, 58–9
 fleet, 56, 315, 446
 food exports reduced, 134
 and France
  Oran affair, 287–9, 293–4
  German attitude to, 33, 200, 214
 German blockade
  German Note, 354–5
  and Irish trade, 325–30, 383, 392
 German threat to, 216
 Hitler Peace Offensive, 73
 Irish citizens in, 77
 and Irish communications, 323–4
 and Italy, 32, 76, 173, 174, 176, 192, 197–8, 436

Jewish influence alleged, 133
 and League of Nations, 82, 83, 105, 108, 376, 378
 nationals in foreign armies, 111, 112
 nationals stranded in Europe, 22
 naval base in Ireland rumoured, 14
 and neutrality, 3, 426
 and Norway, 158–9, 173, 186, 192, 198–200, 209
 and Poland, 39, 114
 political situation, 337–8
 relations with USA, 67, 230–1, 260–1
  aid from, 446, 452
  support for, 66, 211, 350, 395, 404–6
 and Ryan case, 186–7
 Second World War, 273
  blockades Germany, 315
  Chamberlain's assessment, 209–11
  Churchill PM, 203, 209
  defeat seen as inevitable, 249–50, 264–5, 274, 277, 286, 290–1, 304, 305, 310
  driven back, 227–9, 406
  and Finland, 104, 105–6, 134
  and France, 6, 71, 73–4, 96, 260–1, 268, 272–3, 285, 366n, 408
  German blockade, 102, 177, 241, 249, 274, 347, 352–4, 358, 361, 389
  German invasion threat, 230, 233–4, 241–2, 261–2, 317
  and German threat to Ireland, 149–55, 261, 319, 347, 349, 432, 437, 443, 448–50, 451
  neutrals bombed by, 427
  pressures in East, 291, 296
  rationing, 457
  refugees, 188–9
  Russo-German pact, 60–1
  and Scandinavia, 179–80, 192
  strength of, 314–15
  victory hoped for, 416
 and Slovakia, 81
 'small nations' propaganda, 100
 transatlantic air service, 136
 and Turkey, 74
 ultimatum to Germany, 8
 unemployment, 116
 wartime agriculture, 196
British Army, 292, 374
 Dunkirk, 229–30
 equipment, 252, 338

479

Irish liaison, 237, 315, 317
and Irish neutrality, 374–5
in NI, 256, 262, 304, 348, 374, 437
in Norway, 198–200
officer arrested in Ireland, 295–6, 297
recruitment, 2–3, 110–12
uniforms in Ireland, 45, 47, 117–18
British Black List, Paris Legation, 378
British Channel, 353
British Commonwealth Merchant Shipping Agreement, 1931, 51
British Consulate, San Sebastian, 429
British Council, 160
British Embassy, Berne, 415
British Embassy, Paris, 144, 344
British Embassy, Washington, 162, 412
British Legation, Dublin, 323
Press Attaché, 390–1
British Meteorological Office, 372–3
British War Risks Office, 358
Brittany, 274
Brown, Jane, 123
Brown, Sir William, 308, 335–6
Browne, Dr Michael, Bishop of Galway, 267
Bruce, Stanley M., 457
Brussels, 437
Bryan, Major Dan, 414
Buchan, John, 265n
Budapest, 22
Bulgaria, 88, 118, 273, 400
Bullitt, William C., 246
Burgin, Edward Leslie, 168, 175n, 176, 196
Burgos, 10, 187, 190
Burgos Prison, 63–4, 80, 99, 313–14
Ryan visited, 26–7, 123–4
Burke, Thomas, 92, 162
Burma, 296
butter stocks, 166, 169, 307
Byass, Major E.Y., 295–6

C
Cabinet Committee on Emergency Problems, 420, 421, 437–9
Cabinet meetings
memos
Anglo-Irish trade, 167–8
trade talks, 168–9, 170, 171
minutes extracts
belligerent naval craft, 23

British diplomatic representative, 12, 37
British proposals unacceptable, 266
draft trade agreement, 363–4
trade talks, 186
World's Fair, 158
cable communication, 225, 262, 324
'Cabot' flying boat, 32, 33, 34, 46
Cadell, Wing Commander
Irish co-operation talks, 222–6
Cahill, Horace T., 110
Cairo, 273
Calais, 228, 414
Caldecote, Lord, 274–5, 280, 298–9, 300, 308, 334
on air raids, 330–1
Dulanty interviews, 305–7, 309–10, 320–1
efforts re munitions, 307–8
trade talks, 335, 336
Camp de St Avén près Vannes, 362
Campbell, Sir Gerald, 88
Campile, Co Wexford, bombed, 339, 347, 350, 351
cartridge misidentified, 366–7
DEA statement, 370
German regrets, 355, 370
German responsibility proven, 364–5
Canada, 56, 101, 142, 276, 291, 341, 405, 455
air service, 136, 243, 282
High Commissioner for Ireland, 102, 121
and Irish neutrality, 85–7, 88–91, 156, 365–6, 385, 391
Walshe telegram to Hearne, 83–4
Irish trade, 356
refugees, 366
relations with USA, 20, 386
and Treaty ports, 422
Vatican diplomacy, 157
war participation, 264–5
Canadian Broadcasting Corporation (CBC), 90
Canadian Catholic Women's Association, 90
Canadian Club, 90
Canadian Overseas Armies, 90
Canadian War Loan, 140
Canary Islands, 187
Canterbury, Archbishop of, 149, 331
Cape Clear, 58

Index

Cardiff, 426, 427
Cardozo, Harold, 317
Carinthia, 135
Carol, King of Rumania, 273
Casado, Colonel, 122n
Casement, Sir Roger, 65, 78
Catholic Church, 86, 213, 292, 304
  atrocities alleged against, 143–4
  in Fascist Italy, 75
  and IRA, 157
  NI pogroms, 17
  Paris churches sealed, 344
  Poland, 62–3, 143–4, 165
  Portugal, 131, 132
  priests and London blitz, 369
  in US, 109, 125
  and Vichy government, 275, 409, 431
Catholic University of America, 395n
Catholic Youth of Canada, 90
cattle trade, 1, 153, 196, 307, 309, 334, 353
  blockade, 349
  price talks, 335
  by weight, 46, 47
CBS, 274n, 303. *see also* Columbia Broadcasting Company
censorship, 131, 153, 154
  Britain, 201, 306, 417
  Germany, 25–6
  Hempel approach on, 143–4
  necessity of, 3, 11
  Rynne memo on, 28–30
  Spain, 24, 39
Ceuta, 291
Chamberlain, Neville, 9, 69, 142, 151, 191, 275, 305n
  Barnes and Richards case, 121, 146, 147
  British co-operation proposals, 271–2, 280–1
  de Valera contacts, 17–18
  declaration of war, 291
  Finnish-Russian peace, 164
  Hitler contacts, 5, 73
  Hore-Belisha resignation, 133
  illness, 338
  and Irish neutrality, 43
  and Irish representative, 46–7
  and Irish unity, 254
  last visit from Dulanty, 209–11
  letters from de Valera, 37–8, 47–8, 145, 146, 212, 278–9
    Barnes and Richards, 146
  letters to de Valera, 35–6, 42, 45, 48

Munich agreement, 89, 287, 288
Peace Offensive speech, 69–70
retirement, 203, 209, 212, 228n
trade talks, 176
Champs Élysées, 345
Channel Islands, 315
Charles, Sir Noel Hughes Havelock, 197
Charles-Roux, F., 293–4
Chartres, 246
Château du Grand Boucher, Ballan Miré, Tours, 244
Chateau Renault, 246, 247
Chateaudun, 246, 247
Cherbourg, 58
Chernak, Dr Mateas, 115
Chiang, Wei Kuo, 163
Chiang Kai-Shek, Generalissimo, 163
Chicago, Archbishop of, 126
Chicago Consulate, report on 1939-40, 161–2
Chicago Daily News, 406
Chicago News, 303
Chile, 68
China, 81, 99, 118
  Japanese invasion of, 99–100
Chinese Embassy, Berne, 415
Christian Commonwealth policy, 90
Christian Science Monitor, 393
Chungking, 296
Church, T.J., 398
Churchill, Winston, 45, 61, 104, 167, 233, 290, 305n, 310, 338, 402, 457
  Britain in Scandinavia, 199, 200
  and France, 96, 264–5, 268, 273, 275
  and Irish neutrality, 210, 279
  and Irish unity, 254, 282
  and neutral states, 159
  Oran affair, 287, 288, 294
  Prime Minister, 203, 209
  on Treaty ports, 295, 384, 385, 387–8, 390, 395n, 397, 402, 416, 417, 455–6
    Shaw urges takeover, 411n
Ciano, Gian Galeazzo, 113–14, 173, 197
cipher books, protection of, 204
citizenship, 42
City of Limerick, SS, sinking of, 362
Civil Aeronautics Authority, US, 162
civil aviation, 263, 334
Clann na Poblachta, 313n
Clarke, Lt Col
  Irish co-operation talks, 222–6

481

Documents on Irish Foreign Policy, Volume VI, 1939–1941

Class Struggle, 295n
Clipper flying boat, 161, 354
Clissmann, Elizabeth 'Budge', 411, 415
Clissmann, Helmut, 411n, 415
Clonlara steamship, 79
Clover Club, Boston, 108, 110
Clyde river, 361
Coast Watching Service, 385
coastal defence, 16–17, 43, 44, 104
   British aid needed, 202, 237, 252–4
   mutual codes, 224
   weak, 56–7, 282
Cobh, Co Cork, 57, 59, 92, 101, 412. *see also* Treaty ports
codes, 297, 378
   British-Irish, 224
   destruction on withdrawal, 204, 207
   telegrams, 60, 83–4
Colijn, Heindrikus, 82, 177
Collinstown aerodrome, 220
Colombia, 372
Colson, General, 250
Columbia Broadcasting Company, 406, 428
Columbia University, 404
Colville, John, 275n
Commissioners of Public Works, 445
Committee of Imperial Defence, 271
Committee to Defend America by Aiding the Allies, 231
Commonwealth, British, 33, 185, 388
   constitution making, 257
   German trade with, 93
   'inter se' relationships, 137
   Irish links with, 51–2, 142
   plan for France, 260
Communism, 66, 75, 342, 409
Communist Labor Party of America, 295n
Communist Party, of Ireland, 415
Communist Party of Great Britain, 147n
Compiègne, 251n, 260
Conant, Dr James Bryant, 109–10
Conboy, Martin, 333, 430
concentration camps, 80, 429
confidential documents, destruction of, 204–5
Congress of Vienna, 1815, 283
Connecticut, 162
conscription, 21, 73, 111–12
Conscription Bill, US, 350
Conseil National, Berne, 171

Conservative Party, 210
Constitution, 1922, 138, 139, 257–8, 344
Constitution, 1937, 127n, 135–6, 142, 278
contraband control, 95–6, 118, 184
Contraband of War, Memo on, 59
Controller of Censorship. *see* Coyne, Tommy
Conway, John M. (Ottawa), 85, 139, 397, 398
Cooper, Alfred Duff, 167, 306, 338, 416–17
Copenhagen, 55, 415
Corap, General André Georges, 284
Cork, 221, 358
Cornwall-Jones, Major A.T.
   Irish co-operation talks, 217–26
Corriere Padano, 75
Cosgrave, W.T., 396–7
Coulondre, Robert, 6, 8
Courageous, HMS, 73
Courrier de Genève, Le, 171–2
Court of Criminal Appeal, British, 127–8
Coventry IRA bomb, 119–21, 149, 156.
   see also Barnes, Peter; Richards, James
   executions, 162, 183
   sentences, 127–8
Cowles, Gardner, 303
Coyne, Tommy, Controller of Censorship, 28, 29, 30
   letter from Boland, 436–7
Cracow, 97
Craig, James D., 296
Craigavon, Lord, 17, 210, 269, 278, 295, 397n
Cranborne, Lord, 416–17, 456
   Dulanty meeting, 400
   letter from de Valera, 378
Crédit Lyonnais, Tours, 362
Cremin, Cornelius 'Con', 348, 352
   evacuation, 246, 248
   Paris visit, 337, 343–4
   reports to Walshe, 6
Cremins, Francis T., (Geneva), 105
   correspondence
      Lester, 391–2
      Murphy
         Joyce case, 434–5
   memo to Walshe, 81–3
   presents credentials in Geneva, 371–2

482

Index

reports to Walshe, 7, 21, 87–8, 112–13, 118
  Berne Legation, 371–2
  Germany's expansionism, 171–5
  Scandinavian invasions, 176–8
  telegrams
    DEA, 62, 309
    Walshe, 392–3
  20th Assembly of League, 107
Cremins, Francis T. (Berne)
  correspondence
    Murphy, 430–1
      Joyce case, 441–2
  telegrams
    Walshe, 415–16
Creswell, Commander J.
  Irish co-operation talks, 217–26
Crillon Hotel, Paris, 345
Cromwell, Oliver, 455
Cross, Ronald H., 406
Crozier, W.P., 316, 455–6
Cuba, 68, 94
Cudahy, John, 96, 332–3
Cuervo, Colonel Maxim, 124, 190
Curley, Michael Joseph, Archbishop of Baltimore, 126
Curragh, Co Kildare, 220
  bombed, 422–3, 426, 453
currency, 185, 194, 205, 455
Custodian of Enemy Property, 450
Cuxhaven, 39
Cyclops (steamer), 199
Czechoslovakia, 151, 174, 344
  disturbances, 97–8
  and Germany, 6, 22, 39, 74, 159, 164, 214, 285
  and League of Nations, 83
Czestochowa, bombing of, 9

D

Dáil Éireann, 50, 264
  de Valera neutrality statements, 12, 65
    Rynne suggestions, 48–53
  de Valera on Berne Legation, 370
  Defence Conference, 443
  Hamburg broadcast, 69, 71, 77–8
  invasion contingencies, 444
  League of Nations estimate, 376
  support for neutrality, 16, 385, 397, 398–9, 402
Daily Mail, 274, 317

Daily Mirror, 181, 331
Daily Telegraph, 72
Dakar affair, 366
Daladier, Edouard, 6, 9, 69, 70, 96, 164, 284
  fall of, 208
dancing, German ban on, 334
Danzig, 10, 73, 97
Dardanelles, 32
Darlan, Admiral, 216n, 250
de Ansaldo, Madame, 361
de Casas Rojas, Count, 78–9
de Castellane, Marquis, 287
de Champourcin, Michels Jaime, 122, 124, 141, 190, 339n, 340, 354
de Clenzia, Marquesa, 94
de Gaulle, General Charles, 216n, 268, 275, 366n, 399
  captures Gabon, 394
  sets up National Committee, 272–3
  support for, 407, 410
de Grenus, Edmund, 371
de Kerillis, Henri, 203
de la Cierva, Juan, 187
de la Hoide, Miss, 22
de las Barcenas, Domingo, 187
de las Harcehas, Juan, 124–5
de Mamblas, Viscount, 79
de Senaller, Baron, 122–3
de Valdeiglesias, Marques, 170
de Valera, Eamon, 71n, 72n, 86, 110n, 264, 369, 437, 455
  Anglo-Irish relations, 182, 218, 294–5, 299, 317
  anti-Partition campaign, 101, 121–2, 178, 269–70
  Barnes and Richards, 119–20, *145*, 146, 148–9
  British guarantee on invasion, 320
  British proposals, 266–7, 280–1
  Chamberlain retires, 209, 210
  Irish representative, 18
  lampooned in cartoon, 181
  MacDonald talks, 234–44, 252–60, 269–70, 282
  and Maffey, 42–6, 315, 391
  message to Eden, 15–17
  title of British representative, 42, 43, 45–7
  trade talks, 167–8, 169, 189
  Treaty ports, 385, 386, 387, 390, 396–8, 402, 411, 415

483

Cabinet reshuffle, 35
and Canada, 89, 140
correspondence
　Chamberlain, 35–6, 37–8, 48, 212, 278–9
　Barnes and Richards, *145*, 146
　Cranborne, 378
　Eden, 142–3
　Walshe
　　German Note, 329–30
　　Maffey contacts, 297–9, 311–12, 373–5
Finland attacked, 129, 166
and Germany, 184, 319
　Hempel interview, 300–1
　Irish representative, 76
　Legation staff request, 423, 424–5, 428, 432
　on peace with Hitler, 241–2
　invasion contingencies, 442–4
and League of Nations, 105, 129, 163
Low Countries invaded, 212, 215, 233
memos to
　Berne Legation, 370–1
　Gallagher, 322–4
　Walshe, 169, 334
　　British proposals, 271–2
　　Germany and Ireland, 190–1
　　Hempel meeting, 232–3
　　pressure on neutrality, 289–92
　　trade talks, 192–3
　　worsening situation, 249–50, 272–5
neutrality, 12, 101
　and espionage, 240–1
　in favour of British, 47, 281
　MacDonald meeting, 236–44
　treatment of belligerents, 23
reports from Walshe
　Eden meeting, 200–3
and Ryan case, 98–9, 156, 313
telegram to Hambro, 107
and USA, 161, 384, 395, 430
　Christmas address, 130–1
　Gray, 389, 399
　New York Times interview, 304
de Valera Reception Committee, Boston, 109
de Vichenet, Comte Charles de Romrée, 382n
Déat, Marcel, 318, 441

Defence, Department of, 72, 263, 360n, 445
　invasion contingencies, 437–9, 443, 444, 449, 450
　munitions, 144
　preparations for neutrality, 36–7
Defence, Minister for, 315, 317, 424. *see also* Traynor, Oscar
Defence Council/Conference, Irish, 259, 443
defence forces. *see* British Army; Irish Army
Delargy, Professor James H., 184
Democratic Party, US, 350, 405
Denmark, 9, 30, 68, 191, 267, 328, 350
　agriculture, 227
　German invasion, 171–2, 176–81, 186, 198, 235, 443–4
　mobilisation, 55
　neutrality, 49, 51, 54, 289–90
Denny, Harold, 304n
Derry, County, 348
Derry Gaol, mutiny, 130
Deutsche Allgemeine Zeitung, 96, 293
Deutsche Nachrichten Büro, 182n
Deux Sèvres, 362
Devonshire, Edward William Spencer Cavendish, 10th Duke of, 17, 188–9
Devonshire, HMS, 199
Dewing, Major-General Richard H., 223, 224
Diamantis, steamer, 84
Dieppe, 381
Dillon, C.L., 182
Dillon, James, 232–3, 399
diplomatic corps, Dublin, 102. *see also* German Legation, Dublin
　Axis powers, 221
　belligerent states, 4–5, 11
　British appointment sought, 12
　Canada, 121, 137–8
　invasion contingencies, 404, 443, 449
　protection for, 5
　title of British representative, 141–2
diplomatic representatives, Irish, 5, 303, 304
　Berlin, 71
　correspondence mislaid, 76
　emergency instructions, 203–7
　exequatur, 71, 80–1, 119
　financing, 263

Index

invasion contingencies, 449
passport provision, 442
Portugal, 131–3, 132, 133
wartime communications, 4–5, 7–8, 15, 184, 262
  Berlin, 13–14, 41
  USA, 34–5
disabled, evacuation of, 16
Dobrudja river, 88
Dobrzyński, Wacław Tadeusz, 27
Dombaas, Gudorandsdal, 200
Dominican Order, 131
Dominion Affairs, Secretary of State for. *see* Cranborne, Lord; Eden, Anthony
Dominions, 20, 52, 101, 388, 415
  and British trade, 456–7
Dominions Office, 15, 181, 203, 271, 298–9, 378
  attitude to Ireland, 15, 19
  de Valera's title, 42
  and IRA executions, 148–9
  Irish Sea mined, 307
  trade talks, 192–3, 193–7, 335–6
  and Treaty ports, 390
Donegal, County, 315, 348
Donegal Bay, 297n
Donnelly, Maisie, 122n
Dorman-Smith, Sir Reginald, 196
Doyle, Peadar S., 71n, 191
Dresden, 182, 216n
Dreyfus case, 346
Drogheda, Co Louth, bombed, 422
Droitwich, 47
Drummond, Sir Eric (Lord Perth), 17
Dublin, 100, 131, 137, 348, 358, 363, 379, 454
  British Press Attaché, 390–1
  defence of, 243, 258–9
  German bombs dropped in, 422, 426
  German news agency, 182
  invasion contingencies, 404
  IRA arrests, 240
  Maffey diary, 41–8
  papal legate vacancy, 230, 249
Dublin, Archdiocese of, 163, 364, 366, 367
  McQuaid appointment, 383, 386
Dublin Bay, 84n
Dublin Horse Show, 182
Duff, John, 188

Dulanty, John W., 44, 231–2, 274–5, 298–9, 374
  Barnes and Richards, 119–21, 127, 148–9
  Caldecote interviews, 305–7, 309–10, 320–1
  correspondence
    Hore-Belisha, 36
    Walshe, 119–20, 132–3, 144, 300
      meteorological reports, 372–3
  minute from Walshe (facsimile), *145*
  pilot training request, 334
  rank discussed, 16
  reports to Walshe, 166–7, 188–9, 306, 316, 402–3
    air raids, 330–1, 332, 368–9, 380–1
    Barnes and Richards, 120–1, 147–8
    British attitude to Ireland, 454–7
    Caldecote interviews, 305–7, 309–10
    co-operation proposals, 280–1, 281–3
    Cranborne meeting, 400
    IRA threat to Maffey, 141
    last visit to Chamberlain, 209–11
    Machtig interview, 307–8
    political situation, 337–8
    trade talks, 175–6, 308–9, 335–6
  and trade talks, 168, 170–1, 171, 175–6, 308–9, 335–6, 358, 361
Duleek, Co Meath, bombed, 426
Dún Laoghaire harbour, 72n
Duncormick, Co Wexford, bombed, 339
Dunkirk evacuation, 229–30, 242, 338
Durham, 457
Dutch East Indies, 250
Duval, General, 208, 215, 216, 230

E

East Asia, 291
  Monroe Doctrine, 250, 277
East End, London, 369, 390
East Indies, 250
Eben-Emael, fortress of, 208
Economist, The, 294
Ecuador, 40, 108
Eden, Anthony, 101, 160n, 210, 280
  Barnes and Richards, 120–1, 146, 147, 148–9
  despatch from de Valera, 169
  on Finland, 166–7
  and Irish neutrality, 18–20

memo from Maffey, 41–8
title of British representative, 141–2
trade talks, 175–6, 192, 193–7
Walshe meetings, 15–20, 200–3
Education, Department of, 445
Egypt, 18, 93, 94, 250, 273, 400
Eighty Years' War, 285n
Elliott, Major George Fielding, 274, 295, 303
Elser, Johann, 89n
Emergency Powers Act, 1939, 52
Emergency Powers (No. 48) Order, 1940, 444
Emergency Powers (No. 2) Order 1939, 51–2
Emergency Powers (No. 5) Order 1939
Rynne memo on, 28–30
Emergency Powers Orders, 49, 50, 52, 262, 438, 445
Enfield, Co Kildare, 123n
English Channel, 57, 228
English College, Rome, 213
Epernon, 246, 247
espionage, 221
British, 295–6, 298–9
German, 4, 240–1, 243, 259–60
Held, 30, 232, 235, 269
Roos execution, 155
Essary, Fred, 100
Essex, 338
Estonia, 60, 70, 97
Ethiopia, 32
Eugene, Father, 125n
European Boxing Championships, Dublin, 182
European Commission of Human Rights, 127n
European Court of Human Rights, 127n
evacuation camps, 16
Evening Mail, 11, 147
Evening Standard, 274
Excess Profits Tax, UK, 338
executions
Barnes and Richards, 119–21
exequatur, British, 71, 80–1, 119
Export Board, suggested, 335
External Affairs, Department of, Canada, 91
External Affairs, Department of (DEA), 136, 323, 356n, 363. *see also* diplomatic corps, Dublin; diplomatic representatives, Ireland

Anglo-Irish trade talks, 168–9, 170, 360–1, 364
Beckett money lodged, 318–19
and censorship, 28–30
effects of neutrality, 11
emergency orders, 49
and German bombs dropped in Ireland, 350, 370, 427–8
invasion contingencies, 379, 420–1, 444, 448–50
and League of Nations membership, 375–8, 400–1
memos from
British liaison meeting, 315
for de Valera, 370–1
German Legation staff, 423–5
invasion contingencies, 448–50
League of Nations, 107–8
message to Macaulay, 35
monitoring broadcasts, 190–1
passports provision, 442
telegrams
to all missions, 279, 387
Brennan, 299, 305, 350
Kerney, 339, 361, 382, 392
Macaulay, 249, 263–4
MacWhite, 213, 302
Murphy, 293–4, 317, 325, 337, 347–8, 363, 378
O'Donovan, 364, 366, 367, 383n, 427–8
Warnock, 128, 302, 316, 337, 351–2, 412, 437
German blockade, 348–50
German bombs dropped in Ireland, 339, 347, 364–5, 366–7
invasion threat, 227, 302
more frequent reports requested, 382
neutrality, 212, 293
Washington Legation, 140–1, 146
wireless communication, 324
External Affairs, Minister for. *see* de Valera, Eamon
external association, 257

F

Fabry, M., 230
Falange, 122
Falangistas, 341
Falklands War, 202n
Far East, 197, 291

Index

Farinacci, Roberto, 75
Fascism, 31, 74–6, 180, 190n, 197
Fauchille, Paul, 111
Federal Political Department, Geneva, 371, 372
Ferguson, R.C., 417
  letter from Walshe, 231–2
Fermanagh, County, 192, 202
fertiliser imports, 307
Fianna Fáil, 122n, 150, 151, 153, 154
fifth columnists, 220, 221, 235, 240–1, 253–5, 259–60, 269. *see also* espionage
  denied by Hempel, 281
  German methods, 222
  internment urged, 270
Finance, Department of, 131–2, 263, 356n
  invasion contingencies, 444, 450
  and League contribution, 401
  US loan sought, 445
Finat, José, 340–2
Findlay, Sir Mansfeldt de Cardonnel, 78
Fine Gael, 232n, 376n, 397, 398–9
Finland, 27, 68, 117, 121, 154, 157, 172, 412
  and Britain, 121, 134, 199, 214
  and League of Nations, 112–13, 118, 129, 377
  Russian threat, 70, 88, 101
    invasion, 103–8, 134, 152, 443–4
    peace with Russia, 164, 165, 166–7
  Russian war supplies, 175
Finner Camp, Donegal, 297
First Gulf War, 202n
First World War, 7, 21, 25, 45, 55, 73, 134, 231n, 285, 369
  costs, 338
  French weapons reused, 284
  neutrality in, 3, 4, 16, 37, 51, 54, 328
  'Region of War', 276
  sinking of *Leinster*, 84
  submarine crisis, 57
  territorial waters, 58–9
  US troops, 56
  Versailles treaty, 260, 286
Flanders, battle of, 268, 291
flax, 335
flying boats, 32, 46, 92, 161–2, 354n
Flynn, T.J., 263
Foch, Marshal Ferdinand, 106, 286

Food, Ministry of, UK, 166, 168n, 170, 175–6, 308, 335
Food Control Office, Berlin, 134
food rationing, 457
food supplies, 80, 134, 165–6, 194
Forbes, Sir Arthur Patrick Hastings, 9th Earl of Granard, 362
Ford, Henry, 282
Foreign Affairs, Ministry of, France, 246, 248–9
Foreign Ministry, German, 281
Foreign Office, Germany, 135, 333, 382
  Barnes and Richards, 155
  blockade, 383
  contraband control, 93, 103, 184
  on de Valera, 215
  and German bombs dropped in Ireland, 370, 431–2
  Kerry Head attack, 315–16
  Murphy seeks Paris visit, 352, 355
  size of Irish Legation, 416
Foreign Office, Spain, 79, 187
Foreign Office, UK, 59, 150, 271, 303n
  and Irish diplomats, 142
Foreign Relations Committee, US Senate, 405
Forward, 411
Four Power Pact, 174
Foxe, Elizabeth, 189n
Foynes, Co Limerick, 220
  Meteorological Station, 403
  radio station, 34, 50
  submarine spotted, 46
  US cancellations, 161–2
  US service to, 92
France, 29, 58, 94, 214, 216, 234, 241, 369, 381, 389, 406, 416, 440. *see also* Vichy government
  colonial development, 285–6
  constitutional changes, 294
  Cremin report, 6
  de Gaulle charged with desertion, 268
  Dublin Legation, 323
  and Finland, 104, 105–6, 134, 164
  fleet, 242, 259, 273
    destroyed by British, 287–9, 293–4
    Oran affair, 287–9, 295
  government weaknesses, 283–4
  and Ireland, 23–4, 44–5, 304–5
  and Italy, 32, 76, 87, 173, 174, 178, 197–8
  Joyce family in, 430–1, 434–5, 441

487

and League of Nations, 82, 83, 105, 108, 309, 376–7
meteorological reports, 403
nationals in foreign armies, 112
and neutral states, 209
and Norway, 192, 199, 228n
and Poland, 114
Roos execution, 155
Scandinavian blockade, 179–80
sea traffic, 57
Second World War, 10, 20, 61, 65, 86, 96, 203, 208, 239, 291–2
   Anschluss, 97
   armistice, 249, 250, 260, 264–5, 273, 289, 293
   Attachés recalled, 446
   attitudes to, 69–71
   blackouts, 21
   and Britain, 24, 25, 73–4, 150, 151, 152, 260–1, 268, 272–3, 275, 408
   British losses in, 229–30, 252, 285, 307
   British passport holders, 430–1, 434–5, 441
   Cabinet changes, 208
   collaboration, 407, 409–10
   collapse of, 333, 334
   food restrictions, 64, 363
   Franco-German talks, 393–4
   under German control, 285–6, 318, 343–6
   German invasion, 228, 230, 244, 443–4
   Irish passport holders, 22, 351–2, 429, 430, 431
   mobilisation, 6
   munitions, 364–5, 367
   Paris evacuation, 246–9
   shipping, 102
   situation, July 1940, 283–6
   threat to, 216
   ultimatum to Germany, 8
   US support for, 56, 66, 211, 230–1
Franciscan Order, 126
Franco, General Francisco, 64, 95, 187, 317n
   defence of Catholicism, 75
   Irish recognition of, 181
   and Ryan case, 26–7, 98, 122–3, 340–2
Franco-British Union, 260, 273
Franco-German Armistice, 377

Frankfurter Zeitung, 131
Free French, 216n, 268n, 366n
Freeman-Thomas, Freeman, 1st Marquess of Willingdon, 455
Freemasonry, 275
French, Sir Henry, 308
French Army, 284
French Embassy, Berne, 415
French Embassy, Rome, 213
French Indo-China, 250
French Legation, Dublin, 446
French West Africa, 366n
Front Populaire, 275, 304–5
fuel shortages, 106, 134, 410
Funk, Walther, 106
Fusset, Martinez, 27, 64, 80, 98

G
G2 (Irish Army Intelligence), 97n, 182n, 414n
Gabon, capture of, 394
Gallagher, Frank
   memo to de Valera and Walshe, 322–3
   memo to de Valera, 323–4
Gallardon, 246
Gallup Poll, 405, 406
Galway city, 57, 92, 220, 221, 259, 361
   Athenia survivors landed, 97n
   de Valera speech, 210, 212, 215, 227
Galway Diocese, 364
Gamelin, General Maurice, 215–16, 216, 284
Garches, 246
Garda Síochána, 297
Garvin, James Louis, 97
Gasquet, Cardinal, 126
Gayda, Virginio, 31–2, 180
Gazette de Lausanne, La, 159
Gemelli, Fr Agostino, OFM, 126
Geneva, 15, 21, 377, 400, 430
Geneva Legation, 387, 438. *see also* Cremins, Francis T.
   to close, 371
George VI, King, 81, 126, 142, 257
   Barnes and Richards, 148–9
Gerede, Hüsrev R., 65
Germaine, SS, 185
German Academic Exchange Service, 411n
German-American Bund, 66, 67
German-American League of Culture, 66, 67

Index

German Army, 198, 284
  and Irish recruitment, 110–12
German Day, San Francisco, 66–7
German Embassy, Berne, 415, 416
German Embassy, Paris, 345n, 362, 402, 434–5
German Legation, Dublin, 160, 182n, 323. *see also* Hempel, Edouard
  extra staff sought, *418–19*, 419–20, 428, 432
  DEA memo, 423–5
  Press Attaché, 391
  supervision of, 221
German Navy, 104, 172, 198
German News Agency, 182
German Note
  Boland on, 354–5
  Walshe letter to de Valera, 329–30
  Walshe memo on, 325–9
German Official News Agency, 143
'German Plot', 153
German Post Office, 41
German Prize Law, 1939, 352
German Propaganda Organisation, 213
German-Soviet Boundary and Friendship Treaty, 1939, 60–1, 87–8
Germany, 20, 21, 55, 57, 136, 151, 289, 366, 388
  aircraft research, 381
  and *Altmark* incident, 158–9
  censorship, 5–6, 14
  expansionism, 171–5
  foreign nationals in, 22
  and France, 285–6, 291, 318, 406, 408–10, 441
    armistice, 250, 260, 273, 289, 293
    Franco-German talks, 393–4
  hegemony of, 291–2
  and IRA, 223, 313
  and Ireland, 35, 76, 181–2, 182, 190–1, 238
    attitude to, 61, 68–9, 77–8, 117–18, 183–4, 232–3, 333–4, 358
    German bombs in, 339, 347, 350, 422–3, 425–8, 431–3, 452
    Germans in, 240–1, 243, 259–60
    invasion fears, 218–26, 234–44, 267, 269–70, 274, 277, 280–1, 292–3, 299, 304, 317, 319–20, 348, 437, 448–50, 451
      Hempel denial, 300–1, 302
    Irish nationals in, 14, 39–40, 183, 185

neutrality accepted, 12, 26, 33, 34, 52, 53, 278
  submarines, 17, 101
  territorial waters, 23–4, 44–5
and Italy, 113–14, 135, 164–5, 179–81, 197–8, 415
and League of Nations, 378
and neutrality, 53, 54, 278, 289–90
and NI, 236, 272, 275–7, 315
patriotism, 200
Peace Offensive, 69–70
and Poland, 39
and Russia, 130, 241, 273, 296, 395, 400, 416
  Finland attack, 104, 105–6, 108, 117
  pact, 60–2, 64–5, 66, 75, 87–8, 227, 273, 291
and Ryan escape, 340–3
Second World War, 5–6, 24–6, 164–5, 249, 288, 315, 351
  air raids on Britain, 215, 330–1, 332, 368–9, 380–1, 390, 406, 416, 455
  blockade of Britain, 40, 348–50, 361, 383
    British-Irish contacts, 102–3, 107
  blockaded, 174–5, 177, 179–80, 227, 242, 264–5, 283
  British invasion plan, 230, 380
  invades Low Countries, 208, 211, 212, 213
  invades Norway and Denmark, 171–2, 176–8, 198
  invades Poland, 5, 6, 7, 9, 27, 143–4
  living conditions, 106, 383
  military techniques, 237–8
  success of, 249–50
and Spain, 10
and USA, 10–11, 65–7, 350, 440, 446
Gerstenberg, Joachim, 183
Gestapo, 340, 342
Gethsemane, 125
Gibraltar, 114, 197, 287, 291, 366, 415
Giornale d'Italia, Il, 31–2, 433
Giraud, General Henri, 216
Glasgow, 124, 256, 274
Glasgow, cruiser, 199
Glennon, Cardinal John Joseph, 126
Globe and Mail (Toronto), 138–9
'God Bless America' (song), 350
Godfrey, Admiral John H., 373, 375
Godfrey, Cardinal William, 126

Goebbels, Dr Joseph, 159
Goering, Field-Marshal Hermann, 106, 380
Gogarty, Oliver St John, 160
Golden Gate International Exposition, 66
Goral people, 97
Gormanston, Co Dublin, 220, 223
Gort, Co Galway, 267
Görtz, Herman, 232n
Government Information Service, France, 268
Government Telegraph Code 1933, 378
Graf Spee (pocket battleship), 130, 158
Granard, Lord, 362
Grandi, Count Dino, 197
Gray, David, 162, 167, 312, 399, 411
  letter from Walshe, 314
    conversation notes, 387–9
  memo from Walshe, 439–41
  papal audience, 168
  and Treaty ports, 413
Greece, 54, 84n, 94, 178, 383, 407
  and Albania, 400
  Italy invades, 382, 413, 415, 436–7, 448
  and League of Nations, 118
  pro-Axis, 250, 273
Green, Dr Jerome, 109–10
Greenwood, Arthur, 282
Greig, Captain Alexander B., 102
Grew, Joseph C., 99, 100
Grey, Sir Edward, 59
Griffin, Father, 337, 343–4
Guaranty Trust, New York, 93, 362, 363
Gunning, Thomas, 27

H
Haarlem, 208
Hacha, Dr Emil, 164
Hague Convention, 1907, 83, 85, 443, 449, 450
  Articles 10 and 26, 2
  neutrality and recruitment, 111
  Opening of Hostilities, 439
Haldane, Professor J.B.S., 147
Halifax, 139
Halifax, Lord, 9, 126, 142, 203
Hallon, Dr James, 331
Hambro, Carl J. (Geneva), 366
  telegram from de Valera, 107

Hamburg, 67, 134, 381, 383
  air raids, 351
  broadcasts, 69, 71, 77, 78, 183–4
Hanover, 25, 229
Hanson, Richard, 395–6, 397
Harbour Commissioners, 263
Harding, Sir Edward, 17–18, 19, 20
Hardinge, Alexander, 148
Harrison, General, 297, 373, 375
  army liaison meeting, 317
  Maffey/de Valera meeting, 315
Harstad, 228n
Hartmann, Dr Hans, 184
Harvard University, 109–10
Haugh, Kevin, 266
Havana Conference, 323
Havas reports, 155
Havas-Reuter dispatches, 203
Hawaii, 277
Hawker Hurricane aircraft, 380
Healy, Garth, 162
Hearne, John J., 161n, 188
  aide mémoire to Skelton, 121–2
  attitudes to Irish neutrality, 85–7, 88–9, 121–2, 137–40, 422
  correspondence
    Walshe, 100–2, 365–6
    Treaty ports, 395–9
  King interview, 396–8
  memo to Walshe, 88–91
  reports to Walshe, 85–7, 137–40, 264–5, 267
  seeks material for speeches, 90–1
  telegrams
    Brennan, 385
    Walshe, 83–4, 115, 156, 304, 391, 422
Hearst, William R., 66, 211
Held, Stephen Carroll, 232, 235, 240–1, 269, 301
Helsingborg, 427
Helsinki, 104
Hempel, Edouard, 71, 76, 100, 191, 272, 320, 428
  and espionage, 281
  extra staff sought by, 418–20, 428
  memo, 423–5
  and German blockade, 349
  German bombs dropped in Ireland, 364–5, 366–7, 425–7, 431–2, 452
    Walshe meeting, 453–4
  and German Note, 325, 329, 355
  Irish neutrality accepted, 302, 319–20

490

and media reports, 143–4
memo to Walshe (facsimile), *418–19*
and transhipment, 358
Walshe meetings with, 84–5, 232–3, 425–7, 428, 453–4
Hendaye, France, 337
Henderson, Sir Nevile M., 5
Henry II, King of England, 227n
Hepburn, Mitchell F., 137
Herald, 160
Herald Tribune, 303n
Herriott, William Talbot, 316
Hertzog, General, 250
Heyman, Major G.D.G.
  Irish co-operation talks, 217–26
Hickey, James, 190n
High Commission, London, 337–8
High Commissioner, status of, 18, 43, 60
High School, Dublin, 182
Hill, Sir Quintin, 308
Hinsley, Cardinal Arthur, 147, 149
Hitchcock, Alfred, 303n
Hitler, Adolf, 22, 31, 66, 164, 193, 217n, 236, 369, 395
  assassination attempt, 89
  and Britain, 61, 215, 314, 380
  Ciano meeting, 114
  de Valera on peace with, 241–2
  expansionism, 192
  and France, 6, 8–9
    Pétain meeting, 409–10
  and Ireland, 100, 241
  and Italy, 198
    Mussolini, 32, 75–6, 179–81
  Peace Offensive, 69–70, 73, 334
  popular support, 25, 173, 351
  psychological portrait, 12
  Reichstag speech, 64–5, 67
  remilitarisation, 285n
  and Russia, 75
    Molotov meetings, 390, 400
  unmoved by casualties, 455
  and USA, 10, 67, 292
    Roosevelt letter, 181–2
Hoare, Sir Samuel, 1st Viscount Templewood, 250
Hodgson, Sir Robert, 27
Holland, 22, 68, 82n, 94, 203, 227, 241, 269, 294, 328
  and blockades, 349
  and Britain, 229, 291, 292
  financial transfers, 93

German invasion of, 208, 211, 213, 216, 218, 224–5, 235, 236, 251, 259, 284, 421, 443–4
  de Valera on, 212, 233
  expected, 88, 174, 177, 192
  German reaction, 214
  speed of, 228, 238
  and League of Nations, 118
  mobilisation, 55
  neutrality, 3, 4, 9, 47, 49, 51, 201, 209, 289–90, 330
  refugees, 188–9
  sea traffic, 57
  Simon Bolivar (liner) sunk, 96n
Hollywood, 405
Holy See Legation, 62–3, 76n, 125
  communications through Berlin, 13, 14, 26, 41, 184, 227, 229
  Consistory, 125–6
  Macaulay resigns, 367
Home Rule Act, 1914, 280
Hong Kong, 250, 273
Hooten, Professor Earnest, 110n
Horan, Timothy J., 188
Hore-Belisha, Leslie, 133
  letter from Dulanty, 36
hospitals, 16
Hotel Continental, Bordeaux, 248
Hotel de l'Univers, Tours, 247
Hotel Russischer Hof, Berlin, 67
Hotel Terminus, Bordeaux, 248
House of Commons, 43, 384n, 385
  Churchill on Treaty ports, 384, 385, 388, 390, 397, 455–6
Hoysted, Major
  Irish co-operation talks, 222–6
Huddleston, General Sir Hubert, 224
Hudson, Sir Robert, 175n, 192
  trade talks, 196
Hughes, John T., 108–9
Hull, Cordell, 211
  aide mémoire from Brennan, 74
Hungarian embassy, Berne, 415
Hungary, 32, 68, 88, 94, 213, 345
hunger strikes, 102, 121
Hyde, Dr Douglas, 42, 139
Hyde Park, Duchess County, New York, 146

I
Iceland, 366
Imperial Airways, 32, 46, 50

491

Documents on Irish Foreign Policy, Volume VI, 1939–1941

India, 273, 276, 298n, 315, 455
Indo-China, 250
Industry and Commerce, Department of, 356n, 445
  and German blockade, 327, 329–30
  meteorological reports, 372
  refugee question, 188
Industry and Commerce, Minister for, 52, 169, 263n
influenza, 369
Informaciones, 170
Information, Ministry of, UK, 295, 298–9, 300, 314
  media censorship, 306
  and USA, 303, 312
Institut Missionnaire St Augustin, 361
International Brigade, 64n
International Convention for Air Navigation, 1919, 23–4
International Labour Office (ILO), 22, 377
International News Service, US, 92
International Postal Union (IPU), 41
internment, 130, 337, 429
  fifth columnists, 221, 240, 270
  in Germany, 39–40
  in Ireland, 3, 17, 23, 72, 234, 262, 453n
  in Rhodesia, 104
Intransigeant, 230
Inverliffey, SS, sinking of, 48, 185
Iran, 68, 135
Iraq, 93, 250
Ireland. *see also* Anglo-Irish relations; Anglo-Irish trade; neutrality; Treaty ports
  attitudes to Britain, 90, 238
  British representative in, 15–16, 18, 19, 20, 35–6, 37, 61
    title of, 42, 43, 45–7
  defence of, 252–3, 262, 317
  foreign uniforms banned, 117–18
  German threat to Britain, 149–55, 233–4
  international situation, July 1940, 294–6
  invasion contingencies, 234–44, 297, 379, 404, 433, 437–9
    Boland memo, 442–4
    DEA memo, 448–50
    Dept of Taoiseach memo, 444–5

  draft note for foreign governments, 450–1
  propaganda in event of, 420–1
  investments overseas, 357
  and League of Nations, 375–8
  nationals stranded in Europe, 22
  Nazi activities alleged in, 200–1
  relations with Germany, 26, 182, 183–4
    German bombs dropped in, 339, 347, 350, 422–3, 425–8, 431–3, 452
    German nationals in, 14, 17, 18, 73, 243, 323
    invasion fears, 252–4, 267, 269–70, 274, 277, 279–81, 292–3, 304, 317, 375, 437
    representative, 76
  unemployment, 98
  and USA, 161, 452
Irish Air Corps, 16, 201–2
Irish Army, 33, 202, 267n, 308, 367, 372
  British Army liaison, 317
  Curragh bombed, 422–3
  desertion, 112
  HQ-British cable link, 225
  ill-equipped, 236–7
  Intelligence (G2), 97n, 182n, 414n
  invasion contingencies, 235, 297
  Liaison Officers, 348
  mobile columns, 220–1
  ordnance, 364n
  radio transmitters, 225–6
  recruitment, 323
  size of, 385
Irish Brigade, 27n, 123n
Irish College, Paris, 344
Irish College, Rome, 62–3, 433
Irish Convention, 1917, 417
Irish Folklore Institute, 184
Irish Historical Society, Canada, 90
Irish Independent, 144
Irish language, 19, 102, 122
  German broadcasts in, 118, 183–4, 191
Irish Meteorological Service, 403
Irish Military Intelligence (G2), 97n, 182n, 414n
Irish Nationality and Citizenship Act, 1935, 431
Irish Parliamentary Party, 45n
Irish Press, 144, 427, 436–7
Irish Race Congress, Chicago, 161

Index

Irish Red Cross Society, 450
Irish Republican Army (IRA), 22, 99, 137, 252, 255, 267, 298n, 365
  Barnes and Richards executions, 152–3, 154, 155–6, 162, 183
    de Valera appeal, 142–3, *145*, 146
    reprieve efforts, 146–9
    US influence sought, 140–1
  British anxieties, 223–4
  British bombing campaign, 89, 119–21, 127–8, 152, 154, 181
  and Campile bomb, 364
  detention of, 259
  and Germany, 47, 78, 135, 184, 232n, 235, 240–1, 313, 411n
  and Italy, 156, 157–8
  Magazine Fort raid, 130–1
  prisoners, 77, 130, 301
    hunger-strike, 102, 121
  Ryan, 312–13
  and Stuart, 382n
  threat to Maffey alleged, 141
Irish Republican Brotherhood (IRB), 108n
Irish Sea, 57, 274, 353
  mined, 307, 329
Irish Times, 68, 131, 144, 397, 427
  IRA executions, 147
  neutrality, 30
isolationism, US, 66, 405–6
Italian Embassy, Berne, 415
Italian Fascist Party, 75
Italian Legation, Dublin, 323, 436–7
Italy, 68, 94, 136, 291, 394, 454
  on brink of war, 74–6, 197–8, 213
  and Britain, 192
  Fascism, 74–6
  and Germany, 164–5, 179–81, 415
  and IRA, 156, 157–8
  and Ireland, 156, 240, 263–4, 443, 448–9, 451
  likely strategy of, 8–9, 31–2, 74–6, 176
  mobilisation, 198
  neutrality, 77, 173, 174
  radio stations, 25–6
  sanctions, 227, 287, 288
  Second World War, 229, 230n, 273, 289, 333
    armistice, 260
    blockaded, 242
    Greek campaign, 178, 382, 413, 415, 436–7, 448

shortages, 283
South Tyroleans, 135
and Spain, 8, 10
and Switzerland, 21, 176–7
threat to Salonika, 177–8
threat to shipping, 249
and USA, 231
workers in Germany, 159

J

Japan, 56, 68, 193, 231, 250, 376, 440
  Burma road closed, 296
  Manchuria, 163
  Monroe Policy, 277
  neutrality, 9
  and Russia, 40, 273
  and USA, 99–100, 249, 291
Japanese embassy, Berne, 415
Jenkins, T. Gilmour, 308
Jeseossingfjord, Norway, 158
Jesuit Order, 126, 187n
Jews, 262, 345
Johnson, General Hugh, 217
Johnson, Senator Hiram, 211, 405
Johnson Act, US, 211, 405
Joint Defence Council, proposed, 338
Jordan, William Joseph, 456
Journal (Canada), 140
Journal des Débats, 208, 209, 216
Joyce, Giorgio, 435, 441, 442
Joyce, James, 430–1, 434–5
  death of, 441–2
  letter from Murphy, 402
Joyce, Lucia, 402, 430–1, 434–5, 441–2
Joyce, William, 'Lord Haw-Haw', 190n
Julianstown, Co Louth, 426
Jung, Dr Carl Gustavus, 12
Justice, Department of, 445, 449
  refugee question, 188

K

Karelia, 103n
Kearney, John D., 102n
Keith, Berriedale, 294–5
Kelley, Frank R., 406
Kelly, John Hall, 102n, 137
Kennedy, Joseph P., 405, 430
Kerney, Leopold H., 156
  correspondence
    Boland, 24
    Murphy, 429

Walshe, 141
  anti-Partition campaign, 178–9
  memos to Walshe
  neutrality, 14–15
  Ryan case, 26–7, 63–4
  trade negotiations, 78–80
  notes by, 190, 354
  Portuguese representative, 131–3
  reports to Walshe, 7–8, 10, 38–9, 94–5
  censorship, 170–1
  Ryan, 98–9, 122–5, 186–7, 312–14
  Ryan escape, 339–43
  and Ryan case, 26–7, 63–4, 141, 190, 346–7
  telegrams
    DEA, 339, 361, 382, 392
    Walshe, 411
Kerney, Raymonde, 94, 179
Kerry, County, 101, 376n, 417
Kerry Head, SS, attacked, 316, 337, 351
Keyes, Father, SJ, 110
Kiernan, Dr Thomas J., 76
Killary, Co Galway, 57
Kimball, Solon T., 110n
King, Mackenzie, 89, 102n, 137–8, 264, 365, 391
  and Treaty ports, 395–8
King-Hall, Sir William Stephen, 365
Kirkpatrick, Sir Ivone, 303
Klaipeda, Lithuania, 184n
Knox, Colonel, 439
Knox, Frank, 274
Koht, Dr Halvdan, 158, 199, 209
Konigstein Castle, Dresden, 216n
Kriegsmarine, 274n
Krock, Arthur, 429–30

L

La Época, 170
La France au travail, 346
La Pointe, Ernest, 20
La Suisse, 7, 172
Labour Party, Irish, 191n, 397, 398–9
Labour Party, UK, 191n, 203, 282, 331, 417
Lamorlaye, France, 362
Lampson, Sir Miles, 18n
Landon, Alf, 405
Lands, Department of, 445
Land's End, 58, 274
Laon, 215

Latvia, 64, 70, 97
Laval, Pierre, 264, 289, 393–4, 399
  Pétain reconciliation, 441
  unpopular, 407, 409–10
Law of Nations, 53
Le Figaro, 287, 288
Le Havre, 230
Le Jour, 9, 203, 230, 287–8
Le Journal, 8, 208, 215
Le Matin, 9, 230, 346
Le Petit Parisien, 9, 203, 208
Le Temps, 7, 203, 209, 230, 287, 288, 318
League of Nations, 15, 22, 105, 135, 157. *see also* Cremins, Francis T.
  Avenol resignation, 309
  collapsing, 400–1
  Covenant, 22
  Cremins moves to Berne, 391–2
  Cremins report on, 81–3
  de Valera unable to attend, 107
  Finnish appeal, 107–8, 112–13, 117, 118, 129, 134
  Irish membership of, 62, 375–8
    Boland on, 400–1
    Walshe minute on, 407
  Manchuria, 163
  refugee questions, 188
  Secretariat, 377
leases, termination of, 205, 207
Lecomte, Colonel, 172
Leicester Regiment, 199
Leinster, steamer, 84n
Lemass, Sean, Minister for Supplies, 169, 192, 266, 267, 335–6
  MacDonald meeting, 270
  trade talks, 186, 189, 194–7
Lemp, Leutnant Fritz-Julius, 97
Lend-Lease Bill, US, 445–6, 452
Leningrad, 130
Lennon, District Justice, 131
Leopold, King of Belgium, 227, 229
Les Dernières Nouvelles de Paris, 346
Lester, Seán, 82, 83, 309
  League Secretary General, 375, 377
  letter from Cremins, 391–2
Lestocquoy, Eugène, 446
Leydon, John, 168
  letters from Walshe, 95–6, 231–2
  memo on British trade, 165–6
Libya, 75n
Liège, 208n

Index

Liénart, Cardinal, 9
Lille, 9
Lillehammer, 199
Limerick, 316
Limerick aerodrome, *418–19*, 419–20, 423, 424
Limerick Steamship Co, 79, 80
Lindbergh, Colonel Charles A., 217
Lindemann, Professor F.A., 1st Viscount Cherwell, 402
Lippman, Walter, 231
Lipski, Józef, 5
Lisbon, 110, 161, 414–15, 428
  Legation, 131, 133
Lithuania, 64, 70, 82, 184n
Little, Reverend James, MP, 267
Liverpool, 124, 126n, 202, 274, 381
livestock trade, 107, 308
Lloyd, Edward, 308
Lloyd liner *Bremen*, 117
Lobby Correspondents, 321
Local Defence Force (LDF), 438, 444
Local Government and Public Health, Department of, 444
Local Security Force (LSF), 267n, 323
Lodz, 97
London, 124, 160, 172, 202, 415
  air raids, 338, 368–9, 380–1, 383, 390, 406
  Andrews visit, 416
  broadcasts from, 11, 139, 273
  censorship, 312
  French puppet government in, 260
  Gray in, 167, 168
  Irish nationals in, 369
  public shelters, 368–9
  trade talks, 192–3
    minutes, 193–7
  Walshe visit to, 15–20
London Midland and Scottish mail-boat, 326, 349, 354–5
London Naval Treaty, 1930, 84n
Lopez-Pinto Berizo, General José, 27n
'Lord Haw-Haw', 190
Lore, Ludwig, 295, 298
Lorraine, 407, 410
Los Angeles, 322
Lothian, Philip Henry Kerr, 11th Marquess, 12, 167, 405, 406
Lough Swilly, 57, 58, 59, 221, 348
Louth, County, 262
Luetzow, Vice Admiral, 274

Lufthansa, 423
Luftwaffe, 106n, 218, 228, 249, 453n
  blitz, 368–9, 380–1, 390
  bombs dropped in Ireland, 339, 347, 422–3, 425–8, 431–3, 453
  shipping attacked, 316, 362
  successes, 130, 214
Luxembourg, 55, 203, 215
Lynch, David J., 110
Lyons, Louis M., 405n

M

Maastricht, 208n
Macaulay, William J.B., 14, 263–4, 366
  letter to Walshe, 163
  message to, 35
  reports to Walshe, 125–6, 167, 213
  resignation, 230n
  telegram to DEA, 249
MacBride, Maud Gonne, 65, 183
MacBride, Seán, 313
McCormick, Anne O'Hare, 314
McCormick, James. *see* Richards, James
McDaid, Mgr Denis, 62–3, 433
MacDermot, Senator Frank, 399
MacDonald, Malcolm, 266–7, 280, 305, 307
  British proposals rejected, 278–9, 281–3
  de Valera talks, 234–44, 252–60, 269–70
McElligott, James J.
  memo to Moynihan, 356–9
McEwen, John, 196
McGeachy, J.P., 100
McGilligan, Patrick, 69, 71
machine guns, 202
Machtig, Sir Eric, 17, 141, 192, 203
  Dulanty interview, 307–8
  Irish co-operation talks, 217–26
McIvor, Dr Daniel, 140
Mackenzie, Ian, 140
MacMahon, General Peadar
  memo from Moynihan, 36–7
  Walshe memo on invasion contingencies, 437–9
McMurrough, Dermot, 227
McQuaid, Fr John Charles, 383n, 386
MacWhite, Michael
  letters from Boland, 114–15, 119

495

reports to Walshe, 31–2, 157–8, 168,
    197–8
  Fascism, 74–6
  Hitler and Mussolini, 179–81
  telegrams
    DEA, 213, 302
    Walshe, 448, 451
Madeleine church, Paris, 345
Madrid, 27, 75, 178, 382n
  Germans in, 340, 342
  Ryan case, 63, 156
Madrid, 170
Madrid Legation, 7–8, 64, 132–3, 312
  telegram from DEA, 387
Maffey, Sir John, 35, 36, 72, 102, 137,
    143, 200
  Anglo-Irish trade talks, 169
  British Army liaison meeting, 317
  British representative, 37, 60
  de Valera/Harrison meeting, 315
  de Valera meeting, 37–8
  Eden-Walshe meeting, 200–3
  IRA threat to, 141
  memo to Eden, 41–8
  Walshe meetings, 297–9, 311–12,
    373–5, 389–91
  Treaty ports, 416–17
Magazine Fort raid, Dublin, 130–1
Maginot Line, 21, 55, 70, 88, 160, 172,
    284
  broken, 214, 228
  defence of, 215–16
Mahan, Admiral Alfred Thayer, 57
Maher Pasha, Ali, 273
Mahr, Dr Adolf, 14, 41
maize, re-export of, 50
Majestic Hotel, Paris, 345
Malmo, Sweden, 427
Maloney, Dr W.J., 65, 78
Manchester Guardian, 147, 316, 455
Manchuria, 163
Manion, Dr Robert James, 89–90
Mansion House Conference, 1919,
    139
Marin, Louis, 208
Marseilles, 123
Martinez Campo, General, 340
Martinique, 288
Maurras, Charles, 318
Maynard Keynes, John, 381
Meade, Walter, 187
media. *see* press; radio

Mediterranean theatre, 32, 76, 173,
    197, 242, 381, 441
Megerle, Dr Karl, 333–4
Meighen, Arthur, 395n
Mein Kampf (Hitler), 87
Memel wireless station, 184
merchant shipping, 49–50, 51–2, 293
Mers-el-Kebir affair. *see* Oran affair
Mersey River, 361, 426, 427
Meteorological Office, UK, 403
meteorological reports, 372–3, 402–3
Meuse, river, 284
Meyer, Dr David de Waal, 89, 138, 264
Middle East, 296, 362n
Middleton, Drew, 406
Milan, 113, 126n, 135
Milford Haven, 58
Military College, 414n
Minehan, Monsignor, 109
mines, 17, 96n, 172, 261, 358
  Irish Sea, 307, 329
  minesweeping, 58–9
  Norwegian waters, 180, 276
Ministry of Information, UK, 130, 139n
Molotov, Vyacheslav Mickhaylovich,
    103
  Hitler meetings, 390, 400
Monahan, Father, 337, 352
Montana, 162
Monteiro, Armindo, Portuguese
    ambassador to Britain, 133
Montini, Mgr Giovanni Battista, 63
Montmédy, 215
Montoire-sur-Loire, 409–10
Montreal *Gazette*, 267
Moravia, 97, 164, 165
Morgan, J. Pierpoint, 109
Morocco, 133, 187, 291
Morrison, William 'Shakes', 168
Morse Code transmissions, 322–4
Mortished, Peter, 22
Mortished, R.J.P., 22
Moscow, 75
Moscow Radio, 273
Moulins, 343
Mountjoy Prison, 77
Moylan, Seán, 109
Moynihan, Maurice
  on British proposals, 266–7
  Cabinet memos
    Anglo-Irish trade, 167–8, 168–9,
      170, 171

Index

letters from Walshe, 107, 379
  to MacMahon, 36–7
memos
  from DEA, 448–50
  from McElligott, 356–9
on neutrality, 36–7, 48–53
Terms of Reference of trade talks, 189–90
Moynihan, Seán, 131
  letter from Walshe, 404
Muhlhausen, Dr Ludwig, 183–4
Mulcahy, Elizabeth. *see* Clissmann, Elizabeth 'Budge'
Mulcahy, General Richard, 232
Mullingar, Co Westmeath, 295n
Mulrean, Father, 123–4
Munich, 89
Munich agreement, 1937, 167n, 287, 288
munitions, 3, 224–5
  in Finland, 166–7
  French inadequacy, 284
  Irish rearmament, 17, 18
  Irish shortages, 201, 236–7, 243, 244, 252, 258–9, 269, 270, 306, 307–8, 310, 317
    British pressure, 294–5, 311–12
  Italian, 31
  no Irish manufacture, 107, 232
  sought from France, 144
  UK production, 338
  from USA, 20, 99–100, 231, 296, 350, 405, 406, 439, 452
Munitions, Ministry of, UK, 338n
Murphy, Father, SJ, 110
Murphy, Matthew
  reports to Walshe, 65–7, 163
Murphy, Seán
  correspondence
    Cremins
      Joyce case, 430–1, 434–5, 441–2
    Joyce, 402
    Kerney, 429
    O'Byrne
      Beckett, 318–19
    O'Kelly de Gallagh, 361–3
    Walshe
      French public opinion, 69–71
  reports to Walshe, 8–10, 203, 215–16
    de Gaulle, 268
    Dunkirk, 229–30
    French armistice, 250–1

    French situation, 208–9, 283–6, 318, 408–10
  Legation evacuated, 244–9
  Oran affair, 287–9
  Paris visit, 343–6
  telegrams
    DEA, 317, 325, 337, 347–8, 363
      codes destroyed, 378
    Walshe, 60, 310–11, 389, 406, 431, 434, 446
      Franco-German talks, 393–4
      Laval-Pétain reconciliation, 441
      Oran incident, 293–4
      support for Vichy, 304–5, 399, 407
  visiting occupied territory, 343–6, 351–2, 412
Murphy, Sheila G., 143–4, 163n, 364, 367
  Boland minute to, 80–1
Murray, Gladstone, 90
Murray, Senator, 162
Mussolini, Benito, 8–9, 113n, 114, 173
  choices of, 31–2, 75–6, 177
  and Hitler, 174, 179–81
  poised to enter war, 197–8, 213
  US attitude to, 231

N

Nagle, Austen H., 403
Namsos, 228n
Nanjing, 99
Napoleon Bonaparte, 292, 455
Narvik, 186, 199, 200, 228n, 229
National Centre Party, 399n
National City Bank, Dublin, 205, 445
National Gallery of Ireland (NGI), 14, 41
National Labor Relations Board (US), 405
National Museum of Ireland (NMI), 14n, 41
National Socialism (Nazism), 61, 86
  alleged in Ireland, 200–1
  anti-Catholic, 126, 292
  in USA, 66–7
national sovereignty, theory of, 4
Naval Intelligence, British, 201
navicerts, 417, 454
NBC, 295
near East, 173, 174, 176
Neligan, Monsignor, Bishop of Pembroke, 90

497

Netherlands. *see* Holland
neutral states, 9, 51, 289–90
  diplomatic protection by, 204
  duties of, 1–2, 4
  Italy, 31–2
  and nationals of belligerent states, 3, 4
  Norway, 198–200
  recognition by belligerents, 53
  rights of, 4–5, 50
  Spain, 10, 24, 38–9
  Switzerland, 21, 392–3
  trade agreements, 328
  USA, 10–11, 13, 20, 49, 92
neutrality, Irish, 1, 3, 29–30, 42, 53, 292, 450–1. *see also* Anglo-Irish relations: British invasion possible; Germany: and Ireland: invasion fears
  aide mémoires on, 34, 121–2
  Altmark incident, 158–9
  British attitude to, 18–20, 33–4, 90, 100–1, 138–9, 200–1, 210–11, 255, 433, 454–7
    co-operation talks, 217–26
    Maffey assessment, 45, 46
    offers on NI, 238–9, 253–9, 269–72, 275–9
    pressure on, 236–44, 269–70, 271–2, 278–9, 289–92
  British newspaper criticisms, 72, 294–5, 297, 299, 301, 305–6, 308, 311, 320–1, 333, 455
  and British trade, 107
  Canadian attitude to, 83–4, 85–7, 89–91, 115, 137–40, 156, 391
  de Valera support for, 212, 215
    Dáil statement, 48–53
    message to Eden, 15–17
  defence of, 2, 54, 56–7, 59, 209, 211, 262, 295–6, 299, 304
  early stages, 11–12
  in favour of British, 47, 200
  German attitude to, 68–9, 171–2, 173, 175, 177, 183, 209, 232, 235, 256, 293
    attacks on shipping, 316, 337
    doubts, 278
    guarantee, 319–20
    Legation staff request, 418–20, 423–5, 428, 432
    threat denied, 300–1, 302
  and German blockade, 326–30, 348–50

German bombings, 339, 347, 350, 422–3, 425–8, 431–3, 452
German Note, 354–5
importance of geography, 56–8
international recognition of, 52, 60, 62, 415, 416
internment of Axis citizens, 240–1
and Italy, 75–6, 179–81
and League of Nations, 62, 82, 378
meteorological reports, 372–3, 402–3
and munitions offer, 311–12
not negotiable, 322
preparations for, 36–7
public attitudes to, 100–1, 152
reasserted, 279, 280
and recruitment, 110–12
Rynne memos on, 1–5, 32–4, 53–9
situation, July 1940, 294–6
and trade, 3–4, 190, 358
and transhipment, 334, 352–4
treatment of belligerent nationals, 259–60
and Treaty ports, 393
US attitudes to, 290, 303, 308, 314, 385, 387–9, 388–9, 394–5
shipping, 95–6
Neutrality Act, US, 92, 161, 386, 404–5
Nevinson, Henry W., 147
New York, 88n, 94, 162, 303, 333n, 440
  liners stalled in, 117
  messages through, 35, 76
  World's Fair, 158, 161
New York, Archbishop of, 125–6
New York Consulate, report by, 161–2
New York Herald Tribune, 211
New York Post, 295
New York Times, 35, 70, 231, 322, 347, 406, 429n
  de Valera interview, 304
  neutrality, 397
  support for Britain, 314
  on US and war, 211
New York Volkzseitung, 295n
New Zealand, 20, 88, 142, 307, 308–9
  and British trade, 456
Newfoundland, 323
Newry, Co Down, 297, 348
News Review, 200–1
newspapers. *see* press
Nolan, Sean, 415
Norman invasion, 1169, 227n
Normandie (liner), 117

Index

North Africa, 31, 32, 173, 287, 441, 448
North American College, Rome, 213
North Atlantic, 57, 114n
North Sea, 73, 96
North Sea theatre, 57, 274
Northern Ireland, 33, 148, 274, 280, 398, 412. *see also* anti-Partition campaign
  anti-Catholic pogroms, 17
  barrier, 56
  British Army in, 374, 437
  British offers on, 154, 238–9, 253–4, 269–70, 299
    commitment to unity, 270, 271–2
    likely reaction, 271–2
    NI as neutral, 255–7
    rejected, 278–9
    unity declared in principle, 254–5, 257–9
  British troops in, 302, 304, 348
  cannot become neutral, 255–7, 256, 271, 276
  de Valera on, 46
  German plans for, 236, 272, 275–7, 315
  invasion contingencies, 224, 236, 261–2, 397n
  Joint Defence Council suggested, 238–9, 255, 258, 269, 270, 271
  'Plan Kathleen', 232n
  PM visits London, 416
  refugees, 234
  risks of unity, 290
  trade, 184, 356, 357
  in UK title, 46–7
  war production, 256
Norton, William, 190n, 191
Norway, 68, 78, 94, 117, 211, 241, 273, 274, 294, 437
  Altmark incident, 158–9
  Britain in, 198–200, 214, 228, 291, 292
  broadcasting service, 34–5
  and Finland, 134
  German invasion of, 171–2, 176–81, 186, 192, 198, 211, 219, 235, 236, 259, 267, 284, 443–4
    infiltration, 209
    speed of, 238
  government in exile, 228n
  mine-laying, 276
  neutrality, 54, 289–90
  and Russia, 104
  shipping register, 95

Norwegian Legation, Berlin, 186
Nunan, Seán
  memo on cartoon, 181
Nuremberg Trials, 106n

O

O Ceallaigh, Seán T., 161
Observer, 97
Observer Patrols, 323
O'Byrne, Patrick, 246, 248
  letter to Murphy, 318–19
O'Callaghan, Michael, 183
O'Connell, Cardinal William Henry, 109, 110
O'Connell, Kathleen, 161n
  Boland letter to (facsimile), *359*
  Walshe covering note, 119–20
O'Donnell, Blanca, Duchess of Tetuan. *see* Tetuan, Duchess of
O'Donnell, Peadar, 64
O'Donnell family, 414
O'Donoghue, Philip, 127–8
O'Donovan, Colman, 41
  and Consistory, 126
  letter to Walshe, 230
  reports to Walshe
    Irish attitude to Poland, 62–3
    Italy still neutral, 113–14
  telegrams
    DEA, 364, 366, 367, 383, 427–8
    Walshe, 386, 433
O'Duffy, General Eoin, 187n
O'Farrell, Father, 344
O'Grady, Father, 343–4
O'Higgins, Kevin, 232n
O'Higgins, Dr Thomas F., 232, 267
O'Kelly de Gallagh, Count Gerald, 248, 343, 344, 402
  letter from Beckett (facsimile), *447*
  letter to Murphy, 361–3
O'Leary, Grattan, 85, 139–40
Olympic Club, San Francisco, 66
Olympic Games, 104
O'Mahoney, Senator Joseph C., 305
O'Malley, Ernie, 182
Ontiveros y Laplana, Don Juan Garcia, 179
  letter from Walshe, 156
Oppenheim, Lassa, 276
Opposition parties. *see* Fine Gael; Labour Party, Irish
O'Rahilly, Professor Alfred, 440–1

499

Oran affair, Algeria, 287–9, 291, 293–4, 295, 302
Orange Order, 398
Oranmore aerodrome, 220
O'Reilly, Gerald, 354, 414
O'Reilly, John Boyle, 108
Orly aerodrome, 343
O'Rourke, Tiernan, 227n
Oslo, 199
Osservatore Romano, 63, 180–1, 213, 302
Ostia, 113
O'Sullivan, Professor John Marcus, 376
Ottawa, 100, 264, 366
Ottawa, Archbishop of, 90
Ottawa Journal, 85
Ottawa Legation, 137, 140
  telegram from DEA, 387
Oxford University, 331
Oysterhaven, Co Cork, 316

P
Pacific theatre, 99–100, 386, 446
Palais Bourbon, Paris, 345
Palestine, 124–5, 298n
Pan American Airlines, 161–2, 354n, 428
Pan de Soraluce, José, 78–80
Panama, 95
Panay (gunboat), 99
Papal Nunciature, Berlin, 68, 164–5
Papal Nunciature, Berne, 372, 415
Papal Nunciature, Dublin, 386
Papal Nunciature, Paris, 304, 343–4, 399, 407
  evacuation, 244, 245
Papal Nunciature, Vichy, 434
paper supplies, 29
parachutists, 214, 215, 218, 219, 243
  German methods, 222, 224, 235
Paraguay, 94
Paris, 9–10, 11, 167, 284, 288, 410
  churches sealed, 344
  government evacuation, 245–9
  Irish colony, 337, 343
  Murphy visits difficult, 337, 343–6, 347–8, 406, 412, 434
  newspapers, 441
  occupation of, 310–11
  population of, 345
  student demonstration, 394, 407

Paris Legation, 123n, 144, 347–8, 412
  bank account, 362
  codes destroyed, 378
  evacuation to Ascain, 244–9
  France enters war, 8–10
  Irish colony documents, 361–2
  in La Bourboule, 283
  telegram from DEA, 387
  in Vichy, 337
Paris-Soir, 208, 216, 230, 283, 346
Parc Monceau hotel, Paris, 344
Partition. *see* anti-Partition campaign
passports, 429
  Berlin Legation, 182, 185
  destruction of blanks, 205, 207
  Irish passports sought, 430, 434–5, 441–2
  Paris Legation, 337, 351–2, 361–2
  wartime regulations, 52–3
patrol boats, 44
Peace of Westphalia, 1648, 285
Peace Treaties, 1919, 29
Pearse, Patrick, 227
Pêche, 187
Pegasus, HMS, 73n
Pershing, General John J., 231
Persia, 135, 456
  WWI neutrality, 54
Persian Gulf, 273
Perth, Lord (Sir Eric Drummond), 17
Pétain, Marshal Philippe, 264, 446
  armistice, 250–1
  on British aid, 268
  Catholicism, 275, 302, 399
  collaboration, 407
  de Gaulle defies, 272–3
  France's future, 283–6
  Franco-German talks, 393–4
  Irish sympathy with, 304–5
  Laval reconciliation, 441
  meets Hitler, 409–10
Petersen, Dr Karlheinz, 135, 143, 182n
petrol depots, 2
petrol rationing, 21, 31, 456
  France, 346
  Germany, 24, 40
Peyrouton, Marcel, 251, 441
Philadelphia, 440
Phillip, Percy, 70
Phillips, Admiral Sir Tom, 18
Phillips, William, 197

Phoenix Park, 220, 221
  ammunition raid, 130–1
Pilet-Golaz, Maurice, 371
pilot training, 334
Pinto, General Lopez, 187
Pittman, Senator Key, 249, 277
Pius XI, Pope, 126
Pius XII, Pope, 157n, 364
  Consistory, 125–6
  Gray audience, 168
  Irish bishoprics, 230, 366, 367
  and Nazism, 292
  von Ribbentrop audience, 164–5
'Plan Kathleen', 232n
Plate, River, naval battle, 130
Poitiers, 248
Poland, 31, 32, 74, 93, 134, 159, 160, 164, 174, 230, 240, 289, 429
  atrocities, 25, 143–4
  British support, 73, 121, 214, 292
  German nationals in, 114
  invasion of, 5–10, 20, 22, 27, 39, 55, 227, 284
  Ireland fails to support, 62–3
  Irish nationals in, 185
  Irish parallels with, 131
  and League of Nations, 82–3, 118
  protectorate, 64, 97
  and Russia, 60, 65, 70, 87
  workers in Germany, 159
police, Irish, 33
Polish 'Corridor', Germany, 97
Polish Embassy, Madrid, 382n
Pontifical Academy of Sciences, 126n
Portugal, 68, 304, 318, 331, 400, 414–15
  blockaded, 315
  Irish representative, 131–3
Posen district, Germany, 97
Post Office, UK, 226, 324
Posts and Telegraphs, Department of, 445
Prague, 97–8
Prendergast, Jim, 415
press, 15, 34, 41, 427
  British press and Ireland, 72, 191, 200–1, 294–5, 296, 297, 299, 301, 305–6, 308, 311, 320–1, 390–1, 455
  Dulanty-Crozier meeting, 316
  Treaty ports, 416–17
  censorship, 3, 7, 28–30, 37
  Hempel concerns, 143–4
  Italian coverage, 436–7

  and neutrality, 11, 49–50
  in US, 162
press agencies, British, 29
Press Association (PA), 295, 298, 437
Press Information Bureau, 122
Price, Ward, 97
Prien, Kapitänleutnant Gunther, 73n, 104
Prisoners of War Convention 1929, 438, 450
Pritt, Denis N., 147
Privy Council, right of appeal to, 137–8
Procopé, Hjalmar Johan, 103
profiteering, 134
Propaganda Ministry, German, 65, 135
Protectorate of Bohemia and Moravia, 97, 164, 165
Prouvost, Jean, 268
Prussia, 184, 285
Pryce, Major M.H., 297
publishing, 116
Pugeol, General, 250
Pulitzer Prize, 314n, 429n

Q
Queen Mary (liner), 117
Queen's University, Belfast (QUB), 163n
Queen's University (Kingston)
  Alumni Association, 90, 91
Queenstown. see Cobh

R
radio broadcasts, 225–6, 263, 267, 295, 297
  censorship, 3, 5–6, 11, 25–6
  de Gaulle appeal, 268n
  German, 69, 71, 77–8, 118, 183–4, 190–1, 274, 437
  invasion contingencies, 379
  news bulletins, 322–4
  Norwegian, 34–5
  shortwave in morse, 322–4
  wireless sets for Legations, 6
Radio Éireann, 14, 47, 76n, 184
  censorship, 11
  heard in Germany, 25–6, 62, 78
Radio-Paris, 7
railways, 159, 234, 261
Ralston, James Layton, 140

501

Rassemblement National Populaire, 318n
rationing, 457
  France, 394, 410
  Germany, 24, 40, 61, 115–16, 129–30, 383
  Switzerland, 21
Reavy, George, 318n
recruitment, 2–3, 4, 45, 47
  and neutrality, 110–12
Red Cross Convention, 1929, 438, 449, 450
Red Cross Society, Geneva, 45, 345, 370, 377, 438, 443
Redaktion-Irland, 382n
Redmond, John, 45
refugees, 188–9
  British, 42, 373
  France, 247–8
  from NI, 234, 262
Regime Fascista, 75
'Region of War' theory, 275–7
Regional Commissioners, 444
Reichsbank, 106n
Reinhard, Dr Otto, 41
Remembrance Day ceremony, Canada, 88–9
Rennes, 246
Republican Party, US, 350, 405
Repulse, HMS, 73
Rethel, 215
Reuter, 11, 152
Reynaud, Paul, 284
  government of, 208, 216, 251
Reynaud Committee, 260, 268n, 272
Rhine, river, 285n, 286
Richards, James ('McCormick'), 140–1, 152–3
  de Valera appeal, 142–3, 145, 146
  execution, 154, 155–6, 162, 183
  reprieve efforts, 146–9
  sentence, 127–8
Riga, 130
Rineanna airport, 220, 424
Robinson, Paschal Charles, Papal Nuncio, OFM, 126, 163n
Rockall Bank, 97
Rockefeller Foundation, 110n
Romania (Roumania), 9, 21, 32, 68, 94, 174, 177, 224, 250
  Nationality Law, 112
  seeks Italian help, 87–8
  totalitarian state, 273

Rome, 31, 75, 172, 184, 213
  von Ribbentrop visit, 164–5
Rome Legation, 428, 433, 443. *see also* Holy See Legation; MacWhite
  telegram from DEA, 387
Romier, M., 215
Roos, Dr Phillipe, 155
Roosevelt, President, 211, 231n, 274, 365, 444
  ambassador leaves Paris, 246
  Cudahy remarks, 332–3
  Finnish mediation offer, 103–4
  Ford and, 282n
  French message to, 251
  and IRA executions, 146, 162
  and Ireland, 168, 439
    Treaty ports, 387, 413–14
  letter to Hitler, 181–2
  neutrality asserted by, 10–11, 13, 20, 49, 92
  non-belligerent ally, 9, 230–1
  peace message to churches, 125
  ready for war, 429–30
  seeks defence funding, 217
  support for Britain, 167, 386, 405
Rossi, Cardinal, 367
Rosslare, Co Wexford, 59, 349
Rotary Club, Canada, 90
Rothschild family, 345
Rotterdam, 101, 208
Rouen, 230
Royal Air Force (RAF), 32, 49, 58, 71, 362n, 380n, 425–6
  forced landings, 34, 72
  German air raids, 159–60, 381
  German captures, 39–40
  and Irish defence, 221, 223, 243–4
  Spitfires, 330–1, 330n, 380
  strength of, 242
  US planes, 282–3
  weaknesses of, 291
Royal Navy (RN), 44, 49, 59, 219, 294, 315, 388
  and Ireland, 236, 237, 274
  and Irish defence, 220, 221, 223
  losses, 72–3
  North Sea mines, 96–7
  Oran affair, 287–9
  strength of, 282
  weaknesses of, 291
Royal Oak, HMS, 73, 104
Royal Ulster Constabulary (RUC), 297

Index

rubber boats, 381
Rugby wireless transmitter, 324
Ruhr area, 214
Russell, Seán, 313, 382
Russia (USSR), 22, 26, 77, 117, 177, 192, 241, 346
  attacks Finland, 101, 103–4, 105–8, 134, 172, 175
    League appealed to, 112–13, 129
  peace with, 164, 165, 166–7
  and Britain, 201, 274
  and Germany, 134, 173, 273, 296, 390, 395, 400, 416
    pact, 60–2, 64–6, 75, 87–8, 104, 227, 273, 291
  and Italy, 75
  and Japan, 100
  and League of Nations, 118, 129, 376
  and Poland, 83
  transport system, 130
  and USA, 395
Rüter, Dr, 93, 383
Ryan, Fr Arthur Haydn, 163
Ryan, Desmond, 182
Ryan, Eilís, 99, 123, 346–7
Ryan, Frank, 80, 170, 179, 190, 382, 411
  escape, 339–42, 346–7, 361
  Kerney memos/reports to Walshe, 26–7, 63–4, 98–9, 122–5
  Kerney visits, 63–4, 123–4, 312–14
  in Lisbon, 414–15
  official concern, 141, 156
  opposition to release, 99, 186–7
  sentence, 124
Ryan, Dr Jim, 264
  trade talks, 195–7
Rynne, Michael
  invasion contingencies
    draft note, 450–1
  letter to Walshe, 275–7
  memos by
    Horan, 188
    if Britain invades Ireland, 149–55
    if Germany invades Britain, 233–4
    intensified emergency, 261–3
    invasion contingencies, 420–1
    League of Nations, 375–8
    neutrality, 1–5, 11–12, 32–4, 53–9
    situation, June 1940, 260–1
    transhipment, 352–4
  memos to Walshe
    Barnes and Richards, 127–8

  British media and neutrality, 72
  international treaties, 135–6
  neutrality, 48–53
  recruitment, 110–12
  minute from Walshe, 105

S

Saar region, 74
Saarbrücken, 160
St Brice, M., 8
St Colman's Church, Gort, 267n
St Columba's College, 149
St George's Channel, 57
St Jean de Luz, 15, 249, 341, 346
St Louis, Archbishop of, 126
St Patrick's Day, 139, 165, 170
St Sauveur, Marquis de, 362
St Trond, 208
Salamanca, 170
Salazar, António de Oliveira, 132, 331
Salonika, 177–8, 213
Saltonstall, Leverett A., 110
Salzburg, 113
Sambre, river, 215
San Francisco, 303
San Francisco Chronicle, 66, 314
San Francisco Legation, 65–7
  report on 1939-40, 161–2
San Francisco News, 67
San Sebastian, 27, 341, 429
San Sebastian Legation
  report from Kerney, 7–8
sanctions, 227–8, 287, 288
Sandjak of Alexandretta, 76
Sandwell, Bernard K., 139
Sankey, Lord, 149
Saorstát Éireann, change of name, 135–6
Sardinia, 31
Saskatchewan University, 139
Saskatoon, 139
Saturday Evening Post, 138, 178–9
Saturday Night, 139
Saturnia (liner), 114
Sauerwein, Jules, 97
Savoy Hotel, London, 192
Saxony, 184
Scandinavia, 117, 155, 164, 388, 429
  Allied support, 105, 134, 198
  blockade, 174, 179–80
  German invasions, 176
  German trade, 93

503

and League of Nations, 81, 82, 118, 129
and Russia, 108, 113, 177
sea traffic, 57
timber exports, 184
Scapa Flow, 73, 104, 151
Scherl Verlag, 116
Scotland, 56, 196n, 239, 256, 274
Scotsman, 294–5
Scott, Joseph
  letter from Brennan, 322
Scots College, Rome, 213
Seanad Éireann, 16, 444
Second World War, 163n, 202. *see also* Britain; France; Germany; neutrality
  Balkans, 400
  begins properly, 203
  Britain declares war, 291
  British civilian situation, 337–8
  British-Irish mutual co-operation, 217–26
  character of modern war, 111–12
  Eastern Front, 25
  German military campaign, 224, 227–9, 237–8, 253
  German victory possible, 154, 214–15, 249–50, 264–5, 277, 286, 290–1, 304
  imminent, 5–6
  and League of Nations, 376
  Low Countries invaded, 208
  new world order expected, 331, 456–7
  North Africa, 441
  opinions in Berne, Dec 1940, 415–16
  situation, July 1940, 272–5, 294–6
  situation, June 1940, 260–1
  trade costs, 357
  unofficial Anglo-German talks, 310
  and USA, 10–11, 65–7, 211, 383, 446
    mood changing, 230–1, 265, 315, 404–6, 429–30
Secret Service, British, 73, 78, 331, 340
Secret Service, Spanish, 340
seed potatoes, trade, 80
Seldte, Franz, 159
Senate Foreign Relations Committee, 231n
Sensi, Monsignor, 372
Seyss-Inquart, Dr Arthur, 144
Shanghai, 99

Shanley, Representative, 162
Shannon port, 221
Shaw, Captain, 417
Shaw, George Bernard, 411n, 441
Sheehan, Vincent, 303
Sheehy, Dr Maurice S., 395
Sheffield, 416
Sherwood Foresters, 199
Shetland Islands, 151
shipbuilding, 256, 283
shipping, 4, 50, 56, 102–3, 153, 234, 249. *see also* Treaty ports
  Anglo-Irish trade, 194, 195
  boom, 373
  Britain blockaded, 274, 348–50
    German Note, 325–30, 354–5
  British food trade, 165–6, 196
  British losses, 117, 406
  British strength, 454
  crews interrogated, 17
  display of colours, 14, 41, 49–50
  German attacks, 316, 337, 362
  German warning, 84–5
  insurance, 1, 358
  intensified emergency, 262–3
  invasion contingencies, 450
  and Irish neutrality, 4, 23, 104, 293, 316, 445, 452
  USA, 74, 92, 93, 95, 100, 161, 234
  Italian, 114
  searching of, 219
  timber exports delayed, 184
  and trade talks, 358
  transhipment, 336, 352–4
  US destroyers to UK, 439
  use of Irish flag, 14, 41
Shipping, Ministry of, UK, 170, 175, 308, 406
short wave transmissions, 25, 34, 35, 138, 139, 322–4
  in Berlin, 78
  invasion contingencies, 379
Siberia, 342
Siegfried Line, 61, 175
Silvercruys, Baron Robert, 85, 88
Simon, Sir John, 147
Simon Bolivar (liner), 96
Sims, Admiral William Sowden, 57
Sinn Féin, 153
Sino-Japanese War, Second, 99
'situation' code, 8
Skagerrak Strait, 172, 200

Index

Skelton, Dr Oscar D., 90, 91, 140, 264, 365–6, 391
  meetings with Hearne, 137, 138
  memo from Hearne, 121–2
  Treaty ports issue, 395–9
Skerries, Co Dublin, 72n
Slattery, L.M., 40
Slovakia, 159
  Consul sought, 80–1, 114–15, 119
Smith, Paul, 66
Smith case, 302
Socialism, 411
Socialist Party, France, 208
Société Générale, Paris, 363
Sours, 246
South Africa, Union of, 18, 19, 20, 26, 88, 138, 142, 250
  and British trade, 456
South America, 40, 53, 231, 265, 405, 429
  European trade, 446
  German population, 323
  Irish trade, 356
  and League of Nations, 108, 113, 377
  Willingdon Mission, 455
South Atlantic, 114n
South Circular Road bomb, 426
South Tyrol, cession to Italy, 135
Southern Rhodesia, 104
Southern Shanxi, 99
Sovereign Island, Co Cork, 316
Soviets. *see* Russia
Sowby, Reverend C.W., 149
Spain, 51, 68, 73, 136, 214, 275, 291, 337n, 382, 415, 443. *see also* Kerney, Leopold H.; Ryan, Frank
  anti-Partition campaign, 171, 178–9
  Belgian embassy expelled, 382n
  blockaded, 315
  censorship, 39, 170–1
  correspondence delays, 14–15
  and Ireland, 429
    Portugal joint accreditation, 131–3
    trade negotiations, 78–80
  to join Axis, 291
  Kerney cautioned, 382
  and League of Nations, 377
  Legation *see* Kerney, 7–8
  neutrality, 8, 24, 38–9, 383
  trade, 179, 187, 350

Spanish Civil War, 7, 27n, 39, 64n, 123n, 163n, 303n, 313, 317n, 340
  commemorations, 124
  Irish credits frozen, 79–80
Spanish Embassy, Berne, 415
Spanish Embassy, Paris, 361
Special Representative, status of, 18
Spellman, Cardinal Francis Joseph, 125–6
Spitfires, 330–1, 380
sports, 182
Squire, Sir John Collings, 147, 149
Stalin, Joseph, 193
Standard, 47
Stanley, Sir Herbert, 104
State Department, USA, 60, 62, 94, 161, 445
  contraband risks, 95–6
  denounces Japan treaty, 99
  and IRA executions, 146
  map of combat zones, 92
Statesman, 149
Statute of Westminster, 210
Steele, John, 139, 295, 298, 299, 303, 314
Stephenson, John E., 181, 188–9, 217–26, 335–6
sterling holdings, 357
Stewart, Mr, 92
Stimson, Henry L., 274, 440
Stokes Brandt mortars, 367
Stoneman, William H., 406
Stonyhurst School, 187
Straits of Dover, 274
Street, Sir Arthur, 332
Stuart, Francis, 382
Student-Exchange-Service, 182
Styria, 135
submarine warfare, 47, 50, 61, 97n, 102, 117, 160, 198, 228, 274
  German successes, 72–3, 454, 455
  and Ireland, 44, 46, 219, 298n
    detention of German crews, 17
    entry forbidden, 16
    in Kerry, 101
    rescued crew landed, 84
    restrictions, 23, 44–5, 51
  Irish-British trade safe, 100
  Irish ships sunk, 48
  and neutrality, 18, 180
  and port defence, 57–8, 221
  risks to US shipping, 92

Scapa Flow, 104
Ulster coast, 256
Sudan, 224n
Sudetenland, 6, 164
Suez Canal, 32, 173, 197
Sullivan, Mark, 211
Sunday Express, 274
Sunday Times, 274
Súñer, Ramón Serrano, 98n, 122, 340, 341, 342
Supplies, Department of, Irish, 165, 168, 171, 356n
  and German blockade, 329–30
  invasion contingencies, 444
Supplies, Department of, UK, 168n, 170, 175–6, 196, 335
  enquiry re Irish armaments, 231–2
Supplies, Minister for. *see* Lemass, Seán
Supreme Court, Irish, 139
Supreme Court of Canada, 137
Swansea, 316
Swaziland, 20n
Sweden, 104, 112n, 333, 437
  and Finland, 134
  German threat, 172, 177
  and League of Nations, 377
  neutrality, 427
  and Norway, 199
  Russian threat, 105
  WWI neutrality, 54
Swiss Federal Council, 371n, 444
Switzerland, 16, 68, 155, 293, 371, 406, 450
  and *Altmark* incident, 159
  British bombs, 427
  Cremins appointed to, 391–2
  entry and exit, 430, 442
  financial transfers, 93
  Irish Legation, 370–1
  Joyce case, 402, 434–5
  and League of Nations, 81, 82, 118, 400
  mobilisation, 7, 56, 88
  neutrality, 9, 21, 29, 54, 82, 333, 350, 392–3
  and Scandinavian invasions, 171–3, 176–7
  trade agreements, 328
Syrop, Dr Friedrich, 159

T
Tablet, 294
Tacoma (German ship), 130

Tallinn, 130
tank warfare, 237, 243, 259
Taoiseach, Department of the, 421
  memo on invasion contingencies, 444–5
Tardini, Mgr Domenico, 157, 383
Taylor, Myron C., 125, 167
Tegart, Sir Charles, 298–9, 321, 374
Telegrafo, Il, 180, 197
telegram codes, 7–8
telegraphic communication, 324
Telepress, 87
termination payments, 206, 207
territorial waters, 2, 58–9, 84–5, 253, 255
  aide mémoire to belligerents, 23–4
  defence of, 50, 83–4
  forced landings, 45
  German submarines, 44
  Irish ship attacked, 316
Teschen question, 82
Tessin area, Switzerland, 177
Tetuan, Duchess of, 26–7, 63, 64, 98, 122n, 187
Thames Estuary, 361
'Theatre of War' theory, 276
Thirty Years' War, 285n
Thom, Dr Corcoran, 109–10
Thomsen, Henning, 423
Thorvaldsen Museum, Copenhagen, 55
Tientsin, 99
timber exports, 184
Times, The, 149, 160, 294, 299, 303, 437
Tipperary, County, 40
Tokyo, 99, 273
Toronto, 139, 398
Totalitarianism, 275, 302
Tours, 247–8, 249
  Legation evacuation, 244–5
Toynbee Hall, 331
trade, 3–4, 93. *see also* Anglo-Irish trade; transhipment
  British blockade Germany, 40
  defence of ports, 94
  essential supplies, 47–8
  and German blockade, 325–30, 348–50, 383, 389, 392
  German Note, 354–5
  German-Irish, 182, 184
  prices, 390
  Russo-German, 61
  Spain, 78–80, 179, 187
  US-Japan, 100

Index

Tralee, Co Kerry, 316
Transatlantic Air Agreement, 136
transhipment, 192, 358–9, 360–1
  in draft agreement, 364, 390
  proposals, 334, 335–6, 358–61
  Rynne on, 352–4
  violation of neutrality, 349–50, 451
Transylvania, 87, 88
Travel Permit regulations, 52–3
Travers, Father, 246, 247, 337, 343–4
Traynor, Oscar, 264. *see also* Defence, Minister for
Treason Act, 34
Treasury, UK, 335, 454
Treaty ports, 2, 4, 14, 45, 58, 59, 138, 160, 262, 415
  Britain seeks use of, 151–2, 235–7, 252–3, 270, 295, 384–5, 387–8, 390, 395n, 397, 402, 411n, 416, 417, 455–6
  offence to neutrality, 19–20
  reasons for, 149–52
  British attitude to, 58, 59, 212
    Maffey-Walshe conversation, 416–17
  Canadian attitude, 395–9, 422
  Churchill attacks policy, 210
  Churchill speech, 384, 385, 390, 395n, 402, 455–6
  convoys argument, 412
  defence of, 56–7, 221, 282, 358
  diplomatic offensive, 386, 387, 408
  and foreign shipping, 51–2, 219
  German reports on, 333–4
  in intensified emergency, 262–3
  and Irish unity, 255
  and neutrality, 19–20, 393
  no question of return, 101, 121, 280, 413
  Shaw urges capture, 411n
  strategic importance, 56–8
  US campaign for, 384, 399, 411–12, 429–30, 439–41
Trondheim, 200
troop carriers, 218, 219
Tunis, 251
Turkey, 68, 79, 94, 133, 250
  and Allies, 74, 76, 175, 178, 192
  neutrality, 9, 65, 174
Tweedsmuir, John Buchan, 1st Baron, 265n
Twomey, Moss, 313
Twomey, Daniel, 167, 168
Tyrone, County, 192, 202

U
U-boats. *see* submarines
Ukraine, 416
Unden, Bo Osten, 112, 129
undesirable aliens, 262
United German Societies, San Francisco, 66
United Kingdom. *see also* Britain; Northern Ireland
  in title of representative, 46–7
United States of America (USA), 125, 155, 187, 201, 229, 277, 379, 416, 451. *see also* Washington Legation
  and Britain, 150, 296, 395, 404–6, 454–5
  aid sought, 151, 152, 274
  defeat feared, 277, 286
  and Canada, 138, 265
  and conscription, 112
  consulates, 1939-40, 161
  Dublin Legation, 323
  First World War, 56, 57, 58
  Fleet, 439–40, 446
  and France, 251, 260–1, 291
  and Germany, 40, 174, 292–3, 305, 428, 432
  and IRA executions, 140–1, 146
  and Ireland, 34–5, 72, 305, 437
  anti-Partition campaign, 167, 168, 178–9, 322
  assets in, 443–4, 449, 450
  de Valera Christmas address, 130–1
  German bombs dropped in, 347, 349, 432
  invasion fear, 319
  Irish-Americans, 101
  leasing facilities, 388–9
  loan sought, 445
  neutrality, 60, 62, 160, 201, 290, 295–6, 298–9, 301–4, 306, 308, 312, 314, 385, 392, 394–5, 426, 429–30
  possible guarantor of neutrality, 255, 256, 269
  shipping zones, 74, 92, 93, 95, 100, 161, 234
  trade, 356, 357
  Treaty ports, 94, 374, 375, 384, 386, 387, 393, 399, 408, 411–15, 417, 429–30, 439–41
  isolationism, 211, 217, 231, 274

and Italy, 197–8, 448
and Japan, 249
and League of Nations, 309, 376, 378, 400
Lend-Lease Bill, 445–6, 452
munitions, 224–5, 236, 242, 296
  arms embargo, 13, 66
nationals in foreign armies, 111, 112
neutrality, 9, 49, 161, 326, 332–3
  Brennan report, 20
newsagencies, 324
and NI, 17
planes from, 243, 282–3, 284, 291
radio broadcasts, 11–12
rearmament, 217, 231
Russell leaves, 313
and Russia, 103–4
and Ryan escape, 342, 346–7, 415
Second World War, 86, 211, 216–17, 380
  closer to entry, 230–1, 265, 315, 350, 383, 404–6, 429–30, 446
  unprepared for, 211
tariffs, 357
trade, 456
Vatican diplomacy, 157
University College Cork (UCC), 440n
University College Dublin (UCD), 69n
Uruguay, 94, 130
US Congress, 452
US House of Representatives, 211
Ushant, 58, 362n
USSR. *see* Russia
Utrecht, 208

V
Valentia, 323
Vandenberg, Senator Arthur, 231
Vatican, 30, 173, 213, 364, 366, 431, 434. *see also* Holy See Legation
  atrocities in Poland, 143–4
  condemns Scandinavian invasions, 180–1
  Dublin vacancy discussed, 163, 230, 249
  and IRA bombs, 157
  and Irish neutrality, 35
  McQuaid appointment, 383, 386
  sympathy towards Vichy, 305, 431
  and totalitarianism, 302
Vega, General Alonso, 187
Vendôme, 246, 247
Ventry Harbour, Kerry, 72n, 84n

Verdier, Cardinal Jean, 9, 344–5
Versailles, 246
  Treaty, 1918, 286
Viborg, 104
Vichy government, 268n, 275, 293, 317, 346, 362
  armistice, 250–1
  collaboration opposed, 407
  Dakar affair, 366n
  discouraged, 363
  economic system, 318
  Franco-German talks, 393–4
  Irish sympathy for, 304–5
  Laval-Pétain reconciliation, 441
  Murphy on, 408–10
  Murphy visits Foreign Minister, 310–11
  support for, 399, 409–10
  and Vatican, 305, 431
Vichy National Council, 70n
Victoria, Queen, 265
Vigón, General Juan, 340
Vincentian Order, 246
Vintras, Squadron Leader R.E. de T.
  Irish co-operation talks, 217–26
Vistula river, 25, 61
Vladivostok, 160
von Dewall, Walter, 131
von Killinger, Baron, 66
von Neurath, Konstantin Freiherr, 164
von Ribbentrop, Joachim, 8, 66, 114, 164–5, 320
  Norwegian White Book, 198–200
von Rintelen, Emil, Minister Plenipotentiary, 433
Voroshiloff, 75
Voz de España, La, 10, 14, 38

W
Walsh, Eileen J., 69, 183
Walsh, J.C., 333
Walsh, Maurice, 178–9
Walshe, Joseph P., 168, 181, 364
  Anglo-Irish military co-operation talks, 217–26
  and British Representative (Maffey), 42, 45, 46–7, 155–6, 297–9, 311–12, 373–5
  Treaty ports, 416–17
  correspondence
    Archer, 297, 414–15
    Brennan, 91–2, 162, 445–6

Index

de Valera
  Maffey meetings, 297–9, 311–12, 373–5
  Dobrzyński, 27
  Dulanty, 119–20, 132–3, 144, 160, 300
    meteorological reports, 372–3
  Ferguson, 231–2
  Gray, 314, 387–9
  Hearne, 100–2, 365–6
    Treaty ports, 395–9
  Kerney, 141, 178–9
  Leydon, 95–6, 231–2
  Macaulay, 163
  Moynihan, M., 107, 379
  Moynihan, S., 404
  Murphy, S.
    French public opinion, 69–71
  O'Donovan, 230
  Ontiveros, 156
  Ryan, E., 346–7
  Rynne
    Germany and NI, 275–7
  Warnock, 5–6
  on de Valera-MacDonald talks, 269–70
  and German Legation
    extra staff requested, 418–20, 423–5, 428, 432
    Hempel meeting, 84–5
  invasion contingencies, 442–4
  memos by, 281
    on British guarantee, 320–1
    to de Valera, 169, 271–2, 272–5, 289–92, 294–6, 334
      British defeat inevitable, 249–50
      Germany and Ireland, 190–1
      Hempel meeting, 232–3
      trade talks, 192–3
    to Dulanty (facsimile), *145*
    on German bombings, 425–6, 427, 431–2, 453–4
    on German invasion, 319–20
    German Legation staff, 428, 432
    German Note, 325–9
    Gray memo, 439–41
    Hempel interview, 300–1
    to MacMahon, 437–9
    Maffey meeting, 389–91
    troops in NI, 348
    visit to London, 15–20
  memos to
    Boland, 131–2, 400–1
    Cremins, 81–3
    Gallagher, 322–3
    Hearne, 88–9
    Hempel (facsimile), *418–19*
    Kerney, 14–15, 26–7, 63–4, 78–80
    Rynne, 127–8, 135–6, 420–1
      neutrality, 1–5, 11–12, 32–4, 48–53, 72
  minutes
    from Boland, 143–4
    on League of Nations, 407
    to Rynne, 105
  note on Barnes/Richards reprieve efforts, 148–9
  reports to (*see also under* Brennan; Cremins; Dulanty; Kerney; Murphy, Seán; Warnock)
    Cremin, 6
    Hearne, 267
      neutrality, 85–7, 137–40
    MacWhite, 31–2, 74–6, 157–8, 168, 197–8
    Murphy, M., 65–7, 163
    O'Donovan, 62–3, 113–14
  reports to de Valera
    Eden meeting, 200–3
  telegrams from
    Brennan, 60, 292–3, 303, 395, 399, 445, 451
      Treaty ports, 384, 393, 408, 411–14
    Cremins, 392–3
    Hearne, 83–4, 115, 156, 304, 422
    MacWhite, 448
    Murphy, S., 60, 304–5, 389, 399, 406, 431, 446
    O'Donovan, 386
    Warnock, 278, 389
      German bombs dropped in Ireland, 422–3, 426
  telegrams to
    Brennan, 62, 94, 95, 387, 412, 417, 451–2
      US and Irish neutrality, 394–5, 429–30
    Cremins, 415–16
    Hearne, 391
    Kerney, 411
    MacWhite, 451
    Murphy, S., 310–11, 393–4, 407, 434, 441
    O'Donovan, 433

Warnock, 229, 355, 383, 392, 416
  German bombs dropped in
    Ireland, 432–3, 452
  and trade talks, 170
  and Treaty ports, 386
  and US Legation
    Gray conversations, 387–9, 439–41
Walshe, Maurice, 138
Walter Logan Bill, US, 405
War Cabinet, UK, 35, 305, 330, 338, 454
  and Ireland, 310
  and Irish unity, 254, 306
  losses, 332, 369
  and trade negotiations, 309
War of Independence, 148n
War Office, Spain, 187, 340, 341, 342
War Office, UK, 45, 150, 153, 306
  Irish cable link, 225
  Irish talks, 221, 222–6
  munitions, 307–8, 312
War Trade Agreements, 77, 328
Warner, Albert, 406
Warner, Professor William Lloyd, 110n
Warnock, William, 301, 353
  correspondence
    Boland, 13–14, 41, 68–9, 71, 76–7
    Walshe, 5–6
  and German bombs dropped in
    Ireland, 426, 432–3
  German Legation staff request, 419, 420, 423, 424
  and German Note, 354–5
  Joyce case, 430–1, 441–2
  letter to Boland, 67–8
  reports to Walshe, 24–6, 77–8, 133–5, 186, 214–15
    Barnes and Richards, 155–6
    Britain in Norway, 198–200
    British-Irish shipping, 102–3
    Christmas 1939, 129–31
    end of war expected, 164–5
    Finland attacked, 103–4, 105–6
    German situation, 39–40, 96–8, 115–18, 227–9
    German trade, 93
    Ireland in German press, 333–4
    neutrality breaches, 158–60
    public opinion, 72–4
    Russo-German pact, 60–2, 64–5
  telegrams
    DEA, 128, 227, 302, 337, 351, 382, 437
    German blockade, 348–50

German bombs dropped in
  Ireland, 316, 339, 347, 364–5, 366–7
Irish nationals, 351–2
neutrality, 212, 293, 302
Walshe, 229, 278, 355, 383, 389, 392, 416, 420
eye trouble, 382–3
German bombs dropped in
  Ireland, 422–3, 426, 432–3, 452
Warsaw, 39, 63
Washington, 88n, 94, 110, 162, 198, 380, 395n, 406
Washington, SS, 161n
Washington Evening Star, 211
Washington Legation, 449. *see also*
  Brennan, Robert
  dinner for Gray, 162
  invasion contingencies, 449–50
  lack of communication, 34–5
  telegram from, 146
Washington Merry-Go-Round, 405
Washington Post, 160
Washington Times-Herald, 160, 211
Waterford, 262, 339
Waterson, Sidney Frank, 456
weapons. *see* munitions
Welles, Sumner, 99, 100, 164, 332
Wells, Lynton, 303
West Indies, 96n
West Prussia, 97
Westminster, Dean of, 149
'Westphalian System', 285n
Wexford, County, 365. *see also* Campile bomb
Weygand, General Maxime, 106, 215n, 216, 250, 275
  de Gaulle cashiered by, 272–3
whiskey, trade, 80
White, William Allen, 404–5, 231
White Book on Norway, 198–200
Wiedemann, Captain Fritz, 66, 67
Wilhelmina, Queen of Holland, 421
Wilhelmshaven, 39–40, 73
Willingdon Mission, 455
Wilson, President Woodrow, 430
Winchell, Walter, 217
Winnipeg Free Press, 100
'Winter War', 103n
Wireless Board, UK, 225, 226
Wisconsin, 332

Woermann, Dr Ernst, 68, 281, 350, 412
  assures Ireland of German respect, 302
  extra Legation staff sought, 419–20, 423
  and German bombs dropped in Ireland, 337, 355, 365, 367
Wood, Sir Kingsley, 305
Wood, Canon W., 368
woollen goods, trade, 80, 335
Woolton, Lord, 175n, 176, 196, 305, 307, 456
  Dulanty interview, 308–9
World's Fair, New York, 158, 161
Württemberg, 184
Wyndham Club, London, 390

Y
Ya, 170
Yangtze River, 99
Ybarnegaray, Michel Albert J.J., 208, 268
York, Archbishop of, 149
Yugoslavia, 31, 68, 94, 178, 181, 273, 400, 412
  and Italy, 32, 173–4, 198, 213
  and League of Nations, 118
  Nationality Law, 112

Z
Zagret Cable Company, 351
Zakopane, 97
Ziwes, Mr, 248
Zurich, 427
Zvrskovec, Dr, 114–15